THE OXFORD HANDB(

QUAKER STUDIES

THE OXFORD HANDBOOK OF

QUAKER STUDIES

Edited by

STEPHEN W. ANGELL

and

PINK DANDELION

OXFORD

UNIVERSITY PRESS

OXFORD

UNIVERSITY PRESS

Great Clarendon Street, Oxford, OX2 6DP,
United Kingdom

Oxford University Press is a department of the University of Oxford.
It furthers the University's objective of excellence in research, scholarship,
and education by publishing worldwide. Oxford is a registered trade mark of
Oxford University Press in the UK and in certain other countries

First published 2013
First published in paperback 2015

Published in the United States of America by Oxford University Press
198 Madison Avenue, New York, NY 10016, United States of America

British Library Cataloguing in Publication Data
Data available

Library of Congress Cataloging in Publication Data
Data available

ISBN 978–0–19–960867–6 (Hbk.)
ISBN 978–0–19–874498–6 (Pbk.)

To our colleagues, past and present,
at Woodbrooke Quaker Study Centre
and Earlham School of Religion

Contents

PART II QUAKER THEOLOGY AND SPIRITUALITY

PART III QUAKER WITNESS

PART IV QUAKER EXPRESSION

List of Contributors

Margery Post Abbott is the author and co-editor of numerous books including *A Certain Kind of Perfection* (Pendle Hill, 1997), *Walk Worthy of Your Calling: Quakers and the Travelling Ministry* (Friends United Press, 2004), *To Be Broken and Tender: A Quaker Theology for Today* (Friends Bulletin Corp., 2010), and *The Historical Dictionary of the Friends (Quakers)* (Scarecrow Press, revised 2011). Abbott regularly leads workshops and teaches on Quakerism at study centres in the United States and Britain. She holds a Bachelors degree from Swarthmore College and a Master of Urban Studies degree from Old Dominion University.

Richard C. Allen is Reader in History at the University of South Wales. He has published widely on Quakerism, migration, and identity. His most recent works are *Quaker Communities in Early Modern Wales* (University of Wales Press, 2007) and the co-edited *Irelands of the Mind* (Cambridge Scholars, 2008); *Faith of our Fathers: popular culture and belief in post-Reformation England, Ireland and Wales* (Cambridge Scholars, 2009); and *The Religious History of Wales: a survey of religious life and practice from the seventeenth century to the present day* (Welsh Academic Press, 2013). He is currently writing *Welsh Quaker Emigrants and Colonial Pennsylvania* and co-authoring *Quaker Networks and Moral Reform in the North East of England*.

Stephen W. Angell is the Leatherock Professor of Quaker Studies at the Earlham School of Religion in Richmond, Indiana. He is co-editor with Paul Buckley of *The Quaker Bible Reader* (Earlham School of Religion Press, 2006); co-editor with Hal Weaver and Paul Kriese of *Black Fire: African-American Quakers on Spirituality and Human Rights* (Quaker Press of FGC, 2011); and author of *Bishop Henry McNeal Turner and African-American Religion in the South* (University of Tennessee Press, 1992). He is an Associate Editor of the journals *Quaker Studies* and *Quaker Theology,* and he is on the editorial boards of *Quaker Religious Thought* and the *Journal of Africana Religions.*

Simon Best is Tutor for Nurturing Friends and Meetings at Woodbrooke Quaker Study Centre, Birmingham, England and a lecturer within the Centre for Postgraduate Quaker Studies, Woodbrooke and the University of Birmingham. He was awarded his PhD from the University of Birmingham in 2010 with a thesis entitled 'The Community of Intimacy: The Spiritual Beliefs and Religious Practices of Adolescent Quakers'. His publications include 'Adolescent Quakers: a community of intimacy' in Dandelion, P. and Collins, P. (eds.) *The Quaker Condition: the sociology of a liberal religion* (Newcastle, Cambridge Scholars Publishing, 2009); 'Quaker Events for Young People: informal education and faith transmission' *Quaker Studies*; and 'Adolescent Quakers: a hidden sect' in *Quaker Studies*. His research interests include adolescent Quakers, Quaker rites of passage, and the interrelationships between adolescent, young adult, and adult Quakers.

Michael Birkel is Professor of Religion at Earlham College in Richmond, Indiana, where he also directs the Newlin Center for Quaker Thought and Practice. His writings focus chiefly on Quaker spirituality and include: *'A Near Sympathy': The Timeless Quaker Wisdom of John Woolman* (Friends United Press, 2003); *Silence and Witness: Quaker Spirituality* (Orbis/Darton Longman and Todd, 2004); *Engaging Scripture: Encountering the Bible with Early Friends* (Friends United Press, 2005); *The Messenger that Goes Before: Reading Margaret Fell for Spiritual Nurture* (Pendle Hill, 2008); and *Genius of the Transcendent: Mystical Writings of Jakob Boehme* (Shambhala, 2010).

Geoffrey Cantor is Professor Emeritus of the History of Science at the University of Leeds and Honorary Senior Research Fellow at University College, London. Most of his recent research has been directed at elucidating the historical interrelations between science and religion. His publications in this area include *Michael Faraday: Sandemanian and scientist* (St Martin's, 1991); *Quakers, Jews, and science* (Oxford University Press, 2005); *Religion and the Great Exhibition of 1851* (Oxford University Press, 2011); and, with John Hedley Brooke, *Reconstructing nature: The engagement of science and religion* (T&T Clark, 1998).

Max L. Carter is the Director of Friends Center and campus ministry coordinator at Guilford College, Greensboro, NC. His research and writing includes his PhD dissertation 'Quaker Relations with Midwestern Indians to 1833' (Temple University, 1989); *Minutiae of the Meeting* (Guilford College 1999); and *College Spirit* (Guilford College, 2003). He has authored numerous articles for Quaker journals, periodicals, and devotionals. A recorded Friends minister, his interests include Quaker history, intentional communities, and Quaker work for peace in the Middle East.

Elizabeth Cazden is an independent scholar based in Providence, Rhode Island, USA. She studies Quaker history especially in New England, seeking to view the Quaker experience in its economic and social context. A former lawyer, she is the author of *Antoinette Brown Blackwell* (Feminist Press, 1983) and of articles in *Quaker History, Harvard Magazine*, and *Cobblestone,* and on Examiner.com. She teaches writing (adjunct) at Roger Williams University. Her current major research project has a working title of *Slaves Among Friends: Rhode Island Quakers in a Slave-based Economy, 1660–1785.*

Charles L. Cherry is Professor of English and formerly Associate Vice President of Academic Affairs at Villanova University near Philadelphia, Pennsylvania. He has been, since 1991, editor of *Quaker History,* based at Haverford College. He is the author of *A Quiet Haven: Quakers, Moral Treatment, and Asylum Reform* (Associated University Presses, 1989) as well as articles on literature and higher education.

Pink Dandelion is Professor of Quaker Studies at the University of Birmingham and directs the work of the Centre for Postgraduate Quaker Studies, Woodbrooke and the University of Birmingham. He edits *Quaker Studies* and acts as Series Editor for the Edwin Mellen Press series in Quaker Studies. His books include *The Quaker Condition* (Cambridge Scholars Publishing, 2009); *The Quakers: a very short introduction* (Oxford University Press, 2008); (with Jackie Leach Scully) *Good and Evil: Quaker perspectives* (Ashgate, 2007); *Introduction to Quakerism* (Cambridge University Press, 2007); *The Liturgies of Quakerism* (Ashgate, 2005); *The Creation of Quaker Theory* (Ashgate, 2004); the co-authored *Towards Tragedy/Reclaiming Hope* (Ashgate, 2004); and *The Sociological Analysis of the Theology of Quakers: the silent revolution* (Edwin Mellen Press, 1996).

Petra L. Doan is Professor of Urban and Regional Planning at Florida State University in Tallahassee, Florida. A convinced Friend, she attended Westtown School and joined Westtown Meeting in 1973. After earning her BA in Philosophy at Haverford College, Dr Doan completed her MRP and PhD from the Department of City and Regional Planning at Cornell University in International Planning. In addition to numerous publications in the field of planning, her *Friends Journal* article (2002) on 'Gender, Integrity, and Spirituality' (2002) describes her spiritual journey as a transsexual woman. Dr. Doan is a member of Tallahassee Monthly Meeting in Tallahassee, Florida.

Jeffrey Dudiak is Associate Professor of Philosophy at the King's University College in Edmonton, Canada, specializing in Continental philosophy of religion and ethics. His major publication to date is *The Intrigue of Ethics: A reading of the idea of discourse in the thought of Emmanuel Levinas* (Fordham University Press, 2001). His current interest in 'truth' includes work on Quakers and truth. He is also engaged in thinking through a phenomenology of Quaker religious life.

Mark Freeman is Senior Lecturer in Economic and Social History at the University of Glasgow. He has published widely on various topics, including articles in the *English Historical Review*, *Economic History Review*, *History of Education*, and *Quaker Studies* on aspects of modern British Quakerism. He is the author of *The Joseph Rowntree Charitable Trust: A Study in Quaker Philanthropy 1904–1954* (William Sessions, 2004); and co-author, with Robin Pearson and James Taylor, of *Shareholder Democracies? Corporate Governance in Britain and Ireland before 1850* (University of Chicago Press, 2012).

J. William Frost is the Emeritus Howard M. and Charles F. Jenkins Professor of Quaker History and Research at Swarthmore College. He is co-author of *The Quakers*; and author of *The Quaker Family in Colonial America: A Portrait of the Society of Friends* (Greenwood, 1988); *A Perfect Freedom: Religious Liberty in Pennsylvania* (Cambridge University Press, 1990); and *A History of Christian, Jewish, Buddhist, Hindu, and Muslim Perspectives on War and Peace* (Edwin Mellen Press, 2004). He has edited several books and published many articles on Quaker history. His current research interests are William Penn, anti-slavery, and the evolution of the peace testimony.

Mary Van Vleck Garman is Professor of Religion at Earlham College in Richmond, Indiana, USA, where she also teaches in Earlham's first-year writing programme. She is the co-editor of *Hidden in Plain Sight: Quaker Women's Writings, 1650–1700* (Pendle Hill Publications, 1996). Her other research interests include contemporary religious movements, religion in the USA, friendship, and 'Quakeumenism'.

Michael P. Graves is an independent scholar who has served as a Professor of Communication Studies at four institutions, including George Fox University and Regent University. His publications include *Preaching the Inward Light: Early Quaker Rhetoric* (Baylor University Press, 2009), which was named book of the year by the Religious Communication Association. He co-edited a critical volume on Southern Gospel music and has published more than fifty scholarly essays, book chapters, and reviews. His research interests include Quaker rhetorical practice, visual rhetoric, the rhetoric of music, and transcendence and the moving image.

Gerard Guiton is the author of *The Early Quakers and the 'Kingdom of God'* (Inner Light, 2012); and *The Growth and Development of Quaker Testimony* (Edwin Mellen Press, 2005). He co-edited *Overcoming Violence in Asia: The Role of the Church in Seeking Cultures of Peace* (2009) for the Historic Peace Churches and World Council of Churches. Gerard is a spiritual director in private practice, a peace activist, a workshop leader, and a regular contributor to Quaker journals and newsletters worldwide. He is a member of Australia Yearly Meeting of the Religious Society of Friends.

Douglas Gwyn teaches Quaker Studies at Pendle Hill, a Quaker centre for study and contemplation in Wallingford, Pennsylvania. His publications include *Apocalypse of the Word: the life and message of George Fox* (Friends United Press, 1986); *The Covenant crucified: Quakers and the rise of capitalism* (Pende Hill, 1995); *Seekers found: atonement in early Quaker experience* (Pendle Hill, 2000); and *Vision through time: the story of Pendle Hill* (forthcoming). His research interests include Quakers and the Bible, eschatology, and utopian movements.

Betty Hagglund is Project Development Officer at the Centre for Postgraduate Quaker Studies, Woodbrooke/University of Birmingham, UK. Her publications include *Tourists and Travellers* (Channel View Publications, 2010) and a number of articles on Quakers and Quakerism. Her current research interests include Quakers and the natural world in the seventeenth and eighteenth centuries, seventeenth-century book distribution networks, Scottish Quaker history, the Aberdeen Quaker poet Lilias Skene, travel writing, history of the book, Margaret Fell and the Jews, and the nineteenth-century travel writer Maria Graham.

Thomas D. Hamm received his PhD in history from Indiana University in 1985. He is Professor of History and Director of Special Collections at Earlham College in Richmond, Indiana, where he has been on the faculty since 1987. He has written and published extensively on Quakerism since 1800. His first book was *The Transformation of American Quakerism: Orthodox Friends, 1800–1907* (Indiana University Press, 1988).

His most recent is an edited volume, *Quaker Writings, 1650–1920*, published by Penguin Classics in 2011. His current project is a study of Hicksite Friends from 1827 to 1900.

Robynne Rogers Healey is Associate Professor of History and Co-director of the Gender Studies Institute at Trinity Western University in Langley, British Columbia, Canada. Her publications include *From Quaker to Upper Canada: Faith and Community Among Yonge Street Friends, 1801–1850* (McGill-Queen's University Press, 2006); and a number of articles on Quakers and Quakerism. Her research interests include gender and Quakerism, the transatlantic world in the eighteenth and nineteenth centuries, the twentieth-century peace testimony, and Canadian Quakerism.

Gregory P. Hinshaw is an independent scholar. He is a public school superintendent in Indiana and has published in the areas of Quaker history, Indiana history, local history, and history of education. He is presently serving as presiding clerk of Indiana Yearly Meeting and as a member of the General Board and Executive Committee of Friends United Meeting.

Roger Homan is Professor Emeritus of Religious Studies at the University of Brighton. His early work was in the sociology of religion and the history of religious sects. More recently he has been occupied with ethical issues in social research. On these themes he has published extensively in journals. Major book publications include *The Ethics of Social Research* (Longman, 1992); and *The Art of the Sublime* (Ashgate, 2006). Current research interests include religious aesthetics and the applications of ethics.

David L. Johns taught Theology at Wilmington College and Earlham School of Religion and is Vice President for Academic Affairs and Dean of the College at Union College in Barbourville, Kentucky. His publications include *Quakering Theology* (Ashgate, 2013); *The Collected Works of Maurice Creasey* (Edwin Mellen Press, 2011); *Mysticism and Ethics in Baron Friedrich von Hügel* (Edwin Mellen Press, 2005); and a number of articles and book chapters on Quaker thought. His research interests include ecclesiology, ecumenism, modern Quakerism, post-colonialism, and liberation theology.

Elizabeth P. Kamphausen is an independent scholar in Quaker Studies. A birthright and convinced Friend, she earned her MA in Religion from the Earlham School of Religion in Richmond, Indiana. In addition to teaching Quakerism at several Friends' boarding schools, she taught Quaker Studies at Pendle Hill in Wallingford, Pennsylvania from 1994–2000 where she also pursued research in James Nayler's life and teachings. She is currently a Licenced Clinical Social Worker in private practice as well as a hospice counsellor, having earned an MSW from the University of Toronto. She is a member of Tallahassee Monthly Meeting in Tallahassee, Florida.

Emma J. Lapsansky is Professor of History and Curator of Special Collections, Emeritus at Haverford College, in Haverford, Pennysylvania. A University of Pennsylvania PhD (1975), her recent scholarly publications include *Quaker Aesthetics* (University of Pennsylvania Press, 2003, with Anne Verplanck); *Back to Africa: Benjamin Coates and the American Colonization Movement* (Penn State University Press, 2005, with

Margaret Hope Bacon). Her co-authored essay on British abolitionist Thomas Clarkson is forthcoming in a University of Illinois Press anthology. She is currently at work on two research projects: a history of a Bryn Mawr, Pennsylvanian Quaker family; and a study of a mid-twentieth-century Philadelphia Quaker utopian community.

Howard R. Macy is Professor Emeritus at George Fox University in Newberg, Oregon. His publications include *Rhythms of the Inner Life* (F. H. Revell, 1988); *Laughing Pilgrims: Humor and the Spiritual Journey* (Paternoster Press, 2006); and *Stepping in the Light* (Friends United Press, 2007), as well as numerous articles in Friends publications. He currently serves as editor of *Quaker Religious Thought* and continues research interests in the Hebrew prophets, in spirituality, and in the role of humour in Christian living.

Rosemary Moore is an independent scholar attached to the Centre for Postgraduate Quaker Studies at Woodbrooke Quaker Centre, Birmingham. Her publications include *The Light in Their Consciences: Early Quakers in Britain 1646–1666* (Pennsylvania State University Press, 2000); an edition of *The History of the Life of Thomas Ellwood, Written by Himself* (International Sacred Literature Trust, 2004); and (with R. Melvin Keiser) *Knowing the Mystery of Life Within: Selected Writings of Isaac Penington in their Historical and Theological Context* (London: Quaker Books, 2005). She was a cooperating editor for *Protestant Nonconformist Text, vol.1 1550–1700* (R. Tudur Jones, ed., Ashgate 2007).

Mike Nellis is Emeritus Professor of Criminal and Community Justice in the School of Law, University of Strathclyde. He has a longstanding interest in penal reform, and is a board member of the Howard League, Scotland. He was formerly a social worker with young offenders, has a PhD from the Institute of Criminology in Cambridge, and was involved in the training of probation officers at the University of Birmingham. He has written widely on the fortunes of the probation service, alternatives to imprisonment, and particularly the electronic monitoring of offenders.

Edwina Newman is a lecturer with the Open University and a member of staff in the Centre for Postgraduate Quaker Studies at Woodbrooke in Birmingham, England. Her publications include a number of articles on Quakers and Quakerism. Her research interests include the social history of eighteenth- and nineteenth-century Quakerism.

Elizabeth A. O'Donnell is a Former History lecturer in further and higher education, and works as an oral historian for Northumberland County Archives, Woodhorn, Ashington, Northumberland. She has published a number of articles on nineteenth-century Quakers in the northeast of England. Her research interests include the origins of first-wave feminism, abolitionism, and the treatment of young offenders in the nineteenth century.

Laura Rediehs is Associate Professor of Philosophy and Programme Coordinator of Peace Studies at St Lawrence University in Canton, New York. She is currently researching how Quakers have understood knowledge, showing how their 'expanded empiricism' allowed them to accept science while maintaining religious belief. Her research interests also include the debates concerning scientific realism, the history of the concepts of 'subjectivity' and 'objectivity', Kuhnian incommensurability of paradigms, and comparing *satyagraha* with Quaker non-violence.

Arthur O. Roberts of Newberg, Oregon, is a retired George Fox University Professor. Books about Quakers include *Tomorrow is Growing Old, Stories of the Quakers in Alaska* (Barclay, 1978); *Catechism and Confession of Faith*, modern English edition, with Dean Freiday (Barclay, 2001); *Early Quaker Writings*, with Hugh Barbour (Pendle Hill, 2004); *Through Flaming Sword, the Life and Legacy of George Fox* (Barclay, revised edition. 2008). He has contributed articles to several Quaker journals, including *Quaker Religious Thought*. His books of poetry and Christian inspiration include *Heavenly Fire* (Barclay, 2007) and *Exploring Heaven* (Harper, 2003).

Janet Scott was Head of Religious Studies and Director of Studies in Theology at Homerton College, Cambridge and a member of the faculties of Divinity and of Education at the university. She has also worked as Director of the Centre for Ecumenical Studies at Westcott House in the Cambridge Theological Federation. In 1980 she gave the Swarthmore lecture, *What canst thou say? Towards a Quaker theology.* She is a member of the World Council of Churches Faith and Order Plenary Commission and attends WCC Central Committee. She is currently a trustee and moderator of Churches Together in England.

Jackie Leach Scully is Professor of Social Ethics and Bioethics, and Co-Director at the Policy, Ethics, and Life Sciences Research Centre, Newcastle University, UK. Her research interests include the formation of moral understandings by religious and non-religious groups, especially around new technologies; feminist bioethics; and disability. Her publications include *Quaker Approaches to Moral Issues in Genetics* (Edwin Mellen Press, 2002); *Good and Evil: Quaker Perspective*, co-edited with Pink Dandelion (Ashgate, 2007); and *Disability Bioethics: Moral Bodies, Moral Difference* (Rowman & Littlefield, 2008), as well as numerous articles on bioethical issues.

Carole Dale Spencer is Associate Professor of Christian Spirituality at Earlham School of Religion in Richmond, Indiana. Her publications include *Holiness: The Soul of Quakerism: An Historical Analysis of the Theology of Holiness in the Quaker Tradition* (Paternoster, 2007); and a number of articles on Quaker history, theology, and spirituality. Her research interests include Quakers and Holiness, nineteenth-century revivalism, Quakers and Methodism, Quietism, Hannah Whitall Smith, Jeanne Guyon, and Christian mysticism.

Sylvia Stevens gained her PhD from the University of Sunderland in 2005. She is an independent researcher, a member of the Quaker Studies Research Association, and has contributed to the *Journal* of the Friends Historical Society. Her particular research interests focus on the cultural and religious history of Quakerism in the eighteenth and early nineteenth centuries. Her study *Quakers in Northeast Norfolk, England, 1690–1800* is forthcoming from the Edwin Mellen Press.

Nikki Coffey Tousley is a doctoral candidate in Theology at the University of Dayton. She holds a Masters of Divinity from Duke University and an MPhil in Quaker Studies from the University of Birmingham. Her MPhil thesis focused on shifts between first- and second-generation Quaker theology as implied in conversion narratives. Her current work draws on Thomistic virtue ethics and contemporary narrative theology to understand the Quaker tradition, particularly the role of worship and sanctification in eighteenth-century Quaker writing on property on the 'right use of things'.

Lonnie Valentine is Professor of Peace and Justice Studies at the Earlham School of Religion and has taught there for over twenty years. He has an MA in Religion from the School of Religion and a PhD from Emory University. Lonnie served as co-chair of the Religion, Peace, and War Group of the American Academy of Religion and as director of the Peace Studies Association. His publications in reference include 'Western Ethical and Religious Traditions' for the *Encyclopedia of Violence, Peace, and Conflict*; 'Pacifism' for the dictionary of *Contemporary American Religion*; and six entries in the *Oxford International Encyclopedia of Peace*.

Maureen Waugh has a PhD from the London School of Economics. She is a freelance researcher and an overseer in Glasgow Quaker Meeting. She was formerly a lecturer in History at the University of Birmingham and has written on Quaker involvement in the League of Nations in the inter-war period.

Jacalynn Stuckey Welling is Professor of History at Malone University in Canton, Ohio. Her scholarly works include articles and presentations on the intersection of faith and teaching, social reform activities among Gurneyite Quakers in Ohio, the evolution of mission practice among Evangelical Friends, and housing policy for the poor in small cities in the United States. Her current research interests include domestic and international mission practice within Evangelical Friends Church-Eastern Region. Formerly an administrator at a public housing authority in Stark County (Ohio), she is also exploring social policy trends among urban areas in the US industrial belt.

Lloyd Lee Wilson is a recorded minister of the gospel in West Grove Monthly Meeting, North Carolina Yearly Meeting (Conservative). His publications include *Essays on the Quaker Vision of Gospel Order* (Quaker Press of FGC, 2007); and *Wrestling with Our Faith Tradition: Collected Public Witness 1995–2004* (Quaker Press of FGC, 2005); in addition to numerous pamphlets and journal articles. Wilson earned undergraduate and graduate degrees at the Massachusetts Institute of Technology and an MA from the Earlham School of Religion. He is Registrar Emeritus at Chowan University in North Carolina, where he also served as Assistant Professor of Religion and Accounting.

Many of the authors also acted as consultants, reading and commenting on draft chapters. We are also indebted to the following who acted as consultants:

Paul N. Anderson, Allen Austin, Maureen Bell, Irv A. Brendlinger, Peter J. Collins, Patricia D'Antonio, Nigel Dower, David J. Hall, Welling Hall, Roger Hansen, Tom Head,

Sandra Holton, Larry H. Ingle, Nancy Irving, Sunne Juterczenka, Thomas C. Kennedy, Callie Marsh, Johan Maurer, Rachel Muers, Eleanor Nesbitt, John William Oliver Jr., John Punshon, Ben Richmond, Ann Riggs, Ellen Ross, Phil Smith, Ron Stansell, Michele L. Tarter, Christine Trevett.

INTRODUCTION

PINK DANDELION AND STEPHEN W. ANGELL

QUAKERS are a fascinating religious group both in their original 'peculiarity' and in the variety of reinterpretations of the faith since its early beginnings. The way they have interacted with wider society is a basic but often unexplored part of British and American history. This book charts Quaker history and the history of its expression as a religious community.

A BRIEF HISTORICAL OVERVIEW

Quakerism began in England in the 1650s. George Fox, credited as leading the movement, had an experience of 1647 in which he felt he could hear Christ directly and inwardly without the mediation of text or minister. Convinced of the authenticity of this experience and its universal application, Fox preached a spirituality in which potentially all people were ministers, all part of a priesthood of believers, a church levelled before the leadership of God. True spirituality was inward and the outward forms of Christianity, such as set apart ministers, church buildings, sacraments, and 'times and seasons' (the Christian calendar) were anachronistic and apostate. Fox preached that this was an age of a new covenant with God, the beginning of the end of the world. Quakers represented the true church and the only right way to a salvation available in this life, but all could become Quakers. All could realize salvation and consequent perfection. In 1652, we see the beginnings of an organized movement, noted for the depth and quality of its leadership amongst men and women in the north of England, amongst young and old.

To secure and nurture this direct encounter with the Divine, Quakers worshipped in silence. They were active as missionaries and Quakerism became the most successful sect of the 1650s and by 1680 numbered one per cent of the English population. While true worship was inward, the transforming experience many encountered, their 'conviction' or 'convincement', led to distinctive forms of witness. Quakers refused to remove their hats to anyone except when in prayer. They listed days and months by number, not (pagan) names, thus Sunday was first day. They started to wear plain clothes and eschew anything considered superfluous or vain, such as titles or gravestones. They opposed outward war while conducting their own spiritual warfare, the Lamb's War, to bring about an intimacy between heaven and earth on a global scale. They refused to pay tithes to the 'hireling ministry' or for the upkeep of 'steeple houses', and refused to swear oaths after the injunction in the Gospel of Matthew to swear not at all.

The 1650s, with the lack of censorship in England, provided a fertile seedbed for the Quaker movement, but the 1660s brought heavy persecution. From the 1680s, particularly with the invitation to create a Holy Experiment in Quaker Pennsylvania, Quakers emigrated en masse. Quakers became a transatlantic community, joined together by their testimony and also by marriage ties in a group that only allowed marriage to another of the true church. This transatlantic community went through various changes in the 140 years following the establishment of Pennsylvania. Most notable was a 'Quaker reformation' led by John Woolman and others, that created a 'great turning' in the 1750s on the issue of slavery. Many Quakers had been slaveholders in the 1750s and before, but Elizabeth Cazden, among others of our contributors, traces how slavery became a disownable offence in the Philadelphia Yearly Meeting by 1774, and other Yearly Meetings in America shortly thereafter. She also discusses the broader effects that this had on Quakers—for example, the significant amount of anti-slavery work that some Quakers did, but also the strong persistence of racial prejudice in many Quaker quarters, including exclusion of blacks from most American Quaker schools until the mid-twentieth century.

Quakers in America underwent a series of schisms in the nineteenth century, creating in the twentieth century three distinct traditions of Evangelical (in two main groupings), Conservative, and Liberal. In general, as Thomas Hamm has demonstrated so thoroughly in his work, the nineteenth century was a time of great change among all varieties of Quakers. Some changes occurred similarly in all the branches, although at a different pace in each, including diminishing use of plain speech and plain dress and a willingness to read novels and plays and not to see such activity as sinful. Influential in these changes was an 1858 contest in Britain; a prize was offered for the best essay on the causes of decline among Friends. The winning essay by John Stephenson Rowntree decried such Quaker attributes as the over-emphasis on silence, the disuse of the Bible in worship, the downplaying of intellectual qualifications, and the limitations of the travelling ministry, the deficiencies in higher education among Quakers, Puritanical attitudes towards music and the arts, and disownment of those who 'married out of meeting' (Russell 1979, 390). All branches of Friends in America and in Britain instituted reforms in many or all of these areas over succeeding decades. Elizabeth A. O'Donnell explains the great growth of higher education among Quakers from 1830 to 1960; the institution of postgraduate centres of study at Woodbrooke in Birmingham, UK in 1903 and at Earlham School of Religion in Richmond, Indiana, US in 1960 being only two examples.

Of great importance for the future development of Friends was the Friends' international mission movement, explored by Jacci Welling. This nineteenth-century missionary initiative began in earnest in Britain in the 1860s and spread rapidly to America. Missionary movements were undertaken in Asia, Africa, and Latin America. Not all missionary work bore equal fruit, but missions to Kenya and elsewhere in East Africa, beginning in 1903, and missions to Guatemala, Bolivia, and elsewhere in Latin America, beginning about the same time, have borne considerable fruit. As a consequence of the liberalization of British Quakerism, beginning at the Manchester Conference in 1895, British Friends gradually withdrew from international mission work over the next two generations, but many Evangelical Friends in America have maintained a strong missionary emphasis. To a large degree because of these missions, most Friends in the world today are Evangelicals of various kinds. Generally, they have adopted a pastoral system (which appeared among Quakers in America during revivals in the 1870s and 1880s), and their worship includes music, vocal prayer, a sermon, etc. Thus, the successes of missions to Africa, Asia, and Central and South America have given new geographical emphases to world Quakerism. Today, of 400,000 Quakers worldwide, one third are in Kenya, with a further 12 per cent in Bolivia, and silent worship is now a minority practice. The range of styles and types of Quakerism worldwide is huge. There are small isolated groups of primitive Quakers meeting in silence, still preferring plain dress and speech, Conservative Quakers with their own Yearly Meetings, Liberal Quakers whose beliefs extend beyond Christianity to other forms of theism and non-theism, Quaker Meetings with pastors, Friends churches whose emphasis is still predominantly Quaker, and others that have chosen to place community witness before sectarian legacy and identity, and Quaker mega-churches with thousands of participants and large pastoral teams. There are those who emphasize behaviour and witness as the basis of Quakerism, those who define their Quakerism in terms of belief. There are those for whom communion and baptism is purely inward, those for whom the outward elements can be a helpful addition to worship. Buildings vary from rented rooms in community centres to large purpose-built sanctuaries with bell towers. As such, while this book offers an introduction to one religious group, that group is a very broad church and the history and theology of the Quakers raises important insights into the study of religion and society as a whole.

Quaker Historiography

Modern Quaker Studies began with Robert Barclay of Reigate and his unfinished, voluminous 1876 publication *The Inner Life of the Religious Societies of the Commonwealth*. Barclay was an Evangelical Friend who used his own reading of the early history to justify the form of Quakerism he most preferred. However, his history was also to prove seminal for Friends of other persuasions, as they came to review the past. Liberal Friends such as J. W. Rowntree believed an understanding of Quaker history was the key to a (Liberal) Quaker revival. When Rufus Jones (1909, 1911, 1914, 1921) and W. C. Braithwaite (1912, 1919) took on Rowntree's vision for a comprehensive and complete history of

Quakerism as a means to this revival, the Victorian Barclay was the author they used as both a foundation and a departure point for their own interpretation of the essence of Quakerism. Rather than posit Quakerism as essentially evangelical, with George Fox and the early missionaries as proto-pastors, as Barclay had, Jones in particular presented Quakers as essentially, and foremost, mystical.

The work of Braithwaite and Jones formed the seven-volume Rowntree series published between 1912 and 1927. Alice Southern (2011) has explored the agenda behind the Rowntree series—that one aim of these ambitious works was to prepare the way for a liberal transformation in the Religious Society of Friends, while showing how such interpretations might be grounded in an affirmation of early Quaker tradition.

Jones's view has since been much challenged and Melvin Endy summarizes concisely the competing interpretations of Quakerism in his 1981 article in *Quaker History*, between Jones's view that located the beginnings of Quakerism with Christian mystics and the view espoused in various ways by Geoffrey Nuttall (1946), Hugh Barbour (1964), and Frederick Tolles (1960) that Quakerism can be best understood as a wing of Puritanism. This view of a Quakerism rooted in Puritanism, the 'Puritan School', gathered pace in the middle of the twentieth century.

A third strand of interpretation emerged in the mid-twentieth century when Lewis Benson (1944, 1966) argued that to see Friends in terms of mysticism alone was insufficient. Quakerism, Benson said, was about the inward experience of the Light of Christ *and* the universal mission that was led and fed by this experience. His prophetic Christianity was about a dialogical relationship with God, of hearing and obeying, and he framed Quakerism within a more biblical sense of history than had Jones.

In the 1970s and 1980s, in counterpoint to previous 'insider' accounts of Quakerism, Christopher Hill (*The World Turned Upside Down,* 1972) and Barry Reay (*The Quakers and the English Revolution,* 1985) presented Quakerism from a Marxist or materialist perspective. Hill and Reay made the question of the connection between Quakers and the radical Civil War sects a much more vital one. Certainly Rufus Jones and others had discussed the Civil War sects prior to Hill, but Hill made that connection come alive. Reay used hard data and their discussion was presented in an accessible way. Equally materialist was Larry Ingle's 1994 biography of George Fox, emphasizing the social and historical rather than the theological.

Richard Bailey (*New Light on George Fox,* 1992) established Fox's concept of 'celestial flesh' as a way of describing divine in-dwelling. Bailey also offered a theory of the divinization of Fox in the 1650s and 1660s and the de-divinization of Fox after 1670. Fox was brought down to the level of an Apostle, other Friends to the state of believers. His work has been partnered by that of Michele Tarter who has looked in particular at the experience of early women Friends. In this, she is part of a movement that has rightly placed the experience of women at the heart of Quaker history. Other scholars to focus on women's experience include Catie Gill (2005), Elaine Hobby, Sandra Holton (2007), Bonnelyn Kunze (1994), Rebecca Larson (1999), Phyllis Mack (1989, 1992), Elizabeth O'Donnell (1999), Sally Bruyneel (2010), and Christine Trevett (1991, 2000).

If Jones, the 'Puritan school', and Benson were the key Quaker theorists of the first half of the twentieth century, Douglas Gwyn (*Apocalypse of the Word*, 1986 and others) emerged in the second half of the century as the fourth main Quaker theorist of Quakerism. His doctoral work on 'apocalyptic' and his complementary and contrasting approaches to understanding the nature of Quakerism have been seminal to most of the more recent scholarship. Gwyn alone, though with later agreement of Dandelion (*Liturgies of Quakerism*, 2005), and Moore (*The Light in their Consciences*, 2000), argues that early Friends until 1666 felt they were living out a 'realizing eschatology', i.e., an unfolding endtime. In all his work, Gwyn is similarly trying to understand how Friends compensated for the defeat of the 'Lamb's War' and how they sustained themselves following 1666.

Not all scholars agree with this view of early Friends and few place the same emphasis on eschatology that Gwyn does. Carole Dale Spencer (2007) is one of those who wishes to downplay the central emphasis Gwyn gives to eschatology and the apocalyptic in the thought of early Friends. For her, this is only one element of seven, which characterized early Friends' theology, a collective group of characteristics which she sees as unmistakable 'Holiness' in character. Spencer argues that early Friends preached a radical Protestant holiness that in time was reproduced in Methodism. Spencer claims that this Holiness theology is a thread that runs throughout Quaker history. Her work rewrites the family tree of Quakerism as she places the Quaker Holiness Revival of the 1870s as central in the genealogy of the Quaker traditions.

A nascent form of Liberal Quaker theology, with many complexities and occasional contradictions, has been discerned in the work of William Penn by Melvin Endy, Jr. (1973) and Hugh Barbour (1991), among others.

Astute close readings of seventeenth-century texts have yielded large dividends in two recent works. Psychological sensitivity and structuralist readings of primary texts play a large part in Hilary Hinds' (2011) examination of Fox and early Quaker culture. Hinds mines thoroughly early Quaker theology and rhetoric for its broader cultural and discursive significance, e.g., exploring the various ways that early Quakers made their lives preach. Playing off works such as Gwyn and Dandelion (2005), Hinds argues that the careful chronologizing of works such as Fox's *Journal* actually plays an important part in emphasizing the place of the unfolding endtime in early Quaker thought, since it highlighted the intention of early Quakers to witness to the work of the indwelling Christ through their own lives, as they were living them. Using texts of 79 Quaker impromptu sermons (or 'messages') from the seventeenth century, Michael P. Graves (2009) explores the role of memory and what he calls 'metaphor clusters' in making lengthy, compelling extemporaneous sermonizing possible.

In later eras, Quaker publishing has been immense. The role of Quakers in anti-slavery movments has been an especially productive area. John Woolman's life and thought has been probed sensitively by Michael Birkel (2003); Mike Heller (2003); and Geoffrey Plank (2012), and his coworker Anthony Benezet has received welcome attention in Maurice Jackson (2009). Lucretia Mott has received attention from Carol Faulkner (2011); Beverly Palmer et al (2002); and Dana Greene (1980), among others.

Conservative Quaker anti-slavery, in the person of Pennsylvania Quaker Benjamin Coates, is illuminated in a collection of letters edited by Emma J. Lapsansky and Margaret Hope Bacon (2005). A more radical, utopian side of Quaker anti-slavery is thoroughly explored in Thomas D. Hamm's *God's Government Begun* (1995). Issues of American Quakers and racial justice have been further explored in a new narrative treatment from Donna McDaniel and Vanessa Julye (2009); in Thomas Kennedy's study (2009) of the most important Quaker project to issue from the Reconstruction period, Arkansas' Southland College; and in a collection of primary source documents edited by Harold D. Weaver, Jr., Paul Kriese, and Stephen W. Angell (2011). This is but a small sampling of the new publications in the areas of Quaker race, slavery, and anti-slavery. While there is room for much more work, Quaker relationships with aboriginal peoples in parts of the present or former British Empire such as Australia and the United States have occasioned both scholarly works and other works of critical reflection in recent decades (Kelsey 1917; Hixson 1981; Milner 1982; Carter 1989; Swatzler 2000; Brindle 2000; Pencak and Richter 2004; Walker 2006).

New editions of the *Journal* and letters of Elias Hicks (Paul Buckley 2009, 2011) and of Allen Jay (2010) have provided new light on life and thought on both sides of American Quakers' Hicksite–Orthodox divide. More work is needed, though, especially in examining the development of Evangelical Friends. Arthur O. Roberts, leading evangelical Quaker historian and theologian, starts some of that work with his chapter in this volume and forthcoming work by Timothy Burdick looks at shifts in evangelical identity amongst Friends in Oregon (Burdick, forthcoming). Thomas Kennedy's *British Quakerism, 1860–1920* (2001) provides what is perhaps the definitive treatment of the British Quaker generational transformation from an evangelical Orthodox into a Liberal Quaker community.

The theology of Rufus Jones and his ecumenical leadership continues to receive its due share of attention. The searching critiques of Jones by late-twentieth-century Quaker theologians are concisely summarized by Wilmer Cooper (2005) and Endy (1981). But also see new portrayals of Jones's mysticism (Matthew Hedstrom 2003); of his legacy in the continued witness of Douglas Steere, Thomas Kelly, Howard Brinton, and Howard Thurman (Leigh Schmidt 2005; Anthony Manousos 2010; Glenn Hinson 1998; Stephen W. Angell 2009); and of his contribution to reimagining Protestant missions (Angell 2001). David L. Johns (2011) collects the most significant work of important twentieth-century British Quaker theologian Maurice Creasey, into book format for the first time.

Ron Stansell's *Missions by the Spirit* (2009) offers invaluable reflections on the life and contributions of Quaker missionary pioneers in East Africa (Arthur Chilson), Guatemala (R. Esther Smith), India (Everett Cattell), and Bolivia (Jack Wilcutts). Not all individual Quaker mission fields have received suitable scholarly attention, but one that has received illuminating examination has been the Quaker missions that brought about what is the largest national Quaker set of churches as of the publication of this Handbook—the Quaker churches in Kenya. See especially Levinus Painter (1966); Ane Marie Bak Rasmussen (1995); Esther Mombo (1998); Herbert and Beatrice Kimball (2002); Stephen Angell (2006c); and Benson Khamasi Amugamwa (2008).

Varieties of twentieth- and twenty-first-century Quaker engagements with the Bible can be seen in the prolific scholarly contributions of Paul Anderson (e.g., 2000) and Henry Cadbury (e.g., 1953); in Michael Birkel's *Engaging Scripture* (2005); and in an edited volume by Paul Buckley and Stephen Angell (2006), among others. In the present generation, works of Quaker theology and spirituality with creative (and, Quakers would say, Spirit-led) attention to present-day realities and with depth in classical Quaker traditions continue to appear, e.g., Wilmer Cooper (2001), John Punshon (2001), Michael Birkel (2004), Lloyd Lee Wilson (1993, 2005), and Margery Post Abbott (2010). Spiritual classics such as Thomas Kelly's *Testament of Devotion* (1941) and Richard Foster's *Celebration of Discipline* and other works (Foster, 1978, 1981, 1985, 2011) continue to bring Quaker spiritual insights to a wider public.

EDITORIAL CHOICES

Quaker studies is a vibrant field, relating very much to the wider study of Christianity, theology, and social history. The two postgraduate centres at Earlham School of Religion in Richmond, Indiana in the US and at the University of Birmingham in the UK are constantly producing new thinking and writing, and increasing numbers of students and academics are interested in the contribution Quakerism has made to the history of religion.

This led to one of the challenges of editing this volume: how much cutting-edge thinking to include? For example, some traditional categorizations such as Quietism representing eighteenth-century Quakerism are currently in the process of being questioned. The challenge for us was whether to omit the term 'Quietism' as the label for that period or to include it with caveats. At the time of writing, the research awaits completion, and testing by the academic community and so we have taken the latter route. However, it highlights the fact that in a vibrant academic field, even traditional ways of analysing the past are open to constant reinterpretation. We are not claiming the final word. We hope to have been faithful to the best of published scholarship.

The chapters themselves are not always as heavily referenced as a journal article would be, but each chapter concludes with a list of suggested further reading and together with the references cited are compiled into a healthy bibliography. Where possible we have used accessible and in-print editions to help those interested in accessing the primary material.

We have also, of course, needed to assert consistency over the various chapters. You will find different authors emphasizing different scholarly accounts, for example, between Gwyn and Spencer, but we have been firm on matters of style and phraseology. The term 'Inner Light' came into the Quaker vocabulary in the latter part of the nineteenth century and is today used interchangeably with 'Inward Light' by modern Friends. Some have argued it has changed the meaning of the term, shifting the location of the Divine from outward from which Light comes inwardly to an inner deity within or to a change of consciousness. However, 'Inner Light' is also mistakenly used to refer back to early Friends who never used the term. They used 'the Light Within' or 'Inward Light'. Except where explicitly referring to the 'Inner Light' as an idea, we asked authors to use 'the Light Within' to accurately express this key Quaker concept.

We have struggled to include as much material as we would like on Quakerism in the global south in spite of the distribution of Quakerism. This is partly due to the resource gap between north and south, and the lack of good academic research on this new location of majority Quakerism. While we have deliberately tried to emphasize the contribution and experience of women Friends, this is still largely an unwritten story. The same is true of Black Friends, generally.

The Pattern of the Book

This Handbook aims for a broad, thorough, in-depth treatment of the Quaker tradition in all chronological periods, with coverage of Quaker meetings and churches in all parts of the world, and including both men and women. All of the chapter authors were informed from the outset of the editors' wish for both breadth and depth in coverage, and have endeavoured to craft their chapters accordingly.

Recognizing the multidimensional nature of our subject matter, this book consists of 37 individual chapters, for which the editors have devised four main headings: the History of Quakerism; Quaker Theology and Spirituality; Quaker Witness; and Quaker Expression. We invite the readers to dive into the sections and chapters of most interest to them, but also to recognize the complex and holistic nature of the society, church, and movement before them. To the extent that one can sample from all of these main sections, or even read the whole book through, the reader will gain a fuller appreciation of Quakerism in all of its historical and present-day dimensions.

The first eight chapters present the history of global Quakerism from 1647 to 2010. This is initially presented chronologically. Rosemary Moore explores the first period of Quakerism, and Richard C. Allen the years following 1660 to the end of the seventeenth century. Robynne Rogers Healey looks at the eighteenth century, and Thomas Hamm the bulk of the nineteenth, and the various separations that occurred then. After the separations in the nineteenth century, the section ends with an overview of the four main traditions from 1887 to 2010. J. William Frost explores Modernist/Liberal Friends, and Lloyd Lee Wilson the Conservative Tradition. Gregory Hinshaw examines the development of Five Years Meeting into Friends United Meeting, and Arthur Roberts the tradition of Evangelical Quakerism, today represented by Evangelical Friends Church International.

The next nine chapters explore various topics related to Quaker theology and spirituality. After Carole Dale Spencer sets out the theological contexts of the varieties of Quakerism, Stephen Angell examines the key theological issues surrounding 'God, Christ, and the Light', and Nikki Coffey Tousley explores the topics of 'Sin, Convincement,

Purity, and Perfection'. Howard R. Macy unpacks the complex issues around Quakers' relationship to the Scriptures, and Douglas Gwyn looks at the issues of 'Eschatology and time', so key to Quaker origins, and which have gone through various shifts in understanding since. Gerry Guiton illuminates theological aspects of Quaker engagement with politics, while Mary Van Vleck Garman alerts us to the gendered dimension of Quaker spirituality with her chapter on 'Quaker Women's Spirituality'. Michael Birkel then explores some of the practical dimensions of Quaker spirituality in his chapter on 'Leadings and Discernments'. David Johns caps this section with an explanation of Quakers' diverse forms of worship, and interrelates that activity to Quakers' unusual understanding, within the Christian context, to sacraments as 'inward' rather than 'outward'.

The third section incorporates fourteen chapters on Quaker witness. The variety of the witness covered will be disclosed by a glance at the contents: ministry and preaching by Michael Graves; travelling ministry written by Sylvia Stevens; missions from Jacci Welling; ecumenism and interfaith by Janet Scott; plainness and simplicity by Emma Lapsansky; slavery, anti-slavery, and race by Elizabeth Cazden; peace and war relief by Lonnie Valentine; penal reform by Mike Nellis and Maureen Waugh, asylum reform by Charles L. Cherry; education by Elizabeth O'Donnell; business and philanthropy by Mark Freeman; the family by Edwina Newman; sexuality by Petra L. Doan and Elizabeth P. Kamphausen; and youth and young adults by Max L. Carter and Simon Best. Quaker faith and practice is often understood and organized around testimony, witness collectively observed by the meetings as a whole. Several of the most widely observed aspects of testimony, including peace, equality, and simplicity (or plainness), receive their fullest examination in this section.

Our final section, on Quaker expression, includes six diverse chapters. From their earliest days, Quakers were known as 'Publishers of Truth', and the meaning of this expression, in its most literal sense, is explored by Betty Hagglund in her chapter 'Quakers and Print Culture'. Quakers' evolving aesthetics around their meeting houses and churches, and their evolving interactions with art from early prohibitions or discouragements to a cautious or enthusiastic embrace, is explored in Roger Homan's chapter. Philosophical dimensions of Quaker expression are developed in Jeff Dudiak and Laura Rediehl's chapter on philosophy and truth, and in Jackie Leach Scully's chapter on ethics, and Geoffrey Cantor shows us how Quakers have been involved in scientific discovery from shortly after their founding. Finally, Margery Post Abbott invites us to consider what directions the Quakers' future may take. All these chapters have been written by the leading scholars, supported by an equally able collection of chapter consultants (many of whom were also authors) who checked for missing detail and emphasis, given our desire to be global in our coverage. We are very grateful to everyone who contributed with such excitement and enthusiasm. We are also very grateful to Steve Olshewsky for his help with compiling the bibliography, Marylin Inglis for her copy-editing, and colleagues at Oxford University Press for their continued support.

This book offers *the* reference guide to the history and theology of Quakerism worldwide in all its traditions as well as pertinent overviews of how Quakers have responded, for example, in the fields of politics, business, science, education, art, and aesthetics. We hope you will find it as rewarding to read as we have found it to edit.

PART I

HISTORY OF QUAKERISM

CHAPTER 1

....

SEVENTEENTH-CENTURY CONTEXT AND QUAKER BEGINNINGS

....

ROSEMARY MOORE

THE BACKGROUND

....

THE Quakers were one of several religious groups that appeared in England during the civil wars of the mid-seventeenth century. By this time, there was a long history of religious protest in England, since the Elizabethan church settlement was a compromise that had left many people dissatisfied. Some people would have preferred a Presbyterian form, as adopted by Reformed churches of continental Europe, but meanwhile they were willing to live within the existing arrangements, and they bided their time. Others, believing in a congregational form of church government and despairing of a true reformation in England, emigrated to the Netherlands towards the end of the sixteenth century (and the end of Elizabeth I's reign), and set up their own churches. Here some of the British exiles met with Mennonites and became converted to the practice of believers' baptism. Some of these converts also acquired the theology known as 'Arminianism', which taught that salvation was possible for all people.

During the reign of James I, conditions in England eased and these exiles began to return, so that by the 1640s there were a number of self-governing 'separated' or 'gathered' churches. Those who continued to practise infant baptism were known as Independents and were the forerunners of the Congregationalists. Baptists, a varied group, considered that there was no warrant for infant baptism in the Bible. Some retained the Calvinist belief in salvation for a limited number of elect people and became known as Particular Baptists. Others, who believed in the general possibility of salvation, were known as 'General Baptists'. There were also Seventh Day Baptists, who observed Saturday, the Jewish Sabbath, rather than Sunday.

The victory of Parliament in the civil wars at first resulted in the ascendancy of the Presbyterian interest. The Church of England hierarchy was abolished and the regular parish ministry was reorganized on Reformed principles. Nevertheless, there was much local variation; there were no hard and fast divisions between religious groups and denominations in the modern sense did not form until later in the century. Many of the army officers supported the Independents and a number of their ministers were appointed to parish churches. Some Baptists had no objection to a parish ministry, despite their belief in believers' baptism and their emphasis on a spiritual, Bible-based religion, and so some Baptists also became parish ministers. In consequence, parish ministers might be Presbyterian, Anglican, Independent, or Baptist in their religious inclination, and the Book of Common Prayer continued in use in some areas.

The 'separated' churches continued alongside the parish ministry, and varied from congregations with trained ministers to small 'do-it-yourself' bodies led by local men or even by women. Some of them were 'Seekers', people who thought that no true church existed at that time, and looked back to recreate the New Testament church, or forwards to the coming Kingdom of Christ. In addition, besides Protestant churches, the Roman Catholic Church had never been entirely suppressed, and in the north of England especially, it was still strong.

New ideas about religion had been percolating into England from continental Europe for some time. During the twenty years before the civil wars, some theological books teaching spiritual religion and direct contact with God and emphasizing the divine rather than the human Christ, were translated into English. While direct influence is impossible to trace, these ideas formed part of the background against which radical sects, including Quakers, developed during the free-thinking period of the 1640s and 1650s; one result of the civil wars was the abolition of controls on speech, printing, and ways of worship.

Sects and informal religious groupings could now proliferate and disseminate their ideas in quantities of cheap pamphlets. Some introduced ideas of social equality into their teaching of the coming Kingdom of the Lord, that unlearned people could be called to preach the gospel, and even that, 'All the earth is the Saints, and there ought to be a community of goods, and the Saints should share in the Lands and Estates of gentlemen, and rich men' (Edwards 1646, 1/34; Pagitt 1645). Levellers, who advocated major political, economic, and religious reform, were influential in the army, and were finally suppressed by Cromwell. The Fifth Monarchists looked for the coming of the Kingdom of God on earth, and were willing to give it a helping hand, by revolutionary uprising if necessary. In 1649 came the Digger or 'True Leveller' movement, led by Gerrard Winstanley (1609–76), who founded several communistic Digger communities, which rapidly fell foul of landowners and were put down. The Ranters arrived a little later. These were individuals rather than an organized group, who thought that if they were living in the Spirit of God then it was actually impossible to sin, and that therefore they could perform actions with impunity, particularly in relation to sexual behaviour, that were normally considered sinful. Last, in 1652, came the Muggletonians, led by John Reeve and Ludovic Muggleton, who considered themselves to be the two witnesses of

Revelation chapter 11. Besides the sects and groups, there were a number of charismatic individuals with their own followings.

THE ORIGIN OF QUAKERS

Into the midst of these turbulent times Quakerism was born. There are no contemporary records of Quaker beginnings. The main source of information comes from the early pages of George Fox's *Journal* (Fox 1952), and these are missing from the manuscript, which underlies the published version and were in any case composed years after the events they describe.

It is clear that the leading personality among the early Quakers was George Fox, born at Fenny Drayton (then known as Drayton-in-the-clay) in Leicestershire in 1624. He had been a serious child, and at the age of nineteen he left home and travelled the country, an unhappy young man seeking a true religious faith. During this time he visited London, where he had a Baptist uncle; he must have heard about contemporary matters of dispute while there and may have taken part in discussions.

While back in the Midlands, perhaps during 1646 or early 1647, Fox met with 'tender people' and among them was a 'very tender woman' named Elizabeth Hooton (Fox 1952, 9), a former Baptist. Religious meetings were held at her house, and her son Oliver described what happened:

> My mother joined with the Baptists but...finding they were not upright hearted to the Lord...she...left them, who in those parts soon all were scattered and gone. About the year 1647 George Fox came amongst them in Nottinghamshire and then after he went into Leicestershire where the mighty power of the Lord was manifest, that startled their former separate meeting and some came no more, but most, that were convinced of the truth, stood, of which my mother was one, and embraced it'. (Braithwaite W.C. mss 'Children of Light' papers)

'Startled' was a strong word in those days, and the 'mighty power of the Lord' was the 'quaking' that gave Quakers their name. Early Quakers were charismatics. Elizabeth Hooton was the first of the two powerful women who influenced the life of George Fox. She devoted the rest of her life to the Quaker ministry and twice visited New England where she was whipped as a vagabond. She died in Jamaica in 1672, during a third visit to America.

Then came George Fox's breakthrough experience, as he recorded later in his *Journal*:

> But as I had forsaken the priests, so I left the separate preachers also, and those called the most experienced people; for I saw there was none there that could speak to my condition. And when all my hopes in them and in all men were gone, so that I had nothing outwardly to help me, nor could tell what to do, then, Oh then, I heard a voice which said, 'There is one, even Christ Jesus, that can speak to thy condition', and when I heard it my heart did leap for joy. (Fox 1952, 11)

Fox's *Journal* shows that in the years 1647–50 there were increasing numbers of Friends, as he called them, in the English East Midlands. These were religious groups that felt no need for any appointed ministers or pre-arranged services. Instead, they were led in their meetings by what they understood as the power of God, and accepted this power as the ultimate authority rather than the Bible as all mainstream Protestant Christians believed. Presently the Friends, led by Fox, became militant. One day in 1649, coming into Nottingham to attend a meeting, Fox wrote that he 'looked upon the town, and the great steeplehouse struck at my life when I espied it, a great idol and idolatrous temple'. So before the Quaker meeting was over, Fox left and went into the 'steeplehouse'. The sermon was about to start and the preacher told the congregation that the Scriptures were 'the touchstone and judge by which they were to try all doctrines'. Then, Fox wrote, 'the Lord's power was so strong upon me, that I could not hold, but was made to cry out and say, "Oh, no, it is not the Scriptures" and was commanded to tell them God did not dwell in temples made with hands'. Fox was arrested and imprisoned for 'a pretty long time' (Fox 1952, 39–40, 43). In the years following, many of the Friends acted in similar ways and were willing to suffer for it.

After his release from Nottingham gaol Fox moved to Derby, where in the autumn of 1650 he and his companion were charged with blasphemy for claiming to be united with Christ, and again imprisoned. According to Fox's 1659 work, *The Great Mistery of the Great Whore*, the nickname 'Quaker' dates from this year, being first applied by the justice who tried him (Fox 1990 iii, 109; Fox 1952, 4). The term stuck, so that in their books the Friends usually identified themselves as 'those in scorn called Quakers'. This is the first episode in Quaker history for which independent contemporary evidence exists, for the 'mittimus', or charge sheet, was preserved and afterwards published (Anon. 1654, 55; Fox 1995, 52). Elizabeth Hooton was also imprisoned in Derby; a letter she wrote to the mayor of Derby protesting against her treatment has survived (Hooton 1650).

Fox was now becoming known beyond his immediate district. He had already been in correspondence with Richard Farnworth from Tickhill in Yorkshire, who later became one of his chief assistants, and on his release from Derby gaol Fox moved north to the area around Doncaster. Here there were already religious groups with similar ideas to Quakers, opposed to the paid professional ministry and the regular worship of the parish churches. The local leader was well-to-do yeoman Thomas Aldam, but the outstanding personality was Richard Farnworth, probably then aged twenty-three (Hoare 2004, 202–5). He wrote later that he could find no satisfaction in formal religion, but came to see, 'by the breaking forth of the light of God in my spirit, that the steeplehouse was no church . . . that the Church of Christ was made all of living stones' (Farnworth 1654, 3, 8). He became a prolific author of Quaker pamphlets.

A convert from a neighbouring Independent church was even more important in Quaker history. James Nayler (1616–60) had previously served eight years in the army as a quartermaster with John Lambert (1619–84), the most radical of the Parliamentary generals. Naylor was about 35 years old and living at home on his farm when he met Fox. In the early days of Quakerism, Naylor proved to be the Friends' most effective preacher and debater and their most capable theologian. Many contemporaries considered him to be the equal of Fox as a Quaker leader.

THE 'GREAT PEOPLE TO BE GATHERED'

From the spring of 1652 the South Yorkshire groups joined Fox in active travel and preaching, including disrupting church services. Presumably it was the teaching and example of Fox and Hooton (who had joined Fox in Yorkshire), coupled with the quaking or visible 'power of the Lord', that inspired these previously law-abiding people to such activity. Thomas Aldam, Elizabeth Hooton, and several others were imprisoned in York Castle, where they wrote a powerful attack on the parish ministry, *False Prophets and False Teachers*, possibly the earliest Quaker pamphlet, published in late 1652 or early 1653.

Meanwhile, in the early summer of 1652, Fox, Nayler, and Farnworth set out westwards. Their route was not random—Fox had planned the journey so that he might meet people likely to be sympathetic to his opposition to the parish ministry. This was a time of much economic distress, exacerbated by the wars, and the church tax or 'tithe', originally intended for the support of parish ministers but now often in the hands of lay 'impropriators', was a cause of much hardship. Fox included in his journey an area where a tithe strike was beginning, and an early pamphlet gives a flavour of his message:

> They are such priests as take Tythes…they that will not give them they sue at the law…beside the Tithe-corn [they] take ten shillings for preaching Funeral Sermons…and Easter Reckonings and Midsummer dues and money for churching of women, and thus by every device get money and burthen poor people that labour very hard, and can scarce get food and raiment. (Fox 1653, 3–4)

On his way westwards Fox was 'moved of the Lord' to climb a great hill, thought to be Pendle Hill, where he 'was moved to sound [seek to ascertain] the will of the Lord' and the Lord let him see 'in what places he had a great people to be gathered'. Great meetings followed. One Sunday in June, Fox came to an old chapel on Firbank Fell between Sedbergh and Kendal, where there was a big meeting of local Separatist congregations. In the afternoon Fox preached from a rock (nowadays marked with a plaque) to over a thousand people (Fox 1952, 103–9). Two local Separatist preachers, Francis Howgill and John Audland, heard Fox on this occasion and they joined with Fox, probably bringing their congregations with them.

Continuing westwards into Lancashire, Fox and his companions were invited to stay at Swarthmoor Hall near Ulverston, a household accustomed to welcoming travelling preachers. The mistress of the house, Margaret Fell, was the wife of wealthy landowner Thomas Fell, a Judge of Assize and Member of Parliament. Thomas Fell never became one of the Friends but gave them support and protection, allowing them to use Swarthmoor Hall as their base. His wife Margaret, however, was 'convinced'. She was a woman of great ability, and acted as the Quakers' chief administrator, raising funds, disciplining the erring, and storing the voluminous Quaker correspondence. Hundreds of these manuscripts have survived and are available to the modern researcher. She was also the author of several pamphlets and a great correspondent. A collected edition of her letters is available (Glines 2003). After the death of her husband in 1658 she took an even more active part in the Quaker movement, and ten years later she married George Fox.

Most of those who became the first leaders of Quakerism had joined the movement by the end of 1652. During 1653 the Quakers spread across northern England and into Scotland. There were great charismatic meetings, by no means entirely silent, for there could be 'singing in the spirit'. Some Quakers 'walked naked as a sign' or went through the streets in sackcloth and ashes to demonstrate the bankruptcy of society and the coming wrath of God. Naturally, there was fierce opposition from parish clergy. Fox was twice charged with blasphemy, but with assistance from Judge Fell and other powerful people the charges did not proceed. Some Parliamentary supporters among the gentry thought that Quakers could be a useful counterweight to Catholic Royalists. James Nayler was also tried for blasphemy, but succeeded in converting his judge, Anthony Pearson.

Ten years later Francis Howgill (1618–69), one of two Friends charged with the mission to London, recalled those heady early days:

> The Lord of heaven and earth we found to be near at hand, and as we waited upon him in pure silence, our minds out of all things, his dreadful power and glorious Majesty appeared in our assemblies, when there was no language, tongue, nor speech from any creature, and the Kingdom of heaven did gather and catch us all as in a net, and his heavenly power did draw many hundreds to land . . . in so much that we often said to one another with great joy of heart, What, is the Kingdom of God come to be with men? (Howgill 1662, 5)

Other people, however, saw the Quaker activities quite differently. One book described how people 'all over Yorkshire' were being drawn into 'absurd and unreasonable . . . principles and practices; by running up and down the country to act in quakings and trances, and drawing many people after them'. 'Wandering ministers' left their homes to preach and cry in the streets; 'everyone that will, imagining he is called to it'. 'Men, women, boys and girls, may all turn into prophets by [according to] Quakers, and all other preachers and ministers are but deluded and without calling.' They looked for 'extraordinary raptures, inspirations, miracles', and they promised 'the casting out of Devils' (Anon. 1653a, 39, 44). This was the first of a long series of anti-Quaker works, and Quaker writers, in the early days notably Farnworth and Nayler, published many rebuttals.

THE SPREAD OF QUAKERISM FROM 1654

During 1654–5, Quakers spread over much of the rest of England and Wales, in what must have been a carefully planned missionary enterprise, though Fox, in his *Journal*, said only that the Lord had raised the ministers up (Fox 1952, 174). Travelling ministers required immediate inspiration or 'drawings' for their work, but this did not prevent Fox from directing them, for a number of surviving letters refer to his instructions. The preachers went out in pairs, two men or two women together, usually an older person with a younger, the strongest teams going to the main cities of London, Bristol, and Norwich.

At this point one needs to consider the position of the women preachers. Certainly, women preachers and religious leaders were by no means unknown in other religious groups, but these were exceptions and generally, women did not preach or pray publicly, and still less did they travel the country as missionaries. Among Quakers, women were considered the spiritual equals of men, taking literally the text from the Acts of the Apostles 2:17, which is itself a quotation from an Old Testament prophet, 'Your sons and your daughters shall prophesy'. It is likely that this attitude arose from the personal experience of George Fox and the position of Elizabeth Hooton in the early days of Quakerism is significant. Margaret Fell was even more influential, and while she herself was not a preacher, surviving correspondence shows that she thoroughly approved of the women who did travel 'in the ministry', and she also published a pamphlet on the subject, *Womens Speaking Justified, Proved and Allowed by the Scriptures*. Modern reprints are available (e.g. Fell 1989). But equality of women applied only to spiritual matters, and some Quaker meetings proved reluctant to accept women preachers (Cotton 1656, Caton 1658). In domestic matters, Quaker pamphlets show that women would normally be subservient to their husbands (Farnworth 1653, 25; Burrough 1657a).

So the travelling preachers went on their way. Sometimes they were allowed to deliver their message in the parish churches after the minister had finished his sermon. This was permissible until 1655, when new regulations aimed at Quaker preachers restricted the practice. Sometimes they were welcomed by separated congregations, especially by Baptists, and in other places they preached in the open air. Sometimes their reception was hostile, and a number of travelling preachers were put in the stocks and whipped as vagrants or for causing a public disturbance. Women ministers were especially liable to receive such treatment. If taken to court, the men refused to remove their hats to magistrates. Quakers were aware that they might have to suffer for their faith and many did so willingly. Seventeenth-century prisons were very unhealthy places, and the first of a number to die in prison was James Parnell, aged 19, in Colchester in 1656. As more people became Quakers, refusal to pay tithes, leading to distraint of goods, was the most common cause of 'sufferings'. Quakers published many accounts of such troubles, partly to gain sympathy and partly in the hopes of influencing public policy.

Overall, the new movement was stunningly successful, so that by the end of 1654 there were Quaker groups in many areas. The leaders of the London mission, Francis Howgill (1618–69) and a young man named Edward Burrough, found it worthwhile to hire a room that held a thousand people, no doubt squashed and standing, in the Bull and Mouth, an inn near St Paul's Cathedral. The site of this inn is now marked by a plaque on the wall in St Martin-le-Grand.

Many Friends, in addition to the original cohort, were moved to take part in the mission, and Fox tried to control them in a letter to the meetings: 'If any amongst you have movings to do any service for the Lord, when they have done it, let them return with speed to their habitation, and there serve the Lord in their generation' (Fox 1654b). Sometimes things went wrong, as when Burrough wrote to Fox:

> Some have been here, and we heard of some in our passage in Lancashire, which give great occasion [i.e., cause trouble] and make the truth evil spoken of, and we have the worse passage. I lie it upon thee…to take care of it…Call them in when they come out of prison. (Burrough 1654)

Most people who became Quakers appear to have been of the 'middling sort', tradespeople and craftsmen. There was a small but influential number of well-to-do Quakers, and for these people it was important that, unlike some other radical groups, Quakers were not opposed to the right to hold private property. The financial support of the mission was largely provided by Friends in the north, but by 1655 there were signs that London was becoming the Quaker centre. It was London Friends who negotiated with printers, arranged payments for various activities, replied to attacks in the press, and obtained access to the government and to the 'good and great' of the time.

Quakers were in Scotland as early as 1653, but they found it difficult to put down roots (with the exception of Aberdeen later on). A Cromwellian army was quartered in Scotland and Quakers had success with the soldiers, but little with the indigenous population. It was a similar story in Ireland at first, where Quakers arrived in 1654. During the following years Quakers went further afield; they visited Holland in 1655 and had considerable success there before continuing to Germany. Pamphlets were published in Dutch and German. The American mission began in 1655 with the arrival of Mary Fisher (c.1623–98) and a companion in Barbados, and Quakers soon spread throughout the American colonies. Four were hanged in Boston between 1659 and 1661, having disobeyed the sentence of banishment upon pain of death. Other Quakers went east. Mary Fisher, one of the most astonishing of the first Quaker missionaries, having returned from America, joined a party en route to the Middle East, and succeeded in obtaining an audience with the Sultan of Constantinople. Originally a domestic servant, she later married another Quaker preacher, William Bayly, and had several children. After his death she remarried and emigrated to America.

QUAKER TEACHING, PUBLIC DEBATES, AND PAMPHLET WARS

The Quakers were quick to realize the possibilities of the press. Some thirty-six 'books', mostly short pamphlets, were published in 1653, some sixty in 1654, then from 1655 to 1658 there were eighty to ninety publications a year. Fox, Farnworth, Nayler, and Burrough were the most productive authors. The number of Quaker women authors has often been commented on, though in fact, books with a woman as sole or joint author were a small proportion of the total number of Quaker pamphlets, and their works tended to be slighter—presumably because women, on the whole, were less educated than the men at that time.

The tone and content of Quaker pamphlets were always related to the current political situation. In April 1653 Cromwell dismissed the Rump parliament (so-called because it consisted of what remained of Charles I's Long Parliament after Pride's Purge of 1648), and replaced it with the Nominated or Barebones Parliament, appointed by church leaders. The hopes of all radicals were high that year. Quaker pamphleteers produced apocalyptic prophecies of the coming of the Kingdom of God on earth and doom for the wicked, together with diatribes against the parish ministry, and proposals for social reform and justice for the poor. But the Nominated Parliament failed to agree and was dissolved in November. From 1654, with Cromwell confirmed as Protector, Quaker pamphlets tended to become a little more restrained in language and the emphasis began to shift. Their message moved away from the imminent coming of the Kingdom of God on earth, which did not seem likely at that moment, towards emphasizing their belief that the Kingdom was, to an extent, already realized among Quakers, the sons and daughters of God, as Fox termed them. Most typical was the belief that while the Kingdom of God was already beginning to be present in the Quaker movement, a final consummation in the (probably near) future was also to be expected; 'the Kingdom is come and coming' was the typical Quaker phrase.

Not all the themes that made up the early Quaker faith can be described in terms of politics, since the Quaker movement had been born in an immensely exciting, usually communal, experience. It was the charismatic phenomena of their meetings, more than anything else, that distinguished Quakers from the other radical sects with whom they shared many ideas. The Friends had to find ways of accounting for these experiences in terms that made sense within the bounds of current thought and theology. Their emphasis on the present and spiritual Kingdom of the Lord represented one method of rationalizing what had happened to them, and also led to a distinctive attitude to the Bible, which, said Quakers, could only be understood by the Spirit in which it was written. Christ was the Word of God, they said, and the Scriptures were the words of God. Nevertheless, they made as much use of biblical texts as their opponents when looking to support their arguments, and a paper exists giving a long list of biblical texts that appeared to support the Quaker experience of 'quaking' (Anon. 1653b).

Fox often expressed the Quaker experience in terms of sonship to God, a close relationship like that of Christ to the Father. Fox is on record as calling himself 'the son of God' on a number of occasions. At their trials for blasphemy in 1652 and 1653, both Fox and Nayler declared that God was in them, and both, probably, were blaspheming according to the law, despite their equivocations as to what they had actually meant. In later years, Quakers were more careful to express their beliefs in biblical terminology, thus avoiding charges of blasphemy.

The word most strongly associated with Quaker teaching is 'light'. In the first years of the Quaker movement Fox was mainly concerned with the unity between Christ and the believer, and he spoke of 'the Light', sometimes as equivalent to Christ and sometimes as the way Christ made himself known to the believer. It may be that 'the Light' became the characteristic Quaker phrase because it was a safe alternative to 'Christ', to be used with less risk of blasphemy charges. It is possible that some of the light imagery and specifically the phrase 'the Light Within', derives from the proto-Quaker groups already in existence in Yorkshire before Fox's arrival, since it is common in the early works of Richard Farnworth at a time when Fox and Nayler did not use this phrase.

Belief in the spiritual presence of the Kingdom of God was not peculiar to Quakers, but Quakers gave it their own interpretation. One consequence was the possibility of moral perfection in this life, and this included the necessity of practising one's beliefs to the last detail. Therefore, Quakers refused to pay tithes and other church dues. All people were equal in the sight of God, therefore, Quakers did not remove their hats before magistrates and other social superiors, and addressed single individuals as 'thou', not making use of the polite 'you'. For the same reason, conspicuous consumption on the part of well-to-do Quakers was frowned upon. Quakers would not take oaths, and, while they justified this from the Bible (Mt. 5:33–7), the underlying reason probably had to do with equality, since rich people were rarely asked to take legal oaths.

These beliefs and actions led to many attacks on Quakers, verbally, physically, and in print. During the 1650s, over 300 anti-Quaker pamphlets were published. Some were purely derogatory, attacking Quakers as crypto-Catholics, immoral, and engaged in witchcraft. Anti-Quaker titles included *The Quaker Unmasked*, *Quakers are Inchanters and Dangerous Seducers*, and *The Quakers Dream: or, the Devils Pilgrimage in England*. Quakers were vulnerable in that certain of their doctrines and habits, such as their attitude to the Bible and their emphasis on human conduct rather than God's grace, were, to the suspicious mind, reminiscent of Catholicism.

Many pamphlets were written in connection with theological disputes. These were carried out by an exchange of pamphlets, a 'pamphlet war', or by public debates followed by an exchange of pamphlets. Public theological debates were a popular entertainment at this time. Opponents of Quakers were of various theological persuasions, but their attacks on Quakers followed similar patterns: that Quakers used their own idiosyncratic understanding of the Spirit to interpret the Bible; they ignored Biblical commands regarding church services and the upkeep of ministers; and did not respect the civil authorities. In addition, they said, Quaker teaching about 'the Light' was unclear, leading to a misunderstanding of the nature of Christ and his work, to belief in justification by works, and to impossible ideas about sinlessness. Was the Quakers' 'light in the conscience' the same thing as the natural light of conscience? Quakers said not, but found it very difficult to explain exactly what they did mean, and this problem was not resolved until later in the century.

JAMES NAYLER AND THE CRISIS OF 1656

By 1655 there was a major Quaker presence in London, and Francis Howgill and Edward Burrough needed assistance. The situation called for the Quakers' best. Fox had not made a good impression when visiting London, for in that sophisticated milieu he had been considered odd and uncouth. The right person for the job was clearly James Nayler, who arrived in London in June 1655. He enjoyed immediate success as a London preacher and was soon moving in good society, writing to Margaret Fell about a meeting attended by 'Lady Darcy', and other notables including Sir Henry Vane (Nayler 1655). During the winter of 1655–6 Burrough and Howgill departed for a tour of Ireland, leaving Nayler to manage the work in London. Consequently Nayler came under much pressure, but all seemed to be well until summer 1656, when a problem developed in connection with a woman named Martha Simmons. She had been a well-regarded Quaker preacher who had worked in East Anglia with James Parnell, but in 1656 something went amiss, and, according to a report sent to Margaret Fell, 'she was judged by FH [Francis Howgill] to speak in her will', that is, without being truly inspired by God (Hubberthorne 1656). (Richard Hubberthorne was one of the most capable Quaker preachers, close to Fox and Fell, who arrived in London later that year to reinforce the Quaker leadership.) The Quaker belief was that they had the Light of Christ within them, which, being the Light of Christ, could not err nor be divided. If it happened that there was disagreement about somebody's 'light', then it was the practice to follow the advice of local leading Friends, who in the summer of 1656 were Burrough, Howgill, and Nayler.

Simmons, however, refused to accept discipline from Howgill and asked Nayler for support. Nayler appears to have wavered. He then went to stay at Martha Simmons's house and refused contact with his former colleagues. The contents of letters flying to and fro among Quakers that summer seem to indicate that Nayler was suffering some kind of mental disturbance, but it is not possible to know exactly what happened. At the time, George Fox was in prison in Launceston in Cornwall, so was not free to deal with the situation. Leading Friends decided that Nayler must be taken to see Fox, but on the way Nayler was arrested and imprisoned in Exeter. Meanwhile, Martha Simmons visited Fox and told him that he should bow down to Nayler. Fox thought that Nayler had sent her, and as a result, after Fox had been freed and finally met with Nayler in Exeter, there was a complete breach between them.

Nayler was eventually released and was again joined by Martha Simmons. In October, accompanied by Simmons and a group of similarly minded people, Nayler rode into Bristol in a recapitulation of Christ's entry into Jerusalem. Nobody can be sure what was going on in the minds of the participants in these events. There is considerable literature on Nayler and readers who wish to pursue the matter in more depth would probably do best to consult Damrosch (1996) or Neelon (2009).

Nayler was not supported by the Bristol Friends, and the whole party was arrested. He was taken to London and after a famous trial before Parliament, he was sentenced to be whipped, pilloried, branded, and imprisoned. Members of Parliament thought that Nayler was the leading Quaker, and one is reported to have said: 'Cut off this fellow and you will destroy the sect.'

Fox's first consideration after Nayler's trial was to limit the damage. Nayler had been better known amongst the general public than Fox, both as a preacher and as an author. But among established Friends, Fox was considered the leader. Not one of the leading Quakers openly supported Nayler, although Richard Farnworth disappeared from view for several years, perhaps because he was uncertain where his loyalties lay.

Fox was now determined that there should be no further challenge to his position. After his release from Launceston he travelled the country and held several large meetings at which he instructed Friends on their private and religious life, with emphasis on unity and order. The meetings settled down in time, and from now on Fox included London in his itineraries, and, presumably, overcame his earlier problems of acceptance there.

The loss of Nayler and Farnworth made it difficult to keep up the flow of Quaker pamphlets. Burrough now became the leading theological writer, while Fox produced eighteen pamphlets in 1656 and twenty-two in 1657, thus making the public aware of his name. The general public would never again mistake someone else for the Quaker leader. More care was taken with presentation—Fox's early pamphlets had been very rough, but from 1657 onwards they were more carefully edited. There was a noticeable change in the style of all Quaker pamphlets, their tone being moderated, with frequent use of phrases such as 'We believe so-and so' rather than dogmatic declamation. Quakers had become concerned for their public image.

This move towards a gentler, more sophisticated Quakerism was assisted by several new converts, notably Isaac Penington, who with his wife Mary joined the Friends in 1658. Wealthy, university-educated, and an established author of Seeker pamphlets, he became a leading Quaker publicist during the following years.

Nayler survived his punishment and wrote several pamphlets expressing his penitence and his wish for reconciliation with the Friends, but Fox was unwilling to agree. Nayler was released from prison in 1659 and again took part in the Quaker ministry. There was a limited reconciliation with Fox in 1660 shortly before Nayler's death.

The Embryonic Quaker organization

Quaker organization developed from a need to handle matters of discipline and to care for the Quaker poor, especially those affected by persecution. Letters written in 1653 and 1654 refer to the setting up of General and Monthly Meetings in the North, 'to declare what necessities or wants are seen in their several meetings, there to be considered on by friends there met, and as freedom and necessity is seen, so to minister', and with the appointment of people to care for the meeting who before long became known as 'elders' (Anon. 1653/4). There are indications that during the 1650s a regular church order developed, at first in the north and later over the whole country, consisting of local meetings with local leaders, gathering from time to time with other meetings for a 'General Meeting', sometimes holding 'Monthly Meetings' for Business, and guided by experienced Friends, usually those who had first convinced them. This was similar to the practices of the separated churches from which many Friends had come.

The Quaker movement attracted many argumentative and unconventional people and an established church order was especially necessary in connection with marriage. Friends were, with good reason, sensitive to any hint of sexual irregularity, for there were several scandals in the early days. The Nominated Parliament had made provision for civil marriage, but some Friends were not happy about making the prescribed declaration before a magistrate. Fox therefore issued instructions—those who wished to marry were to declare it, 'to the elders of the church where they are, that it may be examined'. If the elders agreed, then the marriage could take place, 'published in the meeting when the church of God is gathered'. Friends could then make their declaration to the magistrate if they wished. However, if the rightness of the marriage was not clear to 'the elders and overseers of the church', it could not take place, for marriage was an affair of the church, not just of the individuals concerned (Fox 1655). These regulations were repeated and refined in a number of later documents. At this date there was no set form for the marriage ceremony, and the couple probably chose their own words for taking each other as husband and wife.

The function of an 'elder', a person appointed to look after the needs of a local church, was known among Friends at least since 1654, but the marriage regulations provide an early instance of the use of the actual word. 'Overseer' was a term used in various ways among Quakers before it settled to its modern Quaker meaning, a person with responsibility for pastoral care. In the 1650s the current use is indicated by a note to leading Friends, appended to Fox's instructions on marriage. They were asked to send copies of Fox's instructions to all meetings 'over which you are self overseers', indicating that there were levels of authority, with a middle rank of 'overseers' between the apex, that is the administration of Fox and Fell, and the local meetings (Fox 1655).

The first of a number of Quaker documents on church discipline, known as the Epistle from the Elders of Balby, dates from November 1656, and its coincidence with the Nayler affair is probably no accident. It has eighteen clauses and a postscript, covering all aspects of church order and also Quakers' private lives in considerable and prescriptive detail. It has been published (Moore 2001; and slightly abbreviated in Jones, R. Tudur 2007, 360–3). The postscript remains part of the current book of discipline of British Quakers:

> Dearly beloved Friends, these things we do not lay upon you as a rule or form to walk by, but that all, with the measure of light which is pure and holy, may be guided; and so in the light walking and abiding, these may be fulfilled in the Spirit, not from the letter, for the letter killeth, but the Spirit giveth life. (British Yearly Meeting 2009, 1.01)

In the early days, financial support for travelling ministers was mainly provided by the Kendal Fund set up by Margaret Fell in 1654 under local treasurership, but with the Quaker movement increasingly centred on London, it became difficult to manage finance from Swarthmoor. During 1657–8 it was decided to cease central funding for ministers except for those travelling abroad, to raise money for local needs county by county, and to transfer responsibility for central funds to London. Records of 'sufferings' were also to be collected by counties before being sent to London, where they could be used for publicity or for petitions to the government. This embryo county organization became the basis for the Quarterly Meetings reorganized by Fox in 1667–8. The new centre of operations in London, replacing Swarthmoor, was the house of Quaker wine-cooper Gerrard Roberts, in the City of London. A regular Business Meeting for London men Friends was set up, probably in 1656, and a paid clerk, Ellis Hookes, was appointed in 1657.

It should be noted that women had only a limited part in these arrangements. Quaker views on the equality of women did not, in general, extend to their taking part in church government. Approved women had authority to 'appoint meetings', but that was the end of it. Women do not appear to have participated in the local Business Meetings. No women are recorded as regional overseers. A Women's Meeting was set up in London around 1657, for the purpose of handling practical matters in the care of poor Friends, but there are no records of Women's Meetings outside London during the 1650s, though they may have existed in some places. Women's Business Meetings did not become a regular feature of Quakerism until some years later, and then at the cost of considerable controversy.

QUAKERS AT THE END OF THE PROTECTORATE

After the Nayler affair Quakers began to settle down. They rarely quaked and their published pamphlets showed a desire to stand well in society. But in August 1658 Oliver Cromwell died and his son Richard, who succeeded him, could not command the same loyalty. During the following eighteen months, the country descended into near chaos. Many Quakers reacted to these events as they had in 1653, the time of Cromwell's dismissal of the Rump and the appointment of the Nominated Parliament—they hoped that political disruption heralded the coming of the Kingdom of God. They were now in a much stronger position than in 1653. Then they had been a relatively small group, confined to the North, but in 1659 their headquarters was in London, near the action. Their leading publicist, idealistic and able Edward Burrough, though still only 25, was a fine public speaker as well as a pamphleteer, but with no deep experience of politics and politicians.

Richard Cromwell resigned in April 1659, and the Rump Parliament, which had never been formally dissolved, was recalled in early May. During the summer of 1659 all the radical sects, Quakers included, felt that the Lord was at last on their side. Quaker pamphlets now began to appear at a rate of several a week, many written by Burrough, while others were issued on the authority of the London Men's Meeting, on behalf of Quakers as a whole. In all, during 1659 they published nearly 200 pamphlets, closely following the changing political situation, with a similar number produced in 1660.

The first pamphlets were full of apocalyptic hope for the coming Kingdom of God, with demands for the toleration of Quakerism. George Fox's contribution was *To the Parliament of the Commonwealth of England, Fifty-nine Particulars laid down for Regulating Things*, which, besides calling for toleration, gave Fox's ideas on future social policy. Examples include:

> 12. Let no one be put to death for cattle, for money or any outward thing.
> 26. Let none be Gaolers that are drunkards, or swearers, or oppressors of people, but such as may be good patterns to their prisoners, and let none lie long in gaol, for that is the way to spoil people, and to make more thieves, for there they learn wickedness together.
> 33. Let all poor people, blind and lame, and cripples, be provided for, that there might not be a beggar in England. (Fox 1659a)

But the government was unstable and militias were being raised in various parts of the country. Fox's opinion was that Friends should not become involved in the coming conflict, but a number of Friends did not take his advice. It became clear that Fox could not command all Quakers everywhere. The Quaker attitude to armed conflict was not fully worked out at this time. Fox was consistent in that he repeatedly advised Quakers not to take part in plots against the established government, but he had also warned Cromwell that his failures in war were due to his disobedience to God, and he praised Quaker soldiers (Fox 1659b, 5). With the government collapsing, it became increasingly difficult for Quakers to know the right course of action. Fox became ill, probably mentally distraught as a result of a sense that the Quaker movement was running out of control. He left London to stay with friends in Reading and for some weeks was out of touch with events.

During the summer and early autumn of 1659 there was growing hostility in the country towards the radical sects, Quakers especially, as they were perceived to be taking positions of power in the militia and in the country. Quaker pamphlets described the increasing severity of attacks on meetings. Burrough's pamphlets from August to the end of the year follow the twists and turns of the increasingly confused situation. In October he was hopeful, 'We look for a new earth as well as a new heaven…the Lord will appear to be the king and judge and law-giver over all' (Burrough 1659a, 3). By November he was in despair of any immediate good outcome, comparing the government to a horn of the fourth beast of Revelation 13 (Burrough 1659b). In December he produced a statement which was published on the authority of the London Men's Meeting, taking the view that the right way for Friends was to stand aside from politics, 'We are not for men or names…We have chosen the Son of God to be our king and…his kingdom is not of this world neither is his warfare with carnal weapons…we are given up to bear and suffer all things…until the appointed time of our deliverance' (Burrough 1659c).

Only in Scotland was there a disciplined army, under George Monck. On 2 January 1660 Monck's army crossed the border into England and marched on London, where he arrived on 3 February. Some Quakers welcomed this development as the action of the Lord in bringing down the present unsatisfactory government. But it soon began to appear that a restored monarchy might provide the only means of achieving a calm and united country. The way was cleared for the Restoration and in May Charles II was proclaimed king. The day of the radical sects was over.

SUGGESTED FURTHER READING

Barbour, H. (1985 [1964]) *The Quakers in puritan England.* New Haven and London: Yale University Press, reprinted with a new preface by the author. Richmond, Indiana: Friends United Press.

Barbour, H. and Roberts, A. (2004 [1973]) *Early Quaker writings.* Grand Rapids, Michigan: William B. Eerdmans, reprinted Wallingford, PA: Pendle Hill Publications.

Braithwaite, W. C. (1955 [1912]) *The beginnings of Quakerism.* London: Macmillan. 2nd edn. prepared by Henry J. Cadbury, Cambridge: Cambridge University Press.

Fox, G. (1995 [1952]) *The journal of George Fox.* J. L. Nickalls (ed.) Philadelphia: Religious Society of Friends.

Ingle, H. L. (1994) *First among Friends: George Fox and the creation of Quakerism.* New York and Oxford: Oxford University Press.

Moore, R. (2000) *The light in their consciences: Early Quakers in Britain 1644–1666.* University Park: Pennsylvania State University Press.

Reay, B. (1985) *The Quakers in the English revolution.* London: Temple Smith.

Trevett, C. (1991) *Women and Quakerism in the seventeenth century.* York: Sessions.

CHAPTER 2

RESTORATION QUAKERISM, 1660–1691

RICHARD C. ALLEN

IN May 1660 Charles II was proclaimed by the Convention Parliament as the lawful monarch of England, Scotland, and Ireland, thereby bringing the eleven years of the Republic swiftly to an end (Keeble 2002; Harris 2005). In an attempt to establish whether his administration would be markedly different from that of his predecessors, Ahivah, a Quaker prophetess, petitioned Charles, presenting herself at Whitehall dressed all in white. In her address 'for the Saints Liberties…within these Realms and Dominions' she described to the king her vision of his return from exile and affirmed that his restoration was lawful and sanctified by God. Nevertheless she cautioned that his return was conditional, and that he would be expected to allow the 'Saints' to gather together and to preach freely. In a call for liberty of conscience for dissenters she stated, 'let the Saints make themselves a body in Christ's fashion' with Charles as their 'Protector'. So, what did Ahivah anticipate the Restoration would mean for itinerant preachers and dissenters in general? She hoped that the king would allow them to preach and instruct constables to protect them so that 'they [Dissenters] be not abused in such conditions, as I myself have been; as being cast into bedlam, for a mad-body, for prophecying the return of your majesty'. A published account of the meeting specifically offered advice to the newly restored king. The author suggested that the Interregnum governments were:

> not faithfull unto God, but grieved the Spirit of the Lord with their hypocrisy from day to day, talking for Liberty, but behold they brought forth oppression, and so became worse then those that went before them, who did not profess so much for liberty in their words, but performed better *things* in their actions.

There was an assertion that, despite the change in fortunes for the king and the Royalists, all kingdoms belonged to God and kings were dependent upon his favour, while governments ought to be 'righteous' and respect 'every man's *conscience*'. As for the Quakers, they sought 'no greater liberty, either in things religious, or in things civil betwixt man and man, than we desire all others might enjoy'. Specifically, if such a government was established then the Friends would willingly 'submit unto Righteousness from the Supream Governour' and would 'yield all due lawful obedience unto him and his Commands' (Ahivah 1660, 2–3). This definitive statement that they were prepared to 'live peaceably with all men, and perswade others unto the same' (Ahivah, 3–4) was shared by Margaret Fell and by many other Friends who either sent petitions and letters to the king, which were approved by leading members of the Society, or wrote directly to Charles in an unsanctioned private capacity (Burrough 1660b, 15; Fell et al 1660a, *passim*; Fell 1710, 208–9; Moore 2000, 177–9). At this stage, these tentative overtures represented the views of some key individuals; notably, as yet there was no mechanism for fully articulating the voice of all Quakers or for enforcing a unified position.

Persecution

The Declaration of Breda (4 April 1660) promised a degree of religious toleration to those who did not 'disturb the peace of the kingdom' and this was formally enacted (Moore 2000, 175). Not everyone supported this. Anglican clergyman, who had lost their livings in the 1650s, sought revenge against dissenters, particularly Quakers, who were thought to be intent on the destruction of the established church as well as social and political upheaval. They accused Friends of blasphemy and questioned their unorthodox theological beliefs and values (Manning 2009, 27–56). Landowners, who had also suffered under Cromwellian rule, similarly sought to punish former republicans and sectaries, and poured scorn on Friends, especially their characteristic plain attire, their refusal to remove their hats, and their use of *thee* and *thou*, which went against the social conventions of the age. Moreover, in the public mind, Quakers were associated with the extremism of the 1650s and their allegiance to the state was questionable. The prevailing view from many quarters was that Friends had not yet turned their swords into ploughshares (ch. 1, this vol.), and it is not surprising that, given the large numbers of radical dissenters, particularly Friends, a fearful Restoration government commenced a purge.

The fear that disillusioned radicals were attempting to overthrow the government was given greater credence with the Fifth Monarchist uprising of 1661. This was led by Thomas Venner who, with a small band of armed men, rebelled against the king. After four days of fighting (1–4 January 1661) the rebellion was crushed and Venner was tried at the Old Bailey and executed on 19 January (Greaves 1986, 49–57). A letter from Nicholas Bowdon on 12 January 1661 expressed his concern about Venner's uprising and Quaker involvement. He stated that 'Quakers and "phanaticks" are in Wiltshire and are believed to number about 10,000' (Sheffield Archives, 1661; Greaves 1986, 54–5). The inflated estimates demonstrated just how entrenched fears were and inevitably the repressive measures (the Clarendon or Penal Code) that followed served only to breed further mistrust on both sides. The lack of a coherent organizational structure gave credence to those who questioned the commitment of Quakers to abandon their previous rebelliousness. Neither ministers nor senior clergymen were convinced by Friends protestations of allegiance to the Crown, and the promise of those early days of the Restoration proved more difficult to realize than anyone anticipated. Meetings were broken up, members were imprisoned, and other punitive measures were imposed (Braithwaite 1979 [1919], 9–10; Miller 2005). Dissenters were restricted by the Corporation Act in 1661 from holding public office unless they took Anglican communion, while the following year the Act of Uniformity made the Book of Common Prayer compulsory. Friends' refusal to pay tithes, church rates, and other levies to the established church, and their unwillingness to swear the Oath of Allegiance (LSF, Great Book of Sufferings (GBS); Champion 1992; Clark 1988), exacerbated suspicions that they did not support the restored monarchy. More directly, the Quaker Act of 1662 punished those who refused to comply by rendering their meetings illegal and persistent offenders were liable to transportation (*An Act*... 1662). To compound matters the Conventicle Act (1664 and re-enacted in 1670) forbade conventicles, unauthorized Meetings for Worship, from being held. No more than five people could gather unless they were from the same family and, upon a third conviction, the sentence of banishment could be issued (Fletcher 1984, 235–46). The Five Mile Act of 1665 forbade itinerant dissenting preachers from coming within five miles of incorporated towns or their former livings. The measure also restricted their right to teach.

The imposition of this punitive legislation was savage and all dissenters were persecuted between 1660 and 1689. The survival of Quakerism, given their 'peculiar social habits, their embarrassing manifestations of scriptural enthusiasm, and their broad range of "testimonies" for Truth', hung in the balance (Horle 1988, ix). Their non-compliance left them increasingly vulnerable to the distraint of property, local harassment, forcible arrest, and long-term incarceration. Yet the penal code was not implemented uniformly and often depended on the tenacity of the authorities, particularly during the uncertainty surrounding the Exclusion Crisis and alleged Popish Plot in the late-1670s and early 1680s, and the Rye House Plot in 1683. Sporadic enforcement of the law often arose because the authorities had mixed feelings about it. The legal process was cumbersome, and local law enforcers were frequently apathetic or sometimes sympathetic to the plight of the Friends who became proficient at lobbying for leniency (Horle 1988, 256–66; Davies 2000, 171–9, 184–9). At times, non-Quaker relatives and neighbours lent assistance, and at state level limited toleration was granted to dissenters. A Declaration of Indulgence was offered on 15 March 1672 that allowed dissenters to worship publicly as long as they licensed their ministers. Friends nevertheless refused to take out licences for meetings since they believed that the state had 'no more right to give, than to take away, religious liberty' (Watts 1978, 247–8). The rapidly changing political situation, increased fear of Catholicism, and the perceived growth in the number of meetings of dissenters forced the king to rescind the measure one year later (Horle 1988, 79–83).

The persecution of Quakers was recorded in considerable detail in the Great Book of Sufferings, including examples of armed constables or soldiers dragging Friends from their homes and even their beds, or apprehending them on the road and seizing their horses and goods. Others were publicly humiliated by being whipped as they were pulled along roadsides, locked in the stocks or pillory, shouted at or physically abused by mobs (LSF, GBS, *passim*; Miller 2005, 72–3, 97–100). Paid informers intimidated local communities (Braithwaite 1966, 107–14), and magistrates or judges exacted severe punishments (Davies 2000, 173–5, 178–84; Carroll 2010, 25, 27–8). Many Friends were tried alongside common felons, vagabonds, slanderers, thieves, and murderers, for their refusal to keep the Sabbath, for attending unlicensed meetings, or seditious practices and treasonous behaviour (Besse 1753, II, 756). The penal code allowed some to indulge their own prejudice Besse, I, 472), while others were fearful that dissenters and republicans sought a return to the 'good old cause' of the Interregnum. Fox's 'Peace Testimony' of 1661 promoted pacifism among Friends, but initially not all Quakers adhered to this belief (George Fox et al 1661; Braithwaite 1969, 101–5; Weddle 2001, ch. 2–3). Moreover, in the last year of the Interregnum there were those who were prepared to raise a militia while others were complicit in the Northern Plot in 1663 (Moore 2000, 169–70, 180–1, 184–5). Post-Restoration, the peace testimony was gradually adopted, but in the pragmatism of Isaac Penington (1616–79) there was an acknowledgement that those who had not been called to the witness for peace, particularly magistrates, could defend the vulnerable (Moore 2000, 181–2). In America, the military involvement of Friends during wartime was quite a different experience. For example, during King Philip's War between 1675 and 1676 the Quaker authorities of Rhode Island, although not directly in charge of the military campaigns, were, at the very least, obliged to provide defence (Weddle 2001, ch. 9–11).

IMPRISONMENTS AND DEATH

Quakers endured their privations with great fortitude. An early Quaker missionary, Francis Howgill (1618–69) who was imprisoned for life at Appleby, Cumberland, in 1663 for refusing to swear allegiance, stated that 'if it [prison] be the place of my laying down the body, I am content' (Backhouse 1828, 84). Howgill, who died in prison after six years, always refused to blame or criticize his captors. In a poignant letter to his daughter in 1666 he explained:

> be sure that thou let nothing separate thy love from God and his people … [who] were ever hated, and belied, and persecuted; and evil-spoken of, always by bad and evil, loose people: these are God's people, and his love, and peace, and blessing, is with them … [He] hath been with me in the midst of many troubles, trials, and sufferings, and hath lifted up my head above my adversaries, because I trusted in his Name; which at times I found as a refuge, and a present help in time of need. (Backhouse, 90, 86)

As many as 450 Quakers died in prison during Charles II's reign, including early leaders such as Howgill, Richard Hubberthorne (1628–62), and Edward Burrough (1634–63), the latter two dying in Newgate prison (Moore 2000, 183–4). Other leading Friends died shortly after their release, notably John Audland of Westmoreland in 1664 and Richard Farnworth of Yorkshire in 1666 (Leachman 2004a; Greaves 2004). George Fox (1624–91) and Margaret Fell (1614–1702) suffered the ill effects of their punishment without complaint and, as John Miller has pointed out, 'suffering was an integral part of early Quaker identity' (Miller 2005, 71). This placed them at odds with their families and neighbours and, for Quaker women this could also result in the temporary abandonment of spouses or children. The death or long-term incarceration of these early leading Friends is significant as it deprived the Society of much-needed direction, yet it did leave those who remained the challenge of negotiating the stormy years of Stuart rule. Alongside Fox, George Whitehead of Westmoreland (1637–1724) provided leadership. Whitehead's contribution, despite periods of imprisonment, was invaluable when both Fox and Fell were arrested in January 1664 and when in May 1665 Fox was held in isolation at Scarborough Castle (Whitehead 1725; Smith 2004). Indeed, Whitehead's 'cautious, careful, conservative nature was well suited to the new age, a leading figure in the shift toward theological orthodoxy and political respectability' (Moore 2000, 228).

The conditions in most mid-seventeenth-century prisons were extremely grim as they were usually dimly lit, poorly ventilated, and inmates were forced to sleep on cold floors or wet straw. Friends were often abused by over-zealous gaolers or fellow inmates. They were also routinely arrested for failing to swear the necessary oaths, or for contravening the Conventicle Acts. Others were prosecuted for recusancy, as illustrated by arrests during the political crises that occurred between 1669 and 1672, 1678, 1687 and 1689 (Besse 1753; Davies 2000, ch. 13). A high proportion of Quakers found themselves before the courts and this reflected the pervasive fear in late-seventeenth-century society. Interestingly, Friends were most likely to be prosecuted in the civil courts for not attending church services (Davies 2000, 172). Notwithstanding the enthusiasm with which punitive measures were embraced in some quarters, there were some instances where Quakers were treated more humanely: sometimes local arrangements allowed gaolers to grant lengthy periods of parole or provided family members with visiting rights (Horle 1988, 265).

REACTION TO PERSECUTION

Members who responded calmly to hostility and brutality, and made no complaint about the intolerance they faced were viewed as courageous and heroic by their fellow members. Friends had also gradually adopted pacifist principles: they refused to bear arms, provide substitutes, or indeed pay for the expenses of the county militia. They also campaigned unstintingly for an end to armed conflict and tried to persuade others to do likewise. There were nevertheless different approaches to pacifism on both sides of the Atlantic as well as the arming of ships by Quaker merchants (Brock 1990; Weddle 2001; Jenkins 1985, 10–19). When constables and bailiffs came to arrest them, distrained their goods, or where acts of intimidation or petty malice were carried out, Friends passively allowed them to go about their business. However, fear of prosecution was a significant barrier to those who were interested in the Society, but could not contemplate the stoicism and personal sacrifice this required. This acted as a drag on recruitment as the leaders were all too aware and they began to seek legal redress by challenging the legitimacy of the penal legislation.

More than other dissenters, Friends successfully exploited the expansion of print culture in the pre- and post-Restoration period and published a substantial number of tracts and other literature to proselytize their ideas (O'Malley 1979, 169–84; Peters 2005). After 1660, Friends sought to strengthen their community by tightening the organizational structure and actively countering the reputation that they were debauched, ungodly, and disloyal to the state (Bitterman 1973, 203–28). Publishing their views was central to this. Although this was a largely effective campaign some of their more implacable opponents accused them of disseminating literature akin to 'High poison taken into the body, and delusions into the soul' (Davies 2000, 110). It was in this period that Friends became more adept at using the law to expose the ambiguities, procedural irregularities, and the impracticalities of the penal code. The Society established a centralized organization which was better able to provide legal advice and support for its members. Indeed, their 'disparate legal tactics...ensured the victory of the "Lamb" over the "Beast"' (Horle 1988, 188). Subsequently, Friends challenged the legality of the Quaker Act and the Conventicle Acts, particularly refuting the allegation that meetings were seditious gatherings (Moore 1995, 126).

MISSIONARIES AND MEETINGS IN EUROPE, THE CARIBBEAN, AND NORTH AMERICA

After the Restoration, proselytizing continued with the missionary work and publications of William Ames (d. 1662), William Caton (1636–65), Stephen Crisp (1628–92), and Benjamin Furly (1636–1714) in Germany and the Netherlands (Bernet 2006, 1–15; Juterczenka 2007, 39–53), and with the favourable reception of William Penn's *No Cross, No Crown* (c.1668) in parts of the Netherlands which led to it being translated into Dutch (Juterczenka 2007, 45). Female Quaker missionaries in the pre- and post-Restoration period were proactive, including Elizabeth Hooton (c.1600–72), Ann Austin, Elizabeth Hendricks, and Elizabeth Johnston Keith. These women sought to influence and attract followers from among European Anabaptist, Mennonite, and Pietist communities, and the 'international Quaker movement...for a short time in the second half of the seventeenth century [was] a field of intense missionary efforts and great expectations' (Bernet 2006, 15). In spite of such efforts the Friends were unable, in most cases, to develop long-lasting meetings as they had done in the British Isles and in North America (Cadbury 1952, 11–12; Bernet 2006, 1; Juterczenka 2007, 40–1).

By the early years of the Restoration there was a growing Quaker presence on Barbados, which was described by one Friend as the 'nursery of the truth'. By the 1680s there were six meeting houses and seven graveyards on the island, but at the same time as they were establishing their meetings, planters were arguing that the Quakers challenged the traditional order of Barbadian society and, of course, the economic basis upon which the future of the island rested. These Friends, some of whom such as Ralph Fretwell and Lewis Morris were large-scale slaveholders, also caused resentment as they refused to contribute to the upkeep of a militia on the island despite the very real threat of a slave rebellion. Consequently, members of the Society were heavily fined for their alleged religious deviancy and unwillingness to support the militia (Gragg 2009, ch. 3).

The missionary activity of Friends in the American colonies has been described as a 'Quaker invasion' and they were subjected to brutal oppression, particularly in Massachusetts and Maryland (Pestana 1991, 25–43; Carroll 2010, 15–31), but post-1660 Friends increasingly became tolerated, albeit grudgingly, with Rhode Island becoming 'the most important Quaker northern colony' (Worrall 1980, 3–25). The establishment of some substantial Quaker communities overseas and the transatlantic networks of Friends allowed for the sizeable growth of Quaker merchant businesses in the West Indies and North America (Greaves 1998; Gragg 2009, 22–37). Yet, despite the growth and prosperity of these Quaker communities, the desire for an independent Quaker territory had by the mid-1670s still not been realized. Increasingly, as Friends toned down their 'reformation of the world', their less confrontational attitude towards the state authorities and clergymen allowed them to direct their thoughts towards a more coherent organizational framework and opportunities to press for a Quaker colony.

'Gospel Order': Organization

In response to earlier allegations of fanaticism, sedition, or worse, leading Friends, particularly Fox, sought to devise some means of restraining the excesses of the few who were already damaging the Society's reputation and so avoid divisions in their communities. The process of bringing order to the Society assumed greater priority after the Restoration. Members were thereby urged to avoid the predilection of early Friends for quaking, offering prophesies, dressing in sackcloth and ashes, or walking naked into towns and churchyards as a sign of God's displeasure. This was not always adhered to. In 1672, the Quaker theologian Robert Barclay (1648–90) processed in sackcloth and ashes through the streets of Aberdeen, an important early centre of Quaker activity (Hagglund 2005, 180–90). Yet, in most cases, Friends' fervour was now expressed in silent worship in their meeting houses. Fox became convinced that the survival of the movement required a more strategic approach. Fox was not just 'a religious visionary...but also a far-sighted pragmatist' and sought to provide 'a system of self-government that ensured the Society's internal cohesion' (Cantor 2005, 21). Thus, in the 1660s he developed an organizational structure based on a pyramidal network of regular meetings for both worship and the conduct of the Society's business. Gradually this meeting structure was introduced in all areas to provide a vital support system. At weekly Meetings for Worship

(First Day Meetings) both men and women were encouraged to reflect upon their lives, while Business Meetings were essentially hierarchical with lines of authority which, in Britain, saw regional meetings look to the London Yearly Meeting for guidance and discipline (Leachman 1998; Beck and Ball 1869).

As part of this process of change, annual gatherings, which had formerly been held in Skipton and Barlby [Balby] in Yorkshire, were transferred to London from 1660 and meetings across Britain sent representatives. In May 1661, the General Assembly of the Brethren was held, but it was not until 1668 that meetings were held consistently, largely because of the high levels of persecution. Quarterly Meetings appointed their own representatives and concerns that affected Friends, particularly those that could not be resolved at the local or regional level, were referred onwards. Yearly Meetings were subsequently organized for Ireland, Scotland, and Wales in the 1670s and 1680s. In America, New England Quakers held their first Yearly Meeting in 1661. During his visit to the West Indies and American colonies in 1671, George Fox sought to replicate the organizational apparatus that was increasingly commonplace among British, Irish, and some North American communities (Fox 1995, 590–664; Pestana 1991, 91–6). As he stressed to the Friends in Barbados, they required 'well-ordering' and the better 'managing of their affairs' (Gragg 2009, 54). These meetings led to a 'highly democratic movement, abjuring a professional ministry or leadership' while combining 'consensual decision making with a strong, hierarchical organizational structure' (Cantor 2005, 22). Delivering these objectives thus led to a remarkable proliferation of meetings with particular responsibilities and a structure that undoubtedly embedded greater solidarity, but may also have stifled individualism.

CENTRALIZATION AND SCHISM

These developments towards institutionalization 'necessitated the assertion of corporate authority over the individual conscience' (Martin 2003, 8) and this provoked resistance from those who were concerned with the restrictions imposed on the individuality and enthusiasm of the early Quakers. John Perrot (d. 1665) criticized the Quaker tradition of removing hats while at prayer, but he was accused of extravagance in his missionary work and of being misguided in his comments about the removal of hats. Perrot had not submitted his opinions to Fox and other principal Friends before his writings were made public, and there was concern that this could stir up the same kind of passions that John Nayler had aroused in 1656.

A meeting between leading Friends and Perrot in late 1661 did not resolve matters, and after his arrest and imprisonment in June 1662 he was officially censured by the Society. Perrot accepted voluntary exile in Barbados but continued his schismatic beliefs on the island by seeking to influence dissenters. The following summer he was allowed to travel to Maryland and Virginia, and called on Friends there to hold meetings when the spirit moved them rather than the formal holding of meetings at allotted times. His return to Barbados in 1664 clearly shows how far removed he was from

Quaker beliefs—he received a commission as captain from the governor of the island, wore a satin coat, carried a sword, and received payments for 'extracting the oaths that the Quakers refused to give' (Smith 2004 [2007]; Gragg 2009, 46–7).

Richard Farnworth and other important Friends met in London in May 1666 and issued 'The Testimony of the Brethren'. This declaration stressed that by isolating separatists such as Perrot and his supporters, particularly from holding positions within meetings and curtailing their missionary activities or restricting the publications of their works, they were safeguarding the integrity of the Society (Moore 2000, 197–203). Even after his death in August 1665 the Perrotian divisions persisted (Carroll 1971; Martin 2003, 32–81), but more positively, the controversy served to convince many Friends of the need for a tighter organization based on 'a hierarchical system of church government, as a surer means of controlling Friends' behaviour' (Martin 2003, 20).

Alongside Foxian centralization, which continued throughout the 1670s and 1680s, the London Yearly Meeting received reports from regional meetings of cases of persecution, the strength of their meetings, and also funds. By the early 1670s other London meetings dealt with poor relief, the discipline of the Society, and ownership of property (Leachman 1998, 73–101). From 1673 the Second Day Morning Meeting of 'Public Friends' was responsible for publishing Quaker tracts and managing the network of preachers throughout Britain and Ireland. In the same year the Meeting of Twelve was established which drew representatives from the six London meetings, and offered poor relief and legal assistance (Horle 1988, 165, 175–6). Three years later the Meeting for Sufferings was inaugurated to lobby the government (Braithwaite 1979 [1919], 281–6; Horle 1986, 17–18). It consisted of ministers, elders, and other invited representatives, and was designed to help Friends negotiate the legal complexities and assist those who faced financial ruin. The committee gave expert legal advice and suggested ways in which the Society could appeal against legal and illegal actions (Greaves 1992, 237–59). With the implementation of the Act of Toleration (1689) this meeting, in conjunction with the Second Day Morning Meeting, helped to manage the business of the Society when the Yearly Meeting was in recess, and continued to give much-needed support to those who were persecuted for the non-payment of tithes.

It is widely acknowledged that women played a crucial role in the foundation and survival of the Religious Society of Friends (Trevett 2000, 87–90; Gill 2005, 153–64). George Fox consistently believed that women should have equality, while Margaret Fell actively sought their involvement in the management of the movement by holding their own meetings (Ingle 1991, 587–8). Although women had held meetings to coordinate charitable work from the 1650s, their involvement in meetings for business and in the general administration of the Society proved to be a source of some tension (Edwards 1955, 3–21). In c.1668 Fox called upon Friends to appreciate that both men and women were 'heirs to the gospel' and 'heirs of this authority', and in the years which followed women's Business Meetings were thereby a natural, if controversial, development (Fox 1995, 528; Trevett 1991, 79, 82). Initially, shared meetings were the norm, but Quakers such as John Banks of Cumberland, were aware that women might be overshadowed by the men. He observed in 1674 that some women 'quenched the notion of the good in themselves by looking out at the men' and, therefore, he advocated separate meetings (Banks 1674, 181–2). Fox felt compelled to censor those among the Friends who accused him of high-handedness and authoritarianism concerning the establishment of women's meetings (Ingle 1991, 590), while, at the same time, Mary Penington (bap. 1623–82) explained that in these meetings women's 'natural capacities' could be given full rein. A network of Women's Meetings had been established by the late-1670s to transact business, but many Friends, including Penington, had a narrow outlook concerning these female roles (Ingle 1991, 590), and the debate itself continued throughout much of the late-seventeenth century (Kunze 1994, ch. 3).

The Wilkinson-Story controversy of the 1670s was an additional reaction against Foxian centralization, the establishment of Business Meetings, and more specifically, the decision to allow Women's Meetings which some Friends considered to be an 'unscriptural and an unnecessary appendage to Quakerism' (Trevett 1991, 80). John Wilkinson (d. 1683) and John Story (d. 1681) of the Preston Patrick Meeting in Westmoreland questioned the legitimacy of these actions, and consequently the Preston Patrick Meeting separated from the main body of Friends. There is evidence that regional supporters of Wilkinson and Story objected to these overarching structures as well as the establishment of the Women's Meeting, but it is also apparent that, as the controversy progressed from the 1670s into the early eighteenth century, the challenge posed by the leading protagonists was primarily against the growing authority of Fox and the London Friends. This can be best illustrated in the views of William Rogers (d. 1711?) who, in 1680, stated that Fox's innovations were divisive (Rogers 1680; Martin 2003, ch. 2). It was, however, agreed that these meetings would work towards mutual goals, and this, at least, guaranteed women an administrative, if unequal, role in the Society although it was not until the mid-eighteenth century that all Monthly Meetings had a Women's Meeting (Wilcox 1995).

Some of these Monthly Meetings oversaw large geographical areas, while others were quite small (e.g. Upperside in Buckinghamshire), and increased in size as local groups amalgamated after 1700. They managed the local meeting's financial, legal, and property transactions, including the provision of poor relief and education, and enforced the code of discipline. The Quarterly Meetings, which were established between 1666 and 1668, received and deliberated upon the minutes of the Monthly Meetings. In conjunction with the Monthly Meetings they implemented the Quaker code of conduct, especially where disciplinary matters needed a firm hand.

WILLIAM PENN, POLITICS, AND THE GRANTING OF PENNSYLVANIA

The 'Testimony of the Brethren', which George Fox fully supported after his release from prison in September 1666, anchored the structural changes. These were decisive points in the development of Quakerism as the 'expressions of the Spirit, which had been implicit in every paper ever written by Quaker leaders on questions of discipline and organization, was formalized as never before' (Moore 2000, 225). Given the level of persecution such measures were necessary to ensure unity and, despite resentment at further centralization, there was greater opportunity for Friends to challenge the law, lobby for judicial changes, and respond to political changes. William Penn (1644–1718), the son of an English admiral, played a significant part in the delicate negotiations with the Crown and carefully articulated Quaker opposition to the penal code. He advanced the cause of religious liberty by his 'forceful polemics' within and outside the royal court (Geiter 2000, 20). In response to the Conventicle Act (1670), which effectively barred Friends from Meeting for Worship, he wrote *The Great Case of Liberty of Conscience*. This direct appeal to Charles II did not, however, mean that his views were publicly accepted and he was subsequently charged with sedition and imprisoned at Newgate. Together with William Meade he was found not guilty by the jury despite the determination of the judge to ensure their conviction (the Bushell Case). This action established the right of a jury to decide court cases independent of the will of the judge, and significantly brought Penn to greater royal and parliamentary attention as a spokesman for dissent. His ability to network effectively with leading politicians—notably the earls of Rochester and Sunderland, as well as Sidney Godolphin (the 'Chits')—gave him access to the Privy Council and the promotion of religious freedom. Significantly, these men were 'neither Whig nor Tory but Court politicians... [who] took their lead from the king, not from party leaders' and this gave him a particular advantage in his dealings at court (Geiter 2000, 28). When James, Duke of York, espoused Catholicism in 1673, there was an attempt to exclude him from the succession, sending shockwaves throughout the kingdom. Friends had to decide on their allegiance and from 1675 the Morning Meeting cautioned members to identify those politicians who would best support toleration. Although his allegiances were never fixed, Penn's frustration with the process of securing a colonial charter directed him towards a more pragmatic political stance. In this respect, he supported the Whigs in the first election of 1679 (Jones 1986, 61). This period marked his growing political significance, but it was his rapprochement with 'the Chits' that enabled him to convince court politicians and ultimately King Charles to grant a special acquisition of land that would become Pennsylvania. Charles nevertheless sought to punish the Whigs, particularly after the Rye House Plot of 1683, and this led to a further wave of persecution for dissenters.

The decision to grant Penn his colony was taken on 28 February 1681, in lieu of a debt of £16,000 owed to Admiral William Penn (Dunn, 1986c, 41–2). The charter of Pennsylvania was signed by the king on 4 March, and proclaimed on 2 April 1681; he called on Penn to 'enlarge our English Empire, and promote such useful commodities as may be of benefit to us and our dominions... in the parts of America not yet cultivated and planted' (Soderlund 1983, 41). The granting of Pennsylvania 'did not owe its origins to the desire for a religious utopia, nor was it just another colonial venture'. The crisis in England over the exclusion and the alleged popish plot that had surfaced in the late-1670s threatened the future of the monarchy. Charles, as a shrewd political strategist, realized that to avoid the same calamity as his father he had to offer a commercial and ideological incentive. Penn drove a hard bargain over the new colony and also sought the three counties below Pennsylvania (Delaware), which were reluctantly granted since these were part of the Duke of York's lucrative proprietorship (Geiter 2000, 44–5).

After these negotiations leading Friends, including Thomas Rudyard, Arent Sonmans, Ambrose Rigge, Thomas Barker, and William Gibson, met with William Penn in London and discussed his plans for settling Pennsylvania. As a result, several Quaker companies were established and the territory was divided up. Acting as trustees for prospective settlers, these Friends conveyed parcels of land to other members who believed that they could create a new Quaker colony that would be politically and economically viable, while also allowing them to practise their religious beliefs unhindered (Pomfret 1956b, 137–63; Frost 1990). A number of Friends had already secured part-ownership of West Jersey (Bodleian Library, 1675; Pomfret 1956a), and purchased East New Jersey in 1682. Burlington, on the east side of the Delaware River, was an established town when Philadelphia was just getting started. Quakers first settled in Burlington in August 1677 and the Meeting records date from 1678. Five or six ships brought 1400 persons to Salem or Burlington prior to 1681, the year prior to the settlement of Philadelphia (Gummere 1883). East Jersey, however, failed to result in a permanent Quaker settlement, and the two provinces were combined in 1702 into New Jersey (Landsman 1986, 241–57). These territories, along with Delaware, gave Friends an ample opportunity to safeguard their communities and to establish 'a single "culture" area' (Tolles 1960, 117) but, according to John Pomfret, 'the temptation for Penn and his Quaker associates to obtain control of the entire area from the Hudson to Chesapeake was too strong to resist' (1953, 252). These developments were sanctioned by George Fox and other leading Quakers who 'stood firmly behind the plan of colonization in America... [and] glimpsed the possibility of a great dominion... that would encompass the fertile valleys of the Delaware and its branches' (Pomfret, 253, 291).

Economic and social factors, as well as an escape from persecution, prompted many Quakers to risk the dangers of a lengthy sea voyage in order to establish settlements for the Friends. The downside to all this activity was that the emigration of individual Quakers or families caused many British Quaker meetings to shrink dramatically. It was reported that in some areas, notably in rural meetings, the 'unsavoury precedings & runneings into Pensilvania... [was] a Cause of great weakening If not totall decayeinge of some meetings'. For these Friends there was a general feeling that they were the 'remnant' of once-vibrant Quaker communities (Allen 2004b, 42). Controversy and political intrigue also undermined the new colony, and some emigrants questioned William Penn's reputation. Indeed, settlers in the Welsh Tract in 1697 called him '*diwyneb*' ('two-faced') for allegedly reneging on his promise to give them land in Philadelphia and along the Susquehanna (Allen 2004b, 39–40), but the reality was that they were no longer a numerically dominant group as, due to the religious toleration enshrined in the frame of government for the colony, larger numbers of other ethnic and religious groups had settled in the province.

Business Networks

Alongside the transatlantic networks that were established and the influx of new Quaker communities in the American and Caribbean colonies (Gragg 2009, 58–71), business networks and entrepreneurial activity increasingly became characteristic of early modern Friends. During the implementation of the penal code many Friends' business interests suffered from their refusal to swear oaths, and merchants 'could not sue for debts, nor carry through their transactions with the customs and excise, nor defend their titles, nor give evidence' (Braithwaite (1979 [1919]), 181), while lengthy imprisonment naturally hampered trade. They, however, gained a reputation for hard but honest bargaining, and many were remarkably successful (ch. 28, this vol.; Walvin 1997, ch. 2; Roberts 2004, 172–93; Raistrick 1950).

Although there is abundant evidence that Friends were capable of establishing good foundations in their business endeavours, they also took their social responsibilities seriously too. In Barbados, Quaker settlers were 'among the most prosperous in the Atlantic world' (Gragg 2009, 63), but in 1669 stated they that 'we have many Poor among us'. Their response, as Gragg shows, was to bequeath money for the poor in their wills, such as Thomas Foster of St Philip who, in 1684, left £200 for the poor in the five meetings on the island (Besse 1753, II, 287; Gragg 2009, 73). Similarly, among the finest exponents of Quaker philanthropy was John Bellers (1654–1725), a London Friend, who wrote a number of tracts towards the end of the century outlining his thoughts on good health, education, and the importance of assisting the poor, which became a charitable model for others in the years after his death (Bellers 1695; ch. 3, this vol.).

Doctrinal Literature

As noted earlier in the discussion of controversies a substantial body of doctrinal Quaker literature was produced after the Restoration, including the publication of tracts directed at their opponents (Underwood 1997, 17–19). Works by George Fox and Margaret Fell as well as other leading members, such as Barclay, Penn, Whitehead, and Isaac Penington, were widely circulated, but there was a distinct change in direction in the theological outpourings of Friends from the 1650s onwards. As Dandelion has observed, Quakerism 'lost its eschatological edge in the 1660s and adopted a pragmatic approach essential for survival' (2007, 47). While Friends still based their theology on the reception of Christ in Spirit, they also stressed the importance of the historic Jesus. During Fox's visit to Barbados in 1671 he wrote to Governor Codrington and the Assembly exonerating Friends from 'false reports... [and the] many scandalous lies and slanders [which] have been cast upon us, to render us odious' (Fox 1995, 602–6). In doing so, he was responding to the accusation that Friends on the island were deviant in their religious practices in denying God, Christ, and the Scriptures, as well as social mal-contents who were inciting a slave rebellion. Fox was attempting to defend the Quaker community, and at the same time outlining their wider social responsibilities and the orthodoxy of their belief system (Fox 1995, 602–4; Gragg 2009, 55). Significantly, other works by Fox, notably his journal and the 'Book of Miracles' compiled after 1675, were not published in his lifetime. Indeed, the 'Book of Miracles' was never published and was ultimately lost, while Fox's journal underwent substantial editorial change by the Second Day Morning Meeting. It was not until Norman Penney's 1911 edition that Fox's almost complete original work was published. This delay may well have stopped further controversies from emerging particularly over the charismatic leadership of Fox himself (Cadbury 1948; Moore 2005, 335–44).

Equally important in defending Quakerism in the 1670s was the work of the Scottish Friend Robert Barclay, particularly *Quakerism Confirmed* (Barclay and Keith 1676; Sell 1992, 210–26) and *Theologiæ verè Christianæ Apologia* published in Latin in Amsterdam and reprinted the following year (Barclay 1676). The latter scholarly text was promoted around Europe, especially in the Netherlands and Germany in 1677 by Fox, Penn, and the Scottish Quaker George Keith (1638?–1716). This was followed by an English version, an *Apology for the True Christianity Divinity* (Barclay 1678). The extent to which there was agreement within the Society and whether Fox agreed with Barclay, has been debated by Melvin Endy and T. Vail Palmer (2004; 2006).

Towards Toleration

Charles II's death in 1685 and the accession of James II heralded new opportunities for dissenters. The following year some charges of recusancy were dismissed (Horle 1988, 88–90), and this period was a turning point in the relationship between the state and dissenters. The pre-eminence of William Penn in royal circles from the late 1670s onwards and his close association with James II during the mid-1680s onwards requires reflection. In May 1686 he was appointed as an unofficial envoy to Holland to assess the depth of feeling of William, Prince of Orange, for the king's proposed measure of toleration. Although there was support for the removal of the penal laws, there was no agreement on the removal of the Test Act, which the prince felt could, under a Catholic monarch, challenge the basis of Protestantism. Indeed, a precedent had been set by Louis XIV's revocation of the Edict of Nantes a year earlier. Despite the muted success of his visit, Penn and fellow dissenters ardently lobbied for toleration. In the spring of 1687 Penn was actively involved in drafting the Declaration of Indulgence for all, including Catholics. For dissenters this gave them the opportunity to hold peaceful meetings if they petitioned the king for relief. Yet there was opposition from Anglicans as well as dissenters who feared that, if this measure succeeded, Catholics would again achieve political power. Moreover, many Friends were concerned about Penn's too-firm an attachment to the king and sceptical that such a measure of toleration was simply based on James's royal prerogative and not parliamentary legislation (Geiter 2000, 56–7). Despite Anglican opposition, the king sought to dismantle the penal code and granted a Declaration of Indulgence on 4 April 1687 and reissued the following April.

The extent to which members actively sanctioned the endeavours of Penn is also open to question and Friends began to suspect him of worldly motives with comparisons being made to the great courtier in the Book of Esther. With the invasion of Prince William in 1688, Penn was arrested in December, accused of having papist leanings, and brought to trial but bailed. Subsequently he was rearrested and his life was certainly in peril during these uncertain years. Viewed as a traitor by William and Mary, Penn consequently lost control of Pennsylvania and only skilful negotiation with the new regime saw him regain royal favour and, in 1694, the restoration of his colony (Geiter 2000, 21, 61–3, 66–8). The Act of Toleration that followed in the wake of William's victory over James II meant that Friends could now license their meeting houses and accept that they had a modicum of safety (Horle 1988, 94–5) but it proved to be double-edged. It certainly provided a much safer environment for Friends to practise their beliefs without the continued threat of imprisonment, although they would not compromise on the issue of oaths and tithes. Conversely, there was also a significant decline in membership post-toleration. It is true that until the early years of the eighteenth century there was recruitment, but as the century wore on numbers declined in many areas (ch. 3, this vol.).

The Keithian Controversy and the Death of the First Generation

Although Quakerism increasingly moved from the radicalism of the 1650s to a position of respectability, serious internal disputes continued to arise. The last major controversy of this period within the Society was centred on George Keith, a Quaker theologian from the Aberdeen Meeting. Like many other leading Friends he was imprisoned several times in the 1660s but continued to proselytize alongside Robert Barclay before making his way to London in 1670 where he joined up with Fox, Penn, and Whitehead. An active participant in the theological debates of the period, Keith was an ever-present spokesperson for the Society and was again imprisoned for his beliefs. In 1684 he was appointed as surveyor-general of East Jersey before relocating to Philadelphia in 1689 where his views led to schism.

Unlike the previous disputes which centred on organizational innovations, during the 1690s Keith asserted the authority of Scripture over the light within and 'to impose creedal affirmation as a requisite of Quaker membership', while other settlers, particularly William Stockdale, defended the current practices (Keith 1692, 6). Keith's campaign may have arisen from local circumstances, particularly his fear that meetings in Pennsylvania could be contaminated by attendees from other religious communities in their efforts to secure the practical assistance of leading Friends in the colony (Martin

2003, 22). He began to question the conviction of Friends, sought greater evidence of their belief in the historical Jesus with personal declarations of faith, and ultimately promoted a written Quaker creed. Fierce criticism quickly emerged in Philadelphia and elsewhere, and this was fuelled in 1692 by his polemic publications against Friends' beliefs. At the Yearly Meeting his actions were condemned as that of a schismatic, while his own disapproval of Quaker magistrates sanctioning force against pirates led to his subsequent arrest and trial. The London Yearly Meeting, conscious that such activity could reignite persecution, censured his views. Given the limited legal position of the Society under the Act of Toleration and questions over the loyalty of some leading Friends to the new political regime, such divisions thrust the Quakers back into the limelight. Keith, however, was determined to expose the heretical views, as he saw them, of Friends on both sides of the Atlantic. The London Yearly Meeting attempted to resolve the problem, but in 1694 they disowned Keith. He responded with accusations that leading Friends, particularly George Whitehead, William Penn, and the late Robert Barclay, were heretics and the controversy continued into the eighteenth century (Martin 2003, ch. 3; Chamberlain 2005 [2004]).

Despite the controversies that surfaced, many historians agree that towards the end of the seventeenth century Quakers lacked the tenacity and dynamism of the pioneers of the Commonwealth and Restoration years. The death of George Fox in 1691 marked the end of the 'heroic age' of the Society, and Fox was deemed irreplaceable by those who had benefited from his charismatic leadership. An entire generation of prominent Quakers was lost after 1689. Robert Barclay (1648–90), Stephen Crisp (d. 1692), Mary Fisher (c.1623–98), Margaret Fell (1614–1702), and many other leading lights of the Society were all dead by the early years of the eighteenth century. William Penn (1644–1718) and George Whitehead (1636–1723) died shortly afterwards and although they were succeeded by devout, spiritual men and women, passion gave way to caution and recruitment suffered. The early leaders had kept the Society together in the most challenging of circumstances, during the worst years of persecution and their deaths left a vacuum that was difficult to fill. Perverse though it may appear, toleration, not persecution, was to prove more damaging in the long term.

Post-Toleration

Local intolerance nevertheless continued to persist: state laws inhibited Quakers from exercising responsible roles in local or national politics; like all non-Anglicans they were still barred from attending English universities; and petty recriminations and accusations that Friends were disturbers of the peace were still voiced or published in broadsides. Regional meetings, as well as the Meeting for Sufferings, reported on numerous occasions that members were subject to harassment for tithes, fined, or imprisoned for failing to adhere to muster rolls or offering substitutes for the military, and chastised if they were perceived to be disruptive (Allen 2003, 23–47). Yet, in contrast, for most dissenters, including Quakers, in the post-revolution years there were growing signs of rapprochement at the national and regional levels where they often assisted in poor relief or acted as churchwardens or constables (Davies 2000, 202–7). As Friends gradually achieved accommodation with the state they acted as a pressure group informing the political debate and moral issues of the age (Greaves 2001, 24–50; Allen 2007, 54–72). Their determination to oppose tithes thereby denying state maintenance of ministers, however, meant that their property was still being distrained well into the eighteenth century and beyond (Ditchfield 1985, 87–114). Equally, their refusal to swear oaths required careful negotiation until eventually they agreed on a compromised solution whereby they could affirm in legal matters. The Affirmation Act of 1696 was an important step in providing relief, but the exact wording of the affirmation was a matter of considerable discussion for the next twenty-six years, until the Affirmation Act of 1722 was accepted by Friends (Morgan 1993, ch. 3–4). The critical watershed for the Society came when the first generation of leading members had passed and missionary fervour declined. The persecution of Friends made them a highly visible and controversial body of dissenters during the Restoration period, but this strangely enough did not obstruct their survival or prosperity at this stage. Once they were no longer the principal target of the authorities, Quakerism became less visible.

Suggested Further Reading

Ahivah (1660) *A Strange Prophecie presented to the Kings Most Excellent Majesty...* London: Aaron Banaster.

Allen, R. C. (2004a) 'Establishing an alternative community in the North-East: Quakers, morals and popular culture in the long eighteenth century', in Helen Berry and Jeremy Gregory (eds.) *Creating and consuming culture in North-East England, 1660–1832.* Aldershot: Ashgate, pp. 98–119.

Allen, R. C. (2007) *Quaker communities in early modern Wales: From resistance to respectability.* Cardiff: University of Wales Press.

Allen, R. C. (2009) 'An alarm sounded to the sinners in Sion: John Kelsall, Quakers and popular culture in eighteenth-century Wales', in J. Allen and R. C. Allen (eds.) *Faith of our Fathers: Popular culture and belief in post-Reformation England, Ireland and Wales,* Newcastle: Cambridge Scholars Press, pp. 52–74.

Beck, W. & Ball, F. T. (1869) *The London Friends' Meetings, showing the rise of the Society of Friends in London,* London: Kitto.

Besse, J. (1753), *A collection of the sufferings of the people called Quakers* (2 vols) London: L. Hinde.

Braithwaite, W. C. (1979) *The second period of Quakerism.* London: Macmillan, 1919, 2nd edn, rept, York: Sessions.

Cadbury, H. J. (1952). 'First settlement of Meetings in Europe', *Journal of the Friends' Historical Society,* vol. 44 (1), 11–12.

Carter, C. F. (1967) 'Unsettled Friends: Church government and the Origins of Membership', *Journal of the Friends' Historical Society,* vol. 51, 3, 143–53.

Davies, A. (2000) *The Quakers in English Society, 1655–1725.* Oxford: Oxford University Press.

Frost, J. W. (1993) *A perfect freedom. Religious liberty in Pennsylvania*. Philadelphia: Pennsylvania State University Press.

Geiter, M. K. (2000) *William Penn*. Harlow: Longman.

Gragg, L. (2009) *The Quaker community on Barbados: challenging the culture of the planter class*. Columbia, MS: University of Missouri Press. Greaves, R. L. (1986) *Deliver us from evil: The radical underground in Britain, 1660–1663*. New York; Oxford: Oxford University Press.

Horle, C. W. (1988) *The Quakers and the English legal system, 1660–1688*. Philadelphia: University of Pennsylvania Press.

Moore, R. (2000) *The light in their consciences: The Early Quakers in Britain, 1646–1666*. University Park, Pa: Pennsylvania State University Press.

Morgan, N. (1993) *Lancashire Quakers and the establishment, 1660–1730*. Halifax: Ryburn.

Trevett, C. (2000) *Quaker women prophets in England and Wales 1650–1700*. Lewistown, NY and Lampeter: Edwin Mellen Press.

CHAPTER 3

....

QUIETIST QUAKERISM, 1692–C.1805

....

ROBYNNE ROGERS HEALEY

THE death of Fox and the passage of the Act of Toleration ushered in the long eighteenth century of Quakerism. Commonly called the Quietist period, this era has been interpreted as one in which exclusivity and sectarianism took precedence over zealous expansion. While silence did come to dominate forms of worship, this was not a period of stagnation or regression. Throughout this century Quakers developed the features that came to define their distinctive way of life. Far more than an insistence on simplicity and spiritual detachment from earthly affairs typified this period—Friends expanded their geographical influence, made important contributions to commerce and industry, and clarified enduring positions, or testimonies, on war and humanitarianism.

The portrayal of Quietist Quakerism as the faith of an 'inoffensive, industrious, frugal, and conscientious people' (Trueblood 1966, 148), has typically been presented as either evidence of the deterioration of enthusiastic Quakerism, or as an unremarkable stage between the 'aggressive' Quakerism of the early and later periods (Braithwaite 1919; Jones 1921; Williams 1962; Trueblood 1966; Punshon 1984). Jones (1921, 33) contends that Quietist mysticism shaped 'the transition from the primitive Quaker movement to "Quakerism"', but unlike the 'characteristically positive' mysticism of the early period, this mysticism was 'negative to a marked degree', based as it was 'on a pervading sense of the wreck and ruin of fallen man'. Braithwaite (1919) was equally as pessimistic. Despite this negative portrayal, Southern (2011) and Pryce (2010) have demonstrated that Braithwaite and Jones were ambivalent about Quietism. In a private letter to Emma Cadbury, Jones wonders at the inconsistency of what he considers an inadequate theology producing outstanding individuals and moments in Quaker history: 'There are two ways to look at Quietism. The fundamental theory of it seems to me a false one but the actual fact of it on individual lives was often very wonderful, and in many cases produced a very high type of saint' (Southern 2011, 37). This incongruity is seen in later works. Punshon (1984) characterizes eighteenth-century Quaker meetings as 'lifeless' and their ministry 'uninspiring' (151) and suggests that the separation of Quakers from the world 'is one of the tragedies of English religious history' (103); at the same time he argues that 'Eighteenth Century Quietism preserved the soul of Quakerism rather than losing it' (102).

Women's historians have a more positive view. Larson (1999) maintains that in contrast to Puritan and Congregationalist women in eighteenth-century British colonies, Quakerism provided an alternative to the models of submission and domesticity. As 'Public Friends', some Quaker women challenged social conventions by delivering public lectures to mixed audiences. Despite a more rigidly applied Discipline, Quaker women in the Quietist era retained an independent spiritual identity and spiritual authority (Larson 1999, 299–303). Eighteenth-century Quaker women were not liberated from customs like their seventeenth-century sisters (Mack 1992) and spiritual equality did not extend to control of property (Frost 1973, 178). Nonetheless, spiritual authority endowed Quaker women with community influence and ministerial functions unavailable to women in most denominations (Bacon 1986; 1988). Moreover, women were at the centre of the domestic enterprise that defined the values of eighteenth-century Quakerism—values that were feminine: 'restraint, benevolence, privacy, domestic order, passivity' (Mack 2003, 164).

Negotiating the space between spiritual authority and spiritual submission was demanding. Ecstatic worship progressively yielded to silence as Quakers sought spiritual awareness by rejecting all temporal desires and distractions. Yet, they also became absorbed in social reform. Was this new? Mack (2003, 163) argues that the 'desire for passivity and self-annihilation, on the one hand, and the urge toward self-transformation and world transformation, on the other' has been a consistent aspect of Christian thought. Quakers struggled to reconcile their beliefs to their world; scholars have struggled to understand the Quietist paradox. Mack (2003, 173) reasons that the 'contradiction between the ideal of self-transcendence and the cultivation of a competent self was resolved by turning the energies of the individual outward, in charitable impulses toward others'. Alternately, Dandelion (2010) suggests that a 'pair of dualisms'—worldly and non-worldly and natural and supernatural—functioned in tandem during the Quietist era, creating separate spheres of Quaker life. Caught between their desire to reform the world and their longing to build a holy, distinct community, eighteenth-century Quakers created a dualistic world in which their mysticism remained isolated from the world they worked to change.

THEOLOGY

The development of Quietist theology was neither sudden nor complete. An overview of the period reveals three theological tendencies among Quakers—Quietism, rationalism, and evangelicalism. While the three emerged and flourished at different times, for much of the period they were able to function side by side. After all, proponents of all three theologies traced their roots back to early Friends. By the end of the century, however, differences between advocates of each theology began to surpass their similarities and fissures emerged within Quakerism.

The death of Fox in 1691 shortly after that of Barclay in1690, and the passage of the Act of Toleration (1689) can give the illusion of a sudden shift in theological bearing. This was not the case. The theology of George Whitehead (1636–1723), who emerged as the unofficial leader of the Society after Fox's death, reflects Barclay's negative view of human nature. Barclay insisted that the working of the Light Within required the suppression of all 'creaturely activity'. It was Barclay's *Apology*, Jones (1921, 60) argues, that was 'beyond question the primary influence which made Friends quietistic'. Whitehead may have deepened the descent into Quietism (Punshon 1984; Barbour and Frost 1994), but its features—the suspension of human reason, planning, and all worldly activity to passive receptivity of divine revelation—were present before he expanded the theology. Already in 1689, the London Yearly Meeting Epistle (LYM 1821, 36) counselled Friends 'as the Lord's hidden ones, that are always quiet in the land...who know when and where to keep silent... keeping out of all airy discourses and words, that may any-ways become snares, or hurtful to truth or Friends'. Whitehead and Stephen Crisp (1628–92) echoed these sentiments in 1692, exhorting Friends to demonstrate their faith by 'a quiet life, and peaceable subjection' to government and to 'all study to be quiet, and mind their own business, in God's holy fear' (LYM 1821, 54).

It is difficult to determine whether Quietism influenced Quakers' position in society or if their position in society shaped the development of Quietism. While the Act of Toleration gave non-Anglicans, except Catholics and Unitarians, a right to worship and hold property, toleration had its limits. Dissenters continued to be barred from universities and public office (they could not serve as sheriffs or members of Parliament, nor could they sit on juries) and, along with other English subjects, they were still required to remit tithes to support the established Church of England. The freedom of worship enshrined in the Act of Toleration was conditional: places of worship had to be registered and meeting in private homes was prohibited (William and Mary 1688). Some high-church Anglicans, suspicious of the anticlericalism and lack of sacraments in Quakerism, accused Quakers of being non-Christians (Punshon 1984, 100–101; Barbour and Frost 1994, 83–84) despite their willingness to profess faith in 'God the Father and in Jesus Christ his Eternall Sonne the true God and in the Holy Spirit one God blessed for evermore' and the 'Divine Inspiration' of the Old and New Testament (William and Mary 1688, 75).

In this new age of limited toleration, Quakers wanted to appear as inoffensive as possible and Quietist theology proved useful to the task. Bell (2008) demonstrates the extent to which eighteenth-century 'mainstream' Quakers were prepared to rewrite theological treatises and histories to fit a revised image of Quakerism as innocuous. This is apparent in Whitehead's introduction to and editing of the 1716 edition of *A collection of sundry books, epistles and papers, written by James Nayler*. Twenty-three of Nayler's tracts—half of what he produced between 1652 and 1656—were considered 'controversial' and excluded from the collection (Bell 2008, 432); those included were edited to remove hints of extremism or doctrine that had come to be considered unsound

(Bell 2008, 439). Under Whitehead's pen, Nayler was reinvented in the Quietist mould from a convicted blasphemer to 'an "everyman" figure of the suffering Quaker' (Bell 2008, 437). Nayler's writings were not the only works to be censored or revised. Fox's *Journal* was altered, Sewel's *History*—the first full-length history of Quakerism written by a Quaker—was translated from Dutch to English and 'corrected' in the process, and Whitehead's own journal left out experiences that might be considered theologically radical. This was, as Bell suggests, a survival strategy. The Morning Meeting's control over the Quaker press and the image of English Quakerism grew throughout the Quietist period (Hall 1992). It is most evident in the 1742 German edition of Sewel's *Geschichte*, a direct translation of the English *History* with almost no reference to the Dutch original. By this point, Bell contends, English Quakerism 'had become the adjudicator of orthodoxy, with English the language of Quaker belief' (Bell, 445). That it took half a century to arrive at this juncture indicates that the transition to Quietism, for which this period is named, was not smooth. Moreover, for all of the formal attempts to present Quakerism in the Quietist mould, the reality of Quakerism was far more diverse. The Keithian Controversy at the beginning of the Quietist era, and the Irish Separation and Hannah Barnard (1754–1825) controversy at its end are the most overt signs of discord occasioned by theological differences.

Jones saw Quaker Quietism as rooted in the continental Quietists of the seventeenth and eighteenth centuries whose spiritual quest was characterized by 'total absorption in God, the annihilation of self, the substitution of divine action for action directed by human will, and the attainment of a perfect and selfless love' (Jones 1917, 8). The direct translation from continental to Quaker Quietism has been challenged since continental Quietists were antinomian and Quakers were not (Tolles 1945, 27; Punshon 1984, 120). Certainly there was a shift to silent worship partly in response to Quietism. As Tousley (2008) and Dandelion (2010) have observed, eighteenth-century Quakers did not claim the same spiritual intimacy with the divine as their predecessors had. The 'meantime theology' (Dandelion, 2010) that developed focused increasingly on introspection. Claims about personal transformation became less certain (Tousley, 2008) at the same time that Quakers abjured anything sensory or worldly as leading to divine revelation.

The Quietist fear of acting ahead of the Spirit cast a shadow of uncertainty on ministry. Instead of the confident vocal ministry of the early period, greater hesitation and even anguish became common resulting in meetings that were ever-more silent. Journals attest to the agony of ministers who felt compelled to speak while at the same time they felt unfit to do so. Williams (1962, 123) provides a number of examples: in 1770 Irish minister John Rutty recorded twenty-two successive meetings in Dublin where the silence was broken only once. In 1785 American minister Job Scott visited fifteen meetings over the space of twenty days, 'not daring to open his mouth in one of them'. Shortly afterwards, Thomas Scattergood visited seven successive meetings and remained silent in each one, despite the eagerness of those in attendance to hear him speak. Rebecca Larson (1999) and Phyllis Mack (2003) relate the experiences of women who also felt conflicted over their motivation to public ministry. Jane Fenn Hoskens' (1694–1764) description of her first attempts to speak is illustrative:

I had not long enjoyed Divine peace, before the old accuser [Satan] began again, telling me I had blasphemed against the Holy Ghost, in that I had deceived the people, in pretending to preach by Divine influence, which he insinuated was a positive untruth; and for me to make a show of worshipping Him whom I had thus belied, was a sin never to be forgiven. (Larson 1999, 77)

This fixation with incorrect 'leading' is also evident in the lives of Lydia Lancaster (1683–1761) and Elizabeth Hudson (1722–83) who both delayed speaking in ministry for years after they first felt called to do so (Larson, 1999). Alternately, Diana Caroline Hopwood was so strongly convicted of her message that she persisted in public ministry despite being reproached by male elders in her meeting (Wright 2003, 41–3).

Rationalism or moderate Quakerism was another distinct emphasis in Quaker belief in this period. Quietism may have dominated the practice of ministry, but Quakerism was not immune to Enlightenment influences and, as Barbour and Frost (1994, 98) maintain, eighteenth-century Friends 'reached no consensus over the relationship of the Inward Light of God to the natural light of reason'. Were reason and religious 'leading' incompatible? Rationalist Quakers navigated the space between the two quite successfully, claiming their roots in the work of early Friends. Fox may have discouraged reliance on 'head knowledge', but he did not disdain education; many early Friends were skilled linguists, mathematicians, natural scientists, and theologians; and, responding to early Quaker detractors, required reason as did addressing the religious controversies (Barbour and Frost 1994, 98). Thomas Beaven's *Essay Concerning the Restoration of Primitive Christianity* (1723) alludes to the careful balance between reason and the Light: 'the *common Reason* of Man stands in Need of Light and Help from *Heaven*... 'tis the *divine Spirit,* which *enlightens* and *influences* the *noble* Faculty of *Reason*' (Barbour and Frost 1994, 99). Rationalist Quakerism was manifest in an ethical life. This emphasis on ethics is apparent in William Penn's 1693 treatise *Some Fruits of Solitude* that discouraged excess of any sort and emphasized the harmony between moderation and Christian virtue (Barbour and Frost 1994, 98). Avoidance of extremes was a key component of Quaker rationalism; it did not deny revelation and could be critical of deism. Like Quietists, rational Quakers became silent in Meeting for Worship. Their Quakerism was moderate and functioned quite successfully between the poles of reason and revelation, Scripture and nature without having to choose one over the other (Barbour and Frost, 1994). Unlike the Quietists whose mysticism was uncompromisingly kept separate from the world (Dandelion, 2010), the rationalists, who included Quakers such as Alexander Arscott, John Bockett, Richard Claridge, and James Logan, were comfortable with their compromise position. It was not until the late eighteenth century that theological divisions on both sides of the Atlantic called into question the rationalist positions of Quakers such as Hannah Barnard and Abraham Shackleton (1752–1818) (Barbour et al 1995, 100–6).

Evangelicalism swept through the English-speaking world in the mid-eighteenth century; in North America the movement was known as the Great Awakening and in Britain it was referred to as the Evangelical Revival. Quietist Quakers were deeply suspicious of this enthusiastic religious movement (Tolles 1945; Hamm 2003), but they were not untouched by it. By the time of the Evangelical Revival, Quakers had become respectable members of upper-middle class society (Tolles 1945; 1948) and, despite differences between Quietists and rationalists, both were generally theologically committed to the inward working of the Light—or the Christ in one's soul—as opposed to the evangelical focus on the atonement of the historic Christ. The emotional excesses of revivalism disturbed established Friends (Tolles 1945). In some ways it is ironic that Quakers, the heirs of an ecstatic faith, were so disparaging of the emotional religion of evangelicals. This is a measure of how the Religious Society of Friends had changed. Quietist and rationalist Quakers had come to believe that the process of salvation was gradual, not sudden (Frost 1973; Hamm 2003; Tousley 2008). Despite Friends' scepticism, evangelicalism expanded its influence in the English Atlantic world. In some cases its influence was very personal as seen in the autobiography of Elizabeth Ashbridge (1713–55) who attempted to reclaim the 'enthusiastic potential in prophesying and writing' and thus recaptured the Great Awakening's 'spirit and practice in her text' despite Friends' rejection of it (Tarter 2005, 187). In other cases its influence was much broader. The issues at the centre of the Irish separation and the Hannah Barnard controversies discussed in Chapter 4 are evidence of the extent to which the London Yearly Meeting had been influenced by evangelical theology by the turn of the century.

Organization and 'Sectarianism'

The survival strategies that Quakers formulated in this period focused predominantly on meeting organization and discipline. What emerged as a response to persecution under the Conventicle Acts became increasingly uncompromising and codified. As organizational structures tightened, Friends' sectarianism increased and the focus of the Meeting shifted inwards to meeting discipline and the family (Frost 1973; Butler 1978; Barbour and Frost 1994). This did not prevent Friends from engagement with the world around them.

The eighteenth-century Religious Society of Friends became more organized, bureaucratized, and hierarchical. One element of this was the codification and collection of rules of behaviour in what American Quakers called the 'Discipline' (Butler 1978, 40), and what British Quakers titled the *Christian and brotherly advices, given forth from time to time by the yearly meetings in London*, but referred to as *The Book of Extracts* (Punshon 1984, 137). The structure of local, Monthly, Quarterly, and Yearly Meetings also afforded the network for maintaining unity among Quakers near and far, and the Queries continued to be used to assess the spiritual condition of the Society. These changed throughout the century to reflect the concerns of Quakers and the local interests of meetings. Jones (1921, 140) insists that the 'custom of answering the Queries in a formal and detailed way was almost certainly a mistake', given the questions implied the acceptable answer and led to formulaic, rather than inspired, responses.

From a Quietist perspective, meeting business was considered an alternate form of worship and all decisions were subject to the direction of the Light Within among spiritually equal Friends. Nonetheless, reason and intellect did play a role in examining evidence brought before the Meeting (Barbour and Frost 1988, 111). And, while spiritual equality was accepted in theory, handling meeting business created a space for elders, ministers, overseers, and clerks to form a spiritual oligarchy (Butler 1978, 40–2; Worrall 1980, 75; Punshon 1984, 143; Barbour and Frost 1994, 77). Moreover, women did not serve on the Morning Meeting or the Meeting for Sufferings, nor was there a Women's Yearly Meeting in London, although there were Women's Yearly Meetings in the colonies and Ireland. London women attended the Box Meeting, but they advocated at length for their own Yearly Meeting (Mack 1992, 319–22). It was not until 1784 that a delegation of British and American Quaker women was successful in convincing London Yearly Meeting men to create a Yearly Meeting of Women Friends. Not every woman supported this cause. Margaret Hoare Woods, a London Friend, preferred subordination to 'female Rights' (Jennings 1986, 30–1). Caution is called for in regarding eighteenth-century Quakers in light of present-day feminist thought. Quaker women had considerable agency (Levenduski 1996), but in truly Quietist fashion, many defined agency not as doing what they wanted to do, but doing what was right (Mack 2003, 156).

The clarification of membership tightened organization. Before 1700 membership was loosely articulated. As Hamm (2003, 30) says, 'Friends knew who belonged and who did not.' Children of Quakers were counted as were those who married Friends and followed Quaker practice. Large-scale transatlantic colonization in the late seventeenth century demanded a more formal process of determining who belonged. Colonial meetings asked London Yearly Meeting (LYM) to insist that Monthly Meetings issue certificates to departing emigrants that testified to their standing in the Religious Society of Friends, their ability to marry, and their credit status (Butler 1978, 28–9). The challenge of poor relief also forced LYM to more precise definitions. Only members were entitled to poor relief; what about those claiming to be Friends only to access this benefit? And which Meeting provided assistance in the case of relocation? These questions were answered in 1737 by the Meeting in a minute on 'Removals and Settlements' (Jones 1921, 108). Membership rolls were created and carefully maintained, and children of members in good standing were to be considered birthright Friends. The consequence of birthright membership was a large number of nominal members who were Quakers by birth not by choice (Jones 1921, 109–110). The Quaker reformation only a generation after this decision is indicative of its impact on the spiritual vitality of eighteenth-century Quakerism.

Another attempt to accomplish uniformity among Quakers in constituent Yearly Meetings was the publication of a collection of Advices, Queries, and rules of discipline. New England Yearly Meeting replaced the advices of Fox and other visitors with a formal Discipline in 1708; the Philadelphia Yearly Meeting approved its first Discipline in 1704, although it was lengthened and arranged more carefully in 1719 (Butler 1978; Worrall 1980; Barbour and Frost 1988) and in 1738 the London Yearly Meeting issued its Quarterly Meetings with copies of *The Book of Extracts*. In 1783 *The Book of Extracts* became the first officially printed Discipline (Jones 1921, 143); shortly afterwards the American Yearly Meetings printed their Disciplines (Barbour and Frost 1994, 108). Prior to mass printing, Disciplines were the property of Meetings and there was considerable disparity in their updating. Nevertheless, implicit in the adoption and circulation of a collection of rules was the assumption that they would be enforced.

Disciplines and *The Book of Extracts* provided guidance to Quietist Quakers eager to create a unique culture as a 'peculiar people'. Testimonies on plain speech (not using heathen calendar names and retaining the informal *thee* and *thou*), plain attire, and simple decoration were considered outward markers of an inward faith. The fact that the Epistles of this period continually warn against 'corrupt customs and vain fashions of the world, in speech, habit, behaviour, or furniture' (LYM 1821, 245) suggests that compliance was more difficult to achieve than to dictate. Margaret Fell (1614–1702) had warned against uniformity of costume in her last Epistle to Friends in 1698: 'It's a dangerous thing to lead young Friends much into the observation of outward things, which may be easily done; for they can soon get into an outward garb, to be all alike outwardly, but this will not make them true Christians' (Barbour and Roberts 2004, 566). Many Quakers agreed. By the end of the century, they themselves distinguished between plain Friends—those who observed the regulations—and gay or fast Friends—those who did not. The marked presence of gay Friends alongside plain Friends at the end of the Quietist period is evidence of the diversity of Quakerism. Even so, Quakers made careful use of visitation and a 'religiously guarded education' to nourish their unique culture (Brinton 1958; Frost 1973).

In mid-century, the Society began a process of internal reform designed to return the Society to its primitive purity. Business and industrial success had created some wealthy Quaker families (Walvin 1997). Some of these Quaker grandees (Tolles 1948) seemed more concerned with the letter, rather than the spirit, of the testimony on plainness, using luxurious materials within the restrictions of simple style. Less prosperous Quakers also disregarded testimonies on plainness, endogamy, or dealing in military wares (Tolles 1948; Marietta 2007). Reformers, men and women alike, looked to the Discipline as the instrument for correcting these errors. Beginning in 1755 Philadelphia, elders, overseers, and 'all others active in the discipline' were urged to 'zealously...repair the breaches' to Quaker practice in the 'hopes of the primitive beauty and purity of the Church [being] restored' (Marietta 2007, 54). Reform quickly spread throughout the Quaker world with committees of visitation diligently ferreting out transgressions of the Discipline. Cases of discipline and disownment escalated dramatically. In 1756, recorded violations of the Discipline increased by 64.1 per cent from 1755, a trend that continued until 1760. And, in the 1760s, 21.7 per cent of Philadelphia Yearly Meeting members in Pennsylvania were disowned (Marietta 2007, 55). Between 1750 and 1790, the Philadelphia Yearly Meeting disowned fifty per cent of its young birthright Quakers (Levy 1988, 16). The fixation with endogamy and premarital sex (Marietta 2007, 3–31) shifted the emphasis to the family as the focus of the Society's purity and the hope for its future (Levy 1988; Marietta 2007), although allegiance to the religious group superseded loyalty to the family (Forbes 1982).

In 1760 the London Yearly Meeting initiated a systematic review of the Discipline's implementation, setting off a period of reform in Britain similar to that in the colonies (Punshon 1984, 142–4). No research on the Quaker reform movement in Britain exists that is comparable to Marietta's study of the Philadelphia Yearly Meeting and, while British reform also resulted in a decline in membership, one difference in the legal restrictions on marriages is notable. The Hardwicke Marriage Act, which came into force in 1754, was the first legislation to attempt to prevent 'clandestine marriages' by delineating the requirements by which a marriage was considered legally valid. Exempted from these provisions were Quakers, Jews, the royal family, and those marriages solemnized in Scotland or overseas (Outhwaite 1995, 85). The precise impact of this statute on the Religious Society of Friends is unknown. Its conditions suggest a legal obligation to enforce endogamy among Quakers, yet the law did not prevent Quakers from marrying non-Quakers. The Discipline, on the other hand, did stipulate that Quakers who married 'one of the World' or 'by the Priest' could be disowned (Punshon 1984, 133).

Reformers did achieve a more purified Society. In the process, however, Quakerism became more sectarian and less tolerant of difference. With large numbers of young people being disowned, the stigma of repudiation declined along with the Society's membership (Worrall 1980, 89). Those who remained in the fold did not retreat from the world as Jones (1921) suggested. Rather, Quietist Quakers developed strategies to negotiate the lines between the dichotomous worlds of the Meeting and the outside world (Dandelion 2010).

EXPANSION THROUGH THE BRITISH ATLANTIC WORLD

A strength of early Quakerism was its constituent local communities, each overseeing its own affairs. Local meetings were connected to the larger Quaker network through epistolary correspondence, Quaker publications, and the travelling ministry. The Quaker world expanded significantly in the Quietist period as Friends fostered established networks throughout the Atlantic world. They joined other Britons who took advantage of the more frequent and faster carrying trade after 1675 (Steele 1986). Quakerism did become a transatlantic faith and it was changed in the process. In spite of LYM's originally successful attempts to control the periphery from the centre (Landes, 2010), Quakerism was lived in its local contexts and transatlantic Quakerism was increasingly shaped by a variety of local expressions.

The Religious Society of Friends adapted easily to expansion to the far reaches of the Atlantic world. Its needs were few. Ministry and business relied on laity, not educated clergy; there were neither tithes to collect nor sacraments to administer; there was no music, rendering instruments and musical training unnecessary; and meeting houses were simple affairs (Barbour and Frost 1994, 57). Many frontier meetings began in a member's rustic dwelling. Isolated frontier settings could be beneficial to a group of

Quietist Quakers distanced from the worldly snares of large urban centres and free to live out their peculiar ways. The dispersal of Quakers across North America necessitated the creation of two more Yearly Meetings: to the New England, Baltimore, Virginia, and Philadelphia Yearly Meetings were added the New York Yearly Meeting in 1695 and the North Carolina Yearly Meeting in 1698. Peripheral meetings could be difficult for Yearly Meetings to monitor. As the Society became more organized, it became more hierarchical. It is a testament to the enduring strength of the local Meeting that control could never be completely uniformly applied despite the best efforts of Yearly Meetings to do so.

A number of factors helped to maintain unity among Quakers despite vast distances and multiple Yearly Meetings. Winchester (1991) suggests three strands that connected Friends—religious, mercantile, and kinship bonds. By the beginning of the period, LYM had established communications with North American and Caribbean meetings and had already taken responsibility for controlling the religious message 'beyond the seas' (Landes 2010, 62–94). Quaker publications, epistolary correspondence, and the travelling ministry were central to this strategy. LYM's Quaker publications were selected by the Morning Meeting and revised and censored before being sent to press (Hall 1992; Bell 2008). Certain titles were sent abroad, especially to areas where Quakerism had been recently introduced. For instance, in 1699 LYM sent books to Boston and its environs as a measure of support and theological guidance (Landes 2010, 66). Frost (1991) cautions correlating the reception of books in the colonies and their being read, although Tarter (2005) affirms the existence of a transatlantic religious reading culture among Friends. The breadth of literature was probably quite limited. With some exceptions, by the 1740s members of most North American meetings 'would have had access to copies of a few journals of English Friends, Sewel's *History*, Barclay's *Apology*, Ellwood's *Scriptural History*, and Penn's *No Cross, No Crown*' (Frost 1991, 15). And even though PYM appointed its own Overseers of the Press in 1691, until 1770 it published little local material. Therefore, until the American Revolution, approved publications largely flowed one way across the Atlantic.

Epistolary correspondence, on the other hand, was exchanged freely between all the meetings. The practice of sending Epistles was well established by the Quietist period. LYM sent annual Epistles to its constituent meetings as well as to the other Yearly Meetings that sent their own annual Epistle to LYM. Epistles combined religious exhortation and practical advice on a wide variety of issues. Faithful attendance at meeting, family governance, and observance of the Discipline were recurrent religious topics. Practically, Friends were instructed to keep clear of the repeated political 'commotions' of the period. All of these Epistles were copied and circulated throughout local meetings connecting Quakers throughout the Atlantic world.

Tolles (1960) contends that the London Yearly Meeting considered the travelling ministry key to 'uniting and solidifying Quaker community' (27). To control the message they shared, ministers were required to have the approval of their Yearly Meeting prior to an overseas journey. Both men and women participated in transatlantic ministry. Women's names are well represented in eighteenth-century meeting records throughout Great Britain, the Caribbean, and North America. This was a diverse group. Jane Fenn Hoskens, an indentured servant in the colonies, Catharine Payton Phillips (1726–94), an English woman of intellectual and literary accomplishments, and Abigail Craven Coles Watson (1684–1752), an Irish woman and wife of a 'gentleman' are representative of the women who crossed the seas in this period (Larson 1999, Appendix I). While ministry and commerce were to be kept strictly separate, many Quietist ministers, especially men, successfully blended the two (Winchester 1991; Landes 2010). Ministerial journeys could last for months or even years, thus necessitating this combination.

Did the transatlantic Quaker network create a homogeneous transatlantic Quaker culture? Undoubtedly, transatlantic religious ties were strong (Tolles 1960). The political lobby between London and American Quakers has been identified as 'one of the most sophisticated' (Olson 1992, 70). Even dreams have been analysed for their transatlantic connectedness (Gerona 2004). Yet, inasmuch as Friends were part of a transatlantic culture, the local nature of lived Quakerism should not be forgotten. Consider the Discipline. Contents were similar between Yearly Meetings, but each Discipline reflected local interests. Concerns about poor relief spurred London Quakers to write their first Discipline and colonial meetings felt compelled to address the treatment of Amerindians and slaves (Barbour and Frost 1994, 108). Spatial distance between Quakers in urban and frontier settings affected the ease of gathering for worship or business. Space allotted to women in meeting houses varied. Bacon (1986) indicates that colonial meetings included roughly equal space for women when they constructed meeting houses while English meeting houses originally allotted a small gallery, loft, or a separate shed for Women's Meetings (46). Lavoie's (2002) more recent assessment of meeting houses in the Delaware Valley reveals that the 'standard' rectangular design that placed equally sized Men's and Women's Meeting spaces side by side originated in mid-eighteenth-century urban Philadelphia (161–3). More isolated countryside meetings in the colonies followed a variety of practices, adding smaller, separate, even unconnected, meeting space designated for women's business (Lavoie 2002, 161–4). In some cases these practices emulated English customs, and in others necessity was the governing factor in determining the size and shape of the meeting house. The difference in the Quaker press on each side of the Atlantic has been noted. The reason for the paucity of books written and printed by Friends in the colonies is not conclusive. Frost (1991) wonders if the vagaries of war, slavery, and Amerindian relations took precedence over the need for local publications? He also suggests that the increase in local publications after 1770 and the failure of the Holy Experiment made Friends aware of the need 'to recapture their history or reform the present' (16). Perhaps Quakers, like other Americans in the New Republic (Davidson 2004), put their press to work in the process of developing an identity that was as much American as it was Quaker.

COMMERCIAL LIFE

Far from keeping out of commercial affairs, Quakers in the Quietist period expanded their mercantile interests, some accumulating great fortunes in the process (Walvin 1997). It has been suggested that Quaker business practices, especially the concern over debt, alongside Quaker networks produced an environment in which Quaker industry could flourish (Tolles 1948; Winchester 1991; Landes 2010). Certainly legislation such as the Navigation Acts favoured the transatlantic trade, but Quakers showed themselves to the entrepreneurs and innovators in a changing economic landscape. They participated in every area of imperial commerce, including the traffic in African slaves and goods produced by slaves (Soderlund 1985).

The eighteenth century was the era of the Quaker business person and merchant, although farmers continued to make up a large proportion of the Society, especially in the colonies. Many professions, including the civil service, were closed to Quakers, compelling them to seek alternate forms of employment. Friends had an interest in science, although the claim that they were vastly over-represented in the Royal Society does not stand up to scrutiny (Cantor 1997). They were well represented among merchants and manufacturers. Innovation and inventiveness is apparent in the Darby family of Coalbrookdale. Covering the eighteenth century, three generations of Abraham Darbys (I, II, and III) revolutionized iron production, paving the way for industrialization in Great Britain (Punshon 1984, 109–113; Barbour and Frost 1994, 86; Labouchere 1988; 1993). The Darbys along with other Quaker families—Reynolds, Lloyds, Champions, and Rawlinsons—dominated the eighteenth-century iron industry. A consequence of endogamy was the strengthening of religious and commercial networks by kinship ties, giving rise to dynastic mercantile families in many areas of industry (Barbour and Frost 1994, 86). The commercial fortunes of Quakers expanded along with the British Empire and banking arose from the need to invest their wealth. The Barclay and Lloyd families are two of the most well known in Quaker banking. Transatlantic trade opened up new possibilities in merchandising such as the trade in cocoa. The renowned cocoa and confectionary families—Rowntrees, Frys, and Cadburys—really made their mark in the nineteenth century. However, the Rowntrees' business got its start in this period beginning with the initiative of Mary Tuke who, in 1725, won the right to be a Freeman and member of the York Merchant Adventurers Company and to trade as a grocer (Punshon 1984, 113–15). She began as a tea and coffee merchant and took on her nephew William, as her apprentice. In 1752 he inherited the shop and in 1785 William's son Henry Tuke (1755–1814) joined him. The scientifically minded Henry had trained as a physician and launched a chocolate factory alongside the grocery. In 1860 Henry Rowntree was hired to manage the cocoa department and two years later he purchased it from the Tukes, going on to make the Rowntree name synonymous with confectionary.

Quietist Quakers wrestled with determining the relationship between worldly and religious activity. For devout Friends, the leading of the Light Within always superseded demands of the world, including those of their families. This created a particularly unique situation for Quaker women. At a time when the separate spheres of private and public were becoming entrenched, Quaker women ministers were at liberty to travel at great distance over long periods of time. The Darbys are a case in point. Abiah Maude Sinclair Darby (1716–94) became the second wife of Abraham Darby II in 1745. She was knowledgeable about the family's iron works and often assisted with its management. She cared for the children of her husband's first marriage and gave birth to six of her own. And, in 1751, she began to travel in ministry, journeying even when pregnant. Her husband supported her labours and occasionally accompanied her (Labouchere, 1988). Abiah, in turn, supported her daughter-in-law Deborah Barnard Darby (1754–1810), who also began to travel in ministry while her children were young. Families and meetings supported divine 'leading' by releasing members from the demands of their day-to-day lives. Labouchere (1993) hints that Deborah Darby may have used ministry to take an annual break from the demands of family life that included her husband's mental illness. Ministerial journeys were no vacation. If this was a motivation, the journals that recount travelling conditions and the spiritual anguish of attending to the Light Within suggest that one burden was merely replaced with another.

Try as they might to separate themselves from the commercial world, Quaker entrepreneurs could not extricate themselves from it. They were surrounded by the wealth of the empire's flourishing mercantile economy as seen in Richard Shackleton's description of Coalbrookdale: 'This is the most extraordinary place I ever was in: there is such a mixture of religion and worldly business, human learning and Christian simplicity... such a wild, native irregularity, subdued and cultivated by art and opulence' (Labouchere 1988, xiii). Quakers did not denounce wealth; they were, however, anxious about its products. Tolles (1948, 143) argues that because of their refusal to isolate themselves from the market, Quakers 'subjected themselves to mental and moral tensions which sometimes became intolerable'. They dealt with these tensions in three ways: some left their faith; others satisfied themselves with being gay Friends; and some, like John Woolman (1720–72), abandoned business entirely (Tolles 1948, 109–43; Punshon 1984, 115–20). Woolman was very devout and has been described in saint-like terms (Trueblood 1966); few were as dedicated to Quietist principles as he was. More standard was the need to settle upon ways to traverse separate spiritual and temporal domains (Dandelion, 2010). Plain clothing and language became a particularly important protective barrier to this end. Simplicity was a costume that permitted Friends to perform in the commercial sphere while maintaining their distance from it.

QUIETIST QUAKERS AND THE WORLD

There has been considerable examination of the paradox central to late Quietist Quakerism: 'an abnormal degree of introspection' coupled with 'a rediscovery of the beckoning social tasks of humanity', and Jones depicts Quietist Quakers as 'an island in a sea which they had never explored or charted' (Jones 1921, 314). Recent interpretations have suggested that Quakers viewed the religious and secular realms as dialectic, but overlapping (Mack 2003; Spencer 2007), or as distinct, but not unfamiliar (Dandelion 2010). Given the pluralities of Quietist Quakerism, it is likely that eighteenth-century Friends justified their engagement with the world in diverse, not singular, ways.

Quakers did not sit as members of the British Parliament in the eighteenth century; they were a major force in colonial legislatures, especially in New England and

Pennsylvania where they dominated the Assembly until the early years of the French and Indian Wars. Whether they sat as elected members or not, Quakers were practiced writers and used their abilities to petition legislatures and the Crown wherever they lived. Friends' political stance on the non-payment of tithes cost many dearly and eighteenth-century Epistles routinely enumerate the 'sufferings' this produced in loss of property or incarceration. Political events in the Atlantic world also compelled Quakers to clarify their position on war and slavery.

Armed conflict was a regular circumstance in the long eighteenth century and challenged Friends' pacifism. Between 1688 and 1763 Britain and its colonies were embroiled in four wars of empire. Added together with the years of the American and French Revolutions, war was a matter of course for half the long eighteenth century. The peace testimony denounced any involvement in war, including profiting from trade in military goods. The line between military and non-military wares could be blurred by those willing to cross it: tradespeople and merchandisers could find ways of filling military contracts and avoiding disciplinary action. Wars offered plentiful opportunities for gain through privateering; its repeated mention in the Epistles indicates that not all Friends remained as clear from the 'commotions' as the Meeting desired. War illuminated the conflict between the affluence and pacifism of Friends. Did one cooperate with belligerents to keep one's property safe, or refuse and suffer accordingly? War also cast a prophetic pall on events that might otherwise concern only the most devout (Marietta 1974). This is apparent in LYM's stern warning in 1776: 'It is worthy of the serious consideration of all, whether the calamities now deeply affecting this great empire, may not have been permitted by divine providence in displeasure, on account of the accumulated transgressions of the people' (1821, 323). Quakers' anti-war stance became well defined by the French Revolution: do not engage in activities associated with war; do not talk about war; pray (LYM 1821, 373–4).

While times of war generated an official Quaker position, war was also very divisive, reflecting the diversity within Quakerism at this time. The war crisis of 1755, in which the Pennsylvania Assembly voted a war tax of £50,000 to defend frontier settlements from Delawares, divided Friends who wanted to reform and purify the Society, and voted against the tax, and those who preferred compromise (Barbour and Frost 1994, 125–6). Neither Philadelphia nor London Yearly Meetings advocated tax refusal, but twenty-one prominent Friends, including John Woolman, issued a declaration urging tax resistance. And when Catharine Payton Phillips visited Philadelphia, she organized for an audience in the Assembly where she spoke out against the tax; she was not the only woman vocal against it (Mack 2003). The tax passed and few devout Friends served in the Assembly after 1756.

During the American Revolution, the American Yearly Meetings adopted an official position of strict neutrality (Mekeel 1979, 162–4; Barbour and Frost 1994, 142–3). As a result, Quakers were branded as Tory sympathizers and individual Friends suffered arrest, confiscation of property, and a few were banished. Most Friends did dissociate from the politics of the Revolution; in fact, Mekeel (1979, 163–4) suggests that the 'complete withdrawal of the Quakers from participation in the political developments which

were transpiring had eliminated their ability to influence events'. Some Friends disagreed
with the Society's official position. A number who broke away or were disowned formed
the Free Quakers (Mekeel 1979, 283–93). Regardless of their individual positions, when
peace arrived, American Quakers came to terms with their new government. A few true
Loyalists returned to England, and some took advantage of free land in Upper Canada,
but this latter group was not politically motivated.

Given the extent to which Quietist Quakers sought to distance themselves from temporal matters, their prominence in the humanitarian initiatives of the eighteenth century is noteworthy. In fact, there is a correlation between a deepening Quietism and
the desire for social reform that calls into question secularization narratives in which
'retrograde' Quakers became more Quietist while 'progressive' Quakers became capitalists and activists unconcerned with religion (Mack 2003). Charitable work, slavery,
treatment of the mentally ill, prison conditions, and Native American relations occupied the minds of eighteenth-century Friends. It seems those most committed to social
reform were also intensely quietist. Even after surrendering control of the Assembly in
1755, Friends remained committed to positive Amerindian relations, especially with
escalating conflict on the frontier. In 1756 they aligned with like-minded Mennonites
and Moravians to form The Friendly Association for Regaining and Preserving Peace
with the Indians by Pacific Measures (Barbour and Frost 1994, 126–7; Hamm 2003, 33).
While short-lived, The Friendly Association marks Friends' first attempt at an ecumenical fellowship to achieve Quaker practice. A few years earlier, in 1751, Pennsylvania
Friends had joined others in founding the first private hospital in the colonies (Barbour
and Frost 1994, 127). English Quakers also sought inter-denominational association
with English Evangelicals in 1787 when they joined together to form The Committee for
the Abolition of the Slave Trade. Cooperating with those outside the Meeting to realize
the tenets nourished within the Society, positioned Friends to have a profound humanitarian influence.

Anti-slavery activism developed slowly over the eighteenth century. Some Friends
expressed unease with the traffic in humans as early as the late seventeenth century, but
the movement did not accelerate until mid-century when Philadelphia Yearly Meeting
agreed to print John Woolman's *Some Considerations on the keeping of Negroes* (1754).
Woolman's publication and his example had a profound influence on the attitudes of
Friends and non-Quakers alike. He is credited with awakening the anti-slavery movement (Barbour and Frost 1994, 145). The figure who spurred the movement to an international level was Anthony Benezet (1713–84) whose attack on slavery, *Observations
on the Enslaving, Importing and Purchasing of Negroes,* was published in 1759. Benezet
corresponded with other abolition leaders; he distributed his tracts to American politicians, members of Parliament in Great Britain, royalty in England, France, and Portugal,
and Anglican bishops. He is, arguably, the leading abolitionist of his day. The renown
of Friends such as Woolman and Benezet should not overshadow the likes of Quietist
Quakers such as Joshua Evans, 'untutored, semi-literate, and virtually uneducated',
who also set an example for Friends by his rejection of goods produced by slave labour
either directly or indirectly (Kelley 1986). New England Yearly Meeting led the way in

making slave holding a disownable offence in 1770 and by 1784 all of the American Yearly Meetings ruled similarly (Hamm 2003, 34–5). Even though they did not sit in Parliament, English Quakers' labours in The Committee for the Abolition of the Slave Trade finally resulted in the passage of 'An Act for the Abolition of the Slave Trade' in 1807.

Assumptions about Quietist Quakerism have produced interpretations of Quakerism in the long eighteenth century that conceal the diversity that was its lived experience. It was more than 'a noble *mood*... too rare and abstract to be translated into real life' (Jones 1921, 56). Nor was it 'a spent force' (637) waiting passively for nineteenth-century rejuvenation (Braithwaite 1919, 637). Certainly the Quakerism of this period differed from that of the founders. The Quietist period did create a more exclusive group, but its influence on worldly affairs far exceeded the limits dictated by its size. The legacy of Quietist Quakerism is paradoxical. The retreat to sectarianism set the stage for the acrimonious schisms of the nineteenth century. Conversely, the focus on humanitarianism—precipitated by Quietism—achieved changes that may not have been accomplished otherwise.

FURTHER READING

Barbour, H. and Frost, J. W. (1994 [1988]) *The Quakers*. Richmond, IN: Friends United Press.

Braithwaite, W. C. (1919) *The second period of Quakerism*. London: Macmillan and Co. Ltd.

Dandelion, P. (2010) 'Guarded domesticity and engagement with "the World": The separate spheres of Quaker Quietism in common knowledge, 16(1), 95–109.

Gerona, C. (2004) *Night journeys: The power of dreams in transatlantic Quaker culture*. Charlottesville: University of Virginia Press.

Jones, R. M. (1917) 'Quietism', *The Harvard Theological Review*, 10(1), 1–51.

Jones, R. M. (1921) *The later periods of Quakerism*. Vols. 1 and 2. London: Macmillan and Co. Ltd.

Larson, R. (1999) *Daughters of Light: Quaker women preaching and prophesying in the colonies and abroad, 1700–1775*. New York: Alfred A. Knopf.

Marietta, J. D. (2007 [1984]) *The Reformation of American Quakerism, 1748–1783*. Philadelphia: University of Philadelphia Press.

Mekeel, A. J. (1979) *The relation of the Quakers to the American Revolution*. Washington, DC: University Press of America.

Vann, R. T. and Eversley, D. E. C. (1992) *Friends in life and death: The British and Irish Quakers in the demographic transition, 1650–1900*. Cambridge: Cambridge University Press.

CHAPTER 4

HICKSITE, ORTHODOX, AND EVANGELICAL QUAKERISM, 1805–1887

THOMAS D. HAMM

In 1875, Philadelphia Friend William Hodgson published the first volume of his history of nineteenth-century Quakerism. The subtitle is revealing: 'A Historical View of the Successive Convulsions and Schisms Therein during That Period' (Hodgson 1875).

At the beginning of the nineteenth century, the Friends were largely unified, but over the next three generations, their separations laid the foundations of modern Quaker diversity. In the 1820s, American Friends divided into Hicksite and Orthodox groups, and in the 1840s and 1850s both groups experienced new schisms. British Friends were more unified, but not immune to conflict. And after 1860, Friends underwent other dramatic changes.

Friends explained this differently. Usually they argued that their group represented continuity with historic Quakerism and their opponents had gone astray. Contemporary historians have refined those judgements, seeing larger cultural influences—evangelicalism, religious liberalism, politics, social and economic change—transforming Quakerism.

PRELUDE TO SEPARATION

Historians, like Friends at the time, disagree on why American Quakerism irreparably fractured in the 1820s. Some blame the growth of evangelicalism rooted in the larger culture. Others see encroachments from Enlightenment rationalism.

Conflict first appeared in the 1790s. In Ireland, Friends such as Abraham Shackleton (1752–1818) questioned parts of the Old Testament. Shackleton argued that it was impossible to reconcile the extermination of whole races of people during the 'Hebrew wars' with the loving God of the New Testament. The Irish Yearly Meeting decided that challenging Scripture was unacceptable and disowned Shackleton. Disownment also befell Hannah Barnard (c.1754–1825), a minister from Hudson, New York, after she voiced similar views while visiting England (Jones 1921, I, 293–305).

With the benefit of hindsight, Friends later saw the roots of difficulty in other events. Some pointed to a growing evangelicalism in certain Yearly Meetings, particularly London. Others saw it in conflicts among American Friends in the 1810s over proposals for a conference of American Yearly Meetings to create a uniform discipline and consider proposals to establish a Quaker college. And others saw it in what they perceived as inroads made by Unitarianism (Ingle 1998, 65–80).

HICKSITE AND ORTHODOX

By 1820, a Long Island Friend, Elias Hicks (1748–1830) had become the most polarizing figure in Quakerism. A minister since the 1770s, Hicks travelled widely among American Friends and developed a pointed critique of contemporary Quakerism. His sympathizers became known as Hicksites, although they themselves eschewed that label.

In some respects, Hicks was an extreme Quietist who feared acting without the guidance of the Holy Spirit. Hicks summed up his vision of spiritual life in an 1827 sermon: 'And this was what I laboured after—to be empty, to know nothing, to call for nothing, and to desire to do nothing'. Hicks concluded that corruption was creeping in among Friends through the ties that some had formed with Presbyterians, Anglicans, and others of 'the world's people' (Gould 1827, I, 47).

Many Friends had such ties, especially in Philadelphia, New York, the United Kingdom, and Ireland. They enthusiastically joined non-Quaker evangelicals in humanitarian, religious, and reform activities, which they saw as forwarding Quaker commitments. But Hicks and like-minded Friends perceived dangers (Ingle 1998, 14; Dorsey 1998, 395–428). Typical was Jesse Kersey (1768–1845) of West Chester, Pennsylvania. 'As certainly as the children of Israel were to dwell alone, and not to mix with the surrounding nations—so was the Society of Friends', he wrote. 'They were called out from the various classes of men, and they were to stand separate in order that the force of their example might have a proper effect upon the surrounding inhabitants' (Kersey 1851, 84–5).

Hicks and his sympathizers worried about more than Quaker peculiarity, however; they feared the growing evangelical influence on American society. Evangelicals made great claims about evangelism and reform, but Hicksites saw 'ever more injustice, hardness of heart, cruelty, pride, envy, detraction, covetousness, malice, bitterness'. They had no difficulty explaining this failure. 'A spuriously ordained man-made ministry', in other words, hirelings, led evangelicals. Their activism had its 'origin from the natural will and wisdom of the Creature' (Kimber 1822, 9). Kersey summed up this critique. It was: 'contrary to the great principles laid down by Christ and his apostles, for any step to be taken with a view to advance the cause of universal righteousness, that is not dictated by the immediate openings and leadings of the spirit of Christ' (Kersey 1851, 213). Instead, Hicks argued, such activities were 'carried on in the very Spirit, power, and contrivance of fallen man,... which abundantly... do[es] the work of Anti-Christ' (Hicks 1834, 182–3).

Such ties, Hicks thought, weakened Friends. He saw problems in biblicism that made the Bible the ultimate authority, rather than the Holy Spirit, and in a Christology that emphasized salvation by the Blood of Christ, rather than through obedience to the Light Within. And he saw it in the increasing authoritarianism of leaders who advocated such doctrines. Thus a reformation was necessary (Ingle 1998, 38–61).

Other Friends, in North America and in Great Britain, saw danger in Hicks's views. As one critic summed up, the 'great object' of the Hicksites was 'to lessen Jesus Christ in His outward appearance at Jerusalem; to preach up the light within, in opposition to the proper divinity of our blessed Lord, and to the entire exclusion of all He did and suffered for us in the flesh' (Luther 1827, 38–9). Add the Orthodox conviction that Hicks questioned the authority of the Bible and conflict was inevitable. Historians dispute the bases of Orthodox Quakerism. Some see it as an evangelical intrusion into the Religious Society of Friends. Certainly, after 1800, some American Friends, and many in England, articulated a Quakerism that echoed the theology of non-Quaker evangelicals. When Hicksites challenged them, they responded that all these doctrines were consistent with early Quaker writings. Both sides claimed to be the legitimate Friends (Ingle 1998, 10–13).

Hicks was not a systematic theologian, and some passages in his published sermons and writings supported Orthodox charges. He rejected the doctrine of Atonement through the physical Blood of Christ. Instead, the Atonement was the crucifixion of self that Jesus modelled through His death. Jesus was not born the Christ, but became the Christ through His perfect obedience to God's will. Hicks's preaching abounded with Scriptural allusions, and he professed that he preferred the Scriptures to any other book. But he said that knowledge of them was unnecessary for salvation, and denied that they were 'the only rule of faith and practice'. He opined privately that the Bible had been, because of disputes over interpretation, 'the cause of four-fold more harm than good to Christendom' (Hicks 1824, 8; Hicks 1831, 140–1; Ingle 1998, 41; Hamm 2002, 180–1).

By the mid-1820s, Hicks's critics had become known as Orthodox Friends. Most active were weighty Friends in Philadelphia, especially the minister Stephen Grellet (1773–1855) and the elder Jonathan Evans. A succession of visiting English Friends reinforced them, particularly Thomas Shillitoe (1754–1836), Elizabeth Robson, Anna Braithwaite (1788–1859), and George and Ann Jones. Convinced that Hicks was dangerous, they attacked (Ingle 1998, 96–121)

By December 1822, there was open conflict. Some Philadelphia Friends publicly denounced preaching by Hicks and Priscilla Cadwalader Hunt (1786–1859), a like-minded minister visiting from Indiana (Hamm 2008, 407–31). Benjamin Ferris

(1780–1867), a Wilmington, Delaware Hicksite engaged in a newspaper debate with a Presbyterian minister, added more fuel to the fire (Anon. 1823). Orthodox Friends blasted Ferris's exposition of Quakerism. Early in 1823, Philadelphia Yearly Meeting's strongly Orthodox Meeting for Sufferings published a short pamphlet of quotations from early Friends on the divinity of Christ. Hicksites denounced it as a blatant attempt to impose a creed (Ingle 1998, 96–121).

Over the next four years tensions grew, as Hicks's letters and sermons circulated as pamphlets. Side issues developed, especially at Philadelphia Yearly Meeting, as both sides tried to use disciplinary and official machinery against opponents. These in turn became part of a print war, as Hicksites accused the Orthodox of seeking dictatorial power and the Orthodox called Hicksites 'ranters' (Ingle 1998, 96–180).

The conflict came to a head in April 1827, during the sessions of Philadelphia Yearly Meeting. Hicksites tried to replace Samuel Bettle, the staunchly Orthodox clerk, with John Comly (1773–1850), a Hicksite. When that failed, they met at Green Street meeting house and called for reorganization of the Yearly Meeting. Hicksites, in Comly's words, had decided on 'a quiet retreat from these scenes of confusion' (Comly 1853, 333). They would, as Philadelphia minister William Wharton wrote, 'rally round our ancient standard the Light of Truth, to *reorganize* the Yearly Meeting upon the basis of brotherly love and condescension' (Wharton, 1828). In October 1827 they held their 'reorganized' Yearly Meeting and about two thirds of the Yearly Meeting's membership joined it (Ingle 1998, 183–200).

What were the fundamental issues? For Orthodox Friends, they were order and doctrine. The Hicksites had 'gone out in open infidelity and deism', challenging institutions such as the Meeting for Sufferings and elders. They were no longer Friends and had to be disowned (Hamm 1988, 17–18). Hicksite thinking was more complex. They emphasized perceived Orthodox abuses of power and unwarranted attacks on venerable Friends such as Hicks. Many perceived themselves as conservatives, defending ancient Quaker ways against innovation. But a liberal strain was also manifest. 'I would not lay a straw in the way of any *honest* enquirer', one Ohio Friend wrote in 1829. 'Why shall I be an enemy to a fellow being,... because he may not believe the justness and correctness of my observations'? (Updegraff 1829). As Wharton told a sympathizer, Hicksites did 'not hold it to be important, for every man's opinion to be precisely the same' (Wharton 1828). This embrace of theological diversity would, after considerable contention, become integral to Hicksite Quakerism. Some Friends simply followed their leaders. As another Ohio Friend observed: 'There were a number of Friends here who would not read or inform themselves respecting the controversy and consequently were very ignorant about it, but when it came from the galleries they must believe what they hear' (Stanton 1830).

Historians have suggested other issues. Contemporary observers, such as Hicks and Halliday Jacakson, noted that urban Friends were more likely to be Orthodox than rural ones (Jones 1921, I, 470–4; Ingle 1998, 46–8). Sociologist Robert W. Doherty suggested that in Philadelphia Yearly Meeting the Orthodox were wealthier, apparently adjusting more successfully to the emerging market economy (Doherty 1967). Others challenge the applicability of this model to other Yearly Meetings (Hamm 1988, 16–17). Larry

Ingle emphasizes questions of power. It is clear that in Philadelphia and New York Yearly Meetings the Orthodox were disproportionately Friends in positions of authority (Ingle 1998, 16).

The Philadelphia separation forced Friends elsewhere to decide which Yearly Meeting was the legitimate one. New England, North Carolina, Virginia, Dublin, and London Yearly Meetings embraced the Orthodox. The recognition by London, the most influential of Yearly Meetings, heartened Orthodox Friends. In New York and Baltimore, Hicksites were the overwhelming majority, a definite minority in Indiana, and close to parity in Ohio (Ingle 1998, 225–46).

The process of division was painful. 'Oh! this separating business, how very closely does it assail our feelings of tenderness and affection', wrote one New Jersey Orthodox Friend in February 1828 (Allinson 1828). The rhetoric on both sides was ferocious. Hicksites were caught in a 'dark delusive spirit', said an Orthodox minister (Hunt 1858, 103). 'Hicksitism and Libertinism, were one and the same thing', preached another (Anthony 1830, 28–9). Hicksites responded in kind. The Orthodox were 'creed Quakers', using 'the most Jesuitical arts' in an 'apostate' and 'antichristian spirit' (Chandler 1827; Foulke 1829; Poole 1824). Orthodox women were 'd-mn bitches', one vicious critic scrawled on a meeting-house wall (Emlen 1828). 'If they could have a law established, to further their designs', wrote one Indiana Friend, 'poor old Elias Hicks and many others, would have to seal their testimonies with fire and faggot' (Morrisson 1828, 38). Both sides went to court over property or to exclude the other side as intruders (Hamm 1988, 18).

This separation still haunts Friends. And after 1830 both sides experienced new schisms.

HICKSITES, 1830–1860

After the Separation, Hicksites embraced three groups. Most were traditionalist Friends who perceived the Orthodox as dangerous innovators. Others, especially in New York, Philadelphia, and Baltimore Yearly Meetings, simply sided with the majority in their local meetings. The third, an articulate group of incipient Liberal Friends, engendered fierce controversy.

The first manifestation was in Wilmington, Delaware. In the 1820s, Friends there, such as Benjamin Ferris, had attacked Trinitarianism and biblical inerrancy, but now concluded they had allowed too much 'free inquiry' (Ingle 1984, 127–37; Webb 1831). They and Philadelphia Friends disowned members who questioned the inspiration of the Scriptures (Hamm 2002, 182–3). In the 1830s and 1840s, many Hicksites, most notably Lucretia Mott (1793–1880), but including New York Friends such as Charles Marriott and Isaac T. Hopper (1771–1852), embraced reform movements. Hicksites were disproportionately represented in the convention that organized the American Anti-Slavery Society in 1833 (Drake 1950, 140; Hamm 1994, 557–69). Four of the five women who organized the first women's rights convention in the United States, in Seneca Falls, New York, in the summer of 1848, were Hicksites or had Hicksite ties (Faulkner 2011, 60–160). Many Hicksites found the non-resistance movement a logical extension of Quaker testimonies (Hamm 1994, 557–69).

Most Hicksites, however, were either apathetic or actively opposed to Quaker involvement in reform. The reasons were complex, but at their heart was a conviction that working with non-Quakers, even in good causes, endangered Quaker peculiarity. Philadelphia Yearly Meeting summed up this view in 1830:

> If we, as a society, so far depart from the teachings of the spirit of truth, as to mingle with other professors in what is called religious concerns,—though professedly to promote the cause of Christ…our individuality, as a people, will be lost, and our excellent testimonies,…will fall to the ground. (Philadelphia Yearly Meeting 1830, 7–8)

Such Friends pointed to the prominence of clerics—'hireling ministers'—in reform movements. Since reform groups often depended on paid lecturers and agents, they were one with 'hirelings'. 'Whoever undertakes to do God's work, in the capacity of an editor, a lecturer, or any other, and receives money for it, is a *base hypocrite*', preached George F. White (1789–1847), a New York minister, in 1843. Such were, White judged, 'more *degraded than the Devils in hell*' (Anon. 1843, 94).

Such conflicts produced ruptures after 1840. Reformers denounced ministers such as White. More conservative Hicksites responded with charges of defamation. In Indiana, they laid down Green Plain Quarterly Meeting, a reform stronghold. Abolitionist Friends found themselves disowned. Reformers formed their own organizations, first called Congregational Friends, later Progressive Friends. In Indiana, Michigan, Ohio, western New York, and southeastern Pennsylvania they attracted hundreds of adherents (Hamm 1995, 66–9; Jordan 2007, 81–103).

The Congregational groups were self-consciously radical. They repudiated practices that they believed hindered free expression: recording ministers, appointing elders, even the concept of membership itself (Hamm 1995, 216–27). They warmly endorsed virtu-ally every reform. Congregational Friends, those at Waterloo, New York, would refrain from 'a rigid uniformity in respect to theological opinions and shibboleths' and would be 'devoted to the culture of a wider charity, a more enlightened and earnest sympathy with the Reforms of the Age, a more generous hospitality for new ideas' (Anon. 1849, 100). 'Fine-spun theological abstractions' were unimportant, Ohio Congregational Friends proclaimed in 1852. Instead Christianity should simply be 'a religion of LOVE' (Ohio Yearly Meeting 1852, 15).

Not all Hicksites who sympathized with the reformers separated, most notably Lucretia Mott. However, even she was increasingly marginalized by more conservative Friends. 'Some of us were prepared for much greater changes or advances than we made 18 years ago', she wrote in 1846, 'but we ignobly compromised…Those who were gained are now our oppressors, we having…cloth[ed] them with office' (Mott 1846).

Conservatives responded in kind. In Indiana Yearly Meeting, former clerk David Evans claimed that Congregational Friends sought 'to form an organization…with a platform broad enough to embrace infidelity and even atheism, and subject to all degrees of anarchy and ranterism' (Dugdale 1850, 1). But Quietism was at the heart of Hicksite conservatism. Progressive Friends, Ferris wrote in 1851, thought that religion should advance as quickly as the natural sciences, constantly revised in the light of new discoveries. Thus they called for 'progress, progress, go ahead, push on, go to work, do something'. This showed that they had 'not learned one of the most essential lessons taught in the school of Christ', waiting for divine leading (Ferris 1851).

By 1860, conservatives had the upper hand among Hicksite Friends. Many reformers had left for Progressive meetings, which, in turn, were fading. Some returned to their old meetings; others became spiritualists or Unitarians. The divisions left some Yearly Meetings badly weakened, especially Genesee, Ohio, and Indiana (Thomas 1920, 21–32). Joseph S. Walton, visiting Genesee Yearly Meeting in 1848, summarized the situation: 'They are too few to divide again...One thing I think is very certain that without a change there will be no meetings of the Society of Friends in these parts' (Walton 1848). Walton was not far wrong; after 1830 Hicksite Quakerism steadily shrank

ORTHODOX FRIENDS, 1830–1860

Orthodox Friends also knew division. As among the Hicksites, Quietists contended with Friends open to the larger world. Most Orthodox Friends positioned themselves firmly within the dominant evangelical religious culture around them.

The sources of this transformation are complex. One acute observer was an English Friend William Tallack, who visited the United States in 1859 and 1860. He sensed that the dominant social forces were assimilation and consolidation. Isolation was becoming impossible. 'From this tendency the farthest west and the wildest backwoods cannot withhold compliance', he wrote, concluding that Friends were no more resistant than their neighbours (Tallack 1861, 31–2).

Orthodox Friends variously manifested this assimilation. Revealing is the diary of Ann T. Updegraff, a young woman in Mount Pleasant, Ohio. In the early 1840s, her reading included the *Oberlin Evangelist* (the Updegraffs were friends of noted revivalist Charles G. Finney), biographies of assorted English Evangelicals and missionaries, and the works of 'the pious Mrs. Hemans'. Any scan of the London weekly *Friend* shows the same tendencies (Hamm 1988, 23–4).

Equally important were ties with non-Quaker evangelicals in religious, humanitarian, and reform work. As early as 1826, Elizabeth Fry (1780–1845), the noted English prison reformer, had written: 'I...can hardly bear to hear Friends make us out to be a chosen people, above others' (Anon., 1848, 70–1). Two decades later, Ann T. Updegraff agreed. 'Alas! for sectarian pride and bigotry. What reason is it that we should not unite in benevolent works, because we unite our efforts with a Christian who has a different name?' (Updegraff 1844).

The great exemplar of Quaker evangelicalism was Fry's brother, Joseph John Gurney (1788–1847) of Norwich. A gifted minister and prolific writer, Gurney had a profound impact on Orthodox Friends. He was known for his work in Bible, anti-slavery, prison reform, and educational societies, and his friendships with Evangelicals such as William Wilberforce. His 1837–40 journey in the United States was what one historian calls 'a triumphal procession' (Hamm 1988, 20–2; Swift 1962).

Gurney embodied the evangelicalism that came to dominate Orthodox Quakerism in these years. Advocating that Friends join 'vital Christians among all the Orthodox denominations', he also reoriented Quaker understandings of vital points of doctrine: the role of the Bible, the place of the early Friends, the guidance of the Light Within, and the nature of justification and sanctification. He envisioned a Quakerism harmonious with non-Quaker evangelicalism (Gurney 1848, iv).

Gurney was committed to Scriptural authority, arguing that only the Holy Spirit should guide Friends in interpreting the Bible. This put him, at least implicitly, at odds with long-standing convictions that the 'standard works' of early Friends were authoritative explications. He cautiously suggested that Friends had misunderstood Biblical teachings on two subjects. One was the Light Within. While he agreed that all people had a certain illumination that allowed them to distinguish good from evil, this hardly compared with the light found in Scripture. The Bible was comparable to the noonday sun, the Light Within to the moon (Hamm 2006, 55–6).

Equally important, Gurney argued that for generations Friends had misunderstood the relationship between justification and sanctification. The former was salvation, a state of acceptability to God; the latter was holiness or sinlessness. Before Gurney, Friends argued that the two were inseparable—one could not be justified unless sanctified. Gurney responded that justification was a simple act of faith in the Atonement, sometimes gradual, sometimes instantaneous. Sanctification was a second, gradual experience, often extending through a lifetime (Hamm 1988, 21–2; Spencer 2007, 140–3).

By 1860, 'Gurneyite' had become the label for evangelical Quakerism in the United States. For some Evangelical Friends, however, even Gurney was not evangelical enough. They included a few Americans, most notably Elisha Bates (1781–1861)of Ohio, who publicly denounced 'heresies' in early Quaker writings and was water baptized (Hamm 1988, 31–2). More numerous were the English Beaconites. The name comes from an 1835 pamphlet *A Beacon to the Society of Friends* by Manchester Friend Isaac Crewdson (1780–1844). He attacked the Light Within as a 'delusive notion' and denied the possibility of revelation outside the Bible. London Yearly Meeting appointed a committee that tried to restore unity by silencing him. Instead, he and his sympathizers withdrew to form a body they called Evangelical Friends. They repudiated the ministry of women and practised physical baptism and communion (Jones 1921, I, 490–92, 505–8; Isichei 1970, 45–53).

Gurney also faced criticism from the still-influential Quietist wing of London Yearly Meeting. Thomas Shillitoe pronounced that Gurney's writings were 'not sound Quaker principles . . . and they have done great mischief in our Society', concluding: 'the author is an Episcopalian, not a Quaker'. When Gurney asked the Yearly Meeting of Ministers and Elders for a certificate for his American visit, opposition was fierce (Jones 1921, I, 508; Swift 1962, 183–4, 213–14).

Gurney's critics found supporters in the United States. By 1845, differences became so sharp that they produced a cascading series of separations that began in New England and affected most Orthodox Yearly Meetings. Thus the Wilburite strain of Quakerism emerged. Most Orthodox Friends, however, found the Gurneyite vision compelling (Hamm 1988, 28–34).

The American Gurneyite mood by 1860 was optimistic. While English Friends worried about declining membership, Americans were comfortable in the knowledge that their faction was in the majority on their side of the Atlantic, and they embraced the overwhelming majority of Friends west of the Appalachians. Gurneyites possessed social and political influence. They could also point to institutions, especially schools, which they had created. They had firmly embraced Sunday, or in Quaker parlance, First Day schools. A major break with past practice came in the 1850s, when Friends transformed older boarding schools into Haverford and Earlham colleges. And the years after 1860 saw unprecedented innovation among Gurneyites (Hamm 1988, 36–48; Isichei 1970, 166–257; Kennedy 2002, 12–46).

HICKSITE FRIENDS, 1860–1887

The future of Hicksite Quakerism in 1860 was unclear: Conservatives seemed triumphant, and the ancient bounds of Quaker peculiarity remained in place. While theological liberals such as Lucretia Mott were highly visible, they were marginalized. Suspicions of ties with non-Quakers remained strong. Yet within a generation, many of the strictures of the plain life would be swept away. Innovations—higher education, circular meetings, First Day schools, and the Friends Union for Philanthropic Labor—became central to Hicksite life. Hicksites viewed themselves as part of a larger movement of religious liberals in American Christianity. The reasons are unclear, but appear to be a combination of cultural adjustment and the death of an older generation of conservative leaders.

The Civil War was a crisis for Hicksites. Yearly Meetings hastened to remind their members of the Peace Testimony. Individuals blasted the Confederacy. Sarah Palmer in Philadelphia was vociferous. 'Quakers are drilling, contrary to all the peace principles of the Sect … I'm opposed to war', she continued, 'but if ever war was holy, this one, in favor of the most oppressed … down-trodden part of humanity, is' (Bacon 2000, 86). This theme—that good might come if the war ended slavery—was common among Friends. Mott agreed. She hated war, but opposed any peace that preserved slavery (Palmer 2002, 312). While we have no statistics, Friends sensed that hundreds of young Hicksites were volunteering for military service, and many weighty Friends urged leniency toward them (Anon. 1866, 393). Dozens of Hicksites went south to work among the freed slaves, often in association with non-Quakers, breaking down another old barrier (Smedley 1987).

This openness to 'the world's people' paralleled a steady relaxation of the strictures of the plain life. Increasingly, the word *plainness* passed out of use, becoming instead a commitment to *moderation* or *simplicity*. By 1882, the *Friends' Intelligencer* noted that few Friends still wore 'the distinctive garb of the Society'. Friends became open to once-forbidden pleasures, such as novels, the theatre, and music (Hamm 2000, 31). Significantly, some Hicksites argued that while simplicity represented 'true elegance' in apparel, traditional plain dress was a 'self-adopted emblem of…self-righteousness' (Johnson 1860, 55; Anon. 1875, 4–5; Anon. 1884, 46).

Hicksite Friends embraced other innovations—striking was the opening of Swarthmore College in 1869. Earlier, Hicksites had viewed higher education with suspicion, and now they had their own college (Biddle 1883, 4–5). Hicksites followed the Orthodox in opening First Day schools. By the 1880s, they had become general in all of the Hicksite Yearly Meetings (Hamm 2000, 32–4). Another parallel with Gurneyite Friends was the use of 'circular meetings'. These were special Meetings for Worship, 'for the purpose of arousing Friends from their supineness', first held in Philadelphia Yearly Meeting in 1864 (Anon. 1864, 264). Hicksites also began to work together across Yearly Meeting boundaries. This began with the formation of a committee on Indian work in 1869. In 1878, Illinois Yearly Meeting proposed regular conferences on 'the subjects of reform that are now agitating the world at large—temperance, arbitration, abolition of capital punishment, etc'. By 1896, the Friends Union on Philanthropic Labor included all of the Hicksite Yearly Meetings. Four years later it became Friends General Conference (Hamm 2000, 32–4).

Equally striking was the growing self-identification of Hicksite Friends as religious liberals. Hicksites never clearly defined what it meant to be liberal, but they pointed to a number of characteristics: an emphasis on freedom of thought and toleration; antipathy to creedalism; identification with non-Quaker liberals; openness to higher criticism and critical study of the Bible; intense criticism of evangelical doctrines of the Atonement and eternal punishment; and continuing revelation and the Inner Light (their favoured term) as the foundations of Quakerism (Hamm 2000, 24–8). Typical was an Ohio Friend Clarkson Butterworth, in 1882. God, he told Friends, wanted righteous living, '*not* by teaching the miraculous conception, water baptism, bodily resurrection, the efficacy of the outward blood and sacrifice, the infallibility of the Pope or of the scriptures or any of those dogmas or notions about which professing Christians have cut one another's throats, and shed rivers of blood' (Butterworth 26 Nov. 1882). A Friend in Burlington, New Jersey, summed up the Hicksite vision in 1880: 'We meet to "Mind the Light", not as it was revealed to Fox, Barclay, and Penn, but as it is to us, by the needs of the present. Man is progressive, and truth a continued revelation, by which we mean, if we seek after and follow the Light we will be prepared to receive newer and higher conceptions of truth' (S. E. 1880, 182).

By 1887, one senses a rising confidence among Hicksite Friends. Their numbers were not growing. Of roughly 20, 000, about 60 per cent were in Philadelphia Yearly Meeting, another 30 per cent in Baltimore and New York, and the rest scattered in Genesee, Ohio, Indiana, and Illinois Yearly Meetings. One visitor observed that the total membership of the last was roughly that of Green Street Monthly Meeting in Philadelphia. But they sensed that the religious world was moving in their direction, toward an appreciation of the truths that Friends had long upheld (Hamm 2000, 18, 31). As Philadelphia Friend David Newport was quoted in 1887: 'He had no idea of a decline of Quakerism; on the contrary, he thought the day of its acceptance had come, and that its grand doctrine was illuminating the darkness everywhere' (Anon. 1887, 829).

GURNEYITE FRIENDS, 1860–1887

Gurneyite Friends saw even more dramatic changes, both in North America and Britain. They produced a new round of separations in North America while laying the foundations for divergence between American Gurneyites and British Friends.

The 1860s saw the emergence of a new generation of leaders in North America, forming a renewal movement. Articulately evangelical, they were committed to Quaker peculiarities: the peace testimony, simplicity in speech and dress, unpaid ministry, women's ministry. But they also advocated reforms that, in their minds, pared away outdated practices. A particular target were rules against marrying non-members. The reformers advocated a more educated ministry and membership, and an end to 'sing-song' preaching. They helped develop the first Quaker foreign missionary work in two centuries. During the Civil War, while committed to the Peace Testimony, they were vocal in their Unionism. They raised money enthusiastically to found schools, orphanages, and hospitals for the freed people; hundreds of young Gurneyite Friends went south as workers (Hamm 1988, 36–70).

While weighty Friends were one in supporting the Peace Testimony, thousands of young Friends deviated and joined the Union army. Significantly, many Monthly Meetings did not deal with them as offenders against the Discipline. This led to a fear that many members did not really understand Quaker teachings (Hamm 1988, 66–9).

The response of Indiana Yearly Meeting, the largest and arguably the most influential of the American Gurneyite bodies, was to hold general meetings. Weighty ministers and elders explained Quaker views on subjects such as peace, the new birth, ministry, and sanctification. The general meetings always included substantial periods of worship, and these attracted the most interest. Therein lay the roots of revolution. Within a decade, the general meeting movement had become a revival movement (Hamm 1988, 71–2).

Beginning about 1868, a competing vision of Quakerism emerged, articulated by Friends such as David B. Updegraff (1830–94) and Caroline Talbot of Ohio Yearly Meeting; Dougan Clark (1828–96), Esther Frame (1840–1920), and John Henry Douglas (1832–1919) of Indiana; Luke Woodard of New York; and Rufus King of North Carolina. They shared a commitment to the interdenominational holiness movement, a powerful movement founded on the conviction that holiness, or sanctification, was a second, instantaneous experience following conversion. Through holiness teachings, they transformed American Gurneyite Quakerism. In Britain, however, while holiness found advocates, its impact was more limited, and the ultimate direction of London Yearly Meeting was very different (Hamm 1988, 75–85).

Since Gurney's day, Evangelical Friends had seen sanctification as a second, but gradual, experience. The holiness movement taught that all that was necessary was to *claim* the experience, on the basis of faith in the Blood of Christ. That done, traditional Quaker ways—the plain life, separation from the world, peculiarity—lost their value. Indeed, in the minds of many holiness advocates, they became 'dead works' that only erected harmful barriers among fellow Christians. As Updegraff summed up:

> Many could not see that the blessing of God rested upon an attempt to convey to perishing sinners 'accurate *information*' about our 'distinctive *tenets*'. I was one of that number and joined with others in imploring that 'the dead' might be left to 'bury the dead', and that we might unite in preaching the gospel and getting converts to *Jesus*. In the providence of God such counsel prevailed, and then it was that our General Meetings became 'Revival Meetings'.

They *were* revival meetings. The traditional methods of evangelical revivalism—impassioned preaching, the mourner's bench, prayer with seekers, music—quickly came into use. From New England to Kansas, dozens of Gurneyite meetings were swept up in the movement. By 1880, the impact was clear: Plainness faded; silence was regarded as inferior to preaching; community was redefined. Gurneyite Friends, for the most part, no longer saw themselves as called to be a peculiar people. Instead, they were part of the larger community of evangelical Protestants. Not all Yearly Meetings were equally affected. Baltimore was largely immune, and Philadelphia Gurneyites watched with a mixture of hope and deep reservations about revivalist methods. North Carolina was initially more restrained, largely because of the influence of Allen Jay. But the others were powerfully moved. 'You cannot understand it here', Barnabas C. Hobbs, the clerk of Western Yearly Meeting, told London Yearly Meeting in 1878. 'No one can without seeing it. Our meetings were shaken as by a vast whirlwind' (Hamm 1988, 85–92).

Opposition also appeared, with major separations in Western, Iowa, and Kansas Yearly Meetings, and a small one in Indiana. In most cases, the separating Friends had shown themselves open to reform, but the revival was entirely too radical. They branded its advocates 'Fast Quakers', outrunning their divine guide. Such Friends found common cause with the older Wilburite groups and laid the foundations for Conservative Friends (Hamm 1988, 92–4, 99–102).

Others with doubts about the revival refused to separate. Relatively few in numbers, they nevertheless possessed considerable influence because of their leadership skills and positions of authority. They included Barnabas C. Hobbs in Western, Joel Bean (1825–1914) in Iowa, Charles F. and Rhoda M. Coffin and Timothy Nicholson in Indiana, Elizabeth Comstock (1815–91) in Ohio Yearly Meeting, Thomas Kimber in New York, and Allen Jay (1831–1910) and Nereus Mendenhall in North Carolina. They found their organ in the Philadelphia Gurneyite weekly, the *Friends' Review*. These Friends, active in the earlier renewal movement, had generally sympathized with the revival. But as it became more radical, their reservations grew. They thought it best, however, not to separate. As Charles F. Coffin wrote: 'Many of us see defects in the church at present, but feel that inside is the proper place to labor for their remedy'. They would provide the space for the emergence of an American modernist Gurneyite vision after 1890 (Hamm 1988, 111–20).

London Yearly Meeting in this period offers both instructive parallels and contrasts. In the 1860s, it was as fervently evangelical as any American Gurneyite body. In the 1870s, it embraced many of the same innovations—general meetings, missions, and conscious identification with other evangelical groups. The factions—fervent evangelicals, moderates, and Quietists—also paralleled North America. Yet its course was ultimately different.

In 1859, British Friends competed to analyse: 'The Causes of the Decline in the Society of Friends'. The winner, John Stephenson Rowntree, argued that Friends needed, in the words of Thomas C. Kennedy, 'more knowledge of the wider world, deeper comprehension of the Bible as a guide to living in that world and stronger appreciation of the necessity for liberty of thought and action for both working through their differences and providing a healing spirit for others'. Over the next three decades, British Friends struggled to realize this vision (Kennedy 2002, 40–1).

Friends in London and Dublin Yearly Meetings did push out in new directions and by 1870 Quaker missionaries were in Africa and India. Another innovation was home missions, combining evangelism with education. Adult schools, which used 'a Sunday morning Meeting to teach reading and Christianity to the unlettered working classes using the bible as primer', by 1870 reached over 15,000 students, more than London Yearly Meeting's membership. Dublin and London Yearly Meetings both established General Meeting committees (Kennedy, 120–2; Hamm 2009a, 149–50).

Still, British Friends' innovations had their limits, and, before 1880, evangelicalism determined those bounds. By 1870, a small group of Quietists had separated and established a General Meeting at Fritchley. More important was a controversy in Manchester. Some young Friends there, led by David Duncan, embraced critical Biblical scholarship. They asserted that parts of the Bible were probably mythical and that it was vital to re-establish, 'absolute freedom within the borders of the Society of Friends'. Other Friends responded with accusations of unsoundness, and a Yearly Meeting committee headed by weighty and deeply Evangelical Friend Joseph Bevan Braithwaite (1818–1905) intervened. It caused Duncan's disownment. He died before he could appeal, which Braithwaite saw as divine judgement (Kennedy 2002, 47–86).

After 1880, however, the courses of London Yearly Meeting and most Gurneyite Friends in North America diverged. Americans had long seen London as the arbiter of Quaker orthodoxy, but the differences are striking: one was the pastoral system, the other was the response to the Richmond Conference of 1887.

In the minds of American Friends, one of the happy results of the revivals was new members and formation of new meetings. The converts, however, usually found silent worship uninspiring, and many fell away, so revivalists argued that arrangements for regular preaching were necessary. As one put it: 'Every analogy of nature teaches us that when life is produced it must be nourished, and if life of the higher order it is a crime not to do it'. In the late 1870s, a few meetings made informal agreements with ministers for support while the minister lived among them. In 1886, Iowa Yearly Meeting formally endorsed the pastoral system, and by 1900 every American Gurneyite Yearly Meeting except Baltimore had followed. The innovation brought controversy; some Friends previously supportive of revivalism declared that it marked the end of Quakerism. But they lost (Hamm 2009a, 147–8).

Even as revivalists prevailed on the subject of pastors, their endorsement of outward ordinances put them on the defensive. Given the Biblical literalism many shared it was not surprising that many, such as the Beaconites, embraced physical communion and water baptism. Indiana Yearly Meeting responded in 1875 by ruling that no one who participated in outward sacraments could remain a minister or elder. By 1880, an open debate had erupted, one that grew hotter when Updegraff himself was baptized. He opened a fierce campaign for toleration, and many revivalists supported him, but others were opponents. By 1886, every Gurneyite Yearly Meeting except Ohio had ruled against toleration. Under Updegraff's domination, Ohio voted by a narrow margin against restricting 'liberty of conscience' (Hamm 1988, 130–7; Indiana Yearly Meeting [Orthodox] 1886, 59).

In response, more moderate Friends called for a conference of the Gurneyite Yearly Meetings to be held in Richmond, Indiana, in the autumn of 1887. Dublin and London sent delegations, and a few important Philadelphia Gurneyites attended. Gurneyites openly debated the ordinances, pastors, sanctification, and other issues. The conference laid the foundations of the Five Years Meeting. It also produced a long statement, the 'Richmond Declaration of Faith', which has become the authoritative articulation of Quakerism for Evangelical Friends (Hamm 1988, 137–9).

In the following year, the American Yearly Meetings officially represented at the Richmond conference (save Ohio) recorded unity with the declaration (Minear 1987, 138–41). London Yearly Meeting, however, refused, even though Braithwaite had been the principal author (Kennedy 2002, 111–18). Its decision is revealing.

By 1888, as London considered the Richmond Declaration, it had begun to diverge from American Gurneyites. Clearly, a revival was not going to sweep through the Yearly Meeting. While something like the pastoral system had been introduced into the Mission Meetings and Adult Schools, resistance to paid ministry in regularly established meetings was widespread. Even some staunch evangelicals were doubtful about the American revival and its innovations (Hamm 2009a, 152–4).

Also critical to the decision was an emerging influential group of young Modernist Friends in the Yearly Meeting. By the twentieth century, they dominated it. In 1884, they found their rallying point in a book by three Friends, Francis Frith, William Pollard, and William E. Turner. A Reasonable Faith attempted to restore the Light Within to the central place in Quaker faith, questioned Biblical inerrancy, and emphasized the love of God in place of a substitutionary theory of the Atonement. While many in the Yearly Meeting were outraged by what they saw as a 'radically unsound work', attempts to condemn it officially failed. The combination of Modernist-leaning Friends, Quietist suspicions of anything that seemed to endorse American revivalism, and even some evangelicals worried about implied creedalism, prevailed to set British Friends on a different path (Kennedy 2002, 86–118).

Summary

By 1887, the Quaker world had begun to assume the lines that distinguish it today. In North America, bitter divisions had produced seemingly irreconcilable Hicksite, Gurneyite, and Wilburite bodies. Gurneyites and Hicksites had softened the strictures of the plain life and allowed their members to move closer to 'the world'. Hicksites and Wilburites agreed on maintaining silent worship, but on little doctrinally. Hicksites had moved towards a vision of Quakerism that they characterized as liberal: at odds with evangelicalism, suspicious of attempts to impose uniform doctrinal standards, and emphasizing the Inner Light.

Gurneyites were by far the largest group, embracing at least two thirds of Friends in North America, nearly all in the United Kingdom and Ireland, and planting the seeds for future growth through missions in Africa, Asia, and Latin America. Their official theology, as enunciated in their books of Discipline and most clearly in the Richmond Declaration of 1887, was firmly evangelical. Yet diversity was beginning to appear. A wave of revivalism in North America had swept away most of the old landmarks and created pastoral Quakerism. Some moderate opposition remained, however—opposition that would provide an opening for the appearance of an American Gurneyite modernism in the 1890s. And in the United Kingdom and Ireland, rejection of pastors and the Richmond Declaration drew a line that would grow in importance.

Suggested Further Reading

Faulkner, C. (2011) *Lucretia Mott's heresy: abolition and women's rights in nineteenth-century America*. Philadelphia: University of Pennsylvania Press.

Hamm, T. D. (1988) *The transformation of American Quakerism: Orthodox Friends, 1800–1907*. Bloomington, IN: Indiana University Press.

Ingle, H. L. (1998 [1986]) *Quakers in conflict: The Hicksite reformation*. Knoxville, TN: University of Tennessee Press.

Isichei, E. (1970) *Victorian Quakers*. Oxford: Oxford University Press.

Kennedy, T. C. (2002) *British Quakerism, 1860–1920: The transformation of a religious community*. Oxford: Oxford University Press.

CHAPTER 5

MODERNIST AND LIBERAL QUAKERS, 1887–2010

J. WILLIAM FROST

THE major theme of most silent Meeting Friends in the twentieth century is their transformation under the impact of liberal or Modernist theology, the social gospel, and war. The resulting synthesis allowed the creation of new meetings, expansion of the peace testimony, reunification of American Hicksite and Orthodox Meetings, but increased estrangement with pastoral holiness and fundamentalist Friends. The focus of this essay is on Friends who worship in unprogrammed Meetings that include the fifteen Yearly Meetings in Friends General Conference, three Yearly Meetings in the far west of the US, Quakers in Great Britain and Ireland, and the small Yearly Meetings in Australia, France, Germany, and South Africa. (Wilburite or Conservative Friends who also worship in silent meetings are explored by Lloyd Lee Wilson in Chapter 8 within this volume entitled 'Conservative Friends, 1845–2010'.)

During the 1960s the Quaker liberals faced challenges based on theology and history and had to incorporate perspectives posed by a radical anti-war movement, black power advocates, women's liberation, and a questioning of moral standards on marriage, sex, and homosexuality. Liberalism remained the dominant perspective, but it was chastened, less certain of the relation of Quakerism to Christianity, and open to alternative religions. Diversity in religious beliefs, declining membership numbers (particularly among the young), and social activism, characterized Friends in 2010.

LIBERAL OR MODERNIST QUAKERS

The initial focus of this chapter is to show why liberalism emerged and how the merger of Modernist theology and social gospel service renewed Friends, preserved silent worship, and expanded work for peace and social justice.

The first generation of Quaker liberals took the insights of German, British, and American Protestant Bible scholars and theologians, and merged them with important themes of Quaker history. They wished to affirm Christianity, remain Quaker, be relevant to society, and accept the findings of science. A younger generation raised with the evangelicals' emphasis on higher education and good works now confronted intellectual challenges to their inherited beliefs. Modernist Christianity sought to incorporate the knowledge posed by the evolutionary science of Charles Darwin, the new psychology of religious experience, and the findings of archaeologists and historians studying ancient Israel. For the liberals the evangelical reliance on an inerrant Bible was no longer tenable because Darwin had demonstrated that humans were a product of evolution. Historical critics had shown the changes in Hebrew religion from the primitive stories in *Genesis* to the profundity of the prophets. Jews seeking to experience the divine and to interpret the acts of God in their history created the Old Testament. The Bible, the history of the church, and the creeds needed to be approached critically. Major beliefs of Christianity should be understood as symbolic statements of truth, not taken as abstract truths binding for all time. Liberals found in religious experience a foundation for religious certainty. Christianity was not a set of doctrines; it was an unmediated life-transforming experience of a living Christ (Barbour and Frost 1994, 219–30; Hamm, 1998, 144–60).

Quaker liberalism began in Great Britain with a group of young men from important evangelical families. John W. Rowntree (1868–1905), Edward Grubb (1854–1939), W. C. Braithwaite (1862–1922) (whose father had largely drafted the Richmond Declaration of Faith), Thomas Hodgkin, A. Neave Brayshaw (1861–1940), and J. W. Graham (1859–1932) were all birthright Friends, and all well educated. They were schoolteachers, lawyers, and businessmen, and essentially self-taught in theology, ethics, and history. Only J. Rendel Harris (1852–1941) had a PhD, an international reputation as a Bible scholar, and university appointments. The only American of comparable stature and who worked closely with the British liberals was Rufus Jones (1863–1948), a New England Friend whose aunt and uncle were Eli and Sybil Jones, important Quaker evangelical ministers well known to English Friends. A lifelong member of New England Yearly Meeting and professor at Haverford College from 1893 to 1933, Jones influenced several generations of Quakers in Philadelphia and Five Years Meeting (Vining 1958).

The first flowering of liberalism in Britain came at the Manchester Conference of 1895, attended by over a thousand Friends, and sponsored by the Home Missions Committee to inform younger members of the principles of Friends and to strengthen public ministry. Of the 139 contributions, one-third by women, most were uncontroversial—twenty-five stressed evangelical themes, while twenty-two espoused liberal ideas (Kennedy 2001, 143–6; Davie 1997, 57–85). Still, the liberals became a visible presence and created a programme of summer schools beginning in 1897 where several hundred Friends gathered to learn the results of the scholarly study of Quakerism, Christianity, and English society—particularly what could be done about war and the presence of widespread poverty. Liberals taught these classes.

The closest analogy to Woodbrooke and the summer schools among the American Hicksite Yearly Meetings was Friends General Conference. The Hicksites in 1881–2 created the Friends Union for Philanthropic Labor to coordinate social policy, an educational conference in 1894, and Friends General Conference in 1902 as an annual meeting for worship, education, and sociability but with no authority over individual Yearly Meetings. The Hicksites acceptance of liberalism came more easily because, unlike the Orthodox, they had traditionally opposed evangelicalism, disliked creeds, and stressed the primacy of religious experience.

A second project initiated by J. W. Rowntree and Rufus Jones was for a series of histories of the Society of Friends. These would ultimately run to seven volumes, four by Jones on the continental roots of Quakers, mysticism, and the history of Friends after the 1720s, two by W. B. Braithwaite (after the early death of Rowntree) on the formative periods of Quakerism, and one by several authors on Quakers in colonial America. These carefully researched books would demonstrate that the anti-intellectualism of the Wilburites and the doctrinal rigidity of the evangelicals distorted the vision of George Fox and the first Friends. Quakerism was not an offshoot of the Puritans, because its origins lay with continental Anabaptists. Early Friends, like the liberals, rejected formal theology and a hireling ministry, made the Bible subordinate to religious experience, opposed predestination as libelous to God and degrading to humans, and sought to end the social evils of society. Unlike the Calvinists, Friends began with a positive view of humanity. History provided modern Quakers with a series of paradigmatic figures: Fox and Penington for direct religious experience, Margaret Fell for women's power, William Penn for religious liberty and political involvement, John Woolman for anti-slavery and mysticism, and Whittier and Mott as the best of nineteenth-century Orthodoxy and Hicksites, for their lack of dogmatism and for their abolitionist activism.

Although the Rowntree books received favourable reviews in British and American Quaker periodicals, more Friends gained access to liberal thought through the articles that Edward Grubb (1854–1939) wrote as editor of the *British Friend* from 1901 to 1913 and Jones composed as editor of the publication renamed *American Friend* from 1893 to 1912. Grubb, in addition to pamphlets and booklets, wrote twenty-one books between 1897 and 1933. A bibliography of Jones's books and articles runs to forty-three pages (Dudley 1946; Rush 1944). Liberal Friends wrote studies of Quaker social thought, dress, the peace testimony, and biographies of major figures. Quaker liberals made sure that any Friend who could read would have access to the new perspectives.

Since its founding, Friends had a suspicion of divinity schools and the academic study of religion as fostering head knowledge. The Modernists saw anti-intellectualism among Quakers as a legacy that hindered ministry in meeting for worship. Thus, in 1903 they established Woodbrooke as a non-degree granting school with good scholars as faculty. Seeking to combine religious nurture and academics, Woodbrooke offered courses in Quakerism, Bible, church history, international affairs, and problems of society. Friends of all ages with varying academic qualifications, international students, and men and women seeking a religious training certificate from Cambridge for school teaching, or a social-work degree from the University of Birmingham came to Woodbrooke. Cooperation with the nearby Selly Oak Colleges, where missionaries of dissenting churches, and later the Church of England studied, allowed development of a rich curriculum, expanded library, and stimulating environment. Woodbrooke was firmly Christian and liberal. For example, J. Rendel Harris, the first director of studies, came from an evangelical background, and led students in prayer, singing hymns, devotional study of the Bible, and recounting religious experience (Davis 1953, 19–30). His successor, H. G. Wood was a noted Bible scholar and theologian.

For liberals the essence of Quakerism, which had created and sustained it, was a direct experience of God called the Light Within, Inward Light, Light of Christ, Christ within, and—a term rarely used before 1900 but increasingly prevalent—'the inner light'. God created and designed all humans with an ability to feel or know the divine. Jones called this mysticism and defined it as a 'consciousness of direct and immediate relationship with some transcendent reality which in the moment of experience is believed to be God' (Jones 1922, 44, 123, 136, 152–3; Jones 1949, 64). Jones agreed with William James that the human/divine encounter was compelling, life-transforming, unverifiable to outsiders, and distorted when expressed in language. Quaker mysticism was not a negative life-denying phenomenon, but a positive falling away of the barriers to this world in an awareness of the presence of the divine that could be created and shared in a meeting for worship and that led to a concern for the wider society. It could be consoling, ethical, and prophetic.

Liberals tended to be philosophical idealists, emphasizing that God was immanent with signs of his presence in the greatest human achievements in music and art as well as mundane activities and family life. All life was sacramental and could lead to God. Creeds could be useful if they were taken as imperfect formulations from the past. It was difficult to pin down the Modernists on what they believed about original sin or the Trinity because they regarded all human conceptions of the divine as flawed. The Bible should be read as an inspired but not inerrant work, as a valuable devotional tool. The first generation of liberals were more inclined to apply historical criticism to the Old Testament than the New and retained a focus on Jesus as the supreme example of a man fully in harmony with God, the person in whom God and man touched and became one, a teacher of the supreme system of morals. His crucifixion and resurrection proved that God entered fully into human life, served to communicate the love of God for humanity, and demonstrated that there was life after death. While affirming the crucial historical role of Jesus of Nazareth, what was important now was experiencing the Inward Christ (Fosdick 1951, 40–7).

As early as the Manchester Conference, Modernist theology became associated with another emphasis, called the social gospel in America and social Christianity in Britain. The connection between the two movements became so strong that even today most silent meeting Friends would not separate them. The social gospel, like Modernism, originated outside the Religious Society of Friends as Protestant clergymen sought to apply the teachings of Jesus to economic and social problems. Repudiating laissez-faire economic theory and paternalistic benevolence of the Victorians, reformers sought insights from the newly professionalized disciplines of history, political science, economics, and sociology.

In the US, the social gospel helped fuel the Progressive Movement that captured both political parties. In Britain the emergence of the Labour Party and Fabian socialists focused attention on the condition of the working class and need for industrial reform.

British Friends before 1914 rarely became socialists and tended to vote Liberal while supporting Lloyd George's reform agenda and those factions opposing imperial expansion and advocating arms limitations. American Quakers since the Civil War voted Republican as the only party advocating Black rights in the South. Friends remained pro-business, supporting as part of the peace testimony arbitration of labour disputes rather than strikes. Philadelphia Yearly Meeting (Orthodox) never endorsed women's suffrage and the Hicksites did not do so until 1918; both Yearly Meetings deplored Quaker Alice Paul's (1885–1977) radical tactics of demonstrating outside the White House during the First World War (Benjamin 1976, 165–9, 184–91). The early Quaker social gospel was a genteel affair advocated by educated men and women.

Friends joined peace societies that advocated arbitration among nations, a world court applying international law and limitations on war obtained through the Hague conferences beginning in 1897. Peace advocates remained middle class, patriotic, reformist, and optimistic. The Modernist Friends rediscovered Fox's 1660 declaration against war and reprinted William Penn's essay advocating a parliament in Europe. The small Australian Friends movement, in an area where conscription was being debated, advised British Friends to oppose universal military service. Still, even in the summer of 1914, few Quakers expected a major war.

The events of August 1914 showed the contrast between Friends and most other churches that rallied to the defence of their nations. The war proved to Friends that acculturation was costly and that they were and should remain a distinct sect. Pacifism has characterized the official stance of Yearly Meetings from 1914 until now, but there have always been dissenters. For example, about one-third of the eligible young men in Britain volunteered for the military. Over 600 young Quakers joined the Friends Ambulance Unit as a way of serving without killing, even though it remained under military control. The Meeting for Sufferings created an emergency committee to help Germans stranded in Britain find housing and work. The Friends Service Council created the Friends War Victims Relief Conference (FWVRC) to send volunteers to France to help civilians in war-devastated areas. Supporting these men required extensive fund-raising in Britain and the creation of a bureaucracy of volunteers to negotiate with English and French governments, armies, and local authorities, to establish priorities in projects, fund supplies, transport workers to France, and coordinate activities with other relief agencies.

American Friends learned from the experience of British Quakers and gained over two years to agitate for peace. When the USA declared war in April 1917 and adopted a draft, a majority of young Quakers joined the military with the support of most of their elders. Either because of tradition or because weighty Friends controlled policy, all American Yearly Meetings endorsed pacifism. Under the leadership of Young Friends, members of all branches joined to create the American Friends Service Committee (AFSC) to provide a vehicle for young men who would join British conscientious objectors (COs) in relief activities in France as 'a service of love in wartime' (Rufus Jones in Frost 1992, 1).

The FWVRC and AFSC cooperated at all levels and the 600 Americans in France continued and expanded the work of building and erecting houses, aiding farmers, and building and staffing a maternity hospital. Many who worked in France or who went to prison for their pacifist beliefs would emerge as leaders of Liberal Friends until the 1950s. The war had radicalized them and they were determined that they would work for peace to make certain that this really was a war to end wars.

Friends created the AFSC and FWVRC as temporary agencies to aid the COs, but at the end of the war the French government, having concluded that the Friends were among the best relief agencies, requested that they take charge of reconstruction in the Verdun area—a scene of utter devastation. When a few Americans were allowed into Germany, the British and American service agencies sent a delegation, headed by Jane Addams, which returned with a report of people facing starvation. Because the Friends had not supported the war (unlike the Red Cross), the German government invited them to dispense food to children. Eventually, Friends would supervise the feeding of over one million German children. Seeing the dire conditions in Eastern Europe, Friends established food-aid projects in Austria, Poland, Serbia, and Russia—even being tolerated by a suspicious Soviet government until 1924.

Quaker aid workers discovered that peace had not dissipated the animosities fostered by the war. They also learned that among a few French and Germans with whom they worked were people who sympathized with their religious views and peace work, and sought continued contacts with Friends. Under the leadership of Carl Heath (1869–1950), a recently convinced member, Friends created 'Quaker Embassies' in Berlin, Paris, and Madrid. Aid workers held worship services on Sunday and during the week sponsored discussions on religious and political issues. Since the seventeenth century there had been small groups of Friends in Europe, and now German and French Yearly Meetings emerged.

In 1915, British Friends endorsed the idea of a conference of all Friends to discuss peace. Delegations from all strands of Quakerism came to London in 1920 and received six impressive studies on major issues. Disagreements on socialism as an answer to economic issues and the value of the League of Nations divided delegates, but they agreed on the centrality of the peace testimony, its basis in the life and teachings of Jesus, its confirmation in religious experience, and the need to expand it to deal with the causes of war in colonialism, racism, economic inequality, and nationalism (Kennedy 2001, 312–87). In retrospect, one can discern a fundamental difference in Quaker understanding of their work for peace. For the absolutists who had suffered in prison, peace became a religious commitment founded on obedience to the Light and personal transformation was the key. An alternative and majority view agreed on the religious basis of the peace testimony but saw it as socially and politically efficacious—a perspective Quakers should offer to other Christian churches and the wider society.

LIBERALISM ASCENDANT 1920–1960

Four developments defined Modernist Quaker life after 1920. Firstly, the gradual ascendency of liberal thought in Britain, in Friends General Conference Meetings, and in East Coast US Orthodox Meetings, but the continuing controversy where conservative evangelicals and fundamentalists remained strong. Secondly, the reunification of Hicksite and Orthodox Meetings in New York, Philadelphia, and Maryland, Baltimore; Yearly Meetings and the Wilburite and Orthodox Meetings in New England and Canada. Thirdly, the creation of new meetings, and finally, the work for a relevant peace witness in a time of totalitarianism and war.

At London Yearly Meeting, Woodbrooke remained a centre of Modernist thought with a strong faculty and visiting Fellows (including a virtual who's who of prominent British and American Quakers) who taught, researched, and produced major books. However, not all liberals endorsed Rufus Jones's identification of mysticism. William Littleboy (1853–1936) of Woodbrooke published 'The Message of Quakerism to the Non-Mystic', a perspective endorsed by Harvard's Henry Cadbury (1883–1974) who refused to call himself a mystic, because they stressed the importance of obedience and service over ecstacy and feelings. 'Action…leads to thought and can also lead to spiritual growth' (Littleboy 1945, 8; Bacon 1987), xiii).

A more far-reaching critique of liberalism came from Lewis Benson (1906–86), a New Jersey businessman, who concluded, on the basis of study of George Fox, that Modernist Quakers had distorted the message of early Friends, by being too accommodating to modern culture. Benson insisted that Fox was not being metaphorical when he claimed, 'that Christ has returned to teach his people', and that Friends needed to return to a Christ-centred, biblically based religion. True Quakerism was neither Protestant nor Roman Catholic, neither Modernist nor evangelical, but the original form of Christianity (Benson 1966, 2–22). Benson and his followers in Britain and America sought to return to a prophetic Quakerism through travelling ministry, preaching, and publications.

Liberals in America—Quakers and other Protestants—found a congenial home in colleges and universities. Friends produced more scholars whose impact went beyond the meeting than ever before in its history. There were Quaker liberals on the faculties of divinity schools at Harvard, Yale, Hartford, and Duke, at secular universities including Cornell and Columbia, and at Earlham and Swarthmore. Haverford College's philosophy department included Rufus Jones and Thomas Kelly (1893–1941) whose *Testament of Devotion* (1941), edited by his colleague Douglas Steere (1901–95), became an instant classic and is still in print. Steere's studies of Christian mysticism, work for unification and the ecumenical movement, lecturing and teaching, continued until his death in 1995. At Swarthmore College, Jesse Holmes (1864–1942) educated generations of young Hicksites in liberal thought and socialism, wrote extensively for the *Friends Intelligencer*, and lectured at Friends General Conference. Anna Brinton (1887–1969) taught classics and Howard Brinton (1884–1973), a student of Rufus Jones, taught science and philosophy at Mills College and Earlham College before moving to Pendle Hill in 1936 as director of administration and as director of studies, teaching there until the 1960s while writing books on Quaker history, education, and worship.

In examining the American liberal intellectuals, two characteristics stand out— most were male and came from Orthodox families. Perhaps their activism resulted from the contrast between their childhood certainties and their adult liberal nuances and careful distinctions. Their accomplishments—writing for scholars and the general public, teaching, participating on meeting committees, attending conferences, working for the AFSC, advocating pacifism in a country often not sympathetic—might have served to reassure them psychologically of the soundness of Modernist Quakerism.

Reunion

A cynic looking at American Quaker history might conclude that although Young Friends had decided to unite even before 1914, they had to wait another forty years for the older generations to die before it could be accomplished. Unification required two developments. Firstly, Hicksites and Orthodox had to stop stereotyping each other as heretics or as intolerant and grasping for power. This could be achieved by getting to know each other better. Secondly, the theological issues had to be ignored or finessed; by dropping or reinterpreting ancient Christian doctrines liberalism did this. Silence in meeting could be reinterpreted to mean silence about doctrine.

The unification of the two New York and two Philadelphia Yearly Meetings came through a series of small steps. New York Friends agreed on a joint depository for the records in 1904, joint work for peace in 1908, joint celebration of the tercentenary of George Fox's birth in 1924, single joint sessions of the two Yearly Meetings in 1928, a merger of Young Friends in 1935, and a joint Service Committee during the Second World War. From 1916 to 1944 a joint committee for Affiliated Service sought to coordinate peace and social justice work. A major obstacle ended in 1940 when Five Years Meeting authorized Yearly Meetings to replace the Uniform Discipline that included the Richmond Declaration of Faith as an appendix. The pastoral system per se was not a key issue, because many New York ministers had trained in liberal seminaries and spoke at Hicksite Meetings. At the Monthly and Quarterly Meeting levels, both groups began worshipping together and when the Yearly Meeting united in 1955, half of all meetings had already affiliated with both Friends General Conference and Five Years Meeting (Van Wagner 1995, 257–75).

The economic and social distinctions among members of the two Philadelphia Yearly Meetings had disappeared before 1900. One sign of similarity was that both Yearly Meetings stopped holding separate Women's Yearly Meetings in 1923 and 1924 (Benjamin 1976, 149–51; Bacon 1986, 197–8). The faculty and students of Haverford, Swarthmore, and Bryn Mawr Colleges met in academic, social, and athletic activities. In 1929 members of both Yearly Meetings created Pendle Hill as a non-degree granting institution to study Quakerism and social issues. Henry Hodgkin (1877–1933), an English Friend who became its first director, believed that since the British had helped cause the separation in 1827, they should now help to heal it. Pendle Hill's faculty, visiting lecturers, board, and students came from both branches.

In Philadelphia, unification came slowly; the two historical societies merged in the 1920s; 1928 brought appointed representatives to attend the other's Yearly Meeting; peace committees joined in 1933, and both Yearly Meetings welcomed a proposal for unification in 1932. By the 1940s the two Yearly Meetings occurred at the same time and they began having joint sessions and merged committees; they established a planning commission in 1946, and in 1950 authorized a joint *Faith and Practice*. Full unification took place between 5,537 Orthodox and 11,633 Hicksites in 1955, essentially the same numbers as at the turn of the century (Hadley 1991, 138–72).

The development of new unprogrammed meetings brought vitality and made Liberal Quakerism a nationwide movement, even though three-quarters of Friends General Conference Friends still live east of the Appalachian Mountains. The new meetings, often found in college or university towns, generally have fifty or fewer members, most of whom joined Friends as adults, live at great distance from other meetings but keep in contact with Friends through the Friends World Committee for Consultation or American Friends Service Committee (Wilson 1993, 63). Members of these new meetings remain unconcerned with the theological issues that divided earlier Friends, emphasizing mystical worship and actively seeking social change. In New England, where there were no Hicksites, new independent meetings in Cambridge, MA, Providence, RI, and Hartford, CT helped merge the older Gurneyite and Wilburite meetings in 1945 into a united New England Yearly Meeting that affiliated with both Friends United and Friends General Conference.

Pacific Yearly Meeting began with the unprogrammed meeting in San Jose, CA founded by Joel (1825–1914) and Hannah Bean (1830–1909) in 1889. It joined thirty other meetings in 1931 to become Pacific Coast Association and that evolved into Pacific Yearly Meeting in 1947, and divided in 1973 to form North Pacific Yearly Meeting and Intermountain Yearly Meeting. Intermountain's meetings have 1008 members scattered through six states, including Texas and Colorado. Another new Yearly Meeting called Southeast covers Florida and coastal areas of South Carolina and Georgia; the even-more recent Southern Appalachian Yearly Meeting and Association has twenty-nine meetings in eight states, ranging from West Virginia to Mississippi.

LIBERALISM AND ITS CRITICS

Silent Meeting Friends during the 1960s faced challenges posed by Afro-Americans, Marxist and anarchist students, anti-war activists, a revolution in moral values, and a rethinking of liberalism's intellectual foundations.

Quakers' long tradition of work against slavery, for black education in the North and South, race relations committees, and protests against lynching should not obscure the facts that in 1900 few black people felt at home in Quaker meetings, most Quaker schools remained segregated, and Philadelphia remained a segregated city with most Afro-Americans confined to menial positions. Beginning in the 1920s, the AFSC sought to further racial harmony through lectures and conferences attended by both races. Integration came slowly: first to all-male Haverford College in 1926 and all-female Bryn Mawr in 1933; co-ed Swarthmore refused to admit black students until it was integrated in 1943 (by a Navy unit). Oakwood School in New York admitted black students in 1933; Media Friends' decision to integrate in 1937 was controversial and the two Philadelphia Yearly Meetings' boarding schools, Westtown and George School, changed their policies after the Second World War: Westtown in 1945 and George School in 1946. Quaker schools in Delaware, Maryland, and North Carolina began integrating only in the 1960s. Even so, Quakers took pride in their race relations, with Bayard Rustin (1912–87) lecturing at Friends General Conference and serving on the AFSC board, which sent Martin Luther King to India to study Gandhi's techniques.

After accepting integration at about the same pace as other liberal northerners, Friends were appalled in 1969 when a group of Afro-Americans seized the floor at Philadelphia Yearly Meeting to demand funds as 'reparations' for past injustices (McDaniel and Julye, 2009, 279–86; 322–36). Marxist students indicted the AFSC as insufficiently revolutionary and Black Power advocates charged that its mostly middle-class staff could not be effective at working against poverty. AFSC workers should resemble not white Quakers but those needing help. Yearly Meetings responded to these demands by creating special funds for projects in black neighbourhoods, but did not accept that these were reparations or should be controlled by outsiders. The AFSC diversified its staff, although at a cost of decreasing the number of Friends, and redefined itself as an agency for social change rather than relief.

Friends resisted when radicals tried to take over Quaker institutions, but they also learned from their critics and sought ways to foster social change that conformed to the Peace Testimony. The AFSC worked to coordinate anti-war demonstrations, Philadelphia Yearly Meeting and A Quaker Action Group defied the Federal government and sent medical supplies to North Vietnam, and Friends on the vessel *Phoenix* sailed into areas where nuclear tests were scheduled. Young Friends in the New Swarthmoor movement experimented with communal residences and in George Lakey's 1971 *Revolution: a Quaker prescription for a sick society*, advocated a peaceful transformation of America.

As an intellectual synthesis based on history, philosophy, psychology, and the social gospel, Quaker liberalism after the 1960s seemed less vital. Its optimistic view of the future, its de-emphasis upon sin, and a desire to be compatible with science seemed dated. Liberalism's historical foundation was undermined by scholars who found little evidence of continental mysticism in early Friends, stressed the close relationship between Quakers and radical Puritans, saw Fox stressing sin and transformation, and Jesus as an eschatological prophet. So early Friends were not mystics (Nuttall 1946, 150–66; Barbour 1985, x–xi). William James's description of religious experience seemed too simple, too Protestant and individualistic, and also pre-Freudian in viewing human psychology. Liberalism also rested upon a philosophy of idealism, but now more influential were logical empiricism and existentialism. Rufus Jones, Thomas Kelly, Douglas Steere, Howard Brinton, and Jesse Holmes would no longer have felt at home in philosophy departments.

A lack of Quaker faculty at divinity schools meant that an institution was needed where Friends could engage in academic study of their religion. Pendle Hill, now defined as a centre for contemplation, had no formal connection with a college. So in 1960 Earlham College created a School of Religion as a place to train pastors and those interested in Quakers' Christian heritage. Several of its graduates have held responsible positions at Pendle Hill and in Yearly Meetings affiliated with Friends General Conference.

Liberation theology became influential among silent Meeting Friends because it emphasized structural violence, base communities, learning from the poor, and non-violence. Relief workers confronted the poverty and oppression in Central and Latin America, and meetings creating sanctuaries for draft resisters or so-called illegal immigrants, invoking liberation theology.

The appeal of feminist liberation theology to Friends is also easy to understand. Women had long enjoyed theoretical equality in Friends meetings, boards, schools, and service agencies, and had since the eighteenth century constituted a majority of those who attended and did the work of meetings. In the twentieth century A. Ruth Fry, Anna Brinton, Carolena Wood, and Hannah Clothier Hull played important roles—particularly in relief work—and yet Quaker attitudes towards women and the family remained very traditional. So Quaker women endorsed complaints against patriarchal religion and obtained more inclusive language in *Faith and Practices*.

Unlike liberation theology and feminism, Quaker Universalism posed a greater challenge, because it began by using perspectives basic to liberalism. Both valued worship in Silent Meetings, disliked creeds, wanted openness and tolerance, and remained ready to embrace findings of scholarship. The difference was that Liberal Friends through the 1960s remained firmly attached to Christianity, engaging in the study of the Bible and church history, and they judged the truths of other religions by the life and teachings of Jesus.

Universalist Quakers vary widely in beliefs. Many call themselves Christians for historical or sentimental reasons, even though most are uncomfortable with the Trinitarian formulation. They reason that Fox and Penn had insisted that even peoples who had never heard of Jesus could experience the Light Within and be saved. So Quakers has a long tradition of universalism (*The Quaker universalist reader: a collection of essays, addresses and lectures* 1986; Sheeran, 1983, 75–8; Trevett 1997, 58–81, 121). Other Universalists wish to jettison the name Christian, emphasizing instead that they are a part of the *Religious*, not Christian Society of Friends. They claim that valuing Christianity over all other religions is arrogant, even imperialist, and needs to be abandoned in the new interconnected world. All religions, they argue, contain truths, are culture-based, advocate a compassionate ethical behaviour, value prayer, point humans to something greater than this transient life, require worship, and seek peace. Because Christianity traditionally devalued women, justified despoiling of nature, allowed holocausts, and led crusades and wars, Quakers should emancipate themselves from it. So Friends should not join and support the World Council of Churches. Instead, they should learn meditation techniques from Zen Buddhists, Hindus, or Sufi Muslims, love of nature from Native Americans, and the centrality of women from goddess cults. The Quaker practice of silent worship and experience of the inner light could serve as a bridge to all the peoples and religions of the world.

Universalists tended to approve of religion in general, stripped of its social/cultural context. Many seem more knowledgeable about other religions than Christianity and unaware that by extracting the best of all religions—that just happens to agree with what they already believe—is itself an act of cultural arrogance. Universalism here seems a logical progression from the Modernists who also discovered in mystical religious experience a way to ignore what they no longer believed.

A final challenge clearly emerging in the 1960s was over personal moral values. Until the mid-century, Friends concentrated more on peace and theology than on personal moral issues. *Faith and Practice* condemned tobacco, alcohol, and gambling; and supported nuclear families, grudgingly accepting that divorce sometimes occurred. Sexual relations to create children should occur in marriage, although in 1924 a pamphlet issued by English Friends allowed a limited use of contraception. By the 1950s meetings advocated education about sex as a way of creating healthy relationships. In 1963 a group of English Friends published *Towards a Quaker view of Sex* that argued that homosexuality as an orientation and practice was a legitimate and not immoral form of sexuality. Highly controversial but influential in Britain, there was virtually no mention of the pamphlet at the time by Friends in America.

If in the 1950s, as the Kinsey Reports asserted, a revolution in sexual attitudes and practices was occurring, Friends did not recognize it until the late 1960s. Then they were confronted by pot-smoking, radical young people shouting 'make love, not war' and engaging in premarital sex and experiments in communal living. The AFSC abandoned its successful youth camps because it could not control the teenagers, and Quaker colleges reluctantly abandoned strict regulations for students. Parents, often because they saw no alternative, acquiesced in the new moral standards and meetings took refuge in vague statements that all sexual relations should be based on love and mutual consent and not be exploitative. Clearness committees expressed relief that young Friends were getting married and ignored that they were often already cohabiting.

Open discussion of homosexuality began in America in the 1970s. Liberal Friends discovered that some of their valued members were gay and were unwilling to condemn these relationships— the issue became not abstract morality but concern for individuals. Gays and lesbians formed an interest group at meetings of Friends General Conference. Between 1972 and 1974 New York, Philadelphia, Baltimore, Illinois, and Pacific Yearly Meetings passed minutes affirming civil rights for homosexuals. The debate soon changed from civil rights to marriages under the care of meeting. By the 1980s meetings began authorizing 'same-sex celebration of commitment', partially because same-sex marriages were not recognized in law. Now there is much diversity, with some meetings holding same-sex marriages, others refusing. In Britain, the Yearly Meeting is campaigning for the legality of same-sex marriage. The debate over homosexuality has damaged relationships between Evangelical or fundamentalist Friends and liberals, and is most intense at Yearly Meetings that belong to both Friends United Meeting and Friends General Conference (Frost, 2001, 52–64. See Doan and Kamphausen's chapter 30 within this volume entitled 'Quakers and Sexuality' for a further discussion on this subject).

Quakerism in 2010: the Impact of Liberalism

The results of liberalism can be seen in a portrait of Silent Meeting Quakers in 2010. Most members in 1900 had been raised Friends; now a majority are convinced (Slack 1967, 20). In spite of their desire to welcome minorities, the Religious Society of Friends remains overwhelmingly white, middle-class, and educated. The Society remains organized around family nurture, but there are increasing numbers of young and old, singles, divorced, and gay and lesbians. The businessmen who dominated nineteenth-century Friends have been replaced by schoolteachers, social workers, government employees, lawyers, doctors, and other professionals. To serve an aging population of members, Quakers have created retirement communities that often have large Meetings for Worship.

Friends have not done a successful job in rearing their children to become active adult members, in spite of their controlling many private primary and secondary schools. As a result, membership in the combined Philadelphia Yearly Meeting has dropped by one-third since unification; Britain Yearly Meeting is down only a little. New liberal meetings now exist in suburbs and college towns, but they are often small. However, Quaker membership statistics are not particularly helpful, because many attenders do not become members and, because Friends dislike overt proselytizing, there is little pressure to change one's status. Local meetings that select people for committees often ignore the distinction. In theory the Yearly Meetings have power, whereas in practice local meetings are practically autonomous.

Contemporary Modernist Quakers still operate within a vaguely Christian framework but refuse to endorse creeds, draw upon the Bible as one of many sources of revelation, emphasize Jesus as an ethical teacher and perfect man rather than a deity, use resurrection as a metaphor, and spend little time on life after death. Most liberals continue to affirm an experience of the divine immanent in daily life and shared in worship.

Changes in Liberal Friends' views of ministry and authority within meetings are reflected in how they create what they used to call Christian disciplines but now term *Faith and Practice*. Formerly, disciplines consisted of decisions of earlier Yearly Meetings, sometimes separated into testimonies or beliefs and organizational practices. These were drawn up by committees of ministers and elders and approved by Yearly Meetings. Today they are formulated by special committees, submitted to Yearly Meetings, then sent to local meetings, returned to Yearly Yeeting, etc. The process can take years. For Britain Yearly Meeting, the book is 600 pages long and incorporates many of the perspectives that Friends have espoused over 350 years of history (Britain Yearly Meeting 2009). The process of creation is now more democratic, inclusive, and representative of the variety of Friends' beliefs. Absent, however, is a sense of a Christian discipline or a normative Quaker faith. The discipline could now be titled *Faiths and Practices*.

Within meetings in 2010, a few members do most of the tasks. One difference is the decline in the status of ministers. Formerly all meetings recognized certain individuals as having a gift for speaking in meeting and recorded them. These people and elders sat on the 'facing bench', an elevated group of benches in front of the meeting. Now most liberal meetings (except New England), no longer recognize ministers or elders. In new meetings, chairs are erected in a circle; in older ones, anyone, including children, can sit on the facing bench. There has also been change in the nature of ministry. Silence in meeting continues and no one is supposed to prepare in advance what she or he says, but ministry is now less speaking under the direct inspiration of the Holy Spirit than seeking for the truths discovered in thought, or study, or by meditating. In some liberal meetings, prayer is frequent, in others rare. It is not uncommon for a meeting to have members who value silence; more prefer much speaking and messages that are generally only a few minutes in length can be evangelical, Quietist, or liberal—a heritage of the nineteenth-century separations. Speaking during worship can be calls to action, political analysis, sympathy for suffering members, biblical exegesis, and testimonies about the inner light. The peace testimony is often stressed, but there are few discussions of alcohol, tobacco, or personal morality. Simplicity is often invoked in preaching about ecology (Hamm 2003, 64–74).

In 1900 all Friends wanted to be Christian; today a substantial minority is uncomfortable with this label and there is a small group of atheists in Liberal Quakerism. A sociological study of Britain Yearly Meeting concluded that almost anything could be said during Meeting for Worship, if it were said in a Quaker way—that is, quietly, not threatening, searching, and respectful. The diversity in theological beliefs was so great that Quakerism had become a manner of behaving rather than a matter of similarity of beliefs (Dandelion 1996, 100–1, 110–20, 310–11). The same seems to be true of liberal Yearly Meetings in America. Quaker Business Meetings originally operated by 'sense of the meeting', that is, Friends by silence and by listening to others, could arrive at a conclusion influenced by the Light. A study of weighty Friends in the combined Philadelphia Yearly Meetings in the 1970s found a division with nearly half believing that decisions were based upon a consensus with no assumption or necessity for divine guidance (Sheeran 1983, 84–9).

Modern Friends are a diverse group with special gatherings for those interested in history, theology, psychology, art, gay and lesbian issues, family life, education, and the arts. Yearly Meetings, Friends General Conference, and retreat centres schedule sessions on an enormous variety of topics, but they concentrate upon spiritual nurture.

In all their diversity, Friends in the year 2010 preserved two liberal foci: Silent Meeting for Worship and living the peace testimony. Most want to affirm their historic relations with Christianity, Quaker traditions, and mysticism, and to do so in a way that positively values their present individualism, work for social justice, and desire to be open to insights from other religions and scientific research. They want a constructive relationship with evangelical and fundamentalist Friends where each values and learns from the other. Liberal Friends still remain confident that the religious experiences they have found in unprogrammed meeting for worship are valuable, will attract new members, and will enable the Religious Society of Friends to endure as a force for good.

Suggested Further Reading

Barbour, H. and Frost, J. W. (1994 [1988]) *The Quakers*. 2nd ed. Richmond, IN: Friends United Press.

Benjamin, P. S. (1976) *Philadelphia Quakers in the industrial age 1895–1920*. Philadelphia, PA: Temple University.

Brinton, H. (2002) *Friends for 350 Years*. Wallingford, PA: Pendle Hill.

Dandelion, P. (2007) *An introduction to Quakerism*, Cambridge, UK: Cambridge University Press.

Faith and Practice London, now Britain Yearly Meeting after 1920s or any American meeting associated with Friends General Conference: Baltimore, New England, New York, and Philadelphia are the largest.

Fosdick, H. E. (ed.) (1951) *Rufus Jones speaks to Our Time*. New York: Macmillan.

Gorman, G. (1973) *The amazing fact of Quaker worship*. London: Friends Home Service Committee.

Hamm, T. D. (2003) *Quakers in America*. New York: Columbia University Press.

CHAPTER 6

FIVE YEARS MEETING AND FRIENDS UNITED MEETING, 1887–2010

GREGORY P. HINSHAW

On 21 October 1902, leading American Quakers adjourned the third Friends Conference in Indianapolis, Indiana, and convened the next morning as the first session of the Five Years Meeting of Friends. It was new territory for American Quakers, organized in an association that looked more like a denomination than anything that Friends had attempted before. The organization was based on the 'Uniform Discipline', a governing document specifying shared practices and referencing shared articles of faith, uniting eleven Yearly Meetings. Among the American Yearly Meetings recognized by Gurneyite Orthodox Friends in 1902, only three were outside the organization and, with a total membership of more than 80,000, the new organization encompassed a large majority of the world's Quakers. The establishment of the Five Years Meeting of Friends was a result of conflict among American Quakers and reflected the efforts of Gurneyite Quaker leaders to stake out a middle ground in the increasingly diverging Quaker world. These compromise efforts would, over the decades, bear considerable fruit and create considerable tension.

THE QUAKER CONTEXT OF 1887 AND BEYOND

The period between 1887 and 1902 was the culmination of the transformation of American Quakerism. The revival period, just entering full force in 1887, largely left the Friends Church in place of what had been the Religious Society of Friends among Midwestern Gurneyites. In nearly every Gurneyite community, meeting houses were renovated or replaced, musical instruments appeared, pastors were employed, and the plain language and plain dress virtually disappeared. The revival movement also carried the Friends message into new communities. Hundreds of new meetings were organized in places where few Friends had lived before, and membership increased in every Gurneyite Yearly Meeting (Hamm 1988).

The major event leading to the creation of the Five Years Meeting was the Friends Conference of 1887, held in Richmond, Indiana. It was this conference that issued the Declaration of Faith, known thereafter as the 'Richmond Declaration of Faith', a document that has bred unity and division among Friends ever since. The events leading to the Richmond Declaration showed exactly how divided American Quakers had become in the nineteenth century.

Several issues led to the calling of a conference of Gurneyite Friends: advocacy for 'toleration' of the ordinances, the employment of paid pastors, the place of the Light Within, and the place of music in worship, among others. Ohio Yearly Meeting's open endorsement of the ordinances in 1886 made the sacraments the most vexing issue for American Quakers during the period, and leading Friends saw the need for concerted action in response (Woodward 1927, 189–92).

While there had been earlier attempts to call Orthodox Yearly Meetings together, no general conference had been attempted since the 1850s. In 1886 Indiana Yearly Meeting issued a call for a conference of all Yearly Meetings to be held in 1887 in Richmond, Indiana. Indiana Yearly Meeting was the largest in the world and, because it had avoided major schisms, it had a reputation for moderation. The call was quickly heeded by all the other Yearly Meetings, and plans were set in order for the meeting (Woodward 1927, 189–92).

The gathering that convened in September 1887 included most of Gurneyite Quakerism's experienced leaders, both men and women, and official representatives from all Yearly Meetings except Philadelphia, which was unofficially represented by four leading Gurneyites. The conference itself was relatively free of drama and was carefully orchestrated to achieve the desired results. The conference did not actually discuss the ordinances beyond adopting a statement recommended by the Business Committee that these questions were settled and 'that there is no occasion for the discussion of them by the conference'. The most enduring act was the writing of the declaration of faith, left in the hands of a committee led by Joseph Bevan Braithwaite (1818–1905), a leading English Friend. Braithwaite, with the assistance of James Rhoads, President of Bryn Mawr College, and James Carey Thomas, a Baltimore Friend, drafted the declaration using a number of existing statements of Quaker faith. The result was a document that carefully balanced revival impulses with many traditional views. The Light Within and the pastoral system were not formally addressed, but the traditional Quaker view of the sacraments was left intact. At the time, the declaration was seen as a victory for those opposed to ordinances. Some of the leaders present at the 1887 conference were hopeful for more centralized authority, and, though the conference asked the Yearly Meetings to consider the subject of a subsequent meeting, no formal organization resulted (Minear 1987, 107–34; Hamm 1988, 137–8; Russell 1942, 489; Elliott 1969, 271–3; Braithwaite 1909, 317–22; Jay 1910, 359–63).

The official reaction of Yearly Meetings to the Richmond Declaration varied, though North American Friends were far more united on it than later generations would believe. London Yearly Meeting declined to endorse it. Dublin Yearly Meeting largely followed London's lead. Philadelphia's Wilburite leaders did not allow any consideration of the conference or the declaration, and, in Ohio, where the leadership was undoubtedly disappointed by the position on the ordinances, the declaration was said to 'reflect the proceedings and views of the conference'. In all the other Yearly Meetings, however, which represented not only the vast majority of Gurneyite Friends but also the majority of the world's Quakers, the declaration was warmly received. In New England, New York, and Western it was 'accepted,' while Baltimore, Indiana, Iowa, and Kansas 'approved' it, and Canada and North Carolina 'adopted' it (Minear 1987, 138–41; Dorland 1968, 267; Braithwaite 1909, 324–6; Kennedy 2001, 111–14; Punshon 1984, 203–4; Williams 1962, 205–6).

Of the issues addressed by the conference, several continued to be troubling over the next few years. Some Yearly Meeting quickly adopted a pastoral system, while in others the arrangements were haphazard. Singing became common, though musical instruments were an issue nearly everywhere. Indiana Yearly Meeting's treatment of the issue is typical. In 1890, in response to the inquiry of one of its subordinate meetings, the Yearly Meetings called the use musical instruments in worship 'a departure from and inconsistent with the views of Friends'. The clear statement did not, however, suppress the movement towards the use of instruments, which were so common by 1920 that several meetings had installed pipe organs. The ordinances continued to create concern, typically when individual members or local meetings participated against the counsel of their Yearly Meetings. An 1891 plan called the Second Friends Conference, which convened in Indianapolis, Indiana, in 1892. London, Dublin, Canada, and Philadelphia Yearly Meetings declined to name delegates, but all other Gurneyite Yearly Meetings were represented. Evidence of how wide the changes among Friends had become was demonstrated by the fact that many of the sessions opened with a congregational hymn. The conference adopted a minute endorsing the pastoral system, appointed a committee to work on the establishment of a publishing house, and began the work of establishing what was organized as the American Friends Board of Foreign Missions in 1894. The conference failed to reach any conclusions on a suggestion from Kansas Yearly Meeting that the name 'Society of Friends' should be officially replaced by 'Friends Church', leaving the decision to individual Yearly Meetings. Iowa, Ohio, and Western joined Kansas in adopting the designation of 'Friends Church' within a few years. The 1892 conference considered and tabled a proposal for a uniform discipline. The conference did, however, make arrangements for a subsequent meeting in five years.

Gurneyite Friends established new Yearly Meetings in several areas during the 1890s. Wilmington Yearly Meeting held in Wilmington, Ohio, was established by Indiana Yearly Meeting in 1892. Iowa Yearly Meeting set up Oregon Yearly Meeting in 1893 and California Yearly Meeting in 1895 (Knight & McNemar 1991, 6; Beebe 1968, 36; LeShana 1969, 119).

The Third Conference of Friends, held in 1897, received propositions in favour of a uniform discipline and a permanent organization of delegated powers. The idea had originated with William Nicholson of Kansas and was strongly promoted by Rufus Jones (1863–1948), then just coming to prominence. A Maine native, Jones had begun a long career at Haverford College, and as editor of the *American Friend*, became America's leading twentieth-century Friend. A large committee, representing every Yearly Meetings and chaired by James Wood of New York, was appointed to draft the discipline. Notably, Jones was corresponding secretary of the committee. The final document was subsequently adopted by eleven of the recognized Yearly Meetings in North America: Baltimore, California, Indiana, Iowa, Kansas, New England, New York, North Carolina, Oregon, Western, and Wilmington. The discipline contained references to three doctrinal documents: the Richmond Declaration, excerpts from George Fox's Letter to the Governor of Barbados (1671), and the 'Essential Truths', the last largely the work of Wood but sometimes credited to Jones. Ohio Yearly Meeting concluded in 1900, 'We do not see our way clear at the present time to recommend the adoption of the proposed Constitution and Discipline for the Friends Church'. Canada Yearly Meeting adopted the discipline in 1900 then rescinded its action in 1902, largely because Canadian Friends felt that their small numbers would preclude full compliance with it. The Wilburite majority in Philadelphia Yearly Meeting did not even consider the matter. Due to the adoption of the discipline, the scheduled 1902 Friends Conference quickly reorganized itself as the first session of the Five Years Meeting of Friends (FYM) (Vining 1958, 17–23, 66–7; Russell 1942, 493–4; Elliott 1969, 273–4; Dorland 1968, 269–70).

MOVEMENT TOWARDS DENOMINATIONALISM, 1902–1917

As Friends launched their new organization, many of the issues that had brought them together seemed settled. With Ohio Yearly Meeting outside the organization, the ordinance question appeared to be solved. In the Midwest and beyond, the pastoral system was securely in place. Even in New England and Canada, the pastoral system became accepted, and in New York only a handful of meetings remained non-pastoral. Baltimore was officially non-pastoral, though a majority of its congregations employed 'workers', who were pastors in duty if not in name. North Carolina faced the most difficult transition to the system; it failed to adopt the Uniform Discipline in 1901, but adopted it in 1902, ordering that it go into immediate effect. The result was the withdrawal of a small group who formed a conservative Yearly Meeting. North Carolina's rural meetings remained slow to adopt the paid pastoral arrangements, and it was not until 1914 that the Yearly Meeting gave even a qualified endorsement of the employment of pastors (Russell 1928, 60; Thomas 1938, 118–21; Hickey 1997, 72–4, 81–97).

The Uniform Discipline also had the unintended consequence of officially ending separate Women's Meetings for business at all levels, which had already begun to disappear in the previous decade. In reality, Women's Meetings had been separate and unequal, though they had given women a larger voice in church business than in nearly any other Christian denomination. The end of separate meetings brought women into what had been the men's meetings, though women clearly played a secondary role for many years. More than a decade would pass before any FYM Yearly Meeting, except Wilmington, had a woman as presiding clerk. This isolated case would not be duplicated until more than fifty years after the Uniform Discipline, and nearly a century would pass before the last North American FYM Yearly Meeting, Indiana, would finally have a woman presiding clerk. FYM by then called Friends United Meeting, would not have a woman presiding clerk until 1990, more than a decade after the first woman had begun service as administrative secretary of the organization (Elliott 1969, 389–401; *Celebrating 50 Years* 2011, 62, 90).

In the first quarter of the twentieth century, FYM assumed responsibility for work in several areas, including foreign missions and peace. The American Friends Board of Foreign Missions, formed in 1894, began work in Cuba in 1900. By 1912 it had taken over the mission work of Indiana, Iowa, Kansas, New York, North Carolina, Oregon, Western, and Wilmington Yearly Meetings, as well as work in East Africa, which had originated under an independent board in 1902. In 1918 New England Yearly Meeting transferred control of its missions in Palestine to the Board. The Peace Association of Friends, formed in 1867, was officially recognized as the Board on Peace and Arbitration of FYM within a few years of the organization of FYM (Jones 1946, 40–57).

The first decade of the FYM was a period of expanding borders. Canada Yearly Meeting accepted the Uniform Discipline in 1907. The 1907 sessions of FYM also brought a request from Iowa Yearly Meeting that a new Yearly Meeting be established in Nebraska, which opened in 1908. It was the only time that FYM would officially sanction the establishment of a new Yearly Meeting in the United States. FYM also joined the Federal Council of Churches in 1907. In many ways, this movement toward unity reflected a progressive impulse toward centralization and organization (Dorland 1968, 270; Russell 1942, 539; Hamm 2003, 54–5).

If the first decade represented the beginnings of denominationalism in FYM, the second decade opened with the first evidence of deep conflict within the organization. The roots of this conflict are complex. The revival period had produced different visions of Gurneyite Quakerism, one more focused on holiness and the other more moderate. As early as 1895 the *American Friend* had published differing views on deep theological issues. The liberal or Modernist group, led by Rufus Jones and others, came to oppose revivalism, to embrace critical study of the Bible, and to seek relationships with other branches of Friends. For Holiness Friends, Modernism was dangerous and even unChristian. Both sides would claim that their views were truest to original Quakerism, though each had clearly been influenced by non-Quaker thinking. As the sides began to formulate and articulate their views, each attempted to gain control of Quaker institutions, mainly Quaker colleges. Modernism largely gained the day in Baltimore, New England, and New

York, while holiness Friends were in the ascendancy in California, Iowa, Kansas, Oregon, and Western. In Indiana, North Carolina, and Wilmington, a careful balance was maintained between a majority who were clearly sympathetic to holiness views and Modernists, usually associated with Quaker colleges. Within a few years, the disagreements would be carried into FYM, as holiness Friends attempted to remove the taint of Modernism from the organization. In many ways, these two views and the conflict between them have continued to influence the organization throughout its existence (Hamm 1988, 146–72).

The 1912 sessions of FYM included a lengthy discussion over the role of the Richmond Declaration and associated documents. California, Kansas, and Western Yearly Meetings requested clarification of the role of these statements. By overwhelming vote, FYM affirmed its role as 'historic statements of belief', but qualified that 'they are not to be regarded as constituting a creed.' In addition, the body approved the creation of a publications board to assume ownership and control of the *American Friend*, which had been owned by a private corporation. The periodical had been formed in 1894 as a merger of the *Friends' Review*, Philadelphia's Gurneyite periodical, and the *Christian Worker*, an organ of Midwestern evangelicals. The journal had been edited primarily by Rufus Jones and was perceived by many Midwestern and Western evangelicals to be unsound. Jones had developed ties with increasingly Liberal English Friends, and his writing had grown increasingly Modernist. In reaction to Jones's Modernism, the *Evangelical Friend* was formed in 1905, though when FYM assumed editorial control over the *American Friend*, the *Evangelical Friend* moved from weekly to monthly publication and ceased altogether in 1914. The first of many efforts at improving the organizational structure of FYM also began during the period (Russell 1942, 537–8; Hamm 1988, 148; Vining 1958, 70, 77–8, 83, 118, 144; Elliott 1969, 278–9; Barbour and Frost 1988, 239).

ECUMENISM AND THEOLOGICAL TENSION, 1917–1941

Beginning in the latter years of the nineteenth century, an ecumenical spirit slowly emerged among American Quakers. Orthodox and Hicksites in New York Yearly Meeting jointly observed their bicentennial in 1895. Several Monthly Meetings held joint anniversary sessions in the early twentieth century as well. Young Friends also served as early points of contact between the branches, while peace work served as the first permanent connections between adult Friends. The First World War did more to speed reconciliation than any other factor during the period. Quaker relief work, in order to be effective, clearly needed centralized organization, so Friends, both Orthodox and Hicksite, formed the American Friends Service Committee in 1917. The committee was widely supported by FYM Friends but proportionally less so than by other Friends, even in the beginning (Russell 1942, 516, 533; Jones 1921, 984).

There were dissenting opinions in the drive towards Quaker ecumenism. Evangelicals had become increasingly alarmed at the Modernism that seemed to be growing in Friends colleges, and seemingly within FYM. The 1922 sessions of FYM marked the crisis point, and for a time it seemed that the organization might break apart completely. In that year California, Kansas, Oregon, and Western Yearly Meetings again requested a stronger reaffirmation of the Richmond Declaration and associated statements. As a result the body adopted a report, largely prepared by Rufus Jones, which gave stronger recognition to the documents and removed the line 'but they are not to be regarded as constituting a creed'. So harmonious was the conclusion of this matter that the body approved the report without a vote and then sang, 'Blest Be the Tie That Binds' and the Doxology (Russell 1942, 538). The apparent settlement did not totally calm the conflict. In Western and Indiana Yearly Meetings, small minorities took issue with Modernist theology, perceived liberalism at Indiana's Earlham College, and the growing tension within FYM. In 1920 Indiana and Western Yearly Meetings appointed a joint committee to investigate Earlham College. A group of ten evangelicals, including several leaders of Indiana Yearly Meeting, attempted to sway the committee against the college, while the college's leaders responded with equal vigour. When the committee issued its final report in 1921, it largely endorsed the college, exonerating it on virtually every disputed issue. In 1924 several Friends withdrew from those Yearly Meetings and later organized Central Yearly Meeting in 1926. The 1926 statistics of Central Yearly Meeting report 326 members, a tiny percentage of the more then 30,000 Friends in Indiana (Hamm 1997, 127–39; *History of Central Yearly Meeting* 1976, 11–12; Hamm 2003, 60).

As early as 1919 formal requests were made within Oregon Yearly Meeting that the Yearly Meeting withdraw from FYM. In 1924 the Yearly Meeting gave an ultimatum that FYM demonstrate significant changes in doctrinal positions or its membership would cease in 1926. When it perceived no discernable changes, the Yearly Meeting in 1926 acted by a 173–130 vote to withdraw, ending its twenty-year association (Beebe 1968, 49–55; Elliott 1969, 280–3; Russell 1942, 540–1). Kansas Yearly Meeting, too, found itself in disagreement with FYM. The Yearly Meeting withdrew all financial support in 1930 and by 1935 no Kansas Friends were serving on FYM boards. In 1937, at the request of seven of its Quarterly Meetings, Kansas Yearly Meeting passed a resolution to formally withdraw from the organization (Elliott 1969, 283–4; Russell 1942, 541).

Perhaps no other person exercised more influence on FYM during the early twentieth century than Walter C. Woodward (1878–1942). An Indiana native, Woodward was raised in Oregon, became General Secretary of FYM in 1917, and later the same year became editor of the *American Friend*. He continued in these two capacities until his death in 1942, twenty-five years later. Woodward was a tireless advocate for expanding the borders of FYM and Quaker thought, and, though many evangelicals perceived him as too liberal, no subsequent leader has ever equalled the influence that Woodward had on the organization (Emerson 1952).

NEO-QUAKERISM, STRONGER UNITY, AND CONTINUING CONFLICT, 1941–1965

Organic union between branches came first in local meetings, just as local meetings were the first places of official contact. Joint Orthodox and Hicksite worship occurred in several places, mostly in the eastern US in the early twentieth century, often because both branches had decreased in size (Russell 1942, 535). The emergence of neo-Quakerism, a term apparently first used by Elton Trueblood (1900–94) to describe the influx of liberal seekers who found a home among Friends, would have long-standing implications for the future of FYM. In 1928 the first officially 'united' Quarterly Meeting, All Friends Regional Meeting, was accepted by both New York Yearly Meetings. In 1936 the American Friends Fellowship Council was formed and affiliated with the American Friends Service Committee. The Council oversaw the establishment of numerous meetings in new areas, composed largely of new Quakers but including some relocated members of older meetings as well. Without exception, these meetings were non-pastoral and unprogrammed. By 1940 more than fifty new meetings had been established. Within a few years, these meetings began to join existing Yearly Meetings. In the East, they were generally united Monthly Meetings, joining both branches. In the Midwest and West, they generally did not affiliate with FYM bodies. The Wider Quaker Fellowship, also formed in 1936, served those of other religious traditions who were in sympathy with Friends' views and work. The influx and influence of these neo-Quakers added vitality and an ecumenical spirit to Yearly Meetings in the East, but widened the cultural divisions with Midwestern and Western Friends, who remained the core of FYM (Russell 1942, 536).

By 1931 an ecumenical spirit was at work in New England and by 1943 serious plans for reunification of the two New England Yearly Meetings, divided for almost a century, were in place. The Gurneyite Yearly Meeting had been gradually moving away from pastoral worship. Union finally came in 1945 and included not only the two Yearly Meetings but also another small association made up largely of new Friends and two formerly independent Monthly Meetings. Despite the fact that the reunited body did not require compliance with the Uniform Discipline, FYM invited it to remain in affiliation. Union in New England was not without its detractors, mainly among members of Rhode Island Monthly Meeting. After years of objection, most of the Monthly Meeting withdrew and joined the Gurneyite Ohio Yearly Meeting (Kohrman 1995, 4–8, 10–11; Cazden 1998, 1–16; Hamm 2003, 61).

A decade passed before Yearly Meetings in three more locations reached complete unity. The 1955 merger in Philadelphia had little impact on FYM, since the Orthodox body in Philadelphia remained outside FYM. The 1955 New York merger met with no apparent resistance. New York Friends had been gradually moving towards merger since the 1920s and had met in joint session for eight years before formal unification. Also in 1955 Canada (Gurneyite), Canada (Conservative), and Genesee (Hicksite) joined to form Canadian Yearly Meeting. The Gurneyite body in Canada had also moved towards being largely unprogrammed, and theological views clearly were becoming more accommodating. Joint Hicksite and Orthodox Yearly Meetings had begun in 1928, and plans for union were developed by 1939. Opposition to union in Canada centred in Pelham Quarterly Meeting. American evangelical pastors had long led the Quarterly Meeting, which had shrunk to only three Monthly Meetings. Pelham Quarter refused to join the united Canadian Yearly Meeting and finally joined Ohio Yearly Meeting (Gurneyite) in 1958 (Van Wagner and Barbour 1995, 266–71; Elliott 1969, 338; Dorland 1968, 342–7).

Formal reunion was delayed for several years in Baltimore, where the Orthodox Yearly Meeting was considerably smaller than its Hicksite counterpart. As in other Yearly Meetings, new united meetings were accepted into membership, and several local meetings reunited. The first joint sessions of the two Yearly Meetings were held in 1931, and formal union was discussed as early as 1956. Outside Baltimore Monthly Meeting, the strength of the Orthodox Yearly Meeting lay in Virginia Quarterly Meeting, the remnant of Virginia Yearly Meeting, where Hicksism had been non-existent. Virginia Friends most strongly opposed reunion, and they successfully delayed it until 1968. As reunion seemed imminent, many Friends of Virginia Quarterly Meeting took action to change their affiliation to North Carolina Yearly Meeting or lay themselves down, ultimately leaving only one old Orthodox Virginia meeting in Baltimore Yearly Meeting. When Baltimore officially united, it did so in a unique manner, allowing each local meeting to determine whether it would be affiliated with FUM, Friends General Conference, or both (Forbush 1972, 132, 149–55).

There is much evidence to show that all of this new-found unity was viewed with equivocation or even concern by much of FYM's Midwestern and Western pastoral core, an opinion that had existed for several years (Woodard 1912; Russell 1942, 537). In 1947 a young Friend remarked, 'The Quaker Mason–Dixon line runs North and South, following a mountain range'. Even as union was being celebrated, an editorial in the *American Friend* cautioned, 'Union cannot be effected by tying the ends of "branches" together—they must grow from the same stalk, the same vine and we are not left in doubt as to what the vine is—Christ himself'. This identification of the increasing differences in theology and practice between Northeastern and Midwestern Friends was recognition of the dichotomy that has remained a main point of tension in Friends United Meeting ever since (Williams 1962, 211–12).

The failure of FYM to adopt a new uniform discipline in the 1940s was another indicator of changing views. The 1902 discipline had been modestly revised over the years, but in 1940 the Five Years Meeting appointed a committee to draft a new document, specifying that when four-fifths of the Yearly Meetings had adopted it, it would go into effect. A final version of the proposed 'Faith and Practice' was finally released in 1945. Several Yearly Meetings and a few Quarterly and Monthly Meetings adopted the document, though the quest for official approval was finally and officially abandoned in 1950, when FYM heard a report stating that 'Practically no two Yearly Meetings have taken identical action with regard to it', signifying that FYM was not the denominational body that many believed. FYM authorized as much of the new document as practical at the national level and left each Yearly Meeting to take its own action. Most adopted at least a portion of the document within the next decade.

International and extension work continued to be a strong focus of FYM, and mission work was supported in East Africa, Cuba, Jamaica, and Palestine. East Africa Yearly Meeting was established as a full Yearly Meeting in 1946, reflecting emerging views on race and colonialism. At its establishment it became the largest Yearly Meeting in FYM and was second in size among Quakers only to London Yearly Meeting. The 1950s brought enduring work in other areas. The United Society of Friends Women, originally formed in 1881, and the Men's Extension Movement (called 'Quaker Men' after 1952) were given official recognition by FYM in 1950. The Young Friends movement had been recognized a generation before (Hinshaw and Hockett 1981, 1–4, 23, 25, 49; Russell 1942, 538). A spacious brick headquarters building for FYM was completed in 1955 on Quaker Hill in the north part of Richmond. It was the culmination of years of planning and a symbol of denominational strength. Publications work also reached high tide in the 1950s, with the production of several levels of Sunday School quarterlies and other publications under the direction of the FYM. No publication was more important than the *American Friend*, which continued to be issued twice monthly with generally declining subscriptions until 1960, when it was combined with *Quaker Action* into *Quaker Life*, a monthly magazine that was successfully designed to have broader appeal. While unity seemed to be growing the East and Midwest, one of the smallest Yearly Meetings, Nebraska, was riddled with conflict. Nebraska Yearly Meeting, with a membership of less than 2,000 in 1956, was the largest Yearly Meeting geographically, spread over five states. A sizable majority of Nebraska Yearly Meeting also opposed membership in the World and National Councils of Churches and had a negative view of FYM. As a solution to the internal conflict, Nebraska Yearly Meeting set off an independent Yearly Meeting, Rocky Mountain, in 1957, but only five local meetings, representing about one-quarter of the membership, remained in Nebraska Yearly Meeting (Elliott 1969, 284–5).

International Focus and Internal Détente, 1965–1987

If there has been any constant in the history of FYM, it has been regular reorganization and a quest for reinvention in the organizational structure. In 1948 a study committee was appointed to review the organizational order. In 1953 a more formal committee was established to bring recommendations for reorganization. In 1955 a formal recommendation was made to change the frequency of meetings, the name of the organization, and from the concept of delegate governance to representative governance. In 1960 a representative system was approved, changing from the parliamentary method that had first been adopted in 1897 to the use of Quaker business practice, and approval was given to change to triennial sessions from quinquennial sessions. In 1963 the FYM in session authorized the Executive Council to choose a new name for the organization. Several alternatives were considered, but the name Friends United Meeting (FUM) was adopted in March 1965 and put into legal effect on 1 January 1966.

A 1970 reorganizational plan, effective in 1971, created the General Board and three new commissions—Meeting Ministries, World Ministries, and General Services—to replace the old system of boards and committees. This structure, with alterations, remained in place for more than thirty years and the general plan continues to govern FUM today. In 1972 the triennial sessions were held outside Indiana for the first time, meeting at Green Lake, Wisconsin. A rotating schedule of locations has been used in the years since.

While FUM was not completely free of internal dissension, many of the deep conflicts abated and a period of more than thirty-five years passed with no major withdrawals from the organization. In 1972 Southeastern Yearly Meeting, a small Yearly Meeting comprised entirely of new unprogrammed meetings, mostly in Florida, was accepted into membership in FUM. It affiliated with Friends General Conference at the same time. It was the first and only North American Yearly Meeting in FUM without direct organizational roots in the Gurneyite movement.

Disunity and the Search for Relevance, 1987–2010

American liberalism seemed ascendant in the 1960s, and increasingly liberal views were espoused among many FUM Friends as a result of unification, new unprogrammed meetings, and the anti-war movement. As the American conservative movement strengthened in the 1960s and gained widespread support in subsequent years, its appeal to many of the core constituencies of FUM was also evident. Most of FUM's North American membership remains disproportionately rural and in congregations that were strongly influenced by holiness views. In reaction to liberal court decisions, an influx of liberal seekers and pacifists, and declining strength of Modernist congregations, evangelicals worked hard to make the views of their Yearly Meetings on a number of religious and social issues clear. Many of these Friends could clearly be considered a part of the 'Christian Right' and were able to more clearly articulate their long-held views through the emerging movement. In the 1980s fissures began to show in the careful balance that FUM maintained through the 1960s and 1970s. Two serious issues have been at the heart of nearly all the organizational tension within FUM: the role of Jesus Christ and the view of homosexuality (Carpenter 1997, 233–4).

The Richmond Declaration and associated documents seem to have established FYM as an evangelical body, but divergent views were present almost from the beginning. Views of Jesus Christ as something less than the divine saviour have always been confined to a minority of FUM's constituency, though unification in the North American

East and growing Quaker ecumenism increasingly exposed the Gurneyite core of FUM to views that ranged from atheistic to universalist.

In 1972 California Yearly Meeting asked that FUM make Jesus Christ central to its work, leading to an extensive study of the place of the Richmond Declaration in FUM. In March 1974 the General Board affirmed that the action of FYM in 1922 to recognize the three historic documents as the 'authorized Declaration of Faith' had never been rescinded. A 1984 *Quaker Life* editorial presciently stated that that the basic issue for Friends in the period up to 2000 would be the place of Jesus Christ. In 1987 Southwest (formerly California) Yearly Meeting requested that FUM affirm its support of the Richmond Declaration of Faith, in part in celebration of the document's centennial. In an excruciating triennial session, FUM was unable to do so. The outcome increased evangelical dissatisfaction, and in 1991 Stephen Main, the General Secretary of FUM, called for a 'realignment' of North American Friends. Ostensibly, two groups would have been formed: one evangelical and one liberal, dividing FUM between the two. Iowa Yearly Meeting hosted a conference on the topic in Des Moines. Of FUM Yearly Meetings, only Southwest and Iowa sent official delegates, though Evangelical Friends Yearly Meetings were represented. The conference took no real action, and Southwest Yearly Meeting, after decades of efforts to make FUM more evangelical, announced its withdrawal from FUM in 1993. As a result, those in California who wished to remain in FUM formed the Western Association of the Religious Society of Friends, a small group that today includes only three congregations (Hamm 2003, 149–50).

The tension over the role of Jesus Christ in many ways appears to be moving increasingly away from universalism. In 1992 a called 'meeting for clearness' issued a statement that affirmed the centrality of Jesus Christ, and at a General Board Meeting in March 1993, a purpose statement was approved and has been used ever since: 'Friends United Meeting commits itself to energize and equip Friends through the power of the Holy Spirit to gather people into fellowships where Jesus Christ is known, loved, and obeyed, as Teacher and Lord'. At a General Board session in Africa in 2007, the Richmond Declaration was fully reaffirmed, yet dissatisfaction remained. In 2008 the superintendents of the five self-styled 'Orthodox' yearly meetings: Indiana, Iowa, North Carolina, Western, and Wilmington, issued a joint letter that expressed concern for the future of FUM because of deep divisions on several foundational matters. In response, the General Board appointed yet another restructure committee that continues to seek ways to improve the organization. As part of this process, the General Board reaffirmed the Orthodox Friends faith of FUM, as well as emphasizing that the Richmond Declaration is an accurate reflection of FUM's theological position.

Homosexuality has been the most troubling issue for FUM in the last generation. Between 1977 and 2004, all the Orthodox Yearly Meetings adopted statements that condemned homosexual behaviour, while the so-called 'united' Yearly Meetings, Baltimore, Canadian, New England, New York, and Southeastern, adopted statements and practices that affirmed persons regardless of sexual orientation. Iowa (1977), Indiana (1982), North Carolina (1990), Wilmington (1997), and Western (2004) adopted statements that they believed sexual relations were acceptable only in the context of heterosexual marriage. The united Yearly Meetings have largely left decisions to their local meetings, though Baltimore (1973) was the first FUM Yearly Meeting to make a statement in support of homosexual relationships, stating, '[W]e hope we will come to respect the decisions of others about their own sexuality.' In 1988 Canadian Yearly Meeting gave local meetings the ability to decide whether same-sex relationships would be recognized. In 1988 the FUM General Board adopted a minute that paid staff of FUM are expected to refrain from sexual activity outside marriage between one man and one woman. At the time even some Liberal Friends regarded the decision as 'hopeful,' since, ostensibly, a celibate homosexual could participate in FUM's programmes. In subsequent years, however, the policy has been a point of major contention. Even in most Orthodox Yearly Meetings, vocal minorities seek to affirm homosexuality, while in united Yearly Meetings vocal opposition to homosexual behaviour has slowly disappeared (Kohrman 1995, 12–13; Hamm 2003, 137–42).

The North American constituent Yearly Meetings have largely moved in separate directions in the last quarter-century of FUM's history. Friends in the united Yearly Meetings have maintained stable membership, though pastoral meetings have almost entirely disappeared from among them through decline and withdrawal (Van Wagner and Barbour 1995, 275; Kohrman 1995, 11). Most have grown increasingly liberal since reunification. One of its strongest pastoral meetings sent a minute to New York Yearly Meeting in 1985, warning:

> We hold it to be true that Jesus is Lord and Saviour and the head of our Religious Society. [We are] deeply concerned about the spiritual welfare of New York Yearly Meeting. Many Friends have not taken seriously the high calling of Christ. Many of our Meetings are no longer gathered in the name of Jesus. As a people, we are confused and lacking in spiritual power. Without Christ—we are truly lost.

For many in the united Yearly Meetings, FUM is perceived to be too conservative and too inhospitable to their perspectives. This sense of frustration led Southeastern Yearly Meeting to withdraw from FUM in 2010. It is an action that is under consideration in at least one other united Yearly Meeting.

The Orthodox Yearly Meetings have faced more serious declines in membership, a trend that began in the 1910s. Iowa has gravitated towards the most evangelical end, while Indiana, North Carolina, and Western, historically the strongest Yearly Meetings in FUM, have all faced internal theological tension. Western has faced serious disagreements over universalism and homosexuality, while Indiana has wrestled with the role of the ordinances and homosexuality. The decline of the North American membership of FUM, alienation in united Yearly Meetings, and suspicion within Orthodox Yearly Meetings have reduced the organization's financial stability and decreased the number of staff working for the organization. Many of the once-strong ministries of FUM simply no longer exist (Hamm 2003, 62, 151–3; Angell 2011, 1–33).

If North American Friends in FUM have seen numerical stagnation and decline, the opposite has been the case in East Africa, transformed from a new mission field in 1902 to the largest group of Quakers anywhere in the world less than a century later. The growth and transformation has not come without tension, though these Friends have remained fiercely loyal to FUM. The tension is not theological, since almost all East African Friends are unqualified evangelicals, but tribal allegiances have splintered the unity of Friends in Kenya and neighbouring countries. As early as the 1930s, tensions were evident between northern and southern tribes in the Western Province, where Friends' work has been concentrated. In 1973 Friends in the north formed a second Yearly Meeting, 'Elgon Religious Society of Friends'. In 1979 East Africa Yearly Meeting tentatively approved a restructuring, leading to the establishment of East Africa Yearly Meeting (South) in 1980. In 1984 the FUM General Board recognized all three Yearly Meetings as legitimate. In the same year, a national coordinating body, called the Friends Church in Kenya, was organized. In subsequent years, a multiplicity of Yearly Meetings have been established in East Africa: Bware in 1994 from Vihiga (formerly East Africa [South]), Central in 1991 from Elgon, Chavakali in 1997 from Vihiga, Chwele in 2003 from Elgon, East Africa (North) from East Africa in 1988, Elgon East in 1993 from Elgon, Kakamega in 1993 from East Africa, Lugari in 1992 from East Africa, Malava in 1992 from East Africa, Nairobi in 1987 from East Africa (South), Tuloi in 2003 from Central, Tongaren in 2005 from Elgon East, Uganda in 1980 from East Africa, and Vokoli in 1996 from Vihiga. An increasing effort has been made to make FUM a true global partnership, rather than an American-centred organization. In March 2005 the 'Africa Ministries Office' opened in Kisumu, Kenya (Smuck 1987; Kimball and Kimball 2002).

FUM mission work in other areas has been less successful. The 1959 revolution largely curtailed the work in Cuba, though Cuba Yearly Meeting continues to function and remains affiliated with FUM. Turmoil in the Middle East has hampered the work of the Monthly Meeting in Ramallah on the West Bank. Jamaican Friends have also struggled but continue to maintain an active organization. New mission work has been attempted in other areas, but with the exception of a small work begun in 1980 in Belize and work in Chicago in 1982, no permanent fields have been opened by North American FUM Friends in over a century (Pedigo 1988, 27).

Despite organizational atrophy and repeated conflict, FUM remains the largest Quaker body of its type and continues to maintain an active presence in at least seven countries on three continents. It is also, arguably, the most diverse body of Quakers in the world, both in terms of ethnicity and worship style, if not in terms of theology. It is this diversity that has bred both conflict and compromise, yet FUM has maintained its Christian faith and witness. The meetings of the Five Years Meeting have made a clear contribution not only to the spiritual life of the Religious Society of Friends but also to the spiritual life of the world. Two American Presidents have held membership in FYM. Nearly all the greatest leaders of twentieth-century American Quakerism, such as Rufus Jones, Thomas Kelly (1893–1941), Elbert Russell (1871–1951), Clarence Pickett (1884–1965), Alexander Purdy (1890–1976), Elton Trueblood, and others, emerged from meetings that were constituents of the Five Years Meeting. Jones's 1921 assessment of the Five Years Meeting is still valid:

The Five Years Meeting, by its unifying, inclusive spirit, has had a steadying and stabilizing influence throughout the Society. It has made the work of all the Yearly Meetings more efficient, while it has encouraged a tolerant attitude of mind and co-operative methods of service…There has always been in all Yearly Meetings of this branch a deep and quiet group of persons who possessed spiritual insight, calm faith and solid experience… [T]hey were resolved to maintain unity and to hold the body together until better days should come. (Jones 1921, 933–4)

SUGGESTED FURTHER READING

Hamm, T. D. (2009) 'Friends United Meeting and its identity: An interpretive history,' *Quaker Life* (January/February 2009): 10–15.

Hamm, T. D. (1988) *The transformation of American Quakerism: Orthodox Friends, 1800–1907.* Bloomington, IN: Indiana University Press.

Hamm, T. D. (2003) *The Quakers in America.* New York: Columbia University Press.

Jones, R. M. (1921) *The later periods of Quakerism.* London: Macmillan.

Russell, E. (1942) The *history of Quakerism.* New York: Macmillan.

CHAPTER 7

EVANGELICAL QUAKERS, 1887–2010

ARTHUR O. ROBERTS

INTRODUCTION

THE adjective 'evangelical' in historic Christian and Quaker contexts derives from a Greek word that translates as 'gospel'—literally, 'good news'. New Testament books narrate and interpret God's actions through the Messiah, Jesus. 'Evangelicalism' denotes movements that emphasize personal, experiential salvation by faith in the atoning death and Resurrection of Jesus Christ, enabling moral faithfulness, and a Spirit-filled life. 'Evangelicals' believe Scriptures infallibly convey 'good news' about salvation. They affirm the deity and living presence of Christ. 'Evangelism' denotes Gospel proclamation. 'Evangelists' conduct such ministry. Their ministries seek to bring people into God's redemptive order. Theologically, most Quakers in the world are evangelical.

In this chapter, 'evangelicalism' describes movements first within the United States among Gurneyite Friends after 1887, mostly within the Five Years Meeting, then worldwide, emphasizing experiential Christian spirituality and reasserting biblical doctrines and moral principles considered historically orthodox and Quaker. The Evangelical Friends Church International (EFCI) constitutes one distinct grouping of Friends and its organizational forms, arising within the context of this era.

HISTORIC CONTEXT

The American Quaker context from which EFCI eventually arose sustained continuity with certain earlier and contemporary expressions. Revival meetings, beginning in Iowa in 1867, with altar calls for conversion and sanctification, had affected American

Friends greatly and they continued into the mid-twentieth century. European outreach and visitation ministry offered a pattern; in England Friends Prayer League members formed a Friends Evangelistic Band in 1919. Led by George A. Fox, young Friends evangelized English villages, often with street preaching. Others worked under London Yearly Meeting's Friends Home Missions Committee. These modes of evangelistic ministry dwindled after Modernist policies became dominant in London Yearly Meeting. Other Christian groups then assumed leadership. The second Fox name became largely forgotten among Friends (Roberts 2006, 34.)

Between 1873 and 1915 John Frederick and Alice Hanson's ministry moved between America and Scandinavia. Their son Isaac Hanson said of such itinerant preaching: 'I never heard better evangelists than the Quaker evangelists. They had the spiritual discernment of George Fox and the evangelistic fervor of John Wesley' (Birkel/Newman 1992, 162).

During middle decades of the twentieth century Irish evangelists John and Dorothy Sinton conducted revivals within several American Yearly Meetings, seeking prayerfully to discern the daily Spirit-anointed message-bearer. Irish Friend Simon Lamb and American Friend Paul Anderson (Northwest Yearly Meeting) helped plan the 1985 World Gathering of Young Friends. In the 1990s American Quakers, including Colin Saxton, ministered among Irish Friends. Irish youth reciprocated by visitation ministry among NWYM churches. One was Aiden McCartney, who helped plan the 2005 World Gathering of Young Friends, in Lancaster, England and Mombasa, Kenya.

The 1887 Richmond Declaration of Faith provided a definitive theological foundation for Evangelical Friends. This document reflects the theological acumen of British scholar Joseph Bevan Braithwaite, James Rhoads of Philadelphia, and others. There were two major precipitating issues for the conference: the Ohio ordinance debate and the challenge of liberal theology. Avoiding extremes, delegates found unity in a reasoned, evangelical document of Quaker faith and practice. The conference sparked the founding of the Five Years Meeting. This text served and continues to serve as a foundational document for Evangelical Friends. As of 2010 within Friends United Meeting (FUM), Iowa, Western, Wilmington, Indiana, North Carolina, and their African Meetings include it as an integral part of books of faith and practice. EFCI Yearly Meetings in the United States include it as an integral part, except Eastern Region that notes it as an historical document (author poll and QuakerInfo.com, 2010). Although not translated or cited in most EFCI non-Western churches, its formulations became definitive. For many world Quakers this document strengthened historical continuity, expressed shared Scriptural foundations, and provided common theological language.

MIGRATIONS AND SETTLEMENTS

The early years of this period in Friends history were marked by Quaker migrations to the western United States. In the 1880s Indiana farmers trekked to Kiowa County,

Kansas, and settled a community, naming it after the abolitionist Laura Haviland (1808–1898). The academy they started eventually became Friends Bible College. These Friends offered leadership within Kansas Yearly Meeting that extended its ministry to Africa. Others settled in Nebraska and started Nebraska Central College in 1899, followed by a Yearly Meeting a few years later. The lure of land further west slowed growth. In 1953 the college merged with Penn College (now William Penn), in Iowa and local pastoral churches joined either Rocky Mountain (EFCI) or Great Plains (FUM) Yearly Meetings.

Earlier pioneers had trekked by wagons, while later Friends travelled by rail. Some came further west to Oregon's Willamette Valley to farm or to engage in business or professions; among them was Henry John and Laura Minthorn. Their orphaned nephew studied at the academy that Friends established at Newberg, Oregon, where Minthorn was principal. The nephew, Herbert Hoover (1874–1964) later became a president of the United States. The academy segued into Pacific College. Idaho's snow-packed mountains fed irrigation systems, enabling deserts to blossom, and farms supplanted ranches. Friends from Iowa and Nebraska grubbed out sagebrush and grew alfalfa and in 1908 they built a meeting house, started an academy, and dubbed their community 'Greenleaf'. These pioneers multiplied, evangelized, spread Meetings across the Northwest, and sent missionaries to South America.

Somewhat earlier Friends from the eastern US had migrated to southern California, encouraged by Aquila Pickering's land company. They planted a Quaker community as well as orchards, and named their town and college Whittier. A son of Quaker settlers Frank and Hannah Nixon, would become president of the United States— Richard Nixon (1913–94). Friends thrived in this 'Golden State'; they built meeting houses, evangelized neighbours, and sent missionaries to Alaska and Central America. The nature of these covenant communities broadened over the decades as the general population grew around them. With a vision 'of people to be gathered to the Lord', Friends found ways to bring neighbours into Christian faith and into their fellowships. So did Evangelical Friends churches in established communities from whence westward migrants came, notably those in Iowa, Indiana, and Ohio.

Patterns of Ministry, Worship, and Fellowship

The pastoral system arose out of the revivals of 1867–77, to nurture converts brought into Quaker Meetings through revivals. Itinerant preachers often became settled pastors as new meetings flourished and needed ongoing care. The term 'Recorded Minister' signified Yearly Meeting approval of men and women, whom Friends discerned that God had ordained, to serve in pastoral ministry—or in callings such as teaching or itinerant evangelism. A pastoral sermon became a norm among these Friends, although sometimes augmented or replaced by vocal ministry of others. Pastoral responsibilities included administering church affairs, visiting the sick, providing spiritual counsel, biblical and doctrinal instruction, and community outreach. In large congregations, multiple staffing became a pattern—youth ministers and directors of education assisting a 'lead' pastor.

During much of the twentieth century, a typical week for pastoral Friends in North America included Sunday School at 10 am and worship at 11 am, an evening youth gathering followed by a worship, and a Wednesday night prayer service. In early decades people often knelt during prayer. Accompanied by organ or piano, worshippers sang traditional hymns such as 'Blessed Assurance' and 'Amazing Grace', while choirs, quartets, and soloists sang specials. Christmas and Easter were celebrated with music, pageantry, and Scripture narration. Women's fellowships and men's groups met. Conference sites, such as Quaker Haven, Quaker Hill, Quaker Knoll, and Quaker Ridge, developed in the early decades, providing venues for youth and adult groups and focused on evangelism, teaching, and fellowship. For many, youth summer camp marked the time and place of conversion to Christ. In latter decades of the century spiritual retreat programmes for adults were added.

Under various pressures—greater mobility, television, multiple affinity circles, pop culture, and electronic media—by the late twentieth century the pattern changed. Wednesday night might feature a fellowship meal followed by topical or Bible study, interest and prayer groups sometimes met in homes or cafes. Sunday schools continued, with fewer adult participants. Larger churches held multiple worship services—including (for some) an option of 'open worship'. With the influx of Hispanic and Asian families many congregations became increasingly multicultural, some even multilingual. Within EFCI, ethnic church planting resulted in Hispanic groups in California, Texas, Kansas, Oregon, Idaho, Pennsylvania, Massachusetts, Maryland, and perhaps elsewhere, and a few Iranian and Chinese churches. Home-based gatherings provided alternatives to structure-centred worship. Modes of worship adapted to cultural changes and formality yielded to informality. Praise choruses accompanied by guitars and drums— highly amplified—were relished by young worshippers and tolerated by oldsters who longed for organ-accompanied hymns with aesthetically matched lyrics and music. Churches sustained Christian nurture and leadership training through various sorts of ministry and service opportunities. Young Friends, although less precise and articulate in theological formulation than their elders, nevertheless affirmed experientially, and testified by word and deed, that the crucified risen Christ is the Light Within.

EVANGELICAL FRIENDS AND THE FUNDAMENTALIST–MODERNIST CONFLICT

The fundamentalist challenge to Modernism significantly impacted Friends. The term 'fundamentalism' derived from a series of papers, *The Christian Fundamentals:*

a *Testimony to Truth*, written by theologians and Bible scholars from North America, Germany, Ireland, Scotland, and Britain, and distributed widely between 1910 and 1915 to Christian leaders and libraries in the English-speaking world (later published in several volumes). 'Unbelief was the antecedent not the consequent of modernists', asserted these writers (*Fundamentals* n.d., Foreword, and vol. I, 99). Fundamentalism was shaped by the Scofield Reference Bible's interpretive notes, and by Ussher's chronology dating the created world from 4004 BC. To many Friends, as to other Christians, Darwinism seemed a threat to Biblical authority, the social gospel a threat to pietistic spirituality. In the First World War era some fundamentalists were pacifists—following the example of evangelist Dwight L. Moody during the American Civil War. J. Walter (1857–1935) and Emma Malone (1859–1924), influential Midwest Holiness Quakers, were among them. Edward Mott (1866–1954), of Oregon Yearly Meeting, grateful that the movement's leaders espoused historic Christian theology affirmed the unity of the historic Jesus and the Christ of faith, citing Barclay and Gurney to show compatibility with Quaker teaching about the 'universal and saving Light.'

> Just as truly as God has written His law upon men's hearts, He has revealed his grace to them through the Light of Christ [referencing Acts 17 and Romans 2]. It is possible for even the heathen who feel after God to find Him if they respond to the Light of Christ. (Mott 1943, 146)

Early types of fundamentalism were supplanted by one stressing certain narrow biblical interpretations, such as no women ministers and dispensational pre-millennialism (rife during the Great Depression). Anglo-Israelism surged. Assorted leaders, including popes and presidents, were dubbed the Antichrist. Rapture dates were set periodically—and reset. With the establishment of modern Israel, Christian Zionism flourished. Although in the 1930s and 40s, especially, some Friends did espouse these views, theologically conservative Friends increasingly distanced themselves from them, preferring to be described theologically as 'evangelical'.

Friends continued to share fundamentalist affirmations of historic Christian theology. Deeming Modernism too dominant and efforts to mend theological differences too compromising of Quaker beliefs, several Yearly Meetings left the Five Years Meeting. In 1926 Oregon withdrew and dissident churches of Indiana and Western Yearly Meetings formed Central Yearly Meeting. In 1937 Kansas withdrew. In 1957 certain Nebraska Meetings separated, joining Colorado and Arizona churches as Rocky Mountain Yearly Meeting. Ohio Yearly Meeting had remained independent. Reasons included disapproval of affiliation with the National Council of Churches, liberal theology of certain leaders, and disagreement over mission policies. In 1993 Southwest Yearly Meeting (formerly California) withdrew, disappointed by failed realignment efforts within Friends United Meeting. Although acknowledging cherished spiritual bonds, they officially noted an 'unwillingness of *some* sections of FUM to affirm a commitment to the orthodox Friends position on the authority of Scripture and the deity of Christ'. They deemed FUM's reaffirmation of Christ-centred commitment and biblical authority as too little and too late. In 1995 the Yearly Meeting affiliated with EFCI, as Evangelical Friends

Church Southwest. Whittier First Friends and Berkeley withdrew, however, and, with a Bakersfield group, retained FUM affiliation as the Western Association of Friends.

To twenty-first-century evangelical scholars, the fundamentalist-Modernist controversy reflected overly rationalistic approaches to reality: liberalism too narrowly restricting truth to scientific hypotheses, fundamentalism too narrowly limiting Biblical truth to factual narrative. These scholars, affirming its divine inspiration and authority, believed that taking the Bible literally means honouring literary form, whether historic data, metaphor, hyperbole, or illustrative story. Although forthrightly affirming the Resurrection as factual, they might receive the Jonah story as instructive fable and deem Genesis compatible with creative evolution. Evangelical Friends broadened their understanding of how truth is revealed through sense, reason, and intuition. Interaction with other Quakers became more congenial. Together they sought a coherent understanding of revelation—God's word of truth spoken through the Bible, directly by the living Christ, *and* through creation. (Certain scientists strengthened this perception of nature as God's other book, notably head of the genome project Francis Collins, and physicists Ian Barbour and John Polkinghorne.)

By the end of the millennium, 'fundamentalism' had become a pejorative term, whether applied to Christian or other groups. It was not an adjective Evangelical Friends applied to themselves. Adding to public confusion, the popular press blurred distinctions, dubbing all non-liberal Christians 'evangelicals'; and theologians employed the term 'Modernism' to denote groups grounded in post-Reformation rationalism, liberal *and* evangelical.

THE BIBLE SCHOOL ERA

In the early twentieth century, Bible schools arose in reaction to ascendant Modernism and Moody Bible Institute served as a model. Concerned Christians felt their colleges had accommodated secular scholarship by asserting reason over revelation, by undermining scriptural authority through higher criticism, by diluting biblical understandings of human sin and divine redemption, and by tolerating 'worldly' conduct. They observed a pattern of Christian colleges turning secular. For some this perception was strengthened by a dispensationalist focus on saving remnant people rather than leavening society with Kingdom values. So rescue missions were stressed more than social reform.

In the early decades of the twentieth century, fundamentalist–Modernist conflicts had an impact on Gurneyite Friends colleges in the US—Haverford in Pennsylvania, Wilmington in Ohio, Guilford in North Carolina, Earlham in Indiana, Penn in Iowa, Friends University in Kansas, Nebraska Central, Pacific in Oregon, and Whittier in California. Bible schools seemed an effective way to train Christian leaders and sustain evangelical teachings. With other holiness Christians, Evangelical Friends were involved in starting several. In Ohio, Walter and Emma Malone founded Cleveland

Bible College in 1892. Scott T. Clark founded Friends Bible College in Haviland, Kansas in 1917. In 1919 several Oregon Friends started Portland Bible Institute and brought in Edward Mott as president. In 1899 a Training School for Christian Workers was started by Whittier Friends, among them Ervin Cammack, California's superintendent of missions (Oliver, Cherry, and Cherry 2007, 241).

The Bible School movement divided Quaker loyalties. From the perspective of twenty-first-century evangelical scholars, this conflict seemed unwarranted. The schools did, however, train influential ministers and missionaries—men and women—who provided evangelical leadership during an era dominated by Modernist theology. As noted below, liberal arts education regained trust and seminaries became venues for ministerial preparation.

Revivalism, Holiness, and Evangelistic Outreach

Evangelical Quakers accepted and experienced with fervour the Pentecostal fulfilment of Joel 2:28, 'I will pour out my spirit upon all flesh; and your sons and your daughters shall prophesy' (KJV). Revivals featured men and women preachers. During middle decades of the twentieth century, Friends participated with Wesleyan Christians in camp meetings, often held in rough tabernacles with straw or sawdust floors, and altar benches where under strong preaching penitents knelt, weeping before God, and then rising to testify spiritual victory. Salvation experience became structured as two works of grace, first forgiveness from sins, then sanctification. This neo-Wesleyan two-step formula seemed rigid to many Quakers. Acknowledging the baptizing power of the Holy Spirit, they reaffirmed early Quaker convictions that salvation includes both forgiveness of sins and cleansing from sinful dispositions—one work of grace—continuing in chapters during one's changed and changing life. In later decades, shaped by the writings of Everett Cattell (1905–81), Thomas Kelly (1893–1941), and Richard Foster (1942–), Holiness language stressed disciplines along one's spiritual journey. Ethical emphasis shifted from prescriptive personal conduct—no movies or dancing—to interpersonal actions: reconciliation, peacemaking, earth care, and justice. But they retained high standards of sexual purity, also emphasizing abstinence from alcohol and addictive substances, and integrity in speech and action. Queries in books of discipline affirmed these principles. The charismatic movement of the 1970s, a new revivalist wave, touched Evangelical Friends somewhat. A few used speaking in tongues as private prayer language. Some young adults drifted away from Friends and into charismatic fellowships. The movement attracted some who might otherwise have found a home with Friends. No major rifts or splits occurred and Friends maintained their style of quiet intercessional prayer for divine healing. Quakers deemed the 'signs and wonders' approach too programmatic, too theatrical, and objected to accompanying fundamentalist tenets, such as limiting ministry to males. John Wimber, a driving force in the Vineyard Fellowship—a charismatic movement that became worldwide—had been brought to faith and into ministerial leadership by California Friends. The Yearly Meeting parted with Wimber over the charismatic issue. Friends, however, were influenced by the movement's church-planting techniques. In the 1970s, the Vineyard casual worship style troubled some Friends, who favoured more order and dignity in worship. Its congregational polity also differed from Quaker covenantal (Presbyterian-type) polity.

In *Holiness: the Soul of Quakerism*, Carole Dale Spencer depicts the multiple strands of Quaker perfectionism—mystical, emotional, volitional, rational (see Spencer's Chapter 9 within this volume entitled 'Quakers in Theological Context'). Given a relativistic ethos at era's end, to re-root biblical holiness doctrines in historic Quaker thought and experience seemed timely to some leaders. There were calls to re-affirm holiness, including one by British Quaker scholar John Punshon, who wrote: 'Perfection matters and we need to remedy its present neglect. The process of gradual sanctification toward a fulfilled (perfect) life is both a great challenge and the medium of a great vision' (Punshon 2001, 293).

As revivalism diminished, evangelism increasingly devolved upon pastors to call for commitment to Christ and dedication to faithful living. Such calls generally came through personal and small group ministry, rather than public evangelism. Preaching was generally expository, often a sermon series on a specific biblical book. Local elders gave spiritual guidance to pastors, nurtured members' spiritual gifts, and sometimes disciplined errant ones. Pastors offered membership classes for converts and transfers from other traditions, providing guidance in Quaker history, faith, and practice. Typically, new members were brought before the congregation at worship as elders prayed and welcomed them into fellowship. Sometimes new members witnessed their commitment to Christ and convincement as Friends. Affiliate membership was offered to Christians unready to accept certain Friends' testimonies.

During the past half-century, numerical decline due to demographic factors—smaller families, urbanization, and aging population, and social factors—secularization and increased mobility was offset by outreach efforts that provided modest increases.

Different church-planting techniques were tried with varying success. One reliable method was for a large congregation to establish a new work. During the past half-century membership numbers within EFC-North America rose from 32,000 to 41,000. The number of meeting points increased. In recent decades membership numbers remained flat or decreased and accurate accounting became difficult. Sometimes annual statistics simply listed attendance figures or 'no report'. Twenty-first-century cultural forces made formal memberships seemed superficial to some. Concerned leaders acknowledged the importance of spiritual fellowship but urged pastors to renew the emphasis upon the covenantal value of membership.

During the middle decades youth participated in public witness through Gospel bands, a form of itinerant ministry. They travelled amongst local meetings to give personal testimony, provide special music, and offer short sermons . The practice waned as churches used local groups or ministerial staff, and as increased mobility facilitated other forms of interaction. Quarterly Meetings yielded to less formal modes of fellowship.

Broadening the Christian Witness

Evangelical Friends missionary witness is described more fully elsewhere (see Welling's chapter 20 in this volume, entitled 'Mission'). Suffice it to note that evangelistic efforts, home and abroad, combined proclamation and service. In early decades Evangelical Friends participated in the American Friends Service Committee, notably assisting in post-First World War relief efforts. Two Northwest Yearly Meeting Friends Lewis Hoskins and Kara Newell served as general secretary. Participation dwindled when Friends judged the agency to lack Christian moorings or Quaker oversight. Other service agencies became venues, including Mennonite Central Committee, Heifers Incorporated, World Vision, and Mercy Corps (Evangelical Friend Fred Gregory served for a time as an executive). In later decades youth participated in Christian Peacemaker Team witness in the Middle East and elsewhere. They acted out what evangelical leader-pastor, missionary executive Jack Willcuts had articulated regarding the practicality of pacifism. He wrote:

> The path of peace as taught by Jesus is precisely the way to live in the sinful world where violence is so near. This brings one to grips with the injustice found in a sinful world, enabling one in the power of the Holy Spirit to witness to a deeper truth that can lead us out of darkness into the Light and Love of God. The Sermon on the Mount is not just a set of idealistic words, it is practical advice on how to live and witness in a very real world. (Willcuts 1984, 62)

Service ministries included local and foreign work camps, missionary internships, and tuition aid to needy youth. The Friends Disaster Service, begun by Dean Johnson in Eastern Region in 1974, became a model for other Yearly Meetings. Verbal witness often accompanied service missions. Building houses in needy countries became a regular commitment for some. Participant faith was strengthened and sometimes conversions occurred.

In the early twentieth century ecumenicity flourished and Friends participated. The YMCA and YWCA bonded youth through healthful activities while the Women's Christian Temperance Union fought 'demon rum' and other social ills. Its adjunct, the Loyal Temperance League, awarded certificates to children who pledged abstinence. Christian Endeavor offered a venue for youth. By mid-century, denominations had developed their own programmes, such as the Methodist's Epworth League and Baptist Youth. 'Friends Youth' was formed, stressing intra-denominational fellowship. The Youth For Christ movement held Saturday night rallies in major cities. Campus Crusade bonded collegians in Christian fellowship. Later, Young Life helped and continues to help high-school students follow Christ. Families participated in Billy Graham Crusades. Yearly Meetings joined the National Association of Evangelicals, although participation diminished as strident fundamentalism surged. Friends participated in Congresses on World Evangelism, including one in Cape Town, South Africa in 2010.

RETURNING TO HOLISTIC EDUCATION

Around the middle of the century evangelical Christians, including Quakers, returned to holistic education. In Ohio, Cleveland's Christian Workers Training School, upon moving to Canton became Malone College. California's Training School became Azusa Pacific. These colleges later became universities. Portland Bible Institute became Cascade College. Support groups focused on Western Evangelical Seminary for ministerial preparation, a Wesleyan/Holiness school. By mid-century, the Oregon Friends had put themselves solidly behind Pacific College again. Renamed George Fox in 1949, the school welcomed alumni of defunct Cascade College. It became a university in 1996 upon incorporating Western Evangelical Seminary. Friends Bible College in Haviland. Kansas (since 1990 Barclay College, with broadened curricula) continued serving Midwest Friends along with Friends University in Wichita. Seminaries and graduate schools offered advanced leadership training for Quaker ministers—Azusa Pacific's Friends Center, George Fox's Evangelical Seminary, and Houston Graduate School of Theology. Some Evangelical Friends studied at the Earlham School of Religion. Malone University offered graduate programmes in theological studies.

As fundamentalist and liberal dogmatisms receded, Evangelical Friends schools were again challenged to sustain a Christ-centred education. Their professors became respected scholars. Ecumenically, a national Christian College Consortium supported efforts to integrate faith and learning. Because Quaker universities enrolled many non-Friends students, they included leadership programmes for Friends youth designed to enhance affinity and ground them in their tradition biblically and rationally.

The Bible school approach remained an option. Alaska Yearly Meeting continued its Training School at Kotzebue. The Instituto Alcanzando al Mundo Alrededor (Houston, Texas) served Friends along the US/Mexico border. The Great Lakes Leadership Training Program coordinated centres in Rwanda, Burundi, and the Congo. Berea Evangelical School of Theology in Manila served Philippine Friends through extension programmes. Asian Friends used inter-denominational institutes. Central American Friends supported Berea Bible Seminary in Chiquimula, Guatemala. Peru Friends had a small Bible seminary. The inter-denominational Bolivian Evangelical University (Santa Cruz) served Friends students. Educational levels varied from culture to culture, and Friends adapted leadership training accordingly.

THE ASSOCIATION OF EVANGELICAL FRIENDS AS AN AGENT OF RENEWAL

This movement originated in a 1927 gathering of eleven Friends in Cheyenne, Wyoming (conveniently reached by railway), convened by Edward Mott of Oregon Yearly Meeting.

Attendees, troubled by Modernist trends within the Five Years Meeting, were determined to 'lift up a standard of evangelical faith' (Roberts 1975, 1). The Depression and then the Second World War foiled plans for further gatherings until 1947, when an inter-Yearly Meeting committee chaired by Byron Osborne of Ohio convened the first general conference, in Colorado Springs. Seven triennials followed in various states, the final one in Indiana in 1968. Participants came mostly from independent Yearly Meetings but also from Friends United Meeting and Conservative Meetings. A stated purpose: to 'articulate the united voice of evangelical Friends', 'to provide a possible means of cooperative promotion of evangelical service in various areas such as missions, evangelism, education, publications, youth work, relief, and peace' (Roberts, 2). A magazine, *Concern*, was published from 1959 through 1962. In one issue Charles Beals chided Liberal Friends for selective use of early Quaker writings and asserted that for Evangelical Friends, the Valiant Sixty represent the roots of their faith. 'I as an evangelical Friends minister,' he added, 'am within the framework of the Quaker heritage' (*Concern* 1960, vol. 2.1, 3–4). In a stirring address Everett Cattell declared the time when Friends were overly dogmatic and spoiling for a fight was over. Now 'the whole Friends Church is caught up in a passion for unity'. This concern had 'kept evangelicals from precipitating a clean-cut cleavage throughout the Five Years Meeting' (*Concern* 1959, vol. l. 3, 3 and 14).

The first president Gerald Dillon articulated ways to strengthen bonds of unity among Friends in 1961: 'continuing this informal organization, encouraging independent Yearly Meetings to find organizational means of cooperation, increased inter-visitation, and revival, penitently gathering about the cross of Christ and discovering a common fellowship' (Concern 1964, vol. 3.4, 16–17). A resolution at the 1965 Association conference concluded: 'We urge Friends to work toward and pray for a more fully united Friends Church, evangelical in nature and world-wide in scope. We pray the Association may be an instrument of the Holy Spirit to bring this about' (Roberts, 1975, 35). A resolution called Friends to a more 'vigorous Christian theology', deplored stereotypes of Quakers, and affirmed the peace testimony. Triennial conferences dealt with issues of doctrine, outreach, and worship. They formulated procedural guidelines and a faith statement similar to the Richmond Declaration, but included a section affirming liberty in non-essentials and denoting baptism and communion as spiritual realities beyond outward forms.

The Evangelical Friends Alliance was organized in 1963. It established commissions to facilitate cooperative ministries. This fulfilled one goal. Stirred by Cattell's passion for unity plea, Association leaders—with others—convened a gathering to fulfil a second goal. The 1970 Faith and Life Conference in St. Louis included all branches of Friends in America. Some 135 representatives from twenty-four Yearly Meetings met to consider 'The Future of Friends'. The Friends World Committee, American Section, facilitated it. In a message delegates deemed prophetic, Cattell summoned all Friends to reaffirm Christ and follow Him as Lord. A 'Faith and Life Panel', selected to discern central affirmations, issued study books, *Quaker Understanding of Christ and Authority*, *The Church in Quaker Thought and Practice*, and *The Day of the Lord*. Friends from different groups contributed. At St Louis the AEF administrative council, after prayerful consideration, concluded its ministry had been fulfilled; its concerns now rested upon constituent groups. Seeds of renewal had been planted, so it disbanded. Arthur Roberts was authorized to write its history. In the 'Introduction' he asserted, 'In political terms the St. Louis Conference marked ascendency of a center party among Quakers, and a shift away from polarities of the 1920s and 30s' (Roberts 1975, 1).

During subsequent decades, optimism receded as Liberal Friends became less Christocentric, and less embracing of an infallible and authoritative Bible. But renewal efforts continued. A series of 'New Call to Peacemaking' conferences arose from concerns by Norval Hadley, an evangelical Quaker leader. The series included a 1978 conference on peace and holiness, cosponsored by the National Holiness Association and historic peace churches. In 1976 a series of youth gatherings commenced. 'YouthQuake!' became international with a third meeting in Oaxtepec, Mexico, in 1986. National pastors' gatherings occurred periodically. In 1977 a Conference for Friends in the Americas convened in Wichita, Kansas. Eugene Coffin gave impetus to the 'Forward Movement' within Friends United Meeting. Stanley Brown of Kansas, president during the final years, summarized participant feedback about the Association's role: its prophetic character and inclusiveness (Roberts 1975, 45).

FROM ALLIANCE TO EVANGELICAL FRIENDS CHURCH INTERNATIONAL

A coordinating council of the Alliance consisted of two representatives from each Yearly Meeting and an Executive Committee composed of the superintendent and a member-at-large from each. Administration was organized into sections, Africa, Asia, Europe, Latin America, and North America. Commissions included missions, evangelism and outreach, youth ministries, publications, and Christian education. During the 1970s and 1980s Dorothy Barratt served as a consultant and editor for educational materials and Barclay Press became a major Quaker publishing house. In addition to Sunday School quarterlies, tracts, books, and devotional literature, it published *The Evangelical Friend* as a national magazine, and upon its demise, *Friends Voice*. It published a devotional monthly, *Fruit of the Vine*. Instructive and inspirational website offerings were provided. In addition to those noted in the bibliography, Barclay Press books relating to Friends in this era (1887–2010) include: California Friend David LeShana's *Quakers in California* (1969)' Oregon Friend Ralph Beebe's *A Garden of the Lord* (1968); Ambassador *of the King*, biography of Kansas missionary Arthur Chilson, by wife Edna, (2009); Arthur Roberts' *Tomorrow is Growing Old: stories of Quakers in Alaska* (1978); Ohio Friend Catherine Cattell's *From Bambo to Mango* (1967); and Burundi Friend David Niyonzima's account of tribal reconciliation, *Unlocking Horns* (2001). Marie Haines' *Lion Hearted Quakers*, first published in 1978, nurtured Quaker children. In the last two decades Betty M. Hockett continued this ministry as author of a dozen children's books.

At Houston, Texas in May 1989, representatives from a dozen nations restructured the Alliance into the Evangelical Friends Church International. Constituent Yearly Meetings approved, although some chose not to incorporate the adjective 'evangelical' within regional and local titles. In 1992 Ron Stansell became International Director. And activities increased to include world and regional gatherings. For example, 'Summit 2010' convened 400 young adult EFCI Friends (aged 16–25) in Colorado to discern how to follow Christ faithfully.

EFCI scholars participated with other Friends in a Quaker Theological Discussion Group. It meets annually and since 1959, has published a journal, *Quaker Religious Thought*, to which these scholars contributed articles. During the past decade Paul Anderson of George Fox University served as editor. Beginning with the 1967 World Conference in North Carolina, Evangelical Friends increasingly participated in gatherings of or sponsored by the Friends World Committee for Consultation. This set a pattern for greater interchanges with other Quakers, especially those within Friends United Meeting, and constituted an acknowledgement of a common Christian and Quaker heritage.

International Characteristics
of Evangelical Friends

The movement of Friends from a transatlantic community to Africa, Asia, and Latin America before 1887 was minimal. Evangelical fervour in Britain and mainland United States in the early nineteenth century fostered zeal to spread the Gospel. This passion took Friends to Palestine, Japan, Pemba, Madagascar, Mexico, Jamaica, Alaska, India, China, and Cuba by 1900 (see Graves' chapter 18 within this volume, entitled 'Ministry and Preaching'). Ministries eventually linked to Evangelical Friends Church International began near the turn of the century in China and India (Eastern Region) and in Alaska and Guatemala (Southwest). Church plants in Bolivia, South America (Northwest) and Burundi, Africa (Mid-America) began in the 1930s. Networks of churches were developed in Honduras, El Salvador, Nicaragua, and Peru in Latin America, and in the Democratic Republic of Congo and Rwanda in Central Africa. Burundi (50,000), Guatemala (25,000), and Bolivia (15,000) are the largest and most developed Yearly Meetings. Other statistics: Honduras (8,000), El Salvador (1,000), Peru (2,000), Nicaragua (200) in Central America; Congo (3,000), Rwanda (4,500) in central Africa; and a small work among Navajo Native Americans in Arizona (50). In addition to Bolivia Yearly Meeting (INELA), at least five independent Yearly Meetings developed in that country, mostly spin offs from unaffiliated Central Yearly Meeting, numbering perhaps 30,000 to 50,000. Although not members of EFCI-Latin America, Bolivia Holiness Friends participated in its conferences and educational work. A Mexico City work started in 1967 was linked with congregations along the Mexico–United States border. New ministries were opened in Coahuila, Aguascalientes, and Sinaloa states of Mexico.

Congregations with Evangelical Friends identity planted in China beginning in 1887 were closed after the 1949 Communist takeover of the mainland. In the 1970s several reopened and flourished as registered Three-Self churches. Meanwhile, in Taiwan a Yearly Meeting developed, numbering 5,000 members. Bundelkhand Yearly Meeting in north-central India remained small (500 or fewer). Eastern Region Friends focused on India during decades following the Second World War, with ministries in five new locations in India (varying from 50 to 1,200 adherents), two in Nepal (totalling over 6,000), in Bhutan (600), in Bangladesh (500), and in the Philippines (2,000). These groups affiliated with EFCI either through EFC–ER or Evangelical Friends Mission (an agency operated by EFC–North America since 1978). Groups in Indonesia (2,000) and Cambodia (400) affiliated with EFCI through EFC–Southwest. A small EFC–Europe Region, formed in 2007, had representatives from congregations in Hungary, Serbia, Croatia, Romania (EFC–ER), Russia (NWYM), and Ireland (EFM). After 1990 EFC–ER started ministries in Jamaica, Haiti, and Dominican Republic.

Officially, in 2009 Evangelical Friends Church International numbered 177,000 adherents, 138,000 from outside North America (a conservative figure). In 2010, these were the EFCI regional directors, named by their delegates: Sabino Chipana, Latin America (from Bolivia); Augustin Simparinka, Africa (from Rwanda); Tony Frei, Europe (from Hungary); John Williams, Jr., North America (from Eastern Region); Derming Duh, Asia (from Taiwan).

International workers affirmed early Quaker insights in diverse ways during and beyond the twentieth century. International director Ron Stansell noted eight guiding principles:

1. A Christ-centred message is ever fresh because Christ the Present Teacher speaks both directly and through Scripture.
2. The authority of scripture is accepted without question by twentieth-century Evangelical Friends, as by early Friends.
3. The Holy Spirit, working in the indigenous church from culture to culture can be trusted to lead rightly. Evangelical Quakers encouraged autonomous, God-dependent leadership.
4. The Holy Spirit leads into new fields, exemplified by Apostle Paul's response to the Spirit's call to Macedonia.
5. The Holy Spirit uses both women and men—including youth—in ministry.
6. God is at work in every culture. 'That of God in everyone' is interpreted to mean not a spark of divinity but God's creative work in culture. The wooing of the Holy Spirit in every heart convinces persons to become followers of Jesus.
7. Christian faith is marked by *personal* transformation of new disciples.
8. Social actions are integrated with personal holiness. The 'Lamb's War' is waged by relief to the needy, education, medical work, economic uplift, and reconciliation efforts among hostile ethnic and caste groups.

Distinctive practices of early Friends were extended to the Global South during the twentieth century. A high level of participation in oral testimony, preaching, and teaching became a norm, although diverse in form. Enthusiastic music and artistic expression, including dance and drumming, was common in Africa and Asia. Oral group prayer in Bolivia, Alaska, and India exemplified distinctive cultural adaptation. Direct personal involvement, however, remained a constant. Friends from the West modelled and practised group decision-making in non-hierarchical contexts that were broadly although not universally duplicated. Often local face-to-face cultural practices were adapted by Friends as ways to discern God's will through group process. Service ministries occurred in the Global South in regions with large population segments marked by poverty and political oppression. Friends in Burundi, Bolivia, Peru, and India were mostly from the lowest economic groups, marginalized people—deprived of basic human rights. Dalit castes in India, Aymara-speakers of the Andean highlands, and the disadvantaged Hutu ethnic group in central Africa, constituted most Friends in those regions. Examples of compassionate service: Guatemalan Friends mobilized to tend the sick and dying during the 1918–19 influenza pandemic, After the 1994 genocide, Rwandan Friends united to care for widows, orphans, and displaced persons, healing horrific wounds of war. Wherever they went Friends carried concerns for education, developing primary and secondary school systems. Frequently converts achieved educational accomplishments at rates much higher than for the general public, and took advantage of secular educational programmes offered. In most nations pastoral and leadership training programmes occurred. Beginning in 1999, Friends in the several Latin American countries held pastors conferences with attendance in the hundreds.

Evangelical Friends collaborated ecumenically. In Africa, Central and South America, Friends missionaries regularly participated in inter-mission programmes, often as leaders. From the 1950s through the 1970s, EFC-Eastern Region assigned most mission staff to inter-denominational work in India. A Christian education curriculum writer, an administrator for a leading Protestant seminary, the director of India's Youth for Christ, and the Executive Director of the Evangelical Fellowship of India were all were Evangelical Friends. Guatemalan Friends were on the ground floor of Theological Education by Extension, a movement that created innovations used in several countries. Friends' missionaries in Taiwan demonstrated harmonious ecumenical relationships.

Non-Western cultures where Friends groups were planted during the twentieth century tended to be strongly male-dominated, far more than in Western cultures. This challenged Friends workers and significant changes occurred. Protesting discriminatory dowries and high preference for male offspring, Nepalese Friends consciously honoured girls and laid aside oppressive practices. Friends' Women associations were set up throughout Africa and Latin America. Husband and wife pastoral teams became common, especially in Central America. Friends' women in Africa rose to places of political prominence, including a Burundi Parliament member. Recording women as gospel ministers, although not universal, became accepted in regions of Africa and Latin America. Among South American Friends open speaking in worship by women was encouraged. Several Indian Friends women accompanied spouses as equals in ministries. While further progress was needed to liberate women into ministry at all levels, in oppressive non-Western cultures Friends extended them respect and honour.

In the process of reaching into the non-Western world, evangelical Quakerism changed demographically: sometime in mid- to late-twentieth century, Anglo-Saxon Friends became a minority. In 2010, the ratio was about three Evangelical Friends from the Global South for every Western-culture one. Friends United Meeting, given its seventeen Yearly Meetings in East Africa with 380,000 members—fervently Evangelical— evidenced an even more disparate ratio. This numerical shift impacted the entire Friends movement. New partnerships evolved. Westerners followed initiatives by non-Western brothers and sisters in education, evangelism, and social development. In some settings shared financing and administrative tasks occurred. (This concern for global identity had given impetus to expanding the Alliance into the Evangelical Friends Church International.) Most new efforts by Evangelical Friends in Asia during the last half of the twentieth century occurred as Western Friends followed Asian Friends' contacts into India, Philippines, Nepal, Bhutan, Bangladesh, Myanmar, Cambodia, and Indonesia.

Non-Western Friends increasingly exercised leadership in regional and world gatherings. Local leaders administered the EFCI regions exclusively. Respected non-Western preachers and teachers travelled within the Global South—and the West—to share vision and expertise. Their witness, with that of Western workers returning from the Global South, highlighted transformational developments integrating the spiritual and the physical, for example, in dealing with sex trafficking, inter-ethnic peacemaking, and goddess worship, issues less fully addressed in the West.

The twenty-first century witnessed a significant development in the worldwide family of Friends: non-Western Friends beginning to develop theological formulation concerning issues in their cultural contexts. These issues included biblical understandings about family (especially in Africa), physical healing, dealing with the demonic, the meaning of suffering, and foundations for social reconciliation. In general, non-Western Friends were less materialistic, more charismatic, more concerned for the second coming of Christ, and more empirical in expectations about heaven. These concerns flowed back to Western Friends, humbled by the suffering and deprivations of groups possessing little or no political clout, challenging them to re-examine these issues.

ISSUES FACING CONTEMPORARY EVANGELICAL QUAKERS

By 2010 considerable ethnic diversity obtained. Although welcomed in principle it challenged bonding between North and South, West and East, especially if Western temperaments, individualism, and orderly habits were to dominate. Differences were striking: communalism versus individualism, poverty versus affluence, ecumenism versus sectarianism. Differences in preaching and worship styles, the ordinance issue—these and other issues, needed reconciliation, according to EFCI executive Ron Stansell, by returning to biblical and Quaker roots and by Spirit-led listening.

Sustaining the Bible as definitive for faith and practice was one concern. Loyalty to Scripture was largely unquestioned in the Global South but challenged by secular thought in the North. In all regions evangelical Quakers faced interpretation issues, and how to let Scripture and the Spirit speak to culture and not let culture dictate how Scripture was interpreted and applied.

Non-Western Friends sought ways to exemplify peace among conflicted subgroups, to express faithful witness within local contexts. The strong faith, moral courage, forgiving spirit, and vigorous evangelistic outreach by these Friends encouraged others to greater Christian faithfulness.

Global South Friends were troubled by perceived spiritual coolness and materialism of Western Friends. They considered unbiblical certain tolerated practices, such as divorce, unmarried relationships, and homosexual behaviour. After a century of significant growth, non-Western Evangelical Friends reflected strikingly different profiles—charismatic, post-Modern, and poor, but spiritually vibrant. Their brothers and sisters in the West, however, were concerned that Global South Quakers—with a shorter Christian heritage—not succumb to seductive forces lurking within their social contexts of money, sex, and power.

Evangelical Friends worldwide were marked by group identity, inter-cultural sensitivity, and joy in spiritual transformations. Twenty-first century North American Friends struggled to sustain numbers and group identity in the face of secularism, moral relativism, affluence, and cultural pressures. It was uncertain whether communication technology strengthened or weakened corporate unity. It had proved difficult for Yearly Meetings to sustain bonds of fellowship among Meetings as diverse as house churches ministering to dozens and mega-churches—such as Yorba Linda, California—ministering to thousands.

Elders prayed for Spirit-guided leadership and revitalization of local Meetings. They sought creative ways through inter-visitation and media to sustain and enhance a historic faith community that had indeed become evangelical in nature and worldwide in scope. Paul Anderson articulated a conviction, that with reliance upon Christ's leadership, individually and corporately, Quakerism would continue to 'further and embody the transforming and healing ministry of Christ in the world' (1987 Williams/Anderson, 293). Fox's vision of 'a people to be gathered to the Lord' continued to inspire. Evangelical Friends saw signs of spiritual renewal in global gatherings and ministries of young Friends, encouraged by their Christian commitment to keep truth and love linked together and working as a team.

SUGGESTED FURTHER READING

Barbour, H. and Frost, J. W. (1994) *The Quakers*. 2nd ed. Richmond, IN: Friends United Press. Chapters 16 and 21, 'New forms of Quaker interaction'.

Dandelion, P. (2007) *An introduction to Quakerism.* Cambridge: Cambridge University Press.

Hamm, T. D. (1988) *The transformation of American Quakerism.* Bloomington, IN: Indiana University Press. Chapters IV and VII.

Spencer, C. D. (2007) *Holiness: the Soul of Quakerism.* Milton Keynes, UK and Eugene, OR: Paternoster and Wipf and Stock.

Stansell, R. (2009) *Missions by the Spirit.* Newberg, OR: Barclay Press.

CHAPTER 8

CONSERVATIVE FRIENDS, 1845–2010

LLOYD LEE WILSON

SINCE its beginning in the mid-nineteenth century, the Conservative movement among Friends has been more important theologically than numerically. Though its adherents have always been a minority among Friends, their witness has upheld important points of faith and praxis in the root of Quakerism that might otherwise have been lost. Even as twenty-first-century Conservatives wrestle to sustain an independent identity among Friends at large, they are seen as an example of how to sustain the early Quaker combination of waiting worship and clear Christian commitment while resisting the most serious incursions of the dominant culture into daily religious life.

Although elements of conservative thought and practice have been present among Friends since the movement's second generation, they came to prominence in the Wilburite–Gurneyite schisms within the Orthodox branch of Quakerism beginning in 1845. The seeds of the separations were already in place among Orthodox Friends at the time of the Hicksite–Orthodox separation of 1827. The seemingly solid front against Hicksite innovation included both some Friends who opposed Hicksite innovation because it was innovation, and a larger portion who preferred the orthodox Christian theology prevalent in Protestant circles outside Quakerism over the liberal theology favoured by the so-called Hicksites (Dorrien 2003, 366). For a number of years these two groups co-existed more or less quietly.

Doherty (1965) argues that a strong part of the attraction of Orthodox Quaker theology was the relatively greater emphasis it placed on right belief rather than right behaviour. It offered relief from the narrow strictures on behaviour that were characteristic of Quakerism of the time. While the Hicksite–Orthodox Separation of 1827 can be seen as a split over doctrine, the series of Conservative separations can be seen as splits mostly (though not entirely) over behaviour, especially in the latter separations.

The sources from which Orthodox theology made its way into the minds of North American Quakers are many, but a major source was certainly the travels of numerous Orthodox-thinking English Friends in the years following 1790. Visitors from London

Yearly Meeting were held in high regard, and their messages heard with interest and respect. In the perspective of an increasing number of equally respected more traditional Friends, however, they were spreading ideas and practices that were contrary to the historic witness and practice of the Religious Society of Friends. Hannah Chapman (Gurney) Backhouse, who visited America in 1830–5, advocated strongly for the establishment of Bible study groups like those popular among non-Quakers. This innovation was accepted and implemented readily in many local meetings, but met with resistance among the traditionalists.

It was the popularity of Backhouse's cousin Joseph John Gurney (1788–1847), the most charismatic and most influential of the English Orthodox Friends to visit America (1837–40), which brought these differences to a head and sparked the first Wilburite separation, in New England Yearly Meeting in 1845. It is called a Wilburite separation because of the role played by John Wilbur, an articulate opponent of Orthodox thought and practice, and by the Orthodox Quaker leaders who attempted to silence him.

John Wilbur (1774–1856) was a lifelong Friend from Rhode Island; he was appointed an elder in his meeting in 1802 and recognized as a minister of the gospel ten years later. He believed it important to stay close to the doctrines and beliefs of earlier generations of Friends. A trip to England (1831–3) convinced him of the dangers of Orthodoxy, and he published a book of letters to George Crosfield (Wilbur1895) that detailed his concerns. When Gurney travelled in the ministry among American Friends, Wilbur openly criticized his doctrines as contrary to settled Quaker belief and practice. This resulted in a protracted conflict with the leadership of New England Yearly Meeting (primarily Orthodox) and eventually to his disownment. Wilbur and his supporters then organized as a separate Yearly Meeting; each group claimed to be the authentic and legitimate New England Yearly Meeting.

John Wilbur and those who agreed with him saw Gurney's errors as being directly opposite to those of Elias Hicks, a central figure in the separation of 1827 (Wilbur 1845, 29). According to this view, Hicks and Gurney each held to one half of the Quaker faith and neglected the other:

> Elias Hicks and Joseph John Gurney have both professed their own views…But the former, however, appears to be wanting in his fidelity as to Christ's personal coming and attributes; and the latter in his fidelity as to his spiritual coming and dwelling in the heart of man. The latter has the fullest faith in his personal coming and atoning sacrifice for the remission of sins; the former as full in his spiritual coming for the renovation of the inner man, and a saving of him from a continuance in sin. But both of these appear to be great debtors to the correct part of each other's doctrine; each apparently holds to half, and each apparently rejects half of the Christian covenant, and therefore holding nothing in common with each other in relation to redemption by Christ. But still, each (professedly) holding to half the covenant in common with Friends. (Wilbur 1845, 246–7)

At the heart of Wilbur's opposition to the Orthodox party was his conviction that any deviation from the faith and practice established by George Fox and the other early

Friends was a mistake (Wilbur 1845, 21, 32, 118). While the teaching of other Orthodox Friends was equally objectionable, Wilbur focused his attention on Gurney because he was the most popular and most influential, and therefore the most dangerous (Wilbur 1845, 27 footnote). His objections to Gurney's teaching—and there were many—always boiled down to 'Gurney teaches A, while early Friends taught B. Therefore Gurney is wrong.' Wilbur identified the most dangerous of Gurney's teachings as these:

> The two or three exceptional doctrines of J. J. Gurney…might be selected from the many, under the following heads: 1st, That the Gospel of Christ, is not *in itself* the power of God unto salvation. 2nd, that men are justified by faith without regard to obedience. 3rd, That was the true light which lighteth every man that cometh into the world, he construes to mean no more than Christ incarnate, 'the enlightener'. Let all imbibe these three items of doctrine and Quakerism would be no more. (Wilbur 1845, 220)

In other words, Gurney said the Gospel (good news) was the knowledge of the incarnation of Jesus Christ conveyed in writing by the Holy Scriptures, rather than the power of God to change individual lives as had been experienced personally by generations of Friends (Wilbur 1845, 288). This changed understanding of the nature of the Gospel led to Gurney's doctrine that one was justified by an intellectual faith commitment alone (Wilbur 1845, 281), or what Wilbur would call justification by faith without obedience (Wilbur 1845, 30). Thirdly, Gurney was abandoning Friends understanding and experience of the Christ Within (Wilbur 1845, 315), or the Seed of Christ (Wilbur 1845, 318), which changed the life of the believer who surrendered to it, in favour of a more general influence of the Holy Spirit towards faith in the Christ incarnate of Scripture.

These may be seen as merely theological amendments, and evaluated as such, but it is their effect on outward behaviour, on praxis, that is crucial. What excited early Friends was not knowledge of Jesus Christ gained from study of Scripture, but the powerful inward experience of the Seed of Christ in themselves through which God could change their own lives, breaking the power of sin that kept them tied to old sinful behaviours. By heeding the guidance of this Seed and allowing its power to be at work in their daily lives, Friends felt themselves freed from the power of sinful behaviour and brought into a right relationship with God. In previous Quaker understanding, a changed life was both sign and substance of their life in Christ, and Christ's life in them. Quaker distinctives such as plain dress and plain speech were important signs that the individual had 'given up' to the guidance of the Inward Christ in all things. Gurney appeared to be abandoning these insights for a more traditional Protestant orthodoxy emphasizing belief rather than praxis.

Wilbur was not alone in his discontent over the innovations being preached by Gurney and other Orthodox Friends. Sarah Lynes Grubb (1773–1842) (daughter-in-law of Sarah Grubb) warned London Yearly Meeting in the 1830s against a 'spirit of subtlety' that would replace the 'inward manifestation of our blessed Saviour the Lord Jesus Christ' with a 'literal faith in Christ crucified' (Grubb 1863, 47). Later that decade Joseph Hoag (1762–1846) prophesied a separation over doctrine in Ferrisburg Quarterly Meeting, New York Yearly Meeting (Orthodox) (Hoag 1861, 387).

Four Yearly Meetings were divided in the first wave, or Wilburite, separations. Wilbur's own New England Yearly Meeting divided in 1845, followed by a smaller schism in New York (1847), a larger and more contentious split in Ohio Yearly Meeting in 1854, and finally the separation of a dozen Friends from Baltimore Yearly Meeting. (The separation in Baltimore was in reaction to that Yearly Meeting's recognition of the Gurneyite Ohio Yearly Meeting rather than the Wilburite Yearly Meeting following the Ohio separation. This group remained viable for only a few years, last meeting in 1868 (Hodgson 1876, 203ff.)) The New York Wilburites divided again in 1859 over an internal dispute concerning the publication of Joseph Hoag's *Journal*, and did not thrive in later years (Bradley 1979). Their remaining numbers eventually affiliated with Canada Yearly Meeting Conservative in 1916.

The story of the split and subsequent history of Ohio Yearly Meeting Conservative has been well told by William P. Taber, Jr. (1985). The issues at stake were essentially those that had precipitated schism in New England between Wilburites and Gurneyites (Hodgson 1876, 192ff). Beginning in 1845, epistles were received from each of the two New England Yearly Meetings, but no decision was made to recognize either body. This status prevailed for several years, with various actions being taken to avoid a confrontation and probable separation. In 1854 Thomas B. Gould of New England Yearly Meeting (Wilburite) attended the Ohio Yearly Meeting sessions, and unlike some similar visitors in previous years, was unwilling to leave the meeting during sessions so Ohio Friends would not have to face their own divided condition. (Eliza P. Gurney, Joseph John Gurney's widow, as well as William and Charles Evans of Philadelphia were also present at these business sessions.) Gould's refusal to leave proved to be the catalyst for separation, as the Gurneyites responded by appointing their own clerk, igniting an open dispute over control of the Yearly Meeting (Kinch, Eileen, personal communication, 29/8/11). Some ten years later the two groups disowned each other and civil litigation between the Yearly Meetings was not settled until 1874 (Taber 1985, 63). In Ohio, unlike all the other separations in this first wave, the Wilburites were in the majority and composed the larger of the two Ohio Yearly Meetings.

Philadelphia Yearly Meeting, at the time the largest and most influential of North American Yearly Meetings, avoided a separation in 1846 and subsequent years by a series of administrative manoeuvres. A majority of the members of the Yearly Meeting were Wilburite in sympathies, though there was a strong and vocal Gurneyite minority. The Yearly Meeting sessions in 1846 were faced with two epistles from New England: one each from the two recently divided Yearly Meetings. Only one of the New England groups could be the true New England Yearly Meeting; reading the epistle from either one would commit Philadelphia irrevocably to that group in opposition to the other and in all probability precipitate a schism in Philadelphia. Philadelphia Friends avoided a separation in 1846 by deferring both epistles to the next year's business sessions (Hodgson 1876, 126-8). Much discussion and deliberation followed over the next several years, but no decision favouring either party could be reached. To avoid a separation in Philadelphia, Friends there eventually determined not to exchange epistles with any other Yearly Meetings at all.

After a pause of over twenty years, a second wave of separations began with the division of Iowa Yearly Meeting in 1877 and included Western Yearly Meeting, Kansas Yearly Meeting, and Canada Yearly Meeting. All four meetings had been established by Orthodox Yearly Meetings after the Wilburite separations were over: Western in 1858, Iowa in 1863, Canada in 1867, and Kansas in 1872. Herbert Standing (1964, 24) points out that the Wilburite separations involved Friends in the New England and Middle Atlantic states or those who had migrated from that region to eastern Ohio, while the second wave primarily involved Friends who had migrated from the Southern states into the Midwest. While some of the issues prompting the earlier Wilburite separations were still a factor, the major issue over which Friends divided in this period was the incorporation by many Friends and Friends meetings of features of the Great Revival into Quaker worship and doctrine, including pre-appointed speakers, group singing, formal prayer, and the mourner's bench in worship; a literal understanding of Scripture and teaching that a person may be a true believer in Christ without taking up Christ's yoke and the daily cross.

At the time of the separation in Iowa, there was already a Wilburite quarterly Meeting there: Hickory Grove Quarterly Meeting, part of Ohio Yearly Meeting. Relationships between Hickory Grove Friends and the members of the Conservative Iowa Yearly Meeting were not close for many years, and at least once Hickory Grove Quarter sent the Conservative Iowa Yearly Meeting a listing of the various ways in which they were not in accord with Wilburite principles and practices (Marsh, 2011, 7). Although the other Iowa Friends were not persuaded to change, by 1917 the divisions had softened to the point that Hickory Grove Quarterly Meeting was transferred as a unit from Ohio Yearly Meeting to Iowa Yearly Meeting (Marsh 2011, 8). Since that time Iowa Yearly Meeting has had roots in both the Wilburite and second-wave Conservative separations.

The theological underpinnings of the nineteenth-century Protestant revival movement were already present among Orthodox Friends. The end of the American Civil War in 1865 allowed Friends to turn their attention to the spiritual condition of the Religious Society of Friends overall, and they perceived that condition was not good. Seeing the success of the revival among other Christian groups, and seeing young Friends joining other churches as a direct result of revival meetings, it seemed to many a logical step to adopt revival practices among Friends, and emphasize its theological presuppositions as a consequence.

Iowa Conservatives meeting in the spring of 1877 identified the points at which they disagreed with the doctrine and practice of the revivalists (Standing 1964, 22–3). These included substituting a dependence on outward means (including a literal knowledge of and belief in the Holy Scriptures) for the experience of the Inward Christ, avoiding the necessity of the daily cross, undervaluing the writings of ancient Friends such as Robert Barclay, the introduction of reading and singing into meetings for worship, and the manner in which General Meetings [revivals] were conducted, such as introduction of a mourner's bench, outward consecration, and excess emotionalism.

The 1878 separation in Western Yearly Meeting was also a reaction to the inroads the Great Revival had made among Indiana Friends, including manner of worship, and doctrines that there is no grace given to man before his conversion to lead him towards repentance, and justification by simple belief or faith alone (Heiss 1963, 4). Differences over practice loomed more important than differences in theology or doctrine. The following year Kansas Yearly Meeting also separated. Kansas Yearly Meeting (Conservative) was laid down in 1928 due to declining membership, and its last remaining Monthly Meeting was transferred to Iowa Yearly Meeting (Conservative).

The separation in Canada began with the withdrawal of individual Friends from the Yearly Meeting in 1878, including the Yearly Meeting clerk Adam Spencer. The catalyst was the proposed adoption of revisions to the Yearly Meeting Discipline which de-emphasized plain dress and muted criticism of the hireling ministry. Other Friends followed suit over the next two years, and Canada Yearly Meeting (Conservative) was formally organized in 1885 (Canadian Yearly Meeting 2004). Canada Yearly Meeting (Conservative) and Canada Yearly Meeting (Gurneyite) began meetings in joint sessions in 1944. In 1955 these two, plus Genesee Yearly Meeting (Hicksite) reunited to form Canadian Yearly Meeting (Canadian Yearly Meeting 2008).

During the period of this second wave of separations, a sometimes-protracted process of mutual evaluation took place between each newly organized Conservative Meeting and each of the others. Communication and visitation between two Yearly Meetings was limited until each had expressed its approval of the other, signified by the annual exchange of epistles between their business sessions. To faciliate communications and encourage Conservative-leaning Friends not belonging to accepted Conservative Yearly Meetings, periodicals such as *The Western Friend*, edited by Cyrus Harvey, were formed. By 1890 all the then-existing Conservative Yearly Meetings had completed the evaluation process and were exchanging epistles with one another. Cyrus Harvey perceived that the Conservative 'circle of Correspondence' was now complete and *The Western Friend* ceased publication (*The Friend* 1890, 343).

After the separation in Canada in 1881, North Carolina was the only North American Yearly Meeting to have avoided undergoing either a Hicksite or Wilburite/Conservative separation. The Hicksite controversy had not entangled North Carolina Friends, and the Yearly Meeting had avoided the Wilburite separations thanks in large part to the work of weighty Friend Nathan Hunt. The Gurney innovations had been sifted and weighed; some had been adopted (First-Day Schools), and some neglected. The effects of the Great Revival were felt among NC Friends as elsewhere, but although the traditionalists considered what to do on several occasions they never reached the point that separation was seen as the right course of action. The final straw was the change in Yearly Meeting structure and governance incorporated in the new Uniform Discipline adopted in 1902 to enable the Yearly Meeting to join the new Five Years Meeting. The North Carolina separation was primarily over orthopraxy—specifically church government—not orthodoxy.

When separation came in 1904, the fundamental issues were proper conduct of worship and ecclesiastical polity, including the assumption of authority to recognize gifts of ministry and eldership by the Yearly Meeting rather than by individual Monthly Meetings. The breaking point was the centralization of authority. The traditionalists could bear with innovations in worship and evangelical practice, as long as they did not have to participate themselves, either directly or through financial support. What they could not bear to lose was the responsibility to discern where gifts of gospel ministry had been given in their meetings, and how best to nurture them. When the larger portion of the Yearly Meeting approved the Uniform Discipline, including these provisions, the traditionalists decided that was beyond the Pale and began to meet on their own (Wilson, 2009).

During this period there were several smaller separations in North America and even two in England. Primitive Friends General Meeting in Fallsington, PA (1860–1947) separated from Philadelphia Yearly Meeting, and Fritchley General Meeting separated from London Yearly Meeting (1868–1968; reunited). In 1909 a group of Friends from Fritchley, England, constituted itself as both Halcyonia Monthly Meeting and Western Canada Yearly Meeting, which closed in 1936. Halcyonia Monthly Meeting, like Pelham Quarterly Meeting, did not join CYM in 1955, when the other Canadian Yearly Meetings united. Halcyonia Friends still meet for worship (Chenard 2005). The Conservative Yearly Meeting of Friends in Christ, which separated in 1993, still meets in England.

Each of the Wilburite and Conservative Yearly Meetings began with a strong commitment to maintaining the 'hedge' between themselves and all other religious groups, intent to maintain the purity of their own faith and practice by staying separated, both from the larger culture and from other Friends. The desire for separation from non-Friends was a legacy from the Quietist period, finding expression in the nineteenth century in statements such as the following extract from the 1840 *Advices* of Ohio Yearly Meeting:

> May all dear Friends keep in the quiet habitation aloof from the noise and commotion so prevalent in the world: for the church of Christ is represented as 'a garden enclosed, a spring shut up, a fountain sealed'. . . . we cannot as we conceive unite with those in these and like concerns [temperance and abolition of slavery] who are not brought into the same belief, without endangering our testimony to this doctrine of the Christian faith; and as we fear will pave the way to abandon the dignified standard to which we are called. (Taber 1985, 58)

Once a separation took place, individuals on both sides perceived those on the other side as no longer Friends, and therefore now on the other side of the hedge. In a meeting not yet divided, the question of which group of a newly separated meeting was the true Friends could itself spark a separation. The separation in New York Yearly Meeting prophesied in 1838 by Joseph Hoag began when Starksborough Monthly Meeting approved the marriage of his granddaughter Narcissa Battey to a member of New England Yearly Meeting (Wilburite) (Bradley 1979, 76). In the minds of many, this violated the principle of separation from non-Friends and could not be tolerated. Friends who favoured the Wilburite position now felt they had to stand their own ground. The unspoken truce was over, and Friends now had to act on their sympathies for one side or the other. In Ferrisburg Quarterly Meeting the Gurneyite faction prevailed and promptly laid down Starksborough Monthly Meeting (which quickly reorganized itself as a Wilburite Monthly Meeting).

The hedge was deemed most important by the first wave (Wilburite) Yearly Meetings, less so by the second wave (Conservative) Yearly Meetings, and least important in North Carolina, the last to separate. Within each Yearly Meeting there was considerable variation among the Monthly Meetings in how important the hedge was perceived to be. For example, Paullina Monthly Meeting in Iowa placed less importance on the hedge than other meetings in that Yearly Meeting (Marsh, C. personal communication, 2/7/11), while Holly Spring Monthly Meeting in North Carolina placed much more emphasis on the hedge than other Conservative Monthly Meetings there. In Ohio Yearly Meeting, Chestnut Ridge Monthly Meeting did not allow its members to own automobiles until about 1932. No other Ohio Monthly Meeting is known to have enforced rules against automobile ownership (Kinch, E. personal communication, 29/8/11). Although the hedge helped Friends maintain their distinctive faith and practice in the midst of strong opposing cultural pressures, that assistance came at a price.

The benefits of a close fellowship among the members of these Yearly Meetings were reduced due to their scepticism about everyone outside their own Yearly Meeting— even those who called themselves Conservatives. This scepticism often expressed itself in concern over outward practice. Were Friends in other Yearly Meetings sufficiently dedicated to wearing the plain dress and speaking the plain speech, even among outsiders? Did all Friends stand during meeting for worship when one Friend knelt in prayer? Were they careful not to accept in transfer the membership of anyone who belonged to a Gurneyite Yearly Meeting? Ohio's acceptance of both Iowa and North Carolina Yearly Meetings as true Friends was delayed for years by issues such as these.

As the youngest of the Conservative Yearly Meetings and because its reasons for separation were different from the others, North Carolina overall was less committed to the hedge than the others. Even so, as late as 1937 one Conservative Monthly Meeting in North Carolina was led to publish a protest against Conservative participation in the newly formed Friends World Committee because that would involve mingling with people who were not true Christians. As it turned out, that opinion did not long prevail and North Carolina Conservatives are now active in a wide range of ecumenical Quaker activities and organizations.

The hedge of separation may also account for the general reluctance of Conservative Friends to be involved in the national political process, except on rare occasions when a fresh statement of Friends principles seemed in order. Thus James Henderson of Ohio Yearly Meeting was led to call on President Wilson in 1915 (Taber 1985, 166–7) and North Carolina Yearly Meeting issued a new statement on the Peace Testimony in 1943, (North Carolina Yearly Meeting (Conservative) 1943) but a careful review of North Carolina Yearly Meeting minutes over a fifty-year span shows very little reference to the political issues of the period. Contemporary Conservative Friends are at pains to point out that 'Conservative' refers to a religious conservation of values and practices, not a political commitment, and that members hold a wide range of personal political views.

The first half of the twentieth century was a period of steady decline in membership for the Wilburite and Conservative Meetings generally. Western and Kansas Yearly Meetings were laid down due to low membership, while New England and Canada Yearly Meetings were absorbed into the reunited New England and Canadian Yearly Meetings, respectively. In the three remaining Yearly Meetings, numerous original Monthly Meetings have been laid down or seen dramatic declines in membership. This may be due in part to a general decline in rural populations, and in part to the failure of Conservative Friends to develop a method of evangelization effective in the modern age. Rural Conservative Meetings have experienced the same outflows of membership as other churches in rural areas: children grow up and leave the farm to seek jobs elsewhere.

Particularly since the mid-1950s, the three surviving Yearly Meetings (Ohio, Iowa, and North Carolina) have experienced growth by accepting into membership relatively new, previously unaffiliated Monthly Meetings. Sometimes this has been facilitated by the presence of one or more solid Conservative families in the new meeting, but often geography has been important too. The absence of nearby FGC-affiliated groups has encouraged these meetings to consider joining a Conservative Yearly Meeting, and several have found ways to do so.

Making provision for a suitable education has been important to each of these three Yearly Meetings. In Ohio and Iowa, this was accomplished through boarding schools owned and operated by the respective Yearly Meetings: Olney Friends School (Ohio) and Scattergood School (Iowa). Their alumni, through lives of service to Friends and to the world at large, testify to the strong influence for good that the schools have had over the generations. At the same time, the very importance of suitable education for children has made these schools lightning rods for Yearly Meeting issues of faith and policy at times: who should be allowed to teach at these schools? What should be taught, what standards of behaviour expected? North Carolina, perhaps due to its late start, never established a Yearly Meeting operated school; the general practice for Friends who could afford it was to send their children to Westtown School on the outskirts of Philadelphia. In the last sixty years, Monthly Meetings in North Carolina Yearly Meeting have been instrumental in establishing and maintaining day schools in Durham, Greensboro, Wilmington, and Virginia Beach, Virginia. The same issues present themselves in the operation of these Monthly Meeting schools as at the Yearly Meeting schools in Ohio and Iowa, but they are addressed and resolved locally, without involving the Yearly Meeting directly.

Olney Friends School, operated by the Yearly Meeting since its inception in 1837, became independent in 1998 when low enrollment and increasing financial difficulties led the Yearly Meeting to end its governance. The school was purchased by a group of supporters, many alumni, who now operate it as an independent Friends school not under the care of any Friends meeting (Olney Friends School, 2011).

The gifts of the Conservative Meetings to the Religious Society of Friends at large have been several: maintaining a clear Christian faith without entanglement in Protestant doctrine; a way of daily life emphasizing one's relationship with God and the guidance available from that relationship, rather than individualism and intellectual activity (willingness not to plan, not to over-analyse); recognition of the reality of differing spiritual gifts and the importance of having the community embrace those gifts; a faith based on personal experience that God intervenes in daily life on a regular basis; and an understanding of the mutual interplay between personal faith and personal behaviour. Conservative Friends have understood that faith necessarily makes certain demands on one's behaviour, and that changes in behaviour will bear sustained fruit only if they are based on one's deeply held faith.

Over several generations Conservative Friends have developed a culture of listening that can (and in some persons does) pervade all of daily life (Taber and Taber, 2004). Experience of and commitment to the guidance of the Inward Christ or Seed of Christ within has led to an orientation of daily activities so as to be more ready and able to feel and follow that guidance. The practices that contribute to this culture of listening include setting aside a period of time each day for silent waiting to listen for this guidance, and a high value placed on 'teachability'—the desire to continue to learn about spiritual matters and to be able to incorporate new understandings into all parts of one's life. The culture of listening has also affected manner of speech, encouraging a careful use of words as imperfect pointers towards a reality than cannot be fully expressed. In this, the apophatic nature of Conservative spirituality can be seen.

Conservative Quakers have valued the corporate nature of faith and of practice, understanding the importance of the faith community to which the individual belongs, and the centrality of both corporate worship and corporate discernment. Conservatives have also understood that the faithful community must recognize and nurture spiritual gifts that have been specially entrusted to individuals. While Conservative Meetings continue their witness against a paid ministry, they also continue to recognize their responsibility to help individuals who have been gifted and called into vocal ministry or other paths of service in the development and exercise of those gifts.

A de-emphasis on the importance of the hedge has opened up numerous opportunities for ministry and service among the larger bodies of Friends over the past half-century. Conservative Friends have served with distinction in leadership positions at the Earlham School of Religion, Friends World Committee for Consultation, the Pendle Hill teaching faculty, and as core teachers in Philadelphia Yearly Meeting's School of the Spirit. Conservative Friends are engaging other Friends in serious theological discussion through publications such as Pendle Hill pamphlets, *Friends Journal* articles, and elsewhere.

Over the past thirty years an increased desire on the part of Conservative Friends to share their spirituality and practice has been met by an increased desire by others to hear what they have to say. The Conservative experience of a deeply Christian faith distinctively different from mainstream North American Christianity, both Protestant and Christian, based on an apophatic path, has been particularly attractive.

In recent years the three Conservative Yearly Meetings have shown a willingness to experiment with new modes of affiliation, including membership of meetings and/or individuals at a great distance from any established Conservative Monthly Meeting. Careful but steady experimentation of the possibilities of modern communications has led to greater visibility of Conservatives in general, while they have maintained a continued emphasis on the importance of personal relationships and time spent gathered in corporate worship. Ohio Yearly Meeting has been most active in accepting individuals, families, and other small groups at a distance into affiliate membership, with varying degrees of success. Iowa Yearly Meeting (Conservative) has accepted the challenge of accepting into membership several smaller Monthly Meetings scattered at great distances across the American Midwest. North Carolina Yearly Meeting (Conservative) has been slower to address the matter, but is also beginning to look for ways to respond to these distant inquirers.

The interest of numerous individuals and even Monthly Meetings in new affiliation with the three Conservative Yearly Meetings has presented both challenges and blessings. A steady influx of newcomers requires a continued effort to teach deep Conservative faith and practice effectively. The old Quaker reliance on religious education by osmosis over a lifetime is no longer adequate to the task. At the same time these newcomers have brought fresh ideas and insights to the Conservative vision that have deepened and enriched the Yearly Meetings to which they have become a part.

Plain dress and plain speech are now the practice of only a small minority of Conservative Friends. There have inevitably been changes in theology over the decades as well. In 2006 North Carolina Yearly Meeting (Conservative) reconsidered a portion of the joint statement it adopted with the other Conservative Meetings in 1912. These included New England Yearly Meeting (Westerly), Canada Yearly Meeting (Pickering), Ohio Yearly Meeting (Stillwater), Western Yearly Meeting (Plainfield), Iowa Yearly Meeting (West Branch), Kansas Yearly Meeting (Spring River), and North Carolina Yearly Meeting (Cedar Grove). At the 2006 Yearly Meeting it minuted that at this time North Carolina Conservatives no longer consider biblical Higher Criticism a 'refined species of unbelief'. A concern for the care of the earth has become a part of the witness of all three Yearly Meetings, tempered with a concern that it be well grounded in Quaker faith and practice, rather than simply 'tacked on' in a faddish way.

Recently, North Carolina Yearly Meeting held a one-day retreat to consider what was essential to its identity as a Conservative Yearly Meeting. The answer that found unity was 'the immediate and perceptible guidance of the Holy Spirit'. What Conservatives find important to conserve, at its core, is a life lived under God's immediate and perceptible guidance, moment to moment. What one is truly guided to give up under that guidance may and must be given up, no matter how cherished a tradition; what one is truly guided to accept may and must be accepted, no matter how unexpectedly new. The desire to share this foundational experience—the truth and trustworthiness of the guidance of the Holy Spirit, is what Conservatives wish to share with others, Quaker or not.

SUGGESTED FURTHER READING

Anonymous (1992) *A short history of Conservative Friends*. Richmond, IN. Available at [http://snowcamp.org/shocf/] [Accessed 12/15/11].

Bradley, A. D. (1979) New York Yearly Meeting at Poplar Ridge and Primitive Friends. *Quaker History*, 68(2), pp.75–82.

Cooper, W. A. (1999) *Growing up plain among Conservative Wilburite Quakers: the journey of a Public Friend.* Richmond, IN: Friends United Press.

Dorland, A. G. (1927) *A history of the Society of Friends (Quakers) in Canada.* Toronto: Macmillan Co. of Canada Lt..

Kuenning, L. (1989) *Quaker theologies in the 19th century separations.* [Online] Available at [http://prwebo.voicenet.com/~kuenning/fot/separations.html].

Marsh, C. (2011) *A Lively Faith: Reflections on Iowa Yearly Meeting of Friends (Conservative).* Philadelphia: FGC QuakerPress.

Taber Jr., W. P. (1985) *The eye of faith: a history of Ohio Yearly Meeting, Conservative.* Barnesville: Representative Meeting of Ohio Yearly Meeting.

Wilson, L. L. (2007) *Essays on the Quaker Vision of Gospel Order.* Philadelphia: Quaker Press of F.G.C.

The websites of the three surviving Conservative Yearly Meetings contain useful information, both historical and contemporary:

Iowa [iymc.org]

North Carolina [ncymc.org]

Ohio [ohioyearlymeeting.org]

PART II

···

QUAKER THEOLOGY AND SPIRITUALITY

···

CHAPTER 9

QUAKERS IN THEOLOGICAL CONTEXT

CAROLE DALE SPENCER

QUAKERISM is an experiential faith that developed, as have all theological traditions, in reaction to and in accord with historical circumstances. Despite a mystical interiority, it was oriented to mission in the world and the creation of alternative communities. For a significant portion of Quakers today the notion of a Quaker theology is an oxymoron. Some may even claim Quakerism is 'atheological' because the tradition has no common unifying vision on its reflections of God, Jesus, scripture, ecclesiology, worship, etc. Several distinctive characteristics of Quakerism allow for it to be even more readily shaped by social and historical trends and conditions than many other religious traditions:

1. Being theoretically non-creedal, its faith is less bound to a written tradition.
2. Being theoretically non-sacramental in its non-use of forms in worship, its theology is less tied to historical liturgical practices, which has paradoxically led to Quakers being uniquely divided by two 'forms' of worship.
3. As a largely experiential faith, its theology tends to emerge and develop from the particular and concrete, including social/political conditions and human needs.
4. As a mystical faith, its primary basis of authority is inner experience, originally called 'the Light Within' or 'the Inward Light of Christ', rather than the authority of scripture or church tradition. In its beginnings, scripture and experience were mutually interwoven.

Such fluidity and malleability have created a theology of paradox and polarities. Each new historical context reshaped Quaker theology, sometimes along two different trajectories, one conserving the earlier tradition and one secularizing the tradition.

The first Quakers focused on the in-dwelling Christ, incarnated as the inward Light or Light Within, more than the historical Jesus, though they would never deny that the Jesus of history was also God incarnate. They proclaimed that Christ must be awakened and experienced inwardly, not simply believed in as a historic figure or event. Quaker preacher James Nayler (1618–60) testified to this 'Divine within' when he wrote: 'None can witness redemption further than Christ is thus revealed in them, to set them free from sin: which Christ I witness to be revealed in me in measure' (Nayler 1653c, 32). This claim is the basis of the original Quaker belief in perfection or union with God.

Isaac Penington (1616–79) wrote: 'It is not enough to hear of Christ, or read of Christ; but this is the thing, to feel him in my root, my life, my foundation; and my soul engrafted into him, by him who hath power to engraft' (Steere 1984, 143). The early Quakers were rediscovering the concept of divinization or *theosis*, the mystical Christology of the early Greek thinkers and medieval mystics (Spencer 2007, 52–3). This mystical understanding of perfection as union with God permeated the devotional literature of radical Puritans in Britain in the early seventeenth century through the translation of the *Theologia Germanica* from Latin into English, as well as the translation of the writings of Jacob Boehme, Johan Tauler, and other Christian mystics into English.

Early Quakers had a deep inner experience of the in-dwelling Christ as the mystical reality that lies beneath ritual and dogma, and viewed the Anglican preoccupation with externals as worshipping the shell and not the Reality. Quakers claimed that the Anglican Church had created a dependency on clergy to mediate God, and like many radical groups in mid-seventeenth-century Britain, they attacked the Church of England as a powerful, hierarchical, and oppressive institution. They mockingly called Anglican churches 'steeple houses'. Since the mid-sixteenth century a strong Puritan movement within Anglicanism had been attempting to 'purify' the church of all its Catholic influences in liturgy, the episcopate, the prayer book, vestments, and music. Quakers went further, rejecting entirely the necessity of outward sacraments, a paid clergy, and compulsory tithes. Other dissenting groups also attacked tithes, but Quakers made it an article of Faith. During the 1640s non-conformist groups rejecting the idea of a national church grew. These groups, including Independents and Baptists, formed a spectrum of English Puritan thought, with Quakers being the final product of radical mystical Puritanism (Nuttall 1946, 151). Other dissenting groups, simply called Seekers, who met in silence without organized churches, and radical political groups such as the Levellers, who believed in natural rights and freedom of religion, provided radical seedbeds for the developing Quaker movement.

Certain elements of early Quaker theology reflect its Puritan/Calvinist heritage, yet at the same time the Quaker movement reacted strongly against the normative Calvinism of the time. While early Quakers had a thorough knowledge and high regard for Scripture they challenged the strict biblicism of the Puritans. Revelation was not confined to scripture but could come directly to individuals inwardly by the same Spirit that inspired the scriptures (Fox 1995, 11). Quakers did not separate Christ the Word from Christ as Spirit. Christ was the Light, which was the way Christ was manifested inwardly to every person and in the created world. They also challenged the Calvinist claims of total depravity, double predestination, and a limited atonement of the elect. While early Quakers did not articulate a particular theology of atonement other than its universality, the cross became a central symbol in Quaker theology. 'The cross' for Quakers was not primarily an objective doctrine (though atonement as salvific would be assumed), but more importantly a daily experiencing of the suffering of Christ. During the period of Quaker persecution, the enacting of the cross was primarily literal suffering, and after the toleration act it became more metaphorical as a mark of discipleship. William Penn wrote, 'The bearing of thy daily Cross is the only true testimony' (Penn 1682, 25). These challenges to the normative Calvinism of the time resulted in Puritan theologians becoming the Quakers' chief opponents.

Because early Quaker writers emphasized Christian experience and practical living over doctrinal assertions, they were less inclined to theologize to create a theoretical foundation for their movement than most Christian traditions. Yet by 1676 Robert Barclay (1648–90), a young, well-educated Scotsman formalized (in Latin) a coherent system of beliefs. In the context of the religious pamphlet wars of that period, early Quaker writings are filled with theological and biblical argumentation in their need to respond to their detractors and defend their orthodoxy. Thus they resorted to theology primarily as apologetics.

Barclay's *Apology for the True Christian Divinity* is the first formal systematic Quaker theology, the most influential, and the only one known to most Quakers (Barclay 2002). But a female theologian, Elizabeth Bathurst (1655–85), overlooked by most Quaker historians until recently, also wrote a scholarly apology for Quaker beliefs called *Truth's Vindication* a few years later (1679). It was widely read and approved by Quaker leaders in the late seventeenth century and reprinted six times throughout the eighteenth century (Garman 1996). Her apology was written to defend Quaker doctrine and to refute high Calvinism, similar to Barclay's purpose. Bathurst also produced a strong defence for the Quaker belief in the equality of men and women in *The Sayings of Women* (Bathurst 1683). The only other document written specifically to address the equality of women is Margaret Fell's *Women's Speaking Justified* in 1666, the most significant theological work of the woman called 'the nursing mother' of the early Quaker movement, and the most prolific female writer (Fell 1667). Fell also wrote the first published statement on the Quaker principle of non-violence, *A Declaration and an Information* (Fell 1660a).

The post-Restoration period, the second generation of the movement, does not exude the same radical edge, revolutionary ideals, or spiritual exuberance as the earlier period, but it was a highly creative period theologically. Though some Quaker historians view it as a period of decline, theological reflection and formulation ensured the survival of the Quaker movement when other radical sects disappeared, and also ensured that its radical social ideals such as the equality of women, and the peace testimony would not be lost, being formally written into its theology.

With Barclay's *Apology*, Quaker theology began to take on its particular shape and form, reacting against the scholasticism and rationalism of the Orthodox Calvinism of its day. Barclay was raised as a strict Calvinist, but in his youth was educated at the Scots College, a Catholic college of the University of Paris in France. He knew well the patristic tradition, the Reformed tradition, and the scholastic style of argumentation. Barclay's theological propositions tended towards a more free-will-oriented Arminianism (a cooperation with the leading of the Spirit rather than predestination). While unique in some of its primary emphasis such as the Light of Christ, contemplative worship, and a non-hierarchical spirit-led leadership, it builds on the Arminian critique of Calvinism, which softened pre-destination and was more universalistic in scope. Scholarly debate on Barclay's relevance to modern Quakerism began to be debated at the turn of the twentieth century with Liberal Quakers generally dismissive of his work as a meaningful expression of Quakerism today and evangelical Quakers appreciative of its basic Christian orthodoxy.

Yet Barclay's view of Scripture was distinctive for its time. He does not claim Scripture as a primary authority; revelation comes through scripture, but is not confined to scrip-ture, allowing for direct revelation to come through the Spirit speaking directly to an individual (yet he is careful to say direct inspiration will not contradict scripture). Primary authority is not the Bible but the Light or Spirit that inspired its words. With the Reformation, and *sola scriptura* still dominating Protestant theology, to suggest otherwise was heretical.

Barclay builds on George Fox's mission 'to direct the people to the Spirit that gave rise to the scripture' (Fox 1995, 34). Up until the strong influence of evangelicalism around the mid-nineteenth century, Quaker theology was unified in the belief that while the Bible is God's revelation to humanity, the meaning and power of the Bible is not revealed until one experiences the Spirit of Christ directly.

The early Quaker movement taught a theology of spiritual empowerment. This empowerment was not just individual but focused on the renewal and revitalization of the community. Early Quaker meetings were groups of the 'perfect,' the holy, not in the sense of sinless, but those in whom the Spirit spoke. Attention to the immediacy of com-munion with God came to the early movement via the medieval mystical tradition, but rather than perfection or union with God being limited to the monastic world, it was freely available to every person living in the secular world. Such was the 'good news' that motivated the great outpouring of Quaker preachers and missionaries. Like their Puritan co-religionists they spurned most of the culture of the secular world, but they were not as world denying as often portrayed. Rather than a stark acceptance or rejection of the world, they focused on what prevented or inhibited growth (worldly culture, customs, arts, sports, frivolities), and what assisted growth (silence, worship, prayer, community, spiritual relationships, disciplines, and observing the natural world). As the immediacy of the experience of Christ declined in succeeding generations, many outward behav-ioural forms replaced the inward experience, and gradually became legalistic codes and sectarian distinctions that separated Quakers from 'the world'.

Early Quakers were thoroughly biblical, evangelistic, even apostolic in their concern for the conversion of individuals and transformation of the world. The world was the place where transformation happened, but balanced between the now and the not-yet, generally referred to as a 'realized eschatology' (Gwyn 1986, xxii).

Initially, military pursuits appealed to the early Quakers as it did to all Calvinists and Puritans as a way to fight evil and bring in God's Kingdom. But gradually a pacifist theology emerged, not only from the experience of the Light of Christ, but also from political disillusionment with the course of the English Civil War. By the 1650s Quakers were articulating a doctrine that individuals at peace with themselves belonged to a spiritual community, which had no use for coercion or violence. By 1661 Quakers issued a statement to Charles II condemning violence under any circumstances.

Anabaptists had been preaching non-violence since the Radical Reformation of the sixteenth century, but a new kind of pacifism emerged with the Quaker 'peace testimony', the first theological statement to combine a rejection of violence with a commitment to social justice and political reform. For example, the Quaker theologian William Penn (1644–1718) wrote a frame of government based on Quaker principles for his colony of Pennsylvania, a new kind of political theology.

After the writings of Barclay, Penn, and Bathurst in the seventeenth century, the Quaker theological tradition became increasingly moribund. Original thinking and theological revisioning were both rare and suspect. But they did develop a kind of mystical theology that became known somewhat disparagingly as Quietism.

QUIETISM

British culture of the late-seventeenth century was vehemently anti-Catholic and Quakers were no exception. Nevertheless, a Quaker mystical theology gradually developed as French Catholic Quietist texts were translated into English, and reinforced Quietist contemplative impulses already current in Barclay and other early Quakers. Quietism became highly controversial and political in France, and was eventually condemned as heresy. Its most prominent woman leader, Jeanne Guyon (1648–1717, was imprisoned in the Bastille. Nevertheless, Quietism had strong appeal to pietistic Protestants, especially Quakers who could identify with Quietist repression and persecution. Quietists taught a form of contemplative prayer in which the human will unites with God's will in a non-differentiated union of pure love (perfection). They believed that God is best known through the prayer of inward silence when all human thought and feeling are quieted. Quaker worship in silence already reflected this apophatic attitude so the attraction to Quietism was a natural one.

Quietism in France, like Quakerism in England, reacted against the philosophical shifts of Cartesian rationalism. Both movements emphasized experience over dogma, lay spirituality, and openness to discerning and responding to God's will. With an experiential ground for authority, both movements extended spiritual leadership to women.

Quakers were the first to translate the writings of Jeanne Guyon into English. In 1698 a treatise attacking Quietism compared Guyon's teachings to the Quakers, entitled *Quakerism, a-la-mode, or A History of Quietism* (Bossuet 1698). By 1813 Guyon's and other Quietist writings were officially published as a devotional manual called *A Guide to True Peace* that quickly became part of the Quaker canon. The goal of prayer in Quaker theology was perfection, or the union of the soul with God. Guyon's writings helped to transform radical Quakerism into mystical Quietism by the beginning of the eighteenth century. Yet it must be noted that while ostensibly an inward-turning, contemplative mystical spirituality, Quietism also contains the seeds of a mysticism of resistance because it instils an indifference to persecution and an absolute devotion to the will of God. This explains why some of Quakerism's most passionate and practical social reformers emerged in the Quietist period, such as John Bellers, John Woolman, and Anthony Benezet who awakened the Society of Friends and the wider world to economic oppression and the inhumanity of slavery well in advance of the 'enlightenment' culture of the time.

An English theologian, the non-juring Anglican priest William Law (1686–1761) began exploring the writings of the Quietists in the eighteenth century. Law's writings also helped shape Quietist Quaker theology. The American Quaker reformer Anthony Benezet (1713–84) recognized the spiritual kinship between Quaker spirituality and William Law's mystical writings. In 1780 he wrote an introduction to Law's *The Spirit of Prayer* and published it bound together with several of his own anti-slavery and anti-war writings (Benezet 1780). Thus Benezet took Law's contemplative mysticism and turned it toward social action. Law's *Spirit of Prayer* provided eighteenth-century Quakers with a fresh language to describe their mystical theology, and Law became the 'de facto' Quaker theologian of the eighteenth century (Jones 1921, 265). After an early anti-Quaker High Church period, Law gradually moved towards Quakerism as he immersed himself in the writings of Jacob Boehme and the French Quietists. Law eventually came to an essential agreement with Quaker principles, including a spiritualized view of the sacraments and the priesthood, a complete opposition to war and the taking of oaths (Law 1776). Though Law lived and died an Anglican, every major tenet of Quakerism can be found in his mystical theology (Hobhouse 1972).

William Law, in his pre-mystical Puritan period, had been mentor to John Wesley (1703–91). Wesley, too, was initially attracted to the Quietists, especially Jeanne Guyon, and included many Quietist texts in his Methodist Library. Early Methodism shared much in common with Quaker theology, such as a belief in universal redemption, and an emphasis on the process of sanctification and perfection. In fact, when Wesley began his field preaching he was derisively called a 'new brand of Quaker' (Baker 1949, 3).

Wesley made a thorough analysis of Barclay's *Apology* and agreed with the majority of its propositions. Although he derisively called it a 'solemn trifle' he considered it important enough to condense portions of it, most notably Barclay's proposition on the universal Light of Christ which he published as his own pamphlet on universal redemption. Early Methodism, like Quakerism, sprouted in the soil of mysticism, but gradually Wesley concluded that the mystic way was not scriptural. Nevertheless, he borrowed much of his teaching on perfection from both the Quietists and the Quakers. Wesley's turn against Quietism helped drive the wedge between mysticism and evangelicalism that fiercely split American Quakerism by the mid-nineteenth century.

NINETEENTH-CENTURY DIVERSITY

In the nineteenth century Quaker theologizing took many divergent paths, creating large-scale schism and defection as well as reformation and renewal. Within each new movement or branch, some historic elements would be conserved (such as silent worship) and others secularized (such as doctrinal beliefs).

At the end of the eighteenth century, revivalist currents in American culture began to spark a renewed missionary zeal within many Quietist Quakers, despite their strict sectarianism. Many of the most active Quaker ministers at this time were converts from other denominations. They brought with them a spiritual passion sparked by the evangelical stirrings that were erupting in the religious culture as a countervailing trend to Deism, scepticism, and Enlightenment rationalism. Quietism was being shaped subtly by the new evangelicalism, a product of the Second Great Awakening in America led by Charles Finney. By 1828 evangelical impulses contributed to the first major split in the Religious Society of Friends. One branch, the Orthodox maintained traditional Christian doctrine, and the other, the Hicksites, claimed the Inward Light as the wholly sufficient authority. Both still worshipped in traditional silence without clergy or sacraments, and both felt they were preserving historic Quaker principles.

Many early Hicksites, including their leader Elias Hicks (1748–1830), were traditional Quaker Quietists whose faith centred on the divine in-dwelling of the mystical Christ. Hicks, a rural travelling minister and self-taught theologian, read the standard Quaker literature, but also some of the leading Enlightenment writers of the time. Hicks is generally considered a mystic because of his primary emphasis on the Light of Christ over scripture and traditional doctrine. Although conservative in many ways, his theology contained a liberal trajectory that upset the delicate balance between the Light of Christ, the authority of scripture, and the outward reality of the incarnation and atonement of Christ that an earlier Quietism had held in tension for over a century. Hicks preached a doctrine of the Light of Christ that he claimed was 'the most rational' that 'no man of right reason could doubt or dispute' (Hicks 1832, 278). He challenged all external authority including the traditional authority of elders, thus he appealed to progressives whose main concern was individual freedom.

Deism and Enlightenment thought made inroads into Hicksite Quakerism despite the long-standing belief that 'Truth' was not discovered by reason, but could only be accessed spiritually by direct revelation. Although early Quakerism implicitly understood God, Christ, and Holy Spirit as divine, they never used the term 'Trinity', nor felt a need to adopt Trinitarian doctrine, so the Deism that became institutionalized in Unitarianism seemed to many the logical conclusion of an enlightened Quaker position. The scientific mindset was appealing to a new breed of intellectual, and educated Quakers and science seemed to be at variance with a religion of divine revelation. The Light of Christ was becoming identified with human conscience, God was no longer immanent in humanity or creation, and mystery was removed from religion, all soundly at variance with the mysticism inherent in all traditional Quakerism.

Another trend influencing spiritually restless and inquiring Quakers in the nineteenth century was the Romantic movement, institutionalized in Transcendentalism. Transcendentalism tends toward pantheism rather than Deism, and is more mystical in that ultimate truth remains a spiritual category and can be accessed by an individual through heightened intuition. Ralph Waldo Emerson

(1803–82), perhaps the first self-proclaimed 'spiritual but not religious' soul in America, when asked to define his religious position answered, 'I am more of a Quaker than anything else. I believe in the "still, small voice," and that voice is Christ within us' (Tolles 1938, 142). Emerson maintained that the essential doctrines of Quakers 'revived, modified, stript of all that Puritanism and sectarianism had heaped upon them' corresponded to Transcendentalist thought (Tolles 1938, 143). Walt Whitman (1819–1892), who had a Quaker background, but never joined the Society of Friends, constructed the values of Elias Hicks, as he interpreted them, into a Quaker Hicksite aesthetic (Cummings 1998, 75). In Transcendentalism, the Quaker Light of Christ (Inward Light of Christ) evolved into a more secular 'Inner Light' of nature mysticism and self-realization.

REVIVALISM

Beginning in the 1830s a third spiritual awakening swept North America, the Holiness Revival, which has been called 'Transcendentalism for the masses' (Smith 1980). The emphasis on personal experience, awakening to sanctification or holiness of life, and initially, on social reform, captivated many Quakers hungry for spiritual renewal in the mid-nineteenth century.

The historic practice of transatlantic travel in ministry continued throughout this period. Joseph John Gurney (1788–1847), an English banker, brought lasting new theological trends into American Orthodox Quakerism through a short but transformative visit to the United States from 1837–40. Gurney's wealth enabled him to study at Oxford with private tutors, privileging him with a scholarly theological education not normally available to Quakers. Since many of his teachers, friends, and associates were Anglican, he brought impulses from the wider world of Christian faith and a moderate, but passionate evangelicalism into the Religious Society of Friends. He retained a deeply Quietist spirituality in worship and prayer, along with a reformer's zeal to bring Quakerism into the modern world through religious education, bible study, missions, and ecumenical endeavours with other Christians. Gurney preceded any strong revivalist impulses among Friends, but he set the stage for a new type of spiritual renewal with his emphasis on the authority of the Bible, and spoke of the Light of Christ specifically as the work of the Holy Spirit. Gurney was a passionate Christian and a powerful public minister, but he was not a mystic (Spencer 2007, 137).

Travelling ministers, such as Gurney, who ventured outside of the Quaker 'hedge' became exposed to the currents of early nineteenth-century evangelicalism and became the new 'evangelists'. Quakers were beginning to read more broadly outside the approved Quaker canon. They were also gradually, but tentatively, joining with other Evangelicals in reform activities, most notably temperance and anti-slavery work, and some even plunged into politics. Many Quakers, feeling the fresh winds of the Spirit, felt they were recovering their own 'first principles.'

In British Quakerism, London Yearly Meeting at the beginning of 1800 was essentially Orthodox and evangelical. Evangelicalism (as it was expressed in that time) meant accepting the traditional Christian tenets of original sin, the incarnation, and atonement, salvation through Christ, the authority of scripture, an expectation of a conversion experience, the encouragement of evangelism to share faith, and sanctification or perfection to live out one's faith.

Quakerism in Britain was only mildly affected by the controversies and splits that had so convulsed American Quakerism. The British response to Hicksism in America was to cut off correspondence with the Hicksite bodies. British Quakerism was sociologically more homogeneous than American Quakerism and closely allied with the prosperous business classes. British Quakers' experiments with Sunday schools, evangelism, and local mission work had some success in gaining converts, but struggled to overcome its tendency towards paternalism and classism. Converts from the working classes who desired more expressive worship with music, teaching, and preaching were provided with their own separate meetings, but never integrated into the established Society of Friends.

By the end of the century evangelicalism in Britain was rapidly being eclipsed by Modernism. Gurney, though a respected religious leader in Britain in his time, was largely forgotten by the turn of the century, but ironically had his most lasting impact upon American Quakers. Gurney adopted a distinctive Wesleyan view of sanctification as a subsequent experience to justification. While this seems a fine point of theological hair-splitting today, it became a matter of heated debate in the explosion of revivalist fervour that burst upon the next generation of Gurneyite Quakers and led to even greater theological and ecclesiastic shifts within the Orthodox branch of Friends in America.

The repercussions of Gurney's visit split the Orthodox into two polarizing camps. The more evangelically oriented, considered progressives and liberals within Quaker Orthodoxy, were called Gurneyites. A smaller faction, who rallied around an outspoken critic of Gurney, Quietist minister from New England John Wilbur (1774–1856), and were called Wilburites. The Wilburites opposed Gurney's evangelical orientation over the mystical, favoured maintaining the Quaker hedge, and adherence to the traditional 'peculiarities' of dress and speech as community identification and coherence. Holding essentially orthodox Christian views, but primitivist and sectarian in lifestyle, they objected to what they perceived as Gurney's emphasis on the authority of Scripture over the reality of the indwelling Christ.

The Holiness Revival of the nineteenth century was an American cultural phenomenon that spread to Britain where it was known as the Keswick Movement. It arose initially within American Methodism through the leadership of individuals who felt Wesley's doctrine of Christian perfection was being neglected. One of the early leaders, a laywoman called Phoebe Palmer, gathered groups of ministers and religious leaders from a variety of denominations to 'Tuesday meetings for the promotion of holiness' in her home in New York. By the turn of the nineteenth century, the Holiness Revival spawned the Pentecostalism movement, which added the element of speaking in tongues to the revival atmosphere. This new spiritual movement drew into its stream some Quaker leaders as well, such as A. J. Tomlinson, an Indiana Friend who founded one of the largest Pentecostal denominations, the Church of God, Cleveland.

As the Holiness revivals spread, churches of all denominations came under its spell. Methodist evangelists led the way but prominent leaders arose within every Protestant denomination. Of all the many Protestant traditions to be impacted by this spiritual renewal movement none was as radically transformed as the Society of Friends. While forces of acculturation played a major role in transforming traditional silent meetings into the Friends Church, the impact of the Holiness Movement accelerated the process exponentially. Within a space of forty years (1860–95) about two-thirds of American Quakers adopted a Wesleyan-style theology reflected in new practices and new ecclesiology, and even new architecture. Plain Quaker meeting houses became Friends churches with pulpits, 'mourner's benches', stained-glass windows, and even the occasional steeple-like artefact. Traditional travelling ministers became settled paid pastors. Worship was no longer centred on silent waiting, but pastoral preaching and praying, with congregational singing, altar calls, and public testimonies as standard participatory practices. The emotional tone of revivals was a sharp change from the silent, decorous meetings of eighteenth-century Quaker Quietism, but the physical manifestations of enthusiasm and ecstasy, such as 'trembling' (from whence comes the name Quaker) seemed to many, the signs of a return to the spiritual power of the radical beginnings of the Quaker movement.

In many Yearly Meetings, Wesleyan theology and the literature of the National Holiness Association superseded the writings of Fox and Barclay. The new theology shaped by the revival atmosphere turned sanctification into a second crisis experience, elicited by an altar call. The phrase 'baptism of the Spirit' a familiar one to all Quakers, was reinterpreted to mean 'instantaneous sanctification,' or 'the second blessing'.

One other theological modification affecting traditional Quaker 'realized eschatology' came through the changing currents of nineteenth-century evangelicalism. While pre-Civil War evangelicalism was largely post-millennial, after the war a gradual shift to a pre-millennial eschatology took place. This change was greatly facilitated by the popularity of prophecy conferences in America in the late nineteenth century. Many Holiness Quakers adopted this new eschatology, a radical shift from an optimistic social vision of working towards a 'peaceable kingdom' in this world, to a focus on saving individual souls from a world viewed as a sinking ship.

The primary theologian of the Quaker Holiness Movement was Dougan Clark (1828–1896), who established the Biblical department at Earlham College, a Gurneyite school in Indiana. His book, *The Theology of Holiness*, became the standard interpretation of Holiness Quakerism, but also grounds for his dismissal at Earlham. Elbert Russell (1871–1951), an anti-revivalist and Modernist, who represented a liberal turning movement among Gurneyites, replaced him in 1895. Clark had become a leader, along with the most prominent of the revival ministers, David B. Updegraff (1830–94), of the most radical wing of the Holiness Movement, the 'water party'. The gradual adoption of Wesleyan theology and the eagerness to conform to mainstream evangelicalism, created a uniquely Quaker controversy among the Gurneyites—the Waterite crisis. The Holiness revivalists were so zealous in their reform of Quietist Quaker practices that for many, all traces of distinctiveness had to be eliminated, even those already being relaxed among Gurneyites, The new practices of outward baptism and communion were promoted as 'toleration' and 'liberty of conscience'. For revivalists the 'peculiar' traditional Quaker practices of outward forms of plain dress, speech, and silent worship, were non-essentials, not supported by Scripture. A movement emerged to rethink the forms that were accepted by all other evangelical Christians—water baptism and communion. For many Holiness leaders these forms seemed to be biblical commands, and beginning in the 1870s a few Quaker ministers submitted to water baptism (Hamm 1988, 130). By the 1880s some of the most prominent Quaker evangelists were baptized boldly and publically, shocking the Orthodox establishment, and creating a strong reaction against tolerating any outward forms of the ordinances. This particular adaptation of allowing the inward sacraments to be expressed outwardly became the most threatening to the Quaker theological tradition of apophatic, inward spiritual experience. Fierce opposition to this most tenaciously held distinction split the revival movement and the more radical wing lost much of its power and influence. Only one Yearly Meeting, Ohio, in 1886 allowed 'toleration' of the 'outward ordinances' (Hamm 1988, 136). Most Evangelical Quaker churches today still uphold the traditional understanding of inward baptism and communion as the only necessary sacraments, but give freedom to those who find outward expressions helpful rituals.

The fierce controversies over the question of ordinances, the meaning of sanctification, the nature of worship and ministry, and the role of Scripture led to a call for the creation of a uniform 'Declaration of Faith'. A conference was organized in Richmond, Indiana, the centre of Gurneyite Quakerism, in 1887. Delegates were invited from all Orthodox yearly meetings (Hicksites were thus excluded). The theological principles formulated at this gathering attempted to balance tradition with reform, restraining extreme holiness theology, and upholding traditional opposition to outward and material sacraments. Its statement on Scripture was more fully evangelical with less emphasis on the primacy of the Light of Christ. Although it did not please many of the constituency, it became the 'uniform discipline' for a centralized body of Gurneyite moderates who became the Friends United Meeting in 1902, setting up boards to work together for evangelism, mission work, outreach, and education. Neither London nor Philadelphia, nor the holiness stronghold of Ohio, adopted the Richmond Declaration of Faith, and remained largely separate from this new modern branch of Quakerism, which, after immense travail, had successfully adapted itself to the evangelical mainstream of American culture while maintaining some historical distinctives. The Richmond Declaration proved one way of creating a new synthesis between the historic Quaker tradition and the demands of a changing culture.

By the end of the nineteenth century, Quakers had created four different spiritual paths or theological approaches. While each path had developed into a formal branch of Friends in America, individuals and meetings pursuing these different approaches could also be found within all branches. The four were:

1. A primitivist path that adhered to historic Quaker traditions, Orthodox in its theology but anti-revival, separatist, sectarian, and inward-turning, emphasizing the traditional Quaker understanding of holiness as a life-long process of following the Inward Light of Christ (Light Within). Called Wilburites in the nineteenth century, they are known as Conservative Friends today.

2. A holiness wing, strongly Wesleyan in its theology, evangelistic and missional, emphasizing conversion and sanctification as a second work of grace, toleration for ordinances (though never as a means of grace), and upholding Scripture as the primary authority, with minimal emphasis on the Light, silence, or inwardness. Gurneyite revivalists were strongest in Ohio Yearly Meeting but spread westwards into Iowa, Oregon, and California. They became the Evangelical Friends Church in the twentieth century.

3. A liberal, social-activist wing, anti-revival, humanistic, rational, and progressive, open to Enlightenment thought and a scientific critique of traditional Christianity. Hicksites in America, and London Yearly Meeting in Britain, and some Orthodox were moving in this direction. They became Friends General Conference in America.

4. An evangelical and ecumenical mainstream, Orthodox in doctrine, open to renewal through innovations such as pastors and programmed worship, and a uniform declaration of faith, but valuing some distinct practices such as silence and traditional Quaker testimonies. They became Friends United Meeting.

MODERNISM AND LIBERALISM

By the turn of the twentieth century, a strong need for a new vision of Quakerism had emerged as revivalists and moderate Gurneyites battled for influence and leadership, and the Uniform disciple did not bring uniformity. While the Gurneyite reformers were finding ways to adapt theologically to a changing culture, they were not yet Modernists. The turn to theological liberalism, progressive revelation, higher criticism of the Bible, and evolutionary theory, began to transform moderate Gurneyites through the influence of Rufus M. Jones (1863–1948), the leading voice for Modernism in American Quakerism in the early twentieth century.

The major life goal of Jones, a theologian, historian, and philosopher, was to create a fresh, new interpretation of Quaker history and theology by penetrating to the heart of the early movement. That heart, Jones declared, was its core belief in what he termed the 'Inner Light .... the doctrine that there is something Divine, "something of God" in the human soul' (Jones 1904, 149). Jones formulated the first theory of Quaker origins as essentially mystical, and Quaker silent worship as group mysticism: 'No other large, organized, historically continuous body of Christians has yet existed which has been so fundamentally mystical, both in theory and practice, as the Society of Friends ...' (Jones,

1921, xiii). In the early twentieth century, psychological, theological, and comparative studies of mysticism were flourishing. Jones determined to preserve the mysticism
inherent in Quaker origins by reinterpreting it in light of William James's psychological theories on religious experience. Jones created an 'affirmative mysticism', a modern humanist construct shaped in part by Transcendentalism. Affirmative mysticism
meant experiencing God within the self and affirming the goodness of the world and
the person. An ethical mysticism, it is expressed in active service as love of neighbour,
which his own life modelled in his establishment and directing of the American Friends
Service Committee. Affirmative mysticism countered what Jones perceived as a self-
and world-denying negative mysticism, which he felt had infected Quaker Quietism
through the 'classic Catholic model' (Jones 1931, 12–13). Jones's 'inner light mysticism'
spread throughout Friends, both Gurneyite and Hicksite, who found it intellectually
appealing and culturally relevant. While Jones used William James and Emerson to
understand human nature, later Liberal Quakers would use Freud and Jung.

Clearly Jones was indebted theologically to Friedrich Schleiermacher (1768–1834)
and Samuel Taylor Coleridge (1772–1834) in founding Modernist Quaker theology solely upon the distinctive character of human experience. In Coleridge's view,
Christianity is not a set of doctrines but a way of life, 'Try it' he wrote in *Aids to Reflection*
(Coleridge 1825, 195). The mantra of Liberal Quakerism in the twentieth century echoed this: 'We believe in life, not doctrines' (Wilson, 1948, 12). This shift, beginning early
in the twentieth century, of Quakerism as a way of life without a need for any shared core
beliefs is reinforced in British theologian Janet Scott's 1980 Swarthmore Lecture. On the
question as to whether a Quaker must necessarily be a Christian she writes: 'what matters to Quakers is not the label by which we are called or call ourselves, but the life' (Scott
1980, 70).

A friend and colleague of Jones who helped usher in the turn to Modernism at the
end of the nineteenth century was Englishman J. Rendel Harris (1852–1941), one of
the few Quaker biblical scholars since Gurney. Harris was a Christocentric mystic, an
internationally known New Testament scholar, and collector of ancient manuscripts. He
was a prolific writer of both scholarly and spiritual works, and a strong Modernist voice
in Quaker studies. Yet deeply affected by the Keswick Holiness movement early in his
life, he felt a lifelong affinity with the holiness tradition, and his spiritual life reflected
an evangelical piety. While he cautioned Rufus Jones against fostering a 'Christless
Quakerism' (Spencer 2007, 203) he publicly promoted evolutionary theory and biblical
criticism. He became the first Director of Studies of the educational experiment known
as Woodbrooke College in 1903, a Quaker study centre in Birmingham, England established to strengthen and enrich the spiritual and intellectual life of Friends.

Another significant theological voice for Friends in the transitional era from evangelical to Modernist Quakerism was Hannah Whitall Smith (1832–1911) who became a
popular evangelical speaker and author of spiritual books. She was, in effect, a lay theologian, since even among the egalitarian Quakers, women did not yet have access to higher
education before 1864. Smith is best known today for her bestselling book of practical
holiness theology, *The Christian's Secret of a Happy Life,* still in print (1875). Smith was

raised as an Orthodox Quaker in Philadelphia, but finding their lifestyle too narrow and confining, and their theology too vague, she left her Yearly Meeting and sought a more vital Christian spirituality elsewhere. She became prominent as a 'Bible teacher' in the Holiness Revival, and a key figure in the beginnings of the Keswick movement in England. She spent the latter part of her life in England, writing books and connecting with people through a vast network of correspondence. She was a figure of startling contrasts and contradictions. A prominent Victorian evangelical, she was also an outspoken feminist and a universalist. Like J. Rendel Harris, she combined her Quaker faith with holiness theology, evangelicalism, mysticism, and modernism, trends deeply dividing Friends. Her autobiography, *The Unselfishness of God*, describes her spiritual journey and the transformation of Quakerism in her lifetime (Smith 1903).

Another significant figure who interjected a renewal of a Christocentric mysticism to Quaker life and faith was Thomas Kelly (1893–1941). Kelly was a student of Rufus Jones at Haverford College who succeeded him as Professor of Philosophy. Though raised in Ohio as a holiness Quaker, he took an intellectual approach to faith after college, relentlessly pursuing the life of the mind until 1938 when, in Nazi Germany, he had a transformative spiritual experience. After his untimely death, his writings were collected and published as a book, *A Testament of Devotion*, which became a bestseller (Kelly 1941). Kelly's life reflects the shifts and reactions to the changing religious landscape in the Quaker world in the first half of the twentieth century. His immersion in the study of the Christian mystics through the influence of Rufus Jones and his broad educational and cultural background combined to enable Kelly to write about the spiritual life in a way that spoke across all of the competing branches of Friends and beyond Quaker circles. Kelly articulated a mysticism that was Christian but not exclusive, contemplative but not otherworldly, and socially relevant and practical.

Douglas V. Steere (1901–95) and Richard J. Foster (1942–), are two contemporary Quaker writers on the theology of prayer, worship, and spiritual practices, who bridge the gap between evangelical and Liberal Friends. Steere was a professor of Philosophy at Haverford, a contemplative and ecumenical Friend, and scholar of existentialist philosopher Søren Kierkegaard. Foster, an Evangelical Friend and former Friends pastor, wrote *Celebration of Discipline*, a groundbreaking work on spiritual formation and practice (Foster 1978). Through his many popular books that include anthologies of spiritual writings from a great variety of spiritual traditions, Foster almost single-handedly retrieved the Christian mystical tradition and the practice of meditation and contemplation from a century of neglect by Evangelical Friends. Foster may be the best-known and most widely read Quaker theologian today, but he is a practical theologian, not an academic.

CONTEMPORARY THEOLOGICAL TRENDS

In many ways, early Quakers understood the Bible in a liberationist way, that it was written for oppressed people, to empower the powerless, laypersons, women, and those on the margins, thus their own experience helped shape their understanding of it. Seventeenth-century Quakers scandalized their contemporaries by affirming the right of women to preach in public. While this tradition of gender equality has always been a strong element of Quaker theology, its practice has not always matched theory. Yet, in all stages of its history and in all of its diverse branches, women have been ministers, leaders, and later even pastors in evangelical meetings. Quaker women were at the forefront of the women's suffrage movement in the nineteenth century and strong advocates for women's rights in the twentieth. Quaker theology was foundational to the women's movement in the writings of its early leaders, Lucretia Mott and Angelina and Sarah Grimke. Most unprogrammed and Liberal Quakers have been deeply influenced by contemporary feminist and liberation theologies. Evangelical Friends vary widely on the importance of feminist theology. However, some evangelicals, both women and men, are strong advocates for gender equality, and write and speak on issues of sexism within Christianity and within their own Yearly Meetings. Many Quaker feminists draw heavily on non-Quaker theologians, especially the pioneering feminist theologian Rosemary Radford Reuther who has written extensively on the feminist theology inherent in the Quaker movement, noting the link between feminism and peacemaking among Quaker peace activists. Her prolific writing on all aspects of liberation theology, including critiques of racism, patriarchy, hierarchy, and domination of nature, resonates with contemporary Quaker thought. Reuther wrote an introduction to an important anthology of seventeenth-century documents written by Quaker women, *Hidden in Plain Sight,* compiled and edited by four American Quaker feminist authors.

Many Liberal Quakers today call themselves Universalists; some are Christian inclusivists in which Christ is the Light in everyone, whatever that Light may be named. Universalists work to promote dialogue between practitioners of diverse religions. For many Universalists, religious experience has a universal character, which is the core of all the world's religions, and all religious experience is culturally determined. Each religion is seen as a different response to the divine reality and is constantly evolving through the flux of history. Particular religious traditions are simply the names and forms in which spiritual experience can be expressed and passed on. Pluralists encourage immersion in the culture and practices of other faiths to experience them directly. Thus many 'hyphenated Quakers' of 'double belonging' have emerged, such as Buddhist-Quakers and Jewish-Quakers. Universalists try to give expression to this intercultural consciousness by the use of generic language to convey truths that can be shared among all religions as they gradually converge.

Postmodern, post-Christian Quakers focus not on religious experience, faith, or beliefs, but on the common ground of global responsibility for the wellbeing of the whole earth, a shift from the mystical dimension to the practical or pragmatic. For them, salvation is human and ecological wellbeing or wholeness (holiness in pluralistic terms). Right action or behaviour (orthopraxy) has priority over right beliefs (orthodoxy). In the post-modern context, universalistic theories of religious or mystical experience are giving way to a common praxis of sociopolitical or ethical engagement.

As Quakerism developed from a Christocentric mystical protest movement in the mid-seventeenth century, its theology has been shaped by the same secularizing, cultural forces affecting all religious movements. Those that left the most indelible impact upon the Quaker movement have been Quietism, revivalism (in its Wesleyan/holiness form), evangelicalism, romanticism, Modernism, post-Modernism, and interfaith spirituality. Worldwide, the majority of Quakers today remain evangelical and pastoral. British Quakerism remains entirely unprogrammed and non-pastoral, and all but a tiny minority are liberals and many are post-Christian, mirroring the sharp secularization of Christianity in Europe. But wide diversity of belief does not mean that liberals have no sources of authority. For British Quakerism, final authority resides with the Yearly Meeting and its book of discipline.

In the United States, about two-thirds of Quakers are evangelical and pastoral, and many churches are generically evangelical having adapted their theology to fit the mainstream Christian culture. For these Friends, identity as Christians comes first, and Quaker identity second, and for some it is only a historical accident. For Liberal and unprogrammed Friends, identity as Quakers is primary, and may or may not include identity with Christianity. Adherence to historical Quaker distinctives, particularly form of worship, the peace testimony, and human equality, are the primary theological commitments for unprogrammed Friends, but these 'testimonies', while having a historical core have been broadly influenced and conditioned by secular culture.

The growing edge of Quakerism is in the Global South, especially Bolivia and Kenya. In Kenya alone, where Quaker missions were planted in the beginning of the twentieth century, there are more Quakers than in all of North America. This shifting of the Quaker centre of gravity to the Global South and Africa in particular, reflects the Christianization of Africa overall, from nine per cent Christian in 1900 to over fifty per cent today. Quaker missionaries introduced a Western, Protestant, evangelical orthodoxy to Kenyans that continues to shape the Kenyan Quaker church at present. An indigenous post-colonial Kenyan Quaker theology is only beginning to emerge. Most Quakers in the Global South are theologically and socially conservative, and almost exclusively pastoral.

As a result of these many adaptations and syntheses over 350 years, Quaker theology today ranges widely and eclectically from conservative evangelical to non-theist. As broad as these polarities are (with the exception of the most extreme poles), three theological commonalities may be claimed for Quakerism worldwide: 1) the mystical seed of direct encounter with transcendence. But how that experience is described and interpreted as Christ, Spirit, Reality, or Light and Love, etc. will be shaped by the language of the particular community; 2) a consensual, voteless form of decision-making used in Business Meetings, having it roots in the commitment to the guidance and leading of the Spirit (Rufus Jones's group mysticism); and 3) a general commitment to the peace testimony and non-violence, though strength of adherence to pacifism will vary widely.

Suggested Further Reading

Barclay, R. (2002 [1678]) *An apology for the true Christian Divinity.* Glenside, PA: Quaker Heritage Press.

Dandelion, P. (2007) *An introduction to Quakerism.* Cambridge: Cambridge University Press.

Fox, G. (1995 [1952]) *The journal of George Fox.* J. L. Nickalls, (ed.), Philadelphia: Religious Society of Friends.

Garman, M., Applegate, J., Benefiel, M., and Meredith, D. (1996) *Hidden in plain sight: Quaker women's writings 1650–1700.* Wallingford, PA: Pendle Hill Publications.

Hamm, T. D. (1988) *The transformation of American Quakerism: Orthodox Friends, 1800–1907.* Bloomington, IN: Indiana University Press.

Hobhouse, S. (1972) *William Law and eighteenth century Quakerism, including some unpublished letters and fragments of William Law and John Byrom.* New York, NY: Benjamin Blom, Inc.

Jones, R. M. (1904) *Social law in the Spiritual World: Studies in human and divine inter-relationship.* Philadelphia, PA and Chicago, IL: The John Winston Co.

Smith, Hannah Whitall (1903) *My spiritual autobiography or How I discovered the unselfishness of God.* New York, NY: Fleming H. Revel Company.

Spencer, Carole Dale (2007) *Holiness: The Soul of Quakerism: An historical analysis of the theology of holiness in the Quaker tradition.* Milton Keynes: Paternoster.

CHAPTER 10

....

GOD, CHRIST, AND THE LIGHT

....

STEPHEN W. ANGELL

SEVENTEENTH-CENTURY VIEWS

....

THE earliest Quakers had a robust view of the power of both the God of the universe and God within each person. 'The Lord God of heaven & Earth' prompted Quaker Margaret Fell (1614–1702) in 1653 to warn Oliver Cromwell to 'harken to the light of god in thy Conscience, which is the Light of Christ: who doth enlighten everyone that comes into the world', (Glines 2003, 36) appealing to John 1:9. Here Fell combined several themes characteristic of the first generation of Quakers. God was seen as all-powerful, everlasting, and unchanging, and in charge of external affairs, all classical theological positions. In a 1653 letter to Anthony Pearson, Margaret Fell made the apocalyptic argument that the 'Lord...is workeing for his owne glory & will set up his owne kingdome....He will breake to pieces at his appointed time all their powers, that is irrected against him and his truth' (Glines 2003, 22). Even after Quaker apocalypticism faded, early Quakers maintained a strong belief in God's outward power. That 'the power of God is over all' was a persistent theme sounded in George Fox's (1624–91) *Journal* dictated in the 1670s, a faith Fox saw vindicated in, among other things, some untimely deaths of Friends' persecutors. This classical theism was not very controversial among seventeenth-century contemporaries. In his 1676 *Apology for the True Christian Divinity*, Robert Barclay (1648–90) required less than 900 words to vindicate his first proposition that 'the height' of human happiness rests upon 'the true knowledge of God' (Barclay 2002, 19–21), far fewer words than those lavished upon any of his remaining fourteen propositions.

More distinctive for early Friends was their advocacy of a divine Light of Christ universally present in all humanity and capable of saving all. Christ's Light served several functions. Friends warned that the first function of the Light was to expose one's sins (John 3:19–21). It brought about a 'day of visitation' in one's soul. If not attended to, it would leave one at the peril of God's wrathful judgement (Fox 1671, 12; Barbour 1964, 94–126). Thus confession and repentance were in order for all, if one were to be obedient to the Light of Christ. Persecutors of Quakers should especially take note. To John Sawrey, a Puritan justice who sought to obstruct Quakers' ministry, Fell urged that 'the Light of Christ in thy conscience if thou harken to it' awaken him to his 'blind fleshly carnall knowledge', so that he would avoid the 'flames of fire taking vengeance on them that know not God' (Glines 2003, 41). Early Quakers located the Light in the 'conscience', not indicating an equivalence (often asserting that while the Light was a supernatural function, conscience was a natural one) but rather a similarity in purpose: both enabled individuals and groups to distinguish between good and evil, but the Light reliably so (Underwood 1997, 102–4).

Most Quakers were Puritan in their disdain of natural reason. In *The Great Mystery of the Great Whore Unfolded,* Fox asserted, 'No man walks by the light of reason but he who is in the faith, who is in the light of the gospel, and all other reason is as the beasts of the field' (Angell 1992, 78). An exception was William Penn (1644–1718), when he addressed toleration tracts to a non-Quaker audience. In *An Address to Protestants,* Penn wrote, 'Since Mankind is a reasonable Creature, and that the more reasonable he is in his Religion, the nearer to his own being he comes, and to the Wisdom and Truth of his Creator' (Penn 1679, 188). After the Toleration Act was passed in 1689, Penn clarified that this 'reason' was 'divine reason' or 'right reason' (Angell 1992, 80–1).

As Fox declared in a 1658 letter to Elizabeth Claypole, however, the Light that discovers sin, 'temptations, confusions, [and] distractions' also leads to the power of an 'endless' life in God (Fox 1995, 347). Once the Light searched out one's sins, one ought not dwell on that sight, but rather turn towards and look at the Light, in which one will find grace, strength, peace, and power. Waiting in the Light, one was able to dwell in, and to walk in, the Light (I John 1:7). Hence the persistent emphasis of Friends on a life of holiness, even the possibility of perfection.

Quakers' Puritan opponents often charged that the Quakers' Light was not Christ, inasmuch as it was a principle and not integrally related to the person of Christ, as known through the Gospels. This was not an easy charge for Quakers to refute. Their image of the Light was biblically derived. However, there was a closer relationship between the Light of Christ with the Gospel of John and the first Epistle of John, than there was with the Christ of the synoptic Gospels. To a Puritan opponent James Cave, Fell wrote that 'we say Christ Jesus…is the light of the world (John 8:12) and the Condemnation of thee and all that is in the world'. Quoting John 12:35–6, Fell asked, 'Doth not Jesus Christ say walke while yee have light, least darknes come, for he that walkes in darkness knoweth not whither he goes, while yee have light believe in the light, that yee may be the Children of the Light?' (Glines 2003, 159, 162).

In her epistles, Fell's use of the synoptic Christ was complex. About half of her appeals to texts from synoptic gospels were introduced with words such as, 'Christ saith', denoting an outward Jesus. In other mentions, she eschewed such prefacing, thus denoting the saints' internal condition, or their expectation of Christ's imminent return. The outward Christ usefully articulated commandments, such as that against swearing oaths (Glines 2003, 153), that the 'world' was inclined to ignore. Still, Quakers such as Fell believed that there was no salvation without an intimate acquaintance with the motions of the inward Christ, the Light. There was substantial internal disagreement on this subject in the 1690s, when George Keith accused other Quakers of ignoring the historic Jesus.

Quakers made complex use of the word 'Seed' in their Christology, like the Light a set of biblical images. Sometimes, the word 'Seed' meant a 'descendant', as in Genesis 3:15, where God tells the serpent that enmity will be put between him and the woman, 'between thy seed and her seed' (AV). For Quakers, such as Fell, this verse engendered a distinction between the 'righteous seed' (the seed of the woman, the seed of God, Christ), and the 'seed of the serpent' (the devil, the seed that crucified Christ, the seed that denies the Light) (Glines 2003, 36, 159). Christ will triumph over the 'seed of the serpent' (Gen. 3:15). In other contexts, 'seed' is used as a botanical metaphor; thus, in Barclay's *Apology*, the seed is that divine aspect that grows to greater Life under the influence of the Light (Moore 2000, 82–3).

Early Friends explored possible aspects of the Light that many contemporaries found blasphemous. Sometimes, they championed a view of the Christ within as 'celestial flesh', a Christopresentist view that maintained both a physical as well as a spiritual presence of Christ within a Friend. James Nayler's ride into Bristol in 1656, for which he was severely punished by Parliament, was a high-profile instance of a prominent Quaker assuming Christological acclaim, but it was not the only such instance. Fox and other Friends also embraced appellations such as Son or Daughter of God that linked them to Christ. In Fox's case, at its most puzzling, this sometimes verged on worship towards Fox, as other Quakers bowed down to what they saw as God in Fox, not to the creaturely (Bailey 1992, 132–3). Fox claimed powers to produce miracles that were possessed by the historic Jesus and his apostles. This type of Quaker spirituality diminished rapidly during the early decades; there is little evidence of it in the writings of second-generation Friends such as Barclay and Penn. Much evidence of the first generation's more extreme identifications with Christ was suppressed, only to be recovered somewhat by Quaker scholars in later centuries (Tarter 2004, 89–94; Bailey 1992).

It was not necessarily believed that all persons had equal access to the illuminations of the Light of Christ within. Each was to be faithful to the Light according to one's 'measure', a formulation influenced by 2 Corinthians 10 and Ephesians 4. If one was faithful to one's present measure, it was believed that a greater measure would be granted by God (Barclay 2002, 120–1).

Quakers placed little importance on the Trinitarian or Christological formulations of the early Church councils. We may take as representative Robert Barclay, who makes no reference to any of the councils held at Nicaea, and only one peripheral reference to the Council of Chalcedon (Barclay 2002). Fox tended to view the Nicene concept of the Trinity with three distinct, separate persons in the godhead as a 'notion,' i.e., a speculative theological concept with little or no experiential grounding (Ingle 1994, 111). Nevertheless, early Quakers, including Fox, generally affirmed that God was Father, Son, and Spirit, and that these three manifestations of God are one, although they rejected the use of the unbiblical word 'trinity'(Underwood 1997, 45–7; Fox 1682, 27–8). Rosemary Moore makes the intriguing suggestion that perhaps Fox's thought was really quaternitarian, focusing on four aspects to the godhead, citing Fox's affirmation that 'the Father and the Son, and the Spirit of truth, and that of God in every one's

Conscience shall bear witness unto us' (Moore 2000, 109). In delving into William Penn's thought, Hugh Barbour determined that Penn believed Quaker trinitarianism was less Nicaean than Sabellian (Sabellius was a second-century Christian theologian who more tightly linked the three aspects of the Trinity than the later doctrine approved in Nicaea) (Barbour 1979, 170).

Early Quakers did not write much about the work of Christ or atonement, due primarily to their de-emphasis of Jesus' historicity. Barclay announced that Quakers do not 'derogate' from Christ's atonement, 'but...do magnify and exalt it', but he quickly returned to the more comfortable topic of the inward Light of Christ (Barclay 2002, 122). In 1668, Penn criticized Anselm's view that through his death Christ paid the debt that humans owed to God. The Light leads humans to an 'actual obedience unto right-eousness', not to a righteousness imputed to us by a good Christ's death on our behalf. In 1696, Penn embraced dual meanings for Christ's atonement. Outwardly Christ 'bore our iniquities', but his atonement also had a strong inward dimension: 'through the offering up of himself once for all, through the Eternal Spirit, he hath forever perfected those (in all times) that were sanctified' (Barbour 1991, I, 220–9; II, 621).

Especially controversial was early Friends' universalism, namely, their insistence that Christ, through the Light, could reach people of every era and country, regardless of whether the gospel was preached to them outwardly. Colossians 1:23, that the 'gospel that you heard...has been proclaimed in every creature under heaven', was oft cited by Quakers in this context (Angell 2006b). Thus Fox refuted a Presbyterian in North Carolina who claimed that American Indians did not have Christ in them. Summoning an Indian, Fox 'asked him if that...when he did wrong was not there something in him, that did tell him of it, that he should not do so, but did reprove him. And he said there was such a thing in him.' This Fox regarded as experimental confirmation of a saving Light of Christ within all (Fox 1995, 642). Penn, in his *Christian Quaker* (1674), expounded the evidence for the Light of Christ in holy persons who lived before Jesus, especially highlighting the Greek philosophers of the pre-Christian era (Barbour 1991, 316–24).

Early Quakers talked about a 'covenant of light', or in Fox's words, an 'everlasting covenant of light, life, and peace'. In contrast with the Puritans' 'covenant of grace', the covenant of light, which came from the 'father of lights' (James 1:17), connoted the inward Christ ready to teach Christ's people himself and to lead them into righteous-ness and truth. The 'covenant of light' leads to a 'Lamb's war', an energetic, non-violent confrontation of oppression, repression, and sin in all social and cultural contexts. This covenant of light and 'life with God' was signified, wrote Edward Burrough, by 'the unity of the Spirit and the bond of peace' (Gwyn 2006 [1995], 106–8).

EIGHTEENTH-CENTURY VIEWS

In her posthumous memoir, Catherine Payton Phillips (1726–94) stated that 'the prin-ciple of light and life we profess, is unchangeably the same' (Phillips 1798, 368). One might amend Phillips' statement, yet it is also a good starting place for looking at eighteenth-century Quakerism. Friends continued in agreement on the centrality of the Light of Christ in their individual and corporate lives. Growing diversity also developed among Friends who embraced evangelical, Quietist, and rationalist theologies, and occasionally all three at once.

Eighteenth-century Quakers often witnessed to a strong conviction about the goodness of God. Travelling minister Jane Fenn Hoskens (1694–1764) called God 'infinite goodness' (Hoskens 1837, 467), and Job Scott (1751–93) 'perfect goodness' (Scott 1797, 7). John Woolman (1720–72) begins his *Journal* with the statement that he 'often felt a motion of love to leave some hints in writing of my experience of the goodness of God' (Woolman 1989, 23). He believed that God intended goodness for his entire creation. Trust in God's providence was a common theme for eighteenth-century Friends. Susanna Morris (1682–1755), crossing the Atlantic Ocean under a call for ministry, wrote, 'The allwise God did give me to believe that he would command the proud waves that they should not come at his servants to hurt them' (Bacon, 49). Job Scott stated that he believed his illness and impending death while travelling in the ministry in Ireland was 'in the ordering of Providence' (Scott 1797, 352). Both rejoicing and suffering should be seen as the results of the dealings of an all-wise God.

Sometimes Quakers did not express joy or even resignation in witnessing God's acts of providence. Elizabeth Ashbridge's (1713–55) prayer that she be delivered from an abusive husband was answered when her husband unexpectedly enlisted in the army and died in this service. She blamed herself 'for making such an unadvised request, fearing I had displeased God by it, and though he had granted it, it was in displeasure, and suffered to be in this manner to punish me' (Ashbridge 1807, 50).

Suffering or bearing the cross was to be expected for Quaker ministers. When ministry in Norwich did not go well for Elizabeth Hudson (1722–83), she was 'tempted to murmur and repine in spirit', but instead identified with the Apostle Paul, who boasted 'of the Cross of Christ, which his experience in the Christian faith convinced him was the power of God to salvation' (Bacon 1994, 163). The cross of Christ for Friends was inward, and it usually signified an acknowledgment that God's ways shown to the faithful Friend were not what he or she would have chosen, but the Friend found release in submitting to God's will anyway. Samuel Bownas (1677–1753) advised the aspiring Friends' minister to endeavour 'to keep thyself under subjection to the mortifying power of the cross, that thy doctrine may be adorned with meekness, and also seasoned with gospel salt' (Bownas 1989, 82). In a letter to Friends' ministers, he urged them to 'examine yourselves narrowly, whether you have kept...to your guide'. For himself, he prayed to be 'preserved in humility, and self-denial, under the power of the cross, the most beautiful ornaments a minister can ever be clothed with' (Bownas 1795, 53–4).

Woolman found himself identifying with a difficult-to-understand portion of Scripture, Col. 1:24, where Paul stated that he participated in the ongoing process of the redemption of the world. Woolman observed that Friends living under the cross would find themselves actively participating in the ongoing redemption of which Paul wrote (Angell 2006b, 42–3).

Eighteenth-century Friends sometimes appealed to the example of the historic Jesus. Woolman observed, 'Jesus Christ, in promoting the Happiness of others, was not deficient in looking for the Helpless, who lay in Obscurity, nor did he save any Thing to render himself honorable among Men' (Woolman 1775, 40). Woolman's purpose in appealing to Jesus was always to have his readers follow Jesus' example. William Boen (1735–1824), an African-American Quaker who, like Woolman, always wore undyed clothes, because indigo, the most common dye for men's clothes, was produced by slave labour, was once asked if he was following Woolman's example. Boen's dignified reply was, 'I am endeavoring to follow the footsteps of Christ' (Weaver et al 2011, 11).

Building upon aspects of Penn's witness, some eighteenth-century Friends held that the Quaker religion was eminently reasonable. One was Thomas Beaven, who wrote, 'tis the *divine Spirit,* which enlightens and influences the noble Faculty of Reason, to the highest Pitch of Knowledge and Certainty in heavenly Things' (Barbour and Frost 1994, 99). Beaven thus optimistically differed from Fox in designating reason as a 'noble Faculty'. Some Friends followed Penn's example even more closely by using arguments from reason to appeal to non-Quakers, but arguing more from their feelings of God when appealing to their fellow Friends. One such, J. William Frost argues, was Woolman, who argued from reason in his anti-slavery tracts, but appealed much more to feelings of God in his *Journal* (Frost 2003b, 180–4).

The Light of Christ was sometimes referred to as a 'principle' that could be named variously, as in Woolman's second essay 'On Keeping Negroes':

> There is a principle which is pure, placed in the human mind, which in different places and ages hath had different names. It is, however, pure and proceeds from God. It is deep and inward, confined to no forms of religion nor excluded from any, where the heart stands in perfect sincerity. (Woolman 1989, 236)

Those, like Woolman, who advocated for a Quaker Reformation in the mid-eighteenth-century, argued more clearly than their Quaker forebears had for a progressive growth in human capacity to understand what the Light of Christ is trying to communicate to humanity. Woolman, commenting on slaveholding by many Friends in the American colonies, wrote, 'It is observable in the history of the reformation from popery that it had a gradual progress from age to age. The uprightness of the first reformers to the light and understanding given them opened the way for sincere-hearted people to proceed further afterward' (Woolman 1989, 147). Woolman implied that progressively greater apprehension of where the Light of Christ is leading would also be available to his contemporaries and to their descendants.

Job Scott, a popular minister who travelled extensively in North America and who died of smallpox in 1793 while travelling in Europe, preached an emphatic and clear spiritualized version of the Light of Christ. By 1770, Scott wrote in his *Journal,* he had become 'fully and clearly convinced...by the immediate operations, illuminations, and openings of divine light in my own mind'. 'This inward something' he identified as 'the true and living spirit and power of the eternal God'. There was no Christian salvation without it. As long as it was resisted, 'separation must infallibly remain between God and the soul'. In a paragraph excised by the proto-Orthodox editor of his *Journal* (1st ed, 1797), but restored by a later Hicksite editor, Scott wrote that 'the death of Christ is nothing at all' without submission to this divine light. 'If thou does not *feel* it [Christ's death], it is nothing.' One should not believe anything from the Scriptures 'without the light and evidence of the holy spirit' (compare Scott 1831, I, 41–4, with Scott, 1797, 29–31). Scott's preaching was unchallenged during his life, but Evangelical Quakers blocked posthumous publication of Scott's full *Journal* for many years.

NINETEENTH-CENTURY VIEWS

Traditional Quaker Quietism and Enlightenment rationalist views came together controversially in the thought of Long Island minister Elias Hicks (1748–1830). Hicks believed in an adoptionist view of Jesus, that Jesus became the son of God when he was baptized by John in the Jordan River, and that the purpose of Jesus' sonship was fulfilled when he had turned people to the Light, or the Spirit of Truth (Ingle 1998, 90–91). He denied atonement theories that placed a decisive influence on Jesus' blood shed for humanity on the cross, opposing evangelical appeals to 'plenary satisfaction' and 'imputative righteousness' (Buckley 2011, 148). He stated that Jesus' blood was no more effective in our salvation than a chicken's blood, a formulation previously used by Scott. While Hicks believed, like Fox, that a primary purpose of the Light is to turn humans away from sin, he also had more confidence in conscience and reason than did Fox. Hicks had both Fox and Woolman in mind when writing that 'in every age where any real reformation has been produced, it has always been by instruments newly raised up by the immediate operation of the Spirit' (Buckley 2011, 56–7). Influenced by Penn's anti-trinitarian arguments in *Sandy Foundation Shaken,* Hicks believed that Trinitarian views 'degrade the divine character... [and] greatly derogate from the unity and majesty of God'. God is 'All-Good and All-Gracious'; he entertained objections of theodicy but saw nothing that fundamentally altered his belief in God's complete goodness. His bottom line was that 'God has manifested himself to every rational being under heaven by the immediate impression of his own Life, Light, and Power, and has manifested himself self-evidently to every rational creature, so that all must know him and his will concerning them' (Buckley 2011, 202).

In contrast, Thomas Evans of Philadelphia published extracts of early Quaker writings designed to demonstrate that Quakers had always believed in the Trinity, 'the Holy Three that bear record in heaven, Father, Word and Spirit' (I John 5:7–8 AV), in a high Christology of Jesus as 'God manifest in the flesh', and a view of the atonement that recognized the efficacy of the blood of Jesus for human salvation (Evans 1828, xv–xvi). But under strong evangelical influence, other Orthodox Quakers diverged more freely from earlier Quaker precedents. Joseph John Gurney (1788–1847) was the most prolific and notable of these. Believing that the Bible was a more important authority for Quakers than the Light of Christ, he set about to resolve what he saw as either the ambiguities or errors of 200 years of Quaker precedent. His *Observations on the Religious Peculiarities of the Religious Society of Friends* (1824, 7th ed. 1834) presented his views in a way fairly harmonious with preceding Quaker tradition. He affirmed that 'the outward knowledge of Christ is not absolutely indispensable to salvation, and that other persons, who are *completely destitute* of that knowledge, may *also* be saved from sin'. Similar to early Friends but unlike Hicks, he distinguished between the divine 'law written on the heart' and the natural conscience. 'The law is the *light;* the conscience is the *eye.*' But he then hastened to downplay the importance of these observations. While ancient philosophers before Christ had enjoyed 'some' divine light 'independently of all outward information', Gurney himself 'would on no account exaggerate either its brightness or its magnitude. The early twilight, and the blaze of noon, equally proceed from the sun; but could they be contrasted, it would be *almost* like the comparison of night and day' (Gurney 1848, I, 27, 33, 65–6). The Holy Spirit guiding the committed Bible-reading Christian was like the noonday sun. Gurney distinguished more starkly between the Holy Spirit and the Light of Christ than preceding Quaker theologians.

In his candid *Brief Remarks on Impartiality in the Interpretation of Scripture* (1840), intended for a small circle of friends but later disseminated widely by his critics, Gurney was sweepingly dismissive of the Light of Christ and openly critical of early Quaker theology and Biblical exegesis. In respect to John 1:9, alluding to Christ as 'the true light that enlightens every man coming into the world', Gurney noted that 'certain' unnamed writers mistakenly supposed that:

> because Christ is called the light (i.e., the enlightener), he is therefore to be identified with the influence which he bestows; in short that the light of the spirit of God in the heart of man, is itself actually *Christ.* The obvious tendency of this mistake, is to deprive the Saviour of his personal attributes, and to reduce him to the rank of a *principle.* (Gurney 1840, 8)

Here, Gurney is closer to seventeenth-century Puritan critics of Quakerism than to the Quaker founders. He recommended the 'Holy Scriptures' as 'a light to which at all times ... we do well to take heed, but they shine only in a dark place until the minds of those who read them are illuminated by the Holy Spirit' (Gurney 1840, 6).

Gurney affirmed that Jesus was divine even prior to his birth (Gurney 1848, II, 227). His description of the incarnate Jesus included some moving devotional passages, describing Jesus' humble origins, his homelessness, his preference of servantship to kingliness, and his further humiliation in 'a public execution, in the form which was appointed for the vilest malefactors ... How unspeakably tender and acute, therefore, must have been his sympathy with an afflicted generation' (Gurney 1848, IV, 46–9).

Some of Gurney's followers gave even less credence to traditional Quaker views of the Light. Manchester Quaker Isaac Crewdson (1780–1844) completely repudiated the doctrine of the Light of Christ, leading the Beaconite secession from London Yearly Meeting in 1836 (Russell 1979, 343–6). During the 1870s Holiness Revivals among American

Quakers, these more extreme Gurneyite views became acceptable to many Orthodox Friends.

Some Orthodox Quakers criticized Gurney's theological innovations, especially opposing Gurney's attempt to downplay the Light of Christ as a central part of Quaker theology. The elderly Thomas Shillitoe (1754–1836) replied to a Gurneyite who denounced belief in an inward light that 'If there is not an inward light with which I have been acquainted these sixty years, I am now, when on the brink of the grave, in a most deplorable condition' (Wilbur 1859, 213). This opposition was eventually led by New England Quaker John Wilbur (1774–1856). Standing firmly by early Quakers' statements on the Light, he asserted that if Gurney's views that the 'true light' signified nothing more than 'Christ incarnate, the enlightener', that 'Quakerism would be no more' (Wilbur 1859, 286).

Abolitionist Lucretia Mott (1793–1880), quoting William Penn's 1679 *Address to Protestants*, urged, 'It is time that Christians were judged more by their likeness to Christ than their notions of Christ' (Penn 1679, 119; Mott 1980, 107). So Mott, like Gurney, found Jesus' humility and purity, 'the excellence of his example', to be moving, but her dictum derived from Penn drew a contrast between deeds and 'opinions and doctrines of Christ' that Gurney would not have embraced. She affirmed that 'Jesus *is* here; he *has* appeared from generation to generation . . . His spirit is now going up and down among men seeking their good, and endeavoring to promote the benign and holy principles of peace, justice, and love.' Influenced by liberal theologians such as Unitarians William E. Channing and Theodore Parker, she boldly affirmed continuing revelation: 'Let us not hesitate to regard the utterance of truth in our age, as of equal value with that which is recorded in the scriptures' (Mott 1980, 107–10; Fager 2004, 8–11). Mott maintained membership in a Philadelphia Hicksite meeting but also nurtured relationships with Progressive Friends, who affirmed 'God as a Universal Father' and sought to 'divorce Religion from Technical Theology'. Disclaiming all creeds, these abolitionists and human-rights advocates affirmed that obedience to God and to the spirit of Jesus led them to 'united efforts for the relief of human suffering' and working for 'the removal of giant wrongs' (Pennsylvania Yearly Meeting of Progressive Friends 1853).

In contrast, Hannah Whitall Smith (1832–1911), a Holiness Revival leader born a Philadelphia Quaker, distanced herself for a time from Friends and their Light of Christ theology, because looking within herself left her mired in her emotions. She found liberation in Bible reading and learning about Christian doctrine, and when she returned to Quakers, her meditation on her Bible reading had led her to an 'unselfish' God who saved all (Smith 1903, 151, 186, 211). Opposing historic Friends' beliefs in the Light of Christ, and staunchly supporting Protestant blood atonement theories was another Quaker Holiness Revival leader, David Updegraff (1830–94), influenced by American revivalists from Jonathan Edwards to Methodist Holiness preacher John Inskip. Updegraff decried 'influential teachers directing men to an imaginary saving light of Spirit within them for "peace", instead of to Jesus Christ who "made peace through the blood of the cross"' (Updegraff 1892, 21). His opposition to the 'delusion' that human beings have the Light of Christ sparked Ohio Yearly Meeting's (Damascus) approval of this statement: 'We do not believe that there is any principle or quality in the soul of man, innate or otherwise, which even though rightly used, will ever save a single soul; ... we repudiate the so-called doctrine of the inner light, or the gift of a portion of the Holy Spirit in the soul of every man, as dangerous, unsound, and unscriptural' (Russell 1979, 506).

The 1887 'Richmond Declaration of Faith' approved by representatives of Orthodox Yearly Meetings did not go so far as the Ohio Yearly Meeting minute, but it did emphasize that there was no saving Light within human beings except the Holy Spirit. It cited John 1:9, that Christ 'is the true Light which lighteth every man that cometh into the world', and then proceeded: 'We own no principle of spiritual light, life, or holiness, inherent by nature in the mind or heart of man. We believe in no principle of spiritual light, life, or holiness, but the influence of the Holy Spirit of God, bestowed on mankind, in various measures and degrees, through Jesus Christ our Lord' (General Conference of Friends 1887, 25, 28). If the key words here are 'by nature', the declaration carries forwards the early Quaker view that the saving Light of Christ (more safely called the Holy Spirit) is not natural, but must be supernatural. Without those words, it would constitute a denial of the historic Quaker view of the Light.

TWENTIETH- AND TWENTY-FIRST-CENTURY VIEWS

Some Orthodox contemporaries of Updegraff such as J. G. Whittier (1807–92), Joel Bean, and co-author of *A Reasonable Faith* (1884) Francis Frith, favoured theories of Christ's atonement as a moral example and retained a strong testimony to the Light of Christ within (Jones 1921, II, 660; Kennedy 2001, 97–105). But a fuller development of a moderate Quaker Orthodoxy would await the next generation of Quaker theologians, most notably, Rufus Jones (1863–1948), birthright Quaker from Maine, prolific author, champion of mysticism, and a professor at Haverford College. Jones was an optimist; he understood sin (in the words of the fourteenth-century writer of the *Theologia Germania*) as that which causes 'the creature to turn away from the unchangeable good' (Jones 1904, 249). To be aware of one's sin is to be conscious of finiteness, yet 'consciousness has an infinite aspect which transcends the finiteness of which it is aware' (Jones 1904, 173).

Jones did not accept the distinction between natural and supernatural expressed in various ways from Quaker origins until the 1887 Declaration. For Jones, the divine and human are deeply intertwined, often very intimately so; (here he was influenced by Romantic poets such as William Wordsworth). Likewise, it made no sense to distinguish between the Light of Christ and conscience; for Jones, unlike many Quaker predecessors, there was nothing suspect about the human conscience, which is the seat of the Light (Jones 1920a). With the ability to discern God's will through conscience, no mediator is necessary: 'The Quaker fulfills the reformation idea that Christianity is to be spiritually apprehended by each person for himself or herself; nothing is to come between the individual and God' (Jones 1904, 170). The term 'inner light', dropping reference to Christ, preceded Jones among some Liberal and moderate Quakers by a few decades, but Jones was the theologian who popularized this term. He used 'Holy Spirit', 'that of God in you', and 'Presence', as synonyms for the inner light (Vining 1958, 258; Spencer 2007, 200–201). The inner light is 'a Divine Life resident in the soul; a source of guidance and illumination; and a ground of spiritual certitude' (Jones 1904, 171).

The greatest evidence of a Christian life lived according to the inner light was a life filled with service to others. Jones helped to found the American Friends Service Committee (AFSC) during the First World War, and his deep involvement with the AFSC would be life long. Ultimately, as one lives a life of love and service, all life becomes holy: 'As we feel out for the Divine Life and the Divine sanction we find ourselves woven into a mighty social tissue through which God's life and purpose and will are slowly expressing themselves and through which every deed of ours proves its fitness' (Jones 1904, 201). However, the Holy Spirit was not so much 'inner' for Rufus as is the Light, but serves to sweep quiet gatherings of Friends into unity. In Quaker meetings (which he termed 'group mysticism') at their best, 'one feels . . . a tide of living Spirit flowing underneath the hushed and gathered group' (Jones 1927, 57). Understanding the Spirit as intended to unify Friends and others, Jones worked tirelessly (and, in the case of American East Coast Quakerism, successfully) to reunite Yearly Meetings sundered by the Hicksite–Orthodox separation.

Amongst Midwestern and Western pastoral Quakers, however, Jones's theology was controversial. For example, William Pinkham admonished Jones to adhere to biblical teachings, stating that in a significant sense, God does not dwell within souls that are in hell, or are unregenerate, or have not exercised repentance towards God and faith in Christ (*American Friend*, 8/1/1895, 746). Evangelical Quakers repeatedly registered similar complaints with Jones.

For Jones, the historic Jesus was very important. While Gurney constantly placed an emphasis on the importance of a closer acquaintance with Christ as redeemer, Jones espoused a fearlessly progressive interpretation of Christianity with Christ as friend. Still, Jones's meditations on the historic Jesus led him to the eternal Christ, 'the living Christ trying to find entrance into the human heart' (Jones 1943, 6).

After Jones's death in 1948, some Quaker theologians sought a balance between the legacies of Jones and his evangelical Quaker critics. One strategy sought to recover early Quaker views on God and the Light, with some modest changes, including a continued emphasis on the historic Jesus. In a 1959 article for the influential journal *Quaker Religious Thought*, Maurice Creasey (1912–2004), Director of Woodbrooke, criticized the 'bifurcation' in Quaker thought between evangelicals who adopted much of the thought of other Protestants, and liberals who placed unwarranted stress on mysticism and divine immanence in humans. He yearned for 'the original Quaker conception of Christ, like that of the New Testament as a whole, [which] with extraordinary profundity and flexibility was able to hold together both . . . the historical and the mystical emphases' (Johns 2011, 110–11).

Many Friends from the Global South, strongly testifying to God's power in their lives, bring together evangelical views of Christ with spiritual insights from early Quakers. Oliver Simiyu relates his struggle to make God the Lord of his life and has been 'disturbed to hear some among us who claim a leading of the Spirit above the Scriptures'(Abbott and Parsons 2004, 53). Gladys Kangahi, celebrating God's answering prayer, exclaims, 'Oh, how wonderful and faithful God is!' Testifying to a powerful sense of the Spirit's movement in the lives of present-day African Friends, Kangahi notes that Friends of all ages 'move as the Spirit leads, and, of course, the Spirit leads all of us differently' (Abbott and Parsons 2004, 5,7). Priscilla Makhino advises people to whom she ministers 'to remain in our Lord Jesus Christ and share God's love with others. I like what George Fox says in his writings: "I turned them to Christ and left them there." I do the same everywhere I go' (Abbott and Parsons 2004, 25).

Many Latin American Friends bear a similar testimony. Diego T. Chuyma, a Bolivian Friend who has an impressive ministry 'witnessing to Christ and leading people to the Lordship of Jesus Christ', recalls his time at Pendle Hill, where he read George Fox's *Journal*, which 'challenged and encouraged [him] to continue in the ministry of our Lord Jesus Christ' (Abbott and Parsons 2004, 37). In order to 'fully serve Christ Jesus' as a Friends minister in Cuba, Ramon A. Gonzalez–Longoria Escalona gave up studies in engineering to undertake a seminary education in Matanzas, Cuba. He recalled the impact that both the Bible and the Holy Spirit has had on his life:

> The Bible has a great impact on my life and work. In it I have found the word of God for today… The Holy Spirit, which inspired the Bible, used it to speak to our condition, our situations; it carries us to an experience of Christ, because it gives the testimony of Christ.… I believe that now, more than ever, we must seek the guidance of the Holy Spirit in our ministry, being attentive listeners but, above all, good agents of His will. (Abbott and Parsons 2004, 242, 247)

Since about 1980, some Quakers, largely from Britain and the United States, have adopted the label 'Universalist' and claim experience of 'a living spirit at the heart of our lives which enables us to tell good from evil and right from wrong'. They state that the name for this experience may differ, adding that the name of that which guides one and whom one worships need not be Christ or Jesus (Hetherington). Thus, Marjorie Sykes (1905–95), a friend of Mohandas Gandhi who joined Quakers in India, saw profound parallels between Christian and Indian spirituality and expressed a great debt to both (Dart 1995, 53–6). In general, Universalist Friends have much interest in the positive spiritual aspects of the world religions, not just Christianity.

Subsequently, a movement of non-theist Friends, again mostly in Britain and the United States, and influenced by secularizing trends prominent in those countries, has wrestled with the tradition of the inner light as manifested among Quakers. David Rush wrote that 'the concept of God in every person is very resonant for me, and akin to my humanistic conviction that every life is sacred' (Boulton 2006, 137). Anita Bower saw such names as 'Inner Teacher' and 'Light' helpful in eliminating 'my childhood "Santa

Clause" god, and meaningful in focusing my meditations and reflections'. But these concepts have not led her to any 'belief in an active power or consciousness existing within and beyond humans, which (or who) provides guidance and strength, and deserves to be worshipped' (Boulton 2006, 139).

Quaker youth and young adults in the twenty-first-century witness to Jesus Christ and the Light in vital, diverse ways. Young Friends in Kenya sometimes worry whether their Quaker elders are sufficiently responsive to the Light of Christ and the Holy Spirit. Liani Phylis states:

> The leaders of the Quaker church still follow the ways and rules of those who established the church a long time ago, e.g., they say that George Fox used to conduct the church slowly and there was no clapping of hands in the church. So they have remembered such steps, thus making the church be like a cult. They aren't to be led by the Holy Spirit, but they follow the culture, thus the church is not growing. (Conti et al 2010, 6)

Perhaps the Spirit is moving more strongly through an African-Christian culture promoting lively worship than through a quieter worldwide Quaker culture.

Evelyn Jadin recalls that, as a child, her meeting taught her about the inner light, but she 'never heard of the Living Christ, let alone experienced it...But this all shifted one Sunday' when she attended a Conservative Quaker meeting in North Carolina. There she was 'enfolded by the silence and brought into a deep communion with those around [me] and the Spirit'. She experienced 'a greater presence standing over and around us all, bringing us together under it. Through this worship I felt the Presence of the Living Christ' (Conti et al 99–100).

Howie Baker, a young adult Friend who has had spiritual encounters with several branches of world Quakerism, has written with assurance that the Light is readily available within each branch. He wonders whether the situation of Quakers today might be like an oft-reproduced pictorial image of Quakers inviting into worship Indians who had been on the warpath (James Doyle Penrose's *Fierce Feathers*). 'We [worldwide Friends] are in the same room and not in the situation we've expected, but *the Spirit is here*. That one fact trumps everything else' (Conti et al 123).

CONCLUSION

Early Quaker Christology was unusual among Christian theologies for its relatively ahistorical concentration on the Light of Christ. Even within the earliest generations, there were shifting understandings: an embrace of apocalypticism turned swiftly into an aversion of the topic, and Christopresentist views that assumed both body and spirit were transformed into Christ the Light quickly became a much more strictly spiritual understanding. Early Friends' spiritualizing and universalizing of Christ through the image of the 'Light', so different from most other Christian theologies, has had a lasting shaping influence among Quakers.

Over succeeding centuries, Quakers produced diverse adaptions of the doctrine of the Light, with liberals such as Mott and Jones breaking down the barriers between the natural and divine on matters relating to reason and conscience, and evangelicals such as Gurney and Updegraff downplaying the Light and circumscribing its function. Adaptations continue to the present, with Africans responding to Christ's Light by embracing a more embodied worship, and North Americans and Europeans often heavily reinterpreting Christian concepts in an embrace of Universalism or non-theism. One might well wonder to what degree any or all such changes are brought about by response to the Holy Spirit or response to an outward non-Quaker culture; indeed, they may be occasioned by some of both, as Spirit perhaps can work through outward cultures. Finally, the current generation of younger Friends reminds us that new generations, in new contexts, will always find a need to appropriate Quakerism anew, and that this continuing process will most likely result in the rediscovery of dormant dimensions of historic Quakerism, even as Quakerism itself is also being pressed in new directions.

Suggested Further Reading

Barbour, H. (1964) *The Quakers in Puritan England.* New Haven: Yale University Press.

Barclay, R. (2002 [1678]) *Apology for the true Christian divinity.* Glenside, PA: Quaker Heritage Books.

Freiday, D. (1984) *Nothing without Christ: Some current problems in the light of seventeenth century thought and experience.* Newberg, OR: Barclay Press.

Moore, R. (2000) *The Light in their consciences: the early Quakers in Britain.* University Park, PA: Pennsylvania State University Press.

Punshon, J. (2001) *Reasons for hope: The faith and future of the Friends Church.* Richmond, IN: Friends United Press.

CHAPTER 11

SIN, CONVINCEMENT, PURITY, AND PERFECTION

NIKKI COFFEY TOUSLEY

Like the Puritans, early Friends stressed human powerlessness apart from grace and justification by faith, yet differed in rejecting imputed original sin, in which Adam's guilt is conferred to all humanity. They found an immediate experience of sanctification that exposed and purged sin, allowing perfect obedience to God's will. The Quaker orthodoxy that emerged in the next century was marked by a rigorous behavioural code, decreasing evangelization, and an understanding of sanctification as a more gradual growth towards perfection. Atonement and salvation were central issues in the separations of the nineteenth century, and the emerging branches of Quakerism developed different theologies of sin and perfection.

FREEDOM FROM SIN IN THE EMERGING QUAKER MOVEMENT

The doctrines of justification and sanctification were central questions of the English Reformation, and the theological landscape in Britain ranged from Calvinist Puritanism, which was pessimistic about human nature and stressed justification by grace alone, to Ranterism, which held out the possibility of complete freedom from sin and, in some cases, from ethical constraints. Friends shared much with their Puritan contemporaries, but differed on the possibility of perfection and the doctrine of original sin. Though often accused of Ranterism, early Quakers were careful, at least in later, less enthusiastic writings, to assert their orthodoxy and distinguish themselves from charges of anti nomianism and licentiousness levelled at Ranters. Separatists of all types rejected the Catholic and Anglo-Catholic traditions as preaching salvation through works. Yet the Quaker theology of justification and sanctification that emerged by the end of the century is similar to the Patristic view of sanctification as growth towards perfection through grace, or deification. Carole Dale Spencer (2007) interprets Quakerism as a holiness movement in which perfection is the central theological commitment.

The earliest Quaker writing was occasional and polemic rather than systematic, and given the inchoate theology of the movement, accounts of conversion, or convincement in the terminology of early Friends, are an important source of theology. Owen Watkins (1972) argues that Puritan conversion accounts serve as a useful source of implied doctrine, as authors interpret their experience in the context of a particular theology. Puritan doctrine dictated a two-fold experience of Law and Gospel, in which the Christian must learn, through experience, that justification cannot be earned. Accordingly, their narratives describe an initial legalistic stage, characterized by the conviction that the author is in bondage to sin, followed by an experience of grace which reveals that as one of the elect, the person is freed and justified in spite of sin, through the imputed righteousness of Christ. Conversion was followed by an ongoing war between flesh and Spirit, and only an exceptional few of the elect were expected to gain victory (Watkins 1972, 11–14, 37–9).

The Calvinist emphasis on grace may have been a relief to some seekers, but for others, doubts about election and the emphasis on spiritual warfare brought anxiety rather than comfort. The first Quaker convincement accounts, published as evangelical tracts during the initial decades of the new movement, often begin by describing such anxiety, which prompts a period of seeking. Finding no answers among the various 'professors' of religion, the seeker has an immediate experience of the Inward Christ or Seed, often referred to as a Day of Visitation. The Light of Christ begins to open their understanding, convicting them of sin, exposing their distance from God, and often revealing the desolation that characterizes the world. The experience may be a response to hearing the Quaker message or a direct experience of Christ before any encounter with Friends. The Day of Visitation prompts a period of spiritual warfare, but the assurance of justification Puritans describe comes only after sin has been conquered.

Friends' spiritual struggle is typically described using biblical metaphors of purification, such as fire or a threshing floor, or Christologically, in terms of the Light that reveals sin or an Inward Cross which requires the crucifixion of self to the world. Early Friends held threshing meetings to winnow out those ready to be convinced, which were characterized by groaning, crying, trembling, and other dramatic manifestations of the Spirit. The struggle with sin culminates in an experience of regeneration, an unshakable unity with the indwelling Christ, through which the now fully convinced Friend is both justified and sanctified, or set free from sin, and has a new, intimate understanding of God's will. Abiding in the love of Christ, the person is transformed, made obedient, and given the power to bear the Cross of Quaker discipline, risking imprisonment, loss of property, and disownment by family and friends. Especially for women, it may also include accepting a call to public ministry (Tousley 2008).

This doctrine of sanctification is inseparable from early Friends' eschatology. Friends held that through Christ the original goodness of creation has been restored and thus every person is called to perfect obedience through regeneration. In his *Journal*, Fox

(1995, 27) describes stepping back into the Garden of Eden, behind the flaming sword set at the entrance when Adam and Eve were banished. This imagery is found in other Quaker writing, and may be a reference to Rev 2:7, which promises that those who conquer with Christ will eat from the Tree of Life. Friends accepted Puritan pessimism about human nature apart from grace, preaching that the Devil is the ruler of the world. Those who rejected the Light of Christ continued within the Fall, but they had been redeemed and called out of the world.

It is clear from the early autobiographical narratives that convincement was expected to be characterized by immediate justification and sanctification; but it is unclear to what degree this claim was to a persistent, sinless perfection. Spencer (2007, 69–73) argues that George Fox's (1624–91) claims to complete perfection were in the context of ecstatic experience, and that he neither made the experience paradigmatic nor made himself the centre of the movement. T. Canby Jones, studying Fox's corpus as a whole, argues that Fox held that sanctification restores to humanity the state of Adam before the Fall, in which the person can choose not to sin, but not to that of Christ, for whom it was impossible to sin (1955, 148–9). Yet in the first two decades, the position of Fox and other Friends is not so clear. Few early autobiographical accounts report inward spiritual struggle following regeneration. More generally, early Friends favoured exhortation over discussion of theological fine points, and the rhetorical moment called for an emphasis on complete victory over sin in anticipation of an impending apocalypse.

Early Friends' confidence in perfection brought charges of Ranterism and blasphemy, particularly when Fox preached that all could be 'sons of God' or claimed infallible knowledge of God through inward revelation. Friends rooted sonship in the scriptural promise of adoption thorough faith, but Fox was accused of claiming equality with Christ. James Nayler's (1618–60) triumphant entry into Bristol in the guise of Christ seemed to confirm the perception that Quakers were blasphemers who claimed a Christly perfection. At least some Friends in the 1650s may have shared with Ranterism the belief that they had reached a persistent state of perfect freedom from sin, though this freedom was marked by obedience rather than licence. As the movement matured, the rhetoric of perfection became more careful, and Friends wrote of experiencing Christ 'in measure' while maintaining that they had found a victory over sin denied by other Christians.

Many of the early polemics by Friends were directed against the clergy, and a common accusation was that 'professors' kept their flocks in bondage by 'preaching sin' and denying the possibility of perfection. For instance, in her 1660 pamphlet 'True Testimony from the People of God,' Margaret Fell (1614–1702) argues that because they are ignorant of their Redeemer living within, ministers 'perswade all people of an impossibility of being freed from sin, but that they must sin all the dayes of their lives, and so keeps people in the fall, in the transgression, under the curse, & death'. She testifies that Christ has broken the power of the serpent and those who live in obedience live in a state of righteousness from which one cannot fall. Christ is the righteous one, the Second Adam, who 'sanctifieth and washeth them that be in the fall; he who never transgressed, redeems out of transgression'. Fell does not necessarily imply a persistent state of sinlessness, but claims that those who have been purified live in 'the holy Order of the Life,

Spirit, and Power of the everlasting God' and can never err so far as to lose their salvation. Descriptions of abiding in God's love, unity with Christ, and drawing on the power of the Lord are common in descriptions of the ongoing lives of the convinced, and would become dominant themes in the next decades of the movement.

Convincement Among Second-generation Friends

Persecution, conflicts over leadership, and the excesses of the 1650s demanded more careful articulation of Quaker theological positions. Friends began to develop more systematic accounts of Quaker doctrine and asserted orthodoxy in response to charges of heresy, though historians differ on the degree to which this represented clarification of existing beliefs or a shift in theology. Quaker writing was increasingly directed towards those already within the community, often in the form of epistles and longer journals. Friends continued to claim victory over sin, but the expectation of an immediate apocalypse was waning, along with the enthusiastic rhetoric of absolute assurance and perfection. Larry Ingle (1994, 103–6) notes that Fox never acknowledged that his early preaching tended toward Ranterism, rather he increasingly emphasized unity and curbed more extravagant claims by the late 1660s.

Despite the growing emphasis on corporate experience, those born within the Quaker community were expected to undergo a personal experience of sanctification. 'Traditional' Quakerism, received from family without convincement, was seen as empty, though the fact that writers address the topic suggests many were members only by tradition. Second-generation journalists fit their experience into the pattern of first generation, but appear less confident in victory over sin. Their accounts tend to emphasize humility, patience, and surrender, rather than the power necessary for evangelism or enduring persecution. Conforming to plain dress and other Quaker peculiarities is a recurring theme, and second-generation writers sometimes display elements of ethical legalism from which the first generation felt freed (Tousley 2008).

Quaker journals written at the end of the seventeenth century cover a wider span of the author's life than early accounts, typically beginning with early childhood experiences of openness to God's presence, reflecting Friends' view that infants do not carry Adam's guilt. The subsequent journey parallels that of earlier Friends, though with crucial differences. The second-generation writers often describe a period of falling away from God, rather than seeking among various traditions. As in earlier accounts, the sense of alienation ends with a Day of Visitation, conviction of sin, and a period of spiritual warfare. This spiritual struggle is often described as an inward Cross and crucifixion of self will, through which the author accepts the outward Cross of Quaker discipline. Purification metaphors of fire and threshing remain common, but earlier imagery of return to the Garden is rare (Tousley 2008).

The experience of purification is followed by a final experience of grace, which brings a sense of peace, but for second-generation Friends, the sense of assurance appears less complete. They are more likely to express feelings of doubt or alienation after regeneration, and may continue to struggle with Quaker discipline, discerning God's will, or answering a call to the ministry. For those who do experience freedom, perfection is rarely an instantaneous release from sin, but the gradually ripening fruit of surrender, humble waiting, and abiding in God's love (Tousley 2008).

As Spencer (2007, 34–5) has argued, this more gradual experience is consistent with early Christian teaching on deification, in which holiness develops through increasing union with and a partaking in the nature of Christ. Isaac Penington (1616–79) (undated, 29), who was convinced in 1658, describes his experience as 'an inward change, by the Spirit of the Living God, into His own nature'. The basic pattern of justification and sanctification continued to characterize the autobiographies of Friends in the eighteenth and nineteenth centuries.

APOLOGETICS AND DEVELOPING QUAKER ORTHODOXY

The most widely read systematic statement of Quaker theology was Robert Barclay's (1648–90) 1678 *Apology for the True Christian Divinity* (2002). Barclay rejects the Augustinian doctrine of imputed original sin, in which Adam's guilt is passed on to infants at birth, as contrary to God's mercy. Yet he maintains a pessimistic view of human nature apart from grace, arguing the mature person is bound to sin after the Fall and has no ability to overcome sin until 'he be disjoined from this evil seed and united to the Divine Light' (Barclay 2002, 85). In a less widely read 1679 apologetic, Elizabeth Bathurst (1655–85) also rejects imputed sin, arguing that while sin comes into the world through Adam, the world is redeemed through the gift of Christ, the new Adam. Thus, guilt is assigned only to those who reject the gift and choose transgression (Bathurst 1996, 362–3). Early Friends had been accused of minimizing the atonement, but both Barclay and Bathurst link the individual experience of sanctification to the substitutionary death and resurrection of Jesus.

Barclay distinguishes between the Seed, which is universal in all humanity, and the indwelling Christ, which is fully present only in those who have submitted to purification of the Cross and 'put on Christ' (2002, 124). He argues that the indwelling Seed of Christ calls all of humanity, even those who do not know the historic Christ. When it is not resisted, the Seed works salvation in individuals by 'bringing them to a sense of their own misery, and to be sharers in the sufferings of Christ inwardly, and by making them partakers in his resurrection, in becoming holy, pure and righteous and recovered out of their sins' (Barclay 2002, 115–16). In response to those who accused Friends of preaching either salvation through works or Ranterism, Barclay and Bathurst agree with

Calvinists that the righteousness of Christ is imputed as a free gift, yet they insist it must also be imparted as real holiness in the life of the regenerated person. Barclay writes in his proposition on perfection: 'In whom this pure and holy birth is fully brought forth, the body of sin and death is crucified and removed, and their hearts joined to Truth; so as not to obey any suggestions or temptations of the evil one' (2002, 205).

Barclay clarifies that Friends neither claim equality with God nor claim that all Christians reach a persistent, sinless state. Perfection requires perseverance and ongoing, daily growth. He writes that holiness is truly present in the regenerate person, but only 'in measure', like gold that remains pure even in small amounts (Barclay 2002, 207). Neither Bathurst nor Barclay rule out apostasy by those who have experienced a measure of perfection, yet both argue that there is a measure of perfection from which a complete fall from grace is impossible. Barclay further suggests the possibility of a persistent state of complete freedom from sin, but says that he must take it on faith because he has not reached that state (2002, 206–7).

Barclay's account of sanctification raises questions about human will, as regeneration is both a gift of grace and requires a human response. Anticipating the critique, he argues that the first moment of justification is not an act of the will, but passivity or the giving up of resistance to the visitation of grace. An unregenerate person has no power to work with grace, but once grace lays hold, becomes a co-worker with Christ (Barclay 2002, 129). Bathurst addresses the question of the will in a less dualistic argument, echoing Augustine's argument that the human will is truly free only when conformed to God's will and released from bondage to sin.

The experience of purification was often described by Friends as a crucifixion of the will, attained through 'death' of the self and crucifixion to the world. William Penn's (1644–1718) *No Cross, No Crown*, written in 1682 as an expansion of an earlier pamphlet, uses the central metaphor of the Inward Cross to outline the main characteristics of Quaker discipline. Like Barclay's *Apology*, it was formative for later Friends. Penn argues that members of the true Church bear the daily cross, or circumcision of the heart, which leads to righteousness. Like Bathurst, he stresses that true freedom of the will is freedom from sin. Those who have been redeemed receive the power to become sons of God, which is 'an inward force and ability to do whatever He requires; strength to mortify their lusts, control their affections, resist evil motions, deny themselves, and overcome the world in its most enticing appearances' (Penn 1991, 19). They are new creatures, with 'a new will; such as does the will of God; not their own' (Penn 1991, 9). Bathurst describes sanctification as conforming to and being guided by the 'perfect Principle of God' in the conscience, so that the regenerated 'come to witness in themselves the fulfilling of his Determination, which is, To finish Transgression, and make an end of Sin' (Bathurst 1996, 378).

The doctrine of perfection formed the basis of Quaker identity, as Friends saw themselves as a community called out of the world to corporate holiness. Oversight of discipline became the work of elders, and the spiritual struggle of second-generation Friends was often over acceptance of the stringent ethical demands or testimonies, which set Quakers apart. As Spencer argues, 'pressing after' perfection necessitates detachment from the distractions and pleasures of the world, and thus is the basis of Quaker simplicity. Perfection also necessitates love of God and neighbour, forming the basis of the Quaker peace testimony (Spencer 2007, 78–81). Other Quaker distinctives, such as the emphasis on discerning God's will, patient waiting, plain speech, truthfulness in business, and refusing oaths are also underlain by the experience of sanctification within the community and the desire for perfect obedience to God's will.

Conformity and Reform Among Eighteenth-century Friends

By the early eighteenth century, Friends had begun to develop the boundaries of sectarian Quietism, erecting a 'hedge' separating them from the world. Their convincement narratives are characterized by an increasing emphasis on humility and receptivity as an aspect of communal holiness. Friends no longer expected the immediate apocalypse, and came to understand the gathered community as the realized Kingdom of God. Some historians, particularly Rufus Jones (in Braithwaite 1921, xliv–vlv) and A. Neave Brayshaw (1982) have interpreted the century as a period of decline and sterile Quietism. The emphasis on communal discipline was at times legalistic, especially for those who did not have experience of regeneration, and led to disownment of those who did not conform. Yet as Marietta (1984) suggests, withdrawal from the world and the desire for perfect obedience made room for prophetic stands on abolition, warfare, and other issues.

Samuel Bownas (1677–1753) (1989), writing in the mid-eighteenth century, stresses sanctification and divine inspiration as the essential qualifications of ministry. Journals typically follow the pattern of the late seventeenth-century narratives, with increasing emphasis on expectant waiting, humility, and discerning God's will. Bownas advises ministers 'in a state of infancy' to avoid either overrunning their guide or saying too little: 'keep humble and low, being honestly given up to be and do just what the Lord by his Spirit would have thee, resignation to the will of God being absolutely necessary for a minister' (1989, 28). In the early stages of her ministry, Jane Fenn Hoskens (1694–1764), an early eighteenth-century convert, was brought to a state of mourning by doubts about taking up the 'mortifications' of Quaker discipline and whether she, as a woman, was truly called to preach. Yet she learned that 'if people would but patiently wait [God's] time, they would be enabled to perform and would find deliverance in a proper season' (Hoskens 1771, 15). For women, particularly, the emphasis on humility and ministry as a gift of grace was freeing, allowing ministerial roles frowned on by the wider society, as their preaching was justified by obedience to God's will.

For Quietist Friends, perfection required the constant discipline of receptive worship and prayer, even after sanctification, as well as reliance on the guidance of elders. Travelling ministers sought to be constantly open to 'motions' and 'openings' of the

Spirit, describing nascent leadings as feelings of 'weight' or 'concern', and tested their leadings within the community. They recount 'exercises' and 'travails' as they struggled with God's will, or 'baptisms', in which God's presence was keenly felt. When they were obedient, they found a sense of peace, but inspiration could be withdrawn if they failed to respond or moved beyond their leading.

John Woolman (1720–72) describes being 'brought low' as he struggled with whether he could accept the hospitality of a slave owner. Praying for assistance, he says, '[I was] helped to sink down into resignation, I felt a deliverance from the tempest in which I had been sorely exercised, and in calmness of mind went forward, trusting that the Lord, as I faithfully attended to him, would be a counsellor to me in all difficulties' (Woolman 1989, 59–60). He resolved to leave money for the slaves, regardless of the response of his hosts. This humble waiting is a significant shift from the bold rhetoric of the first decades of the movement, though both were understood to be the fruit of union with God. Expectant waiting was an aspect of early Quakerism, but eighteenth-century Friends increasingly stressed passive, receptive mysticism as the basis of obedience. They drew more explicitly on mystic writers such as Thomas à Kempis, William Law, and the Catholic Quietists, whose works they translated and republished. Quietists, on the edge of Catholic orthodoxy, practised an apophatic mysticism rooted in poverty of spirit and the 'prayer of quiet', which resonated with Friends.

Although perfection continued to be rooted in the individual experience of sanctification, corporate holiness was increasingly emphasized. The absence of persecution and increasing financial prosperity had led to a relaxing of discipline in the early eighteenth century, particularly within the colonies where Friends had political power. A holy community was the ideal, but at least some members were 'traditional' Friends, without the experience of sanctification, and too conformed to the world. By the 1740s a movement for reform began in Pennsylvania under ministers such as Anthony Benezet (1713–84), John Churchman, Isaac Pemberton, and John Woolman. Elders took on a larger role in visiting Quaker families, admonishing or disowning many who did not conform to Quaker discipline. The reformers' insistence on communal purity was also a call to be disentangled from even indirect involvement in warfare, slavery, avarice, and other forms of oppression. Benezet, writing during the American Revolution, calls the nation, not just Friends, to Christian perfection, pacifism, and the duty to love God and neighbour (1778, 6). Although he was thoroughly Quietist in his emphasis on purity and submission to God, Benezet reached beyond the Quaker hedge and anticipated the late nineteenth-century social gospel movement in his emphasis on social responsibility for sin. The reforms spread to Britain, though 'gay' Quakers who rejected Quaker dress and other disciplines were typically marginalized rather than disowned, and the hedge was less rigidly defined (Brayshaw 1982, 181–4).

By the late eighteenth century, Friends began to be influenced by external revival movements, which again fostered an instantaneous experience of justification and sanctification. In the early 1790s, Quietist Job Scott (1751–93) rebukes revivalist Friends who seem too confident in salvation, instead stressing gradual growth to perfection, and the possibility of apostasy even for those who have experienced sanctification. He argues that the historical atonement is efficacious only through the suffering of the Inward Seed and crucifixion of self-will (Scott 2001, 32). True religion proceeds 'no further than God is livingly the continual mover, worker, and efficient cause of all that is rightly wrought therein; nor on the other hand, any further or faster than man comes under the holy influence of the spirit, grace, or power of God' (Scott 2001 [1824], 6).

Spencer (2007, 119) describes the character of the late-eighteenth and early-nineteenth century as 'Evangelical Quietism', which emerged from, but also began to break down, sectarian Quietism. Younger Friends raised in the Quaker hedge looked outwards for signs of renewal and revival. Though some authors argue that non-Quaker revivalism brought a foreign element to Friends, Spencer suggests their evangelism was equally an outgrowth of the revivals of the mid-eighteenth century and a recovery of aspects of the holiness of early Friends. This synthesis would not hold, and the Quaker orthodoxy of the eighteenth century broke down over the next century, beginning with the Hicksite separation.

Hicksite Conscience and Ethical Perfection in the Nineteenth Century

The doctrines of sin, justification, and perfection were not central to the Orthodox–Hicksite schism, except to the degree to which these issues relate to debates over the nature of Christ and authority within the community. The roots of the Hicksite and Orthodox schism are complex, but the eighteenth-century emphasis on communal holiness and oversight by elders contributed to the divisions. At the beginning of the schism, Friends on both sides accepted the doctrine of perfection as formulated by eighteenth-century Friends (Barbour 1994 [1988] 173), but the trajectory of Hicksite thought was to emphasize natural moral conscience apart from grace and sanctification.

As Ingle argues, the primary point of contention between Hicksite and Orthodox Friends was the atonement. Elias Hicks (1748–1830) agreed with Barclay's rejection of imputed original sin and held that all are called to partake in the Divine nature after the manner of Jesus (Ingle 1998, 89–92). Yet he went further, arguing against the necessity of a substitutionary sacrifice and treating Jesus as moral exemplar rather than as saviour. Hicks's journal exhibits the general pattern of earlier convincement accounts, although he does not describe his experience in terms of an Inward Cross or new birth (Hicks 1969, 13–15). There is little sense of personal struggle with sin in his narrative, although his preaching included themes of fallen humanity, new birth, and the need for humility and diligence in the moral life.

A common theme in Hicksite accounts is the 'law written on the heart', which judges and instructs those who are obedient to and tendered by the Light of Christ. Like their Quietist ancestors, Hicksites emphasize humility, waiting, and obedience; however, rationalist imagery of illumination or opening of the mind predominates rather than biblical themes of purification or partaking in Christ. John Comly (1773–1850) describes his struggle with sin as a conflict between his animal and spiritual natures, writing that in early manhood 'the passions and propensities of animal nature more and more appear, and produce sore conflict in the sincere enlightened mind' (1853, 22). Attending to teachings of the Divine Light allowed him to overcome his animal nature and brought peace and consolation. With time, Liberal Friends no longer saw a clear distinction between the Seed and the fully indwelling Christ described by Barclay. As a result, they developed a more positive view of human nature in which the Light is present as conscience in all rational creatures, without the need for purification. As Wilmer Cooper writes, 'a faith that stresses the inwardness of religion…can lead to a sense of self-sufficiency in moral action and away from any sense of need for moral and spiritual redemption, including the need for a saviour' (1990, 56).

Despite rejection of the theology of sanctification, Hicksite theology retained the Quietist emphasis on openness and obedience to the Light as the basis of social change. Lucretia Mott (1793–1880) maintains the divinity of Jesus, but argues that his example of non-conformity and reform is primary. Like Benezet, she extends hope of perfection to the world, reflecting a modern concern with human progress in which Friends and other reformers as the vanguard (Mott 1980, 108). She writes that the authorities of Jesus' time were emerging from barbarism and 'not prepared to exhibit all those great principles in the near approach to fulness (sic), to the perfection called for at our hands. There is this continued advance toward perfection from age to age'. She cites the self-denial and righteousness of contemporary reformers as evidence of increasing perfection, criticizing those who rely on Scripture rather than the Light and thus justify slavery, intemperance, and war (Mott 1980, 110–11). Liberal and Orthodox Friends on both sides of the Atlantic were influenced by the late-nineteenth-century Social Gospel movement, interpreting pacifism and other Quaker testimonies in light of its optimism, hope in progress, and recognition of the social nature of sin.

ORTHODOX THEOLOGY IN THE NINETEENTH CENTURY

On the other side of the Hicksite–Orthodox schism, Elisha Bates' (1781–1861) 1824 systematic account of Quaker doctrine, written in response to Hicks, remained close to Barclay in its theology of sanctification. Bates describes sanctification as deep purification inseparable from justification, emphasizing watchfulness and growth toward perfect obedience (Bates 1875 [1824] 110–24). Yet tensions arose by mid-century as Friends influenced by revivals began to preach instantaneous conversion and the Wesleyan doctrine of sanctification as a second experience. It seemed to more traditional Friends that an instantaneous experience of conversion undermined real growth in holiness, despite revivalist claims to perfection.

John Wesley largely appropriated Barclay's account of perfection, but argued that sanctification is a separate work of grace, subsequent to justification. He affirmed that conversion was insufficient without 'entire sanctification', but was dismissive of Quietist mysticism and accused Friends of failing to follow their own ethical standards (Spencer 2007, 81–2, 271–83). As Methodists became more conformed to society, their message was taken up by the Holiness movement, which also maintained entire sanctification as a 'second blessing' and emphasized experiences of the Spirit. To revivalists, traditional Quakerism seemed spiritually dead, endlessly waiting when God was immediately available to those who had been sanctified (Hamm 1988,85).

For Evangelical Friends, the death and resurrection of the historic Christ was more central than the Inward Christ. Joseph John Gurney (1788–1847) emerged as the leader of mid-nineteenth-century evangelical Quakerism, advocating biblical orthodoxy and the atonement as a substitutionary sacrifice, as well as accepting the Augustinian doctrine of imputed original sin (1848). Unlike most evangelicals, Gurney de-emphasized conversion and sanctification, and his journal lacks a sense of transformation. Spencer argues that Gurney was closer to rationalism and Calvinist orthodoxy than to early Friends, as he critiqued mysticism and understood justification as an act of faith in which the righteousness of Christ is imparted to the believer (2007, 143). Although Gurney did not reject sanctification as necessary to salvation, critics accused him of preaching justification without holiness.

John Wilbur (1774–1856) agreed with Gurney that Hicks erred in minimizing the atonement, but thought Gurney failed to attend to the Inward Christ as the source of perfection. At the centre of the 1854 Orthodox–Wilburite schism was the role of humble waiting, purgation, and union with God, which had characterized eighteenth-century orthodoxy. Wilbur objected to Gurneyite revivals, Bible study, and Sunday schools as foreign to Quaker tradition and a distraction from the waiting obedience necessary to sanctification. Thomas Hamm writes that Wilbur 'feared that contact with the world, even with the most benevolent and humane intentions, would distract Friends from the great struggle of the soul toward holiness' (1988, 28). Wilburite Friends insisted on strict conformance to discipline as a matter of communal purity, and maintained the Quaker distinctives of plain dress and speech longer than other Friends.

By the late nineteenth century, Holiness Revivals led to further tensions between Holiness advocates among Friends and moderate Gurneyites. The best-known Quaker Holiness narrative is by Hannah Whitall Smith (1832–1911). Smith found little comfort in expectant waiting as a young Friend, and turned to revivals for assurance of justification. After several years, she began to long for victory over sin and experienced the 'second blessing' in which 'we abandon ourselves to the Lord for Him to work in us, both to will and to do of His good pleasure, that we take Him to be our Saviour from the power of sin as well as from its punishment, and that we trust Him to give us, according to His promise, grace to help in every time of need' (1903). Smith was influenced by Methodist and Quaker teaching on sanctification, and she stresses the receptivity of Quietism. Her experience of sanctification was gradual, but dependent on prior belief in justification through the atonement.

Separation of justification and sanctification became the dominant theology among evangelical Quakers due to the preaching of Holiness Friends such as David Updegraff (1830–94). Updegraff drew more heavily on revivalism than Smith, and saw justification and 'entire sanctification' as instantaneous experiences of the Spirit linked to Pentecost. He writes that the Christian must 'consecrate and hallow himself to God, and earnestly implore the baptism with the Holy Ghost, who will indeed "cleanse the thoughts of his heart by His inspiration, that he may perfectly love Him and worthily magnify His name"' (Updegraff 1892, 139). Like earlier Wilburites, moderate Evangelicals grew concerned that Holiness Friends relied too much on emotionalism and had strayed from Quaker orthodoxy, trivializing the conversion experience and making prayerful waiting on God unnecessary. Some openly opposed the revivals, while others merely cautioned against the excesses (Hamm 1988, 114–20). From a Holiness perspective, moderates appeared to minimize the doctrine of perfection, instead emphasizing ecumenicism, Modernism and the Social Gospel (Spencer 2007, 250–2; Hamm 1988, 165–6).

Moderate Evangelicals were initially a minority in America, but dominated the Orthodox wing by 1887, when they drafted the Richmond Declaration to affirm orthodoxy in the face of revivalist innovations. The Declaration follows Barclay in rejecting imputed original sin and affirming fallen human nature. It insists that justification and sanctification are inseparable, avoiding the language of 'second blessing', and reaffirms the need for submission to God and openness to purification. It was an uneasy compromise. Ohio Yearly Meeting (Orthodox) did not unite with the Declaration. Holiness Friends remained in other yearly meetings, eventually separating from Five Years Meeting to form Evangelical Friends Alliance, though the doctrine of sanctification was not central in this division. Both bodies affirmed the Richmond Declaration.

Like the Quietist reformers, most Evangelical Friends were committed to social change and missions, linking holiness to social transformation; however, for some Holiness Friends the expectation of the imminent Second Coming meant evangelism rather than social reform was primary (Hamm 1988, 119). Hamm argues that where eighteenth-century Quaker philanthropy was grounded in the desire to be disentangled from all obstacles to holiness, Evangelicals saw good works as the fruit of salvation (Hamm 1988, 22, 31). Wilburites maintained the Quietist view, seeking to be disentangled from the seeds of greed and war, but arguing Friends should not be involved with those who did not wait to discern the will of God.

FRIENDS IN THE TWENTIETH CENTURY

Sanctification and perfection were less central to the development of twentieth-century Quakerism. Rufus Jones (1863–1948) was the primary voice of twentieth-century Liberal Friends, although he came from a moderate Evangelical background. Like Hicks, he was optimistic about human nature and retained the Quietist emphasis on union with God. Yet he went further in rejecting the necessity of sanctification and disjoined the Light from the purgation of the Inward Cross. In this perspective, sin becomes a human struggle 'to emerge from the biological processes of nature' and be governed by conscience and rationality rather than instinct (Cooper 1990, 60). Nineteenth-century British Friends were moderate Evangelicals, but the 1895 Manchester Conference marked a shift towards liberalism, including a more optimistic view of human nature and natural human conscience. Convincement narratives are rare among Liberal Friends, who more often talk of finding a like-minded community than conversion, although journaling has been revived as a spiritual exercise.

The theology of sanctification among Evangelicals has changed less in the twentieth century, although tensions led to the withdrawal of Yearly Meetings influenced by the Holiness movement in 1947. Spencer points to Everett Cattell's (1905–81) *The Spirit of Holiness* as the primary contemporary articulation of Holiness Quakerism. Cattell's argument that love is the essential quality of Christian perfection resonates across Quaker divisions, although it does not reach the mystical depths of traditional Quaker experience (Spencer 2007, 232–4). The Richmond Declaration remains the primary statement of moderate Quaker evangelicalism, although the rejoining of separated yearly meetings has sometimes strained the moderating position. Conversion narratives, especially in the form of oral testimonies, are integral to evangelical culture, and both Holiness and moderate Evangelical Friends typically stress the moment of conversion and a personal experience of justification through grace.

For both Evangelical traditions, missions continue to be seen as a fruit of perfection, and the majority of non-Western Friends holds either a Holiness or moderate Evangelical view of sanctification. Early twentieth-century Kenyan missionary Arthur Chilson (1872–1939), who trained at the Holiness Friends Bible Institute, taught sanctification as a second work of grace and emphasized the power of the Spirit, which appealed to many African Friends. More moderate Friends within Five Years Meeting found him too revivalistic and refused support for him to return to Kenya. The resulting controversy led to the development of more Pentecostal Holy Spirit Churches separate from Friends, and the remaining Kenyan Meetings allied with Friends United Meeting (Stansell 2009, 13; Rasmussen 1995, 59–62). Pentecostal practices such as speaking in tongues have also resulted in tensions among Latin American Friends, where missions were primarily under the care of Holiness Friends. Yet the majority of Friends in the region continues to identify with the Holiness tradition (Calvert 2005, 9–10).

Conservative Friends, heirs of the Wilburite tradition, maintained the Quietist consensus and sense of separation from the world, although elements of liberal theology and activism are now been accepted by many Conservatives. Conservative Friends Lloyd Lee Wilson (1947–) and Wilmer Cooper (1920–2008) have been influential in articulating traditional Quaker theology of surrender, purification, and union with God to other branches of the Society, with emphasis on the communal nature of obedience. Cooper has argued that integrity is the testimony that underpins all Quaker ethics, including the more commonly identified testimonies of simplicity, equality, and peace:

> Undergirding [the Quaker testimonies] is the concern that our outward lives
> bear witness to truth discerned inwardly...If our inward leading is to be 'doers of
> the truth', then integrity needs to be at the center of our being, at the center of our
> consciousness, and at the center of our outward witness. (1991, 10)

Such dialogue across the Quaker divisions has been fruitful in recapturing the fullness of
Quietist orthodoxy. Thomas Kelly (1893–1941), like Jones, was a liberal from a moderate
Evangelical background, but moved to a mediating position. His *Testament of Devotion*
returns to the self-renunciation and absolute reliance on grace found in earlier Quaker
writings. Kelly places holy obedience centrally, writing with great beauty about the joy
and union with God that grows out of submission and the crucifixion of self-will.

Progressive optimism about the possibility of overcoming social sin persists among the
liberal and moderate Evangelical traditions, as well as among some Conservatives. Such
Friends may not describe their experience in terms of sanctification, but typically emphasize moral integrity and openness to truth, which has roots in early Quaker perfection. Yet
in the wake of the First and Second World Wars and the Holocaust, Friends such as Elton
Trueblood (1900–94) and Douglas Steere (1901–95), returned to a less optimistic view.
Trueblood, a moderate Evangelical, argued the necessity of reclaiming discipline in all religious traditions in response to the evils of the age. He writes in 1948 that great sensitivity
to social wrongs stems from a recognition of God's sovereignty: 'The world is helped when
any man or any group demonstrated the power which this connection makes possible'
(Trueblood 1948, 100). More recently, Holiness Friend Richard Foster (1942–) has taken up
this call for discipline rooted in obedience and the desire for perfection (Spencer 2007, 235).

SUMMARY

The teaching on sin, purification, and perfection that emerged in the late seventeenth
and eighteenth centuries set the bounds of Quaker Orthodoxy:

- There is no imputed original sin, however, the world is under the power of sin and
  there is no possibility of righteousness after the Fall, apart from grace.
- Righteousness is imputed as a gift and inheres in the person only insofar as there is
  a partaking in the Righteousness of Christ. Yet justification and sanctification are
  one grace, and there is no justification without inherent righteousness.
- The Inward Christ is present universally as the Seed in all of humanity, but is only fully
  present through the purification of the Inward Cross and crucifixion to the world.
- Perfection is not a static, sinless state and requires ongoing abiding in and union
  with God, through which the will is conformed to the Divine Will in perfect Love.
- Perfection is communal, and corporate perfection is the basis of the Quaker
  testimonies such as simplicity, truthfulness, and perfect love, expressed as pacifism.

In the nineteenth century, divisions among Friends broke down this orthodoxy. Hicksites maintained the tradition of expectant waiting but sought natural ethical perfection without the necessity of sanctifying grace. Revivalist Friends emphasized an instantaneous experience of justification at conversion followed by a second experience of sanctification, but rejected or minimized Quietist spirituality. The separation of justification and sanctification in Holiness teaching divided Evangelicals, and the Richmond Declaration reaffirmed the traditional view that they are one work of grace. Holiness spirituality and more moderate, modern Evangelical streams coexisted within the meetings that later formed Friends United Meeting and Evangelical Friends International, although the latter retained more of the Holiness tradition and early Friends doctrine of perfection. Wilburite Friends came closest to retaining the Quietist orthodoxy.

SUGGESTED FURTHER READING

Barclay, R. (2002 [1678]) Propositions 4–8 in *Apology for the true Christian Divinity*. L. Kuenning (ed.) Quaker Heritage, Glenside, PA.

Hamm, T. D. (1988) *The transformation of American Quakerism: Orthodox Friends, 1800–1907.* Bloomington: Indiana University Press.

Marietta, J. D. (1984) *The reformation of American Quakerism, 174--1783.* University of Pennsylvania, Philadelphia.

Spencer C. D. (2007) *Holiness, the soul of Quakerism: An analysis of the theology of holiness in the Quaker tradition.* Milton Keynes, Paternoster.

Tousley N. (2008) 'The experience of regeneration and erosion of certainty in the theology of second-generation Quakers, No place for doubt?' *Quaker Studies*, 13, 1, pp. 6–88.

CHAPTER 12

··

QUAKERS AND SCRIPTURE

··

HOWARD R. MACY

In the religious turmoil of seventeenth-century Britain, Quakers developed a distinctive approach to the Bible that witnessed to their experience with Scripture and to their experience of God. The vitality of their experience led to a paradoxical approach, full of tensions, which eventually brought diversity and division.

The tensions explored central questions in religious life: What are the sources of religious authority? How are God's purposes and presence known and conveyed? How do individuals and communities receive and use God's revelation to guide their lives?

This chapter presents the historic roots of the Quaker approach to Scripture and how this changed over time. It explores not only how these changes emerged from within the Friends movement but also how the wider religious culture influenced Quaker witness and practice. At some points it will help to distinguish descriptions of Scripture from practices in using it. It will also help to recognize that individual use of Scripture in any particular period is not uniform and may vary among users, depending on a variety of factors including temperament, training, and purpose.

Scripture Among Early Friends

···

Early Friends lived in a culture shaped by the ideas and passions of the Reformation. The Bible had come to replace the hierarchical Church as the basis of Christian authority. Though there were continuing struggles about the role of the Church, *sola scriptura*, Scripture alone, had become the dominant principle for authority. The big idea paired with this principle was the priesthood of the believer, the idea that everyone could come directly to God without human intermediaries. Applied to the Bible, this meant that all Christians should be able to read and interpret the Bible on their own. In the sixteenth century, these paired convictions led to the translation of the Bible into readers' ordinary languages, notably German and English, and Gutenberg's recent invention of the moveable-type press made wide distribution of the Bible possible, even when it was illegal.

By the turn of the seventeenth century, ordinary people had ready access to inexpensive editions of the Bible, notably the Geneva Bible, and wide circulation grew after King James I supported an 'Authorized Version' (King James Version) of the Bible in 1611. Readers used their Bibles to introduce individual interpretations of all kinds, many of them outside the confines of the Church of England. Diligent reading and study of the Bible became a cultural norm, both within the established Church and within various separatist movements.

George Fox (1624–91) and other early Friends embraced the importance of Scripture in knowing God and guiding their lives. Yet they cherished Scripture in the context of their direct encounters with God and of their conviction that the Spirit that inspired Scripture was also inwardly teaching them. Valuing the Bible and relying on the Spirit's direct teaching are both complementary and paradoxical convictions that shaped Friends' use of Scripture.

EARLY STATEMENTS ABOUT SCRIPTURE

George Fox knew the Bible thoroughly and used it lavishly—its words, phrases, images, and stories flood Fox's speaking and writing. Those who knew Fox well mused that if all the copies of the Bible were lost, the whole of its text could be recovered from Fox's memory. While he directed people to the inward teaching of Christ, the Present Teacher, he also affirmed importance of the Bible:

> These things I did not see by the help of man, nor by the letter, though they are written in the letter, but I saw them in the light of the Lord Jesus Christ, and by his immediate Spirit and power, as did the holy men of God, by whom the Holy Scriptures were written. Yet I had no slight esteem of the Holy Scriptures, but they were very precious to me, for I was in that spirit by which they were given forth, and what the Lord opened in me I afterwards found was agreeable to them. (Fox 1995, 34)

In his *Letter to the Governor of Barbados*, Fox also speaks of the importance of the Bible to Friends. He writes that they are inspired, that 'they are to be read, and believed, and fulfilled,' and that are profitable for teaching. He continues, 'And we do believe that the Scriptures are the words of God... We call the Scriptures, as Christ and the apostles called them, and as the holy men of God called them (vizt) the words not *word* of God' (Fox 1995, 604).

Similarly, in his *Apology* the young theologian and scholar Robert Barclay (1644–90) argued that the Scriptures come from God and have unmatched value. In Proposition Three about inspiration and the Scriptures, Barclay writes:

> From the revelations of the Spirit of God to the faithful have come the scriptures of Truth, which contain [(1) faithful historical accounts, (2) prophetic accounts, and] (3) a full and adequate account of all of the chief principles of the doctrine of Christ

which were spoken, or which were written, by the motions of God's Spirit at various times in treasured declarations, exhortations, and maxims which were given to certain churches and their pastors. (Freiday 1967, 460)

As he begins his discussion, Barclay directly addresses the misunderstanding or false accusations of other Christians: 'In spite of what has been said, we consider the scriptures undoubtedly and unequivocally the finest writings in the world. Nothing else that has been written is preferable or even comparable' (Freiday 1967, 46).

In a similar way, Elizabeth Bathurst (1655–85) wrote *Truth's Vindication* as 'a gentle stroke to wipe off the foul aspersions, false accusations, and misrepresentations, called upon the People of God call'd Quakers' (Garman et al 1996, 340). Her first chapter countered the 'great Slander' that the Quakers 'do not own' the Scriptures. She responds that Quakers 'do believe the Scriptures, so far as Scripture it self requires Faith in it self'. She argues that Quakers, in keeping with Scripture, reserve the phrase 'Word of God' to refer to Christ, who is the Word (Garman et al 1996, 349–50).

Witness to the importance of Scripture was common among early Friends. At the same time, however, even as they pointed to the Bible's unique importance, they also proclaimed the presence and reliable authority of the Spirit's inward teaching apart from Scripture. As seen in the quotation above, for example, Fox witnessed that Christ the Present Teacher led him to insights inwardly, not rising from the reading or study of the Bible, that he later found consistent with Scripture. In confidence of the reliability of the Spirit's direct teaching, he also did not look to the Bible as the final authority against which all leadings or openings should be tested (Palmer 2011, ch. 3, 9).

Similarly, Barclay argues from Scripture for the primacy of the Spirit as the foundation of both ancient and contemporary revelation:

> Nevertheless, because the scriptures are only a declaration of the source, and not the source itself, they are not to be considered the principal foundation of all truth and knowledge. They are not even to be considered as the adequate primary rule of all faith and practice. Yet, because they give a true and faithful testimony of the source itself, they are and may be regarded as a secondary rule that is subordinate to the Spirit, from which they obtain all their excellence and certainty. We truly know them only by the inward testimony of the Spirit or, as the scriptures themselves say, the Spirit is the guide by which the faithful are led into all Truth (John 16:13). Therefore, according to the scriptures, the Spirit is the first and principal leader (Rom 8:14). Because we are receptive to the scriptures, as the product of the Spirit, it is for that very reason that the Spirit is the primary and principal rule of faith. (Freiday 1967, 460)

Isaac Penington (1616–79) makes a similar witness: 'And the end of words is to bring men to the knowledge of things beyond what words can utter. So, learn of the Lord to make a right use of the Scriptures: which is by esteeming them in their right place, and prizing that above them which is above them' (*Christian Faith* 1960, no. 204).

In their original setting, Quakers were asserting the importance both of Scripture and of direct inward experience. They declared 'both/and' in a time when the principal of *sola scriptura* threatened to diminish the importance of vital inward experience, particularly among those who insisted that truth was revealed only in biblical times and was found only in Scripture. It was an important paradoxical witness. To anticipate what happens among Friends, however, we should note John Punshon's observation that Barclay's use of the word 'secondary' opened the way for a diminishing of the importance of Scripture. 'Secondary', he points out, often means derivative, subordinate, or of lesser importance. '...Calling the Bible a "secondary" authority has led over time to many Friends not regarding it as an authority at all' (Punshon 2006, 271, 253).

EARLY PATTERNS IN USING SCRIPTURE

One way in which Friends used Scripture was to demonstrate that Friends teaching was consistent with the Bible and, often quite pointedly, that Friends interpreted the Bible more faithfully than their detractors. As John Nickalls points out, 'No one, in fact, knew his Bible better than Fox did, or could quote it in argument more devastatingly' (Fox 1995, xxvii). So when Fox entered into public dispute about what the Bible said and invited people to look in the Scriptures while he taught, he usually prevailed.

Robert Barclay also used the Bible to make his case. For example, in the quotation above he argues for the Spirit as the primary rule of faith 'because we are receptive to the scriptures'. Also, in his *A Catechism and Confession of Faith*, Barclay answers all of the catechetical questions by simply quoting portions of Scripture. He does this, he says, to disprove the 'grossest slander cast upon these people [Quakers] that they vilify and deny the scriptures and replace them with their own conjectures'. To make his point, in answer to the catechetical questions he offers only the words of Scripture, 'without addition or commentary... [and with] no quibbling, no academic subtleties' (Barclay 2001, 16). He invited his readers to be fair in deciding whether he had used the Bible properly.

Barclay is best known for his *Apology*, a thorough work that builds notably on his theological training. His command of Scripture, historical theology, and argument are impressive, and the *Apology* has served Friends well ever since. Others with university and theological training, such as William Penn and Samuel Fisher, also used that in explaining Quakers to those outside the movement.

Certainly it was important to appeal to biblical texts in making their witness to people who relied heavily on Scripture. But for Friends, the Bible was more than a book of texts or principles. Friends engaged Scripture not only to learn about God, but also to encounter God. More precisely, they believed that they could only rightly know the Scriptures by first 'com[ing] to the spirit of God in themselves' (Fox 1995, 136) and relying on the Spirit to teach them through the Scriptures. Their experience of Christ as the Present Teacher continued in the use of the Bible. In the process of reading, everyone could be taught inwardly. As Thomas Kelly described it:

We can go back into that Life within whom Amos and Isaiah lived, that Life in God's presence and vivid guidance, then we understand the writings from within. For we and Isaiah and Hosea feed on the same Life, are rooted in the same holy flame which is burning in our hearts. (Kelly 1988, 32)

Early Friends also learned to read the Bible with empathy, entering into its teaching and narratives and its community of faith as fellow travellers. Barclay refers to the Scriptures as a 'looking-glass', a mirror, that reveals our own journey and teaches us through 'the conditions and experiences of the saints of old' (Freiday 1967, 59). As nearly as they could, through the Bible they were entering into the story and the outlook of the earliest Christians (Birkel 2005, 1ff).

T. Vail Palmer demonstrates that the earliest Friends' use of Scripture reflected this reading with empathy. The sermons, teaching, and letters of leaders such as George Fox, Margaret Fell, and Edward Burroughs were filled with allusions, images, and phrases from the Bible, but not used in a way that was simply quoting text to prove a point. Instead, out of their deep personal engagement with Scripture, they gathered up phrases and metaphors and melded them into new syntheses as they spoke in the power of the Spirit that inspired and taught them the Scriptures (Palmer 2011, ch. 3). Palmer's reading suggests that this strikingly inward interweaving of Bible and experience diminished over time, even though Friends continued to use the Bible steadily.

Changes in the Eighteenth and Nineteenth Centuries

Friends continued to value Scripture as they moved into the eighteenth century and many relied on it to inform their teaching and ministry. A few, notably John Woolman (1720–72), seemed to approach the empathetic reading of Scripture—Michael Birkel shows how Woolman experienced the Bible as reflecting and interpreting his experience. The Bible also shaped Woolman's understanding and bold ministry, especially through his engagement with the prophet Jeremiah (Birkel 2003, 39–56). Palmer finds that Woolman's direct, generous use of Scripture seems less than that of early Friends, but that other Friends used the Bible as a source of texts to support their testimonies or more as a textbook for doctrine and ethical teaching (Palmer 2011, ch. 4). Despite varieties in method, the Bible stood as an important source for Friends and they encouraged each other to read and understand it.

During the eighteenth century Friends began to loosen their strict boundaries against outside groups and, in the process, took on some of the varied influences of that time. Three strands of religious thinking particularly influenced Friends: Quietism; rationalism in religion, under the growing influence of the Enlightenment; and evangelicalism, particularly flowing from the work of John and Charles Wesley.

Friends' witness to the inward work of the Spirit to teach and apply Scripture provided fertile ground for the radical inwardness of Quietism in Europe, particularly in France. Many Friends gladly read Madame Jeanne Guyon, Miguel de Molinos, and François Fénelon and they even published an anthology of their writings in *A Guide to True Peace*, a little book still available from Quaker publishers. Quietism influenced Friends' reading of Scripture in at least two ways. One direction was to rely on the Spirit-directed, internal understanding of Scripture and to demean external influences. Job Scott writes about reading Scripture in this vein:

> The safe state is that of a careful, inward waiting for direction... God alone can give the right turn and direction to our minds... Haste is almost always dangerous, but waiting on the Lord for clearness, direction and qualification is always, and never, if rightly exercised, fruitless. (Scott 1824, 32)

For others, the importance of the Bible as a source seemed to diminish and the direct inward teaching by Christ, or the Light of Christ, was not only superior but sufficient. Friends had mixed practice at this point. Some were sceptical about the value of Scripture, even to the point that some refused to use the Bible at all. On the other hand, many in this stream still valued the Bible highly, encouraged reading it frequently, and used it in sermons and writing. At the same time, more traditional Friends showed concern that the reading and knowledge of Scripture had been seriously eroded (Hamm 2002, 185).

Another influence among Friends grew out of rationalism, one that looked at the Bible more analytically and, in particular, insisted that the biblical text show an internal consistency. In this spirit, several prominent Friends began to question the authority or inspiration of certain parts of the Bible. In the late eighteenth century, Abraham Shackleton was among the first to argue that the loving God seen in the New Testament could never have required that the Israelites undertake wars of conquest as reported in the Old Testament. In 1799 Hannah Barnard (1754–1825) joined in this judgement, rejecting the idea that 'the great and merciful Creator ever commissioned any nation or person to destroy another' (Ingle 1998, 9). Rational analysis of the Bible was in its early stages and would flourish in the nineteenth century. It would continue to influence Friends in the decades to come.

Friends touched by the other stream of influence—evangelicalism—responded sharply to challenges towards the reliability or authority of the Bible. One of the most notable was Henry Tuke (1755–1814), who in 1805 published his book *The Principles of Religion, as Professed by the Society of Friends, Usually Called Quakers*. In its first half-century Tuke's volume appeared in twelve English editions and in editions by several North American Yearly Meetings (Williams 1987, 145–6). He argued that Friends doctrine was based on Scripture and, using the Bible, tried to address the various issues that Friends such as Shackleton (1752–1818) and Barnard regarded as inconsistencies in Scripture.

In addition to addressing questions of doubt and reinterpretation of Scripture, Friends influenced by evangelicalism organized to distribute the Bible more broadly among Friends. Emerging Quaker leader Joseph John Gurney (1788–1847) had early on joined with Christian friends such as William Wilberforce and others in the work of the British and Foreign Bible Society, founded in 1804 (Jones 1970, I, 496). When the American Bible Society was founded in 1816, many American Friends helped lead its efforts (Jones 1970, II, 886). However, in 1829, directly after the Great (or Hicksite) Separation, Orthodox Quakers in the United States began a work of their own, the Bible Association of Friends in America. The leaders of this work were concerned that some American Friends were 'scantily supplied with copies of the Bible', thinking that 'no supply of the Bible can be considered as *adequate*, which does not put a copy into the possession [of] *every person capable of reading it*'. They especially emphasized that each child should have a copy of the Bible 'printed on good paper with large type' and that parents should model and teach its value (*Appeal* 1832, 4, 7). Their appeal attributes the short supply of Bibles both to availability and to the economic conditions of some Friends. But these leaders also show their conviction that ignorance of and indifference to the Bible's content, along with levity and scepticism, had led to false teaching and to the denial of basic truths.

The travels of Stephen Grellet (1773–1855) and Elias Hicks (1748–1830) in 1808 illustrate the complexity of the problem of Scripture at this juncture of Quaker experience. Grellet and Hicks travelled together in ministry in New York Yearly Meeting to encourage local meetings to live faithfully as Quakers. In the course of their travels, Grellet come to believe that Hicks 'tended to lessen the authority of the Holy Scriptures', and he 'frequently, fervently, and earnestly laboured with him' to turn away from that teaching. Hicks did not respond well to this concern and ten years later, Grellet was one of the leaders who confronted Hicks publicly about his teaching (Grellet 1874, I, 142).

Hicks himself warned about the misuse of Scripture by Friends who were tending to take the Bible as 'the only rule of faith and practice' (Hicks, 1861, 175). He also insisted that he delighted in reading the Bible, a fact attested by those who knew him well:

> As to the Scriptures of truth...I have always accounted them, when rightly understood, as the best of books extant....and [I] have made more use of their contents to confirm and establish my labours in the gospel, than most other ministers that I am acquainted with .... I have read them as much as most other men, and few, I believe, have derived more profit from them than I have. (Hicks 1861, 215)

Friends were moving in conflicting ways away from a balanced tension that valued both Scripture and the teaching of the Spirit. Put perhaps a bit too broadly, those who emerged from the Hicksite stream came to value the inward and experiential as a primary authority; those in the Orthodox stream came to give the Scriptures as external authority a more prominent role. Both streams claim fidelity to the early Friends tradition.

Evangelically influenced Friends used another new initiative to renew interest in and knowledge of Scripture, that of organized Bible studies. While they continued to emphasize the importance of families reading Scripture together each day, a practice that had long been affirmed in Yearly Meeting 'Advices', this approach to Bible study set a new direction. In one innovation, they followed the lead of Protestant groups that quickly spread the use of Sunday Schools, a robust and new method initially begun in 1780 by Robert Raikes especially to reach poor children. Friends preferred to call them 'First Day Schools for Scriptural Instruction' (Hamm 1988, 26). Walter Williams traces the first such school to Levi Coffin in 1818 in Deep River, North Carolina (Williams 1987, 193), but the use of this model spread broadly in the 1830s and beyond. Hannah Backhouse (1787–1850), a well-regarded English Friends minister and first cousin to Joseph John Gurney, led in this development when she travelled among Friends in the United States from 1830 to 1835. During these years, especially in ministry in Indiana, Backhouse set up numerous weekly 'Bible meetings' in which participants would read and study Scripture and would share portions of the Bible which they had memorized. Before she returned to England in 1834 she wrote a manual, *Scripture Quotations for the Use of Schools,* to help Friends continue the development of this movement (Jones 1970, II, 887–8).

Friends in England showed similar innovations in teaching the Bible. Joseph Sturge (1793–1859) began the Adult School movement in Birmingham in 1845 and two years later invited Quaker teachers to a conference on Bible teaching that resulted in the founding of the Friends' First-day School Association (Jones 1970, II, 955–6). Both initiatives grew and prospered in the ensuing decades.

Though many Friends led in these new directions, the most prominent leader was Joseph John Gurney, an influential minister in Britain who travelled in America during 1837–40. A banker by trade, he had a fine theological education and studied the Bible devoutly, even learning to read it in its original languages. He promoted systematic teaching of the Bible in meeting schools and helped by providing materials he had created for England's Ackworth School for that purpose (Jones 1970, II, 889). His encouraging ministry to Friends in Indiana led them in 1847 to found Earlham College, where studying the Bible was an important part of the curriculum.

Many interpreters believe that Gurney also led Friends more fully to a new way of thinking about Scripture, one that gave prominence to the Bible over the work of the Spirit. One of the key evidences of this is a statement that grew out of a controversy about the Bible in London Yearly Meeting in 1836. The statement, which Gurney heavily influenced, came from Westmorland Quarterly Meeting and was endorsed by London Yearly Meeting. The substance and specific language of it shaped Friends' witness for decades to come, as, for example, in the Richmond Declaration of Faith of 1887, to be discussed later. The core of it reads:

> It has ever been, and still is, the belief of the Society of Friends, that the Holy Scriptures of the Old and New Testaments were given by inspiration of God: that therefore the declarations contained in them rest on the authority of God Himself and there can be no appeal from them to any other authority whatsoever: that they are able to make us wise unto salvation through faith which is in Christ Jesus; being the appointed means of making known to us the blessed truths of Christianity: that they are the only divinely authorized record of the doctrines which we are bound as Christians to believe, and of the moral principles which are to regulate our actions: that no doctrine which is not contained in them can be required of any one to be

believed as an article of faith: that whatsoever any man says or does which is contrary to the Scriptures, though under profession of the immediate guidance of the Spirit, must be reckoned and accounted a mere delusion. (Jones 1970, I, 510)

Some Friends objected to these new developments in emphasizing Scripture for several reasons. They worried, for example, that Friends' cooperation with other Christians in these enterprises would distort and diminish the distinctive Friends witness. So John Wilbur (1774–1856), a leader among Friends who objected, warned against such 'departures' by 'joining with hireling clergy' and 'Bishops, priests, and people of divers other denominations' in working to spread the Scriptures (Jones 1970, I, 512). Opponents of these new directions were also troubled by how much, especially in teaching the Bible in schools, Friends relied on materials prepared by scholars and ministers outside the Friends' tradition.

Even more importantly, these Friends objected to the nature of Bible study itself. They believed that the approach to study used in the new movements abandoned some of Friends' key insights about how they valued and used Scripture. They felt that study of this sort brought external means and abandoned the work of the Spirit in interpreting the text. As Rufus Jones notes: 'The prevailing theory, in conservative circles, was that this revelation of truth was too sacred to be openly discussed and argued about. It was to be read with reverence and awe...not to be 'worked over' by the intellect' (Jones 1970, II, 885). Before 1860, Friends did not read the Bible aloud in meetings for worship; speaking directly out of the Spirit's guidance would not need this aid. So this move to public discussion and systematic study of the Bible seemed like a betrayal of core Quaker values. In a letter, John Wilbur even spoke of it as the work of the devil to study 'to preach the letter only instead of Christ Jesus in the demonstration of the spirit and power' (Jones 1970, I, 515).

This sharp rejection of the emerging approaches to Scripture among Friends, along with a variety of other issues, eventually led John Wilbur and those who joined him to separate from other Friends in the Orthodox Quaker stream. The Wilburite Separation culminated in 1854 and became a movement that Friends have called 'Conservative'; (see Wilson's chapter 8 within this volume entitled 'Conservative Friends 1845–2010').

CHALLENGES TO THE BIBLE IN THE NINETEENTH AND TWENTIETH CENTURIES

Several factors emerged to challenge traditional understandings of the Bible in the nineteenth century. This prompted a variety of responses that continued into the next century. The main sources of challenge were new scientific theories and broad changes in analysing and interpreting Scripture.

Early in the nineteenth century, the science of paleontology began to show from the fossil record that ancient creatures had existed that long outdated known human history. At the same time, geologists were working out a sequence of the earth's geological strata and argued that the development of the earth was long and gradual. These two related streams of thought brought into question the common interpretation of the Bible that the world was created about 6,000 years ago.

In 1859, Charles Darwin published his *On the Origin of Species* in which he argued for the evolution of species through the process of natural selection. Within twenty years, his theory was widely accepted in the scientific community and by the general public. This theory, in effect, challenged traditional interpretations of the Bible's teaching about creation.

The nineteenth century also saw the emergence of archaeology, though it wouldn't mature as a science until early in the twentieth century. Nonetheless, important ancient sites, such as Nineveh, were excavated and their treasures taken to museums around the world. Among the remarkable discoveries were ancient texts contemporary with the events of the Bible. By the 1870s scholars had deciphered the ancient writing systems of cuneiform Akkadian and hieroglyphic Egyptian, and this revealed much about the life of ancient Israel's neighbours that had previously been unknown. The texts included ancient laws, historical annals, economic texts, and various religious texts, not least some creation stories, flood stories, and myths about the gods of Israel's neighbours. Insight into these texts also raised questions about traditional interpretations of some biblical texts.

Another challenge to traditional interpretations came from the work of what was then called 'higher criticism'—new approaches to interpreting the Bible based on analytical methods emerging from the Enlightenment. One of the most controversial subjects in the in the nineteenth century was the question of who wrote the Bible. For example, the new methods led to the conclusion that Moses was not in fact the author of the Pentateuch—the first five books of the Bible—as had been traditionally thought, and that the Book of Isaiah came from multiple authors and times. Not only the conclusions, but the methods themselves sparked strong debate since many readers of the Bible worried that the underpinnings of their faith, strongly reliant on biblical teaching, were being threatened.

People who cherished Scripture tended to respond in two ways to these new realities. Many people of faith challenged the validity of the new scientific theories, considering them wrong since they disagreed with what they understood to be the plain teaching of the Bible. They also rejected the new approaches to analysing Scripture, regarding them as arid and dangerous, not arising out of genuine faith. Friends, too, had to respond to these new challenges, and they tended to divide into those who would reject the new directions and those who, while desiring to remain faithful to Scripture, were willing to explore new ways of interpreting and studying it.

Many of the Friends who had been influenced by Joseph John Gurney not only developed new practices among Friends, but also continued to cooperate with other groups in the evangelical stream. In America they shared in the work and energy of the Great Revival and came to share in theology, notably in teaching about Holiness, and in adopting new methods. So it is not surprising that these 'Revival' Friends also shared evangelical responses to the challenges of new scientific theory and new methods in biblical study. They largely resisted and attacked the new approaches. David Updegraff (1830–94), a prominent leader among these Friends, warned against 'higher criticism' and how it brought 'fearless attacks of unsoundness in high places'. At this point there were few trained biblical scholars in this group of Friends, and such training was looked at with suspicion (Hamm 1988, 109). In his history (decades later), Walter Williams (1884–1973), an Evangelical Friend from Ohio, expresses a similar spirit when he says: '... considerable numbers of Friends on both sides of the Atlantic were drinking of the waters of knowledge, sometimes polluted with doubt, from the fountain bearing the high-sounding name: *Modern Biblical Scholarship and Progressive Religious Thought*' (Williams1987, 211). These responses persisted for decades and, among some, found similarity and support in the fundamentalism that emerged among American Protestants.

A defining moment in American Evangelical Quakerism came at a gathering of Friends in Richmond, Indiana in 1887. This was a diverse group, but all from the Gurneyite stream. They agreed on a statement entitled the 'Richmond Declaration of Faith', a statement that is still widely used among Friends even though the religious context has changed over time. The statement itself was decidedly evangelical, but more moderate in tone than emerging responses among some Friends and in the larger Protestant culture. The statement affirms the inspiration and authority of Scripture, but it does not use the words 'infallible' or 'inerrant' that were becoming important to other evangelicals at the time. This may well be in part because Friends' confidence in the Spirit working through Scripture undercuts the worry that we can only know God through a text that is perfect in every way. One of the principal contributors to the statement was Joseph Bevan Braithwaite, an Evangelical Friend from England.

Others Friends gradually accepted and engaged in the new approaches to science and biblical study. English Friends moved in this direction earlier than their American counterparts, and they influenced changes in America. The Modernist or liberal stream included freedom of thought, a growing sense of progressive revelation, coupled with a sense that modern methods of study could deepen one's understanding of the Bible. When English Friend David Duncan used methods of 'higher criticism' in the 1870s, his work was unwelcome. However, within thirty years, the directions he had pioneered had become commonplace in England (Dandelion 2007, 117–18).

In England in 1884, three young Friends published the book *A Reasonable Faith*, which stirred discussion about moving towards more liberal approaches. In 1893, London Yearly Meeting opened the way for such movement, recognizing the need to meet the younger generation and to stir Friends from a kind of lethargy (Russell 1979, 501ff). John Wilhelm Rowntree (1868–1905), still in his twenties, was one of the most compelling English leaders. He influenced London Yearly Meeting's decision in 1893 and two years later emerged as a leader among young liberals at the conference at Manchester that attracted a thousand people to address the topic of Friends and modern thought. Friends organized a series of summer schools to bring qualified scholars to teach about the new movements in Bible, science, and theology. The first of these was at Scarborough in 1897, with more than 650 people attending (Punshon 1984, 241), and they continued for a couple of decades. In a similar move, Friends established Woodbrooke in 1903 as a study centre near Birmingham (England) that invited people to come for short and longer periods of study (Brayshaw 1953, 317ff.). Among the scholars and thinkers who influenced this movement were Rowntree, H. G. Wood, Rufus Jones (1863–1948), Rendel Harris, and Caroline Stephen.

Rufus Jones's participation in these events in Britain nurtured a strong friendship with John Wilhelm Rowntree and convinced him to seek similar changes among American Friends. His leadership and advocacy, along with scholars such as Elbert Russell (1871–1951) of Earlham College and Mary Mendenhall Hobbs (1852–1930) of Guilford College, did bring more Modernist approaches to Scripture, trying to acknowledge the advances in science, and to discover the value of new approaches to biblical texts. Summer schools were offered at Earlham (the Earlham Bible Institute) beginning in 1897 and at Haverford College, beginning in 1900 (Russell 1979, 508–9) Friends established a similar institution, Woolman School, at Swarthmore in 1917, and it continued for ten years. It was succeeded in 1930 by Pendle Hill, a study centre similar to Woodbrooke, in Wallingford, near Philadelphia (Punshon 1984, 276).

About the same time, and in contrast to these summer schools and study centres, Evangelical Friends also established schools to teach Bible and to prepare people for the work of public ministry. In 1892, Walter and Emma Malone founded the Cleveland Bible Institute, later to become Malone University. In 1917, Scott T. Clark founded the Kansas Central Bible Training School in Haviland, Kansas, where it became a two-year, then the four-year Bible college, Friends Bible College, and was renamed Barclay College in 1990. Other Friends colleges, such as Pacific College, now George Fox University, also had a strong commitment to Bible teaching, but teaching that continued traditional views and resisted changes introduced by Modernism.

In the early twentieth century, especially in America, the conflicts between Modernism and Fundamentalism raged and affected all Christian groups. How people regarded and treated the Bible was, of course, one of the central issues. Friends had their own history of conflict and change, but the larger controversies influenced Friends as well.

Also in the early twentieth century, Friends, mostly from evangelical roots, established new missions in a variety of places, notably Kenya, India, China, Guatemala, and Bolivia. From these early efforts vigorous Yearly Meetings have grown, the missions have expanded into new areas, and the membership of Friends in the Global South now far exceeds the membership of Friends in America and Britain. Virtually all the Yearly Meetings that grew out of this mission effort now belong to either Friends United Meeting or Evangelical Friends Church International, both of which still point to the Richmond Declaration of Faith to characterize themselves. The Yearly Meetings that arose from the missions' effort generally share the outlook on the Bible that their founding Yearly Meetings held. They distribute and teach from the Bible. Several maintain Bible schools or Bible institutes to prepare leaders for public ministry. Such teaching was also offered to those who could not be resident students through programmes such as Theological Education by Extension. Often the Bible has been the primary resource for both teaching literacy and providing religious instruction. As Esther Mombo of Kenya notes: 'The Bible became central to the work of evangelism and literacy, which went hand in hand' (2006, 87). The Bible was the basic textbook. People learned it well, often memorizing much of the Scriptures, and passed its message to one another in story and teaching.

DIVERSITY IN MODERN PRACTICE

Beginning in the last quarter of the nineteenth century, Evangelical Friends in America gradually adopted practices of programmed worship and pastoral ministry. These practices are now the norm among these Friends and are also the most common forms in the Friends movement. In this context, Friends give the Bible a prominent place in their attention and activities. The statement about the Scriptures in Northwest Yearly Meeting's *Faith and Practice* illustrates the importance of the Bible for these Friends:

> We believe the Holy Scriptures of the Old and New Testaments were given by inspiration of God. They are the divinely authorized record of the doctrines that we as Christians are bound to accept, and of the moral principles that are to regulate our lives and actions.... Interpreted by the Holy Spirit, they are an unfailing source of truth. We believe the Spirit will not lead person or groups contrary to the teachings of the Scriptures ('God's Revelation').

Such regard for Scripture shapes the life of these Friends meetings. Prepared sermons are a regular part of worship, and members expect that such preaching should be 'biblical', some even expecting that it should be 'expositional' in style. Most Friends churches have Sunday Schools for both children and adults. The classes may use curricula developed specifically by Friends or developed with like-minded groups, such as other groups in the historic Holiness movement. In any event, the lessons are based on particular biblical texts. Most of these Friends churches will also have a variety of other activities based on the Bible: Vacation Bible Schools, youth Bible quiz teams and contests, Bible study groups, and strong encouragement of personal Bible reading. Many Friends also give copies of the Bible to children and youth in their meetings.

Friends in the 'liberal' tradition continue a sharply different view of the authority and singular importance of the Scriptures. Excerpts from Philadelphia Yearly Meeting's *Faith and Practice* illustrate the contrasts:

> Friends' appreciation of the Bible and other scriptures springs from our faith that there is in everyone the capacity to be open and responsive to the experience of the Divine...Like Fox, Friends since have found the Bible to be the record of direct experiences of the Holy Spirit, serving as an important touchstone against which to test our leadings...Friends know from experience that knowledge of the Bible widely shared in a Meeting deepens the spiritual power of both spoken ministry and inward listening...Given the Bible's importance in shaping the ways Friends have expressed their experience of the presence and leading of God and its power to illumine our worship and our vocal ministry, we are encouraged to know it well. We

do not, however, consider scriptures, whether Hebrew or Christian or those of other religious faiths, to be the final revelation of God's nature and will. Rather, we believe in continuing revelation ('Friends').

The practices of individuals and meetings vary widely. Some individuals know the Bible very well, even committing large portions of it to memory; others scarcely know it at all. Some meetings encourage the use of Scripture and may even offer some teaching to deepen members' understanding. Other meetings marginalize or neglect it in practice. Some members have come to Friends partly in reaction to personal experiences in which they felt the Bible was misused or even used abusively. So they and their meetings are sometimes cautious about using the Bible.

Some leaders among Liberal Friends actively encourage the steady reading and study of the Bible. Chuck Fager, a writer and publisher among Liberal Friends, often invites serious Bible study in works such as *Reclaiming a Resource*. Joanne and Larry Spears have taught and written about a method they call Friendly Bible Study to help guide groups into attentive, spiritual listening to biblical texts.

Conservative Friends continue to hold that they are the most faithful to early Quaker faith and practice. After reporting the work of Fox and Barclay, Stanley Pennington summarizes, 'Barclay affirms the great benefit for Friends in the ongoing use of Scriptures, as a resource for us as we seek to know and follow the presence of the Living Word of God'. He then points to Ohio Yearly Meeting's *Book of Discipline*, Advice No. 16: 'Be diligent in the reading of the Bible and other spiritually helpful writings.' Many individuals and families practise daily reading of the Bible. In their gatherings for business and worship, Conservative Friends do use forms of reading Scripture, generally accompanied by a period of waiting worship. Some meetings have Bible study groups to read and explore the Bible (Pennington 2010). Also from this tradition, Lloyd Lee Wilson urges the importance of daily Bible reading, directed Bible study, and 'soaking' Bible reading in his lecture 'Why do you still read that old thing?'.

A notable trend in the twentieth century came as Friends of all sorts engaged in and even embraced biblical scholarship. Instead of regarding seminary education as suspect, many came to welcome it and even regard it as necessary. Seminaries typically include the academic study of Scripture, and Friends came increasingly to accept that study and the Quaker leaders who had become outstanding biblical scholars. Recognized leaders and scholars included Moses Bailey in Old Testament studies and Henry Cadbury, Alexander Purdy, and George Boobyer in New Testament studies. In recent decades, among the many fine scholars who have emerged among Friends, a growing number of specialists in biblical studies have given new leadership.

The shape of biblical scholarship in the academy has also changed in recent decades, with new approaches to analysis displacing the historic centrality of 'higher criticism' with its focus on authorship and sources. Instead, new methods have emerged drawing on insights and methods from literature, the social sciences, feminism, and other creative and interdisciplinary approaches. They have broadened and deepened our understanding of Scripture and the community of faith from which it first came. This new diversity in methods has also helped lower defences against critical analysis.

Recognizing that sound scholarship is making a substantial contribution to Friends colleges, seminaries, and serious journals, it is useful to note that, for a variety of reasons, much of this work does not find its way into the life of many Friends meetings. Friends who want to learn these methods and results more deeply often still rely on special schools, workshops, and conferences, and now sometimes through study on the Internet with extension courses available through programmes such as those at Earlham School of Religion, the first Quaker seminary.

Reflections on the Path Ahead

The Bible will continue to play an important role in Quaker life and practice. The current differences among Friends take their shape from long history and habit, and it seems unlikely that these differences will change markedly in the near future. Virtually all Friends claim to value Scripture's witness and they encourage active engagement with the Bible as a part of faithful living. Friends have tended to stray from the difficult tension of the paradox of God speaking to us through both Scripture and the Spirit. To hold that point of paradox, Evangelical Friends could steadily encourage the Spirit-led reading of the Bible. Liberal Friends could embrace the Bible's role more fully as an authoritative guide. All Friends could do more to deepen Bible literacy.

Michael Birkel's *Engaging Scripture: Reading the Bible with Early Friends* is one indication that the renewed interest in reading Scripture through the lens of spirituality may open new paths (or recover older paths) for Friends. Another fresh path may come from listening to those who teach and minister out of the Friends meetings in the Global South. Cross-cultural listening could well deepen the understanding of Friends in Britain and North America. New insights could come from Friends in Africa, Asia, and Latin America who may hear and live out the Bible more ably than those steeped in traditions of Western Europe. Their treasure of cultural practices, social organization, and varied histories can deepen our understanding of the biblical texts. The work of Friend Esther Mombo of Kenya is one example of how throughout the Global South the gifts of traditional cultures combined with contemporary scholarly tools are bringing fresh and valuable readings of Scripture.

Suggested Further Reading

Birkel, M. L. (2005) *Engaging Scripture: Reading the Bible with early Friends*. Richmond, IN: Friends United Press and Earlham Press.

Buckley, P. and Angell, S. W. (eds.) (2006) *The Quaker Bible reader*. Richmond, IN: Earlham Press.

Freiday, D. (ed.) (1967) *Barclay's Apology in modern English*. Hemlock Press.

Hamm, T. D. (2002) "'A Protest against Protestantism': Hicksite Friends and the Bible in the nineteenth century' *Quaker Studies* 6 (2), pp. 175–94.

Jones, R., (1970 [1921]) *The later periods of Quakerism*, 2 vols. Westport, CN: Greenwood Press.

....

CHAPTER 13

QUAKERS, ESCHATOLOGY, AND TIME

....

DOUGLAS GWYN

ESCHATOLOGY involves various beliefs and expectations regarding 'last things'—the end of personal life or of world history. Eschatology also implies teleology: it usually asserts that some divine end, or purpose, will be fulfilled in the way things end. Eschatology sometimes recapitulates protology: for example, the belief that the end will re-instate in some way the paradise of humanity's beginnings. Hence, eschatological beliefs frame 'time' and 'world' in decisive and meaningful ways. The end of the world may imply that the physical world will be destroyed and/or profoundly altered. Similarly, the end of time may imply that time will be experienced very differently and/or be replaced by timelessness, eternity. Or eschatology may concern simply the end of *a* world, the passing of a given social system, or a given historic era. Eschatology is a way of thinking about ultimate reality in temporal terms. It is a metatemporal outlook, comparable to metaphysical views.

Eschatological beliefs typically inspire believers to act in certain ways. They may experience the end-time as a present reality that inspires and empowers a very different way of living. Or they may see the end-time as a future event. In the meantime, believers act in ways they believe will be rewarded by God in the end. Either way, the sense of an end deeply affects personal morality, group social practices, and political options. Eschatological beliefs inspire social and political attitudes and actions ranging from revolution and resistance, to progressive reform, and conservative reaction.

Eschatology typically includes a meantime belief in divine providence. God acts in history to shape events towards divine ends. God also redeems, leads, consecrates, and provides for individuals and communities of faith as agents of divine purpose in society and history.

As we shall see, Quaker eschatology was non-violently revolutionary in its earliest phases. Its mode shifted to countercultural resistance in the latter seventeenth century and extending through the eighteenth century. Over the course of the nineteenth century it bifurcated into progressive-reformist and reactionary modes. Those trends extended into the twentieth century, producing Modernist optimism and fundamentalist pessimism regarding society and its destiny. The late twentieth century witnessed a post-Modern eclipse of time by space in both progressive and reactionary Quaker eschatologies. New communication technologies have created an instantaneous global grid in which the new is replaced by an omnipresent now. We will devote greater attention to seventeenth- and eighteenth-century Quaker eschatologies, as they are the most distinctive.

Pre-Quaker Eschatologies during the English Civil Wars

Two civil wars (1642–8), followed in 1649 by the beheading of King Charles I and the declaration of an English Commonwealth, induced a protracted state of crisis in England. While most people would have preferred to retain familiar ways, the rending of the English religious and political fabric inspired considerable eschatological speculation, religious experimentation, and political agitation. Oliver Cromwell had recruited men to fight for Parliament's cause by suggesting that they were fighting for the Kingdom of God. Radical preachers and political agitators in Parliament's army and elsewhere proclaimed their visions for the fulfilment of that hope. Levellers advocated a republican government, wide-ranging political reforms, and religious freedom to usher in the millennial 'rule of the saints' in Britain. Fifth Monarchists attempted violent insurrections in 1657 and 1661 to attain the same end. Diggers initiated farming communes for poor people and advocated an end to private property as the beginning of God's true commonwealth in England. Seekers awaited a new, purified Church that would transcend proliferating religious conflicts and inaugurate a new age of the Spirit. Others expected a physical return of Christ to rule as the rightful King of England and then the world. Women prophets emerged in Independent and Baptist congregations, announcing imminent transformation.

But as more conservative forces in Parliament and the Army took control of the nation by 1650, radical groups saw their eschatological hopes fade. Ranters raged against the emerging Puritan establishment. They enacted a libertine inversion of Puritan morality and declared that good and evil were all the same, and that heaven and hell exist only here on earth. But most chastened radicals quietly awaited further developments. (These pre-Quaker eschatologies are followed in Gwyn 2000.)

The Apocalyptic Spirituality of the Early Quaker Movement, 1650–1666

The Quaker movement blossomed around northern England in 1652 as a resurgence of radical ideas and experiments, albeit refocused and empowered in new ways. Its central founding figure, George Fox (1624–91), had been imprisoned for a year at Derby in

1650 for preaching moral perfection in Christ. Previous radicals had suffered imprisonment as a defeat. Fox declared his imprisonment Derby's 'day of visitation' from the
Lord, a spiritual crisis for a town imprisoning an innocent minister of Christ. He debated
with local clergy in his cell and sent letters to town leaders. He even wrote to the parish
bell-ringers (timekeepers): 'time will come that you will say you had time, when it was
past. Oh, look at the love of God now, while you have time' (Fox 1995, 55–6). In various
ways he sought to shift human consciousness from regular, chronological rhythms to a
transformative encounter with 'the mighty day of the Lord'.

In a similar, counter-intuitive manner Fox counselled disillusioned radicals to
'stand still in the Light' of Christ, which would reveal their false, socially constructed
selves and socially received world. This Light, which Fox insisted abides in each person's conscience, was apocalyptic in the root sense of the Greek *apokalypto* ('to reveal'
or 'to take away the veil'). It demystified and delegitimized the alienated relations of
the social world and one's place in it. This apocalyptic revelation 'ended the world' as a
self-evident, self-authenticating realm. Early Friends gathering in this revelation began
to enact new moral behaviours, socially equitable relations, and non-violent initiatives
for social change to initiate the Kingdom of God in provisional ways. They understood
their de-alienated social patterns as a living 'testimony' that 'reaches to the witness of
God in every one'. Spoken and acted testimony could turn others to the Light of Christ
in their own consciences and begin the same apocalyptic 'end of the world' in their experience and transformed lives.

George Fox equated standing still in the Light with taking up the Cross. Following
Paul's witness in Gal. 6:14, Fox wrote to Friends in 1653: '[The] cross must be taken up
by all, who follow Jesus Christ out of the world which hath an end, into the world which
is without end; and all the evil things of the world must be denied... where the world is
standing, the cross is not lived in' (Fox 1831, VII: 66).

Fox summarized his message with the words: 'Christ is come to teach his people himself by his power and spirit and to bring them off all the world's ways and teachers to his
own free teaching' (Fox 1995, 104). This was a message of Christ's return, not as a physical descent from the sky but *via* the Light in each person's conscience. This apocalyptic
revelation was radically grounded in the present. Whatever fulfilment might come in
the future, the present apocalypse was the only one to be known and entered. Friends
were discouraged from speculating about the future. In a letter to his parents in 1652
Fox wrote, 'Look not back, nor be too forward, further than ye have attained; for ye have
no time but this present time: therefore prize your time for your souls' sake. And so grow
up in that which is pure, and keep to the oneness' (Fox 1831, VII: 19).

The movement grew exponentially in its first four years, gathering thousands of radicals across England and Wales. It exerted vigorous resistance to the national Church,
whose clerical teaching and liturgical calendar Friends believed kept the world turning and alienated men and women from the day of the Lord, Christ's return in their
consciences. They called their movement the 'Lamb's War', drawing upon imagery
from the Book of Revelation. The faithful follow Christ the Lamb into spiritual warfare against the demonic forces of Satan/the dragon. Friends understood the beast and

false prophet raised by the dragon in Revelation 13 to be the state-enforced Church and its enfranchised clerical class. Friends were pioneers in greater social equality and fair trade practices. But the Lamb's War focused its non-violent struggle primarily against the state-enforced Church as the greatest impediment to Christ's reign on earth. Fox believed that a coerced faith alienates the conscience from the Light and teaching of Christ within. All other social ills follow from that basic deformation of consciousness. Friends testified to Christ as the rightful new sovereign in England, ruling from the grassroots through freely gathered communities of men and women who follow the Light Within. In contrast with the hollow victory of the English Civil War, the Lamb's War pursued the peaceable Kingdom by non-violent means of struggle.

Thus, early Quaker pacifism was highly conflictual. In a 1652 epistle to Friends, Fox wrote:

> That which is set up by the sword, is held up by the sword; and that which is set up by spiritual weapons is held up by spiritual weapons, and not by carnal weapons. The peacemaker hath the kingdom, and is in it: and hath the dominion over the peace-breaker, to calm him in the power of God ... The days of virtue, love, and peace are come and coming, and the Lamb ... will overcome with the sword of the spirit, the word of his mouth; for the Lamb shall have the victory. (1831, VII:20)

Fox's 'come and coming' language (echoing Jesus' usage in John 4:23) suggests that early Quaker apocalyptic might be termed a 'realizing eschatology'. Quaker spirituality and social practices enacted Christ's return as a present, unfolding reality, expanding in circles of participation and social influence.

Early Quaker spirituality fused temporal and eternal realities. Fox wrote in 1653: 'The first step of peace is to stand still in the Light ... here is God alone glorified and exalted, and the unknown truth, unknown to the world, made manifest, which draws up that which lies in prison, and refresheth it in time, up to God, out of time, through time' (1831, IV:17–18). It also fused personal eschatology (life after death) with the revolutionary struggle of the Lamb's War. As the movement elicited growing state persecution and mob violence, several leaders died. Early leader Edward Burrough succumbed in a London prison in early 1663. Fox wrote to comfort Friends: 'Be still and wait in your own conditions, and settled in the Seed of God that doth not change, that in that ye may feel dear Edward Burrough among you in the Seed ... with whom he is: and that in the Seed ye may all see and feel him ... and so enjoy him in the life that doth not change, but which is invisible' (Fox 1995, 437). Thus, faithful attentiveness to the Light/Seed of Christ's presence unites one in eternal oneness with the faithful in all ages. Fox taught that these faithful are found beyond the bounds of Christendom, since anyone who turns to and follows the Light in their own conscience enters the eternal oneness.

Another key early leader, James Nayler (1618–60), enacted a variation on early Quaker apocalyptic. In 1656, as the Quaker confrontation with religious and political establishments reached a boiling point, Nayler and a group of followers performed in the streets of Bristol a sign of Jesus' entry into Jerusalem. Nayler rode on a horse while his followers sang 'holy, holy'. The action was intended as a sign of Christ's return as the Light/Seed in the flesh of common men and women like themselves. That was a basic conviction of the movement. But the Nayler group evidently expected something important to precipitate from the event. Nayler did not believe himself to be Christ, but writings from his four intense years of itinerant Quaker ministry suggest that he aimed to expend himself so completely that only Christ would show through in his words and actions. Parliament chose not to recognize the difference. A long show trial convicted Nayler as a blasphemous false-Christ and meted upon him a savage punishment. Parliament's action aimed to stigmatize the Quaker movement generally. These events in the last weeks of 1656 sparked a more decisive reaction against Friends, intensifying state persecution and mob violence.

Another variant on early Quaker eschatology was Margaret Fell's (1614–1702) outreach to the Jewish community in Amsterdam. Fell was Fox's feminine counterpart in early leadership and a gifted administrator of the movement. Her writings are similar to Fox's on the apocalyptic revelation of the Light. But evidently she also shared with some contemporary groups the millennial expectation that the last days would feature a general conversion of the Jews. Jews had been banned from England since the late thirteenth century and Fell was among those who petitioned for their readmission.

She also wrote to the Jewish community in Amsterdam. Her 1656 tract, *The Call to the Jews out of Babylon*, calls Jews to turn to the Light Within. Her supporting texts are drawn exclusively from Hebrew Scripture, without use of New Testament texts or references to Jesus as the Messiah (Bruyneel 2010, ch. 4). Her aim appears to have been less a Jewish conversion to Christian doctrine than a Quaker–Jewish convergence in following God's Light Within. So Fell's outreach combined the Quaker existential grounding in personal experience of the Light with contemporary non-Quaker millennial expectations about the conversion of the Jews. But such speculations were generally avoided by Friends. The present apocalypse is the only apocalypse one can know. Predictions about the future only divert attention from the present work of the Light. Although Jews were readmitted to England by the end of the 1650s, Fell's outreach produced no recorded results.

As persecutions against Friends intensified, the Commonwealth also stalled and collapsed; the Stuart monarchy and episcopal state Church were restored in 1660. Fox's *Journal* records that as he watched the Commonwealth falling apart in 1659:

> I saw how the powers were plucking each other to pieces. I saw how men were destroying the simplicity and betraying the Truth...the powers had hardened themselves, persecuting Friends, and had many of them in prison, and were crucifying the Seed, Christ, both in themselves and others...So God overthrew them, and turned them upside down, and brought the King over them. (Fox 1995, 353–4)

Note the implication here: the failure of God's Kingdom on earth was not a matter of mistaken Quaker expectations but recalcitrant human alienation and persecution. Friends were prepared to suffer greatly for their witness to the day of the Lord, but they could not guarantee the outcome. Human freedom can turn back God's Kingdom, but God is not mocked. Fox saw providential judgement in the fall of the Commonwealth.

The Restoration of the monarchy and the state Church unleashed much harsher and more systematic persecution, while Friends maintained a stubborn prophetic witness. They refused to meet secretly, as most non-conforming groups did. In 1660 Dorothy White could still witness: 'This is the acceptable Day of the Lord...the warfare of the Lamb is begun'. But already the focus was starting to shift from outward expansion and revolutionary social transformation to resistance and the internal consolidation of the movement. White continued: 'Thus is the Living God purifying his Temples; and he is making a Glorious Situation, a Heavenly Habitation, and an Everlasting dwelling place in the Sons and daughters of Men; for God is now come to dwell in his people' (*A Visitation of Heavenly Love*, Gwyn 1995, 237).

From Apocalyptic Movement to Resistant Sect, 1666–1750

By 1666 it was clear that the Restoration regime had pulled England back from the end-time to a stabilizing meantime, which proved increasingly prosperous (albeit harshly exploitative and imperialistic). Friends gradually shifted their mode from a revolutionary grassroots movement to a hedged sect maintaining countercultural spiritual and social practices within a secularizing society. They began organizing themselves more fully for the long term with parallel men and women's tracks of monthly, quarterly, and Yearly Meetings. Fox promoted the parallel meetings as a restoration of the relations of Eden: 'man and woman were helps-meet in the image of God...before they fell, but after the fall in the transgression, the man was to rule over his wife; but in the restoration by Christ, into the image of God, and his righteousness and holiness again, in that they are helps-meet, man and woman, as they were before the fall' (1831, VIII:39). The men and women's meetings modelled that more egalitarian relationship. Thus, Friends enacted a counter-restoration, a countercultural sectarian response to England's Restoration regime. Eschatology merged with protology (doctrines of first things) in a recovery of pre-patriarchal wholeness.

Quaker eschatology also shifted from a rapidly spreading apocalyptic social crisis to a stable, microcosmic order, a sustainable sectarian 'city set upon a hill' within a violent, unjust, and nascent imperialist regime. Like Paul, who saw that 'the present form of this world is passing away' (1 Cor. 7:31), Fox wrote that governments and other forms of organization begin and end in time. Quaker organizational practices ('gospel order') are not Christ's government itself, but create the space for Christ/the Light/the Spirit to lead directly among the people. This government will stand when all others have passed away (Fox 1995, 528).

Friends settled into a highly disciplined religious society in eighteenth-century Britain and America. Their microcosmic eschatology can be heard in the spiritual autobiographies, recorded sermons, and other writings of various Quaker ministers. For example, John Griffiths describes life in the Cross as a new creation:

> Everything that appertains to the creaturely will and forwardness of desire to chuse and act for itself, must die upon the cross; therefore there must be a remaining chaos without form and void, to endure all sorts of storms and tempests, until the effective Word saith, 'Let there be Light.' (1764, 138)

James Gough witnessed in his own personal transformation: 'My mind was moulded into a divine frame, a new creation of pure love to God and to men, and wherein the heavens and the earth in sweet harmony, seemed to show forth a power, wisdom and goodness' (1781, 24). Mary Neale testified: 'I know there is a kingdom of heaven, because I already feel it within me, Christ in me ... and because he lives, I live also; not merely an animal life which must perish, but a life hid with Christ in God' (1795, 154).

The disciplined community of faith, separated from the world, living in plainness and simplicity, discerning Christ's leadership in its midst, was understood as an embodiment of God's righteousness on earth. Distinct dress and behavioural codes clearly delimited the Quaker community as a 'peculiar people': that is, a people of God's possession (1 Pet. 2:9). To be sure, there were some abiding disagreements on the requirements of Kingdom behaviour. But as Joshua Evans wrote, using Isaiah's eschatological vision (Isa. 11:9), 'love will surely harmonise the true disciples together, and nothing shall be found to hurt or destroy in all God's holy mountain' (1837, 36).

While these Quietist Friends were not as bold as early Friends in confronting the world, they believed their plainness and ethical stands would exert a leavening influence in the wider society. Thomas Chalkley (1675–1741) exhorted Friends: 'Ye are the Light of the world; a city set upon a hill cannot be hid. When divinely enlightened by the grace and spirit of Christ, [Friends] ought to exert themselves to their Master's glory and excite others, and stir them up to their duty' (1866, 467).

Compared with early Friends, the eschatology of Quietist Friends is muted. The image of a 'city set upon a hill' suggests a static spatial teleology (a sanctified communal space in which God's will is realized) more than a temporal eschatology (a sense of God's will revealed in historical events).

FURTHER WITHDRAWAL, 1750–1800

Not all was well on 'God's holy mountain'—a core group of reforming ministers and elders on both sides of the Atlantic believed that Friends were slowly succumbing to the violent and exploitative cultural mainstream of Anglo-American society. They pressed for still more stringent discipline, a tighter definition of the Quaker sanctified communal space. The precipitating event in the colonies, especially in the Quaker-governed colony of Pennsylvania, was the French and Indian War. The British Crown ordered its colonies to collect taxes to prosecute the war. The Quaker-led legislature of Pennsylvania faced a crisis of conscience. Up to that point, Friends had maintained peaceful relations with Native American tribes and avoided military preparations. Rather than abandon the peaceable Kingdom and contribute to Britain's imperial designs, they withdrew from colonial leadership.

The crisis of the war raised larger questions regarding Quaker involvement in rapid, exploitative colonial expansion. The New Jersey Quaker minister John Woolman (1720–72) was a leading voice in this new socio-spiritual reading of the times. In 1759, in view of the war, he drafted an epistle (signed by seven other reforming leaders) warning of God's righteous judgements in history:

> Let us not forget that the Most High hath his way in the deep, in clouds, and in thick darkness—that it is his voice which crieth to the city and to the country, and oh, that these loud and awakening cries may have a proper effect upon us, that heavier chastisement may not become necessary! For though things as to the outward may for a short time afford a pleasing prospect, yet while a selfish spirit that is not subject to the cross of Christ continueth to spread and prevail, there can be no long continuance in outward peace and tranquility. If we desire an inheritance incorruptible and to be at rest in that state of peace and happiness which ever continues... let us then awfully regard these beginnings of his sore judgments, and with abasement and humiliation turn to him whom we have offended. (Woolman 1989, 100–1)

One of the most serious Quaker moral lapses was slave ownership. Notwithstanding their egalitarian social codes, a significant number of colonial Friends owned slaves. Leading Friends had condemned slave ownership from the beginning, but no Quaker body had found unity to condemn and repent of it. Woolman was the most articulate reformer in working to end these practices. He revived the eschatological language of early Friends in prophesying against this blight on colonial America:

> I have seen in the light of the Lord that the day is approaching when the man that is the most wise in human policies shall be the greatest fool, and the arm that is mighty to support injustice shall be broken to pieces. The enemies of righteousness shall make a terrible rattle and shall mightily torment one another. For he that is omnipotent is rising up to judgment and will plead the cause of the oppressed. (Woolman 1989, 160)

During the latter eighteenth century, Friends found unity to renounce any further trading of slaves and then to manumit their slaves. Friends on both sides of the Atlantic withdrew further from the cultural mainstream through their progressive tightening of discipline. As a result, disownments soared. Philadelphia Yearly Meeting declined in membership by half between 1750 and 1800. Thus, by intensifying the sacred space of Quaker faith and practice, the reformers also facilitated the decline of American Friends, from the third-largest religious group in the early colonial period, with political control or major influence in four colonies, to a small marginal sect (for a larger study of this phase, see Marietta 1984).

But the core eschatological/teleological theology and social values of Quaker faith and practice demanded such renunciations, even as they lessened Quaker influence on the wider social order. The American Quaker abolitionist Anthony Benezet (1716–84) reflected with resignation on the example of Christ in transforming the world: 'It's a fundamental truth, that Christ overcame by patient suffering, leaving us an example…that we should follow his steps, but this mode of conquest is so contrary…very few indeed are willing to be pilgrims and strangers in their passage through life' (quoted in Damiano 1988, 224).

NEW ALLIANCES AND SEPARATIONS, 1800–1900

By 1800 extrinsic religious and social influences began to permeate the Religious Society of Friends. Most notably, the dynamism of Wesleyan preaching impressed some Friends feeling stifled by the rigour of reformed Quakerism. They were drawn to Methodist doctrinal clarity and social reform. They found ready allies in work to abolish slavery, reform prisons, and offer educational opportunity more widely. But other Friends were concerned by key theological differences with Wesleyanism, regarding the doctrine of atonement in particular. Evangelicals preached the justification of sinners through acceptance of Christ's death on behalf of all. They went further, to assert that sanctification, holiness is attained by a second often sudden work of the Spirit.

By contrast, Friends had traditionally taught that the benefits of Christ's death accrue only as one takes up the Cross and is gradually transformed by the sanctifying power of the Light's step-by-step leading. There is no justification in Christ without the progressive sanctification of one's actual life in the Light. Job Scott wrote early in the nineteenth century, in response to this growing controversy among Friends: 'The work of redemption goes on no faster or further than in exact proportion to the degree in which we are influenced by and through this efficient operation of the spirit and grace of God, whereby he worketh in us to will and to do his own good pleasure' (Scott 1824b, 6).

This difference in atonement theology has major implications for eschatology. Once justification is based on a propositional belief about the death of Jesus in the past, rather than a present participation in his Cross, the Kingdom of Heaven on earth typically becomes a matter of speculation about the future. Likewise, once sanctification becomes a sudden gift of the Spirit, rather than a step-by-step re-examination and reform of various attitudes and behaviours, then hope for the creation similarly becomes a miraculous quick-fix by Christ returning in glory. These eschatological implications played out among Orthodox Friends during the nineteenth century.

Tensions over the incursions of evangelical Wesleyan theology grew among Friends on both sides of the Atlantic in the early decades of the century. They led to separations in America during the 1820s into Orthodox and Hicksite Yearly Meetings. The vast majority of Friends on both sides were traditionalists, with little or no differences in theology or practice. The innovators in the Orthodox branch were the evangelical revisionists. The innovators in the Hicksite branch were early liberals, who found their theological and social allies among Unitarians. They rightly identified the mutating influence of evangelical theology on the Orthodox party, but they wrongly identified the existential grounding of traditional Quaker theology with liberal Humanism.

Liberal Humanism among Hicksite Friends was slower in developing, but it had its own implications for eschatology. Liberal Hicksites tended to assume that the universal presence of the Light in all people, closely identified with human reason and a gradual perfectibility of the human condition, would eventually supersede traditional Christianity, just as Christians believed their faith had superseded Judaism. This liberal dispensationalism partook of a progressive view of history. Each new revelation is clearer and brighter, elevating humanity to higher vision and achievement. With the widening vistas of scientific discovery and economic advances, liberal eschatology becomes almost entirely teleological. Human enlightenment and social improvement will proceed indeterminately. These were not the convictions of early or traditional Friends, who were radically Christian, maintained a severe sense of human sinfulness, and remained existentially grounded in what may be known of God and history in the present. At this point in Quaker history, further developments in eschatology are almost entirely the result of imported theologies. As Friends found new allies in the wider religious culture, their own traditions soon became opaque and uninteresting to them.

These trends advanced on both sides of the Atlantic, but most dramatically in America, where evangelical theology and spirituality displaced traditional Quakerism in varying degrees. Up to the time of the American Civil War, Orthodox Friends generally endorsed a post-millennial eschatology. Along with most American Protestants, they expected that Christian mission and social reform would steadily improve the world until the millennium was achieved. At the end of a thousand-year 'reign of the saints' Christ would return. For example, in 1858 the Quaker evangelical Dougan Clark, Jr. wrote that personal sanctification is 'working at the level which is destined, with God's blessing, to reform and elevate and evangelise mankind'. All Christian denominations have a role to play in bringing the millennium, when 'the empire of love shall have become universal on earth'. Friends have a special role to play, based on their principles of peace and universal love—key characteristics of the millennium (Hamm 1988, 62). Thus, Orthodox Friends shared with their evangelical allies an optimistic, progressive sense of history, couched in millennial terms.

But the traumas of the American Civil War, the growing exodus from rural America to towns and cities, the accelerating arrival of non-Anglo-Saxon migrants, and the social blights of rapid industrial growth elicited a reactionary shift in evangelical theology (Punshon 2001, 322–3). Revivalism and Holiness theology rapidly pervaded most of the Orthodox branch during the 1870s. With that came a pre-millennial eschatology: the world is getting worse and will continue in moral and social decline until Christ returns and begins the millennial rule of the saints on earth. This theology was therefore sceptical of social reform as anything more than a meantime palliative to human suffering. Pre-millennial pessimism regarding the social and spiritual condition of humanity, along with its emphasis on the imminent return of Christ, became standard in Quaker revival preaching by the 1880s. The nearness of Christ's coming served as motivating rhetoric to pressure sinners to repent and accept Christ as their personal Saviour.

Holiness Friends engaged in a narrower range of social reforms than post-millennial Friends, mainly temperance and education. Some attacked Quaker work for peace, arguing that peace could come only after Christ's return. Until that time revival and missions were the most worthwhile work for Christians (Hamm 1988, 108). Thus, pre-millennial theology helped turn Evangelical Friends from progressive reform towards reactionary conservatism. John Punshon (2001, Chapter 9) is correct in suggesting that early and traditional Quaker theology is amillennial: it simply does not engage with the passage in Revelation 20:4 that speaks of a thousand-year rule of the saints.

The Richmond (Indiana) Conference of 1887 produced a Declaration of Faith aimed at halting the polarizing drift between post-millennial reformers and pre-millennial revivalists. The statement makes no mention of the millennium, but emphasizes that 'when [Christ] at last appears we may appear with Him in glory. But all the wicked, who live in rebellion against the light of grace, and die finally impenitent, shall come forth to the resurrection of condemnation' (General Conference 1887, 33–4). Here eschatology is stated entirely in personal terms—saved or condemned—without reference to the destiny of the wider creation. Eschatology serves a consequential ethic: eternal reward for believers; eternal punishment for infidels. By contrast, early and classical Quaker ethics, informed by a realizing eschatology, had fused means and ends in the present life of the Seed within.

By the end of the nineteenth century post-millennial Quaker reformers were merging with new Modernist and social-gospel currents of Christian thought. While earlier reformers attacked social problems as impediments to the spread of the Gospel, the new liberal Modernists wanted to remake society according to the teachings of the New Testament. Thomas Newlin suggested in 1897 that earlier generations had failed to realize that 'a new society was quite as emphatic in Christ's teaching as a new man'. Rufus Jones (1863–1948) enthused in 1895 that 'the Spirit of God is in His world, shaping history…putting down evil, and making for righteousness, silently guiding the forces in the great battle of Armageddon'. Here 'Armageddon' is not a future cataclysm but the march of liberal progressive triumph over sin and social blight. Liberal Friends 'saw a vague, endless progression ahead, as the world grew better and better' (Hamm 1988, 157). As noted above regarding Hicksites, here teleology completely defines eschatology. Divine ends eclipse the sense of an End.

Among British Friends evangelical trends didn't advance as far. Moderate evangelical reformers wrested control of London Yearly Meeting from Quietist leadership by the middle of the nineteenth century and dominated British Quakerism for the rest of the century. But an 1895 conference of Friends in Manchester showcased the liberal-Modernist currents that had been building among British Friends for decades. These converged with Modernist elements among Orthodox Friends and the slowly building Liberal Quakerism of Hicksite Friends in America. Rufus Jones was the energetic synthesizer of these Anglo-American trends over the next decades.

MODERNISM AND ANTI-MODERNISM,
1900–1970

The early-to-middle twentieth century witnessed the further development of these trends. An American Friends Peace Conference was held in Philadelphia in 1901 to consider the prospects for more proactive Quaker peacemaking. Modernist Friends now participated in ecumenical 'peace societies' in America and Europe, bringing their long-time pacifist experience to bear on the challenges of a new century. The Conference epistle suggested that Friends are 'in a position today to speak with greater intelligence and wisdom and therefore with greater power, than ever before in history'. Stephen Smith suggested that such efforts would hasten the day when 'the kingdoms of this world should become the kingdoms of our Lord and his Christ' (Rev. 11:15; Proceedings 1902, 11). Rufus Jones suggested a developmental scheme of history. Just as the spirit of fighting is strong in childhood and we gradually wean ourselves from it, so 'Christian civilisation' is on a similar path of development. 'The warmer currents of the Gulf Stream are slowly flooding the world' (1902, 29–30). The conference chair Susan Janney queried more cautiously, 'Whither do we seem to be tending? Are we looking forward or backward; toward a higher evolution of industrialised civilisation, or toward a revival of 'reactionary militarism' in our social and political life?' (1902, 213). Ultimately, she endorsed the former as the dominant, long-term trend.

British Friends also breathed a new Modernist confidence that with the advances of science and technology, the spread of Christian civilization, economic development, and the rigorous questioning of traditional dogmas, history had stepped aboard an escalator of nearly inevitable progress. A 1900 London Yearly Meeting statement enthused, 'Men of faith, living at the dawn of revelation, reached out after God, even amid the institutions of polygamy, slavery, and blood-revenge. We, in like manner, are to be faithful to the guidance of the noontide light, shed on us in the face of Jesus Christ' (London Yearly Meeting 1925, 45–6).

Meanwhile, pre-millennialist revival Friends grew increasingly anti-Modern in the early twentieth century. They were drawn into the broader fundamentalist grounds well rejecting Darwinian evolutionary theory and historical criticism of the Bible. Many were also influenced by fundamentalist schemes of world history organized into 'dispensations', featuring elaborate endtime predictions. Tensions grew between Modernist and anti-Modernist factions in the Five Years Meeting of Orthodox Friends. For example, Earlham College in Indiana, founded by Orthodox Friends, came under attack in the 1920s for teaching evolution and 'higher criticism' of the Bible.

But Holiness Friends were by no means preoccupied with sheer reaction to Modernism. Following their own pre-millennial agenda, they launched major missions in East Africa, the Caribbean, and Latin America in this period. These enjoyed great success, particularly in Kenya and Bolivia. Today, the largest population of Friends in the world is in Kenya. Bolivia is the third largest Quaker centre, after the United States.

Pre-millennial preaching of a world locked in sin and heathenism, to be transformed by the second coming of Christ, was part of the Quaker missionary message and remains the predominant eschatological teaching among Evangelical Friends in North America, East Africa, and Latin America.

Two world wars and the advent of the atomic bomb chastened liberal Modernist confidence in the steady progress of divine purposes in human history. Even the irrepressible optimist Rufus Jones concluded during the Second World War: 'I cannot deny the fact of evil, nor can I accept any of the explanations I have heard given of it. It remains an unsolved problem, a huge mystery' (1943, 106). As the post-war nuclear arms race accelerated and the annihilating potential of atomic warfare loomed, eschatology gained a new, scientific plausibility. The end of the world seemed all too imaginable. Concomitantly, teleology became more debatable. Would humankind destroy itself, in spite of God's will? Following the First World War, the Protestant neo-Orthodox movement berated the optimistic 'culture-religion' of liberal Christianity. After the Second World War, neo-Orthodoxy found its Quaker equivalent in Lewis Benson's critique of Liberal Quakerism (1966) and his efforts to reproclaim the founding message of Quakerism. Although Benson identified 'Christ is come to teach his people himself' as the core of George Fox's preaching, he did not explore its eschatological meaning.

POST-MODERN QUAKERISMS, 1970–PRESENT

Post-war developments slowly reframed time and space in Quaker consciousness. The end of Europe's colonial era, then the stalling of American imperialism in the Vietnam War, and the globalization of capital through transnational corporations: these and other factors created the conditions for a new, multicultural sensibility. Christianity became less the standard of faith among Liberal Friends, more open to comparison and combination with other religions and spiritualities. Feminist consciousness grew as women entered the job market in greater numbers. These and other forces combined to challenge the Christocentric, Eurocentric, and androcentric frameworks within which 'progress' had been reckoned.

As capitalism globalized and modernization penetrated all continents, the Modernist opposition between 'new' and 'traditional' broke down: the 'new' was everywhere, and in a sense disappeared. Spatial awareness eclipsed temporality as the horizon of fulfilment. The search for truth was less 'onwards and upwards' than a broadening enterprise. By 1985 British Friend John Lampen summarized: 'Can we settle the question "Is the Society of Friends Christian or not?" In the historical sense the answer is Yes: but that does not preclude the possibility that we may now be called to a new and wider perception of the Truth' (Britain Yearly Meeting 2009, 17:03). A 1994 statement called for a 'broader approach to religion' (Britain Yearly Meeting 2009, 27:4).

Consequently, the complex conversation among differing religious, racial, gendered, and cultural identities foregrounded process over progress. As Pink

Dandelion (Dandelion, Gwyn, Peat 1998, 188) summarizes the new sensibility: 'seeking is more important than finding... authenticity is to be found in a process, not outcome, or that the desired outcome or truth is already manifest in the search, not in further fruits'. Indeed, as cybernetic technologies facilitated communicational processes, teleological ends were eclipsed by technical means. 'Quaker process'—both traditional and new approaches to seeking truth together—became the *sine qua non* of Liberal Quaker faith: doing good by doing it well. Meanwhile, the Internet created an instantaneous global now, a timeless simultaneity that eclipses both eschatology and teleology.

Evangelical Friends were also affected by the subtle yet profound shifts of post-Modernity. Pre-millennial eschatology was still affirmed, as in a 2004 statement by Friends Church Southwest:

> We believe in the Second Coming of our Lord Jesus Christ and all the great events of the end times prophesied in Scripture ... We believe in the great resurrection of both the saved and the lost. We believe everyone will stand before Christ in the final judgment to receive their just due ... At that time Christ will reign fully over the restored universe and God the Father will be fully glorified. (Dandelion 2007, 197)

But pre-millennial expectations were largely eclipsed by the new technical means to pursue evangelism and mission. Techniques of church growth, such as telemarketing and cyber-evangelism, claimed the attention and energies of Evangelical Friends much more than end-time expectations. Consequently, Evangelical Quaker missions have expanded rapidly into new countries, such as Indonesia, Nepal, and the Philippines. Moreover, coordination and innovation no longer extend only from the historic 'centres' in North America to the 'peripheries' of mission fields. For example, Friends United Meeting has reorganized its governance as a full partnership between North American and East African Friends. Friends in Guatemala have initiated their own mission to Cambodia. In sum, rapidly evolving means (technologies) reshape ends. The End is not renounced, but is 'lost in space'.

However, with the severe global economic contractions that began in 2008, tightening financial means have begun to restrict the global visions of Liberal and Evangelical Friends alike. Moreover, the deepening environmental crisis, like nuclear warfare before it, revives the plausibility of eschatological foreboding. The sense of an end (the end of a long era of economic growth, and the growing evidence of ecological collapse) invades the present, creating a *kairos*, a sense of moment, what Fox called 'the day of the Lord' or 'the day of visitation'. Within the spatial coordinates of post-Modernity, *kairos* finds revived meaning in terms of place. That is, the grid of space, organized and rationalized by global capitalism, is ruptured by the reassertion of particular places. Localist food-sourcing, reduced travel, the nurture of local cultural traditions, etc.—all these have both reactionary and progressive potentials. 'Time will tell' how Quaker eschatologies and teleologies constellate in this new situation.

CONCLUSION

The evolution of Quaker eschatologies/teleologies after the early apocalyptic phase may be charted along perpendicular axes, as shown in Figure 13.1. Here the horizontal axis is a gradient from less to more strongly eschatological from left to right. The vertical axis is a gradient from less to more strongly teleological from bottom to top.

It will be noted that early Quaker apocalyptic eschatology is not seen on this graph. It could be argued that it should appear in the upper right corner, both highly eschatological and highly teleological. But because it remained resolutely present/Presence-centred (except for Fell's brief millennialism), I would argue that it belongs at the crux of the two axes. So the four quadrants of the graph represent four different departures from the radical apocalyptic spirituality and revolutionary practice of early Friends.

Quietist Friends in the eighteenth century perfected the faith and practice of early Friends. But (partly owing to their rigorously hedged sectarianism) they found little opportunity to influence the culture around them. As we noted above, their eschatology became predominantly a teleology, a fairly stable realization of God's will in a stable religious community.

In the nineteenth century, as Orthodox Friends found evangelical allies in the wider culture, they saw new opportunities to engage with society and history. They partook of a general Protestant post-millennial hope in progressive reform, moving towards fulfilment in Christ's eventual return. So their position, while speculative, combines Quietist Quaker high teleology with renewed eschatological expectation grounded in actual social reform. Modernist Friends in the late-nineteenth and twentieth centuries furthered the trend.

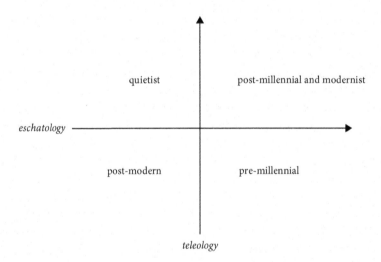

FIGURE 13.1 Interactions of Eschatology and Teleology in Quaker History

The shift among Evangelical–Holiness Friends after the American Civil War to a pre-millennial eschatology marks a dramatic shift towards pessimism about the world and scepticism regarding social reform. Pre-millennial theology is strongly eschatological in its expectations of the second coming, last judgement, and eternal reward/ punishment. But, given its strong emphasis on personal salvation, its teleology is limited, mainly individual. Personal behaviour in this life will have eternal consequences. Concerns to reform society or preserve the environment are much reduced. Christ will come and remake all things.

Finally, the post-Modern Quaker eschatologies of the latter twentieth century are minimally eschatological and minimally teleological. Among Evangelical Friends, pre-millennial eschatology has been marginalized by intensified efforts and great expenditure to advance the Great Commission. But even those teleological ends are driven more by technological and financial means than renewed vision. Meanwhile, among Liberal Friends, 'Quaker process' papers over perplexity regarding historical progress. Means become ends, and the End becomes something 'those Evangelical Friends' believe in.

Thus, eschatology and teleology may be seen as dialectically related, each qualifying the other, and shifting in relationship as the Religious Society of Friends has faced changing socio-historical situations without and conflicts within. The early, apocalyptic formation remains the most distinctive and socially dynamic constellation of Quaker eschatology/teleology.

Suggested Further Reading

Bruyneel, S. (2010) *Margaret Fell and the end of time: the theology of the mother of Quakerism.* Waco: Baylor University Press.

Dandelion, P. (2007) *An introduction to Quakerism.* Cambridge: Cambridge University Press.

Gwyn, D. (1986) *Apocalypse of the Word: the life and message of George Fox.* Richmond, IN: Friends United Press.

Gwyn, D. (1995) *The covenant crucified: Quakers and the rise of capitalism.* Wallingford, PA: Pendle Hill.

Gwyn, D. (2000) *Seekers found: Atonement in early Quaker experience.* Wallingford, PA: Pendle Hill.

Hamm, T. D. (1988) *The transformation of American Quakerism: Orthodox Friends, 1800–1907.* Bloomington: Indiana University Press.

Punshon, J. (2001) *Reasons for hope: the faith and future of the Friends Church.* Richmond, IN: Friends United Press.

CHAPTER 14

....

THE KINGDOM OF GOD, QUAKERS, AND THE POLITICS OF COMPASSION

....

GERARD GUITON

IN 1651 George Fox (1624–91), the principle founder of the Quaker movement, declined an army commission because he 'lived in the virtue of that Life and Power that took away the occasion of all wars [and also because he] was come into the Covenant of Peace which was before wars and strife were' (Fox 1995, 65). This declaration affirmed a commitment to non-violence but, more importantly, to that from which it arose—the Kingdom of God as enunciated by Jesus, his inspiration, or in his own words, the 'Covenant of Peace', the 'Life and Power'.

For Fox, that of the omnipresent Kingdom was in every person in his/her 'own measure' (1698, 12–13). It could, when revealed through them with the help of God/Love, forge a world in which a true 'King' would reign—that is, a lasting and loving relationship between 'all people' with its attendant unity, peace, truth, equality, simplicity, justice, and compassion. Thus separation from God, the early Quakers' understanding of the cause of sin, would be defeated.

So, what did Jesus and the Friends mean by the 'Kingdom' and what influences contributed to their formulation of it? Is the Kingdom important for present-day Quakers and others? This chapter attempts to answer some of these questions and for this purpose it divided into three sections. The first offers a brief biblical exegesis of the Kingdom and thence a delineation of what is here called Jesus' politics of compassion. The second section provides an early Quaker hermeneutic of the Kingdom through the writings of three prominent Friends, Francis Howgill (1618–69), Isaac Penington (1616–79), and Fox himself. Finally, the third section presents four examples of a contemporary Quaker orthopraxis of the Kingdom, which may contain elements of such a politics.

THE KINGDOM: A BIBLICAL EXEGESIS

The importance of the Kingdom for Jesus' witness is underlined by the frequency with which the terms 'Kingdom of God' and 'Kingdom of the Heavens' occur in the New Testament: 162 times in total and 104 times in the Synoptic gospels. Fifteen of Jesus' parables are concerned with the Kingdom. In addition, he testified to it through prophetic teachings and healings, and in the way his life and manner of death unveiled Yahweh's plan of salvation—wholeness and unity in God (Mk.1: 14–15).

As with all prophetic pronouncements in the Hebrew tradition, the proclamation of God's Rule is countercultural. It differs radically from what passes as religion and politics, including their accepted structures. From this tradition and his own experience, Jesus believed the Kingdom was already incarnate in the world (Lk. 17: 20–1) as God's self-revelation.

From Scripture we understand the Kingdom as a 'mystery' (Rom. 16: 26) In other words, it continues to be revealed through the personal insight and experience of anybody who is truly in the Christ/Spirit. It seems natural that such people spread the Kingdom. In doing so they are exemplars of the 'great commission' (Mt. 28: 16–20).

It is through God's grace that such people manifest the Kingdom, which always rises above time and place, besides being experienced existentially in the now. Hence, the Kingdom demands an immediate and radical response as it calls people from the past through remembered witness, but also from the future when all that is of God will be consummated in Love 'in the fullness of time' (Eph. 1: 10). It is, therefore, visionary and universal.

The Kingdom, including its Sermons on the Mount and Plain as well as the Beatitudes, makes serious though not impossible demands (Mt: 5–7; Lk. 6: 20–49). Jesus expected their literal implementation. The practicalities of the Sermon on the Mount's transformative initiatives for reconciliation and healing, for instance, still provide the bases for the on-going and non-violent revolution he inaugurated (Stassen 2009, 74).

While it is *God's* Kingdom, God 'works' with people for their spiritual rejuvenation, for moving the Kingdom's presence into their daily experiences in order that they encourage its understanding and enactment in others. This mutuality is aptly demonstrated by Jesus' table fellowship. He offered an open, joyous, and inclusive table to everyone, symbolizing equality and the restoration of relationships in community (Mt. 8: 11), instead of a restricted and segregated table to which the socially rejected, isolated, and Gentiles were not invited.

In this respect, the biblical saying in English, 'the Kingdom of God is come near to you' (e.g. Luke 10: 9), loses some of its original impact. Translated from the Greek *engiken*, 'near' implies a future state but the Hebrew *karav*—'It's here!' or 'It's arrived!'—conveys the urgency and joy of God's immediate presence now. This 'It's here!' Kingdom can always be a true, secure, and everlasting home if people live it.

The reported activity of Jesus in practising healings, exorcisms, teaching a new ethic for living, and offering a new hope in God to the poor and oppressed, demonstrates the *karav* of Love's Kingdom particularly among the sick, marginalized, and those who stand against 'empire' with all its exploitative practices and destructive might (Eph. 6: 12).

Compassion as Revolutionary Politics

The Kingdom is thus life-giving and seeks to relate the self to the common good based as it is on justice, peace, equity, compassion, and joy; the Gospels speak of the growth and sustainability of community as a sign of unity with God. 'Good works' are important to this process as can be seen in Matthew's Gospel, Luke's Acts, and James's Epistle. Interestingly, in Peter's conversation with Cornelius, the Greek for 'doing good' (*euergetōn*) is applied normally to the action of kings (Acts 10: 38).

Jesus saw spiritual matters within a rabbinical tradition typified by its use of parables as social commentary and as a means of encouraging people to break the spiral of violence created by exploitation and other evils. It was a tradition in which healing, for instance, involved redeeming (e.g. of debts), ministering to the poor, liberation from bondage of all kinds, and salvation. Jesus' own parables and miracles created opportunities for him to likewise teach about righteousness, including justice, in ways that also challenged conventional thinking and acting. His sense of urgency was clear; the time for righteousness was *now*: in such *kairos* moments there is never any time to lose.

Jesus, therefore, could denounce the corruption he believed lay at the heart of Israel and the paucity of righteousness that accompanied it. For this task he may have been fortified by a passage in First Maccabees in which God's Kingdom would be victorious over Mammon. He also understood the 'Messiah' as this-worldly, the one anointed to carry God's justice and love to all people. And he would have seen how the prophets were God's messengers in this respect, ready to remind everyone of their easily neglected covenantal obligations with respect to justice, peace, and mercy. The prophets spoke truth to power, particularly when demanding radical social and political change (Isa. 1: 16–17; Jer. 8: 19; Mic. 2: 1–5). It was the false prophets, uncritically supporting the status quo, who failed to mention social justice.

From their other Semitic and Egyptian neighbours, the Hebrews learned how poverty was contrary to the will of the gods. The duty of the divinely appointed ruler was to protect the poor and oppressed. These non-Israelite practices helped the prophets, scribes, and rabbis discern insights into poverty and its cruel impact on people, insights that were eventually incorporated into the Talmudic codes with which Jesus seemed familiar. As in the Egyptian 'religion of the poor', for example, God was believed to favour the needy, the oppressed, the miserable, the lower classes, the beggars, the humble, and the quiet in the land (Ps. 35: 20), while the exploitative practices of the rich, the proud, and haughty were to be condemned.

The Book of Daniel may have given Jesus a clear idea of a 'Kingdom' contrary to the kingdoms of the world (Dan. 7: 7). Relying on the Semites' concept of divine justice, the Book introduces the truly peaceful and compassionate 'Son of Man' who inaugurates an everlasting Kingdom of righteousness and justice that covers all peoples, nations, and languages (Dan. 7: 14). The Hebrew and Aramaic words for 'Kingdom', *malkuth* and *malkuta dišemaya* ('rule of God'), infer the superiority of God's omnipresent caring and peaceful workings compared with the transient power and jurisdiction of an earthly king.

The way in which the Law Codes legislated and the Psalms promoted social and economic parity may have also helped Jesus formulate his revolutionary views about the Kingdom. The Codes are found in Exodus 20: 22 and 23: 33 (Book of the Covenant), Deuteronomy 12–26 (Deuteronomic Code), and in the Holiness Code of Leviticus 17–26. For instance, at the end of the sabbath year (the seventh year of the seven-year agricultural cycle), personal debts due that year were supposed to be nullified and forgiven. The Jubilee, falling on the forty-ninth or fiftieth year of the sabbatical cycle, proclaimed liberty throughout the land to all its inhabitants. Every household was to welcome absent members, property had to be returned to the original owner or his heirs, Hebrew slaves freed and debts remitted (Lev. 25: 8–55).

The great books of the Pentateuch, too, may have inspired Jesus. Deuteronomy (33: 5), Numbers (23. 21) and Exodus spoke of Israelite deliverance from their plight as outcasts of Egyptian society, the Exodus being divine affirmation that justice and liberation were inherent in the Divine plan.

Perhaps, too, the Book of Judges held importance for him. Anti-monarchical and opposing centralism and empire (Joshua 24: 1), it displayed sympathy towards those who dispensed God's justice and who continued to advance the struggle for Israel's liberation from oppression. The Talmudic tradition itself fundamentally opposed privilege, hierarchy, and violence (Lk. 4: 16–30); it recognized only God as sovereign, something confirmed by the 'enthronement' psalms (Mt. 4: 10; Pss. 22, 29, 47, 93, and 96–9).

In proclaiming a Kingdom that was within everybody (Lk. 17: 20–1), rather than being 'entered' into by means of legalistic formulae, Jesus confirmed people's innate goodness and ability to contribute to God's work. But for the 'Kingdom' to be authentically present within and among people (to be 'at hand'), personal transformation (*metanoia*) was first necessary. It involved repentance (a 'turning round'), a surrendering of one's agenda (e.g. fear, pride, destructive ego), and absolute trust in God (Mk. 1: 16–17). A *kenosis* (an 'emptying') would follow, leaving room for God alone. No *metanoia*, no Kingdom.

Jesus' confidence in the capacity of ordinary people to spread the Kingdom also assumed they would take responsibility for their own spiritual welfare. The hereditary priesthood quickly understood this and its revolutionary implications. Their fears were justified when Jesus forthrightly condemned their own priestly class, the so-called 'royal priesthood' (Mt. 23: 1–36), in the spirit of Judges. He was in no doubt that when people were truly of the Kingdom they were also true 'kings', that is to say, they enjoyed true freedom as priests and prophets of God's peace, justice, and compassion.

Once Jesus' ideas are understood in terms mentioned so far, there is no mistaking their political breadth—class and economic status, social and priestly hierarchy, ethnicity, political and military power, sexuality, age, gender, and physical ability confer no advantage in the Kingdom for all are equal before God (Jas. 2: 1–13). As a result, his revolutionary politics can be understood today as urging all people to:

1. Treat all people and their needs as sacred, and to care for the wellbeing of others with steadfast love; to build harmonious relationships and loving communities, being with and of one another (Rom. 12: 4–5).
2. Be constantly in the service of humanity, especially in giving voice to the voiceless, sight to the spiritually blind; at the same time, expose the structures and works of oppression and warfare.
3. Advocate and demonstrate simplicity and non-violence, thus keeping one's heart and mind free of the seeds of war (Rom. 12: 14–21).
4. Create alternatives to violence; be a means of transformation and healing.
5. Save one's anger for highlighting and healing the mistreatment of others.
6. Advocate and demonstrate social and economic equity, particularly in the form of a fair and accountable redistribution of land and wealth.
7. Never elevate Caesar and other icons above God or Love/Kingdom (Mt. 22: 15–22).
8. Speak Truth to power, including political, military, business, and ecclesiastical power.
9. Be radically egalitarian and inclusive by never condoning prejudice and violence caused by hierarchy, gender, sexuality, age, appearance, social status, and class bias (Mt. 5: 5).
10. Be constantly in prayer, and value silence and stillness.
11. Be willing to live the Kingdom as a priority and as already present.
12. Let one's life speak, therefore—to live as the 'first-fruits of the Kingdom'—and be willing to die like Jesus for Love if necessary (Jn. 15: 12). His death was a plea to unite and continue the peaceful spiritual and thus political revolution.

Jesus' internalization of the Torah, by which the Mosaic Law metamorphosed into the Law of the heart, was an inversion but also a fulfilment of much of the existing Law, and a rediscovery of Jeremiah 31: 33–4, which was also a favourite of the Friends (Dewsbury 1653, 4) to whom we now turn.

THE EARLY QUAKERS' KINGDOM HERMENEUTIC

Any investigation into the early Quakers' theology of the Kingdom must account for the easy and fluid way they moved between its alternative expressions, something that can confuse readers unaccustomed to seventeenth-century religious language. The following equation acknowledges the profound connection between the expressions, a connection that may help illuminate our understanding of their holistic worldview:

Kingdom = Light = 'Christ's Doctrine' = the Christ =
the Life = Spirit = Love = 'in Jesus' = Truth = the Word = the 'Day' =
the Power = Virtue

The Kingdom was the focus and orthopraxis of the early Quakers as it was for Jesus, a focus underlined by the fact that of over eight hundred tracts from the approximately one thousand published between 1652 (the year of their first known publication) and 1663, nearly ninety per cent refer to the Kingdom or its equivalent expressions. Without the Jesus Way of the Kingdom there would be no Quakerism.

The Friends claimed to have rediscovered the Kingdom for their own time and for all time. It was a this-worldly reality and it opened up for everyone the possibility of perfection (spiritual maturity) and thus salvation—again, wholeness and unity in God. Consequently, theirs was a time to be 'prized' for in the now a wondrous opportunity had arrived for a wholehearted welcoming of the Light of the Christ (Nayler 1653a, 16), the basis for redemption. Their discovery was enough to propel Fox to entreat the 'scattered ones over the world' to gather with haste into the Way of Jesus which embodied the Kingdom [Mt. 11: 28]. In doing so they could 'continue afresh' in a mutual relationship with God but outside the apostate Church 'built by the will of men' (Fox 1658b, 1).

From the moment of its initial appearance as 'the doctrine of Christ' in the first-acknowledged Quaker tract, *False Prophets and False Teachers Described* (1652), the Friends used about forty equivalent terms for the Kingdom including 'Sovereignty of God', 'New Creation', 'Christ's Kingdom', and the 'Garden of God' (Guiton 2012, 21, 152–3). It was also present in such phrases as 'where Zion is known', 'in the Life of our King', in references to the mustard seed, and as an antonym of such terms as 'Satan's kingdom', 'the wisdom of the world', and many others. As the above equation intimates, the Kingdom was also the Truth, the Word, the transforming power of Divine Love that was in their 'flesh and bone', and it came as the 'Day of the Lord' and 'Day of Visitation' (Fox 1658b, sig. A2).

Rather than signifying a physical End time or Jesus' bodily Second Coming (widely held beliefs in their time), the 'Day' was the birth from 'above', a messenger, a corrective, a mediator, and was always revelatory. Its realization within would come by God's 'wrath' or 'sword', that is to say, the innate desire for purity in everybody (Nayler 1716, p. 12). It came with a great price since the Way, being 'narrow', was painful and many would fall on stony ground. But if the heart were true, sin would be washed away in the 'Fountain of Life', in the 'Blood of the Lamb'—in other words, through the Inward Light of the Christ which the darkness could not 'comprehend' (Dewsbury 1655, 13–14; Fox 1656, 9). By being 'open' to the 'Day', people could experience it as pure Divine Light and those born of it would see the 'Day' with the spiritual eye since the spiritual person was an image of God.

The 'Day' was a call to bring forth the Kingdom before which individuals would stand in 'humility'. In holding up their 'transgressions' to the Inward Light they would judge themselves but only through the Spirit, the 'Life and Power' (Fell 1660, 7). Thus, as a 'holy nation' [Rev. 14: 4–5], the trumpet of celebration could sound and 'Jerusalem' (or 'Zion') would be conquered. On the outer level, the prophetic oracles helped them bring forth God's indictment of unjust earthly kings and their officers, a judgement designed to eradicate oppression and suffering.

The Friends' identification with the Christ in Jesus as well as Jesus himself gave them a 'foundation' or 'rock' (Fox 1698, 46; [Mt. 7: 20–5]) for spreading the Kingdom in the fear-ridden and dangerous circumstances of their post-civil war times. Inspired by the Gospel way of priesthood mentioned previously, the Friends considered themselves a 'royal' or 'second' priesthood. It was a vocation that included a spiritual anointment as a means of fulfilling the Christ's desire for reconciliation, healing, and wholeness among all people. This vocation would empower them to live harmoniously with each other as brothers and sisters, as sons and daughters of God, and become what they were always intended to be [Isa. 2: 2–5; Eph.1: 3]. The Friends were in no doubt that when people were authentically in the Kingdom they were the perfect priests and prophets (Nayler 1653a, 11; Smith 1657?).

Francis Howgill

For Francis Howgill, as with all the 'royal priesthood', the previously hidden 'Day' 'was [already] come' and would remain an ever-revealing reality, a mystery initially gifted to 'a remnant' [Rev. 12: 17]. This Kingdom was an everlasting, spiritual rule of God [Dan. 7:14] replete with 'purity' [2 Pet. 1:11] which:

> comes to be felt working in the heart, and as it is loved and obeyed, it leads and converts the heart, to the Lord, and draws towards itself, out of unholiness, and from under the dark power' (Howgill 1658, 3, 38–40).

The Kingdom was home to those who were formerly exiled, to those spiritual refugees who now knew the balm of God's righteousness/justice and peace of conscience. And he added joy, felicity, pleasantness, virtue, eternal life, assurance of God's love, comfort and consolation, eternal dignity, quietness, grace, and hope (Howgill 1658 [Rom. 14: 17–18]). It was, he continued:

> eternal brightness shed abroad through all things which pierces through and searches the [most] secret place, even that which is invisible, and makes manifest all things. And the nature of everything by the Day of the Lord comes to be seen, and it appears in the heart. [People are] to wait for the day to dawn [for] that which makes evil manifest and brings it to light. (Howgill 1659, 147)

The Kingdom was the 'pure Light' with its justice and possibility of spiritual and moral regeneration. It was also free grace, 'God's appearance', and satiated the hunger within. It set people on a different path in the world and thus nearer to God. Describing his own experience in finding the Kingdom at long last, Howgill was amazed at the depth of oneness with others with whom he was now 'caught up as in a net':

> And from that day forward our hearts were knit unto the Lord, and one unto another in true and fervent love, not by any external covenant or external form but we entered into the covenant of Life with God. And that was as a strong obligation or bond upon all our spirits which united us one unto another in the unity of the Spirit and of the bond of peace. (1662, 6)

In this way the covenant of death was 'disannulled' by the 'power and arm' of God, and the new 'babe' was born 'from above'. The begotten of the Kingdom were 'heirs to the promise' of God's Kingdom' when unveiling the New Covenant within to the world (Anderdon 1659, 5). This same Light or grace was realized in all but 'not in the same measure', for some were more prone to evil than others.

Words, continued Howgill, could never fully describe the indescribable. They were mere sounds, veils that covered the true beauty and meaning of this spiritual 'habitation', this 'treasure house of wisdom' (Howgill 1661, 3). All who believed of God received this wisdom of Life, Power, and Virtue and would be filled with Divine Love, the 'word of the Kingdom, the word of Power', the 'word of Life', Howgill continues. To be of the Kingdom was to live in the Spirit as a prophet in the manner of Jesus. The Kingdom's 'fullness fills all things', Howgill proclaimed, and in its many mansions there would be an eternal welcoming for the children of the resurrection, the poor in spirit who would experience 'birth immortal' (Howgill 1661; [2 Tim. 1: 10]).

Their self-description as Children of Light [Jn. 12: 36] was a natural expression of their belief that in them 'primitive Christianity', the Jesus Way, was being revived. Thus as the Children they would be saved from death and quickened into the Life to be whole. The Life (i.e., the Kingdom) was hidden, however, from those who led sinful lives. For Howgill and Friends, their own generation and particularly its Calvinists resembled the Pharisees in the way they perceived the Kingdom as an 'earthly and literal' place (1658, 39), but also in their pessimistic view of humanity, of God as a remote Other, in their legalistic observances and ties to the State.

According to the Quakers, Christ's doctrine was always a stranger to such people who continually used abstract formulations to confuse and persecute—what the Friends called 'notions', ideas 'out of the Life' (Penington 1659b, 13). Howgill believed that, despite their constant self-examination and scruples, these latter-day 'Pharisees' failed to see that the Kingdom, being within as the Friends understood Jesus to have said, meant one needed absolute honesty to 'dig deep, sweep clean, and search narrowly' to discover the pearl in the field, the mustard seed, the lost piece of silver (Fox 1990, 26–7). These represented the advent of the Kingdom, the anticipation of the inner and outer worlds turned upside down. This in turn demanded faithfulness, and a patient waiting in the peace and righteousness of the Spirit. Accordingly, Howgill quoted the Sermon on the Mount to assure his readers that anyone who cared to seek would find: 'so first every one must come to feel in [them] the Kingdom [and they] that believe [are] entered into the rest'—'blessed are the poor in Spirit' therefore (1658, 39–40; see Mt. 5: 3).

Howgill also emphasized 'blessed are the [actual] poor for theirs is the Kingdom of God' from the Sermon on the Plain [Lk. 6: 20]. Using both references, he was referring not only to those in need of God (Mt. 5: 3) but also to people especially deserving of justice and material welfare. As the Kingdom was revealed through God's power, glory, and grace to those who waited, it could be fully experienced and enacted on earth when a loving unity, equity, and true justice, including land redistribution (Parnell 1655, 1–17), existed among people and thus between humanity and God (Howgill 1661, 2–5, 38–43). For this they strove by means of a 'Lamb's War', a spiritual war for salvation, against injustice on an inner and outer level (Nayler 1657; [2 Cor. 10: 3–4]).

George Fox

In the early passages of his *Journal* when Fox talks of Light, Life, and Love, he draws our attention to the Kingdom and its contradiction—the world of Mammon, sin, the 'dark world', the kingdom of Satan. From page 12 this contrast continues until the well-known passage in which an 'ocean of Light and Love' covers 'an ocean of darkness' (Fox 1995, 19). This contrast is not merely between goodness and sin, but the joy of being 'in the Life' as opposed to being separated from Love/God. In a manner akin to Paul of Tarsus, he tells us that in experiencing the 'paradise of God', all 'things were new, and all the creation gave another smell unto [him] than before beyond what words can utter' (Fox 1995, 27; [2 Cor. 12: 1]). After this, he emerges restored into the New Covenant. There is a hint in this passage of the exilic journey—from Egyptian slavery or the prodigal son returned to the bosom of the Lord [Lk. 15: 11–32].

On page 34, God lets Fox see 'the divine mysteries of his own everlasting Kingdom'. In *To All that would Know the Way to the Kingdom*, he describes the Kingdom as a guide, teacher, and something that is always present (1653, 3). It stands in contrast with the temporal world but could not be divorced from it. In *A Testimony of the True Light*, the Kingdom is the Light which shows up sin (Fox 1656, 13), a theme developed in *A Distinction between the Phanatick Spirit* in which the 'rage, fury, madness, and foolishness' of the 'fanatic spirit' is exposed and defeated by the 'love, joy, peace, gentleness, righteousness, and true judgment' of the 'spirit of God' (Fox 1660, broadside). The Kingdom here acts as a corrective by which people were kept from their 'wandering minds' so they would remain within the compass of God's love ('in the fear of God'). It was something that would lead from the false to the true Church (Fox 1660).

According to Fox, those who failed to understand the full implications of the Kingdom rejected the teaching of Jesus as the Friends understood it from Matthew 5. This apostasy resulted in division and violence among God's children. Thus, early in his ministry, Fox linked the Kingdom to the pursuit of inner and outer peace. Violence was a flagrant contradiction of Jesus' great commission that the true Church, the Kingdom, and its peoples (rather than that built by 'the will of men'), was to be carried to 'all people' for their transformation into the peaceable Light.

Thus, it was impossible to enter the Kingdom without being 'born again' into an Eden-type 'innocency' as a Child of Light, by which he meant being prepared to undergo an inner crucifixion and resurrection so that a new person and a new order of being would incarnate ('convincement'; [2 Cor. 5: 17]). Such a person would dwell daily in God's presence and be attentive to the inner rhythms of the soul that always sought to pursue its God-destiny. In facing down the darkness within, s/he would be led to perform works of justice and peace that would instil compassion into the body politic for *its* transformation [Jas. 1: 20]. Thus, the Kingdom would be experienced where God/Love happened, incarnate among people (Mt.10: 7–8).

An Answer to the Arguments of the Jews outlines how Jesus' spiritual Kingdom, mentioned 235 times in its 52 pages, is the culmination of all history. Judah's own story, Fox argues, is that of an evolving understanding of God's sovereignty and its inevitable fulfilment in the person of Jesus as he reflected the Christ. The long pre-incarnation shadow disappears as the Light of Christ shines freely, its promise of Love expressed in Jesus' birth, teaching, healing, suffering, death, and resurrection, all of which enable humanity to fulfill its own destiny of wholeness and unity in God (Fox 1661, 10).

The Friends believed that before the Kingdom's advent, humanity had been in captivity (Blackborow 1658, 9). And yet, when the Light did periodically shine through the prophets, the reign of darkness was already threatened. The spiritual Kingdom constituted true freedom, the freedom of the Messiah who 'dashes to pieces' that which was contrary to it (Fox and Hubberthorne 1661,20). Outward kingdoms were drenched in blood and would continue as such without the Light. For these reasons the Kingdom was different not only in its everlastingness but also because in the now of this compassionate Spirit, in its immediacy, time disappeared; at that point there was no beginning and end (Fox 1995, 283; Nayler 1656, 56–9). By rising above time and space, therefore, it could reach in any era into the hearts and minds of all for their transformation into the Life and its child-like Edenic purity. This gave the Kingdom its unique 'Power', and whosoever was in this 'Power' was truly a follower of the Jesus Way in deeds rather than in mere words.

For Fox and Friends, 'Children' and 'Kingdom' were inseparable. As in Jesus' era, seventeenth-century children often came last in the pecking order but in the Kingdom the least would be first. Fox insisted that the Friends should stand as an example to others as Children of the Kingdom and the Light by virtue of their own spiritual awakening and right walking. They were to prove to a hostile world that the Kingdom was one of peace, righteousness, justice, forgiveness, and meekness, and that violence was a stranger to it. In the Kingdom everyone, even enemies, was a neighbour. It was the 'place' where the poor and despised would find justice and sanctuary; 'The trimmings of the vain world', cried William Penn, 'would clothe the naked one' (Tucker 1971, 8). Dwelling in the Light was the sure way of experiencing God, of being in the Presence.

Isaac Penington

While in *The Way of Life and Death*, Penington states unequivocally that the Kingdom was neither 'literal, traditional, nor fleshly' or 'received by natural understanding' (1658, 46), his *Expositions with Observations*, a pre-Quaker meditation on the Sermon on the Mount (he became a Quaker in 1658), emphasizes the Christian orthodoxy of the 'blessedness' of the poor in spirit who would inherit the Kingdom. The right to this large, rich inheritance of 'these perfectly poor ones' was written in their nature, in their 'poverty' (Penington 1656, 52). They who ignored Jesus' Beatitudes, who propagated false teaching while 'expounding the Scriptures out of the Life', barred themselves from the Kingdom and thus brought divine judgement upon themselves (Penington 1659b, 13). The scandal of poverty, both material and spiritual, 'angered' God who demanded the healing of the broken Christ.

Of its nature the Kingdom was cleansing. Penington's *Some of the Mysteries of God's Kingdom Glanced At* helps us grasp the fundamental place of Love at the heart of his movement's Kingdom experience, what may be called its Kingdom-as-Peace Testimony message. It was important to know, he wrote, that God brought forth the 'weak' and 'foolish' who were offensive to the powers of their present age (Penington 1663, 3–4). The Kingdom appeared where the eye of humanity least looked for them (Penington 1660, 28–9).

In *The Axe Laid to the Root* we learn that all followers of the Jesus Way are the true Church. As such they have the Spirit in their midst and the existential Jesus as their comforter and companion. Jesus' Love is the guide, the very means of life itself, the standard that is over all. The tract highlights the Kingdom as an ever-present event with a constant promise for the future (Penington 1659a, 4–5).

However, Penington also warned about the corruptibility of the Kingdom. Repeating Fox, while it could cut through the sin of church-centricity like a two-edged sword, there was a particular need to be aware of the false Church. The wolves within it led people into the 'thick night of darkness' that 'overspread the beauty' of the Kingdom, particularly in the way they promoted the letter of Scripture rather than its Spirit. More importantly, he and the Friends countered the Calvinist belief that the outward Church was the Kingdom of God on earth. Rather than being other-worldly, there was no relation between the Kingdom and the true Church that did not intersect with the world.

PRESENT-DAY QUAKER ORTHOPRAXIS OF THE KINGDOM

If the Kingdom, its politics of compassion, and their early Quaker hermeneutic rose above time and space, their manifestation may be expected in other eras. With this in mind, this section introduces four brief examples of the work of individual Quakers and Quaker organizations that may characterize the above politics:

- During the apartheid years, South African Quakers underwent a torturous journey from their reluctance to involve themselves in politics (during the 1950s and early 1960s), to a dogged corporate opposition to institutionalized racism and militarism. They did so with the help of Friends worldwide. With only about a hundred members, the Friends supported the oppressed majority in a variety of ways, particularly during the emergency years of the 1970s up to the all-party elections of 1994. Hendrik van der Merwe, the founder of the Centre for Intergroup Studies (now the Centre for Conflict Resolution) at Cape Town University, used his pre-eminence among the Afrikaner community to initiate meetings between the African National Congress (ANC), the government, and the media. He actively supported the Mandela family, visiting Nelson in prison.

The Quaker cosmologist George Ellis, Templeton Prize winner in 2004, with a long history of peace and anti-racist activism, received the Star of South Africa medal from President Mandela in 1999 and the Order of Mapungubwe (South Africa's highest honour) from President Mbeki in 2006 for his anti-apartheid work. His wife Mary Roberts Ellis, worked assiduously as a physician for the people of the Ciskei and Transkei. There are many other examples of South African Quakers who, throughout that time, personally engaged with Steve Biko and other ANC leaders while demonstrating within and among themselves a loyalty to the Quaker Testimonies of Peace, Truth, Simplicity, and Equality despite attacks from hostile forces (Guiton 2005, 176–7).

- British Quaker Peggy Preston worked as a nurse in a slum near Johannesburg during the 1950s. Before her expulsion from South Africa for anti-apartheid activism, she assisted Desmond Tutu and Trevor Huddleston, the inspiration for the priest in Alan Paton's *Cry the Beloved Country* (1948). Years later Preston was gaoled in Israel: 'We were well aware that our treatment was totally different to that given to Palestinians or peace movement Israelis'. After many other actions for peace, she joined an international 'Gulf Peace Camp', which situated itself between the two main battle lines prior to the outbreak of the 1991 Gulf war (ibid., 120).
- US Quaker Tom Fox (1951–2006)a worked for the Christian Peace Teams assisting families of imprisoned Iraqis, escorting shipments of medicine to clinics and hospitals, and helping to form Islamic Peacemaker Teams. In 2005 he and three colleagues were kidnapped by Islamists. His co-workers were released in March 2006 but Fox's bullet-riddled body was later found on an Iraqi roadside. Anticipating his capture and even murder, he had urged his friends not to take revenge on those responsible.

- The Friends Peace Teams, founded in 1993 by the late US Friend Elise Boulding (1920–2010), comprise Friends from the two main traditions of Quakerism— unprogrammed and pastoral. The African Great Lakes Initiative (AGLI), covering the region containing Burundi, Congo, Kenya, Rwanda, Tanzania, and Uganda, is its largest programme. In the wake of the Rwandan genocide of 1994, AGLI, together with Burundi and Rwandan Quakers, established what is now the Healing and Rebuilding Our Communities Programme. According to David Zarembka, AGLI's coordinator, the Programme addresses the needs of traumatized people, encourages rapprochement between Hutus and Tutsis (formerly murderous opponents), and reaches out to other areas of conflict such as Kenya (Zarembka 2012, 10–11).

These activities are a tiny sample from a worldwide endeavour by the Religious Society of Friends towards furthering justice, peace, and compassion. It has been an endeavour that since the Society's founding has led Quakers to work actively for religious tolera-tion, gender equality, and equality for other discriminated groups as well as penal, church, and governmental reform. The Society has also engaged in peace initiatives including conflict resolution and mediation in places such as Northern Ireland, draft and war tax resistance, anti-slavery work, and justice for Indigenous Peoples, refugees, and other marginalized peoples. To these may be added care for the insane, war relief, education reform, employment creation schemes, health care, honesty in business, and simplicity in lifestyle and other areas. In 1947 the Nobel Peace Prize was awarded to Friends worldwide for the work they had done, particularly relief work, between the two world wars and post-1945. Further, Quakers work actively towards the preservation of the planet in sustainable ways.

These and other activities reveal a capacity for the Friends to witness to the Kingdom's revolutionary politics of compassion in many and varied ways despite their small number worldwide (about 360,000). It is a witness that since the 1650s has consistently demanded a visible, authentic, and life-enhancing socio-political and economic restruc-turing of relations among the people of God, particularly with the weak and vulnerable. It involves a non-violent struggle with the 'principalities and powers' at their core (Fox 1658b, 1, 3–6), one that continues to challenge the politics of fear and despair, milita-rism, oppression, privilege, and wealth.

That the above activities derive from the Testimonies, themselves born of the Kingdom, might suggest a widespread knowledge of the Kingdom among Friends and others, particularly the mainstream churches. Such an assumption would be wrong. As the Gospel of Thomas tells us, the Kingdom 'is spread out over the earth but people do not see it'. Education programmes creating the link between the Kingdom and such activities might prevent the secularization of the latter.

To conclude: the Kingdom, its Sermons, and Beatitudes as well as their Quaker inter-pretation act as an eschatological continuum. They are a voice of redemption and lib-eration together with the hope they carry for wholeness and unity in God. The early Quakers' politics of compassion, born of their 1650s Kingdom experience, maintains an urgency and vitality to this day. This Kingdom politics lies at the heart of the modern Society's public Testimonies to Peace, Truth, Simplicity, and Equality (some would add Community and Earthcare).

Despite evidence of individualism and postmodern relativism within the body of Friends, the Kingdom is its life-generating and inclusive common language, and its orthopraxis for the furthering of justice, peace and compassion within their Religious Society and respective civil societies as well as internationally.

An early Quaker brings this essay to a close with the theme that began it—the Kingdom's power as the omnipresence of God/Love. Despite being 'few in number in respect of others', wrote Robert Barclay:

> and weak as to outward strength, which we also altogether reject; and foolish, if
> compared with the wise ones of this world, yet neither the art, wisdom, nor violence

of men or devils shall be able to quench that little spark, that hath appeared, but it shall grow [irrespective] of whatever shall stand up to oppose it. (1678, 392)

Suggested Further Reading

Fox, G. (1654) *To all that would know the way to the Kingdom*, N.p.

Guiton, G. (2005) *The growth and development of Quaker testimony*. Lewiston, NY: Edwin Mellen Press.

Guiton, G. (2012) *The early Quakers and the 'Kingdom of God'*. San Francisco, CA: Inner Light Books.

Howgill, F. (1658) *Some of the mysteries of God's Kingdom*. London: Simmonds.

CHAPTER 15

QUAKER WOMEN'S LIVES AND SPIRITUALITIES

MARY VAN VLECK GARMAN

WOMEN have played crucial roles in every stage of Quaker history. Scholars have usually attributed their unusual levels of participation to the much-admired Quaker tradition of 'equality'. This chapter will summarize and celebrate Quaker women's lives of faith, and will suggest another way of interpreting their remarkable accomplishments. The work of previous scholars suggests the need for this alternative. In 1915 Mabel Brailsford published the first history of Quakerism that focused exclusively on women. Earlier historians had mentioned women, but focused on men; the exceptions were biographies of certain prominent Quaker women. Scholars have reopened debates about the participation of women in particular events in Quaker history, such as Christine Trevett's research into early Quaker women and her study of the James Naylor incident in 1656, Michele Tarter's investigation of Quaker women and embodiment, or Phyllis Mack's study of prophetic women, including Quakers, in the seventeenth century.

Beginning in the 1960s and 1970s, feminists discovered the treasure trove of writings by Quaker women, and produced articles and books that opened new areas for research. Church historian Rosemary Radford Ruether argued that early Quaker women represented an early modern feminism because of their skill and insight as interpreters of Scripture. Theologian Grace Jantzen claimed that early Quaker women originated key aspects of the Quaker theological vocabulary, which she designated the 'symbolic of life' (Jantzen 2010, 87). Future examinations can rely on primary documents written by Quaker women, which are now available in print and online versions, often in Spanish as well as English.

BEGINNINGS

Early Friends believed that God was at work in the world in identifiable ways and was restoring all creation, including political, social, economic, and ecclesiastical structures, to their pre-Edenic state. They believed that God intended humanity to live in peace, joy, love, and faithfulness, and they claimed that God could be known directly; that is, without mediation. Of particular interest to Friends were the relationships between men and women, which had been broken in the fall from grace. Quakers, as a sign to the rest of the world, were called to work in partnerships that crossed the prevailing gender, class, and racial boundaries. By challenging the world's patterns of behaviour, early Friends intended to demonstrate God's overpowering and transforming love in the midst of daily life and work.

In the seventeenth century the preaching, teaching, and witnessing of Friends evoked brutal responses from ecclesiastical and civil authorities. Public beatings and mass jailings were intended to harm, humiliate, and intimidate. Some of the harshest attacks targeted the bodies of Quaker women, whose public acts were considered particularly obnoxious because they challenged the prevailing gender ideology of female physical weakness and intellectual inadequacy.

On two occasions in 1654, four young Quaker women, Elizabeth Fletcher, Elizabeth Leavens, Elizabeth Williams, and Mary Fisher (c.1623–98), were treated 'savagely' by university students after they gave public witness at Oxford and at Cambridge. Two years later in Boston, Mary Fisher and Anne Austin were detained, and 'stripped naked, under pretence to know whether they were witches', and were 'so barbarously misused, that modesty forbids to mention it'. Ann Austin (who had borne five children) claimed 'she had not suffered so much in the birth of them all, as she had done under their barbarous and cruel hands' (Besse 1733, vol. 2, 177–8). Many other women suffered assaults and imprisonments, which confirmed the Quaker conviction that the corrupt world needed redemption. Quaker women often travelled with companions, and kept journals that told of their inner struggles and outer challenges. Among those who heeded God's call were Katherine Evans (d. 1692) and Sarah Chevers (d. 1663). In 1657 they travelled together to Salisbury, where they were 'stripped and whipped' (Bell, Parfitt, and Shepherd 1990, 45–6). Two years later they set out for Jerusalem, but were intercepted in Malta by the Inquisition. Officials arrested them on suspicion of blasphemy, and imprisoned them for three years. The account of their 'cruel sufferings' reveals the depth of their religious lives as they found strength in God and in their friendship (Garman et al 1996, 171–203).

As the suffering continued, Quaker women responded collectively. Several accounts exist of the origins of separate Women's Meetings. In one, Sarah Blackborrow (d. 1665), at the suggestion of George Fox, gathered a group of women in 1656 to organize relief efforts. They determined the needs of individuals and families, raised money, and dispensed aid. Some male Friends were uneasy about the Quaker women acting independently, and steps were taken to bring their activities under male authority, and to ensure that any decisions they made were ratified by the men's Meeting.

Early Quaker women also affronted ecclesiastical authorities and cultural expectations by publishing their ideas. They called their readers to radical 'overturning', which for them meant both inner experiences and external acts. In a startling collective effort, they resisted paying tithes for the support of the state church, and published their petitions to Parliament in 1659 under the title, '7,000 Handmaids'. Those who signed the petitions portrayed themselves as faithful prophets, echoing 1 Kgs 19:18.

Each petition included a statement explaining the signers' theological reasons for refusing to pay the tithe. They claimed that 'Christ Jesus the everlasting Priest is come' (Garman et al 1996, 64), so the system of tithes has been 'disannulled', since they were 'made by Colledges of men' (Garman et al 1996, 93) and not by God. Several of the petitions included practical suggestions for redistribution of the money. Instead of paying the state to subsidize ministry, they wanted to 'let Christ send forth his Ministers and Labourers'. They knew these suggestions were radical, but reminded their readers of the power of the Lord God, 'which comprehends the whole world which hath no end' (Garman et al 1996, 118).

Among the signers of the petitions was Margaret Fell (1614–1702), who has been called the Mother of Quakerism for her pastoral, practical, and prophetic activities. Her home, Swarthmoor Hall, became the centre of the movement. From there she corresponded with Friends, offering spiritual encouragement and practical aid. She also used her social position to influence those in power to show mercy to Friends. After she became a widow in 1658, Margaret Fell was jailed for her refusal to submit to the civil authorities. She responded with a defiant claim: 'Although I am out of the King's protection, yet I am not out of the protection of the Almighty God' (Garman et al 1996, 249).

Another petition-signer was Dorothy White (c.1630–85), who published at least twenty tracts during the formative years of the Quaker movement. She identified herself as a prophet by echoing Joel 2:1, declaring that she would 'blow the Trumpet of the Lord God Almighty over all Mountains' in her desire to bring glad-tidings to the poor and the meek (Garman et al 1996, 139). She emphasized the connections between witnessing to the world and 'coming home to within'. In one remarkable sentence that described the 'Glorious Day of the Lord', she used the word 'all' six times, concluding with the plea '...all must feel the overturning of the Mountains which have stood in opposition against the Appearance of the Lord of Glory' (Garman et al 1996, 142).

The sometimes-strident tone of the prophetic tracts by Quaker women is balanced by their use of love-centred language. They regularly addressed religious seekers as 'dear Lambs' and invited them into a 'Life of Love'. Sarah Blackborrow, in 'A Visit to the Spirit in Prison' called herself '...a lover of your souls, but a Witnesse against your deceits' (Garman et al 1996, 49).

Suffering continued in North America during the 1660s. Among those martyred was Mary Dyer, who refused to be intimidated by multiple threats and subsequent banishments and returned to Boston to witness. In June of 1660 the colonial powers, having previously killed two of her male companions, hanged her on Boston Common. Elizabeth Hooton (c.1600–72), convinced by the preaching of George Fox, became a preacher herself and was repeatedly persecuted. In 1661, upon her release from a Boston jail, she was abandoned in the forest without food or shelter. To prevent her from establishing a house in Boston where Quakers could meet, in 1665 she and her daughter were jailed, and then whipped ten times through three different towns (Besse 1773, 229). She claimed in letters to Friends that the wild beasts of the woods treated her better than the 'Savage Professors' (that is, believers) of New England.

Even at the end of her life Elizabeth Hooton was sustained by her sense that God was with her. James Lancaster, in his *Journal*, described her final moments in Jamaica in 1672: 'And she … fastened her arms about me and said, "Blessed be the Lord God that made us partakers of those heavenly mercies…"' (Manners 1914, 73).

Other Quaker women turned to theological writing as a way to serve their faith community. Elizabeth Bathurst's (1655–85) *Truth's Vindication* set out to answer the accusations made against Friends. Her theological skilfulness matched her passion for the Principle of Truth, which she connected to the impartial love of God for 'all Mankind'. She portrayed Friends as lovers of Scriptures, and invited her readers to note the plethora of words used to describe 'the Saviour of the World'. She rejoiced in this linguistic variety as evidence of God's love for all humanity, no matter what their circumstances (Garman et al 1996, 400–1).

Joan Vokins, in her account of a journey from England to New York in 1680, gave voice to fear and doubt: 'Oh how long did his tender Spirit strive with me before I gave up to go to Sea? How did his long Patience wait and suffer?'. She identified her particular sin to be 'Self-righteousness' by which she meant fear of acting in public on behalf of her own desires, not God's calling. She resolved her dilemma by realizing that the best way to serve the 'Living and True God' was to serve God 'in Spirit and in Truth' (Garman et al 1996, 259–60). Here she drew upon the words of Jesus to the Samaritan woman, who recognized his true identity despite her dubious reputation (Jn 4:24). Vokins' journal summarizes the struggles and joys Quaker women came to know in the early years, and points to the next era of Quaker women's experiences.

TRANSITIONS

During the eighteenth century, Quaker women published theological treatises and made journeys to preach and teach the Gospel. While at home they nurtured their families, offered hospitality to travellers, and built friendships that sustained them and their communities.

The writings of Ann Docwra (1640–1710), draw on the symbolic language and biblical imagery of the early days of the movement. Her central concern was the establishment and nurture of true 'Spiritual Community' among Friends in light of the changing political situation in Britain in the 1680s. In language that echoed Sarah Blackborrow and Elizabeth Bathurst, Docwra reminded her readers that those guided by this inner witness would discover that it is 'sufficient to preserve a Nation, or People in Peace'.

Docwra had worked out her own theology, and expressed tolerance towards others' views. She believed that some had looked for the true source of Spiritual Community in the wrong places (e.g. in rituals and ceremonies of the church), but she praised their impulse to undertake this search, since they have 'the love of God in their hearts'. She referred to the king's Declaration of Liberty (1687) as 'God's own work', which God accomplished within the king's heart. She wished the king further guidance from God, since only 'Divine Love and Charity' could bring the nation into 'Unity as Love God about all, and their Neighbour as themselves.'

Ann Docwra argued that laws designed to impede freedom of worship and beliefs were contrary to the Gospel, and also to the Book of Common Prayer. The true relationship between Church and State, she claimed, would guarantee that all could 'sit down under their own Vine, and under their own Fig-Tree' (Mic. 4:4) …having nothing but love' in their hearts for 'the whole Creation' (Docwra 1683, 1–3).

Quaker women continued to travel far and wide during this period, and accounts of their journeys are available because of the work of twentieth-century scholars. Margaret Hope Bacon selected and edited three journals by Quaker women who travelled and preached among Friends in the colonies and in Britain. The introductory chapters and annotations reveal the ways each of these women came to a deeper sense that 'she is fully capable of serving as a channel of the divine spirit' (Bacon, 1994, 19). Rachel Labouchere's book on Deborah Darby (1754–1810) is part of a series that explores the ministries and travels of Darby women within Britain and to North America. Labouchere drew extensively on journals and letters, which included details about daily life and insights into Deborah's struggles over deciding whether to 'leave my near connections and run the Lord's errands' (Labouchere 1993, 58). Although she spent many months travelling, Deborah Darby and her family were also well known for their hospitality, offered to travelling Quakers throughout this period. Rebecca Larson has described a dynamic transatlantic culture (Larson 1999, 8), created and sustained by travelling Quaker 'yoke-mates' who visited, preached, and witnessed to the power of God's loving Spirit. By the mid-1770s Quaker women had gained respect, which helped to legitimize public acts by all women in the colonial culture (Larson 1999, 279).

These travelling ministers set out on their journeys to preach the Gospel, and also to reform those who were drifting away from the traditional faith and practice of Friends. Deborah Darby found the 'Life of Religion' to be low in Glasgow in 1786 (Labouchere 1993, 73). The erosion was similarly perceived among those on the North American 'frontier', where Catherine Payton discovered Friends in Bucks County to be 'too generally in a dull and sluggish state' (Payton 1797, 127).

Freed from the acute demands of the early decades, Quaker women turned their collective attention to the spiritual needs of their Society, focusing on the younger generation. Excerpts from minutes and epistles demonstrate both spiritual wisdom and practical advice. The women of London, for example, sent out 'A Living Testimony …to the faithful' in 1685, and an 'Epistle of Love' in 1686, designated to be 'read among them in the fear of God' (Garman et al 1996, 519–23). They began with expressions of love and encouragement, offering the 'Dear Friends and Sisters in Christ Jesus' the hope that they will be 'strong in the power' of God's might (Garman et al 1996, 519). The duties of the Women's Meetings are then spelled out: to help families that are poor, and to see that their children are raised to become diligent and capable servants of God (Garman et al 1996, 524). They considered themselves 'meets help' with their 'Brethren in the Truth' (Garman et al 1996, 528).

Hints that separate Women's Meetings continued to be controversial can be found in the 1685 letter, which referred to some who 'willfully, scoffingly, maliciously and revilingly call Women's Meetings an Idol and an Image'. The epistle writers countered that the 'Spirit of Grace' poured out on the '*Daughters, Servants, and Hand-maids*' as well as on the Sons (Garman et al 1996, 525). Separate Women's Meetings remained part of Quaker history in both Britain and the United States until the late nineteenth century.

REFORM AND DEBATE

Circumstance in the nineteenth century provided Quaker women with opportunities to engage in social reform movements, even as their public leadership was limited. Elizabeth Gurney Fry (1780–1845), born in 1780 into a prosperous English family, exemplified this ongoing dilemma. Her religious upbringing placed her between two groups. 'Plain' Friends advocated strict adherence to traditional practices, while the 'Gay' Friends were influenced by social trends and fashions, and theological innovation. Fry became known as an indefatigable reformer who travelled widely in Britain and throughout Europe, advocating radical changes in the treatment of prisoners.

Lucretia Coffin was born in 1793 into the Quaker community on the island of Nantucket off the coast of Boston. She devoted herself to the anti-slavery movement and also advocated women's rights. In Philadelphia she and James Mott led the effort to build a site for the 1838 meeting of the Female Anti-Slavery Society. After many threats, triggered in part by the sight of white Quaker women walking arm in arm with black women, a mob destroyed the newly built Pennsylvania Hall, and attacked the local African Methodist Episcopal (AME) church and a black orphanage.

Lucretia Coffin Mott's (1793–1880) gifts in ministry were recorded by her Meeting and stenographers frequently took down her spoken ministry. In 'Likeness to Christ', she remarked that pious people were always asking her, 'what if Jesus should appear among us?' Her response was vehement: 'He *is* here; he *has* appeared … and from generation to generation and his spirit is now manifest, in the humble, the meek, the bold reformers, even among some of obscure parentage.' Her Christology, which proclaimed that Christ's actual presence is revealed in the lives of bold activists or humble slaves, offended some Friends. They feared that Lucretia Mott was too influenced by the radical views of the 'worldly' reformers of the day. When she refused to temper her public comments, her standing as a minister among Friends was called into question. Elizabeth Gurney Fry also faced criticism from within her faith community for her forthright public engagement (Isba, 2010, 203–4).

During the nineteenth century intense theological differences preoccupied Friends in the United States, resulting in a series of schisms that were both theological and cultural. Interpretations of those events have ranged across a wide spectrum, but only Nancy A. Hewitt has investigated the impact of the separations on Quaker women's lives. She analysed letters, journals, and other writings produced by Quaker women during these decades, and concluded that the upheavals of the nineteenth century were not 'tragic' for Quaker women. Instead, the debates offered them fresh opportunities to develop their eloquence as speakers and their facility as theologians (Hewitt 1989, 104). Thomas Hamm's study of Priscilla Cadwalader Hunt (1786–1859), whose life and ministry he painstakingly reconstructed, demonstrates the rich possibilities available to scholars of this era.

Near the end of the nineteenth century Friends gathered in Richmond, Indiana (1887) and in Manchester, England (1895) to consider the future of the Religious Society of Friends. The ways women were involved illustrate the paradox of gender that persisted.

In Richmond, Mahalah Jay (1827–1916) of Indiana Yearly Meeting served as one of the clerks, and of the eighty-six delegates from North America, thirty-two were female. Despite this, 'The role of women' was not among the six official agenda items. Evangelist Esther Gordon Frame (1840–1920) was undaunted. As Friends serve all around the world, she argued, they would discover that women everywhere were in bondage. To neglect their empowerment would be to waste one of God's resources! Similarly, Mary W. Thomas, from Baltimore Yearly Meeting, called for full partnership between men and women in any work undertaken by Friends. Despite the eloquence of these and other Quaker women, no official mention of women appeared in the decision minutes at Richmond in 1887. The pattern continued for future meetings of this group, which eventually became Five Years Meeting. Whether they debated the emerging pastoral system or the growing Quaker involvement in international missions, the question of women as public leaders stayed off the official agenda while remaining on the minds of those present.

Eliza Armstrong Cox (1850–1935) and other Midwestern Quaker women forced discussions of the 'woman question' by founding, in the late nineteenth century, a women-only organization that was patterned after the missionary circles of other Protestant groups. Some Friends claimed that separate organizations for women violated long-standing Quaker commitments to male–female partnership. Others acknowledged that combined organizations inevitably resulted in male-only leadership. Meanwhile, the United Society of Friends Women thrived. It became a national and then international organization, fostering friendships across theological divisions.

The second conference of Friends, held in Manchester, England (1895), followed similar patterns of women's involvement. The first and last addresses to the conference were made by women, seven other women presented papers during the conference, and sixteen took part as respondents to papers delivered by men. Nevertheless, none of the 'six questions' on the agenda focused explicitly on women. Although some women spoke up, noting that they out-numbered men in their Meetings, they continued to be excluded from leadership positions.

In her opening address Matilda Sturge praised George Fox for realizing that 'the light had been there before he recognized it'. She admired Fox's style of leadership: he never 'directed men to himself' but always pointed towards the Divine Source (Report of the Proceedings 1896, 289).

Sturge went on to claim that the Bible was, 'the record of the revelation, not the revelation itself'. She urged Friends towards a new balance, arguing that, 'we live in an age of science' which meant seeing the Bible as 'a literature and not a book'. At the same time she reminded Friends that the Spirit always led believers back to Christ. Most of all, she called Friends to recommit to work on behalf of others, against the lure of complacency. She asked them to remain close to the one 'who is our Teacher, our Saviour, and our Guide' (Report of the Proceedings 1896, 30–3).

A young lecturer in Classics, Anne Wakefield Richardson gave the final paper at the Manchester Conference in 1895. She confessed that she spoke with reluctance about the 'woman question', since Quaker women tended to think of themselves as partners with men rather than distinct from them. She went on to argue that she had became convinced that it was appropriate to speak out because she feared that silence on the topic would contribute to the trend towards consigning this question to the secular world.

Emma Cook Coffin summed up the situation for Quaker women in the United States as the new century began. Born in 1854, she had served as pastor and evangelist among Friend in Iowa, California, and Indiana between the 1890s and the 1930s. She published an article in the July 1920 *American Friend* that concluded that there were fewer opportunities for Quaker women in public ministry, even as women in other Christian groups were even being ordained (Coffin 1920, 680–1).

British Quaker women faced a similar dilemma. Sandra Stanley Holton and Margaret Allen have looked at the efforts to merge the men's and women's yearly meetings in Britain. Their analysis of the arguments around that issue challenged the suggestion that Quaker women enjoyed 'full equality' with men, and so 'did not need' the women's movement. Pam Lunn makes a similar point in her article, which focuses on the suffrage movement in Britain in the early twentieth century. She exposes the myth that Friends as a body were 'always' at the forefront of liberal political causes. Many Friends claimed that 'women in our Society are already equal' or that equality for women was never part of the Quaker message—that men and women were essentially different. Some also argued that suffrage was a political issue and not the proper concern of Friends. Lunn goes on to be highly critical of Friends who became preoccupied with the question of militancy, while refusing to take a stand for suffrage. She attributes those views to class preferences of many Friends, who 'saw no reason' for 'their' women to vote, and plenty of reasons to keep 'those women' from voting at all!

Missions, Service, Leadership

Although travelling in the ministry has been common among Friends since the earliest decades, organized foreign missions, which included establishing institutions for preaching, teaching, and healing, began in the nineteenth century and developed in the twentieth century. Rufus Jones has argued that his aunt Sybil Jones (1808–73) was 'the mother of the Quaker missionary movement'. She and her husband Eli Jones took their first missionary journey in 1840, and during the next thirty years they travelled extensively, 'to acquaint people with Christ's saving power'. Sybil described her ministry most often in terms of her identity as a woman. During their first trip to the Middle East (1867–9) she noticed that some people attended services just to hear a woman preach! When they visited the boys' school in Ramallah, a 15-year-old girl approached them asking them to establish a school of girls (Jones 1937, 3–4). She always addressed women with a 'sister's love' and included in her Gospel preaching a call to a 'standard of equality of sex in social life, religion, and the ministry of the Word'.

Quaker women from both Britain and the United States served overseas through-out the next century. Rachel Metcalf, the first British Friend to journey to India, began in 1866, and her work was continued by Esther Baird and Delia Fistler from North America. British Friends began mission work in Africa in the early nineteenth century, as an extension of their anti-slavery efforts. The memoir of Hannah Kilham's work in Gambia and Sierra Leone in the 1820s reveals her strong belief that all missionary work should be based on language learning and local empowerment. Another British Quaker woman called to serve far from home was Marjorie Sykes (1905–95), who left England for India in 1928. She taught English at the Bentinck School, became fluent in Tamil, and participated in the small Quaker worshipping community.

The impulse to organize international relief efforts also blossomed in the twentieth century, as a group of Friends in the United States, mostly men, founded the American Friends Service Committee in June of 1917. One month later, a working party of six women joined counterparts from Britain in the crucial work of feeding children and establishing health clinics in Russia. During the next several decades Friends deepened their involvement in offering relief to suffering around the world, and also provided opportunities for service to Quaker women.

Carolena Wood of New York Yearly Meeting travelled to France and then Germany in 1919 with Jane Addams and Alice Hamilton. The resulting relief programmes were funded by money raised by Quakers, and fed hungry, desperate German children and adults. Alice Shafer from Illinois, drew inspiration from hearing Carolena Wood speak of her work. She went to Berlin in 1939 to work with the Quaker International Centre, and returned to Germany after the Second World War, staying until 1949. Shafer went on to work for UNICEF, serving children all around the world and inspiring other Quaker women to give their lives in service.

Quaker women served as missionaries throughout the world in the twentieth century. Their stories, and those of the women who became Quaker because of their work, exist in library archives such as the Herbert and Beatrice Kimball Collection at Earlham College. Future scholars will make remarkable discoveries about the lives of missionaries and those who came to Friends on the mission field.

Edna Chilson, for example, served with her husband Arthur in Kenya for twenty years. Her reports, letters, and furlough talks invite speculation about the relationships between African and North American Quaker women. Pearl Spoon, born in Kansas of

Native-American heritage, served as teacher and administrator in Kenya at the Girls School, and was mentored by her pastor Roxie Reeve. Pearl Spoon spoke out on behalf of Africans during her furlough in the United States in 1953. She called on Friends to continue their support and to make specific changes: 'The attitude of the present day missionary going to Africa must be to work *with* the African, not *for* him', she urged (Spoon 1953, 312). Pearl Spoon's work in Kenya continued until her retirement in 1965.

Salome Nolega David (1931–), continued in the tradition of Roxie Reeve and Pearl Spoon. She graduated from the Friends Girls School where she was known as a 'friendly, bright, energetic, ambitious' student leader. She overcame her financial struggles by taking on extra work responsibilities at the school and later attended the Kikuyu Girls Secondary School. Scholarship help made possible her enrollment at Berea College in Kentucky, and when she returned to Kenya, Salome David taught at several colleges, keeping her focus on the training of young girls. She was actively involved in East Africa Yearly Meeting, and in the Friends World Committee for Consultation. On 12 June 1978, Salome Nolega David addressed a special session of the United Nations General Assembly on disarmament. In her address she spoke explicitly as a Quaker, reminding the Assembly that Friends had a long-term commitment to 'working for peace and human dignity, and against war and the preparation for it'. She called on the nations of the world to be stewards of the whole earth: 'what steward would risk turning such a gem (as the earth) into a radioactive cinder?' She connected the call for disarmament to a call for economic justice, pointing out that the needs of ordinary people were being 'sacrificed to military hardware'.

SPIRITUAL LIVES IN THE TWENTIETH CENTURY

In the 1960s and 1970s, Quaker women responded locally and internationally to the movement known as 'women's liberation'. Elise Boulding (1920–2010), Quaker sociologist and activist, wrote a series of essays that expressed her concerns for spirituality within the family, linking it to international disarmament. In a lecture delivered on 25 March 1956 at the Arch Street Meeting House in Philadelphia she declared, 'If the call to live in the Kingdom means anything it surely means helping by our lives to create the conditions for the Kingdom to come in all the world'. Helen Hole, Provost at Earlham College and Professor of English, wrote extensively on education, emphasizing the need for Quaker schools to remain faithful to both social activism and spiritual contemplation. She warned Friends against complacency and challenged them to remember that 'Deep within us are things we'd rather not look at: ambition, pride, interest in our own status and fear of anything that may threaten it, fear that our weaknesses may be found out'. A writer and minister among Friends, Elizabeth Watson drew on literature to express her spirituality. In *Guests of My Life* she demonstrated how poetry saved her from despair after the sudden death of her daughter. She spoke out powerfully for the rights of gay and lesbian people, and joined her voice with those Friends who felt the threat of ecological disaster.

Among pastoral Friends in the United States, Emma Coffin's predictions of 1920 became the reality. A biblical/theological/statistical study done in 1974 revealed that only 10 per cent of the pastors associated with Friends United Meeting were female (Coffin 1975, 17). The Earlham School of Religion, founded in 1960 in part to train Friends pastors, enrolled few women in the earliest years, and it would be a decade before the numbers of women students began to increase. Nevertheless, 'the woman question' remained on the minds of many Friends. In 1975, which was designated by the United Nations as 'International Women's Year', entire issues of *Quaker Life* (August 1975), *The Evangelical Friend* (October 1975), and *Friends Journal* (December, 1975), focused on the women in Quaker history, with some attention to feminism. The authors represented a wide range of views. While most spoke positively about individual Quaker women, especially those from the past, not all were supportive of 'feminism', which they defined as a secular movement for women's social and political equality.

A lively discussion ensued in subsequent letters to the editor. One writer wondered why Quakers as a group have been 'slow to respond' to the women's movement. Several others responded that Friends 'didn't need' feminism because of the strong heritage of gender partnership. Another writer wished that women would 'concentrate on more important issues'.

While none of the respondents objected to the presence or hard work of women in Quaker organizations, for some 'the woman question' had become part of the larger debate, sometimes called 'the culture wars'. At issue were biblical authority, gender identity, sexual freedom, and interpretations of the past. To complicate matters even more, by the 1980s and 1990s, strong Quaker leaders in Africa, Latin America, and the Caribbean, both women and men, began to join these debates. The distinctions between 'liberal' and 'conservative' lost meaning, as post-colonial Friends spoke from their minds and hearts about their experiences with God's overturning power and love.

In 1986 the annual Swarthmore Lecture of Britain Yearly Meeting became the occasion for profound consideration of gender ideologies. Departing from the usual format, the Quaker Women's Group wrote their lecture collaboratively over several years, and then incorporated music, readings, and other non-traditional communication media into their presentation. Reactions varied widely, from heart-felt appreciation to outright rejection. The long-term impact of this event continues to unfold. Within just a few years, though, an international gathering of Quaker women was organized in response. Invitations were extended to Quaker women all around the world to attend a conference at Woodbrooke in Birmingham, England in the summer of 1990. The International Conference of Quaker Women attracted seventy-four women from twenty-one countries. The out-going epistle, written in Spanish and English, expressed the hope that 'through our work we would be better able to perform the service God has given each of us to do, and to assist our sisters everywhere to do so as well'.

The ambiguous relationship between feminism and Quakerism was not resolved at the Woodbrooke conference, but a renewed sense of Quaker sisterhood was created. Personal relationships developed across theological divides during the ten-day conference and afterwards. The publication of the proceedings in 1991 and the circulation of video excerpts (narrated in English and Spanish) brought the plenary addresses to wider audiences. The 'Multwood Group' in Portland, Oregon, which had been meeting together across theological divisions for years, published their collective discoveries and insights (Abbott 1995).

The public leadership of Quaker women has ceased to be a matter of debate for many groups of Friends. Several national and international organizations have had female executives, and many programmed meetings in the United States interview and hire female pastoral candidates. Other Friends link the 'woman question' to the ongoing debates about biblical authority and cultural influence, and as a result the public leadership possibilities for some Quaker women continue to be limited.

Final Comments and an Alternative

In every era Quakers have had to determine when to conform to 'the world', and when to remain aloof from prevailing attitudes and practices. The preaching, publishing, and confronting done by Quaker women in the earliest decades were crucial to the 'overturning' that lies at the heart of Friends' message. Early Friends were willing to violate the prevailing gender ideology as a sign of their commitment to God. As the state-sanctioned persecutions ended, the need to be 'peculiar' began to weaken. Friends developed sturdier organizational structures and more systematic articulations of their theological beliefs in the eighteenth century. At the same time, the gender ideology of the Victorian world gained strength. Especially in Britain the presence and work of women in the Religious Society of Friends remained significant, but their public leadership was increasingly curtailed, and their theological creativity was muted. Perhaps because of the revolutionary and frontier experiences, Friends in the United States negotiated their gender dynamics somewhat differently.

During the nineteenth century the public leadership of women in anti-slavery efforts and the participation of Friends in the drive for women's suffrage, triggered heated debates. Some Friends advocated gender partnerships in relation to social causes, while others considered Quaker women's public leadership to be offensive or a distraction from more important causes. These views were transplanted around the world when Friends engaged in missionary activities in the nineteenth and twentieth centuries. Esther Mombo, in her study of the East Africa Yearly Meeting, has argued that 'additional oppressive forms' were imposed upon female converts during the first fifty years of Friends work there. Despite being 'marginalized' by an imported gender ideology, Mombo has concluded that these African Quaker women heard 'the message of true Quakerism', and have recently claimed a stance of partnership for their future (Mombo 1999, 25).

Quaker women in the twenty-first century continue the journey begun by their foremothers. Especially impressive are the young women who seek ways to bridge the historic and current divisions among Friends. The World Gathering of Young Friends in 2005, the growing presence of Convergent Friends, and the recent publication of *Spirit Rising* all point towards an exciting future. How questions of gender ideology will be negotiated remains to be seen.

As suggested in the opening paragraph, 'equality' does not adequately describe the sources of women's empowerment throughout Quaker history. The term remains susceptible to the redefinitions of each generation and culture, which has meant that in some eras Quaker women have been declared 'equal' to men while being excluded from full leadership in the Religious Society of Friends. To solve this dilemma, Friends could revive the word 'helpsmeet'. This term, with its biblical resonance, more fully describes Quaker partnerships of the past. Current and future Friends can benefit from exploring the virtues of being 'helpsmeet' to one another. Such relationships, based on shared spiritual commitments, are characterized by encouragement, accountability, and mutuality, even in the face of resistance from those in power—in the surrounding society or in the Religious Society of Friends.

Such a shift in terminology could underpin ongoing research into the lives of Quaker women. A model for this approach can be found in Sandra Stanley Holton's study of the 'Priestman–Bright circle' in Britain in the eighteenth and nineteenth centuries. Holton draws on evidence from a variety of disciplines (history, religion, politics, economics) and weaves together stories of kinship, social commitment, and shared religious values (Holton 2007, 7).

Regarding one another and those from the past as 'helpsmeet' will challenge scholars to re-examine the lives and stories of prominent Quaker women. Scholars can also discover and reveal the stories of women whose faithful lives as Friends have been overlooked or misunderstood.

SUGGESTED FURTHER READING

Bacon, M. H. (1994) 'Wilt thou go on my errand?': journals of three 18th century Quaker women ministers: Susanna Morris, 1682–1755; Elizabeth Hudson, 1722–1783; Ann Moore, 1710–1783. Wallingford, Pa: Pendle Hill Publications.

Bell, M., Parfitt, G., and Shepherd, S. (1990) A biographical dictionary of English women, 1580–1720. Boston: G. K. Hall.

Brailsford, M. (1915) Quaker Women, 1650–1690. London: Duckworth and Co.

Brown, E. P. and Stuard, S. M. (eds.) (1989) Witnesses for change. New Brunswick, NJ: Rutgers University Press.

Garman, M., Applegate, J., Benefiel, M., and Meredith, D. (1996) Hidden in plain sight: Quaker women's writings 1650–1700. Wallingford, PA: Pendle Hill Press.

Jantzen, G. (2010) 'Choose Life! Early Quaker women and violence in modernity' in A place of springs: Death and the displacement of beauty, pp. 75–92. London, New York: Routledge.

Larson, R. (1999) Daughters of Light: Quaker women preaching and prophesying in the colonies and abroad, 1700–1775. Chapel Hill, North Carolina: University of North Carolina Press.

Mack, P. (1992) Visionary women: Ecstatic prophecy in seventeenth-century England. Berkeley: University of California Press.

Meredith, D. (ed.) (1991) Proceedings of the First International Theological Conference of Quaker Women, held at Woodbrooke, England, 24–31 July 1990. Birmingham: Woodbrooke.

Mombo, E. (1999) 'Haramisi and Jumaa: The story of the Women's Meetings in East Africa early Meeting, 1902–1979', Woodbrooke Journal, Autumn, pp. 1–26.

CHAPTER 16

....

LEADINGS AND
DISCERNMENT

....

MICHAEL BIRKEL

INTRODUCTION

....

DISCERNMENT has long been a concern in Christian spirituality. It rose to particular prominence in ancient Egyptian monasticism of the fourth century AD, when the quest for inward freedom from self-defeating behaviours and from self-deceiving perceptions came into apparent conflict with the structured life of a solitary or a coenobite. Especially for the spiritual guides (abbas and ammas, spiritual fathers and mothers) who undertook the care of souls in delicate spiritual formation, it was essential to know when to apply the rules and when to set them aside. As the Apostle Paul noted, the letter kills but the Spirit gives life (2 Cor. 3.6), a passage often cited by early Friends (Fell 1660b, 18; Penington, Fox, and Fell 1784; Penn 1726a, 2:242). Discernment was about knowing what to do when. It might mean relaxing a rule of fasting to honour the obligations of hospitality:

> There once went out an order in Scetis that they would fast that week before celebrating Easter. However it so happened that in that week some monastics came from Egypt to abba Moses, and he cooked them a little vegetable stew. And when his neighbours saw the smoke, they informed the clerics of the church that is in Scetis and exclaimed, 'Look, Moses has broken the rule, and cooked food in his cell.' The clergy said, 'When he comes up here we'll have a word with him.' But when the Sabbath came, the clerics saw the great holiness of his life, and they said to him, in front of everyone, 'O abba Moses, you have broken a human commandment but you have mightily kept the commandment of God.' (Migne 1844, 73:944)

This story is taken from the *Words of the Elders* (*Verba seniorum*), an early collection of monastic wisdom. John Cassian, who was steeped in the insights of these ancient Egyptian monastics and interpreted them for a Latin audience, devoted the second of his twenty-four *Conferences* to discernment (Cassian and Boniface 1997, 77–112). Benedict, whose *Rule* came to shape Western Christian monastic life enormously, endorsed Cassian, and thereby the latter came to exert a significant influence in Christian spirituality throughout the medieval period and beyond Benedict and Fry,1982, 297).

A second great stream of reflection on discernment in Western Christianity flows from Ignatius of Loyola, the founder of the Society of Jesus (better known as the Jesuits), in the sixteenth century. In his *Spiritual Exercises*, Ignatius offered rules for discernment. These provide a framework for examining one's inner motivations, to determine the will of God as one faces a decision. Ignatius spoke of these internal movements as good and evil spirits, and these manifest themselves through consolation and desolation. Consolation ultimately brings joy, but some apparent joy is false consolation. Desolation reveals itself through doubt, confusion, and depression, but not all sadness or disappointment is desolation. The task of discernment is to distinguish true from false consolation and desolation. In the final analysis, consolation brings people into a greater sense of divine love and presence, while desolation moves people into isolation from God (Ignatius and Ganss 1991; Silf 1999).

Quaker spirituality offers its own contributions to the history of discernment. As a religious community that has relied greatly on the belief that God can lead individuals and communities into new forms of action and reveal new truth, Quakers of necessity have had to reflect on how to determine if a sense of divine leading is genuine. The openness to new truth requires a vulnerability that can result in misperception. Each era of Quaker history reflects its own particular concerns as well as its changing relationship to the wider world.

SHOWING VERSUS TELLING

Until the twentieth century, Quakers were hesitant to articulate guidelines for discernment. Friends have so highly valued the experience of direct guidance from the Spirit of God that they have been reluctant to frame specific rules for determining whether an apparently divine impulse is in fact reliable. This reluctance to hinder the freedom of the Spirit to lead in fresh and new ways has resulted in a historical tendency among Quakers to show rather than to tell. While the Jesuit founder Ignatius of Loyola conveniently distilled his insights into 'rules for discernment', the student of early Quakerism must search through a library of documents to find examples of discernment and then seek to discover patterns that can be offered as general principles.

LEADINGS

Among Friends, the testimonies are the enduring ethical principles that shape behaviour. Over the centuries, the nomenclature and enumeration of the testimonies have evolved, but today many Friends identify testimonies of peace, simplicity, equality, and integrity. These are guiding principles held by the community, but the individual expression of those testimonies varies. Among Quakers, a leading is often a specific guidance of divine inspiration that embodies one or more of these principles. An example may help to clarify the distinction between a testimony and a leading. From the days of George Fox, Friends had opposed violence and participation in warfare. This principle came to be expressed as the peace testimony. A century later, in a time of war on the Pennsylvanian frontier, some Friends such as John Woolman felt a leading to resist the payment of taxes to support war. While war tax refusal has not become a universal expectation among Friends, an important minority has felt a leading similar to John Woolman's, and that leading has, on the whole, been honoured by the wider community. Leadings come to individuals, but historically it has been the group that has judged whether or not they are genuine. This relationship between individual and community has had a complex history in Quakerism as Friends have sought to navigate the Scylla of deadly rigidity and the Charybdis of formless anarchy. The freedom that must be real enough so that there can be genuine openness to leadings, even to new moral and spiritual truth. This freedom needs to coexist with a structure that is powerful enough to sustain the tradition that has valued that very freedom.

Because Quakers hold that anyone can be led to speak in Meeting for Worship, they also speak of a leading in terms of an inner urge to share words from the silence during worship. Just as with leadings that result in particular ethical actions, a leading to speak in worship must be weighed and measured. Like the ancient monastics mentioned earlier, Friends from their beginnings were aware of the need for interior vigilance, to sharpen one's awareness of the ever-present possibility of self-deception. For Quakers, discernment is the means to distinguish between an interior direction of divine origin and an impulse of lesser derivation, such as a desire to look clever or feel important.

Additionally, any experience perceived as the direct guidance of God can be described as a leading, for example, the sense of being called to undertake a religious visit to other Friends near or far, as was often recorded in the journals of Quaker ministers.

EARLY FRIENDS: MARGARET FELL

Patricia Loring has described Quaker spiritual practices as a spirituality of listening (Loring 1997, 2). Early Friends developed practices of awareness and self-watchfulness that aided discernment. The letters of spiritual counsel written by Margaret Fell (1614–1702) offer a vivid description of this interior listening.

These letters instruct their readers in a process for mindfulness: wait, see, mind. Often there is a pattern in her counsel: to keep low, to wait, to mind the Light, to see, to be faithful and obedient. Each person is given a particular measure of the Light. Margaret Fell says repeatedly in her letters that Friends are to be faithful and obedient to their particular measures, so that they may distinguish between a leading of the Light and a selfish motivation. Such obedience, however, even when costly, is not in the end a dismal task. It leads to peace, joy, and unity with God and with others. It is the path to spiritual freedom:

> My joy and life is, that you would take heed to your own measure received, and be true and faithful to that which is able to save your souls, that eternal pure redemption you may come to witness and the unity of the faith. (Fox 1995, 212)

Many of her letters urge the same practices: keep low, wait, mind the Light, be faithful:

> In the bowels of everlasting Love I write unto you, and in the name and power of Jesus Christ I exhort you, that as you have received Christ Jesus, so walk in him, as you have received the truth, so abide in the truth, that the truth may make you free, as you have received the Light from Christ Jesus, the fountain and fullness of all Light and life, so abide in the Light, dwell in the Light, walk in the Light, have your being and habitation in the Light. Life and immortality moves in the Light, so wait every one in your measure for the manifestation of God. (Fox 1995, 258)

She counsels her readers to distinguish inward truth from outward form:

> Therefore let the eternal search and try every particular, and see what you are covered withal. Yea, let the living principle of God in you all, examine what you enjoy and possess of him which is eternal, and what is of him will stand in his presence, who is a consuming fire unto all that is not of him, and what you do enjoy of that, which is eternal of God, begotten of him by the immortal word, abiding, and being faithful in that, ye shall witness a growth in that which is eternal. (Fox 1995, 95–6)

Although expressions vary in minor ways from writer to writer, Margaret Fell serves as an eloquent example of characteristic early Quaker understanding of leadings and discernment.

THE EIGHTEENTH CENTURY

The eighteenth century saw the rise of what Howard Brinton called the flowering of Quaker culture, a golden age, particularly in the Quaker colonies of North America (Brinton 1952, 181–7) The charisma and turmoil of the early decades of Quakerism gave way to enduring structures and increasing inwardness. The first period of Quakerism may be described as one of robust confidence. Friends in the 1700s were more guarded, more cautious, more suspicious of their own motives—in short, perhaps more intro-spective but less self-assured. Quakers who travelled in the ministry often wrote spir-itual autobiographies or journals, and four of these will serve as representative sources for understanding discernment in this era.

Josiah Langdale (1673–1723) first came to know Friends when he hired himself out as a labourer to Quaker David Milner in 1689, in the year that the Toleration Act was passed, which formally concluded the persecution of religious Dissenters to the state church, although their civil rights were still limited. (Admission to university, for example, was granted only in the nineteenth century.) By then the early excitement of the Quaker movement had yielded to a quiet and rather separate existence. Langdale joined Friends and was eventually acknowledged as a public minister.

In his journal, the writing of which was cut short by his early death, he reflected on the inner work of discernment to test a leading to speak in Meeting for Worship:

> Great dread and fear seized upon my soul and spirit lest I should go beyond the word of the Lord, and speak in my own name, will and time, and so lose the savour of love and life that season the offering which is prepared of the Lord ... I saw by the Light and Spirit of Christ Jesus that a minister of the word of God must wait for the word and counsel of God, and have the word before he can minister to edification and comfort of the people. I saw likewise by the same spirit that if a minister did not keep down in his mind to the word of life and dwell with it he would be liable to receive false conceptions, and have false impressions in his mind, and so take hold of the wrong thing, and be deceived ... I likewise saw that, if a minister waited for the word, and had the word of the Lord, he would speak such things as were suitable to the states of the people he ministered among ... and his words would be felt by them, and they would be benefited. (Langdale and Skidmore 1999, 21–2)

The repeated claim to have seen by the Spirit echoes the language of the Book of Revelation, and suggests that even as Quakers grew less boisterous and apocalyptic, they understood their work in the ministry as prophetic. Langdale's words are reminiscent of Margaret Fell's: keep down, be low, wait. Some qualities are different. Unlike Margaret Fell, who wrote:

> Now, Friends, deal plainly with your selves, and let the eternal Light search you, and try you, for the good of your souls; for this will deal plainly with you; it will rip you up, and lay you open, and make all manifest which lodgeth in you; the secret subtlety of the enemy of your souls, this eternal searcher and tryer will make manifest. Therefore all to this come, and by this be searched, and judged, and led and guided; for to this you must stand or fall. (Fox 1995, 212)

Josiah Langdale's words focus more on edification, comfort, and benefit. Another important sign of a leading, even if discernible only after the event, is that the words of ministry must speak suitably to the inward states of those present. The message must be understood and felt by the gathered community. Under the guidance of the Light of Christ, the minister can see—or feel—into the condition of the worshippers and offer words appropriate to their needs. Other Friends spoke of this experience as coming to 'a feeling sense of the condition of others' (Birkel 2003, 35).

Other Friends of the eighteenth century chronicled their own, similar struggles to discern divine will. Susanna Morris (1682–1755), describing her efforts to be open and faithful to leadings in her travels in the ministry, wrote of a journey in 1744:

> I think we are never safe unless we feel the plough of God's power and the manner thereof so operating in us as to break us into tenderness, then it is that we know how to demean ourselves before him who can and does work such a change that for any of ministers are truly made able to speak for the encouragement of the true travellers, and point out the way to the kingdom. (Bacon 1994, 64)

Elsewhere she wrote of the need 'to wait for his appearance in their own hearts, and know his word there a hammer to break them into tenderness; the offering of a broken heart and a contrite spirit is what the Lord accepts of in our days' (Bacon 1994, 67).

Elizabeth Hudson (1722–83) wrote similarly of the struggle to subdue 'creatureliness' in order to discern a leading to speak in worship:

> I have oft compared the ministry to a fountain or spring of water and ministers to pipes through which the water is conveyed to divers parts of a city, some greater, some lesser according to the distance the stream is to be conveyed or the body of water is to convey, and very frequently we see one pipe so fixed as to be in some sort dependent on another and if any impediment happens to either it frustrates the grand design of conveyance, and no pipe is so small or minute but there is some service or part to act and its not acting that part may possibly disconcert the whole as to incommode a great part if not the whole city. (Bacon 1994, 157)

These pipes are 'in themselves as dead inanimate matter until this divine fountain of Eternal life circulated or flowed in and through them' (Bacon 1994, 157). The minister's pipe must be 'free from all impurity of our frail natures', permitting the 'Holy Current of living ministry' to ebb and flow in its own course:

> neither endeavouring in our own wills or wisdom to raise it beyond its limited bounds or raising or tuning the voice to make others believe it higher tide with us than it really is, for by so doing we only muddy the water and offend our sensible hearers, rendering that which simply dropped would have administered life, a messenger of death. (Bacon 1994, 158)

The minister must, to return to Margaret Fell's words, be low and absolutely attentive to the leading, with a persistent openness. The result of such painstaking vigilance and obedience is, in a phrase used by both Susanna Morris and Elizabeth Hudson, 'sweet peace' (Bacon 1994, 87, 190, 209)—yet another echo of Margaret Fell, who noted how a genuine peace is a sign of discernment (Fox 1995, 241).

John Woolman (1720–72) left some valuable reflections on ministry that pertain to discernment (Woolman 1922, 314–15). His essay, embedded in some editions of his *Journal*, offers an understanding of the role of community in discernment, the concept of a feeling sense of the condition of others, the notion of participation in the sufferings of the body of Christ. His words reflect the eighteenth-century uncertainty that was a retreat from early Quaker confidence.

He begins with a reminder of the need for observant waiting because without such vigilance the minister can stray from a leading or 'opening':

> The work of the ministry being a work of Divine love, I feel that the openings thereof are to be waited for... Oh! how deep is Divine wisdom! Christ puts forth his ministers and goeth before them; and Oh! how great is the danger of departing from the pure feeling of that which leadeth safely!

Genuine ministry to others is rooted in a spiritual revelation of the condition of others, not in the possibly self-centred programmes of the minister herself or himself: 'Christ knoweth the state of the people, and in the pure feeling of the gospel ministry their states are opened to his servants.' To come to this knowledge, one must undergo interior purification: 'Christ knoweth when the fruit-bearing branches themselves have need of purging'. Interior vigilance requires a moment-by-moment openness to being led, as the leading may change in response to new circumstances:

> I have sometimes felt a necessity to stand up; but that spirit which is of the world hath so much prevailed in many, and the pure life of truth hath been so pressed down, that I have gone forward, not as one travelling in a road cast up, and well prepared, but as a man walking through a miry place in which are stones here and there, safe to step on; but so situated that one step being taken, time is necessary to see where to step next.

Echoing the Apostle Paul on wisdom and folly, strength and weakness, he notes that this total openness and radical obedience may appear foolish to some:

> Now I find that in a state of pure obedience the mind learns contentment in appearing weak and foolish to that wisdom which is of the world: and in these lowly labours, they who stand in a low place, rightly exercised under the cross, will find nourishment.

Reflecting on Matthew 6.22 (If your eye is single, your whole body will be full of light) and Colossians 1.24 (I now rejoice in my sufferings for you, and fill up that which is behind of the afflictions of Christ in my flesh for his body's sake, which is the church), he reflects on suffering:

> The gift is pure; and while the eye is single in attending thereto the understanding is preserved clear; self is kept out; and we rejoice in filling up that which remains of the afflictions of Christ for his body's sake, which is the church.

Genuine openness to being led in vocal ministry requires vulnerability. As one stays close to the Guide, the message may suddenly change, and the resulting utterance may appear ineloquent to those who are worldly wise. Those who tire of appearing weak may undergo a powerful temptation to 'kindle a fire, compass themselves about with sparks, and walk in the light—not of Christ who is under suffering—but of that fire which they, going from the gift, have kindled'. Worshippers who have likewise abandoned the 'meek, suffering state' may feel warmed by this unholy fire:

> In this journey a labour hath attended my mind, that the ministers among us may be preserved in the meek feeling life of Truth, where we may have no desire but to follow Christ and to be with him; that when he is under suffering, we may suffer with him; and never desire to rise up in dominion, but as he by the virtue of his own Spirit may raise us. (Woolman 1922, 314–15)

THE NINETEENTH CENTURY

Nineteenth-century Friends largely persisted in the historical Quaker reticence to discuss specific methods of discernment. In the eighteenth century some Friends managed to hold together the theological strains that resulted in schism during the 1800s. Thereafter each division tended to highlight a particular focus, which is apparent in how members of each group wrote about leadings and decision-making. The rationalists among the Hicksite branch emphasized the use of reason as a divinely bestowed gift. Quietist Wilburites showed an enduring suspicion of 'creatureliness'. Evangelical Gurneyites stressed the role of sacred scripture to provide spiritual guidance.

Throughout the nineteenth century, however, Friends of all parties continued to read *A Guide to True Peace*, a short treatise on inward prayer drawn from the Continental Quietist tradition. This brief book consists chiefly of passages from three seventeenth-century writers: Jeanne Guyon (1648–1717), François Fénelon (1651–1715), and Miguel de Molinos (1628–96). These three Roman Catholic writers were at first warmly received by church authorities but eventually were deemed heterodox, in part due to ecclesiastical rivalries and politics. Two English Quakers, William Backhouse and James Janson, anonymously published *A Guide to True Peace* in 1813, and after the schism both Orthodox and Hicksite Friends continued to reprint it. The book may therefore serve as an example of a common view of discernment shared among Quakers in the nineteenth century.

Like most Catholic spiritual writers of the seventeenth-century, Guyon, Fénelon, and Molinos show the influence of Ignatian spirituality, in particular its concern to distinguish between true and false consolation. In *A Guide to True Peace* this is combined with language that Quakers would have recognized as familiar, the concept of experiencing a leading from the Spirit:

> There are many who, when they experience meltings of heart, shedding of tears, and other sensible delights, imagine that they are the favourites of the Almighty, and that then they truly possess him; and so pass all their lives in seeking after those pleasurable sensations; but they should be cautious lest they deceive themselves, for these consolations, when they proceed from nature, and are occasioned by their own reflections, or self-admirings, hinder them from discerning the true light, or making

one step towards perfection. You should therefore be attentive to distinguish those meltings of the affections from the operations which purely proceed from the Divine Spirit; leaving yourselves to be led forward by him, who will be your light in the midst of darkness and dryness. (Fénelon 1816, 45–46)

True to the legacy of eighteenth-century Friends, *A Guide to True Peace* preserves the emphasis on resignation. Although this term had its own resonance in the French tradition of Guyon and Fénelon, as well as writers from earlier in that century such as François de Sales and Jeanne de Chantal, Quaker readers would likely have heard the word in their own spiritual dialect.

> Resignation is casting off all selfish care, that we may be altogether at the Divine disposal…This virtue is practised by continually losing our own will in the will of God…devoting the present moment to him…Surrender yourselves, then, to be led and disposed of, just as he pleaseth. (Fénelon et al 1816, 74, 75)

In some Quaker circles, by the end of the nineteenth century, there emerged an openness to the rise of liberal Protestant thought. An emphasis arose on individual spiritual experience as authoritative, partly in response to the weakening sense of Scriptural authority as biblical texts were submitted to new forms of critical scholarship that questioned the Bible as a reliable historical record. This move reflected the liberal interest in contemporary scientific method. At the same time, it opened the door to an appreciation of mystical experience as personal experience par excellence. Additionally, liberals focused more on changing this world for the better than on the evangelical thrust on saving souls for the next. All this resulted in new ways of talking about discernment and leadings.

The Modernist Impulse of the Early Twentieth Century: Rufus Jones

Rufus Jones (1863–1948) was probably the most influential Quaker since George Fox, who is often considered the founder of Friends. Jones's lifetime straddled two centuries and he witnessed enormous changes. He began life as a farm boy in rural Maine but spent much of his life as a professor of Philosophy at Haverford College in Philadelphia. He was a teacher, a prolific writer, a person who gave much service to Quakers in North America and elsewhere, and for many years was the chairperson of the American Friends Service Committee, a relief and social change organization that was awarded the Nobel Peace Prize in 1947. Rufus Jones had his own intense mystical experiences, but he preferred to focus on the mystical qualities of everyday spiritual life. A person of many interests, he also kept informed of developments in science and in the emerging field of psychology, especially the notion of personality. For all these reasons, he is an apt representative of Quaker thought on leadings and discernment for his era.

Jones wrote that the challenge of the idea of a direct revelation from God is that the ultimate authority can seem to rest with the individual who claims to have had the experience. That can open the door to unstable or unethical people making claims to religious authority. Rufus Jones, focusing on the Quaker tradition, suggests several tests to determine whether a perceived opening is in fact genuine spiritual guidance. The early Friend Robert Barclay said that such real guidance would not be contrary to Scripture. Extending this idea of consistency of divine guidance, Rufus Jones suggests that 'the surest test of Divine guidance is to be sought in life-results' (Jones 1904, 166). Using a biblical concept, he says that it will bear the fruits of the Spirit: love, joy, peace, endurance, gentleness, goodness, faith, meekness, and self-control (Gal. 5.22–3):

> We must not look at the *origin* of an intimation for its justification. We shall ask how it will further life and tend to construct a permanent character.
> The question will be, not where did it come from, but will it unify and construct the life, will it lead to a richer personality and more trustworthy and reliable character? Does it function toward the power of an endless life and produce *fitness* for such a life? This is to be the mark and brand of every spiritual illumination.
> It must contribute to spiritual *growth*. It must make more efficient that God is actively present and vitally dynamic in this particular human life. The best proof that the seed which one plants is an acorn is that it grows into an oak. (Jones, 166–7)

So the first test looks to the results of a leading, while the second test lies in the evaluation by the group. When the worshipping community is gathered in the sense of divine presence, they arrive at a 'high level of social communion' in which 'the spirit of the group can with almost unerring accuracy test the value of the "opening" which finds utterance' (Jones, 173).

A third test lies in transformation of the group, not the individual alone: 'Will obedience to this prompting construct not only a better person, but a better social group, a truer and a diviner fellowship?' (Jones, 179). The goal is concrete social improvement, 'a truer social order' (179), rather than only a private, inward peace and joy.

Rufus Jones was a serious student of psychology, especially of William James. The hesitation to focus on origins may be a response to the ideas of Sigmund Freud, although Jones does not mention him by name. Jones wrote that leadings or openings seem always to come from beyond the threshold of normal consciousness. By 'unconscious', he meant something positive, though not all psychologists in his day would have agreed with him on this.

The focus on results may bear the influence of William James's pragmatism, though it also has roots in historical Quaker practice. Yet is worth noting how this differs from John Woolman quoted above. As with other spiritual traditions, Quakers have employed different tools of discernment. Some look forwards, to where a leading may take self and others. Others look, as it were, backwards, to trace the roots of a motivation in the effort to avoid self-serving self-deception.

Reticence Revisited

The late twentieth and the early twenty-first centuries witnessed a resurgence of interest in spirituality in Europe and North America, and Quakers were willing participants. Additionally, the historic reluctance to spell out what might be called guidelines for spiritual practices were relaxed, perhaps in part due to conversation about the inward life with those who are not Quaker. Another influence in this regard may have been the large number of those who have become Quakers as adults. With many new members who had not grown up among Friends where so much was assumed to have been learned by exposure to Quaker practices, there was a perceived need to spell out what in earlier times had only been hinted at. In short, Quakers began to tell as well as to show.

Hugh Barbour and Paul Lacey turned to the earliest generation of Quaker writers and articulated tests for leadings. These tests include patience (since self-will is impatient), integrity, or moral purity (not 'fleeing the cross' by announcing a difficult leading for others that one would not willingly undertake oneself), consistency of the Holy Spirit who inspired leadings, and unity with biblical precedents and with one's community (Barbour 1985, 119–23; Lacey 1985, 15–18). Similarly, the present author looked to eighteenth-century sources and distilled some guidelines on the inner dynamics of discernment. Despite the yearning to be spectacularly and unambiguously knocked off a horse like the Apostle Paul on his journey to Damascus (Acts 9.1–9), most leadings emerge unromantically from the stuff of ordinary life, though perceiving them requires acute attention. Because some seem to feel that God speaks only through misery or guilt, it is good to recall that a spiritual leading can begin in joy as well as sorrow; either can be centred in love. Discernment demands ongoing vigilance and the particulars of a leading may develop as circumstances change. Because of the human propensity for self-deception, the wisdom of the larger community enhances clearness. Like Ignatius of Loyola, eighteenth-century Quakers noted the difference between a superficial peace that merely avoided conflict with others and a deeper peace that transcended any surface inconvenience (Birkel 2004, 59–67).

Others have written from various perspectives and for different audiences. Lloyd Lee Wilson has drawn his inspiration from the Quaker Quietist emphasis on surrender (Wilson 2006), akin to the French mystical emphasis on resignation, or the German mystical tradition of yieldedness (Boehme 2010, 95–6). Like him, William Taber wrote from his centre in the tradition of Conservative Friends, exploring new metaphors for the intuitive process of collective discernment (Taber 2010). Paul Anderson has written from the Christ-centredness of his Evangelical Friends tradition, while mathematician Peter Eccles has taken the modern scientific perspective as his point of departure (Anderson 2006; Eccles 2009). All these have directed their words towards a primarily Quaker audience.

Still others have composed their works largely for non-Quaker audiences (Bieber 2010; Fendall, Wood, and Bishop 2007; Palmer 2008; Bill 2008), even for the world of business and management (Snyder, Hillman, Peterson et al 2001). Persons from outside the Quaker community have written about discernment, either focusing chiefly on Quaker understandings of discernment (Sheeran 1983) or drawing on Quaker practices and integrating them into the wider Christian tradition (Farnham, Hull, and McLean 1996). All these labours attest to the liveliness of the topic of discernment, both among Quakers and more broadly.

CONTEMPORARY PRACTICES

When Friends gather in what they call Meeting for Business to consider and decide about practical matters, they practise corporate discernment. In Meeting for Worship Friends have historically experienced a powerful sense of unity; likewise when they gather to attend to business, they aspire to unity. Majority rule therefore does not suffice, so they do not vote in Meetings for Business. Instead, they wait for 'the sense of the meeting', a decision in which all present can come to unity.

Meeting for Business begins in silent worship and prayer. The intent of all those present should be to be open to divine guidance, the leadings of the Holy Spirit. The opening stillness is a time to release personal predilections about matters on the agenda and to become receptive to new insights.

The presiding officer is the clerk, whose responsibilities include preparing the agenda, recognizing those who desire to speak to a matter, and to keep the meeting centred in a worshipful state. Beyond that, the clerk has limited evident authority, since the power to make decisions resides with the whole community. Yet the clerk is expected to exercise thoughtful leadership, often through modelling an awareness of the whole and through setting a pace that is neither rushed nor lethargic. Her or his primary task is to listen with a discerning mind and to seek to sense when those gathered are in unity on an issue and then to articulate that unity. The clerk then tests this 'sense of the meeting', and if those present agree, the clerk asks for approval of a proposed action. The decision is expressed in a minute framed by the clerk, among some Friends, or, among others, by a recording clerk who is charged with that task.

The experience of coming to unity can be a sacred moment, especially if the decision concerns a weighty matter. It can be a revelatory moment, when the community feels confirmed that it has been truly guided by the Holy Spirit. It might be compared with the words of consecration among Christians who observe the eucharist with a belief in the real presence of the body of Christ. For these believers, the sacramental words both acknowledge that the body of Christ is present among the worshippers, as the Apostle Paul declared to the early Christian community: 'You are the body of Christ and individually members of it' (1 Cor 12.27), and these words effect a change in the bread and the cup so that they bear or become the body of Christ. Similarly, when dealing with a weighty matter, when the clerk precisely expresses the sense of the meeting, this acknowledges a unity that is already there and can effect a change of sacramental quality. The words themselves bring those present into a sense of their unity and draw them into a deeper sense of unity that parallels the experience of sacramental communion. As a result, Friends find themselves drawn closer to one another and to the Spirit of God that leads them.

Of course, the items of the agenda are often much more mundane and do not result in such a powerful spiritual experience. At other times unity is not achieved: those present do not come to a common agreement. On such occasions, the clerk's task of discernment is more challenging. The clerk may suggest a third path that points the way out of the apparent impasse. The clerk may invite all to sink again into worshipful silence, so that Friends may re-examine their attachments to particular outcomes and refocus their attention to the divine presence. The clerk may sense that the weight of the community is towards a particular decision and that this inclination is Spirit-led, and so may ask if those who are not in unity with the proposed action are nonetheless in unity with the community and therefore willing to move ahead. Those who disagree with the proposed action may choose to stand aside, neither endorsing the proposal nor standing in the way of collective approval. If they choose to do so, then they are obliged to abide by the decision and not to subvert the sense of the meeting after the Business Meeting is concluded. At other times, unity may not be possible, and the matter is laid aside for the time. It may be that some in the community are stubborn or self-indulgent, or it may be that a few hold a truth that the many need to hear. More time is needed to determine this, and the matter may be taken up again at a later meeting.

To conclude, Friends frequently find that genuine openness to corporate guidance can lead to insight that is superior to the previously held opinion or judgement of any single member. Such communal discernment provokes a deeper sense of unity with God and with one another.

CLEARNESS COMMITTEES

A contemporary tool for discernment among Quakers is the use of the clearness committee. The historical predecessor of this practice was a committee that met with a couple who desired to be wed, to verify that they were 'clear' of other marital obligations, and therefore suitable for marriage. Over time, it became the practice of the committee to take on a more explicit counselling role, posing gentle but thoughtful queries and listening to the couple to hear how prepared they were in terms of personal maturity to take on the challenges of married life together. During the twentieth century, Quakers broadened the use of the clearness committee, adapting this form to assist people in discernment in other areas of their lives.

A significant difference in this recent adaptation of the clearness committee is that, as most often practised, it is not the charge of the committee to make a decision or render a judgement as was the historical concern with readiness for marriage. Instead, discernment resides with the person facing the decision, and the purpose of the committee is more akin to group spiritual direction (Dougherty 1995) in which the task is to ask questions that provoke deeper reflection.

The practise of clearness committees has grown beyond the bounds of the Religious Society of Friends, and many non-Quakers have found the practice helpful or have adapted its form to suit their purposes for discernment.

LATIN AMERICA AND AFRICA

The success of Evangelical Friends missions in the twentieth century has resulted in the majority of Quakers living in the Global South, especially in Bolivia and Kenya, where discernment comes to life in new ways.

Emma Condori Mamani, a rising leader among Bolivian Friends, notes that 'discernment' as a term is not used by Friends in her homeland. Instead, they speak of seeking God, which involves much prayer. They recognize the answer when they hear the voice of God within the heart and mind. When seeking an answer for an individual question, Friends may go to the pastor, but often they do not bother to do this because he will only tell them to pray. It is not common to seek advice from elders. Instead, Friends turn inwards to seek direct guidance from God. Emma Condori observes that the balance of individual and community differs among cultures. In the United States, for example, the culture is very individualistic, and so Friends seek others when they practise discernment, as is done in clearness committees. In Bolivia there is a stronger sense of community, and this is balanced by a focus on individual prayer when seeking to hear God's voice (Condori 2011).

John Muhanji, a leading voice among Kenyan Friends, reports that when missionaries brought Quakerism to Kenya in 1902, there was no teaching of distinctive Quaker practices, such as discernment. The initial focus was on understanding God and Christ, and Scripture translation followed, leading to an emphasis on schools and literacy. Thereafter the immediate needs were health care and industrial development, especially farming and housing. 'The testimonies were taught as history, not as living practices.' This is changing as the vast growth of the Kenyan Friends Church brings a need for practical applications in discernment. Rooted in traditional African esteem for elders, Friends use the committee 'for the soul' (yo mwoyo), in which elders will sit with and pray with those seeking guidance, for example, to get married, to seek further studies, or to undertake pastoral ministry. Elders for these committees are chosen for their integrity, life experience, and their capacity to see beyond mere appearances. Given the ongoing challenges in the Kenyan Church for transparency and accountability, John Muhanji emphasizes integrity as a prerequisite for discernment (Muhanji 2011).

For all the turns and developments of Quaker history, the counsel of early Friends such as Margaret Fell—to turn inwards, to maintain a humble attitude, to wait patiently, to see, to test, and to act in faithfulness—endure as the heart of the Quaker practice of discernment. The insights of later generations have enhanced but not overturned those of the earliest Friends. A recognizably Quaker contribution to the understanding of discernment has thus far stood the test of time.

Suggested Further Reading

Birkel, M. L. (2004) *Silence and witness: The Quaker tradition*. Maryknoll, NY: Orbis Books.

Birkel, M. L. (2008) *The messenger that goes before: Reading Margaret Fell for Spiritual nurture*. Wallingford, PA: Pendle Hill Publications.

Fendall, L., Wood, J., and Bishop, B. (2007) *Practicing discernment together: Finding God's way forward in decision making*. Newberg, OR: Barclay Press.

Lacey, P. A. (1985) *Leading and being led*. Wallingford, PA: Pendle Hill Publications.

Loring, P. (1992) *Spiritual discernment: The context and goals of clearness committees*. Wallingford, PA: Pendle Hill.

Morley, B. (1993) *Beyond consensus: Salvaging sense of the Meeting*. Wallingford, PA: Pendle Hill.

Sheeran, M. J. (1983) *Beyond majority rule: Voteless decisions in the Religious Society of Friends*. [Philadelphia, PA]: Philadelphia Yearly Meeting of the Religious Society of Friends.

Taber, W. P. and Birkel, M. L. (2010) *The mind of Christ: Bill Taber on Meeting for Business*. Wallingford, PA: Pendle Hill Publications.

CHAPTER 17

WORSHIP AND SACRAMENTS

DAVID L. JOHNS

INTRODUCTION

WORSHIP is at the heart of Quaker identity. Whether one examines Friends in their first decades in Britain, or in their migration into the Carolinas and Pennsylvania, their movement to New Zealand and Costa Rica, or whether one considers their enormous growth in Kenya, Guatemala, and Bolivia, one will see that worship plays a fundamental role. This role is and has been connected to the group's theological formation, how it understands God, the world, and its vocation. However, because Quaker worship has developed along different paths it has been at the centre of group conflict and division as well as cohesion.

Friends believe that the presence of the living Christ can be known and, through the Spirit, teach, lead, and communicate with humanity. On one hand, this is no more than many Christian groups would claim, even in the century of Quakerism's birth. Yet, Friends emphasize that this is possible apart from the ordinary means used by many others. Thus, while in the twenty-first century most Quakers throughout the world worship in a similar way to free-church traditions, there remains a conviction that the conventions of water, bread, wine, clergy, scripted liturgies, images, holy days, and so on, are unnecessary for this presence of Christ to be known. In fact, these can stand in the way of spiritual growth and obedience to God. But does the claim that something is not necessary mean that it cannot be effective, or that it is harmful, or that it is redundant? Not surprisingly, there has been disagreement throughout the history of the Religious Society of Friends regarding how these questions are to be answered and tension persists between the various responses.

Quakers attributed their views concerning worship, sacraments, and ecclesial life to new revelations or 'openings', and the fervour with which they maintained these was certainly driven by spiritual conviction. However, they also reflected the political disruption within Britain during the mid-seventeenth century. Society was unravelling all around them including those institutions that promised stability. As a consequence, Quakers moved religious authority, sacrality, and stability inwards; external authorities and those spaces generally considered sacred became places of confrontation. Likewise, since the apostolic era, interim ecclesial systems and practices existed in order to care for the Church in Christ's absence. However, since 'Christ is come to teach his people himself', everything has changed. In this covenantal theology, the 'Day of the Lord' had come and the old order was being dismantled. Why practice a ritual such as the Eucharist 'in memory' of Christ when Christ is actually present? Or, why, through bread and wine, 'give witness to the Lord's death til he comes', when witness could be focused not on death but on Christ's living presence? (1 Corinthians 11:26).

Nearly from the beginning of the movement, arguments have been offered for the practices and views of Quakers on worship and the sacraments, including experiential and scriptural. None have had the compelling weight and spiritual urgency as the conviction that the new covenant of Christ's reign had begun and had reordered the communal life of the faithful. This conviction was operative for only a few decades of Quaker existence before it waned with institutional establishment. However, it is responsible for a set of practices that continue to characterize the movement.

Giving Shape to Quaker Worship

When Friends thought about worship their frame of reference included an assortment of Christian expressions: prayers, antiphonal readings, and singing, the Psalter, sermons, Eucharist, offerings, seasonal liturgies, processionals, and so forth. Even though the Book of Common Prayer was under fire from the Puritans, many Quakers would have been familiar with it and with the more abbreviated Directory for the Publique Worship of God (Senn 1997, 510–17). Yet, because there was such strong religious dissention, nearly every worship practice at the time also had its negation or its antitype.

Early Quakers stripped worship to the bone. On the surface, little remained of Anglican or Catholic worship, at least in terms of recognizable forms. The elements used in Puritan worship were far fewer than in other churches: 'long and exhortatory prayers and even longer more didactic sermons [but] no organs, little singing, no pictures, few stained-glass windows' (Senn 1997, 515). But Quakers were determined to reduce worship even further to the fundamental simplicity of waiting together for the Spirit's direction in a silence that reflected the silence of heaven (Revelation 8:1). It could be argued, of course, that this austerity was due to their limited access to the customary spaces and objects of liturgical worship. However, their reasoning was more complicated and woven together with a vision of history and Church.

A number of dissenting groups such as the Seekers experimented with minimalist structure. While there was little that formally united them, they were informally united by their conviction that the churches, liturgies, sacraments, and clergy were not legitimate. By the late 1640s two distinct trajectories were evident among these Seekers and the Quakers managed to synthesize both of these in their own preaching (Gwyn 2000, 96–100) The first was a restorationist impulse that believed God was calling the Church back to a purified Christian faith and practice. Ritual in the churches emerged after the apostolic period, they claimed, and thus they felt justified in dismissing such practices in their effort to retrieve 'primitive Christianity'. The direct operation of the Holy Spirit in the assembly and the experience of the indwelling Christ carried more weight than any official ecclesial practice or doctrine. The faithful community was to be marked by purity of life and worship.

The second trajectory was new covenantal that looked towards a new dispensation rather than backwards at restoration. God's intention was to move the faithful into an unfolding future, not to restore a golden age. Official liturgies, clergy, sacraments, and the like, would be unnecessary in this new era. All that these 'forms and shadows' accomplished previously would be known in 'substance and reality' through an inward experience of Christ that was direct, compelling, and not mediated through customary forms.

The fusion of these trajectories meant that Quakers emphasized both a visible church community marked by holiness and conservatism of practice, similar to the Anabaptists, and also a mystical, inward church community that believed it was guided by direct, knowable, and continual revelation. But whether restorationist or new covenantal, both stood in contrast to many of their established religious contemporaries and their vision of Church and world.

Worshippers 'felt the apocalypse breaking forth in their very bodies'; the old order was being dismantled (Gwyn 2000, 299). In this spirit, George Fox (1624–91) made the sweeping claim that the Church's history from the apostles to his own time was the 'long night of apostasy' and consequently he dismissed much of it (Ullmann 1959,52). This impulse has been called a 'realizing' eschatology, neither an anticipation of the end nor an acknowledgement of static completion; rather it was a conviction that the end was unfolding in the present moment. It was no longer necessary to anticipate the coming of Christ but to announce, 'Christ is come and doth dwell in the hearts of his people and reigns there' (Fox 1995, 261). This perspective directed Friends away from interim thinking and reoriented them towards an end-time hermeneutic through which they read historical events, the Scriptures, and through which they shaped their understanding of worship and sacraments.

Religious offices and liturgical practices are provisions between Ascension and Parousia; most notably, the priesthood reflects the assumption that an intermediary is necessary in place of the anticipated Christ. However, in the new covenant, the real substance is revealed and, according to nineteenth-century Quaker Job Scott, 'When the resurrection of Christ the life is fully known in us, all mere signs are, and in the very nature of things must be, entirely superseded' (Scott 1860, 40).

EXPRESSIONS OF QUAKER WORSHIP

In the first decades of the movement, a meeting for worship could be a surprise to the newcomer. These Friends acknowledged ministry, but did not regard particular persons to be ministers, there was no officiating clergy in these gatherings (this came later in the nineteenth century). Prayers and vocal ministry were usually present, but there was no apparent delegation of these tasks, at least initially. The Eucharistic meal was absent as were fonts for baptism; however, these worshippers claimed to commune continually with Christ and to have been baptized with the Spirit, the one 'true baptism'. And all of this was framed by waiting on the Spirit's direction.

Equally surprising were those things that were actually present in this worship but unexpected. Most notably, for example, was the presence of women's voices, a sound all but absent in most Christian churches in the seventeenth century. In 1666 Margaret Fell penned a compelling argument for women's vocal ministry and by the late nineteenth century, Ohio Quaker Ann Branson casually noted in her journal conversations she had with others about the legitimacy of women preaching (Fell 1666, 15; Branson 1892, 281, 379). But not only did women preach in the local assemblies and sit among the elders in Friends' meeting houses, they were soon instrumental in important transatlantic preaching missions (Larson 1999, 5–12).

Also present in some of these meetings for worship were physical expressions such as tears, trembling, groaning, and sighing. Before the meeting concluded with 'a sweet sound of thanksgiving and praise', those gathered wrestled with the 'inward travail' of seeking to 'overcome the evil in themselves'. While George Fox claimed the name 'Quaker' came from a magistrate he admonished to 'tremble at the word of the Lord', Barclay cites the conduct of worshipers gripped by the power of God as the origin of the movement's name (Barclay 2002, 302).

In general these meetings did not descend into chaos or antinomianism, although from the beginning Friends recognized the propensity for precisely this. Robert Barclay (1648–90), along with William Penn (1644–1718) and George Fox, worked to bring a sense of propriety to the group by declaring that Christ's government among them was a gospel order. This comprehensive programme of eldership assured corporate accountability over individual leadings, spiritual discernment in both the gathered meeting and the home, as well as social testimonies in public conduct (Cronk 1991, 297).

Friends worship today falls into three general categories: unprogrammed, programmed, and semi-programmed. There can be overlap between the categories and in some cases a programmed meeting might worship in an unprogrammed fashion on a given week; however, by and large these categories express the patterned practices of Friends. No group of Quakers, however, worships in precisely the same manner as the earliest Friends since there have been developments in all strands of the movement (Punshon 2001, 195ff).

Unprogrammed worship is sometimes referred to as 'open worship' or 'traditional' Friends worship. At its most basic, there are four simple movements or stages: gathering, settling into silence, expectant waiting, and closing. Each of these is more or less informal and generally there is no announcement of passage from one to the other. The meeting room is usually adorned simply and does not necessarily reflect the architecture and furnishing of most worship spaces (see, Lapsansky and Verplanck 2003). In earlier periods, benches were situated at the front of the room where elders sat facing the other attenders; although this is still done in some meetings it is not the overwhelming contemporary practice. In other spaces there may be a circle of chairs, a small table with a Bible and vase of flowers, but because there is no prescription for the use of space there can a plethora of local expressions. Likewise, though it is usual for meetings to last about an hour there is no prescription for the flow of time. Meetings were considerably longer in earlier centuries and have shorted approximately one half hour each century. In the early twenty-first century, some in Philadelphia Yearly Meeting experimented with unprogrammed meetings lasting several hours (Martin 2003).

Unprogrammed worship has been called 'silent worship,' but this is misleading. While Meetings for Worship may in fact pass without vocal ministry, the purpose of the assembly is to wait. A phrase used with some regularity in recent decades is 'waiting worship', or 'expectant waiting'. Either reflects more accurately both the method and the theological intention of this style. Both suggest that the silence of unprogrammed worship is not passive inaction but an active discipline of waiting with expectation for the Spirit who animates the faithful.

A period of expectant waiting will often be punctuated by vocal ministry. This may take the form of a brief homily, meditation, prayer, or an observation on a spiritual, personal, or public theme. When one senses a leading to speak, she or he rises and offers the message. In some Conservative Friends meetings in Ohio Yearly Meeting, speakers retain an earlier style of sing-song cadence in their delivery.

In the mid-nineteenth century, Josiah Forster stated that music and singing formed 'no part of the worship of God in spirit and in truth, under the new covenant' (Forster 1860, 45). Three years after writing this, Friends Scripture School Press in New York published *Hymns for First Day School*, a collection not only to use in meetings for worship, but 'sufficiently general to be attractive to the children at home' (Friends' Scripture School 1869, inside cover). It is true that Quakerism has not had as rich a tradition of hymnody as Methodism, but singing spans the unprogrammed to programmed continuum and, in fact, it has been unprogrammed Quakers who have published more hymnals and song books than the rest. For instance, Friends General Conference published *Songs of the Spirit* in the 1970s and after years of research and discernment, published the widely used *Worship in Song* (1996), which contains traditional Protestant hymns as well as specifically Quaker songs honouring the lives of George Fox, John Woolman, Margaret Fell, Lucretia Mott, and the Valiant Sixty. In the 1970s Zephaniah Cunningham of Jamaica published *A Quaker Hymn Book*, a collection of original sacred lyrics set to traditional tunes. Many programmed meetings have for decades incorporated hymnals from other denominations into their worship. One notable twentieth-century hymnal produced by programmed Friends is the *Himnario: Corazón y Vida*, still available after its first printing in 1923 by La Junta Annual de los Amigos in Chiquimula Guatemala; nevertheless, there is little distinguishing this hymnal from those used by non-Quakers.

The movements of unprogrammed worship are believed to be prompted by the Spirit immediately, that is to say, in that particular moment. Whatever form vocal ministry takes, priority is given to this immediacy as being more genuinely Spirit-led than messages or actions planned in advance and outside the setting of the gathered worshipping community. Ironically, in terms of form, unprogrammed worship is at least as formalized as programmed worship that may experiment with the inclusion or exclusion of any number of worship elements.

Programmed worship usually resembles other free-church-style worship, but its movements are different from that of unprogrammed Friends. There is a gathering and a closing, but between the two there can be a wide variety of conventions such as hymns, preaching, Scripture reading, public prayers (extemporaneous or written), and so on. Depending upon the local meeting, there might be children's messages, dramatic presentations, choirs, altar calls, and in some parts of the United States and east Africa, for instance, even the practice of communion or baptism. Since drumming and dancing are part of Rwandan culture they are sometimes included in worship in Friends meetings there as well.

The worship space in programmed meetings is often less ornate than other Protestant churches. For example, it would be rare to find paraments or iconography. That said, the similarity between it and other area churches is greater than that of an unprogrammed meeting house. It will include a pulpit or lectern of some sort, musical instruments, and possibly seating for a choir. It is not unusual to see some type of religious art in these spaces such as a cross, a portrait of Jesus, or banners excerpting a biblical text.

Quite often programmed meetings identify someone to serve as pastoral leader and 'release' him or her for ministry, that is, provide financial support to make the work possible. The person serving in this capacity generally carries less organizational authority than a Presbyterian or Anglican counterpart, although in some east African or some US Evangelical Yearly Meetings, this is not the case. As in other denominations, a Friends pastor tends to the spiritual development of the meeting's membership and, therefore, is involved in preparing for and presiding during worship. The pastor generally offers a sermon, although is free and even encouraged to abandon this message if she or he senses the Spirit leading otherwise.

Semi-programmed worship combines elements of both; in fact, many programmed meetings in the United States are actually semi-programmed. The operative difference is that in addition to hymns, prayers, and a sermon, worship will also include periods of unprogrammed worship ranging from a few moments to ten or fifteen minutes or more. Other liturgies, including the Roman Catholic Mass, may allow brief periods of silence, actually so directing the officiating clergy in the printed rubrics. However, silence in semi-programmed worship intends to be active listening for the voice of the living Christ, inviting that presence into the gathering, and communing together (Revelation 3:20).

Worship and its practices were at the heart of some of the movement's earliest controversies. One in particular actually resulted in a push towards gospel order. John Perrot argued that Friends worship, already sparse, was filled with unnecessary ritual. For example, the custom of shaking hands to close worship was an unnecessary ritual. Perrot gave priority to spontaneous individual leadings even to the point of rejecting established times for assemblies in favour of waiting for divine prompting. Perrot believed this was spiritual integrity; Fox denounced him as a 'disorderly walker' like James Nayler. In short, after 1666 the authority of the gathered meeting carried greater weight than any individual, and Fox supported extending gospel order to assure the priority of communal discernment (*HDF*, s.v. 'Perrot, John;' Dandelion 2005, 50; chapter 2 this volume).

A commitment to corporate discernment continues and is particularly evident in Friends' approach to conducting business. For most, regardless of worship style and theological temperament, the spirit and intention of worship extends into deliberation and decision-making. These 'meetings for worship for business' ideally proceed with careful listening for the Spirit's direction and frequent returns to silence. This process is for the business of Monthly, Quarterly, and Yearly Meetings, but individuals seeking clarity and counsel on a particular matter may do so through a 'committee for clearness' that in many respects follows the pattern of meetings for worship and for business.

SILENCE, SPACE, AND TIME

In worship, both space and time are marked in ways that bring the sacred and temporal together. This is done variously depending upon the tradition. In many Christian churches, certain spaces are consecrated for sacred use or are identified as having special importance. Days and seasons progress on the liturgical calendar according to the story of faith. Certain days (Easter for instance), evoke memories of crucial moments in the life of Jesus and are regarded as holy. Quakers, on the other hand, shifted the location of sacrality from external spaces to internal ones, and they collapsed sacred time into the temporal. Church buildings were meeting houses, not churches and certainly not sanctuaries. The nomenclature of 'Church' was reserved for the faithful people of God. It was not unusual to claim that a meeting house was not where God dwelt; any number of seventeenth-century Christians would have affirmed the same. However, by relocating sacrality to internal spaces they opened the entire world to being an appropriate place for worship. Perhaps as importantly, they redefined the character of those spaces previously regarded as sacred. In the years of early enthusiasm, Quakers were known to disrupt the worship of other Christians. Sanctuaries were no retreat from the prophetic witness of the Lamb's War. It is true that some Quaker spaces have attained a kind of iconic status, such as the meeting houses at Jordans Friends Meeting in Buckinghamshire, or Arch Street Meeting in Philadelphia, or Vihiga in Western Provence, Kenya. In these cases, their status is due to their historical and nostalgic value rather than to any attribution of divine power.

Collapsing the sacrality of time into the temporal meant that Friends did not acknowledge the liturgical seasons and the holy days that punctuate the year for most Christians. By the middle of the twentieth century, however, it was not uncommon for some Quakers to commemorate liturgical days such as Christmas, *Semana Santa*, or festivals such as anniversaries or *quinceañera* (Ullmann 1959, 58–9). It is difficult to conclude whether these changes are rooted in theological modification or cultural accommodation, although the latter seems likely. Historically the rationale has been to acknowledge that every day, every season is holy and that no time is by nature more or less sacred than another. It is possible, of course, to consider all time to be insignificant due to its ordinariness; however, the intention of this practice was positive, attempting to elevate all history (and with it, all creation) to the level of sacrality one might attribute to a high holy day.

Because Friends resisted distinguishing specific times and spaces as sacred they likewise resisted naming a special class of persons for a set apart sacred ministry. A consistent feature throughout the history of the movement is that the living Christ is the one who presides at worship and is the one who 'indeed is your Shepherd' (Forster, 48). Even though Friends have 'recorded' those who exhibit special gifts for ministry, they remain particularly confident in the Spirit's ability to choreograph their assemblies.

On one hand, silence complements such a notion. Even so, silence is not an end in itself but a framework providing space for a range of activities that is believed to be incited by the present Christ. 'Worship is not a law of silence, but a holy dependence of the mind upon God', according to Barclay (Barclay 2002, 303; Bauman 1983, 9, 20, 21, 23). Humans, as it were, stand out of the way and permit the presider of the meeting to speak and inspire. A deepening suspicion of 'creaturely activity' during the Quietist period often stretched silence to the point where it became oppressive and resulted in sombre introspection and a hesitation to speak (Dandelion 2005, 48–50). However, at its best, silence was the condition in which divine activity could occur. 'Silence of this kind involves anticipation, an eager waiting, a deep listening. This is the silence of the Quaker faith' (Australia Yearly Meeting 2003, 2.5).

Group silence has been idealized both by those outside and within Quakerism. Quiet meditation can be a welcome retreat from over-activity, but Friends have understood their silence to be active. First, there is the challenge of being still. Then there is the question of what to do with the silence. In the mid-nineteenth century, London Yearly Meeting directed that silence ought not to be spent in 'indolent or vacant musing but on patient waiting in humble prayerful expectancy before the Lord'. One hundred years later, Rachel Needham counselled that silence is time to 'face ourselves', to worship God 'on your own terms', and 'to think unguided by the world' (*Quaker faith and practice* 1995, 2.14; 2.17). Finally, there is the challenge of knowing when to break the silence to speak. Margery Post Abbott notes that to discern this is 'to describe how we sense the movement of the Spirit' (Abbott 2010, 148).

Silence by itself is ambiguous and can symbolize any number of realities, not all of which are of religious importance (Johns 1998, 31). It can range from the silence of the heavens mentioned in Revelation 8:1, an experience of awe in the presence of God, to disinterestedness, a 'dead form', or 'an occasion for slumber' (*Quaker faith and practice*

1995, 2:17). Much depends upon the intentionality of the group itself and whether it enters the silence as retreat from the world or as self-fulfilment, or whether it enters it ready to do the people's work.

Of course, dimensions of early Friends worship did bear a resemblance to their contemporaries. Quakers gathered into groups for their meetings and the act of gathering is an ecclesiological conviction. There are those within Quakerism and Christianity more broadly with a propensity toward individualism. Nevertheless, Friends share in common with other religious groups a commitment to worship as a corporate phenomenon.

Likewise, their worship included prayers and sermonic messages. To aid in the formation of religious imagination and doctrinal understanding, catechisms were written and used, for example those by Robert Barclay and George Keith, although over time the use of Advices and Queries eclipsed their use. However, the environment in which prayer and preaching were offered and the regulations for how these might be practised and by whom, differed considerably from other religious communities. The role of women in preaching, teaching, travelling, and in governance, for instance, was unheard of among most of their early contemporaries.

One needs to understand well a set of practices in order to move beyond them. As with their approach to language, Friends nuanced worship; by doing so, their practices functioned as part of a broader theological critique and confessional witness. But while critique and witness represented a nuanced understanding, their articulation of this was frequently pointed and harsh. Ten years after Fox's Pendle Hill vision, Esther Biddle (1629–96) who claims to have been 'once of this Religion which is now in power', states that 'I am at Liberty from this vain Religion, which never profited me at all...I shall never conform to this worship while I have breath, but shall bear my Testimony against it, for I know the powerful God is risen to throw it down, and woe be to all that uphold it'. Whether for spiritual reasons (which would have been Friends' own assessment) or for reasons of cultural–religious disestablishment, Biddle reflected the attitude of many Quakers at the time towards other religious bodies. Their liturgical worship 'the Lord of Heaven loaths... abhors'; on their altars they sacrifice 'unto Devils and not unto the living God', and so on (Biddle 1660, 14, 15, 16–17). This is no different from the way Fox himself narrates his own disaffection in what has become a foundational text for Quakers: 'When all my hopes in them [the religious professionals] and in all men were gone, so that I had nothing outwardly to help me, nor could I tell what to do, then, oh, then, I heard a voice which said, "There is one, even Christ Jesus, that can speak to thy condition".' (Fox 1995, 11).

In contrast, similar to her contemporaries, Biddle is rapturous when describing her own experience with the Quakers:

> I never went to any Meeting since I knew the Truth, even from the first Meeting to this day, but I was filled with the Living Power of the Lord; Oh! The sweet showers that doth descend from the presence of the Lord, and the pleasant rains that falleth from his Throne like silver drops, it doth distil upon our Hearts, whilst we are in our Meetings in the Name and Power of Jesus...I had rather die the cruelest Death that ever was, or can be devised by man, than to neglect or abstains from Meeting together in his Name....(Biddle 1660, 21)

Barclay recounts his early experience of worshipping with Quakers as one in which the impulse towards good was recalibrated, as it were, to flourish: 'For when I came into the silent assemblies of God's people, I felt a secret power among them which touched my heart; and as I gave way unto it, I found the evil weakening in me and the good raised up.' Like Biddle, this increased his desire to associate with them '...so I became thus knit and united unto them, hungering more and more after the increase of this power and life' (Barclay 2002, 300).

QUAKER SACRAMENTAL PRACTICE

Early Quakers believed God was greater than temples made by humans and also contended that God could be known and experienced apart from the means generally employed by others, including the sacraments. 'For the kingdom of God stands not in meats and drinks, or any outward washings, nor comes in the way of man's observation, but in a heavenly seed, and in the Holy Spirit and power of life' (Penington 1997, IV:133). Consequently, most Friends have not incorporated into their worship the rites of baptism or communion. In the 'old dispensation' worship was outwards and used objects and rites to assist humanity until the full light of God was revealed, but as Caroline Stephen stated, 'we believe that the coming of Christ put an end to the old dispensation of outward observances' (Stephen 1891, 14; Garman et al 1996, 52). In the new era, worship is 'in spirit and in truth' (John 4:24), a phrase that frequently appears in Friends' writings. The symbols and representations of Christ, so important in the past, are no longer satisfying now that the living Christ is come.

With notable exceptions almost exclusively among programmed Quakers, this conviction has remained consistent for the majority of Friends throughout their history. It may well be one of the few remaining distinctives of the movement. Yet, its tenacity is less a matter of shared belief or *esprit de corps* than it is a widely shared experience of the real presence of the living Christ in the gathered assembly.

There were some important turns in the nineteenth century, however, that represented a loosening of traditional theological perspectives. Joseph John Gurney advocated an approach to Quaker faith that included programmatic religious education and the primacy of Scripture as a religious authority, ideas that, according to critics, elevated human learning and de-emphasized the guidance of the spirit of Christ in worship (London Yearly Meeting 1836, 13–14; Wilbur, 592). He was active in writing London Yearly Meeting's 1836 Epistle, which for the first time offered evangelical views as official Friends' teachings. This was met with strong objections from John Wilbur in New England as well as objections from Thomas Shillitoe, Ann Jones, and Sarah Lynes Grubb in London Yearly Meeting.

Until the twentieth century one could be disowned from some meetings for the unorthodox practice of taking the sacraments. David Updegraff (1830–94), a Quaker Holiness minister from Ohio, however, tried the patience of many of his nineteenth-century contemporaries by not only renouncing a traditional spiritual interpretation of the sacraments, but by receiving water baptism himself, and persuading others to follow suit. Inspired by mid-century revivalism, he, along with several other Friends including Esther Frame and Dougan Clark, taught a Holiness message of second blessing. Traditionally, in order to justify their opposition to the water rite, Friends argued that Spirit baptism was in fact the 'one baptism' mentioned in the New Testament. The new revivalists associated this with the experience of sanctification and thus created a new openness to the practice of baptism (Hamm 2003, 50–2).

Ohio Yearly Meeting permitted or at least tolerated the practice; later, in the twentieth and twenty-first centuries, many congregations throughout the Evangelical Friends Church–Eastern Region (formerly Ohio Yearly Meeting) have come to accept and practise both water baptism and communion. Friends pastors in Rwanda interpret Matthew's Great Commission text as a directive to provide water baptism for new members. Another Evangelical Yearly Meeting, Friends Church Southwest, approved in 1994 the use of the sacraments in their meetings; however, they established detailed guidelines for doing so in order to maintain the spirit of the original Quaker witness.

Friends often refer to worship itself, particularly unprogrammed worship, as being communion (or, communion *in the manner of Friends*, to distinguish it from the Eucharist):

> In silence, without rite or symbol, we have known the Spirit of Christ so convincingly present in our quiet meetings that his grace dispels our faithfulness, our unwillingness, our fears, and sets our hearts aflame with the joy of adoration. We have thus felt the power of the Spirit renewing and recreating our love and friendship for all our fellows. This is our eucharist and this is our communion. (*Quaker faith and practice* 1995, 26.15)

Quakers in Switzerland Yearly Meeting expressed what is held to be true among others as well, that this sense of knowing and communing with God extends beyond Meeting for Worship into other dimensions of life: 'Communion may come through the sense of divine presence among us...The whole of life may be filled with a sense of communion so that the touching of spirits which is felt at the First Day Meeting may no longer seem so very special' (Switzerland Yearly Meeting 2009, 77).

As with worship in general, Quaker perspectives on the sacraments were influenced originally by a new covenant/end-time reading of history and Scripture. The faithful were to observe the memory of Jesus only until he comes again (1 Corinthians 11:26), after which remembering would be redundant. Quakers understood this quite concretely. For example, Job Scott compared the physical elements of the sacraments of bread, water, and wine (as with the Protestants, Quakers spent little time considering the five additional sacraments acknowledged by Roman Catholics) with a photograph of a friend who lives nearby; 'at the very best, they are but shadows of the good things' (Scott 1860, 23).

Although the enthusiasm of end-time thinking passed quickly, a pervasive binary of inner/outer persists and has informed Quaker rationale concerning the sacraments from the time of Fox to the present (Creasey 1962; Johns 2007; Thomas 2002, 22ff). The distinction between new covenant/old covenant is fundamental, yet the list of others is extensive and includes, for example: Spirit/flesh; Light/darkness; real/shadow; spiritual life/empty ceremonies; spiritual/carnal; supernatural/natural; and true worship/vain customs. All these and others can be gathered under the larger dichotomy of inner/outer. This binary has created confusion in Quaker thinking about many issues, including worship and sacraments. According to Maurice Creasey, Fox, Nayler, and others used the terms 'inner' and 'outer' to describe their experience of a 'transforming and personal acquaintance with and relation to Christ in the Spirit', in contrast with a form of faith that was conventional, formal, and consisted principally as a body of teachings and ethical practices (Creasey 1962, 5). However, these efforts to convey a spiritual insight were translated into a philosophical idiom in the writings of Penington and especially in Barclay, who described inner and outer in terms of revelation. Thus, insights that come through outer means such as study, Scripture, history, tradition, and so on, were regarded as being of lesser value than those that were inner and spiritual, those that come directly or 'immediately', that is, apart from the mediation of human intellectual or bodily knowing. A lingering difficulty in Quaker theology is how to regard those other-than-inwardly mediated dimensions of religious life.

Clearly, a significant justification for Quaker sacramental practice has grown out of this thinking, but their reading of the Scriptures also supported their position. Quakers provided, on the one hand, nuanced spiritual interpretations of the biblical texts, and yet, on the other hand, readings so literal as to construct their communal practice upon a text's silence. For instance, Penington observed that when Jesus directed his disciples to baptise he never specified 'with water', but rather 'in the name...' 'There is one faith, one baptism. Is not the one faith inward and spiritual? Is not the one baptism so also?' (Penington 1997, IV:125; Stephens, 14). Additionally, they suggested that because sacramental practices have caused contention throughout the Church's history, they cannot be regarded as a reliable basis for faith. More to the point, they argued that rites in general reflect the old covenant and that this 'law was given by Moses, but grace and truth came by Jesus Christ' (John 1:17; Penn 1726, II: 862).

Fox was convinced that true sacramental practice was inward and spiritual; anything else was barren and harmful. Barclay reluctantly and only in passing acknowledged that the sacramental practice of other Christians might be spiritually beneficial. While recognizing that others found value in these practices, Gurney was certain that when they 'draw yet nearer in spirit to an omnipresent Deity, they will be permitted to find, in *the disuse of all types*, "a more excellent way"' (Gurney 1979, 168, emphasis is his; Barclay 2002, 407).

Cooper outlines three emphases among contemporary Quakers in relation to sacraments: obstacle, non-necessity, and sacraments reconsidered. The first reflects Fox's view mentioned above and contends that focusing on shadows and types distracts one from the living reality of Christ. The second, if not cognisant of the earlier new covenant/

end-time theology of Friends, expresses its sentiment. East African Quakers state in their *Faith and Practice*:

> ... this baptism is a spiritual experience of dying to self and being reborn by the power of the Resurrection of Christ (1 Peter 3:21 and Romans 6:4). Without this experience, a water baptism or other ceremony does not suffice, and with this experience baptism is not necessary. Similarly, our communion with Jesus Christ cannot be simply an outward re-enactment of a literal eating of His body and drinking of His blood, but a full remembrance of his sacrifice through prayer and waiting upon the Holy Spirit. (Friends United Meeting in East Africa 2002, 2–3; Anderson 2007, 30–45)

Although it is difficult to know for certain, this position likely represents the mainstream in contemporary Quaker thinking.

The third emphasis, sacraments reconsidered, represents those who are rethinking the function of sacraments and sacramental life. This includes Friends considering the use of sacraments or those who have actually incorporated them into public worship (for example, some in Yearly Meetings such as Indiana and Rwanda), or others who are re-evaluating the coherence of the traditional Quaker theological rationale (Creasey 1963, Johns 1998, Kolp 1984). In this spirit, Nancy Bieber concludes that however communion is practised, its meaning for Friends will be deepened by exploring why it continues to be meaningful to most of the world's Christians (Bieber 1997).

Quaker perspectives on the sacraments have proven challenging in ecumenical contexts, whether with Honduran pastors in a predominately Roman Catholic cultural context, or with formal involvement in organizations such as the World Council of Churches. The WCC's 1982 publication of *Baptism, Eucharist, and Ministry* prompted formal responses to the council's assertion that Christian unity be defined and expressed as an 'eucharistic fellowship' (London Yearly Meeting 1987; Friends United Meeting 1981). John Punshon objected to this interpretation and argued instead that Quakers seek unity not in liturgical and confessional practice but rather in discipleship (Punshon 1987, 36).

It is true that Quakers have historically defended their position rather consistently by rejecting the use of sacraments or, like Gurney, by suggesting that spiritual maturity will naturally vindicate the truthfulness of their convictions. However, Friends' increasing involvement in ecumenical affairs as well as the growing influence of global Quakerism may well mean that more attention is directed at tackling abuses and addressing oversights rather than to simple rejection.

Conclusion

Nothing reveals more about a religious community than its worship. Books of *Faith and Practice* state aspirations and public presentation of ideals. Worship, on the other hand, reveals the push and pull of deep conviction with nagging doubt, of unflattering struggles for power, and of human efforts to manage the unmanageable. It is understandable why so much drama has been associated with it through the centuries. Worship matters.

When new covenant/end-time thinking dissipated, Quakers found themselves, as they often do still, maintaining a form of worship and a view of sacraments lacking sufficient theological basis. That is not to say that these practices are without merit. Many Quakers would state that they have been beneficial and even a prophetic witness to the world. However, it does mean that Friends can often be strict traditionalists when defending certain practices and non-practices; this is true across the liberal to conservative spectrum.

What conclusions can be drawn from examining Friends' worship? First, Quakers have tried to witness to the power and presence of the living Christ. As much as possible, they have stripped worship to it most elemental movements to avoid distraction while listening for the voice of God. Second, they have tried to remain open to anyone in their assemblies who is led by the Spirit to offer ministry, even those whose voices are not always present in other contexts. Third, their understanding of revelation and the cosmos is such that time and space have collapsed into the holy and in every corner of creation the Spirit speaks.

Quaker worship evolved as it did for many reasons, some of which have been discussed here. As a living tradition there is more to be said that is not yet known. However, it is quite likely that as the demographics of the movement continue to shift toward the Global South, the shape of worship will be increasingly textured by the practices, music, liturgies, and theologies from cultures quite unlike those of its founding. Whether this expands Quakerism's self-identity in a unifying way or results in conflict and division will largely depend upon whether each group can recognize in the worship of the other the free and surprising Spirit of God it sees in its own.

SUGGESTED FURTHER READING

Bauman, Richard (1983) *Let your words be few: symbolism of speaking and silence among seventeenth-century Quakers.* Cambridge and New York: Cambridge University Press.

Bieber, Nancy (1997) *Communion for a Quaker.* Pendle Hill Pamphlet no. 331. Wallingford, PA: Pendle Hill Publications.

Dandelion, Pink (2005) *Liturgies of Quakerism.* Aldershot: Ashgate Publishing, Ltd.

Friends United Meeting (1981) *Friends and the Sacraments.* Richmond, IN: Friends United Press.

Hall, Francis (ed.) (1978) *Quaker worship in North America.* Richmond, IN: Friends United Press.

Johns, David L (1998) 'Ritual management of absence and presence: the liturgical significance of silence', *Quaker Religious Thought*, 28: 31–42.

Kolp, Alan (1984) 'Friends, sacraments, and sacramental living', *Quaker Religious Thought*, 20: 36–52.

Martin, Marcelle (2003) *Invitation to a deeper communion.* Pendle Hill Pamphlet no. 366. Wallingford, PA: Pendle Hill Publications.

PART III

QUAKER WITNESS

PART III

SOCIETY WITHOUT GOD

CHAPTER 18

MINISTRY AND PREACHING

MICHAEL P. GRAVES

THE earliest Friends preached impromptu in various settings and to a variety of audiences, claiming the 'Inward Light' of Christ immediately moved them. Of course the Quakers have not been alone in their adherence to impromptu preaching, which was also an important practice in the history of African–Americans, some Appalachian Baptists, and many early Mormons (Davis 1985; Dorgan 1987; Jackson 2010). Early Quaker men and women preached in a variety of venues, including streets, fields, churches of competing sects, and their own meeting houses. They spoke to varying purposes, including prophecy, evangelism, exhortation, and instruction. The typical pattern in their meetings was to convene in silence, waiting for the Spirit to speak either to individuals in silence, or through others who rose to speak under the unction of the Spirit. During the 1670s and, significantly, after the Act of Toleration in 1689, there was a collective effort among Friends towards a more conservative impromptu preaching style, the essence of which is captured in Samuel Bownas's *A Description of the Qualifications Necessary to a Gospel Minister*, published in 1750, a date in the chronological centre of the eighteenth-century Quaker Quietist period. A vestige of the early Quaker approach to impromptu sermonizing remains extant among some twenty-first-century Friends, although the nineteenth century saw a growing diversity among Friends' approaches to ministry and preaching style, a diversity that has continued to grow in the twenty-first century. This chapter deals with the evolution of Quaker vocal ministry from the mid-seventeenth century to the present day. The focus of this chapter is on the message and its delivery rather than the reception by hearers.

THE EARLIEST YEARS, 1648–1689

Very few sermon texts exist for the period 1650–86 (all from George Fox (1624–91) in 1653 and the 1670s). Surviving sermon texts from Fox's preaching includes two rhetorically adroit sermons preached in Barbados in 1671, which saw Fox suggesting that slaves be released from servitude after thirty years of service and that interracial marriage serve as a possible alternative to sodomy (Graves 2009, 181). Both of these sermons are lengthy, rivalling Puritan sermons of the period. Neither, however, is as lengthy nor complex as his important address to the Yearly Meeting in 1674, where he develops the sequential imagery of the Creation–Fall–Restoration sequence (as opposed to the Creation–Fall–Redemption sequence of the Puritans), which suggested that humans might be fully *restored* to the sinless state of Adam and Eve prior to the fall. The sermon is also important because it reveals Fox defending the organizational move in the direction of separate-gender Business Meetings (Graves 2009, 227–56). Fox's sermons, although not organized in a manner that would satisfy seventeenth-century rhetoricians, reveal the skill of a powerful leader to address issues of consequence to Friends.

In addition to Fox's surviving sermon texts, the investigator can also discern how early Friends preached from reports of sermons in their journals and references to preaching in their epistles and tracts. Through perusal of these documents, the reader is able to discover the development of a Quaker homiletic, particularly through such writers as Fox, Margaret Fell (1614–1702), Rebecca Smith, and Robert Barclay (1648–90).

Fox's own habits of preaching as reported in his *Journal* served as a model for others. His approach was, first of all, to instruct hearers to turn to the Inward Light of Christ. Second, he placed emphasis in his preaching on the interpretation of Bible passages, particularly from the Old Testament, as events and persons seen as types that anticipate analogous examples of New Testament fulfilment in Christ and the Church, as well as significant applications of the types to the immediate lives of his hearers (Fox 1995, 108–109). Third, Fox interpreted Scripture in ways that discredited other dissenters and the Established Church, which frequently included pointed attacks on their preplanned and rehearsed sermonizing. In sum, in the *Journal* Fox modelled at least three possible approaches to sermon content for other preachers to follow.

Margaret Fell defended women's rights to preach in her now-famous *Women's Speaking Justified* (Fell 1989, originally published in 1666), which is significant because the ranks of Friends' vocal ministers, or Public Friends, have always included women. In additional works, Fell attacked ministry as practised in Anglican, Puritan, and Presbyterian circles (Fell 1664) and specifically rejected any notion of preparation for a specific preaching event (Fell 1667).

In addition, Puritans, Presbyterians, and Anglicans all demanded a well-educated clergy, but Fox, Fell, Robert Barclay (the Quaker apologist), and numerous other Quaker writers, such as Quaker preacher Rebecca Smith, in her *The Foundation of True Preaching Asserted* (Smith 1687), absolutely rejected university training or ordination to become a minister, a universal and continuing theme among Quakers through to the nineteenth century.

For a number of reasons, the confidence of early Quakers in their 'revivalistic' fervour to convert the world had begun to change by 1676, the year that Robert Barclay published his *Apology for the True Christian Divinity*, a justification of Quaker theology that included 'propositions' dealing with immediate revelation, the ministry, and worship. Barclay argued that silent group waiting was the core of worship, but allowed that speaking prompted by the Spirit might also be helpful to the gathered meeting—when the uttered words were accompanied by 'the evidence and demonstration of the Spirit and of power' (Barclay 2002, 289). Barclay's work was hugely influential on the majority of Quakers during the eighteenth and nineteenth centuries. His lesser-known *Immediate Revelation*, written in 1676, but not published until 1692, set out a theorized psychology of how immediate revelation works (Graves 2009, 113–29).

As the last three decades of the seventeenth century unfolded, Quakers continued to accumulate a fairly consistent body of written advice for novice impromptu preachers. As noted above, even prior to the Act of Toleration in 1689, Quakers were beginning to lose the radical evangelical and 'revivalistic' edge of the earliest Friends, and their advice to neophyte preachers became increasingly conservative. Bristol Quaker Charles Marshall (*c.*1637–98), wrote his influential 1675 public letter, *An epistle to Friends coming forth in the beginning of a testimony*, which advocated a conservative 'passive' approach to content, but also a passive approach, almost a reticence, to the actual prospect of speaking in a Quaker meeting (Marshall 1675, 5–6) Marshall's conservative approach tended to have a dampening effect on impromptu preaching and paved the way for the Quietist period that followed.

The Early Quietist Period, 1687–1700

Barclay's pronouncement that silent group waiting was the core of acceptable worship, but that speaking prompted by the Spirit might also be helpful to the gathered meeting under certain conditions is the most obvious signal of a turn from early Quaker self-identification as soldiers in the 'Lamb's War', ministers who preached direct and energetic messages to convert crowds, to seeing themselves as a 'Remnant' to be preserved in and from the 'world'. The term 'Remnant' encouraged a ministry that sought to bring hearers into a life of discipline and holiness. In addition to Marshall's key letter, writings by Stephen Crisp (1628–92) and George Whitehead (1636–1723) also reveal a very conservative approach to vocal expression in meetings. Crisp, one of the ablest Quaker preachers of the seventeenth century, advises readers to 'wait', be patient, and never utter an angry word in meetings. Whitehead's 1674 tract, *Enthusiasm Above Atheism: Or, Divine Inspiration and Immediate Inspiration,* offered a spirited defence of the impromptu inspired tradition, but in a 1704 published letter, he 'saw great danger in any Person striving to inlarge [sic] in declaration beyond their ability and gifts' (Whitehead 1704, 36–7).

Marshall's Bristol colleague, Benjamin Coole (d. 1717), reasserted the role of inspiration in preaching, and countered Marshall's emphasis on passivity with an explication of the balance between 'passive' and 'active' roles in a Quaker meeting, the former dealing with receiving from the Lord directly, and the latter describing the role of vocal ministry undertaken only after discerning whether the message heard in a passive state is for the minister him/herself, or for the meeting to hear audibly (Coole 1696, 26 and 66; Graves 2009, 106–8).

This brief review of seventeenth and early eighteenth-century Quaker writing about impromptu preaching reveals that Quakers early on attempted to lead their fledgling preachers down a conservative path of fruitful vocal ministry. By their published guidance they may have acted in ways that seemed overly cautious and paradoxical to their commitment to an ostensibly impromptu and immediately 'inspired' vocal ministry, a 'prophetic' strain of sermonizing that might at any moment, under Divine encouragement, fly in the face of the reticent, conservative decorum offered by the published (and spoken) advice of elders.

The Second Day Morning Meeting, which had been founded in 1673, played a key role in the supervision of both vocal ministry and publications during the early Quietist period. John Punshon writes that during this period (and deepening in the eighteenth century), the path to ministry ('recording') became increasingly arduous, while the position of elders grew in importance. Eventually, the role of overseer was added to the top of the powerful regulatory hierarchy (Punshon 1984, 140–3).

Regardless of the dampening trend on vocal expression, sixty-seven sermon texts survive from this period, including exhortations from Quaker notables Robert Barclay, Benjamin Coole, and Charles Marshall, each with a single surviving sermon. George Whitehead has two surviving sermons to examine, while William Penn has eleven, and Stephen Crisp has thirty-two extant sermons. Collectively, the sermons reveal certain characteristics, which were examined in *Preaching the Inward Light* (Graves 2009). Generally, the most significant earmarks of Quaker sermons from this period include: (1) propensity to quote Scripture extensively, especially with emphasis on the application of Old Testament typology to their audiences; (2) presentation of mosaically structured messages that combine and juxtapose theological terms together and rehearse five key conceptual metaphors—i.e., 'light/dark', 'voice', 'the seed', 'hunger/thirst', and 'the journey'; (3) reliance on the use of spatial terms—e.g. 'inward', 'outward', 'upward', etc.; (4) extensive use and refinement of rhetorical questions, some used much as the 'queries' later were; (5) and the use of personal testimony from the preachers. In the hands of Crisp, Barclay, and Penn, the impromptu sermon becomes a work of art, given the growing constraints on ministry in meeting. Some of the sermons are self-reflexive. For example, Crisp's sermon delivered 14 March 1687 at Grace Church Street Meeting, London, deals with the topic of the 'possibility of God speaking directly to people, thus becoming at that moment the Word of God to them' (Graves 2009, 266). Crisp's sermon is a notable rhetorical performance for a businessman without formal education. The university-educated and intellectually gifted William Penn (1644–1718) was, as one might expect, a master of the Quaker impromptu sermon, as he demonstrated at the memorial service of author and minister Rebecca Travers (Graves 2009, 293–308).

In sum, the early Quietist period was a remarkable moment in the development of Friends ministry. This second generation of Quakers developed a culturally centred type of vocal ministry that was strikingly different from Anglicans, Puritans, Baptists, and Presbyterians. Surprisingly, Quaker insistence on utter reliance on inspiration nevertheless produced a significant body of surviving sermons that are, decidedly, 'sermons'. They also began to develop a homiletic for excelling at the impromptu style and how to pass this style on to the younger generation. Their published guidance may have seemed overly cautious and paradoxical to their commitment to an immediately 'inspired' vocal ministry, one that might possibly, under Divine encouragement, question the reticent decorum found in the published advice of elders.

THE QUIETIST PERIOD, 1700–1826

The conservative and cautionary approach to preaching, the beginnings of which are noted above, eventually found ultimate expression in Samuel Bownas's (1677–1753) significant 1750 book, *A Description of the Qualifications Necessity to a Gospel Minister*, which contained essentially a manual on impromptu preaching. The book, written from the perspective of Bownas's long experience as a public Friend, also reflects the accumulated teachings of previous ministers and elders (including their warning to be certain that the message one hears inwardly is in fact a message to be uttered aloud). Bownas believed in a long 'developmental' process of becoming a vocal minister. He reiterated Fox's admonition for elders to be tender when rebuking young preachers, those who seem to go beyond the Spirit's leading (Bownas 1750, 20–1). Bownas also added significant reflections and advice not discovered in earlier Quaker writings about vocal ministry. For example, regarding delivery skills, Bownas warned against speaking too fast or too loud, and not to use the apparently popular 'sing-song' chanting style (1750, 38, ff.). The origins of this approach to the canon of delivery are obscure, but Thomas Hamm reports that as late as the mid-nineteenth century, the 'sing-song' delivery style was controversial among American Quakers (Hamm 1988, 59). Bownas saw it as self-serving and an impediment to the message.

On the canon of style or language, Bownas favoured terseness rather than copiousness: 'guard against superfluous words…which add nothing to thy matter, spoiling its coherence and beauty and expression' (1750, 42). Here he passed on to later generations adherence to the well-known Quaker 'plain style'.

Bownas added to these pieces of advice strong admonitions not to imitate other preachers, either in composition or delivery. Novice preachers were even cautioned against using their own original content on more than one speaking occasion (1750, 58–9), advice that, if followed, surely reduced the novice preacher's fund of available material (or 'commonplaces', in ancient rhetorical parlance) for potential use in the travelling ministry.

Bownas's most significant original contribution to the development of a Quaker impromptu homiletic was his elaboration of a checklist on the 'Matter and Manner of Expression', which was an accumulation of six ways the young minister might expect the Spirit to work in any given sermon. Bownas included the following categories: parables, allegories, narration of history, personal testimony, relation of another person's testimony, and application of biblical typologies (1750, 48–59). Whereas with Fox and other early Quaker writers and speakers, we must deduce their approaches to preaching from their habitual practice and written hints, most of which were not directed towards establishing a formal theory of homiletic. In contrast, with Bownas we encounter a theorizing rhetorician intent on setting out a typology of 'means of expression'. Unfortunately, Bownas's typology is overlapping and sometimes puzzling in arrangement and content, but that did not prevent the book from achieving wide popularity among Friends (Graves 2009, 144–53).

Quietism is a generally under-researched period of Quaker history, according to Dandelion (2007, 77). Surprisingly, it is not as 'quiet' as one might expect from the name. At least seventy-five sermons survive from the period, sermons that hold the promise of offering windows into how Friends in the eighteenth century engaged in impromptu preaching (Graves mss). These seventy-five sermons indicate that a substantial body of stenographic impromptu sermons exists to be carefully examined and compared rhetorically. Of importance, the collection includes two or more sermons by three men and two women, which offers the analyst an opportunity not only to compare and contrast each individual's sermonizing, but also invites comparison and contrast across preachers, including comparisons of content and stylistic choices between genders. Most of this careful analytical work remains to be undertaken.

The surviving sermons of eighteenth-century Quakers have not been systematically collected, catalogued, and examined rhetorically as those from the period 1687–1700 (Graves 2009, 318–20). The current one-volume histories of Quakers by Barbour and Frost, Punshon, and Dandelion make frequent and insightful references to Quaker ministry, but rarely mention specific sermons or make comments on the rhetorical choices made by the ministers. Similarly, in Rebecca Larson's respected volume on Quaker women ministers, *Daughters of Light: Quaker Women Preaching and Prophesying in the Colonies and Abroad, 1700–1775* (1999), she relies on journals and letters to tell the story of ministry by women during the period. Larson mentions two 1765 sermons by Rachel Wilson preached in the colonies, but offers no analysis of the sermons or commentary on Wilson's rhetorical habits.

Lucia K. Beamish goes further than Larson by referencing sermons by Stephen Crisp (1967, 24–6), Francis Stamper (1967, 31–2), and Richard Ashby (1967, 32–3), all from the earlier period, but failing to comment on Ashby's sermon preached in 1710, which is extant. Encouragingly, Beamish also provides brief commentary, mostly theological in nature, on twelve sermons by Thomas Story (1670–1742) (1967, 33–8) and three sermons by Samuel Fothergill (1715–72), mentioning Fothergill's 'love of exhortation by means of queries' (1967, 95), his preference for the Old Testament over the New Testament, and his habit of taking 'a recondite passage from Scripture and build[ing] a sermon on it' (1967, 97). Beamish also mentions the ministry of several eighteen-century women Friends ministers, including Catherine Phillips, Mary Moore, May Drummond, Mary Kirby, and Lucy Bradley (1967, 84–91).

Analysis of these seventy-five eighteenth-century sermons indicates that they continued the tendencies in content and form of the early Quietist period discussed above. In the new century, the public Friends sought to preserve a separated, holy remnant, while at the same time holding forth a positive testimony to the outside world. These preachers were markedly Christians, employing the standard lexicon of Christian theology: 'justification', 'sanctification', 'redemption', etc. They exhorted on matters of morality and Quaker 'peculiarities', such as plain speech and dress. They stressed *purity* and how it might be attained. Everywhere, the personal *experience* of spiritual reality—their own and that of others—was overtly championed.

In terms of rhetorical strategies, the surviving sermons continued to feature extensive quotation (from memory) of Scripture and frequent application of Scripture to the personal lives of the hearers, especially when the passages deal with moral strictures and attaining personal holiness. Like earlier Quaker sermons, most of these sermons did not rest on a base of theological argument. Rather, the conceptual spine of the sermons largely remained the conceptual world of the five key Quaker metaphors from the earlier period: light/dark, sound/silence, seed, hunger/thirst, and journey/pilgrimage. Spatial terms were prominent in the sermons, as preachers in the century attempted to move meetings towards the 'inward' reality of spirituality empowered by the 'Inward Light'. The 'outward' material matters were important as regards Quaker distinctives, but otherwise seen as transient and definitely not to be esteemed. In abundance, the ministers used rhetorical questions to prompt self-examination, much like the 'queries'. As noted above, Beamish observed Fothergill as focusing many of his appeals in the queries, questions individuals and meetings employed to facilitate introspection and behavioural self-scrutiny. Finally, the ministers chose personal testimony as a crucial rhetorical choice in many of the sermons.

There are some surprises among the sermons from the Quietist period. For example, in 1760 Fothergill addressed a meeting of elders in Lancaster, England. His brief discourse in the similitude of a vision or dream dealt with the 'home gathering of many' going to meet their eternal reward (Fothergill 1812, 1). In the extant sermons, it is rare to find preachers relating visions, and that alone raises the critic's interest in this text. More significantly, the text itself is of rhetorical interest. Its construction around a vision of the end—the apocalypse—with the division of earth's people into the 'number ascending up clothed in white' and 'a number left behind', employed classic biblical imagery and language. The clincher was that Fothergill's exordium postulated that some of the very elders seated near him in the meeting were among those unfortunate souls who would be 'left behind'. Direct confrontation such as this was rare and begs for rhetorical analysis. Possibly Fothergill, a 'publick Friend' and himself an elder, may have been asserting the power of the inspired preacher over the dampening power of the uninspired elder.

THE DIVERSIFICATION OF MINISTRY AND PREACHING AMONG FRIENDS, 1826–1900

Rising evangelicalism, along with the simultaneous development of deism and rationalism, began to affect Friends during this period, resulting in seemingly irreconcilable conflicts. Most importantly, a period of strong theological disagreement began to emerge among Friends in the 1820s, which eventually resulted in the 1827 schism in Philadelphia Yearly Meeting known as the Hicksite Separation, a rending of the Quaker fabric that influenced Quaker theology and sermonizing on both sides of the Atlantic throughout the nineteenth century and affects Quakerism to this day. Subsequent years saw further, less catastrophic, but significant 'separations', such as that between Wilburites and Gurneyites. Arguably, emerging diversity was the most important characteristic of Friends history in the nineteenth century.

The historical, theological, and sociological contexts of nineteenth-century Quaker sermons are complex and variegated. Sorting through the threads of discord is well beyond the scope of this essay, but a general overview of the most important diverse paths appears necessary for this discussion. The various paths of disagreement, diversity, and schism have been clearly presented by historians and sociologists. Friends were influenced from two sources, according to Punshon: Deism and the rise of Evangelical Revival, the former questioning the deity of Christ, the authority of Scripture, and the need for personal salvation, while upholding Friends' traditions such as group silence and the quest for inward experiential spirituality. On the other hand, ardent Quaker Evangelicals saw sin as 'total distortion of the human personality'; the Bible as 'inspired and infallible'; personal conversion as absolutely necessary; 'mission' or evangelization as a high priority, as their name suggests; and the possession of a 'personal faith that is doctrinally sound', for example, the belief 'that Christ has accepted the penalty for your sin' (Punshon 1984, 165).

However, Quakers influenced by Deism and rationalism—the latter existing as an approach that placed 'reason above faith, or rational authority above scriptural' (Dandelion 2007, 84)—resisted the rise of evangelicalism. Dandelion writes that 'Deist, rationalist, and extreme Quietist ideas flew in the face of growing evangelical influence'.

There are many paths of nineteenth-century Quaker diversity, but one schism is particularly important to this essay. In the 1830s, Orthodox Friends aligned themselves to one of two camps. Dandelion writes: 'These two positions were epitomized by John Wilbur and Joseph John Gurney and they became the leading protagonists in a second wave of schism that rent Orthodox Yearly Meetings' (Dandelion 2007, 95). Eventually, Orthodox Yearly Meetings separated into Wilburite and Gurneyite Yearly Meetings, beginning in 1845 (Punshon 1984, 197). In America, the Gurneyites were strong in the burgeoning West. Thomas Hamm observes: 'What is indisputable is that between 1830 and 1860 a majority of Orthodox Friends moved significantly closer to the dominant evangelical religious culture in the United States' (Hamm 1988, 20). Later in the century these Evangelical Friends were greatly influenced by the Holiness Revivals led by preachers from other denominations and, largely because of the influx of newly converted members produced by the revivals, eventually themselves embraced a system of 'released' ministry—essentially a pastoral system—which ultimately resulted in 'programmed' worship services (Dandelion 2007, 102–12; Punshon 1984, 199–202). Hamm carefully details the steps in this turn and its effects on Quaker theology and practice (Hamm 1988, 85–130). (Compare Carole Dale Spencer's scholarly account of the Quaker roots of holiness in *Holiness: The Soul of Quakerism* (2007).) This truncated review of Quaker schism is important because the known extant sermons of the period include the essential 1826 sermons that played a role in fomenting the Hicksite Separation as well as the core of Joseph John Gurney's sermons in America, sermons that both revived the Evangelical branch of American Orthodox Friends and provoked the intense response of the Wilburites.

As noted above, the accumulated corpus of seventeenth-century and eighteenth-century sermons is relatively large given their impromptu nature. However, the number of extant Quaker sermons from the nineteenth century is even larger. Research on the period has uncovered 186 Quaker sermons, existing both in print and manuscript notes from auditors, plus forty-nine published speeches by Lucretia Mott, most of them sermons (Mott 1980), bringing the total to approximately 230 sermons. Most of these sermons are from auditors' notes, but a few are from the preachers' later reconstructions of what they said. Arguably, further search at Quaker research libraries, with particular attention to handwritten journals and commonplace books, will produce a total approaching 300 or more sermons with fairly complete texts to analyse. The majority of the sermons in the final total will probably be sermons delivered by American ministers largely for two reasons: (1) the Holiness Revivals in America in the second half of the century encouraged preaching rather than silence; and (2) the turn towards the pastoral system in many American Gurneyite Quaker meetings fostered sermons that were prepared ahead of time and sometimes written out. Arguably, because prepared sermons by definition are not impromptu, the close of the nineteenth century also heralded the end of the Quaker impromptu sermon, at least as it might be said to resemble the typical length and complexity of Quaker sermons from the 1650s to the mid-nineteenth century. Furthermore, doctrinal differences among Friends virtually dictated a varied approach to sermon content.

The list of preachers includes significant Quaker luminaries Stephen Grellet, Ann Jones, Elizabeth Fry, Joseph John Gurney, Lucretia Mott, Sunderland Gardner, Sarah Grubb, Edward Hicks, Elias Hicks, Jesse Kersey, Samuel Tuke, and Robert Barclay of Reigate. This list also offers the rhetorical analyst the opportunity to examine, for example, how select ministers over several decades managed theological disagreement and sociological change through rhetorical agency. In particular, the sermons of the Hicksite Separation are well represented in the surviving sermons by Hicks, Kersey, and others. Similarly, Joseph John Gurney's important 1837 visit to America is at least partially recorded in five of his surviving sermons. Also of note, Robert Barclay's extant sermons provide one example of preaching at a 'Mission Hall Service', which Punshon describes as developing from an educational programme to address illiteracy by British Friends, a Quaker experiment with ministry among poor, under-educated non-Quakers (Punshon 1984, 192). The list of sermons also reveals some chronological gaps in the record of English and American Quaker preaching, particularly in the last two decades of the century when English Quakerism took a turn toward Modernism (Dandelion 2007, 117–28), and American Quaker Evangelicals embraced the pastoral system and 'programmed' meetings. It makes sense that programmed meetings should yield a significant number of sermon texts waiting to be discovered in archives. In sum, much of the basic work of collecting nineteenth-century Quaker sermon texts from both sides of the Atlantic still lies ahead.

Despite the fact that so many sermon texts are currently available, preached by significant Friends ministers, some of them well known, scholars have paid a modicum of attention to actual nineteenth-century Quaker sermon texts, although some authors have commented helpfully on Quaker preaching. For example, Beamish mentions the preaching of Mary Stokes (later Dudley), Thomas Shillitoe, David Sands, and Stephen Grellet (Beamish 1967, 102–16).

Perusal of the sermons indicates that the interweaving of Scripture and the free play of theological concepts, exhortations to find spiritual meaning in silence, the interlacing of Quaker metaphors, and reliance on rhetorical questions—all characteristics discovered in earlier periods—survive in some of the later sermons. For example, an 1853 sermon by Sybil Jones (1808–73) of Maine delivered in Birmingham, England, found Jones weaving together a series of scriptural quotations beginning with the Lord's Prayer, quoted in toto, followed by her own opening prayer. Her sermon featured an interlacing of exhortations to 'draw near in silent waiting' and 'silent adoration', peppered with direct quotations from the Psalms and the Book of Revelation (Jones 1853, 1). As evidenced here, she relied on the power of the Quaker metaphor family of sound/silence, but she also employed the light/dark family: 'the Sun of Righteousness may disperse the mist and darkness now prevailing'. Later in the sermon she employed the journey metaphor, as in the following: 'pass through the wilderness of this world' and the 'foot of a mountain of great difficulty' (Jones 1853, 2). Her evangelical orthodoxy was overtly revealed late in the sermon with these words: 'may sinners come, more and more, unto Zion, and ask, what shall we do to be saved? Let these come unto Jesus, "the Lamb of God, who taketh away the sin of the world", who died and rose again, the just for the unjust' (Jones 1853, 2).

The contrast in styles and approaches in nineteenth-century Quaker sermons is readily seen by turning to Joseph John Gurney's (1788–1847) sermon preached in Liverpool on 6 May 1832. Here Gurney employed some of the stylistic strategies of his Quaker predecessors, such as the rhetorical question, which he used with great skill: 'Where is our penitence, then, friends? where is our broken heart? where is our humiliation? where is our trembling? where is our godly fear? Are you baptized into the name of the Father? Why do you not then tremble? Why are you not amazed? Why are ye not broken down under the sense of the terrors of his law? Why are ye not humbled under the blessed tidings that "God is love?"' (Gurney 1832, 3). Here we see a classic appeal by a Quaker preacher to have the hearers enter into an *experiential* spirituality. The thematic heart of Gurney's sermon, though, was focused on apologetics, particularly on defending the divinity of Christ, one of the points of contention in the debates leading to the Hicksite Separation:

> [T]he doctrine of the divinity of our saviour is not a doctrine of speculation . . . it does not belong, as some suppose, to the mere theory of religion, and therefore may be laid

on one side without inconvenience and without mischief; or, if not disbelieved, be disregarded as a matter of theory alone. My friends, there never was a greater proof of human blindness and ignorance than this particular error. (Gurney 1832, 5)

On the Hicksite side of the ledger, Edward Hicks (1780–1849), Elias Hicks's cousin, delivered one of the most interesting extant nineteenth-century sermons. Edward Hicks, America's best known 'folk artist', is famous for his paintings depicting the 'Peaceable Kingdom' described in Isaiah 11:6–7. Hicks painted sixty-two versions of the Peaceable Kingdom over his lifetime and finished the final painting only hours before his death. Carolyn J. Weekley interprets the evolution of Hicks's Peaceable Kingdom paintings with his effort to cope with the devastating effect of the Hicksite separation on his spirit. Of great importance, Weekley has linked Hicks's evolving visual work with a complex and lengthy 1834 sermon he delivered at Goose Creek Meeting in Loudon County Virginia (Weekley 1999, 223–32). In the sermon, Hicks set forth a detailed biblical hermeneutic of the Isaiah 11 passage according to the ancient framework of the four temperaments: sanguine, choleric, melancholic, and phlegmatic. Hicks moved skilfully through the four temperaments, revealing links to the various animal images that found visual expression in his series of paintings, but also making direct application to his hearers. He ended the sermon by exhorting his hearers to be like the choleric figure of the Ox who, by metaphorical extension, bowed his head to the yoke and submitted to Christ, whose yoke is 'easy' (Weekley 1999, 232).

As is evidenced in this brief notation of three sermons, the impromptu sermon not only survived well into the nineteenth century, but also offers rich veins still to be mined, both theologically and rhetorically, in the extant nineteenth-century Quaker sermons.

Ministry and Preaching among Friends, 1900–2012

The scholarly commentators on twentieth- and twenty-first-century Quakers address the fact that Quakers are diverse both in their theology and *acted* theology. Hamm employs the amusing but accurate title 'Quaker Faiths and Practices' to begin his description of how the schisms of the nineteenth century evolved into Friends' diversity in the twenty-first century. The extreme manifestations range from silent or unprogrammed meetings, which may go for weeks without any sort of vocal ministry, to gatherings of up to 3,000 people at evangelical mega-church meetings, often amplified with 'praise bands' and enthusiastic singing, gatherings where paid pastors are expected to hold forth weekly with prepared sermons that both call the unsaved to repentance and build up—or 'edify'—the congregation through exposition of the Bible (Hamm 2003, 64). Taking a different tack, Dandelion analyses the worship practices of British Friends as 'liturgies' that tend to conceal unexplored theological differences through a mask of silence. He writes: '... the silence of liberal-Liberal Friends can conceal diversity, both of theology, and of the theology of worship' (Dandelion 2005, 112).

There are great differences among 'audiences' or hearers of messages across the sweep of contemporary Quaker ministry experiences. At one extreme, the college- and seminary-educated pastor preaches the sermon and virtually no one in the congregation expects to be allowed, let alone encouraged, to stand and deliver an immediately inspired message, however brief. However, among some Evangelical Friends in smaller meetings or churches, a vestigial version of the silent meeting may take place during a 'programmed' service. This is a brief period of time—one to perhaps five minutes—sometimes known as 'Friends Communion', during which members may rise to speak to the meeting. In most evangelical meetings, hearers expect to listen to a prepared sermon by a designated pastor.

At the other end of the sociological spectrum, for Friends worshipping in unprogrammed meetings, though anyone may rise to speak in theory, in reality only a small proportion of members actually speak. Though they may not be 'recorded' ministers, they are arguably operating rhetorically in the tradition of 'Public Friends'. The meeting participants do not expect a sermon, as such, and would probably be surprised and dismayed if one were preached.

Clearly, there exist radical differences in approach to vocal ministry among contemporary Friends, and skilful analysts and writers have already mapped their varied treks and commented on their present status (Hamm 2003; Dandelion 2005; Punshon 1984). Accordingly, the final section of this chapter reviews the state of knowledge about Quaker sermons in the last hundred years and sketches out some of the implications on preaching entailed in the diversification of Friends.

One cannot accumulate knowledge about a subject such as preaching without primary sources, in this case sermon texts (or recordings). However, the basic work of systematic collection lies ahead, although there are positive signs of interest in such a task. For example, Peter Sippel's helpful 'Quaker Homiletics Online Anthology' lists nineteen sermons from the twentieth century divided into Conservative, Liberal, and Evangelical traditions. Sipple's list includes sermons by important Quakers such as Rufus Jones, John Wilhelm Rowntree, Matilda W. Atkinson, J. Walter Malone, D. Elton Trueblood, and others. Sippel's work is a good start towards a checklist of modern Quaker sermons. To Sippel's list we must add sermon collections, such as those by Arthur O. Roberts (1967, 2006b). However, the bulk of the 'heavy lifting' of sermon collection awaits the researcher.

It is likely that there are thousands of extant Quaker sermons from the twentieth and twenty-first centuries, many of them preached not only in the continental United States, but also in Alaska, Bolivia, Peru, Guatemala, Cuba, East Africa, and other places where Gurneyite Friends sent missionaries. Most of these sermons were not delivered in English. In these locales, worship tends not to be confined to an hour or so, and sermonizing by a pastor, together with vocal testifying by other Public Friends, may go on for hours (Dandelion 2007, 211). Additionally, there may exist notes taken down from speakers speaking spontaneously in unprogrammed meetings in countries around the globe where English is not the primary language.

In America, an appreciable number of sermons may be available for study in the offices or archives of large West Coast Friends churches, where sermons are routinely recorded, as well as in other sections of the United States (such as Richmond, Indiana), where manuscripts or recordings may be available from church or meeting offices or directly from pastors. Internet websites of Friends meetings or churches may also offer the researcher some additional documents or recordings. As mentioned above with respect to the eighteenth and nineteenth centuries, the excellent Quaker research libraries on both sides of the Atlantic continually add to their collections of primary source materials, including sermons, in print, manuscript, and recordings.

It is important to point out that the bulk of these modern sermons eventually discovered and catalogued will not be traditional Quaker impromptu sermons, or what William F. Rushby calls 'the Free Gospel Ministry' of itinerant public friends (Rushby 2000), although a vestige of this earlier form of preaching may be present among Conservative (Ohio) Friends.

As should be clear from the discussion above, the vast differences in ministry and preaching among present-day Friends is not simply a matter of presentational mode, but of theological content as well. Evangelicals tend to downplay traditional Friends' teachings, such as the peace testimony, in favour of a more generalized contemporary evangelical theology. The result is Meetings for Worship that are little different from non-Quaker evangelical services. On the other hand, Liberal Friends who meet in silence, many of them adhering to some traditional Friends' teachings—such as the peace testimony—tend to forsake the traditional Friends' teachings regarding Christ and the Bible as presented by contemporary Evangelical Friends.

One might conclude that in the modern age, Quakers of all stripes have largely forsaken their rich heritage of impromptu preaching and reached for the possibility of rhetorically rich contemporary sermons prepared, and perhaps 'inspired', prior to the meeting, or more brief and potentially 'inspired' messages arising from the immediate inspiration arising in the context of profound group silence.

CONCLUSION

Early Friends acted upon and experimented with the outrageous notion that the Spirit, the Inward Light, might immediately speak through individuals in meetings or in the public square. The history of their ministry and preaching has produced a substantial corpus of 339 known sermon texts, sermons preached as a result of this radical notion of immediate inspiration, some of impressive duration given their impromptu nature. However, as a result of schismatic changes in the formerly universally accepted doctrine among Friends, as well as the adoption of the pastoral system and the development of programmed meetings among many Evangelical Friends, the twentieth century has witnessed the near extinction of the practice of impromptu preaching (except among Conservative Friends and, in an abbreviated form, among unprogrammed Friends worldwide).

While the corpus of extant sermons remains incomplete at this time, we cannot draw any hard and fast conclusions about sermon content and style over the entire period covered in this chapter. However, we can venture the following tentative conclusions. The earliest sermons were multi-thematic mosaics, which occasionally commented on quasi-secular topics, a characteristic of some of the later sermons as well, although the sermons of Evangelical Quakers such as Fothergill and Gurney tended to zero in on a single topic and ventured into apologetic argumentation. In all periods the impromptu sermons showed a propensity of the ministers to quote passages of Scripture verbatim throughout the sermons, often achieving a seamless interplay of Scripture and their own words. Several of the sermons from the second and third periods begin with and focus on a text from Scripture, a choice that was rare in the earlier period, but quite common among contemporary Evangelical Friends. Most of the sermons continued to interweave language drawn from the five conceptual metaphor clusters so prominent in the early period, although Evangelical Friends of the twentieth and twenty-first centuries tend to focus on specifically biblical metaphors or those drawn from contemporary culture and experience. Also, the sermons in all periods tended to exhibit the use of spatial terms and reliance on, or at least use of, rhetorical questions.

All Quaker sermonizing, regardless of the chronological era or culture had and has the potential to soar to rhetorical heights or fall flat. As Seth B. Hinshaw has observed: 'At its best, Quaker ministry has reached spiritual heights unexcelled in human experience— powerful prophetic utterances directly inspired by the Spirit of God. At its worst, it has been wretchedly empty' (Hinshaw 1987, 118). Whether 'prophetic' or 'empty', Quaker sermons from any period, from programmed and unprogrammed meetings, from theological liberals and evangelicals, all enact variations of their roots, a distinct genre of sermonizing that can be examined, critiqued, and appreciated within the constraints of its own theologically evolving and socially energized context.

SUGGESTED FURTHER READING

Abbott, M. P. and Parsons, P. S. (eds.) (2004) *Walk worthy of your calling: Quakers and the traveling ministry.* Richmond, IN: Friends United Press.

Bauman, R. (1983) *Let your words be few: Symbolism of speaking and silence among seventeenth-century Quakers.* New York: Cambridge University Press.

Beamish, L. K. (1967) *Quaker Ministry, 1691–1834.* Oxford, England: By the Author, 76c Woodstock Road.

Bownas, S. (1989) *A description of the qualifications necessary to a Gospel Minister.* Wallingford, PA: Pendle Hill.

Fell, M. (1989) *Women's speaking justified.* C. Trevett (ed.) London: Quaker Home Service.

Fox, G. (1995) *Journal of George Fox.* J. L. Nickalls (ed.) Philadelphia: Religious Society of Friends.

Graves, M. P. (2009) *Preaching the inward Light: Early Quaker rhetoric.* Waco, TX: Baylor University Press.

Hinshaw, S. B. (1987) *The spoken ministry among Friends.* Davidson, NC: North Carolina Yearly Meeting.

Larson, R. (1999) *Daughters of Light: Quaker women preaching and prophesying in the colonies and abroad, 1700–1775.* New York: Alfred A. Knopf.

Rushby, W. F. (2000) 'Cyrus Cooper's memorial and the Free Gospel Ministry', *Quaker History* 89 (1), pp. 28–46.

Spencer, C. D. (2007) *Holiness: The Soul of Quakerism: An historical analysis of the theology of holiness in the Quaker tradition.* Milton Keynes: Paternoster.

....

CHAPTER 19

TRAVELLING MINISTRY

....

SYLVIA STEVENS

FROM the early years of Quakerism in the late 1640s to the present, some Friends have felt called upon to travel beyond their own home meetings to witness to Quaker beliefs and nurture Friends in distant meetings. Whereas Michael Graves considered how Quakers delivered their message in ministry and preaching (in chapter 18 within this volume entitled 'Ministry and Preaching'), this chapter describes the procedures that have evolved to recognize and support those who undertake the role within the unprogrammed and pastoral traditions. It explores how these ministers—also sometimes referred to within the Society as 'Public Friends'—carried out their calling, and examines the theological, social, and cultural implications. For Friends, who for much of their history had no paid ministry, travelling ministers played a particularly important and transnational role. Anyone, man or woman, could speak in a meeting for worship if they felt divinely prompted to do so. Gradually a procedure evolved by which their home meetings recognized, authenticated, and supported those who were gifted in offering vocal ministry. Notwithstanding changes in theological perspective and modifications in procedure, the work of those who exercise a travelling ministry continues to be valued.

SPREADING THE MESSAGE C.1646–1666

....

In the late 1640s George Fox (1624–91) was making his way through the English Midland counties against a background of religious and political turmoil, proclaiming that men and women should put their trust not in the teaching of Church of England priests or of the followers of Separatist congregations such as the Baptists and Independents, but directly in Christ himself (Fox 1995, 11). Elizabeth Hooton of Nottinghamshire (c.1600––71/2) who left the Baptists to join with Friends in about 1647 ignored the opposition of her husband and became the earliest Quaker woman preacher on record. Hooton's position as a woman preacher was contentious and her temerity in reproving a priest in 1650 resulted in imprisonment in Derby gaol. Further imprisonments would follow but she continued her preaching, sailing for America with Fox in 1671, and dying in Barbados in 1679 (Trevett 1991, 16–22).

Early Quaker preachers had no formal system of support, but that gradually changed after the Quaker message took root in the northern counties of England between 1651 and 1654. In 1651 George Fox travelled to Yorkshire and in the following year to Westmorland (now Cumbria). In these counties, sometimes referred to by modern Friends as the '1652 country', Fox converted a sufficient number of men and women to provide a core of followers able and eager to proclaim the truth of their religious experience. Fox recalled that in 1654, when Friends' meetings 'were settled in the north...a matter of seventy ministers did the Lord raise up and send abroad' (Fox 1952, 174). The parallel between this missionary surge southwards with the biblical account of Christ sending the seventy apostles forth to preach, as recorded in Luke 10:1, would have been immediately apparent. Fox mentioned Francis Howgill and Edward Burrough who travelled to London, John Camm and John Audland to Bristol, Richard Hubberthorne and George Whitehead to Norwich, and Thomas Holme who went into Wales. The biblical parallel did not have to imply numerical exactitude—some earlier editions of the *Journal* give the number as 'above sixty'—rather it drew attention to the missionary endeavour, undertaken in pairs. Nonetheless, researchers have found it instructive to list participants and the places to which they travelled.

In 1907, under the title *First Publishers of Truth*, Norman Penney edited a set of manuscripts that gave accounts of the establishment of Friends' Meetings in England, Wales, and Scotland. Nearly a fifth of the 200 people named were women (Penney 1907). Ernest Taylor drew upon this for his account of the preachers, in which he listed sixty-six men and women, most of whom set forth in 1654. He also included Margaret Fell, who provided essential support but whose own journeys were undertaken in later years (Taylor 1994, 40–41). This spreading out of Quaker witness prompted Fox to write a paper in 1654 expounding belief in the justification in the Light of Christ and urging those who spoke in faraway places to 'see that it be in the life of God' (Fox 1952, 174–5). Some women preachers, of whom Ann Audland is an example, not only spoke in public but defended their right to do so in published writings.

Care was taken of the ministers' practical as well as their spiritual needs. Friends expressed contempt of the arrangements for providing ministers with a regular income and frequently referred to the recipients as a 'hireling ministry', but recognized that householders should provide free hospitality to those who visited them to give spiritual ministry. Since hospitality alone was insufficient to cover the needs of those who were unable to pursue their livelihoods while travelling, Friends contributed to the fund established at Kendal for providing help to those who travelled in the ministry or were imprisoned, and for general administrative purposes. For several years Margaret Fell, whose home at Swarthmoor Hall became a centre for travelling Friends and who kept up a prolific correspondence with them, took charge of this fund (Braithwaite 1979, 135–6).

Characterized by their opponents as subversive disturbers of the peace, these early Quaker missionaries often drew crowds estimated in hundreds to their preaching, particularly when it took place in the streets and marketplaces. So large were the 'threshing' meetings in London that Francis Howgill wrote of the great difficulty of separating those who had been reached by his and Edward Burrough's preaching from the uncommitted crowd. Similar crowds attended John Camm and John Audland in Bristol (Braithwaite 1981, 160, 169, 182). Others who undertook journeys around this time included William Caton, who accompanied John Stubbs to Kent and in 1656 was in Scotland with Stephen Crisp. In common with travelling preachers from other Nonconformist groups, those who went beyond their own parishes might find themselves arrested as vagrants. As Richard Vann has described, Ann Blaykling, when apprehended by the civil authorities in Norfolk in 1655, carried not only information on the state of the roads but a list of places and the names of possible contacts (Vann 1969, 10–11). However, although many Friends' Meetings were established as a result of this surge, some cities that would be important Quaker centres in later years, for example, Norwich and York, gained fewer early adherents than might have been expected from the size of their populations. Stephen Crisp's work in northern counties was successful but in Scotland his faithfulness and that of William Caton did not bear immediate fruit (Burnet, 1952, 45–6). However, as the new message spread the number of those convinced who themselves felt called to proclaim it increased. Among them was the young James Parnell, who worked in the eastern counties until he was imprisoned in Colchester for causing a disturbance and died there in 1656.

To claim direct revelation from God was to place oneself alongside Ranters and Muggletonians rather than Presbyterians, Independents, and the moderates among the Baptists who enjoyed a measure of freedom to practice their religion. Quakers who disturbed church services, went naked, or wore sackcloth and ashes as a sign of impending divine judgement were, as Richard Allen has demonstrated with reference to Quakers in Wales, widely perceived as deviant (Allen 2007a, 88). Such behaviour was repudiated neither by Fox, who had similarly acted out his message, nor by other leading Quakers. When James Nayler (1618?–60) entered Bristol on horseback in 1656 surrounded by followers in a manner that re-enacted Christ's entry into Jerusalem, his action provoked arrest on a charge of blasphemy and caused deep division among Friends. As Erin Bell has ably demonstrated in her account of the 'rehabilitation' of Nayler, in the eighteenth century members of the Second Day Morning Meeting in London, anxious to meet the needs of their own time, made numerous decisions relating to accounts of this episode and to the texts of Nayler's own works (Bell 2008). Later generations of travelling ministers would know of him through these edited works of a penitent predecessor.

Travel within England, Scotland, and Wales presented hazards in the form of poor roads and attacks by robbers. To undertake travel overseas was to face the likelihood of a long wait for favourable winds followed by the possibility of capture by pirates, and uncertainty as to one's reception on arrival. With great fortitude several Quaker men and women faced these challenges. In 1653 William Edmundson (1627–1712), who had settled in Ireland, was visiting the north of England when James Nayler's preaching convinced him. His home in Lurgan became the centre for a slowly growing Meeting. The first ministering Friends to visit from England were James Lancaster, Miles Halhead, and Miles Bateman in 1654, followed shortly afterwards by James Tiffin (Braithwaite 1981, 211). Edward Burrough (1634–63), who visited Ireland in 1655 with Francis Howgill (1618–69), convinced the Baptist John Perrot (d. 1665). In 1657, together with Beatrice

Buckley, Mary Fisher, and others, Perrot set out for Turkey. From Leghorn Mary Fisher made her way to the camp of the sultan at Adrianopolis, where she gave the message that she had felt called by God to deliver (Barbour and Frost 1994, 315). Kenneth Carroll has described Perrot's subsequent journey to Rome with John Luffe, and his imprisonment (Carroll 1971). The first journeys to Protestant Europe and America began in the second half of the 1650s. William Caton (1636–65) and William Stubbs in 1655, followed by William Ames, spread the Quaker message to Holland, long a refuge for Puritans from England, and the European area most receptive to the early Quaker preachers.

As Hugh Barbour and J. William Frost have pointed out, 'in general Friends made converts only when there were substantial numbers of English people'. Since Ireland, the West Indies, and North America were being colonized, Quakers travelled to and found followers in those areas. Their account of the arrival of Quaker preachers in America provides a succinct analysis of the differing Protestant religious and political establishments that Friends encountered, varying from the extreme punitive response in Massachusetts to the more tolerant attitude in Rhode Island (Barbour and Frost 1994, 49–59). Mary Fisher and Ann Austin arrived first, reaching Boston in 1656, but were soon expelled. Eight more Friends who arrived shortly afterwards were also expelled. In Massachusetts the differences between the ruling Congregationalists and the Quakers seemed irreconcilable, and the persistence of Quakers in returning time and again in defiance of banishment was so strong that between 1659 and 1661 the English Quakers Marmaduke Stephenson and William Robinson, Mary Dyer from Rhode Island and William Leddra from Barbados were executed.

Persecution, but Expanding Settlement 1666–c.1691

In England eschatological expectations continued to fade as it became clear that plague and fire had not heralded the dawn of a millennium. Members of the government and Church of England clergy still hoped that all Protestant Dissenters could be drawn back into one national Church, but, as Richard Allen has shown in chapter 2 within this volume entitled 'Restoration Quakerism, 1660–1691', extremely repressive legislation—the Clarendon Code—was introduced between 1661 and 1664 in an endeavour to enforce their vision. There was intermittent respite from the effects of these and subsequent laws, but it could not be relied upon to last. Quaker ministers continued their evangelistic work and took the consequences; Richard Hubberthorne died in prison in 1662, as did Edward Burrough in 1662/3, and Francis Howgill in 1669, while William Dewsbury (1621–88) survived but wrote towards the end of his life that he had been a prisoner in Warwick for nineteen years, four of them in close confinement (Braithwaite 1979, 25, 37, 449). Even from 1689, with the passing of the 'Toleration Act' that permitted Protestant Dissenters conditional freedom to worship, contemporary Friends could not be certain that the Act would not be repealed. For Friends from England, Ireland, Scotland, and Wales, who felt divinely led to travel overseas, the Quaker settlement of Pennsylvania in the 1680s would in due course provide a welcoming destination additional to the already receptive colonies such as Rhode Island and, by the mid-1660s, New York and Maryland.

These were years during which, in an effort to ensure the continuation of Quaker witness and to protect Friends who were suffering persecution, George Fox, William Dewsbury and other leading Friends endeavoured to establish a structure of Monthly, Quarterly, and Yearly Meetings upon a firmer basis than the informal and irregular gatherings, such as those at Kendal and Skipton, that had hitherto sufficed. Fox visited Ireland in 1669, and in 1671, accompanied by twelve other Quakers, embarked on a journey to Barbados, Jamaica, and America that continued until 1673 (Barbour and Frost 1994, 316). In addition to holding public meetings, he spent much effort writing and speaking on the need to strengthen organizational structure.

In 1669 Fox gave advice to Friends in the ministry: 'All ye that believe in the light, as Christ hath commanded... that minister abroad, or go abroad in cities, towns, countries [counties], or nations, do not judge one another, nor reflect upon one another in public meetings; for that hurts the hearers.' He expected to be informed about their journeys, complaining to ministers in Pennsylvania and New Jersey in 1685 that 'I was glad to hear from you, but you gave me no account of the increase of truth amongst you, nor what meetings you have had amongst the Indian kings... nor of your visiting Friends in New England, Virginia and Carolina [sic]' (Fox 1990, 13, 291). In an epistle probably dating from about 1675 the long-experienced minister Charles Marshall advised those who were taking their first steps as ministers to 'wait diligently... to know the appointed time' to give their message (Marshall 1704, 193).

By the time Fox died in 1691 the organizational structure, with some regional variations, was recognizably in place across the Quaker world and would greatly facilitate the practical arrangements necessary to support those who travelled as public Friends.

A PERIOD OF UNIFIED ORGANIZATION AND CONSIDERABLE QUAKER UNITY 1692–1805

Once Friends were certain that they had a call to travel beyond the area of the Quarterly Meeting in which they lived, they applied to the men's Monthly Meeting for a certificate that could endorse their concern and their home reputation, and indicate the proposed direction of travel. If they proposed travelling overseas, they sought the approval of their Quarterly and Yearly Meeting, or, if Yearly Meeting was not sitting, the senior Meeting of Ministers and Elders (in the case of London Yearly Meeting this was the Second Day 'Morning Meeting'). William Penn followed this procedure when he applied to go to Pennsylvania in 1699 (Morning Meeting 1699, 298–9). Ministers presented their certificates to the Meetings they visited for endorsement by the clerks. They were helped with expenses where necessary, and given hospitality by the Meetings they visited, whose members would provide guides to take them on the next stage of their journeys. When Rachel Wilson (1720–75) was about to embark on the return journey to England at the end of 1769 Friends arranged for the supplies she would need and for the conveyance of her luggage (Somervell 1924, 66–7). On return home ministers would give a report on the journey.

The request for a certificate was not always granted, but the refusal did not necessarily imply disapproval. When Sarah Collier, for example, told Gainsborough Monthly Meeting in 1718 that she intended to visit Lincolnshire and Norfolk, members thought it unnecessary to give her a certificate because she was 'no stranger' in the areas she intended to visit (Brace 1951, 117). In the light of her experience and bearing in mind the lack of archival records of meetings of ministers in quarterly meetings within London Yearly Meeting before 1750, the activity of its travelling ministers in the period between 1692 and about 1750 may be considerably under-recorded. In England parish overseers were liable to send strangers back to wherever was deemed their place of settlement. Carrying certificates therefore protected ministers from charges of vagrancy as well as reassuring Meetings of the standing of their visitors.

Ministers visiting London gathered to decide who would attend which Meetings on the following Sunday (or First Day). In 1722 William Gibson, a London Friend who had, some years previously been granted a certificate to travel by the Quarterly Meeting but whose qualification to do so had come into question, entered his name in the Book of Ministering Friends, an action to which the members of the Morning Meeting objected. Gibson appealed to the Quarterly Meeting and Yearly Meeting. In recounting the incident Norman Penney and Isaac Sharp, the editors of *JFHS*, quoted the minute of Yearly Meeting 1723 that the 'Sole Right to disown a Minister or other Person belongs to Monthly, Quarterly, Halfe Yearly or Yearly Meetings. After the following 8th of 7th month [September] no minister's name should be entered in the book until he or she produced a certificate from the home Monthly or Quarterly Meeting' (Penney 1903/4, 22–6).

Although they were not specifically named as elders, Philadelphia Yearly Meeting called for the appointment of two or more 'prudent solid Friends' to sit in these meetings in 1714 (Jones 1911, I, 538). In London it was in 1727 that the Yearly Meeting minuted that Monthly Meetings should 'appoint some serious, discreet, and judicious friends, who are not ministers, tenderly to encourage and help young ministers' (*Extracts* 1783, 99), and gave them the right to attend meetings of ministers.

In addition to delivering their message at appointed gatherings ministers frequently felt the need to pass on their experiences more widely, whether orally, in manuscripts intended to for family reading, or in published form. Abiah Darby and Joseph Oxley, for example, produced accounts for their families (Labouchere 1988; Pike and Oxley 1837). Often written up late in life and published after the author's death, the journal bore witness to God's work in his or her life and, in the words of John Griffith, would become 'a lasting memorial and testimony to the truth' that might 'afford profitable way-marks to some weary travellers, who are seeking a city…whose builder and maker is God' (Griffith 1779, [1]–2). In using the evidence of such journals as his, the researcher has, of course, to bear in mind that most had been assembled well after the events and had passed through the hands of either the Morning Meeting or the established editing groups within other Yearly Meetings.

Not all ministers active during the years 1692–1805 who left accounts of their lives recorded in detail their calling to the ministry but those who did so frequently described feelings of unworthiness and hesitation. Lydia Lancaster (1683–1761), for example, became aware of what might be required of her at the age of 14, but endured ten years of 'a long howling wilderness' until she yielded and gave her first ministry (Skidmore 2003, 10). The length of her delay may be at the extreme, but the reluctance is understandable. In meetings for worship the worshipper had to test whether the inward message that he or she perceived was one for him or herself or should be shared, in speech or prayer, with the whole meeting. For the young Joseph Oxley (1715–75) the first act of obedience was simply to stand up with head uncovered in silent prayer and then resume his seat (Pike and Oxley 1837, 231–2). Those newly undertaking, or relatively inexperienced, in travelling in the ministry were comforted to have the nurturing company of a more experienced minister. John Griffith recalled his anxiety when he was living in Pennsylvania and, feeling called upon to visit New Jersey, embarked upon the process of gaining a certificate without knowing who his companion would be. Fellow minister John Churchman recommended him to William Brown, who likewise had been seeking a companion (Griffith 1779, 43–4).

In 1702 the London [Morning] Meeting of Ministering Friends drew up wide-ranging guidance for ministers relating to their exercise of their gifts and to their conduct. They were, for example, to refrain from restlessness when listening to another minister, to avoid long preambles, misquoting of Scripture, affectation of speech and 'hurting Meetings towards Conclusion by unnecessary additions'. In conduct they were expected to be 'Examples of Meekness, Temperance and Charity'. The advice that men and women should not travel as companions sought to pre-empt gossip but some of the issues are open to the interpretation that male, predominantly London-based ministers sought to ensure conformance with their authority. The women were not to 'hinder their Brethren' in public meetings, and men were to have 'Charity towards' the women; none were to circulate manuscripts and thus arouse expectations that publication would ensue before the texts had been approved by the Morning Meeting; and the practice of prophesying against any 'Nation, Town, City or Person' was now cautioned against as action typical of those who 'follow their own Spirits' (Morning Meeting 1702, 74). Richard Allen (2007b, 54–72) has examined the mixed reactions of Friend to the 'tempestuous' preaching career of the Norwegian Quaker Christopher Meidel (c.1659–c. 1715). Although controversial within London Yearly Meeting, preaching in streets and marketplaces did persist. Mercy Bell was neither encouraged nor specifically forbidden when she walked the London streets in 1753 calling for repentance (P[hipps] 1754). Abiah Darby, on the other hand, wished that she had been encouraged to go into the marketplace when she visited Great Yarmouth in 1762 (Labouchere 1988, 115). With minor amendments the advice of 1702 or their equivalents in other Yearly Meetings operated throughout this period and across the Quaker world for, as Rebecca Larson has stated, 'From Charleston to Dublin, "Children of Light" identified themselves as one community linked by shared beliefs, instead of geographical boundaries' (Larson 1999, 40).

Margaret Hope Bacon cited sources in the Quaker collection, Haverford College, that list some 141 American Friends who travelled to Britain or Europe between 1685 and 1835, and 185 as the number of British Friends travelling to the American colonies and United States between 1656 and 1843 (Bacon 1994, 7–8). Numbers in such accounts need to be treated with caution, family and business reasons for travel, for example, may have overlapped with ministerial callings resulting in discrepancies between lists. Nevertheless, bearing in mind that each minister came with the recommendation of his or her Meeting, and that some made more than one journey, they do demonstrate the potential influence that ministers could exercise. In addition to holding specially appointed meetings to attract members of the public, they would attend meetings for worship and business, and might also carry out visits to families. The latter particularly might occasion an unplanned 'opportunity' for worship with an individual. Vocal ministry might also reach hearers in ways of which the speaker was unaware. On a religious visit during which she stayed with the Darbys at Coalbrookdale in 1746, Mary Kirby (1709–79) announced that one then present would be called to preach the gospel. Abiah Darby knew herself to be the one intended (Labouchere 1988, 42).

It is only possible to give a few examples here to indicate the spread of the travellers in Ireland, Europe, the West Indies, and the American colonies and United States. John Dickinson (1659–1741), who travelled through England, Scotland, and Wales, also visited Ireland twelve times and America three times as well as Barbados, Holland, and Germany (Wilson and Dickinson 1847). In addition to travelling in England, Joseph Gill of Dublin (1674–1741) visited America where he attended well over 300 Meetings (Harrison 2008). Elizabeth Ashbridge (1713–55) and Jane Fenn Hoskens (1694–1764), born in England to Anglican parents, became ministers when living in America; Hoskens visited Ireland in 1728 (Larson 1999). Susannah Morris paid two ministerial visits to England (Bacon 1994). Four ministers, American John Churchman (1705–75), John Griffith (1713–76), who had settled back in England, and the English Samuel Fothergill (1715–72) and Catharine Payton Phillips (1726–94) may be mentioned as among those notably active in the reform movement that took hold within the Quaker movement in the 1750s (Marietta 2007; Skidmore 2003).

THEOLOGICAL, POLITICAL, AND SOCIAL ISSUES, C.1646–1805

Early Quakers felt that George Fox's message that Christ had returned to be their inward teacher carried the implication that they were participating in an end-time and that it was incumbent upon them to spread this teaching. Many English Protestants held apocalyptic views in the 1650s but these faded as the upheavals of civil war and the disasters of plague and the fire of London passed without heralding a second coming. After the passing of the Lord's Day Act of 1656, tackling clergy following sermons and Sunday travel were further restricted (Braithwaite 1979, 450–1).

Performing healings and denouncing the wickedness of individuals and cities, characteristic of the early years, persisted despite the sufferings endured under penal legislation. As has been mentioned, there was at the time no guarantee that the benefits obtained under the terms of the English Toleration Act of 1689 would continue. When in the epistle of 1695, Friends at London Yearly Meeting encouraged 'you, whom the Lord hath gifted with a public testimony for his name and truth, will, in this day of liberty, be diligent to visit the heritage of God in their meetings' (London Yearly Meeting 1818, 88), they were aware that there were many people, especially among the clergy who argued that Quakers were not orthodox (Trinitarian) Christians. Nevertheless, men and women in the eighteenth century were increasingly influenced by the cult of sensibility that associated women with emotion and may have affected the adulatory manner in which ministers such as Edmund Peckover were sometimes received (Fothergill 1971, 113).

Robert Barclay's *Apology* (2002), considered in chapter 2 within this volume entitled 'Restoration Quakerism, 1660–1691' and in chapter 3 within this volume entitled 'Quietist Quakerism, 1692–c.1805', was the dominant theological work in this period. It underpinned, for example, the work of Joseph Phipps (1708–87) and was quoted by the travelling minister Mary Brook (1726?–82) in an appendix to her pamphlet on Quaker worship (Phipps, 1767; Brook 1774). On Quietism, Robynne Rogers Healey is surely correct in her argument that a more nuanced view is called for than that put forward by Braithwaite and Jones (see chapter 3 within this volume entitled 'Quietist Quakerism, 1692–c.1805'). Ministers who travelled under concern felt that their service, with all its attendant personal sacrifices, entailed surrender of the self to the promptings of God inwardly experienced. In an age when Quietist texts were widely read by Protestants (Barry 1998, 276) doubtless many may have read them and reflected that reading in the tone of their journals. Whether less literate ministers did so may be open to question. As demonstrated by the life of John Woolman (1720–72), a minister tireless in his witness against slavery and on behalf of the poor, a Quietist religious orientation and wide reading were not incompatible with engagement in the world (Heller 2003). In common with many of their contemporaries, these Public Friends believed in personal Providence but, with the exception of the study of dreams undertaken by Carla Gerona (2004), those of whom became the subjects of the witness stories that circulated orally, in manuscript, and, to a limited extent in printed form in the eighteenth and early nineteenth centuries is under-researched.

The guidelines for ministers given by writers such as Charles Marshall and set out by ministers and elders were much in accord with the work of Samuel Bownas (1676–1753), who, out of long experience as a minister, wrote a treatise on ministry (considered in chapter 18 within this volume, entitled 'Ministry and Preaching'). Published after his death, it was enlarged in 1767, and remained much appreciated. He stressed the need for would-be ministers to have a degree of sanctification, showing the fruits of a well-lived life themselves before giving ministry to others. He provided guidance on content and expression, and caution regarding the temptations that might befall ministers. He was particularly anxious that none should hastily judge inexperienced ministers (Bownas 1750).

Politically, the situations within this largely unified Quaker world varied greatly. From its foundation until they began to withdraw from government—which a few did in the 1750s although Friends still constituted half the Assembly in the 1760s—Friends in Philadelphia Yearly Meeting played leading roles in Colonial Pennsylvania, and to a lesser extent in New Jersey and Rhode Island. At the other extreme, within London Yearly Meeting any political influence that Quakers exercised on Parliament was done through lobbying. In some other Yearly Meeting areas Friends could participate at national level but had less control than in Pennsylvania. There is no study of the reform movement within London Yearly Meeting comparable to that undertaken into the colonial northeast by Arthur J. Worrall and Philadelphia Yearly Meeting by Jack Marietta (Worrall 1980; Marietta 2007). In England most men's experience would have been as participants in parish affairs. Travelling ministers helped to draw the Quaker world together but these significant disparities need to be borne in mind.

TRAVELLING AMONG HICKSITE, ORTHODOX, AND EVANGELICAL FRIENDS, 1805–1887

Thomas Hamm has examined the divisions that took place among Friends in this period and provided the historical background against which the account of travelling ministry as an aspect of Quaker witness has to be set (see chapter 4 within this volume entitled 'Hicksite, Orthodox, and Evangelical Quakerism 1805–1887'). Geographically, too, the Quaker world was changing. In the 1780s London Yearly Meeting made its last contacts with the few remaining Friends in Tortola, one of the Virgin Islands, but ministers were visiting new groups sympathetic to Friends in mainland Europe at Congenies and, from 1790, Pyrmont (Jones 1921, I 238). By 1887 several new Yearly Meetings holding diverse theological views would have been established, for example in Canada and Van Dieman's Land (later Australia) and Midwest America. The reception of travelling ministers became a means of spreading separation.

In the same decade that travelling ministers in England and North America were caught up in these schisms in the Quaker world (see chapter 4, this volume), James Backhouse (1794–1869), described by Rufus Jones as one of the 'forerunner[s]' of Quaker missionary work', felt called to preach to prisoners and travelled to Australia with George Washington Walker as companion (Jones 1921, II, 880). For some of the time, he was accompanied by Daniel Wheeler (1771–1840), another of Jones's 'forerunners'. Backhouse in turn joined Wheeler for some of his missionary travels in the South Seas. Backhouse's later ministerial journeys included a visit to Norway.

Mention has been made above of the place of Providence in the lives of ministers. In 1751 American minister Elizabeth Hudson (1722–83) thanked Providence when Edmund Peckover appeared unexpectedly at a meeting in England where she had been feeling distressed (Bacon 1994, 258–60). The account that Rufus Jones gives of the call to travel overseas felt in 1850 by Sybil Jones (1808–73), including the appearance at a Monthly Meetinmg that she was attending of the English minister Benjamin Seebohm (1798–1871), which she interpreted as a sign of divine favour, has the characteristics of the eighteenth-century experience. Hesitating over a calling to undertake work in Africa, and drawn to seek the advice of Seebohn, Jones had known only that he was 'somewhere in America'. Sybil Jones and her husband Eli (1807–99) travelled in America and Europe, but the extensive journeys they undertook in Liberia, Lebanon, and Palestine (they were responsible for founding Quaker schools in Brummana and Ramallah) were missionary in character (Jones 1921, II 894–5; Barbour and Frost 1994, 340).

A reinvigorated sense of calling to evangelize new territories may have been a mark of Orthodox Quakerism, but outward-looking involvement in important social issues was a feature of both Orthodox and Hicksite branches. As Beverly Wilson Palmer has noted in her edition of *Selected Letters of Lucretia Mott* (1793–1880), Mott, some of whose close family members were Orthodox, was 'deeply disturbed' by the Separation (Wilson 2002, xiv). She and her husband remained Hicksite even when opposed by some within her own Philadelphia Yearly Meeting. A travelling minister, she stood out as an abolition-ist and supporter of women's rights who, in common with those Orthodox Friends who were involved in social issues, was willing to work with members of other denominations.

Friends who supported a Gurneyite evangelical stand sought to renew and modernize Quakerism, while being aware of similar movements taking place within other denomina-tions. From about the mid-1860s the external Revival movement in America, (considered in chapters 4 and 9 within this volume) exerted a major influence upon Gurneyite Friends. Once again travelling ministers became very involved. A member of Ohio Yearly Meeting, David Updegraff (1830–94), experienced conversion under Methodist influence in 1860 and sanctification in 1869. According to Thomas Hamm, 'More than any other person Updegraff brought holiness teachings to Friends', gaining many converts (Hamm 1988, 78, 82). Later he played major roles in challenging the Quaker belief that water baptism was unnecessary and in the movement to introduce a paid pastoral ministry. As a trav-elling minister he aggravated the controversy within Iowa Yearly Meeting in 1881 over an article published by Joel Bean that was critical of revivalism. Joel Bean (1825–1914), himself a minister who had travelled to Britain and who held office within Iowa Yearly Meeting, withdrew to California with his wife Hannah (1830–1909), but the controversy pursued them well beyond 1887. Updegraff had a vigorous opponent in the Conservative recorded minister Cyrus W. Harvey (1843–1916) who defended inward (religious) expe-rience as against the 'outward' acts that he saw as characterizing Revivalist worship.

Issues and Assessments, 1805–1887

Although the issues of authority and procedure raised in England and America by the Wilkinson-Story and Keithian controversies lingered into the eighteenth century, neither had caused the long-standing diversification within Quakerism that resulted from the separations in America during the nineteenth century. 'Transatlantic' Quakerism narrowed as Yearly Meetings ceased to communicate with others of a different persuasion or 'branch'.

Issues of belief surrounding Quaker worship and ministry were raised when some ministers advocated the Bible rather than the Inward Light of Christ as the primary authority. The introduction of an individual pastorate similar to that in other Protestant denominations evolved gradually following the American revivals of the 1870s and 1880s, which drew in large numbers of new members with no background in Quakerism. These new members found it hard to understand the lack of reliably regular teaching available to them (Hamm 1988, 124–30; Dandelion 2007, 110–12). The adoption of the pastoral system did not diminish the sense of being called to fulfil the role, indeed in the view of proponents it enhanced it (Hamm 1988, 126), but it did carry the implications of regular preaching by the same person and of permanent financial support. Itinerant ministry, with its emphasis on testing the concerns of individuals to undertake religious visitation to specific areas, sometimes for long periods but with the intention of returning to their home Meetings, continued to be practised by those Meetings that did not appoint pastors.

Only a few travelling ministers can be mentioned here, and there has been little room to indicate the complexities of their beliefs and actions. During this period, individual travelling ministers had to make difficult judgements as to where they stood on theological issues and then to resolve the tension between witnessing to their belief in whatever situations they found themselves and adhering to the advice on ministerial conduct that their Yearly Meetings enjoined. Anna Braithwaite, Thomas Shillitoe, Joseph John Gurney, Cyrus W. Harvey, David Updegraff, and Joel Bean all felt compelled to be clear about truth and proclaim it, but, as the examples of John Wilbur and Joseph John Gurney, and Updegraff and the Beans indicate, personal hurt and animosity might creep in. Ministers such as Lucretia Mott also had to endure the pain of differences within the family circle. Drawing on background sources and a wider range of examples than can be included here, Thomas Hamm has concluded that Hicksite women were 'battling their way into pursuits hitherto exclusively male' (Hamm 1988, 47). Mott was an outstanding example.

Travelling Ministry among Modernist, Liberal, and Evangelical Friends 1887–2010

It is indicative of the extended geographic spread, theological diversity, and varying extent of involvement in social concerns that one chapter in the historical section of the this volume is devoted to the period between 1692 and 1805, whereas four are needed to cover the years between 1887 and 2010. The present section focuses on ways in which these changes have affected travelling ministry as a form of Quaker witness.

Opposition continued between those who sought to accommodate new research, especially in biblical criticism, and those who regarded such an approach as inimical to their beliefs and experiences. In some Yearly Meetings—mostly those that could be described as liberal or Modernist and held silent, unprogrammed meetings for worship—there was a move away from the traditional recording of ministers. London Yearly Meeting discontinued the practice in 1924. Some Friends feared that without such status, entry to hospitals and prisons would be more difficult, but status itself made others uneasy, 'much more responsibility for the care of the Ministry should be taken by the Monthly Meetings' (London Yearly Meeting 1924, 255). It is clear from the edition of *Christian Practice* issued in 1925 that the intention was to widen participation in vocal ministry, not to deny that some men and women had a particular gift for it (London Yearly Meeting 1954, 17–26). Other Yearly Meetings, for example, North Carolina (Conservative) and New England, have kept the practice of recording without a break. Provision continues to be made within Britain Yearly Meeting for supporting Friends who have a concern to travel in the ministry and is occasionally followed. However, just as Modernism has produced a tendency towards understanding ministry as arising from shared perceptions rather than direct inspiration (see chapters 5 and 9 within this volume, entitled respectively 'Modernist and Liberal Quakers 1887–2010' and 'Quakers in Theological Context') so within Britain Yearly Meeting, some members may have reservations about words such as 'concern' and 'calling' in relation to such ministry when it refers to spiritual rather than social issues.

As well as giving advice to encourage Friends to discern and develop a call to ministry and to recognize the diversity of practice travelling ministers may encounter, many Yearly Meetings provide Friends whose concern to travel in the ministry has been approved with supporting minutes of liberation. Many now also have advice and arrangements for Friends who are travelling abroad for other reasons (Britain Yearly Meeting 2009, sections 13.28–13.30; Ireland Yearly Meeting 2000, 15; Baltimore Yearly Meeting 2001, 63–4).

Missionary activity continued among Orthodox, Evangelical, and (to a lesser extent Modernist) Friends, leading to the establishment of long-term appointments of staff and, in due course, the establishment of new Yearly Meetings. By 2005 the Quaker world spread across the Americas, Europe, Asia, and Africa (Dandelion 2007, 177–9). A parallel increase in the volume and nature of work undertaken within Yearly Meetings to further the witness of their own members similarly led to an increase in long-term appointments, and movements developed in support of communication and coordination between Yearly Meetings, for example, Friends United Meeting and Friends World Committee for Consultation. An analysis of visitors to Britain Yearly Meeting over the years between 1995 and 1999, undertaken in preparation for this chapter, revealed over 180 visitors representing forty countries, some of whom were attending in an official capacity, but as the Yearly Meeting does not keep copies of the certificates it endorses, only the minutes of the originating Meetings might reveal the extent to which visitors may heve been exercising a 'travelling ministry'.

Suspicion of intellectual study diminished over this period, which saw the development of Quaker centres of learning that provided for academic and general study, including support for vocal and practical ministry. Earlham School of Religion (established in 1960) for example, has the training of pastors within its remit. Woodbrooke Quaker Study Centre's well-established course for Liberal Friends on 'Equipping for Ministry' interprets the term 'ministry' broadly, providing in 2011 opportunities to explore the Quaker tradition, 'Experience of the Spirit', and 'Engagement with the World'.

In *Walk Worthy of Your Calling*, Margery Post Abbott has noted a shift in the way that much travel in the ministry originates: 'most of my travel in the ministry has been on the modern model of response to invitation' (Abbott and Parsons 2004, 16). That this model was operating in London Yearly Meeting is apparent from the experience of Elfrida Vipont Foulds (1902–92) for whom the process of discernment in 1950 came after the invitation to represent the Yearly Meeting at the gathering of Friends United Meeting in Richmond, Indiana (Hartshorne 2010, 68). Margery Post Abbott and Peggy Senger Parsons' compilation spans all aspects of travelling ministry, from calling and nurture to 'classic' travel and 'New Forms of Ministry in an Age of Institutions'. Contributors, drawn from Conservative, Liberal, and Evangelical Quaker backgrounds and countries, including, as examples, Diego Chuyma from Bolivia, Oliver Kisaka Simiyu from Kenya, William Taber from Ohio, and David Niyonzima from Burundi.

To what extent travelling ministers in the twenty-first century have succeeded in conveying their messages and unifying Friends will be for future members and researchers to evaluate. Thus far travelling ministry as a form of Quaker witness has recognizably survived the tensions that such endeavours contain between transmission of values and adaptability.

Suggested Further Reading

Abbott, Margery P. and Peggy S. Parsons (eds.) (2004) *Walk worthy of your calling: Quakers and the traveling Ministry.* Richmond, Ind: Friends United Press.

Braithwaite, William C. (1981 [1955]) *The beginnings of Quakerism* (2nd edn.) York: William Sessions.

———(1979 [1961]) *The second period of Quakerism* (2nd edn.) York: William Sessions.

Hamm, Thomas D. (1992 [1988]) *The transformation of American Quakerism: Orthodox Friends, 1800–1907.* Bloomington and Indianapolis: Indiana University Press.

Ingle, H. Larry (1988) *Quakers in conflict: the Hicksite Reformation* (2nd edn.) Wallingford, PA: Pendle Hill Publications.

Jones, Rufus M. (1921) *The later periods of Quakerism.* 2 vols. London: Macmillan.

Larson, Rebecca (1999) *Daughters of Light: Quaker women preaching and prophesying in the colonies and abroad, 1700–1775.* New York: Alfred A. Knopf.

....

CHAPTER 20

MISSION

....

JACALYNN STUCKEY WELLING

AT the opening of the twenty-first century, global membership in Friends Meetings and churches stood at nearly 350,000. Of those, less than five per cent were associated with Britain Yearly Meeting, the founding body of Quakers (Friends World Committee for Consultation 2007). A Friend in the twenty-first century was more likely to be a person of colour or gather in a pastoral meeting where the style of worship might be more exuberant than quiet. Indeed, the largest concentration of Friends in the world is found not in Europe or North America, but in East Africa. The global expansion of the Religious Society of Friends was largely due to evangelistic outreach by Quaker missionaries who ventured into seemingly remote corners of the world. Since the eighteenth century, however, mission also encompassed social activism and reform. This chapter explores the missionary activities of the various branches of Friends, including the initial impetus for itinerant ministry beyond the English Midlands, and an evolving sense of mission work over time. Mirroring transformative theological, intellectual, and social trends within Quakerdom, mission in a Friends' context eventually comprised a wide range of endeavours, including global witness, philanthropy, and social reform.

BACKGROUND

....

George Fox's (1624–91) own mystical religious experience—through which he came to comprehend experientially that the divine Light of Christ was equally accessible to all people—impelled him to bring to others the good news of the Light Within (Fox 1995, 11). Fox and his coreligionists believed that those who heeded the Light Within could enter a state of spiritual perfection, but also held that the Light might dim for those who ignored or rejected its leadings (Russell 1942, 48–9). Children of the Light, as they were often called, therefore felt an urgent call to share the Gospel message with men and women who had yet to experience the Light of Christ, including those who did not live within the bounds of historically Christian lands within Europe, northern Africa, and West Asia (Dandelion 2007, 22–3).

A significant moment in the missionary trajectory of the Religious Society of Friends came in 1652 in England's Lake District, an area that was Christian by tradition but no longer vibrant in the faith (Barbour and Frost 1994, 6). Already a travelling minister, Fox came upon nearby Pendle Hill and felt divinely called to climb it and, as he later recalled, the 'Lord let me see in what places he had a great people to be gathered' (Fox 1995, 103–4; Braithwaite 1955, 78–9). An inspired Fox descended into the local villages, where hundreds were drawn to his teachings. Thereafter, a number of newly convinced men and women from the region followed the biblical example of the early disciples and travelled in pairs throughout England, testifying to the direct availability of God's truth and speaking of Christ's coming Kingdom. (In Quaker parlance, 'convinced' is somewhat akin to 'conversion' within some Christian sects.)

Like the seventy-two who were sent by Jesus to the villages of Palestine, these first Quaker missionaries—sometimes called the 'Valiant Sixty'—travelled lightly, preached zealously, and endured harassment and persecution from those who doubted the verity of Friends teachings or felt threatened by the socially levelling effects that Quaker testimonies (such as peace-making and equality) might have on society (Barbour and Frost 1994, 29). Nevertheless, these first Friends missionaries remained undaunted and thus expanded the circle of Friends throughout Britain by publicly bearing witness to the Light Within (Braithwaite 1912, 151).

Early Missionaries

Friends did not restrict their evangelistic sights to Britain, but preached in the colonies along the western Atlantic littoral or pressed eastwards to continental Europe and places more remote. Evangelism was not without its challenges. Quaker messengers were first introduced to the travails of life on the road while preaching in the villages and towns of England. Mary Fisher (c.1623–98), who would later travel to the Americas and western Asia, was arrested and whipped on orders from the mayor of Cambridge after engaging in a heated theological debate with young university students in 1653 (Besse 1773, 84–5). Courage in the midst of persecution and adversity was typical of the early missionaries who travelled to the British West Indies or American mainland. Quakers who dared to travel to colonial Massachusetts were flogged, fined, imprisoned, or, in the case of four Friends, executed (Jones 1911, 76–84). Impassioned Quaker evangelists were nonetheless resolutely convinced of the rightness of their message and the importance of sharing the Truth with others.

Europe, Africa, and Asia were less fertile fields than was British America. George Fox, who later sojourned in British America from 1671–3, penned epistles (letters of greeting and counsel) to the sovereigns of the Ottoman and Chinese empires, and the Roman Catholic Church. Quaker evangelists set off for the Ottoman empire in 1657 and distant China in 1661. Most were turned back, although the indomitable Mary Fisher did testify to the Ottoman sultan in 1658 (Barbour and Frost 1994, 315). Friends were most successful in Holland and northern Germany, especially in areas that tended to be Protestant rather than Catholic strongholds. Missionaries in Holland established local Meetings of Worship and founded a fledgling Yearly Meeting in the seventeenth century (Bernet 2006, 15–18). Historian William Braithwaite characterized Friends' earliest evangelistic labours outside North America and Holland as nothing more than 'forlorn hopes', but they illustrate the resolve of early Quaker missionaries (Braithwaite 1912, 401 and 429).

HOLY EXPERIMENT AS MISSION

British America was the most fruitful mission field for the first generation of Friends. Meetings were established in the West Indies and North American colonies, particularly in Pennsylvania and east and west Jersey (Jones 1962, 143–4). (The first Yearly Meeting in North America, however, was held in Rhode Island in 1661.) William Penn (1644–1718), who was granted a vast expanse of colonial territory by the British Crown in the late seventeenth century, envisioned a sanctuary for an array of persecuted peoples. Penn's 'Holy Experiment' was a haven for oft-maligned Quakers and other religious groups and represented a different kind of mission—one that did not focus solely on preaching and evangelizing, but on social reform. Penn hoped that settlers would live in harmony amongst themselves under the principle of mutual toleration, not only with each other but also with Native Americans. Although Penn was hopeful that the concept of a 'divine universal light' would resonate with Amerindians, Friends were never particularly successful in drawing native peoples into membership. Instead Penn promoted the development of his vast holdings and the colony became an important commercial venture (Hinderaker 1997, 102). However, Penn cultivated a warm relationship with Native Americans from which flourished a lasting good will between Friends and indigenous peoples (Jones 1962, 498). As a result, significant pockets of Quaker settlement, as well as influence, extended deeper into North America.

QUIETIST MISSION AND REFORM

Penn's Holy Experiment was a precursor to a broader understanding of mission among Friends, one that accompanied a new phase within the Society. By the end of the seventeenth century, itinerant proselytizing gave way to a different type of mission activity, shaped in part by a trend known as Quietism, in which Friends drew inwards, turned away from the larger society, and renewed their emphasis on the leadings of the Light Within (Kennedy 2001, 16–17). This new phase emerged in both British and

Anglo–American Quakerism and was accompanied by a social exclusivity that discouraged others from entering the fold (Hamm 2003, 15; Vipont 1954, 113). In doing so, noted one historian, Friends shifted markedly from a 'Society seeking to establish God's Kingdom on earth to a peculiar people abjuring earthly pleasures in their quest for the Kingdom of Heaven' (Kennedy 2001, 17). While Quietism did not diminish Friends' concern about the spiritual welfare of non-believers, years of persecution had sensitized them to the plight of the disenfranchised. Quakers increasingly championed social causes and the relatively small body was disproportionately represented among humanitarians on both sides of the Atlantic. Quietist Quakers were involved in a variety of social concerns, including prison reform, peace, temperance, anti-slavery activities, and aid to Native Americans (Hamm 1988, 10; Isichei 1970, 212).

More than any other Quietist Friend, John Woolman (1720–72), an eighteenth-century travelling minister, exemplified Quaker concern for others. Deeply sensitive to the circumstances of those in bondage, 'whose souls were as precious as our own', Woolman implored slave-owners to acquit themselves of the wickedness of slavery. During a stirring session at Philadelphia Yearly Meeting in 1758, Woolman appealed to the delegates to consider the denigrating effects of treating people as chattels, admonishing them to manumit enslaved individuals (Heron 1995, 9; Jones 1962, 396). Over time, Friends throughout the colonies eventually espoused an anti-slavery stance, and slaveholding became grounds for disownment and an anomaly among Quakers. The Quietist emphasis on inward purity, the belief that slavery was spiritually corrupting for both the captive and the master, and a growing chorus of voices who shared Woolman's view contributed to Friends' staunch opposition to slavery by the early nineteenth century (McDaniel and Julye 2009, 30–2).

In addition to abolitionism, Quietist Friends focused on a variety of philanthropic activities. Central among those endeavours was mission work among Amerindians. Because Friends on both sides of the Atlantic had long opposed the maltreatment of indigenous peoples and had advanced tribal interests in treaty negotiations with those of European descent, Native Americans were more open to cooperating with Quakers than other religious sects. In 1756, Philadelphia Friends founded the Friendly Association for Regaining and Preserving Peace with the Indians by Pacific Measures to advocate for Native Americans, the first time European–American Quakers organized formally to defend the rights of the original residents of the Americas (Hamm 2003, 33; Jones 1962, 503). Later, Friends established mission compounds to aid various Amerindian nations, sometimes partnering with federal agencies. Although Native Americans usually resisted assimilation and conversion was limited, Friends missionaries introduced European–American plough agriculture among men and tutored Native American women in the domestic arts. While cultural privileging often shaped the form of Quaker mission activities, Friends' emphases on the spiritual equality of all and a desire to evangelize softened social distinctions between the two peoples (Swatzler 2000, 13 and 70).

Although the nineteenth century was marked by divisions within Quakerdom that eventually had an impact on mission practices, a burst of philanthropic activity among both Quietist and increasingly evangelical-leaning Friends ensued (Dorsey 1998, 403).

Philadelphia Quaker women operated charitable organizations for those on the margins of society, including a relief agency for the labouring poor and an evening school for African–American women (Haviland 1994, 422). In Dublin, Irish Friends opened soup shops, distributed clothing, and offered vocational training during the Great Famine in the 1840s (Preston 2004, 105–8). Friends remained at the forefront of abolitionism, founding anti-slavery societies, publishing newspapers, boycotting slave-made goods and services, and harbouring runaway slaves along the Underground Railroad (McDaniel and Julye 2009, 123–5). During the Civil War, Indiana Friend Levi Coffin (1798–1877) served as agent for the Western Freedmen's Aid Society in Cincinnati, an organization founded to bring aid and comfort to refugees of slavery. North American and British Friends offered significant material assistance to runaways and freed individuals as they fled Southern plantations. Nearly five hundred Friends volunteered to teach at the scores of schools established by Quakers in Virginia, South Carolina, Mississippi, Louisiana, and Arkansas in the post-Civil War era (Smith 1969, 159; McDaniel and Julye 2009, 154). Thus Friends' pattern of humanitarian service to others became a permanent expression of Quaker mission (Isichei 1970, 218).

HOME MISSIONS

In the latter half of the nineteenth century, Quakers continued to take on humanitarian and evangelistic projects. Friends in Britain established a distinctive First-Day School initiative that focused on outreach to adults. The first Adult Day School of note was established by Joseph Sturge in Birmingham in 1845. The purpose of adult schools was to teach basic literary skills and offer religious instruction to working-class labourers. Although few pupils became Friends, by 1900 there were 191 Adult Schools. These schools also offered an avenue of purposeful service for young male teachers. Moved by their interactions with the working poor and concerned about the disproportional impact of industrialization on the most vulnerable, young Friends became more sensitive to the need for change in British society (Kennedy 2001, 44–5; Isichei 1970, 263–5). Industrialist George Cadbury (1839–1922) credited his experiences as an Adult School teacher for spurring him to develop a model factory town for his workers on the outskirts of Birmingham in 1878 (Dellheim 1987, 19–20).

Another offshoot of the Adult School movement was the Home Mission Committee, which oversaw evangelistic and pastoral work within Britain. Home mission workers carried the faith to the unchurched, conducted Bible studies, and established new meetings. In doing so, Home Mission staff often came into direct contact with the social ills of British society. A growing awareness of society's problems led to internal conflict over the future direction of the Home Mission Committee. Evangelical-leaning elder members believed that conveying the Gospel message was paramount, while their younger counterparts, influenced by the latest in scientific thought, favoured a programme of social reform. The discussions brought to light both generational and ideological differences.

In 1895 the Home Mission Committee sponsored a conference in Manchester to sort out the divergent visions for the future of domestic mission work (Kennedy 2001, 123). The Manchester Conference was a key turning point in the history of missions among British Friends. The leading lights at the Conference were decidedly liberal and the most influential (Kennedy 2001, 127–30). One of the speakers, William C. Braithwaite, argued that Friends must go beyond 'sentimental' philanthropy, stating 'I am convinced that both the pressure of social problems and the growth of the scientific spirit have been of signal service to Christianity... We have a unique opportunity and if so, a unique responsibility' (Kennedy 2001, 146). Another central figure at the Manchester Conference was John Wilhelm Rowntree, who believed that Friends must not only embrace new theological trends, but also demonstrate the relevance of their faith to the world, and offer solutions to society's problems (Packer 2003, 245). Thereafter, British Friends increasingly participated in ecumenical reform movements, such as the interdenominational Conference of Christian Politics, Economics, and Christianity (COPEC) held in Birmingham in 1924, to address the social conditions of the industrial age (Parker 2005, 34). While British Quakers did not abruptly abandon evangelistic ministry, their home mission activities shifted progressively towards social reform.

American Friends also established home missions committees. Indiana Friends offered aid to the poor, sheltered destitute women and children, and lobbied for prison reform (Swain 2001, 196–8). Friends from several Yearly Meetings formed the Associated Executive Committee of Friends on Indian Affairs (AECIA) in 1869 to coordinate their evangelistic and educational activities among Native Americans in the Central Plains region, many of whom had been resettled from their homes in the East (Illick 1971, 287–8). In 1892, Emma (1859–1924) and Walter Malone (1857–1935) founded Friends Bible Institute in Cleveland, Ohio, developing a programme of study that included assistance to the impoverished in adjacent neighbourhoods. The Malones' mission focus, however, primarily centred on evangelism rather than on Social Gospel initiatives and reflected a pre-millennial eschatological urgency common among Victorian-era evangelicals. Therefore, preaching the Gospel was of paramount importance to Emma and Walter Malone, superseding even humanitarianism. Thus, they prepared their students for pastoral service in the United States and, perhaps more significantly, for mission work abroad.

British Foreign Missions

The foreign missionary enterprise, which peaked between 1890 and 1930, was one of the greatest undertakings in modern history, drawing thousands of men and women, mostly from Britain and North America, to Africa, Asia, and Latin America (Hutchison 1987, 1; Neill 1964, 251). The history of the missionary movement is complicated, evoking images of 'paternalism and an arrogant, insensitive preaching', as Quaker William Barton noted (Institute of Quaker Studies 1971, 43–4). However, missiologist Ron

Stansell suggests that evangelical missionaries 'tended to be far more culturally sensitive and politically savvy than the colonialists and empire-builders, with whom they are usually lumped' (Stansell 2009, 4; Sanneh 2008, 218). Second-generation Friend David Niyonzima of Burundi concurs, arguing that Christian missions fostered unity and reconciliation among the peoples of his country, which were often in conflict (Niyonzima and Fendall 2001, 53). Stansell also posits that Friends missionaries 'saved the Quaker movement from a great eclipse' by facilitating the establishment of vibrant Quaker meetings and churches in East Africa and Central America, among other non-Western regions (Stansell 2009, 7).

Inward-looking Quakers from Britain and North America were latecomers to the missionary movement, although Friends established mission stations in Africa, Asia, and Latin America by the early twentieth century (Jones 1946, 21; Hamm 1988, 58). Quakers typically adopted the Protestant missionary strategy when configuring their missionary tasks, which included evangelism, education, medicine, and vocational training (Barbour and Frost 1994, 209–10; Institute of Quaker Studies 1971, 45). Even so, Friends' emphases on spiritual equality and social justice often created a different dynamic at many of their mission stations. Furthermore, as one historian notes, the democratized nature of evangelical Christianity, which was expressed in a number of Quaker missions, often rendered greater authority to and empowered indigenous Christian leaders 'of marginal status, ordinary education, or limited means'—the type of person for whom Friends had long advocated (Case 2012, 257).

British Friends established the independent Friends Foreign Mission Association (FFMA) in 1868, although their formal entry into foreign mission work came two years earlier when Rachel Metcalfe arrived in India. Like other Friends missionaries who followed her, Metcalfe felt divinely called to service abroad (Milligan 1968, 6; Greenwood 1978, vol. 3, 29). Although the harvest of converts was fairly small in India, missionaries planted colonies for low-caste weavers and helped them locate markets to sell their homespun goods. Vocational training became a mainstay at several Friends missions (Greenwood 1978, 24–8). In addition, British Friends provided shelter and schooling for orphans and were deeply involved in famine relief in India. Those on the margins of society were more likely to convert than India's elites, in part because Christianity transcended caste barriers and social restrictions that bolstered class standing (Greenwood 1978, 38; Stansell 2009, 146, 170).

Additional FFMA mission fields were planted in Madagascar in 1867, in Palestine in 1869, and in China in 1886. Friends' missions bore much fruit in Madagascar, planting nearly one hundred churches and claiming thousands of converts, scores of village schools, boys and girls high schools, and a hospital. The mission later merged with the Church of Jesus Christ in Madagascar. For a time, the Friends hospital was the only place on the island where one could seek medical attention (Milligan 1968, 7). Resistance to the Quaker faith tended to be fairly strong in some areas, so British Friends gradually shifted from evangelism to a greater emphasis on more practical work, especially in the field of education. Few converted to Quaker Christianity in Palestine, but parents clamoured for highly coveted spots at Ramallah Friends School for their children. Directed by Palestinian Christians during its first decade of existence and later overseen by Friends United Meeting in the United States, Ramallah School was a collaborative effort among local Palestinians and Quaker missionary educators. British Friends partnered with other Protestant groups to found West China Union University in Chongqing in 1905. The Chinese were also slow to embrace Christianity, but not Western schools and medicine. In 1906, British Friends opened Chongqing International Institute, a Quaker centre that offered educational and public health programmes. Although evangelism was a central component of their work in China, an array of social programmes converged with pastoral outreach.

With the outbreak of the First World War, British Friends largely abandoned evangelism for relief. During the war, they formed an ambulance committee, sent aid to refugees on the Continent, and offered assistance to foreigners stranded in internment camps. In time, the rhetoric of 'mission' was replaced by an emphasis on 'concern' or 'service' in Britain, as reflected in the founding of the Council for International Service (CIS) in 1919 (Milligan 1968, 23, 39). Relief work and peace-making became the primary focal points of mission. After the war, Quaker centres were established in major cities as international institutions for peace-making (Yarrow 1978, 23–4). In 1927, FFMA merged with CIS to form the Friends Service Council, signalling a break from nineteenth-century conceptions of missionary enterprise.

After the First World War, Friends provided food, clothing, shelter, and livestock to rejuvenate war-ravaged communities. During the Spanish Civil War, British and American Friends organized feeding centres and children's homes for the youngest victims of armed conflict (Milligan 1968, 36; Fyrth 1993, 154–5). By the time the Nazi regime rose to power, British Friends were veteran aid workers. They were insistent, however, that the Friends Service Council represented a religious community rather than a professional relief organization. Yet Friends were so adept at meeting the material needs of victims of war that the organization was awarded the Nobel Peace Prize in 1947, sharing it with the American Friends Service Committee. Committed to reconciliation in the post-Second World War era, British Friends established peace camps in Wales, eastern Europe, and Kenya and emerged as global peace-makers.

REVIVALS AND MISSION IN THE AMERICAS

Missionary practice in the United States and Canada generally followed two tracks, one similar to the social witness trajectory found in Britain and the other shaped by the Holiness Movement (Hansen 2005, 45–6; Stansell 2009, 7). The nineteenth-century Holiness Movement was rooted in Wesleyan perfectionism and the belief that one could be instantly sanctified by the baptism of the Holy Spirit. It was also influenced by the Higher Life conferences held annually in Keswick, England, which affirmed missions and global witness as manifestations of being filled by the Holy Spirit (Wacker 2001, 1–2; Spencer 2007, 165–9). A Christ-centred message was paramount to Holiness missionaries, one that was never 'eclipsed by a secularized message of social reform'. This is not to suggest that the Quaker tradition of humanitarianism was abandoned, but Holiness evangelists primarily attended to 'the message of a Jesus who transforms sinners' (Stansell 2009, 268).

American Friends partnered with their English coreligionists in India, Palestine, and Madagascar as they began to organize their own missionary associations in the 1860s and 1870s. Indiana established its first mission in the Mexican coastal state of Tamaulipas in 1871. Before the end of the century, New York Yearly Meeting established a school in Tamaulipas, and Western Yearly Meeting extended the Friends' evangelistic reach to north central Mexico. Iowa Yearly Meeting ministered to Jamaicans of both African and South Asian descent. Quaker women from Philadelphia and Canada sponsored educational initiatives in Japan. Kansas, California, and Oregon Yearly Meetings organized mission work among indigenous people in Alaska, and Ohio Friends evangelized in China and India. In 1894, several of these Yearly Meetings created the American Friends Board of Foreign Missions (AFBFM). When Five Years Meeting (now Friends United Meeting) was established in 1902, the AFBFM became its official board of missions and gradually assumed oversight of missionary activities among most evangelical-leaning individual Yearly Meetings (Rasmussen 1995, 20).

In the twentieth century, new mission fields opened in Cuba, Guatemala, Bolivia, Burundi, Honduras, and British East Africa, the latter being the most fruitful in the history of Friends mission work (Abbott et al 2003, 182–3). Friends African Industrial Mission (FAIM) was initially conceived by Willis Hotchkiss, an alumnus of J. Walter and Emma Malone's Friends Bible Institute, who had served with Africa Inland Mission. Hotchkiss returned to his alma mater and recruited Arthur Chilson and Edgar Hole to join him in British East Africa. In response to their pleas for aid, nine Yearly Meetings formed the FAIM Board in 1901 to oversee a new work. The central purpose of the mission was the 'evangelization of heathen', but its vocational component became a key feature. Hotchkiss, Chilson, and Hole arrived in present-day Kenya in 1902 and established a mission at Kaimosi. Hotchkiss believed that the mission should provide the Luhya people of western Kenya with the financial means by which they could support themselves and the Church. Chilson focused on the industrial wing, including the building of roads, houses, dams, and mills. Hole oversaw the development of the educational branch of the mission, considered a critical evangelizing tool. Later, medical work was established, churches planted, and additional mission stations launched nearby (Rasmussen 1995, 47–8).

The American Friends' interactions with the Luhya people were often shaped by their own cultural backgrounds. Hotchkiss characterized the social order of the Luhya people as 'barbarianism pure and simple with its social anarchy, lawlessness, and consequent instability of character' (Stansell 2009, 27–8). Even so, the Americans never doubted that the minds and hearts of the Luhya were capable of transformation. Hotchkiss would later write, 'Most missionaries wanted African Christians to remain essentially African rather than become an imitation European' (Stansell 2009, 31). Indigenous understandings of spirituality fused with and often strengthened Christian faith in East Africa, as was evident during a revival in 1927 when many of the attendees began 'speaking in tongues' (Rasmussen 1995, 78). Missionary Helen Kersey Ford observed, 'From burdened hearts, [Kenyans] sought forgiveness with tears such as the missionaries had rarely seen in Africa' (Kimball and Kimball 2002, 33).

Over time, interest in Western education and practices invigorated the Kenyan mission, which grew from a handful of converts in its early years to several thousand by the 1930s (Rasmussen 1995, 20, 47–8). Chapels, primary-level 'outschools', secondary schools, and medical programmes were organized. Friends Bible Institute (now Friends Theological College) was founded in Lugulu in 1943 and transferred to Kaimosi in 1950. East Africa Yearly Meeting was officially set off in 1946 and fully independent by 1962. Although some of the older missionaries were reluctant to relinquish their administrative control, subsequent missionary sojourners increasingly envisioned their role as one that offered professional support rather than oversight of the mission (Rasmussen 1995, 103). East African Quakers eventually became missionaries themselves, establishing mission fields in Uganda and Tanzania, and more locally in the Kenyan regions of Turkana and Samburu (Kimball and Kimball 2002, 59, 65, 73). Over a dozen East African Yearly Meetings were established in the following decades and Kenya hosted the largest concentration of Friends in the world by the close of twentieth century.

Although few Quaker missions approached the level of activity in East Africa in size or scale, the American Friends Board of Foreign Missions and its Yearly Meeting partners established mission programmes elsewhere, including the islands of the Caribbean. Friends first came to the region to escape religious intolerance in the late seventeenth century and George Fox preached among them in 1671–72 (Langford 1997, 8). Nearly two centuries later, Iowa Yearly Meeting dispatched Eli Sharpless to the Caribbean region to 'labour there as an evangelist' in 1881 (Langford 1997, 19–20). Iowa Quakers established a mission field in Jamaica in 1883 and AFBFM later founded a mission in Cuba in 1900. However, a number of challenges, including the presence of other Christian churches on the islands, delimited new areas of entry. The Jamaica mission, which was fully transferred to AFBFM oversight in 1910, established meetings for worship and industrial schools, as Friends had done elsewhere. Of particular note was a short-lived ministry among the South Asian population, a marginalized group descended from indentured servants brought to Jamaica from India in the late nineteenth century. Happy Grove School was originally conceived as a residential industrial school for Hindu and Muslim Indian girls to help them assimilate culturally (Langford 1997, 44–5). Happy Grove later extended its reach to other Jamaican children, eventually becoming a co-educational institution. Friends' mission schools here and elsewhere were particularly well regarded by middle-class parents who enrolled their children in Quaker centres of learning, although most converts were disproportionately poor (Hilty [1977], 310). Relatively few who attended Friends' schools became Quaker, yet many self-identified as Christian (Langford 1997, 130). Yearly Meetings were established in Cuba and Jamaica in 1927 and 1941 respectively, and still maintain their association with Friends United Meeting (FUM).

Non-Evangelical Friends were also engaged in mission activities although these more likely exemplified a social witness track, an alternative to evangelistic mission work. Philadelphia Yearly Meeting supported mission work in Japan and the ministry of William Cadbury, who practised and taught medicine in Guangzhou, China (Restaino 1994, 1–2). Especially after the outbreak of the First World War, Philadelphian and those Friends who had been influenced by Modernist trends increasingly focused their attentions on peace-making and social reform. Rufus Jones, a prominent Quaker and respected intellectual, cofounded the American Friends Service Committee (AFSC) in 1917 for those seeking alternative service as conscientious objectors during the Great War. Under Jones's leadership, the organization continued its relief work after the war and beyond. AFSC offered assistance to refugees of the First World War and the Spanish Civil War, established work camps in major American cities during the Great Depression, formed a cooperative community in the heart of Appalachia, provided aid to oppressed Jews during the Nazi regime, and offered assistance at Japanese internment camps during the Second World War, as discussed more extensively in chapter 14 in this volume entitled 'The Kingdom of God, Quakers and the Politics of Compassion'.

The humanitarian reach of the American Friends Service Committee and the British Friends Service Council held appeal in Europe, Africa, Asia, and the Americas, prompting the formation of new meetings. The increasingly international composition of the Religious Society of Friends led to the founding of the Friends World Committee for Consultation (FWCC) in 1937. The purpose of the organization was to transcend differences of geography and theology and promote unity and fellowship among Friends from around the world. In 1948, FWCC established its presence in the United Nations, eventually forming the Quaker United Nations Office. Although not engaged in traditional missionary work, these organizations remained missional in their commitment to Quaker principles.

'Women's Work' in Friends Foreign Missions

Women played a significant role in Friends foreign missions, whether married or single. In the United States, women were at the forefront of the organizational work of missions abroad. Protestant women missionaries comprised over half of the staff at most mission compounds, though they were often expected to defer to the temporal and spiritual authority of their male counterparts (Hunter 1989, 29). Quaker women's missionary societies, including what is now known as the United Society of Friends Women International (founded in 1881), were among those which offered support and funding for missionary programmes. Women's mission work was thought to be especially vital in the nineteenth century given male evangelists' limited access to local women (Semple 2003, 6). Sarah Jenkins of Ohio accentuated the importance of a female missionary presence in foreign places in 1889, arguing that 'Christian women only can grapple successfully with the evils that surround their sex in these dark lands' (*Friends Missionary Advocate* 1889, 85). For this reason, Ohio Yearly Meeting's China mission, founded by Esther Butler in 1890 in Nanjing, was staffed exclusively by women during its first ten years of existence. Women served as superintendents of the China mission from its founding until 1930, long after male missionaries had joined the staff in Nanjing and a second station in Luho. Similarly, the Yearly Meeting's second mission field, this one located in India, was established and directed by women. Delia Fistler and Esther Baird arrived in India in 1892, founded the first Ohio Friends mission station at Nowgong in the central part of India in 1896, established a second mission station at nearby Chhatarpur in 1919, and served as superintendents of the India mission successively. Some women were more gifted administratively and in ministry than others, but this was also the case with their male counterparts (Nixon 1985, 43, 118). Regardless, female Quaker missionaries, who typically outnumbered male colabourers in the field, served in key roles as ministers and mission practitioners. Female staff in various Friends compounds in Asia, Africa, and Latin America founded orphanages, day and boarding schools for children, Bible training institutes for female evangelists, industrial schools, hospitals, and nurses' training schools.

Roxie Reeve, for example, opened the Girls Boarding School in Maragoli, Kenya, in 1921 to prepare young girls in household management and 'mothering skills' (Thomas 2000, 6–7). Yet, Reeve challenged Western notions of patriarchy and domesticity in favour of a more egalitarian interpretation of women's roles via her own life example as an independent working woman. Many of Reeve's students modelled life choices similar to hers, entering the professions, becoming entrepreneurs, taking up leadership roles in their communities, and embracing the Quaker testimony of equality (Thomas 2006, 15–16). In 1951, a Women's Yearly Meeting was established in Kenya through which women organized village meetings, Bible studies, and lessons in the domestic arts. Furthermore, Kenyan Friends women called for equal standing for men and women, often while attending United Nations and other international conferences (Painter 1966, 108–109; Angell 2006c, 121–2).

R. Esther Smith (1870–1947), a missionary from 1906 to 1947, also exemplified the Quaker commitment to equality in her role as field superintendent of California Yearly Meeting's mission in Guatemala (Stansell 2009, 93–4). As was the case in other mission fields, her tenure was not without its challenges. Quaker missionaries were accused of nefarious activities, such as kidnapping children, duping Catholic Christians, and spying for the US government. The schools were understaffed and access to critical supplies was limited. Nevertheless, a revival in September 1918, not dissimilar to the Evangelical revival that burst forth in Kenya ten years later, spurred growth in numbers in the Guatemala mission and contributed to the expansion of Quakerdom in Honduras and Bolivia (Stansell 2009, 101–3). Friends women, whether American or indigenous, played a critical role in that growth.

INTERNATIONALISM AND MISSIONS

By the mid-twentieth century, missioners had fine-tuned their strategies, with some broadening their social programmes and others extending the scope of their evangelistic ministries. As nationalist movements surged, aboriginal leaders pressed for greater involvement in mission functions or the formation of their own Yearly Meetings. Mid-India Yearly Meeting, set off in 1907, was among the first Yearly Meetings established outside Europe and North America. The educational missions at Ramallah in Palestine and Brummana in Lebanon formed the basis of Middle East Yearly Meeting in 1929. As already noted, East Africa Yearly Meeting was set off in 1946. Non-Western Friends established mission fields of their own, such as Japanese Quaker missionaries who ministered to Japanese expatriates in California in the early twentieth century, engaging in what one Quaker scholar called a 'reciprocal model of missions' (Angell 2006a, 3–4). A spectrum of newly established Yearly and local Meetings also emerged on continental Europe in the twentieth century. The growth of international Quakerism accelerated after 1950, with Yearly, Regional, and local Meetings organized in East Asia, India, Australia, New Zealand, and Central and South America.

Friends organizations such as American Friends Service Committee and Britain Yearly Meeting's Quaker Peace and Social Witness (formerly Friends Service Council), remained committed to issues of peace, justice, and social action at home and abroad. Through its Quaker Peace and Social Witness Relief Grants Fund, British Friends funded mine-clearance projects, micro-credit loans, wellness and health services, vocational training, peace initiatives, and disaster relief, among other programmes. Irish Quaker Faith in Action (IQFA) sponsored similar projects in Ireland, Haiti, and South Africa to offer 'practical and spiritual support to the Christian concerns of Irish Friends' (Irish Friends in Action 2011). Evangelical Friends missionaries in India founded or directed ecumenical organizations that were sometimes transnational in scope. Everett Cattell helped organize the Evangelical Fellowship of India in 1951, Clifton and Elizabeth Robinson began to serve with International Christian Leadership (ICL) in 1955, and Anna Nixon developed the Christian Education Department of ICL in 1962 (Nixon 1985, 426).

As Liberal Friends shifted deliberately towards social action after the First World War, Holiness Friends increasingly focused on evangelistic undertakings. After Quaker missionaries were expelled from the People's Republic of China, Evangelical Friends re-established their mission in Taiwan in 1953, focusing on evangelism and church planting. While many Evangelical Quaker missions continued to support vocational programmes, schools, hospitals, and dispensaries, they emphasized 'soul saving' in their ministries. Evangelical Friends Alliance (EFA), comprised of several Holiness-leaning Yearly Meetings, merged the missionary labours of its constituent bodies in 1978 with the creation of its own sending agency—Evangelical Friends Missions (EFM). EFM nurtured existing missions, cultivated new areas of ministry in Asia, Africa, Europe, the

Caribbean, and the Americas, and emphasized discipleship and pastoral training in its mission strategies.

Friends United Meeting fused the traditional evangelism focus of its early missions and the social action emphasis that arose later. The organization maintained or expanded its long-standing educational and medical programmes in Kenya, Jamaica, and Palestine. In the 1960s, FUM launched educational and support programmes for orphaned and dislocated children in Belize and renewed ties to Cuba Yearly Meeting. FUM's Christian peace-making teams sought to reduce violence and foster reconciliation in troubled areas globally.

THE FUTURE OF MISSIONS

The nature of Friends mission by the end of the twentieth century embodied a broad range of evangelical ministries and social programmes. Perhaps more significantly, Asian, African, and Latino Quaker missionaries—who partnered with their European and North American counterparts—emerged as the primary evangelists and activists as the centre of Christianity moved to the Global South and East. New mission fields were often founded or superintended by non-Western missioners. For example, Jamie and Lydia Tabingo began evangelizing in the Philippines in 1978, John and Sangi Vanlal of India commenced work in Nepal in 1983, and Isaiah Bikokwa expanded the scope of Sambura Friends Mission in Kenya in 1995 (Kimball and Kimball 2002, 73). South Indian Friends preached in Bangladesh, Aymara Quakers reached out to various tribal groups in Bolivia, and a number of Quaker seminaries trained indigenous pastoral leaders. As the global labour force migrated across porous national borders, Friends missionaries served diverse populations in areas that had once been fairly homogenous. In Hong Kong, Friends missionaries shifted their outreach from local Chinese to Filipina domestics and migrant labourers from South Asia and East Africa. Missionaries of European descent increasingly served in support, rather than leadership positions, as technical experts, engineers, medical specialists, cross-cultural interpreters, peace-makers, and administrative consultants to indigenous Quaker ministers and activists.

Negotiating local customs with a faith that was both Christian and culturally relevant was often difficult or complicated for both local leaders and foreign missionaries. In the early years of Quaker foreign missions, smoking, drinking, and dancing were banned, and marriage practices and sexual mores were often contested. In the East Africa mission, for example, converts who practiced polygamy were disciplined or ousted from the community of Friends (Rasmussen 1995, 70; Stansell 2009, 31). Less mention was made of homosexuality, which was typically closeted both within and outside of Europe and North America (see chapter 30 in this volume entitled 'Quakers and Sexuality'). Evangelically inclined Yearly Meetings maintained a traditional view on sexuality in their home churches and the mission field. However, local expressions of worship, including dancing, were commonly practised.

Dynamic social activism characterized mission in Liberal Friends meetings and was ascendant in evangelical circles. Canadian Yearly Meeting advocated for aboriginal rights and promoted environmental and sustainability issues. Friends General Conference launched its Ministry on Racism Programme to foster racial reconciliation and promote greater diversity within its Yearly Meetings. Britain's Quaker Social Action sponsored programmes to ease economic deprivation in east London. Several evangelical Yearly Meetings supported disaster services and offered aid to those affected by local and international calamities. One church meeting formed a Justice League whereby members might 'come alongside the oppressed and impoverished' (First Friends Church 2011). In addition, the number of short-term mission and service trips proliferated in North American meetings in the early twenty-first century. Although the trips were primarily evangelistic in nature, most included a service component as well.

Since the founding of Religious Society of Friends, its adherents have recalibrated the meaning of mission over time, from local preaching to global activism and evangelism. These endeavours fostered the geographic expansion of Quakerdom well beyond the United Kingdom and Ireland, resulting in a culturally diverse membership. Friends' missional activities contributed to a wider range of Friends' religious beliefs, a heightened awareness of social injustices, an international reputation for doing good, and the growth of evangelical Christianity globally. Thus missions functioned in part to ensure that Quakerism remained a vital expression of Christian faith and global service well into the twenty-first century.

Suggested Further Reading

Kimball, H. and Kimball, B. (eds.) (2002) *Go into all the world: a centennial celebration of Friends in Africa*. Richmond, IN: Friends United Press.

Langford, M. J. (1997) *The fairest island: history of Jamaican Friends*. Richmond, IN: Friends United Press.

McDaniel, D. and Julye, V. (2009) *Fit for freedom, not for friendship: Quakers, African Americans, and the myth of racial justice*. Philadelphia: Quaker Press of Friends General Conference.

Nixon, E. A. (1985) *A century of planting: a history of the American Friends Mission in India*. Newberg, OR: Barclay Press.

Niyonzima, D. and Fendall, L. (2001) *Unlocking horns: forgiveness and reconciliation in Burundi*. Newberg, OR: Barclay Press.

Rasmussen, A. M. B. (1995) *A history of the Quaker movement in Africa*. London: British Academic Press.

Stansell, R. (2009) *Mission by the Spirit: learning from Quaker examples*. Newberg, OR: Barclay Press.

Swatzler, D. (2000) *A Friend among the Senecas: the Quaker mission to Cornplanters' people*. Mechanicsburg, PA: Stackpole Books.

Thomas, S. S. (2000) 'Transforming the Gospel of Domesticity: Luhya Girls and the Friends African Mission, 1917–1926', *African Studies Review* 43: 1–27.

Tonsing, B. K. (2002) *The Quakers in South Africa: a social witness*. Lewiston, NY: Edwin Mellen Press.

....

CHAPTER 21

QUAKERS, OTHER CHURCHES, AND OTHER FAITHS

....

JANET SCOTT

THE FORMATION OF QUAKER IDENTITY

THE formation of identity for religious groups (and individuals) is influenced by what they are not, as much as by what they are. In order to distinguish and establish a group there is a need to separate it from what surrounds it. This was true for Quakers in England in the seventeenth century. At the same time as Fox was preaching his vision of Christianity (what Penn called 'primitive Christianity revived') he was excoriating the practices both of the Church of England and of the dissenting clergy. As well as having a positive theological foundation, much of traditional Quaker practice can also be seen as 'over-against' the practices and rituals of the Church of England.

A tendency to be negative towards other churches was reinforced by the treatment that Quakers received from them. In England, Friends conducted arguments in words and writing with Anglican, Presbyterian, and Baptist clergy. Mary Fisher (1623?–98) and Elizabeth Williams preaching in Cambridge were pelted with filth by students and whipped at the market cross. When Mary Fisher later travelled to Turkey to preach to the sultan, she was well received and was better treated by the Muslim Turks than by her fellow Christians. She wrote, 'the Seed of them is near unto God, and their kindness has in some measure been shown towards his servants' (*Quaker Faith and Practice* 19:27). With the restoration of the monarchy in 1660 there was a clampdown on dissent, and Quakers with other dissenters were imprisoned for holding meetings for worship, for preaching in public, and for refusing to swear oaths on the Bible.

Elsewhere, there was also persecution. Katherine Evans and Sarah Cheevers were imprisoned by the Inquisition in Malta for three years . They reported that when they were taken to attend Mass they turned their backs on the altar. In North America in the Puritan colony of Massachusetts the legislature determined to banish Quakers on pain of death. William Robinson and Marmaduke Stephenson were hanged, and Mary (d. 1660) was banished but was hanged when she returned. A statue of her now stands in Boston close to the place of her death.

Even after the Act of Toleration in 1689 there was still discrimination in England. Quakers who refused to pay tithes to the Church of England had their goods distrained. As dissenters, men were not able to attend the universities at Cambridge and Oxford, which were religious foundations (no women of any church could attend until the 1870s). Nor could they take any political or civic role. As Quakers engaged in the long struggle for religious freedom, their attitudes were shaped not only by their religious views but also by the power relationships that pitted a minority Society against an Established Church. Nevertheless, although they opposed the other churches as institutions, seeing these as being in error, they saw that individuals within the churches might be members of the invisible church of all those who answered God's call in their hearts. A key text is that of Robert Barclay in his *Apology*:

> There may be members therefore of this Catholick Church both among Heathens, Turks, Jews, and all the several sorts of Christians, Men and Women of Integrity and Simplicity, who tho' blinded in some things in their Understanding, and perhaps burthened with the Superstitions and Formalities of the several Sects, in which they are ingrossed; yet being upright in their Hearts before the Lord, chiefly aiming and labouring to be delivered from Iniquity, and loving to follow Righteousness, are by the secret Touches of this Holy Light in their Souls, inlivened and quickened, thereby secretly united to God, and therethrough become true Members of this Catholick Church. (2002, *Prop. X*)

Thus, the concept of 'that of God in everyone' tempered the opposition to the institutional churches with the recognition that individuals may be 'walking in the Light'. This laid a foundation for better relationships at a later date. The same theological concept applied to members of other faiths—and people of no faith. However, in Britain, the number of member of other faiths was very small and they were also oppressed minorities. So although the theology was the same, the attitudes were not. Quakers could afford to be positive towards those with little power whose presence rarely impinged on their lives.

This inheritance of background and attitudes has meant that for some Quakers, especially in Europe and the East Coast of North America, it has sometimes seemed easier to be accepting of other religions than of other churches. However, in other parts of the world, where Quakerism has grown in different circumstances, and where identity has formed vis-à-vis different groups and cultures, the attitudes and relationships will also be different, even where the theology is the same.

From Separation to Positive Influence

As the eighteenth century began Quakers in Britain were becoming a 'peculiar people'. The plain language and simplicity of dress, the separation in worship, the retention of Puritan habits, the organization, and discipline set them apart from their neighbours. However, as the Industrial Revolution gathered pace, Quakers were engaged in the world. In trade, banking, manufacture, science, and technology, they were involved in the life of their neighbourhoods and becoming a trusted and respectable group. While Quakers changed under the influence of Quietism, the Church of England was also changing, being challenged by the growth of John Wesley's Connexion, which in time developed into the Methodist church. The Methodists' Arminian theology, the emphasis on holiness, the involvement of laity in leadership and, at least initially, the leadership of women, all had some compatibility with Quaker thought and practice.

The Methodists and the growing evangelical wing of the Church of England shared an interest in social reform and as Quakers began to develop social concerns they found allies in other churches. Elizabeth Fry was able to draw on women beyond the boundaries of the Society to assist with her work in prisons. Most notably, the campaign to end the North Atlantic slave trade drew on the services of William Wilberforce, an evangelical Anglican, to speak for the cause in Parliament. Although social contacts were limited, not least because of the danger of 'marrying out', which would lead to disownment from the Society, Quakers began to work with members of other churches. Their theology, without losing its distinctiveness, was influenced by evangelical thinking. Quakers were influential in the setting up of the British and Foreign Bible Society.

In the second half of the nineteenth century, the Quaker rules relaxed at the same time as changes in the wider society allowed dissenters into Parliament and the universities. Contacts with other churches increased as, for example, some Quakers read theology at university, there was an influx of 'convinced' Quakers with backgrounds in other churches, and there was marriage between Quakers and members of other churches.

In North America, though the Quakerism was initially similar, the context was different. A significant factor was the colony, later state, of Pennsylvania founded in 1681. For the first and only time Quakers were a majority and had power, though this did not last long. Their belief in religious freedom meant that they allowed members of other churches to settle in the state. Quakers then became a minority though retaining some influence.

Another significant factor was the presence of the Native Americans. Penn sought to be at peace with the indigenous peoples and to deal fairly with them though this approach was not universal amongst Quakers. The opportunity of close contact with living religions based on tradition and practice and not on written texts provided a different experience from any available in Europe but was taken by very few Quakers.

A third factor was the presence of slavery and the long campaign against it, though this was not uncontroversial. As in Britain, Quakers worked with members of other churches. However, there was a significant difference in that the American Quakers had direct contact with slaves rather than a distant sympathy. These factors of power and race shaped the context and development of Quakerism in North America and helped to fuel the splits in the nineteenth century.

A fourth factor was the sheer size of the country and in the nineteenth century the move westwards. New Yearly Meetings were set up and there were divisions among Quakers on theological as well as social issues. In the second half of the century, the practical problems of expansion combined with a revival movement amongst Quakers. Influenced by the Holiness movement and camp meetings held by other churches, Quakers especially in the West brought in large numbers of converts. The problems of teaching these numbers the faith and of worshipping in the traditional way with so many unaccustomed to the silent way, led to the introduction of programmed and semi-programmed worship and the use of appointed pastors. Since initially there were no trained Quaker pastors, men from other church denominations were appointed, sometimes with little knowledge of the Quaker tradition. Thus, in some meetings, the Quaker tradition became more adapted to a general Protestant practice, often with an evangelical theology.

While this was happening in North America, Quakerism was beginning to spread into other parts of the world. In the 1830s William Backhouse was travelling in Australia, particularly in Tasmania, setting up meetings. The first Quaker arrived in New Zealand in 1840. The Friends Foreign Mission Association was founded in 1868. Missionaries worked in India, China, Madagascar, and the Middle East amongst other places. In the early years of the twentieth century the first Quaker mission to Kenya from the US took the pastored and programmed form of worship to Africa. More recently, Evangelical meetings have sent missions to Central and South America, especially Bolivia (see chapter 20 in this volume by Welling, entitled 'Mission').

These missions raise the question of whether the missionary should focus on Christianity or on Quakerism. Though conceptually and traditionally Quakerism is Christianity, in practice the two can be separated. This question of the Quaker interpretation of Christianity becomes more acute when Quakers begin to look more closely at relations with other religions.

THE GROWTH OF THE ECUMENICAL MOVEMENT

The evangelical push towards mission had the perhaps surprising result of hastening the development of ecumenical relations, both inter church and inter faith. The need for missionaries to cooperate in the field brought members of different churches closer together: living in lands where other religions dominated brought the need to develop a greater understanding of them. Missions also contributed to a growing global consciousness. These elements came together in some significant world conferences.

The first of these conferences was the World Parliament of Religions held in 1893 in Chicago in conjunction with the World's Fair. The parliament attracted mostly North Americans with some Europeans, and mostly Christians, though other religions including Hinduism, Judaism, Buddhism, and Islam were represented. The working method was through speeches and papers read to plenary sessions: there were also accompanying denominational Congresses, which were much smaller in numbers. Quakers were represented by two groups, each with a separate Congress. The Hicksites were perhaps more prominent with a speaker to the full parliament and a three-day Congress. The Orthodox held a one-day Congress. Most of those who gave papers were from the US though the Hicksites had one speaker from Ontario, Edgar M. Zavitz, and the Orthodox heard a paper from Joseph Bevan Braithwaite of London Yearly Meeting though it was read for him by a Quaker from Indiana.

The Hicksites prepared for the Congress carefully. A committee of Quakers from Chicago was set up and it had an advisory council from the seven Hicksite Yearly Meetings, which took part. This council is seen as the origin of the Christian and Interfaith Relations Committee (CIRC) of what is now Friends General Conference.

Both Quaker Congresses tackled similar subjects: both had papers (given by women) on women in the Society and both considered mission, though in the Hicksite case, a paper of Joseph J. Janney on mission was firmly linked to the importance of peace. Only the Hicksites looked at 'The Grounds of Sympathy among Religions', a paper by Aaron M. Powell.

What may be called the keynote addresses reveal a tension in Quaker theology, which to some extent still persists. Howard M. Jenkins in addressing the full parliament on the religious principles of the Society placed his emphasis on the Inner Light, a concept which allows for a more inclusive attitude towards other religions, though he also spoke of Christ's rule in daily life. James Wood, addressing the Orthodox Congress on 'Our Church and its Mission' stressed that Quakers fully accepted the foundation truths of Christianity, and emphasized the high priesthood of the Lord Jesus Christ and the priesthood of all believers (Hanson 1894, 1122–9).

The 1893 parliament is recognized as the beginning of the modern interfaith movement. What it most illustrated, however, was the need for churches to work together: it might also be argued that within and alongside that, it showed the need for Quakers to begin to reconcile their differences with each other.

The next conference of major significance was the Edinburgh World Missionary Conference of 1910, which brought together representatives of missionary societies and is seen as the start of the modern ecumenical movement, particularly in the boost it gave to the movement for consideration of questions of faith and order in the churches. Between these two conferences, in 1895 Quakers in Britain held the Manchester Conference, which signalled the growing acceptance of modern thought and began the shift towards a more liberal theology within London Yearly Meeting. The establishment in 1903 of the college at Woodbrooke in Birmingham and the founding in 1907 of the annual Swarthmore lecture given at the Yearly Meeting were both part of this shift.

The Edinburgh conference, like most ecumenical events in the first half of the twentieth century, was mainly men, mainly white, and mainly from the Global North (North America and Europe). Of the roughly twelve hundred delegates about twelve are identifiable as representing Quakers though the journal *The Friend* (vol. 50 (1910), 432–41, 451–4) estimates that more than sixty Quakers were present for at least part of the conference. As a result of the conference, churches began to form organizations that would allow them to work together in missions, in peace, and on social questions. They also began to plan for a conference on faith and order. Though delayed by the First World War these movements became established and were included inthe World Council of Churches (WCC) when it was founded in 1948 following the Second World War.

Other conferences of note are the All Friends World Conference of 1920, which for the first time brought together representatives from many Yearly Meetings, and the second Friends World Conference in 1937, which set up the Friends World Committee for Consultation (FWCC). This gave Quakers a world body, which though it has no authority over Yearly Meetings, allows and has allowed Quakers to be represented at the WCC, both at the assemblies and at the central committee, as a Christian World Communion.

The setting-up of the WCC caused a theological problem for Quakers that was resolved in different ways in different Yearly Meetings. The basis for membership of the WCC was as a 'fellowship of churches which accept our Lord Jesus Christ as God and Saviour'. London Yearly Meeting turned down an invitation to join, not only because it considered the basis to be a creed and therefore at odds with the testimony that faith cannot be based on words, but also because it considered the basis to be unsatisfactory. Quakers in North America, however, had a different attitude. Five Years Meeting (now Friends United Meeting, FUM) accepted membership, seeing the basis as an affirmation of faith rather than a creed: Philadelphia Yearly Meeting (YM) (Orthodox) joined as did Canada YM: Madagascar YM joined before 1968 when it ceased to be a member having merged into a United Protestant Church. Friends General Conference tried to influence the WCC to change the basis so as to recognize churches that did not express faith in a form of words, but joined even though they were unsuccessful (CCR 1978, 8–9). At the 1948 Amsterdam assembly, Quakers were represented by Howard Brinton (PYM), Bliss Forbush (FGC), Algie I. Newlin (FYM), and H. Barbara Walker (Canada YM). Thomas S. Brown and D. Elton Trueblood attended as alternates. London YM had a member present in the person of Percy W. Bartlett who attended as the representative of FWCC.

In 1955 the two Philadelphia Yearly Meetings merged and the combined Meeting gave up its separate membership of WCC. In the same year the three Yearly Meetings in Canada merged to form one Canadian YM and kept membership even though they were also members of FUM. Canadian YM with its membership of fewer than 2,000 may well be the smallest church to be in full membership of the Council. As the WCC has grown with many new member churches from the Global South it has changed its constitution so as to require new full member churches to have over 50,000 members. This ruling means that no other Yearly Meeting will be able to join as an individual church because the Quaker method of church government that potentially involves all members requires the size of a Yearly Meeting to be manageable. If any Quakers join in the future under the current constitution it would have to be in larger groupings. Quaker ecclesiology is at odds with WCC practicalities. However, Quakers in Kenya have been able to become members through FUM when membership of that body included their Yearly Meetings. At the 2006 assembly, FUM was represented by young Kenyan pastor Jane Mutoro, who was then appointed to the WCC central committee.

Though their representation has been small, Quakers have continued to be faithful in their attendance at WCC assemblies and commissions, and where possible, the central committee. Their contribution has been significant. In the 1990s Barbara Bazett of Canadian YM, working with the Mennonite Fernando Enns, encouraged the development of the Programme to Overcome Violence. This, in turn, led to the Decade to Overcome Violence approved at the 1998 assembly, which culminated in the International Ecumenical Peace Convocation in 2011. In the process leading to that Convocation, Mennonites, Quakers, and Brethren (the Historic Peace churches) held a series of international peace theology consultations.

Eden Grace (1968–) of New England Yearly Meeting, serving on the WCC central committee from 1998 to 2006, was appointed to the Special Committee on Orthodox Representation. She was able to contribute her knowledge of Quaker business methods to the discussion about how decisions were taken at WCC meetings and influence the move to consensus decision-making, which was adopted at the 2006 assembly. In more subtle ways these and other Quakers have been able to demonstrate by their presence that a church can be represented by women and by lay people. However, there is a problem with this. Since the WCC has made rules for itself about the proportions of women, young people, and lay people to be on its commissions and committee, and since the Orthodox churches tend to name mostly ordained men for their share of places, young Quaker women are much more likely to be nominated for places than Quaker men, however well qualified.

Connection to the WCC has not been without its costs for Quakers. Some Evangelical Yearly Meetings have left FUM because of its membership of WCC. Evangelical Quakers in general consider the WCC to be too political. This does not, however, prevent them from being ecumenical albeit in a more limited way. Evangelical Friends Church International has links with other evangelical churches and is a member of the National Association of Evangelicals, which is affiliated with the World Evangelical Alliance.

NATIONAL AND LOCAL INVOLVEMENT

The involvement of Quakers in national and local ecumenism, whether interchurch or interfaith, depends on several practical factors in addition to the theological issues. It may fairly be said that all Quakers are conscious of the peace testimony and so wish to develop good relationships with their neighbours. In many cases this will involve working together on social issues. However, it will not always translate into membership of formal structures. Where there are formal structures, the representation of Quakers may be through formal appointment, or at local level may be by enthusiasts who have a particular interest or expertise. Many Quakers have little connection with interchurch or interfaith work though they may wish it well.

Significant factors include the size of the nation, the size of the Yearly Meeting, the number of Yearly Meetings in a nation, the strength of the national formal structures, the religious make-up of the nation, particularly whether it is predominantly Christian or another faith or faiths.

Thus, for example, Quakers in India are not in a position to be strongly involved in ecumenism. They have several Yearly Meetings, some unprogrammed, some evangelical, none with more than a few hundred members or strong enough to represent Quakers at a national level. The number of Christians in India is a small proportion, approximately 2.3 per cent of the population. The main ecumenical activity in the nation has been the establishment of the Church of South India, and the Church of North India, each formed after Indian independence and each bringing together three or four mainstream Protestant churches. The emphasis of these churches is on mission, both church growth and service in the form of schools, hospitals, and other social projects, rather than on further ecumenism. Many Christians are of Dalit ('untouchable') origin, though in becoming Christian they reject the caste system. In parts of India there is hostility to Christians and persecution, through legal and physical attacks by members of other faiths. In these circumstances there is little or no opportunity for interchurch or interfaith work at national level, though in some places Quakers are able to participate in local social projects with other Christians or with their Hindu or Muslim neighbours. Quakers do retain an affection for Mohandas Gandhi and remain connected with his work.

By contrast, Australia has one Yearly Meeting to cover the whole nation, with a structure of Regional Meetings, each of which approximates to a State or Territory. The YM belongs to the Australian Council of Churches and is represented by the YM Clerk and another appointed Quaker. The Australian Council of Churches, though it has a formal basis, developed a clause that allowed the membership of churches with no creed but would work in the spirit of the basis. Quakers also belong to state Councils of Churches and in some cases play a prominent and active role. They also belong to both national and state interfaith groups. Interestingly, the most prominent 'other faith' in Australia, that of the Aboriginal peoples, is not regarded by Quakers or other churches as an interfaith matter. Quakers see their work with Aboriginal people as a matter of social justice.

Those nations where there are large numbers of Quakers have different challenges. In Kenya, there is a growing number of Yearly Meetings within one nation. To be represented nationally on the Kenyan Council of Churches, the YMs have had to group together as the Friends Church Kenya. Local ecumenism is less possible because of the way that the original missionaries divided the country into areas. Thus, many villages in western Kenya are almost entirely Quaker. The predominant Muslim presence in Kenya is in coastal areas distant from the Quaker areas, thus there is little interfaith contact. It is mainly in the capital Nairobi and other large cities that Quakers have to cooperate with members of other churches and faiths, for example working for peace when there was inter-tribal violence following the elections in 2010. However, there is also competition, especially for membership of the young, with the growing Pentecostal churches where worship is lively. For Quakers in Kenya, as for other Christians, faith is developed in a context of tribalism and the still persisting concepts and traditions of the pre-Christian culture and local religion. This is compounded by the influence of colonialism and Western culture that is both resisted and accepted. Where Western influence is resisted, indigenous elements resurface within Quakers and other churches. This can lead to a strong national sense but can affect a sense of global ecumenism.

In the US there are many YMs within one nation. This is more complex than Kenya because of the theological differences, so that it is impossible for all Quakers to be represented together at the National Council of Churches. However, Quakers have been involved from the beginning, through Philadelphia YM (which has now ceased to be a separate member) and through the groupings of FUM (Friends United Meeting) and FGC (Friends General Conference). For FUM, involvement is difficult as councils of churches are variously seen as too political or too intellectual, and has become minimal. Interfaith work is seen as detracting from Christian mission. These are issues that can be divisive, and FUM has to prioritize holding together its constituent meetings. FGC is able to be more involved formally through its Christian and Interfaith Relations Committee (CIRC). Even here there are tensions. Some Quakers are attracted to inter-church work because they are looking for Christian fellowship: others have a more universalist perspective and are attracted to interfaith work. It can be difficult to navigate between the two. Nevertheless, CIRC provides a mechanism not only for some Quakers to be represented nationally in interfaith and interchurch work but also for responses to documents such as the 2006 WCC paper, 'Called to be the One Church'.

These examples show the difficulty of generalizing about Quaker involvement. Where there is one YM in one nation, Quakers may have national involvement, as for example in Canada. But in New Zealand the national ecumenical structures are not strong, so Quakers are more involved in interfaith work and in interchurch bodies that deal with social and ecumenical issues. Where there are YMs, usually of evangelical foundation, in predominantly Roman Catholic countries, as for example in the Philippines and Central America, there may be some fellow feeling with Protestant churches, but these YMs are still more concerned about mission and church growth than ecumenical work. Where a YM is in a country of another faith, there may be friendly contact as with Buddhists in Japan, or cooperation in peace work as with Muslims in Indonesia.

In Europe there is a variety of circumstances. Most YMs in mainland Europe are small so have to choose where to focus their energies. The Netherlands YM, for example, is involved in interchurch work through the organization Church and Peace. In the Scandinavian countries the vast majority of the population belongs to the state church, usually Lutheran. Here, Quakers often belong to both the state church and the YM so that they can worship more frequently than the times a small meeting can meet. In these nations the state churches are more interested in international ecumenism as in the Porvoo agreement between the Lutheran and Anglican churches: where there is any national Council of Churches, Quakers play a very minor role. Switzerland YM has a unique place. Its Geneva Meeting is located close to the WCC and is in the same building as the Quaker United Nations Office. The emphasis is more on cooperation on social issues and peace than on theological issues.

The British Isles contain two out of the three examples where YMs cross national boundaries (the other being Central and Southern Africa YM that covers seven countries). Ireland YM covers the whole island containing both Eire and the six counties (Northern Ireland). It is represented on both interchurch bodies and on Churches Together in Britain and Ireland (CTBI). The 'Troubles' in Northern Ireland and the conflict between Catholics and Protestants have meant that Quakers have been heavily involved in peace work and conflict resolution. As a result the Quaker presence in interchurch bodies has been greatly valued.

Britain (formerly London) YM covers three nations, England, Scotland, and Wales, as well as several offshore islands. The YM was involved in the British Council of Churches from its inception in 1942, and now belongs to its successor bodies, CTBI, Churches Together in England (CTE), CYTUN (Churches Together in Wales), and ACTS (Action of Churches Together in Scotland). As one of the largest Yearly Meetings in the world, Britain YM has the financial and people resources to take an active role. Quakers have variously served as president of CTBI, president of CTE, trustees of CTBI, ACTS, and CTE, and moderator of CTE. In addition, many Quakers are active at local and intermediate levels on interchurch bodies. When the current bodies were reconstituted in 1990, a clause based on the Australian one allowed churches without creeds (such as Quakers) to become full members without subscribing to the basis provided they were accepted by other churches as acting in the spirit of the basis. Though the YM's application to join was gladly accepted by other churches, it caused controversy within the YM itself.

Britain YM also belongs to the InterFaith Network in Britain and many local meetings belong to local interfaith groups. However, it has been noted that though interchurch groups deal, at least for some of the time, in discussion and dialogue on faith issues, the interfaith groups tend to focus on community and social issues, and there is little real interfaith dialogue. Though called 'interfaith' they are more truly 'inter-community' groups. The growth of interfaith work in the YM has also been more focused on justice issues than theological ones. Members of the YM were involved in the Kindertransport bringing Jewish children to Britain before the Second World War. The YM currently administers the Ecumenical Accompaniment Programme in Palestine/Israel on behalf of the WCC. However, a Swarthmore lecture on Quakers and other faiths dealing with theological issues due to be given in 1948 was rejected by the lecture committee as not suitable (though it was given under other auspices): not until 2003 was there a Swarthmore lecture on other faiths.

The interchurch and interfaith activity of the YM is held together by a committee. Initially appointed in 1914 as a Commission on Faith and Order, in 1942 it became the Committee on Christian Relationships (CCR), and in 1994 the Committee on Christian and Interfaith Relations (CIR). Britain is the only YM with this capacity as an individual YM to prepare responses to documents and to issue them backed with the authority of the YM. An example of this is the response to the WCC text, 'Baptism, Eucharist and Ministry', which was prepared by CCR and approved by the Yearly Meeting in 1986 (CCR 1986).

THEOLOGICAL ISSUES

Quaker involvement in interchurch and interfaith relationships has raised questions regarding Quaker theology and how Quakers understand themselves. In the first place there is the question of how to understand the variety of Quaker faith and practice. Much of it can be seen as accidental, the product of historical, geographical, or cultural circumstances. Other aspects can be seen as differing developments of the original tradition, each a valid representation. These approaches can be helpful for those who have to represent Quakerism to others, especially at an international or world level. Nevertheless, it must be admitted that there are cases where disagreements between Quakers about their faith are substantial. Yet as Quakers and others have discovered at events such as the Global Christian Forum, when people tell each other their faith stories, there is a growth in sympathy and understanding, and recognition of the Holy Spirit at work in each other's lives. Further, when Quakers find themselves amongst people of other churches and faiths they often discover that however strong the differences, they are recognizably of one 'family' of faith with an understanding of their Christianity that becomes apparent in ecumenical contexts.

Most interchurch structures have a 'Basis of Faith' to which member churches sign up. As has been shown earlier Quakers have reacted in differing ways to these. What underlies Quaker attitudes is the belief that faith cannot be adequately expressed in words and that therefore to demand adherence to a creed is to misunderstand the nature of Christian discipleship. It is possible for those Yearly Meetings with the Richmond Declaration of Faith (1887) in their discipline to regard this as a description rather than a prescription of Quaker faith. It could be argued that those who have stood out for an exception to be made for Quakers are too tender and have understood the basis (the purpose of which is to define who can belong to the organization) to be something that was never intended. On the other hand, it could equally be argued that being prepared to be on the margins is making a witness to the other churches of an understanding of the true nature of faith.

Such witness has also been faithfully maintained on those questions that to other churches provide the heart of the ecumenical agenda, the nature of sacraments, and the ordained ministry. In 1982, the WCC Faith and Order Commission published the so-called Lima text, 'Baptism, Eucharist and Ministry' (WCC 1982). Three YMs responded —Canada, Netherlands, and London. All can be found in the WCC published collections of responses. London YM also published its response separately as 'To Lima, With Love'. Several sections of this subsequently appeared in the Britain YM 1994 book of Faith and Practice (Britain Yearly Meeting 2009). These responses upheld the nature of sacramental living as being inward rather than outward, and that the outward symbols of water, bread, and wine are not necessary. Again, even those few Quaker churches that are willing to practise baptism with water or to hold a Lord's Supper, teach that this is a matter of choice and not necessity. The WCC has so far acknowledged the Quaker (and

Salvation Army) position that in its Canberra statement of 1991 it stated that it gladly recognized that those churches that did not practise outward baptism shared in the spiritual experience of life in Christ. This recognition has been repeated in all subsequent statements on baptism, though often as a footnote. The churches have perhaps not yet realized how revolutionary are the implications of this recognition.

Like other dissenting churches in the seventeenth century, Quakers placed an emphasis with regard to ministry on the priesthood of all believers and the shared ministry of the whole people of God; in interchurch contexts Quakers continue to emphasize these elements. Nevertheless, a form of threefold ministry developed in recorded ministers, elders, and overseers as gifts were recognized that would help to build up the church. In the twentieth century some unprogrammed meetings gave up the recording of ministers. Where there are no recorded ministers (largely in Europe and the Antipodes) this coincides with a well-educated population and membership, and societies where equality is regarded as of great importance. The tasks of ministry are shared amongst all the members. Where there are recorded ministers and pastors (the two often but not always coincide) these roles are seen as carrying responsibilities on behalf of the membership. Pastors are not ordained in any way that would be recognized by other churches, and they still come under the authority of the elders. One distinguishing feature of Quaker ministry in whatever role is that it is often a temporary appointment. Quakers have to learn the discipline of relinquishing any authority or office they may have held. The equality of women and men amongst Quakers, however variously it has been interpreted at different periods of time, has meant that often in meetings of church leaders, Quakers have been the only women and the only lay people present.

Over the past decade the WCC has produced two more documents to which Quakers have responded. The shorter one, 'Called to be the One Church' was issued by the WCC assembly in 2006. The longer one, initially called 'The Nature and Purpose of the Church' (now represented as 'The Nature and Mission of the Church') (WCC 2005) received responses from FUM, CIRC, and Britain YM. Although these were written independently of each other they make similar points and the family resemblance is apparent. All refer to the church as a community led by the Holy Spirit and all draw on the same Quaker tradition and ecclesiology.

The impact of the interchurch movement on Quakers has led, at a time when theology is perhaps a minority pursuit, to a need for a clearer articulation of their faith. It has also encouraged changes and developments in theology. In responding to 'The Nature and Mission of the Church', Britain YM realized that in practice it had changed its view of other churches. For more than a century it had acted as if the Holy Spirit was active in other churches, in contradiction to Barclay's seventeenth-century description of other churches being 'in the Fall' and apostate. This acknowledgement, in effect a change in doctrine, was incorporated into the final response to the WCC.

The traditional Quaker understanding of the ultimate authority in the church being the presence of the Risen Christ known through the Holy Spirit, rather than any body of doctrine, Scripture, or hierarchy, means that Quakers are open to receiving new insights and to interpreting their tradition in new ways. This does mean that they have to have careful checks and testing of what appears to come from the Spirit. It also means that meetings move at different speeds or see different sides to contemporary questions. The question of the relation to other faiths is one such issue that Quakers would benefit from discussing together. The tradition is clear that 'the Light enlightens everyone' (John 1:9) and that the Light is the Light of Christ. What is not so clear is whether other religions are to be seen in Christian terms or whether together with Christianity they are to be seen as aspects of some greater Truth. Some individual Quakers come from traditions other than Christianity and do not see the need for themselves personally to become Christian in order to be Quaker: there are Quakers therefore who are Buddhist, Hindu, Jewish, or Muslim, and in some meetings this causes no problem. Quakers have the task of holding to the truth known to them while demonstrating that Truth is not a proposition that can be put into words but a relationship of love, peace, and justice that has to be lived. Thus in looking for the truth in systems of faith they are also critiquing where these systems (including their own) fall short of their vision of Truth.

GOING FORWARD

In both interchurch and interfaith relations, Quakers are generally reacting to an agenda set by others. Questions regarding sacraments and the ordained ministry that are of the utmost importance to other churches have little real relevance to Quakers. The methods of interchurch dialogue also do not reflect Quaker concerns. Quakers have taken no serious part in bilateral dialogues though they contribute to multilateral consultations. They are not partners to any major covenants. In interfaith relations their concern has been mostly with peace and issues of social justice rather than with theological discussion. Even where there is such material it seldom goes beyond descriptions of different positions with the aim of mutual understanding.

Quakers could begin to develop and put forward their own agenda, recognizing the challenge implicit in their tradition. As a church that places emphasis on the guidance of the Holy Spirit, they can ask how other churches recognize that guidance. They can encourage those working on theological issues to explore how it can be that the same Holy Spirit appears to have led and to be leading different churches to different conclusions on the same issues. With a tradition of a realized (or realizing) eschatology, they can ask what church traditions and practices belong to the Kingdom of God and what is an interim measure. They can take the concept of *koinonia*, which featured strongly in the WCC Faith and Order conference of 1993, and ask that the aspects about relations with other faiths and about community with the whole earth be developed further. They can raise again the question of the nature of the unity that churches seek.

In the seventeenth century, Thomas Story wrote that the unity of Christians consisted 'in Christian love only'. With the exception of the Yearly Meeting in Madagascar that disappeared into a united church in 1968, Quakers have resisted organizational unity or uniformity but have sought to build good relationships. It may be time to ask what a

Christian unity based on love might look like. One approach to this may be similar to the 'receptive ecumenism' recently promoted by the Roman Catholics. This looks for and appreciates the gifts that other churches bring. Do Quakers recognize the gifts that the Spirit has given to their church and are they prepared to be accountable to others for how they use them? Equally, do they recognize the gifts that others have to offer and are they prepared to ask the uncomfortable questions about how these gifts can be received and appreciated within their meetings?

Though this approach has been developed within Christianity, Quakers may well be in a position to extend it to other religions as well. While it is comparatively easy to see that classical Theravada Buddhism with its meditative practice can share gifts with the unprogrammed stream of Quakerism, to enter into this exploration will raise difficult challenges. For example, do Quakers with their Puritan background have the courage to learn from the many Hindu images of God without losing hold of the insight that God cannot be depicted? Can they see that the Hindu approach may be another expression of the same truth?

To undertake this exploration requires an understanding of Christian love. It is, of course, about comfort and nurture, and the encouragement of human flourishing. It is also about social justice and about the challenge of transformation. Above all it is about dwelling in the God who is Love and who demonstrated the nature of that love in self-sacrifice. Quakers have the burden of maintaining the truth as they see it, of continually being the ones who say that there is another way. They have to find the strength that comes from faithfulness, leaving success or failure in the hands of the God who calls them to the task.

Suggested Further Reading

Brinton, H. (1951) 'American Friends and the World Council of Churches' *Friends Quarterly*, 5, pp. 70–8.

Hanson, J. W. (ed.) (1894) *The World's Congress of Religions*. Chicago: W. B. Conkey Co.

London Yearly Meeting (1979) *Unity in the Spirit: Quakers and the Ecumenical Pilgrimage.* London: Quaker Home Service.

London Yearly Meeting. (1987) *To Lima with love*. London: QHS.

Nesbitt, E. (2003) *Interfaith Pilgrims*. London: Quaker Books.

World Council of Churches. (1982) *Baptism, Eucharist and Ministry*, Geneva.

World Council of Churches. (2005) *The Nature and Mission of the Church*, Geneva.

CHAPTER 22

....

PLAINNESS AND SIMPLICITY

....

EMMA J. LAPSANSKY

Soon after creating the Religious Society of Friends, its architects sought to systematize and articulate a coherent body of beliefs and disciplines by which to circumscribe membership in its communities. Early Quakers aimed to declare themselves 'Christian'. However, they also sought to distinguish themselves from what they considered to be the corrupt Church of England, the stultifying rigidity of Puritanism, and the undisciplined anarchy of other religious rebels. Consequently, these Friends began to delineate a body of theology that included divesting themselves—as individuals and as a community—of what they described as 'needless', 'vain', or ostentatious possessions and behaviours. In the early years, this concern was manifested in choices such as the refusal to acknowledge social deference by doffing a hat or using the formal 'you' when addressing people of higher social standing.

Though, over time, the definitions of simplicity widened, neither early Friends nor their religious descendants have succeeded in establishing a unified definition of the boundaries between 'needful' versus ostentatious consumption. Over time, the terms 'simplicity' or 'plainness' came to be used to convey what remains—even today—an imprecise idea. This chapter engages some of the dimensions of Friends' ongoing search for clarity on guidelines for simplicity.

INTRODUCTION: IN SEARCH OF MODESTY

....

Of all the testimonies Friends have adopted to differentiate Quakerism from other forms of Protestantism, and the stripping of worship to its uncluttered essentials, the concept of 'simplicity' has remained among the most elusive and difficult to define. At its core, the goal of simplicity was—and is—to guide Quakers in how to turn away from 'worldly' distractions, and to situate themselves in a deeply worshipful posture, with distracting influences kept to a minimum in order to receive Divine messages, which—Friends believe—are delivered in a 'still, small, voice'. This goal calls upon Friends to eschew 'excess' in their lives, lest the acquisition, maintenance, and protection of what William Penn (1644–1718) termed 'more than is necessary or appropriate' (Frost 2003a, 21) result in vanity or other distractions that may interfere with concentration on that Divine voice. Yet interpretations of practical applications of the concept have remained in flux through changes in time, geography, and theological interpretations.

Though there are multiple facets to Friends' concern with 'simplicity', often the conversation has turned on what seem to be easily visible aspects: material possessions, ostentation, and vanity. Balanced along the thin edge of a theology that requires being 'in the world, but not of it', adherents of the Religious Society of Friends (Quakers) have long grappled with the issue of how much and what kind of material consumption might compromise their posture of uniqueness and religious integrity. Quakers do not have monasteries into which the dedicated can withdraw in a neatly bounded asceticism. And unlike Mennonites and other sects that embraced similar codes of dress and behaviour, Quakers lacked designated authorities who could impose uniform, uncontestable boundaries. Rather, intra-community discernment and discussion remain the only guides to what is appropriate.

But the problem is not just about external possessions. As Quakers seek the 'divine' connection within themselves and others, discerning what disciplines and behaviours promote the desired quality of interior worship also becomes a matter of deep concern. Over time, many Quakers have embraced the idea of 'simplicity' or 'plainness' (sometimes described as 'humility' or 'modesty') as one strategy for nurturing a posture that promotes balance between secular and sacred lives. But, like much of Friends theology, which is grounded in the New Testament focus on visionary experience and continuing 'revelation', simplicity and plainness have been subject to a diversity of interpretations. Though scholars differ on how and when the words 'simplicity' and 'plainness' were first used to signify Friends' intention to live lives that were uncluttered by outward distractions (Frost 2003a, 22–3; Hamm 2003, 101) one way to explore the diverse meanings of these concepts is to examine some of the changing meanings and emphases across time and geography.

SEVENTEENTH CENTURY: 'USEFUL' AND 'SOBER'

The discourse about simplicity was enjoined at least as early as the 1650s, when British Friends set the standard of turning their backs on the tradition of churches with stained-glass windows, altar furnishings, ordained-and-robed clergy, and prepared prayers, sermons, liturgy, and pageantry. Such standardized rituals, early Friends argued, not only invited vanity, corruption, and stagnation into religious worship, but also distracted worshippers from experiencing for themselves the immediacy of the Lord's presence. Worship should be spontaneous, and should bring each individual into direct contact with the Divine Spirit, without intermediary people or prescribed ceremonies.

By the 1670s Quakers in Britain aimed to codify some of the nuance of a 'simple' approach to religious posture. Though at first neither the words 'plain' nor 'simple' were used frequently, as early as 1699 William Penn, admonished his children to embrace 'truth-speaking, ministry, plainness, simplicity, and moderation in apparel, furniture, food, salutation' (Frost 2003a, 23). In *No Cross, No Crown*, published thirty years before, Penn had warned that Friends should steer clear of what was 'vain', 'costly', 'useless', or not 'sober', and he admonished that material goods should be 'simple and plain'. Ornate clothing and furniture, which reflected 'pride' rather than 'humility', were to be avoided. Likewise, games, poetry, comedies, plays, and riddles were among the distractions that should be replaced with 'the best recreation [which] is to do good' (Frost 2003a, 21–3).

Developed in the context of the social realities of seventeenth-century England—agricultural enclosure, widespread homelessness, and conspicuous consumption on the part of the wealthy—Penn's recipe for a Christian society included a radical social component. Though a well-educated member of the upper classes, Penn argued that luxury goods, available only to a small wealthy minority, created artificial and dangerously irreligious social distinctions. Moreover, said Penn, luxury goods impoverished society as a whole by deflecting workers' energies to creating extravagant items instead of creating products that would increase trade and thereby provide work to help the poor rise from poverty. Out of this line of thinking, Penn suggested that clothing should be 'plain and modest', but these terms were not specifically defined except to indicate that choices should not be dictated by popular or 'worldly' fashion. Friends, advised Penn, should adopt a posture of 'non-conformity to the world' which included 'simple and plain speech...' (Penn 1877, 134).

Indeed, much of what passed as definition for 'plain' was arrived at only by triangulation. For example, another social reality of William Penn's world was the tradition of social hierarchy that required deference to those who were above one's own station in life, and the accompanying acceptance of the idea that certain human beings were more valuable or important than others. Friends' adoption of practices to counter the notion of hierarchy included the refusal to follow the social convention that designated the use of 'you' as showing deference versus 'thee/thou' as indicating social equality. This resistance to hierarchical language came to be known as 'plain speech'. Plainness also came to include refusal to doff a hat as a gesture of subservience, and refusal to address people by socially defined honorary titles. At various times, these and other behaviours were described as measures of Quakers' participation in the 'plain' life, or what would come to be called the 'holy conversation', i.e., a life stripped bare of useless behaviours that seemed to contradict the Truth that in God's eyes, all souls were equal. Thus, the theory of 'plainness' was reasonably clear, but aspects of practice were more blurred.

Penn's contemporary, Robert Barclay, also from an economically and educationally privileged background, added yet another level of complexity to the question of what constituted 'plain' or 'simple'. In his 1678 *Apology for the True Christian Divinity*, a treatise widely quoted and revered by many generations of Quakers, Barclay echoed Penn's concern that Friends should eschew vanities and excesses. For Barclay, however, this dictate was variable:

> ...two things are to be considered, the condition of the person, and the country, he lives in. We shall not say, that all persons are to be clothed alike, because it will perhaps neither suit their bodies, nor their estates. And if a man be clothed soberly

and without superfluity, though they may be finer, than that which his servant is clothed with, we shall not blame him for it. (Barclay 1678, 446–8)

For Barclay, one measure of proper plainness, it seemed, was to keep a low ratio of means-to-consumption—a definition that seemed less well defined than that of William Penn.

Hence, the seventeenth-century English Quakers' attempts to codify humility were mired in ambiguity. Account books from the 1670s show that the Quaker role model Margaret Fell (1614–1702), a woman of considerable means, clothed herself in high-quality, brightly coloured fabrics. She insisted that to make inflexible rules about such outward things as clothing and possessions would reduce true faith to a 'silly, poor gospel' of conformity to lifeless rules. On the other hand, in 1686, Fell's less-well-known comrade Joan Vokins advocated conformity to modest consumption. She admonished her children to 'be careful and take heed that you do not stain the testimony of Truth... by wearing needless things and following the world's fashions in your clothing or attire, but remember how I have bred you up' (Vokins 1691). Presumably Vokins, whose 1680s ministry travels had taken her to the New England and mid-Atlantic regions of America as well as to Ireland, was summarizing for her children a message that she had already carried far and wide. By the end of the 1680s, George Fox, George Keith, and several groups of American Friends would expand the issues to question of whether human exploitation such as the keeping of slaves, might also violate the tenets of a 'plain' life.

Despite the attempts of these early Friends, future generations were no more clear about methods to actualize seventeenth-century Quaker values, and several modern historians have continued to try to illuminate what early Quakers meant when they commended a member's 'holy conversation' (Levy 1978, 152–3; Specht 2002, 45–7). In addition to issues of hierarchy/social equality, exploitative labour practices, and 'useless' material goods, some tension about modesty versus ostentation seems to have been partly a reflection of seventeenth-century rural English Friends' disdain for more affluent urban Quakers. All of these themes—and some new ones—reappear in future generations' deliberations about what constitutes 'simplicity'.

Eighteenth Century: Appropriate Uses of Means and Time

Whereas the majority of seventeenth-century English Friends had been rural and of limited means, Friends' routines of hard work, high integrity, and restrained consumption had resulted in an increasing number of well-to-do Quakers. A number of scholars have explored the religious implications of the ways that transatlantic capitalism coupled with the Protestant ethic resulted in unanticipated wealth—and unanticipated tensions (Weber 1930; Bailyn 1964). Many Quakers in Britain and America, looking to their forefathers, experienced more than a little anxiety about their new-found affluence. How would one practise a 'plain' lifestyle if one continued to accumulate excess economic means?

When the 1689 Toleration Act freed British Friends from persecution for their beliefs, the enticing excitement of a new reformist radical religion faded somewhat, and Friends found themselves struggling to meet the multiple challenges of declining membership and a decrease in converts as well. One strategy was to focus on the children of current members, to establish schools to protect them from corruption, to encourage parents to shield Quaker children from worldly temptations, and to define for children a set of high-minded guidelines and rewards to inspire their loyalty. By the 1730s, London Yearly Meeting had instituted the concept of 'birthright Friends', a status of belonging that was bestowed on children by virtue of being born to Quaker parents. By implication, the job of those parents was to raise those children to embrace Quaker values— including the value of 'plainness'. A parent's role, then, was to adopt a ceaseless posture of 'holy conversation', a consistent comportment that modelled rather than preached Friends faith and attentiveness to God's wishes—including 'simplicity'.

However, the contours of the simple life, never having been well delineated in the first place, now needed to be honed against Quakers' increasing affluence. Twentieth-century historian Frederick Tolles referred to these eighteenth-century newly wealthy Quakers as 'Quaker grandees', who formed a transatlantic 'Quaker mercantile aristocracy' (Tolles 1963, 63–84). These affluent young American Quakers travelled frequently to England, where they indulged in opulent shopping sprees, their parents' attempts to dissuade them from excess notwithstanding. Indeed, their parents, themselves struggling to set limits on self-indulgence, often chose to rely on Robert Barclay's (1648–90) guidance that social hierarchy was inevitable, and that the simple life should be gauged by a considered means-to-expenditure ratio. Such a guideline, that allowed for the purchase of expensive, high-quality products, so long as consumption stopped short of 'frivolous' decoration or living beyond one's means, seemed to satisfy many Friends (Tolles 1963, 27–8, 109–43). However, a number of Conservative Quakers were concerned that more clear-cut boundaries should be set. English-born Thomas Chalkley (1675–1741) and American Friends such as John Pemberton publicized their anxiety that the very process of acquiring, using, and protecting worldly possessions would threaten the moral fibre of Quaker individuals and communities. Chalkley challenged fellow Quakers with the question 'what service will… be the riches of the rich' in death. Pemberton reminded them 'that when one feeds himself with the vain pleasures of the world, the spiritual senses become stupefied…' (Chalkley 1866, 440; Pemberton 1785, 8–10).

One Quaker who rose to prominence partly as result of this concern with restraining Quaker excess was John Woolman (1720–72), who is best known for his soul-searching *Journal*, and for his 1754 treatise on *Some Considerations on the Keeping of Negroes*. Woolman's concern with social and economic fairness, including the abolition of slavery, is present throughout his journal, which has been continuously popular with Quaker readers since his death. Woolman, like Chalkley, carried his reform ministry throughout the Atlantic world. In shunning dyed fabrics because dyes were made by slaves, and because dye workers were made ill by the chemicals, and in refusing to use silver table service, on the grounds that slaves were forced to dig such precious minerals and gems for the rich, Woolman echoed William Penn's concerns about the labour 'wasted' on frivolous products. Woolman carried the concern even further, sometimes refusing to ride in stagecoaches, because this mode of transportation demeaned and injured horses, and he travelled abroad in steerage with the crew rather than in the more luxurious passenger accommodations. Woolman often visited slaveholders and attempted to dissuade them from living a life of ease by bondsmen, and when served by a slave, he insisted upon paying the slave (Woolman 1989, 11).

In the example of John Woolman, widely known across the Quaker world, was rekindled another dimension of 'plain-ness': conscious and consistent self-examination for signs of one's participation in subtle forms of social exploitation. This line of reasoning articulated by Woolman was soon enjoined by scores of Quakers in England and America, who admonished their peers about the perils of wealth and began to develop guidelines for managing 'excess wealth' (Marietta 1974, 230).

One manifestation of Woolman's commitment to simplicity was his decision to retire, as a young man, from his lucrative retail business, because he felt that it demanded too much of his time, distracting him from the more important matter of fulfilling his religious responsibilities. Travelling widely through America, England, and Europe, Woolman and his comrades become the inspiration for later Quakers who would aspire to 'retire at age thirty to a life of genteel leisure and public service'. Historians have noted how the eighteenth and nineteenth centuries ushered in the context within which 'propertied self-sufficiently and performance of public service... [became]... the classic goals of the benevolent genteel and successful philanthropic Quakers' (Frank 2002, 121–5). So, too, would the guidelines modelled by Woolman reflect Penn's concerns that true religion should lead to avoiding clothing and consumer goods that required 'wasted' effort in caring for them, effort that might better be used for 'the best recreation' of doing good for society.

By the end of the eighteenth century, Quakers developed a strategy that drew on the social philosophies of William Penn, Robert Barclay, and, perhaps especially, Woolman. The strategy involved making a conscious choice to not only adopt simplicity in one's own life, but also to donate a sizeable segment of one's resources to charitable causes. Thus, as many British and American Friends joined the fight against slavery, others such as Peter Collinson and John Fothergill devoted their excess wealth to establishing philanthropic institutions such as schools, hospitals, and orphanages.

This adoption of strategies of committed philanthropy, often done anonymously so as to avoid the appearance of self-aggrandizement, occurred in the context of a discourse grown tense as Pennsylvanian John Churchman (1705–75), a supporter of Woolman, excoriated Friends for being 'delighted in the pursuit of worldly treasures'. Reacting with horror to the fact that London Friends had speculated in American land, Churchman and his peers reminded their community that Quakers should be 'particularly careful to have our minds redeemed from the love of wealth'. The desire to protect such wealth, argued these Friends, was the cause of war (Marietta 1974, 233–4).

The discourse acquired even greater urgency after the1750s, with the emergence of the issues that precipitated both the Seven Years War and the American Revolution. In America, a growing gap between the poor and the wealthy heightened class tensions. In addition, debates and finally war over England's right to tax that wealth, led some prominent Quakers to withdraw from positions of public authority rather than participate in warfare (Tolles 1963, 17–18, 27–8, 231–46). When, during the American Revolution, many Friends had their property confiscated because of their refusal to support the war, some interpreted this as God's message, expressed by Quaker abolitionist schoolmaster Anthony Benezet that 'it is in nothingness God is found' (Marietta 1974, 241). Thus by the end of the eighteenth century, frugal living (accompanied by vigilance about the social implications of one's economic behaviours), and the redeployment of time and effort to charitable causes, had become a *sine qua non* of Quakers' 'holy conversation'.

NINETEENTH CENTURY: SCHISMS AND REDIRECTIONS

Nineteenth-century Friends looked back nostalgically to their forebears who appeared to have found ways to discern and operationalize aspects of the holy conversation. John Woolman, with his staunch conviction about what was Truth, and his commitment both to living that Truth and to speaking it powerfully to others, was frequently held up as a model. In addition, Thomas Clarkson's (1760–1846) *Portraiture of Quakerism*, published in Britain in 1806, helped to codify the unostentatious lifestyle. Though Clarkson was not a member of the Religious Society of Friends, his *Portraiture* deeply influenced how Quakers and non-Quakers alike measured Quakerliness. Clarkson devoted significant attention to Quakers' 'Peculiar Customs'—including 'Plain Dress'—explaining that:

> [Quaker] men wear neither lace, frills, ruffles, swords, nor any of the ornaments used by the fashionable world. The women wear neither lace, flounces, lappets, rings, bracelets, necklaces, [or] ear-rings... Both sexes are also particular in the choice of the color of their clothes. All gay colors such as red, blue, green, and yellow, are exploded. Dressing in this manner, a Quaker is known by his apparel through the whole kingdom. (Clarkson 1806, 242)

Yet, even as Clarkson was describing how to recognize a Quaker, the nineteenth century ushered in factionalism among Friends who had begun to point accusing fingers at each other, insisting that the Religious Society of Friends was losing its moorings to its original theological foundations. Some elements of the controversy were familiar: were

Friends avoiding conspicuous consumption? Might one meet the guideline of plainness by purchasing an item of very high quality, but without decorative adornment? Was the most important means test an 'appropriate' ratio of means-to-expenditure? Might significant time and/or money donated to charity count as one measure of participation in the 'holy conversation?'.

But while the issues were recognizable, the language and tone of the debate were new. The debates at first coalesced around two New York Friends, Hannah Barnard (1754–1825) and Elias Hicks (1748–1830). Barnard travelled in England and Ireland, while Hicks, a New Yorker, travelled mostly in the United States. But the message they carried to their Quaker comrades was similar: over time, they argued, Quakers had lost the purity of their original spiritual energies. Distracted by secular temptations, modern Friends had allowed their faith to be diluted. As early as 1795, Elias Hicks, upon visiting a northern New York meeting, lamented that the Quaker children there had 'almost all gone out of plainness'. Though Hicks did not always specify exactly which aspects of loss caused him the most dismay, he indicated that he had preached to the parents to exercise 'more diligence and circumspection... in disciplining their children to live 'more agreeabl[y] to the simplicity of our holy profession' (Buckley 2009, 62).

Hicks, originally from a rural area, was wary of urban Quakers, whose wealth, he suspected, dimmed their religious vision. He railed against what he saw as over-reliance on the Bible and early Friends' writings, instead of reliance on the authority of the spontaneous Light Within. Identifying slavery as a stark indication of sinfulness in society, Hicks and his followers made anti-slavery activity a central tenet of their religious practice, embracing plain clothing as one symbol of their disapproval of slave labour. Many Friends, particularly wealthy ones in eastern US cities, aggravated by Hicks's zeal, labelled his followers 'Hicksites', and shunned them as heretics, redefined what it meant to be an 'orthodox' Quaker, even establishing 'guarded' educational institutions to shelter young Friends both from Hicksites and from other temptations of modern world.

Meanwhile, Hicks's disdain for urban Quakers was not unfounded. Indeed, during the first half of the nineteenth century, many American 'Orthodox' urban Friends had relaxed their rules against fashionable clothing and possessions. And it was not only urban American easterners whose vision of Quakerism was shifting. Moving to the western frontier, American Orthodox Friends became more willing to adorn their worship houses so that they resembled those of the other Christian communities they encountered there. Formal pastorates and systematically evangelical mission projects followed in time. Though in Britain the tensions did not rise to the level of schism, some prominent nineteenth-century Quakers also embraced more formal worship services and missionary zeal.

Friends such as British-born Joseph John Gurney (1788–1847) were drawn to other aspects of non-plain religion. The wealthy Gurney, whose aristocratic background and love of music made him suspect among some Friends, travelled throughout England and the American West, promoting Friends' alliances with religious sects that supported more elaborate worship rituals than had heretofore been advocated by Friends. By the 1860s, music, paid ministers, and revival meetings had, for many Quakers in the American Midwest, overridden the traditions of unadorned meeting houses and silent, spontaneous worship services. Expensive, if somewhat conservative, clothing and material goods now became part of the lives of such as Gurney, who remained devoted to Quaker theological and philanthropic values, but whose consumption patterns earned them the moniker 'gay' Quakers, i.e., Quakers whose high-style tastes could hardly be called 'plain' (Dandelion 2007, 95–9; Hamm 1988, 15–22).

Though in England the debate about theology and worship practice was more muted than in America, in other parts of the world, Quakerism acquired a diversity of beliefs and worship styles as revivalist Quakers from Britain and from Midwestern America introduced a version of Quakerism that was more traditionally Christian (i.e., including sermons and music) into Africa, the Middle East, Asia, and Central America. In these settings, debate about simplicity and plainness took a back seat as evangelicalism became the central theme of theology and worship.

Even as Friends' reality was becoming more diverse, however, popular culture— statuary, cartoons, and especially literature—gave rise to a stereotypical 'plain' Quaker as a vessel of virtue and uncorrupted (if rigid) social conscience. From novels such as Herman Melville's *Moby Dick* (1851), Harriet Beecher Stowe's *Uncle Tom's Cabin* (1853), and Sarah Stickney Ellis' *Friends at Their Own Fireside* (1858), readers in Britain and America formed a seemingly indelible image of the 'plain' Quaker, morally stolid and ascetic, dressed in drab clothing and wedded to 'plain speech' (Cummings 1996).

By the late nineteenth century, however, it was mostly Hicksite and 'Conservative Friends' who maintained external markers of plainness, and by the early twentieth century, only small groups of Quakers, scattered mostly in rural areas of the western United States and Canada, remained committed to outward expressions of the plain life, holding to dark-coloured, homespun clothing, and avoiding politics, voting, theatre, art, and alcoholic beverages. By that time, most other Quakers in England and the Americas had deemed such disciplines 'dead formality and ceremony', though urban Quakers in East Coast America often continued to send their children to Quaker schools and to address each other using plain language (Hamm 1985, 85).

The attention to 'plainness' as a guide to Friends' faith did not die but was transformed into a focus on simplicity. Most Friends across the world had settled on the definition expressed in the 1877 edition of the Baltimore Yearly Meeting *Discipline*, which espoused the vague guideline of 'simplicity in deportment and attire, avoidance of flattery and insincerity in language, and... non-conformity to the world... ' (Baltimore Yearly Meeting 1877, 65). And Friends continued to caution themselves to avoid 'a life of ease and self-indulgence' (Baltimore Yearly Meeting 1877, 62).

SINCE THE 1920S

The First World War accelerated a trend that had been growing since British Friends formalized their Friends Service Council, an international war-relief service that had begun as early as the 1870s. Building on this model, the 1917 founding of the American

Friends' Service Committee ushered in a fresh interpretation to the concept of simplicity. This emerging focus on the importance of 'right sharing' harkened back to the ideas of Penn and Woolman, who maintained that the creation and procurement of luxury goods are inherently exploitative of the poor, and therefore constitute economic injustice that is destructive to world peace and to Christian community life.

In the ensuing years, British and American Quakers joined forces to develop social service programmes that went beyond William Penn's concern of helping society's disadvantaged. Relief work during and after the First World War, support for peace negotiations and the development of the United Nations, and assistance for disenfranchised minorities became the focus of many Quaker communities. The new twist on Penn's theme was to *identify* with those who had been wounded by society. Terms such as 'voluntary poverty' appeared in Quakers' vocabulary, and by the 1930s activists such as Mildred Binns Young (1901–95) not only wrote about the value of such a choice, but also chose to make their lives in communities alongside the disadvantaged (Young 1939 and 1941).

Similar human rights programmes followed. Support for workers' cooperatives and education in Appalachia, coupled with deep involvement in the United States racial-justice work led many Friends to reduce their own consumption in order to support philanthropic causes. In Pennsylvania, the home office of the AFSC, and in other areas around the world, a concept developed of 'Live simply, that others may simply live'. Housing and industrial cooperatives, based on the democratic Rochdale principles developed in nineteenth-century England, sprang up in the 1940s. The area of Monteverde, Costa Rica, was developed as dairy farm land and wildlife preserves by American Quakers whose pacifist values led them to defy the American draft during the 1950s. By the 1960s, an increasing awareness of the lopsidedness of industrialized countries' consumption led Quaker meetings in western Europe and the United States to turn their attention to combating conspicuous consumption and planned obsolescence. In 1982, North Carolina Yearly Meeting (Conservative) noted that '... the testimony of outward simplicity began as a protest against the extravagance and snobbery which marked English society in the 1600s'. However, this group argued that in modern times simplicity should 'not mean drabness or narrowness' but rather should be 'a testimony against involvement with things which tend to dilute our energies... and an appreciation of all that is helpful towards living as children of the Living God' (PYM, 2002:158).

By 2002, Philadelphia Yearly Meeting's *Faith and Practice* suggested that 'Friends in comfortable circumstances need to find practical applications of the testimony of simplicity in their earning and spending... balancing the social value of self-sufficiency against the social value of... help for those more needy' (PYM, 2002:80–1).

Since the late nineteenth century, then, the concepts of 'plainness' and 'simplicity' have broadened and changed to embrace more expansive interpretations than were the guidelines of Founding Friends. Subsumed under more wide-ranging modern concerns to which many Liberal Friends are committed—human rights and social justice, preservation and sharing of natural resources, evading the constrictions of technology and/or capitalism, and the development of 'global community'—the concepts of plainness and simplicity in the twentieth century have, for many Friends, merged into concerns about responsible 'stewardship' of the world's finite resources. Expressions such as 'right shar-ing of world resources' or 'living simply so that others may simply live', have, in many Friendly communities, come to express values that originated in early Quakers con-cerns about simplicity and plainness.

By the twenty-first century, while most Quaker discipline guides include the testi-mony of 'simplicity', many have muted specific recipes for achieving it. A few Friends communities remain who are explicit about prohibiting such adornments as jewellery, make-up, and sexually provocative dress; the modern trend bends towards focusing on other elements of faith, such as the role and importance of Scripture, baptism, holy communion, or other aspects of Christian theology (Dandelion 2007, 221–40). Only a minority of present-day Friends, mostly Conservative Friends, use 'plain speech' or plain dress as markers of their faith. Nevertheless, the struggle to define a lifestyle that is sufficiently uncluttered to allow for hearing the 'still, small voice' of the Divine, remains a continued focus of Quaker faith. Additionally, especially for modern Liberal Friends, William Penn's suggestion that Friends maintain 'non-conformity' remains an impor-tant marker of Quaker identity and of Quaker plainness in Europe and the Americas. However, in the Quaker communities of Africa, the Middle East, and Asia, where capi-talist consumption is somewhat less pronounced, honing a definition of 'simplicity' takes a back seat to other religious concerns.

Recent Decades: an Acceptance of Diversity

Since its inception in the mid-seventeenth century, the Religious Society of Friends has differentiated itself from other religious communities by a commitment to a constel-lation of tenets that has included non-violence, spiritual equality, and an avoidance of external or 'worldly' distractions and fads. However, the focus on avoiding fads has lent itself, over time, to a diversity of definitions and strategies, and to an elusive vocabulary that embraces 'plainness', 'simplicity', and 'non-conformity'. Evolving from concepts drawn out of seventeenth-century British realities, these definitions, strategies, and vocabulary have both retained a core meaning and diversified as the realities of Quaker constituencies have diversified over several centuries, continents, and cultures.

Suggested Further Reading

Barbour, H. and Frost, J. W. (1988) *The Quakers*. New York: Greenwood Press.
Durham, G. (2011) *Being a Quaker: a guide for newcomers*. London: Quaker Quest.
Heron, A. (1995) *Quakers in Britain: a century of change, 1895–1995*. Kelso, Scotland: Curlew Graphics.

Gummere, A. M. (1901) *The Quaker: a study in costume.* Philadelphia: Ferris and Leach.

Ingle, H. L. (1986) *Quakers in conflict: the Hicksite reformation.* Knoxville: University of Tennessee Press.

Martinie Eiler, Ross (Spring 2008) 'Luxury, Capitalism, and the Quaker Reformation, 1737–1738', *Quaker History* 97:1, 11–31.

O'Donnell, P. (2003) 'Quakers as Consumers: Introduction', in Lapsansky, E. J. and Verplanck, A. A., *Quaker aesthetics: reflections on a Quaker ethic in American design and consumption.* Philadelphia: University of Pennsylvania Press, pp. 16–40.

Slaughter, T. (2008) *The beautiful soul of John Woolman, apostle of abolition.* New York: Hill and Wang.

CHAPTER 23

QUAKERS, SLAVERY, ANTI-SLAVERY, AND RACE

ELIZABETH CAZDEN

INTRODUCTION

POPULAR histories and some scholarly ones have often portrayed Quakers as consistently opposed to slavery, active in abolition efforts, and committed to racial equality. Even Quaker historians stressed Quaker anti-slavery rhetoric, ignoring inconvenient contrary facts or treating them as isolated slips between theory and practice. Accounts drawn from Quaker minutes and tracts have lacked the economic and social context and parallel non-Quaker discourse. Complicating the narrative, the term 'Quaker' often includes individuals (both slave traders and abolitionists) who never joined, left, or were disowned.

More recent scholarship has presented a more complex portrait of Quaker engagement with slavery and with interracial relationships. Many Quakers—past and present—have shared the racial and class values and practices of their surrounding communities. White Quakers' goals have fluctuated between integrating people of colour into the broader society and empowering African-American self-help efforts. Friends who championed abolition and racial equality were often marginalized. This chapter will present that fuller narrative, focused on Quakers in Britain and America and leaving for other chapters the multi-racial experience of Friends in Africa, Latin America, and Asia.

QUAKERS IN THE SLAVE-BASED BRITISH ATLANTIC EMPIRE, 1650–1750

The Quaker movement expanded geographically within an economic system dependent on enslaved African labour. By the 1650s, with labour scarcer than either land or capital, African workers were essential to profitable development of sugar plantations in the British West Indies, tobacco farms in the Chesapeake region, and wharves, shops, and farms in the northern colonies. The network of Quaker evangelism followed the trade routes.

Quakers' belief in spiritual equality did not immediately make slavery abhorrent. Theologian Robert Barclay (1648–90) insisted that salvation was available (though not guaranteed) to all, 'whether Jew or Gentile, Turk or Scythian, Indian or Barbarian' (Barclay 2002, 115). George Fox (1624–91), citing Scripture, affirmed that enslaved Africans and their English enslavers were ' all of one Blood & of one Mold' (Frost 1980, 47). Both Fox and his companion William Edmundson (1627–1712) preached to enslaved Africans in the West Indies.

But Friends did not object to social hierarchies; the Leveller–Digger impulses of the English Civil War quickly yielded to a desire for respectability. During Fox's 1671–2 visit to Quaker communities in the Caribbean, he stayed with plantation owners, noting with satisfaction that 'many persons of quality' became convinced (Fox 1995, 609). Intent on shielding Friends from persecution, Fox wrote to the governor of Barbados, presenting Friends as law-abiding citizens, with submissive enslaved Africans whom they taught 'to be sober and to fear God' (Fox 1985, 605). Fox's writings, especially *Gospel Family Order,* reinforced a biblically based ethic of mastery in which (male) family heads were responsible for the spiritual, moral, and temporal welfare of all in their households, including slaves (Frost 1980, 36–9; Frost 2012, 14–15). He encouraged Friends to treat their slaves according to the Golden Rule, an ameliorative approach shared with some other English Protestants (Frost 1980, 51–2). Even these efforts created conflicts; Friends in Barbados and Virginia were persecuted for teaching black people to read and taking them to worship.

A few Friends questioned whether slavery was consistent with the Gospel. In 1676, following King Philip's War, William Edmundson asked New England Friends, 'many of you count it unlawful to make slaves of the Indians: and if so, then why the Negroes?' (Drake 1950, 10). In 1688 a group of German-speaking Pennsylvania Friends wrote an anti-slavery minute, but the Monthly, Quarterly, and Yearly Meeting found the matter too weighty to resolve. In 1693 minister George Keith (1638?–1716), who would later leave Friends to work for the slave-holding Society for the Propagation of the Gospel, published a tract asserting that slavery violated the Golden Rule; that the Bible commanded Christians not to return escaped captives into bondage; and that Friends should avoid slaves as prize goods taken in war. But these messages had little effect.

Early Quaker perceptions of slavery may have been shaped by their own sufferings narratives. In 1658 Massachusetts authorities ordered several Friends to be sold into slavery in Barbados for refusing to pay fines, though no captain proved willing to transport them. After the 1664 Conventicle Act, English authorities threatened to ship Quakers to the colonies as temporary slaves, a punishment inflicted on Irish rebels. In the 1690s Friends, like other European travellers, were sometimes seized by Barbary pirates for ransom. In the seventeenth century, 'slavery' and 'captivity' were not restricted by race, and the legal distinction had not yet hardened between temporary captivity and lifelong hereditary chattel slavery.

By 1700, many Quakers came from (or moved into) social and economic elites with deep investments in the slave-based economy. In the West Indies, it was plantation owners who joined the Society. In Pennsylvania, William Penn's large landholdings relied in part on enslaved Africans. Landed gentry and merchants held leadership posts in meetings and colonial governments in Pennsylvania and Rhode Island. Quaker merchants in England and the mainland colonies profitably supplied foodstuffs to Caribbean plantations; more than a few owned shares in slaving voyages. Smaller shopkeepers imported sugar to accompany tea, coffee, and chocolate, rapidly becoming daily middle-class habits. Commercial and kinship ties between Quaker merchants in Britain, North America, and the Caribbean facilitated both travel in the ministry and the accumulation of wealth based, at least indirectly, on slave labour.

The Quaker administrative hierarchy, like British imperial structures, favoured men of wealth. The London Meeting for Sufferings, which lobbied on Friends' behalf and regulated Quaker practice, was dominated by large landowners, merchants, and early industrialists (Vann 1969b, 118–21). Its appointed correspondents for each colony were primarily merchants with colonial investments and business connections; their counterparts in the colonial Yearly Meetings came largely from the same mercantile elite.

Not surprisingly, while a few Quaker ministers criticized growing luxury and consumption, the official advice issued from London to Friends everywhere focused instead on the minutiae of Quaker practice: marriage procedure, removal certificates, and wills. Friends holding slaves were to 'treat them with humanity, and in a Christian manner', advice that differed little from that provided by Congregational or Anglican ministers such as Morgan Godwin (Frost 1980, 131). Servants (including slaves) should 'behave themselves in due subjection, humility and plainness, as becomes their profession and places' (London Yearly Meeting 1703). Friends should take slaves to Meetings for worship or set up separate Meetings (overseen by white ministers) to instil virtues such as sobriety and diligence, not to convert them to Quakerism. As in other churches, meetings mostly provided limited and segregated roles for people of colour, including separate seating and sometimes a separate burial area.

Between 1710 and 1717, a number of meetings, perhaps stirred by a cluster of slave rebellions, debated the propriety of slavery and especially the slave trade among Friends. A few vocal Friends including William Southeby (fl. 1696) of Pennsylvania, William Burling (1678–1743) of Long Island, and visiting English Friend John Farmer (b. 1667) condemned slave-holding, but were disowned for speaking and publishing without permission or otherwise challenging the Meeting's authority. A few Monthly Meetings brought forward anti-slavery minutes, with little effect. Meetings occasionally policed the boundaries of acceptable treatment; one New England meeting disowned a woman in 1711 for condoning a harsh beating, and another clarified that branding slaves was not agreeable to truth (Dartmouth, 5th mo. 1711; Rhode Island, 10th mo. 1715).

On occasion colonial Friends asked advice about slavery from London Yearly Meeting; London answered sparingly and only when asked directly. When Pennsylvania Friends expressed concern about the increased imports of Africans, London asked them to consult with other colonial Meetings, though concurring that importing Africans was 'not a Commendable nor allowed Practice' (London Yearly Meeting 1713). Neither party addressed trade with sugar plantations. Between 1698 and 1712, the Quaker-dominated Pennsylvania Assembly imposed heavy duties to discourage slave imports. Each time the Crown, protecting the lucrative slave trade, vetoed the colonial law; London Meeting for Sufferings declined to use its lobbying power to support the Pennsylvania anti-import campaign. In 1727 Philadelphia Yearly Meeting again asked London Yearly Meeting whether trading in slaves was consistent with Friends' principles. London replied that it was not. However, the advice was apparently not conveyed to any other Meetings until the 1750s when it appeared in Books of Extracts.

London, intent on preserving its carefully cultivated relationship with Parliament, also repeatedly reminded Friends to maintain unity, exercise patience, and not discuss controversial political questions. Philadelphia Yearly Meeting similarly cautioned Friends to 'forbear judging or reflecting on one another either in public or private' concerning slave ownership (Drake 26–7). Among Friends, as among their Congregational and Anglican peers, moral discomfort about slavery coexisted with a reluctance to challenge it.

Between 1729 and 1741 a new wave of anti-slavery agitation appeared. Philadelphia printer (and non-Quaker) Benjamin Franklin published strident tracts by Ralph Sandiford (1693–1733) and Benjamin Lay (1677–1759), resulting in disownments of both men for disorderly walking and publishing without the Meeting's consent. During Philadelphia Yearly Meeting in 1738, Lay dramatically stabbed a book containing a bladder of pokeberry juice, representing the blood of enslaved Africans. Lay has often been treated as an abolitionist martyr, silenced by Quaker oligarchs who opposed his message, an assessment at odds with his previous disownments for unrelated disruptive behaviour (Mielke).

Two other anti-slavery tracts, both published with permission, were better received. Nantucket carpenter Elihu Coleman (1699–1789) published a paper maintaining that slavery was contrary to nature as well as Scripture, and prevented slaves from following the will of God (Drake 1950, 37–9). In 1741, English minister John Bell (1681–1761) published an epistle to colonial Friends arguing that Friends' religious beliefs prohibited using force to control their slaves and living in luxury that required excessive work by enslaved labourers. While Bell advocated kind treatment, not manumission, he suggested that slavery harmed the moral character of slave owners. His epistle circulated widely, and provoked several meetings to strengthen their advice that Friends not import slaves from the West Indies.

Later in the 1740s, New Jersey minister John Woolman (1720–72), already uncomfortable with treating humans as chattel, travelled in the southern colonies observing slave-worked plantations and honing his moral objections to slavery. Unlike the fiery Lay, Woolman was esteemed for his charitable and kindly spirit. He was also politically astute enough to refrain from publishing his views until the Yearly Meeting's Overseers of the Press would approve (Frost 2012, 26–7).

THE TURN AGAINST SLAVERY, 1754–87

The official Quaker turn against slavery happened quickly, at mid-century. Caribbean Meetings were in severe decline, as persecution convinced Friends to either relocate or change denominations. The Seven Years' War disrupted shipping between the northern colonies and the West Indies, and Friends everywhere grappled with renewed persecutions for refusing to fight or to pay militia taxes. Some, viewing the war as punishment for years of laxness and luxurious living, called for a return to perfectionism and discipline. Many in Britain and the colonies concluded that trying to ameliorate slaves' living conditions and provide religious instruction failed to mitigate slavery's moral evils. In America, Great Awakening revivals, while tangential to Quakerism, stirred up discussions that led some to conclude that slavery was incompatible with Christian piety.

During the 1750s, Philadelphia Yearly Meeting Friends revisited the question of slavery as part of a general reform movement. Changes in Yearly Meeting leadership, particularly in the powerful Overseers of the Press, enabled anti-slavery voices to emerge without fear of censure. In 1754 the Overseers, among them Philadelphia schoolmaster Anthony Benezet (1713–84), authorized publication of Woolman's tract, *Some Considerations on the Keeping of Negroes*. The Yearly Meeting issued 'An Epistle of Caution and Advice, concerning the Buying and Keeping of Slaves', likely written by either Woolman or Benezet (Frost 1980, 167; Brendlinger 2007, 119–22). Although copies were apparently not sent officially to other Yearly Meetings, they circulated through the transatlantic Quaker network, and English reformist minister Samuel Fothergill took copies home with him.

By 1757 London Yearly Meeting, also promoting general reforms, took official notice 'that some under our name both in this nation and the Colonies abroad are concerned for Filthy Lucre Sake in Dealing with Negroes', and directed that its previous minutes condemning the trade be compiled and sent out as directives to Friends everywhere (London Yearly Meeting 1757). Meeting for Sufferings discovered, however, that the only such document was the 1727 advice to Philadelphia Friends. Accordingly, the 1758 London printed epistle included a strident condemnation of 'that iniquitous Practice of *dealing in Negroes and other Slaves*' and admonished Friends everywhere to 'keep their Hands clear of this unrighteous Gain of Oppression' (London Yearly Meeting 1758; Frost 1980, 174).

Colonial Yearly Meetings responded with a wave of minutes prohibiting slave trading and urging Friends to manumit their slaves. Later in 1758 Philadelphia Yearly Meeting excluded slave traders from participating in Business Meetings, a step short of outright disownment. The London Epistle strengthened the hand of reformers like John Woolman, who travelled throughout the colonies encouraging slave-holding Friends to manumit their slaves either immediately or in their wills. When he arrived in Rhode Island for New England Yearly Meeting in 1760, Woolman discovered that a Friend had slaves for sale, direct from Africa, near the meeting house (Woolman 1971, 109). The Yearly Meeting approved a new query on slave holding, and the Monthly Meeting quickly disciplined the offending merchant, Peleg Thurston.

In 1761 London Yearly Meeting clarified that engaging in the slave trade was grounds for disownment. British meetings, however, rarely if ever disciplined slave traders, of whom there were a considerable number, including members of the Meeting for Sufferings (Gary 1935, 194–6; Brown 2006, 100). Nor did British meetings discipline West Indies plantation owners. Slavery was treated as an American problem.

This anti-slavery push focused on separating Friends from the stain of the world's ways, not on eliminating the slavery system. Consistent with discussions throughout the British empire favouring gradual emancipation, and with an ethos of trying to reclaim sinners, Friends relied on individual moral suasion. Between 1758 and 1784 every North American Yearly Meeting prohibited Friends from trading in slaves and from holding persons in lifetime bondage. Monthly Meetings were directed to visit all slave-holding families to persuade them to manumit their slaves and to discipline those who refused.

Manumission proved thornier in practice than in theory, however. New England's 1770 minute required manumission of all 'of an age and condition suitable for freedom', addressing fears of local officials that freed people of colour, especially children and the elderly, would require town relief. Local meetings varied in diligence and enthusiasm for carrying out the Yearly Meeting directives. Some Friends freed their slaves under visiting committee's watchful eye. Others refused, stalled, or presented excuses; among those, some—but not all—were disowned. Of those disowned, some joined other churches, while others continued to attend worship, to dress, speak, and behave as Friends, and to be regarded as Quakers by outsiders. Meeting disciplinary actions against Friends for slave holding continued in some places into the 1840s, and even then may have missed some owners (Mangus 1999, 40–1). Hence summary statements that the Religious Society of Friends was entirely free of slave holding by 1776—or even by 1840—must be read with caution.

The Movement to Abolish Slavery, 1787–1833

Even while Friends struggled to end Quaker slave holding, some, like Anthony Benezet, realized that ending the slave trade and slavery itself would require government action. By 1766 Benezet directed his writing at political leaders in Britain and the colonies, drawing on first-hand accounts of the Africa trade and Scottish Enlightenment writings to argue that slavery was inconsistent with the Gospel, reason, and 'every common sentiment of humanity' (Brendlinger 2007, 15–17, 123–214). At the urging of John Fothergill, London's Meeting for Sufferings agreed to reprint and distribute Benezet's work. Attracting the attention of non-Friends such as Thomas Clarkson, John Wesley, Granville Sharp, and William Wilberforce (1759–1833), Benezet's writings contributed significantly to the formation of the transatlantic anti-slavery movement. Until 1780, however, despite pleas from Philadelphia's Meeting for Sufferings, London Yearly Meeting refused to campaign publicly for abolition of the trade, although it praised the efforts of American Meetings to do so.

A number of influential American Friends joined with other like-minded citizens in anti-slavery societies, including Moses Brown (1738–1836) and Thomas Hazard in Rhode Island, Robert Pleasants and Edward Stabler in Virginia, and William Dillwyn, Samuel Allinson, and David Cooper in New Jersey. Under pressure from these advocates, Pennsylvania enacted the first gradual emancipation statute in 1780, freeing children born after a given date. Other northern states followed, by either judicial decree or legislation. Some also restricted or taxed imports of slaves. As these state laws proved unenforceable, anti-slavery activists increasingly looked to national legislation. Friends and Meetings, especially in Philadelphia where the new Congress met, lobbied persistently for a ban on slave imports and an end to slavery (diGiacomantonio 1995).

By 1782 London Yearly Meeting, too, had a shift in leadership to younger well-educated Friends. At Yearly Meeting sessions in June 1783, with a number of American reformist ministers present, London Friends finally agreed to a petition to the House of Commons, drafted by Anthony Benezet and signed by 273 individuals, calling for an end to the British slave trade (Brown 2006, 1, 413–14; Brendlinger 2007, 215–20). It was favourably received but led to little action. For the next few years English Quakers systematically distributed anti-slavery literature (primarily Benezet's works) among the public as well as public officials. Anti-slavery activism came to define Quaker identity, although anti-slavery sentiment also grew somewhat fashionable in British society and probably did not represent the majority position among Friends. In 1787 New England Quaker Patience Brayton, on a religious journey to Britain, addressed a petition to King George III asking him to end the slave trade and free slaves throughout the empire.

In 1787 members of London Yearly Meeting's anti-slavery committee joined with non-Friends such as Evangelical Anglican William Wilberforce, for whom abolition became part of a broad reform campaign. Quakers wrote articles and letters, often anonymously, arguing against slavery on moral and practical grounds, while strategically allowing others to assume the visible leadership. Unlike the individual moral suasion of the 1750s, the new campaign was a highly organized lobbying effort—the first of its type—with petitions circulated and signed by thousands of ordinary men and women. A campaign to boycott slave products such as cotton, sugar, and indigo had little effect on the sugar trade—sugar consumption in Britain almost doubled between 1785 and 1805—but encouraged ordinary Britons, especially middle-class women, to join the campaign (Jennings 1997, 68–9). Friends can therefore claim some credit for the legal prohibitions on slave trading enacted in Britain and America in 1807–8.

FRIENDS RELATIONS WITH FREE
AFRICAN–AMERICANS, 1780–1835

As the number of free African-Americans increased, American Friends' focus shifted from manumission to support for former slaves. During the 1780s, many Meetings negotiated appropriate compensation, based on years of service, for people formerly enslaved by Friends. Some provided land for former slaves to use or hired them in their businesses. Quaker networks assisted free people of colour threatened with re-enslavement, including providing documentation of their free status, as well as those escaping into freedom.

Few African–Americans, either freed or enslaved, formally joined Quaker Meetings (Cadbury). Some Friends believed that people of African descent naturally preferred vigorous preaching and loud rhythmic music to Quaker worship based on silence. Friends such as Moses Brown of Rhode Island encouraged and supported independent black-led churches. But some African–Americans, such as Sarah Mapps Douglass (1806–82) of Philadelphia, wanted to join Friends but complained about having to sit in the back or in the gallery (Bacon 2001, 28–31). In an era when reform ministers stressed strict adherence to the discipline and separation from non-Quaker activities, Meetings carefully scrutinized all membership requests. African–American applicants sometimes experienced extra scrutiny and debate. Many attenders, regardless of race, never requested membership, although they attended Meetings regularly, used Quaker speech and dress, and considered themselves part of the Quaker community. When African–American/Wampanoag whaling captain and merchant Paul Cuffe (1759–1817) spoke from the floor of New England Yearly Meeting in 1810, it was likely the first time anywhere that a person of colour had done so (Wiggins 2001, 21).

Despite these barriers, some African–Americans formed close friendships and spiritual connections with white Quakers. Paul Cuffe was welcomed into Quaker homes throughout the United States and England; his friendship with Newport watchmaker Stephen Gould encouraged Gould to volunteer his time to a local African–American school (Wiggins 2001, 22). In Philadelphia, James (1788–1868) and Lucretia (1793–1880) Mott welcomed African–Americans including Robert Purvis (1810–98) and Sarah Mapps Douglass into their Philadelphia home (Bacon 2003).

Many Friends promoted education for former slaves and free blacks. 'Education' could include basic literacy, bookkeeping, vocational skills, and exhortations to thrift, diligence, and integrity, believed essential for both material success and ethical living. In 1750 Anthony Benezet opened what was likely the first Quaker-run school for black people in his Philadelphia home; by 1800 Philadelphia Friends supported seven such schools. Paul Cuffe founded an interracial school near his home in Westport, Massachusetts.

In the 1820s, as part of broader philanthropic efforts, many Friends, sometimes working with non-Friends, formed new organizations to help free people of colour, many stuck in menial jobs and miserable housing. In many communities, Quakers provided money and varying degrees of oversight for schools for African–American children staffed by African–American teachers. In Philadelphia, Friends in 1832 established the Institute for Coloured Youth. Prudence Crandall (1803–90), raised a Friend, ran a school for African–American girls in Connecticut in the 1830s.

In eastern Meetings, schools for African–Americans were distinct from schools established to provide a 'guarded education' to Quaker students. New England Yearly Meeting's boarding school (now Moses Brown School) turned away two children of colour in 1865, although the local public schools were already integrated (Chace 1937, 181). The fear that integrated schools would lead to 'racial amalgamation' seems to have been a major factor. In the Midwest, however, Quaker schools were open to non-Quakers and without regard to colour. Some white patrons paid tuition for African–American students.

Even as they promoted abolition, however, many Quakers remained embedded in an economy grounded in enslaved African labour. 'Free produce' campaigns had minimal impact on commerce. Quaker-owned shipping firms sent packet boats loaded with southern cotton from New York to Liverpool. English Quaker manufacturers shifted from woollen goods to cotton, joined by New England mill-owners. Only a few Friends expressed unease with relying on slave-produced cotton or tried to find supplies grown with free labour. At least one Quaker-owned mill in Rhode Island specialized in 'Negro cloth,' a cheap wool-cotton blend used for slave clothing on Caribbean plantations.

Some Friends, including Benjamin Lundy (1789–1839) of Ohio, William Thornton of Tortola, and John Fothergill in England, promoted colonization programmes to help freed African–Americans resettle in Africa. Merchant Paul Cuffe initiated a colony in Sierra Leone that could trade with America in goods rather than people. As the colonization movement became dominated by whites who opposed a racially mixed society, many African–Americans and their Quaker abolitionist friends abandoned it. However, a few, notably Benjamin Coates (1808–87) and Elliot Cresson of Philadelphia, continued to support emigration, convinced that white Americans would never admit African-Americans to full citizenship (Lapsansky-Werner 2007).

RADICAL ABOLITIONISM, GRADUALISM, AND THE CIVIL WAR, 1830–1865

The 1830s brought renewed campaigns on both sides of the Atlantic to legally abolish slavery. In England, Friends such as Liverpool merchant James Cropper, who imported sugar from India rather than the Caribbean, led the successful push to abolish slavery in the British empire. Like the earlier Quaker schemes, the 1833 law provided for gradual emancipation over five years. But to some, gradual emancipation now seemed far too cautious. In 1824 British Friend Elizabeth Heyrick (1769–1831) published a widely circulated pamphlet calling for immediate and complete emancipation. William Lloyd Garrison (1805–79) and others, both black and white, took up the cry for immediate and unconditional abolition, urging supporters to 'come out' from churches that hesitated.

Among American Friends, still smarting from the 1827–8 Hicksite–Orthodox schism, the new demand provoked sharp conflicts. Radical abolitionists labelled the gradualists as 'pro-slavery' and charged that they valued profits from the slavery economy more than moral principles. The 'pro-slavery' charge was at best exaggerated, as meetings continued to petition Congress to end slavery in the District of Columbia, restrict the internal slave trade, disallow slavery in newly settled territories and states, and weaken fugitive slave laws. Others protested local restrictive 'black codes'. The gradualists, for their part, accused the radicals of abandoning Quaker methods of working and fomenting dangerous and potentially violent unrest. The two major sticking points, played out in disciplinary proceedings, were participation in non-denominational abolition societies and use of Quaker meeting houses for public abolitionist meetings.

The more radical Quaker abolitionists affiliated with Garrison and with interdenominational anti-slavery societies, many stemming from Quaker work from the 1780s. The Garrisonian American Anti-Slavery Society, organized in Philadelphia in 1833, was at least one-third Quaker, mostly Hicksites. Its leaders included James and Lucretia Coffin Mott of Philadelphia and New England poet John Greenleaf Whittier (1807–92), who also wrote pamphlets, articles, and poems advocating immediate emancipation. Lucretia Mott and other Quaker women with experience running Business Meetings also provided needed leadership to female anti-slavery societies. Although a significant percentage of the most radical abolitionists were (or had been) Quaker, those activists were a small and non-representative minority within the Religious Society of Friends.

In the British and American campaigns that outlawed the slave trade in 1807–8, and in the British campaign to outlaw slavery itself, prominent Quakers had worked without objection within a larger abolition movement. But many American meetings now viewed the mixed societies with suspicion. In addition to mixing Quakers and 'the world's people', anti-slavery societies brought together black and white, men and women, an 'amalgamation' some considered unwise if not scandalous. Radicals pointed out on the other hand, that New York Yearly Meeting (Hicksite) left them little choice as it condemned abolitionists for working with non-Quaker groups while refusing to approve a Quaker Committee on Slavery (Moger 2003). Nevertheless, 'mixing with the world's people' became grounds for discipline and even disownment.

A second dispute was whether anti-slavery societies could use Quaker meeting houses for their lectures, many by Quaker speakers. Some Friends viewed the paid speakers as the prohibited hireling ministry. The burning of Pennsylvania Hall by an anti-abolitionist mob, and threats to other buildings, may also have weighed on Friends. Many Meetings barred their doors. Both New England and Indiana (Orthodox) Yearly Meetings ordered local Meetings not to allow any anti-slavery events because of their 'hurtful tendency'. Many Friends who in other ways supported abolition, such as Stephen Gould of Rhode Island, nevertheless supported the ban.

During the 1830s and 1840s, many radical abolitionists in both Hicksite and Orthodox Meetings, including Arnold Buffum, Sarah Grimké (1792–1873), Isaac T. Hopper (1771–1852), and Abby Kelley Foster (1811–87), were either disowned or resigned their membership in frustration. Eventually anti-slavery Friends from at least five Hicksite Yearly Meetings formed new groups, known as 'Congregational' or 'Progressive' Friends, which were more committed to abolition and other social reforms. James and Lucretia Mott remained within Philadelphia Yearly Meeting (Hicksite), but formed close ties with the Progressive Friends.

In Indiana (Orthodox), clerk Elijah Coffin (1798–1862) opposed black voting, integration, and especially 'racial amalgamation', and encouraged disownment of abolitionist Friends. In response, in 1843 abolitionist activists including Charles Osborn (1775–1850) and Levi Coffin (1798–1877) formed an Anti-Slavery Yearly Meeting that drew about ten per cent of the Yearly Meeting's membership (Jordan). London Yearly Meeting sent a committee, including Joseph John Gurney (1788–1847), to adjudicate the dispute. Despite London's stated support for abolition, and Gurney's own involvement in ecumenical abolition societies, the committee sided with the main Indiana body, pleading for 'true gospel unity' and instructing the separatists to return (Jordan). Indiana Anti-Slavery Yearly Meeting, unrecognized by London or by its Hicksite counterparts, dwindled as members either left Friends or rejoined the main body; it was formally laid down in 1857.

Friends in the southern states struggled to live faithfully by their anti-slavery beliefs in an economy dominated by slave-worked plantations, where state laws barred them from freeing, educating, or providing religious instruction to slaves. An estimated 45,000 Friends migrated, some accompanied by newly freed African–Americans, from Virginia and North Carolina into the 'free soil' of Ohio and Indiana (Barbour 1985b, 86). Those who remained suffered boycotts and intimidation by their slave-holding neighbours. North Carolina Yearly Meeting reluctantly agreed to take title to hundreds of slaves, to allow them to live as free while preventing their re-enslavement by non-Quakers. A few Friends, such as Samuel M. Janney (1801–80), sought to attract northern anti-slavery settlers into southern states to demonstrate the viability of farming without enslaved labour.

An unknown number of Friends violated the Fugitive Slave Law to help freedom-seeking African–Americans travel through northern states to Canada. Quaker ship captains carried concealed freedom-seekers from the Carolinas to northern ports. Lucretia Mott aided the famous escape of Henry 'Box' Brown in a crate from Virginia. Thomas Garrett (1789–1871) of Wilmington, Delaware, provided shelter, money, and shoes to groups led by Harriet Tubman. Levi and Catharine Coffin—models for the Quakers in *Uncle Tom's Cabin*—assisted so many people that he became known as 'the President of the Underground Railroad'. Although only a small percentage of Friends directly assisted freedom-seekers, many African–Americans reported feeling safe asking for help from anyone in Quaker costume (McDaniels and Julye 2009, 98).

During the American Civil War, Friends faced conflicts between their commitment to abolition and their opposition to war. Some Friends abandoned the peace testimony, enlisting or accepting conscription into the Union Army; others violated meeting discipline by paying $300 for a substitute. Some meetings, especially early in the war, disowned those who served or paid. Others, however, declined to do so when so many Friends had assisted in some way (Mangus 1999). When the Union blockaded southern cotton exports, English Quaker John Bright (1811–89) persuaded fellow mill-owners that ending slavery was worth temporary damage to the cotton trade, and lobbied successfully against England recognizing or assisting the Confederacy (Barbour 1985b, 120, 125).

QUAKER ASSISTANCE TO AFRICAN–AMERICANS, 1865–1920

During and after the Civil War, many Friends worked with the government Freedmen's Bureau and other churches and philanthropic associations to provide food, clothing, medical care, and schools to newly emancipated African–Americans in the southern states. Friends in the United States, Britain, and Ireland raised hundreds of thousands of dollars for this effort, with relief committees and sewing groups in virtually every American meeting. Some Friends bought up land in southern states and made it available at minimal cost to newly freed African–Americans; others helped former slaves relocate outside the southern states. Hundreds of Quaker men and women went south to nurse the sick, distribute supplies, and set up schools. Friends also funded African–American teachers, many of them trained in Quaker-run schools.

Although these schools for freed slaves taught religion, few envisioned their African–American students joining the Religious Society of Friends. Many believed, as one Friend complained in 1871, 'that *the coloured people* are too emotional and impressible ever to become Friends' (Kennedy 2009, 40). One notable exception was the Southland Institute (later College) in Arkansas, founded by Indiana Yearly Meeting (Orthodox). By 1868 directors Alida (1823–92) and Calvin Clark sent a steady stream of membership applications to her home Meeting in Richmond, Indiana, which accepted them despite the hesitations of the Yearly Meeting Freedmen's Committee. The Clarks soon requested that Daniel Drew (c.1842, fl. 1867–1907) be recorded in the ministry, likely the first African–American to be so recognized; ten others followed. In 1872 Indiana Yearly Meeting recognized Southland as a Monthly Meeting. It grew to over 500 members, almost all African–American, but was laid down when the school closed for financial reasons in 1925. In Cleveland, Ohio, Walter (1857–1935) and Emma (1859–1924) Malone also evangelized among African–Americans and welcomed them into their Cleveland Bible Institute (now Malone University).

The content in schools for children of colour varied considerably. Some, like the Institute for Coloured Youth (now Cheyney University) under the leadership of African–American Fanny Jackson Coppin, provided a strong college-preparatory education. In other Quaker-run schools, however, the curriculum was limited by doubts about African–Americans' intellectual capacity and an emphasis on moral values that would discourage violence and civil unrest. By 1900 Friends in the United States and in the new Friends Africa Mission largely adopted the Tuskegee model of African–American education advocated by Booker T. Washington, with 'industrial training' for boys and 'domestic training' for girls to prepare them for the jobs most readily available in a segregated society.

INTEGRATION AND THE CIVIL RIGHTS MOVEMENT, 1920–1980

Following the First World War, a number of American Friends took up concerns about race relations. The American Friends Service Committee (AFSC), the Five Years Meeting, and other Quaker organizations held conferences on racial prejudice. Quaker periodicals carried articles and letters addressing the need to identify and eliminate attitudes of racial prejudice among Friends. A few Friends, notably lawyer L. Hollingsworth Wood (1873–1956) of New York Yearly Meeting (Orthodox), worked with interracial organizations such as the National Urban League and the National Association for the Advancement of Coloured People (NAACP).

These sentiments were far from universal, however. In a few places Quakers were openly hostile to African–Americans. During the 1920s an unknown number of Midwestern Quakers belonged to the Ku Klux Klan; at least two, Daisy Douglas Barr (1875–1938) and pastor Ira Dawes, held leadership positions. Indiana Yearly Meeting (Orthodox) in 1922 felt compelled to advise members not to join or assist the Klan, due to its secrecy and its 'fostering and fomenting race hatred' (Indiana Yearly Meeting [Orthodox] 1922, 126).

Even Meetings with more tolerant attitudes had few African–American participants. Differences in social class, culture, and education complicated the racial divide of a largely segregated society. In 1900 Friends in the United States, regardless of branch, were overwhelmingly rural and white. Meetings followed their members, a number moving from urban neighbourhoods with increasing African–American populations to predominantly white suburbs. New unprogrammed Meetings, comprised of well-educated professionals and businesspeople, were established primarily in college towns and suburbs, where there were few people of colour. One 1937 report noted:

> [T]here are practically no Negro members of the Society in the U.S.A., nor apparently are Negroes generally encouraged to join. They are not employed in Friends' businesses; they are welcomed with hesitancy in Friends' homes—it is nearly impossible for their children to attend our secondary schools—and [they] are dissuaded from locating in Friends' neighbourhoods. (Friends World Committee for Consultation 1937, 88)

Friends' concern for race relations was often couched as 'our' concern about 'them'.

Throughout the country concerned Friends joined, and in some cases led, community campaigns to promote desegregation and racial justice. Fair-housing campaigns challenged racial restrictions on housing; Friends recruited people willing to sell to African–Americans, challenged racially restrictive covenants, and acted as testers to investigate suspected discrimination. Friends initiated several new multi-racial and cooperative housing developments. In the 1940s AFSC hosted interracial gatherings at Davis House in Washington, DC, though it was forced to move the programme to a different location due to neighbourhood opposition. Friends Committee on National Legislation and influential women Friends, including Emily Green Balch (1867–1961) and Hannah Clothier Hull (1872–1958), supported the NAACP's campaign for a Federal anti-lynching law.

Education remained a key focus for Quaker race relations work. A number of individual Friends and AFSC advocated for peaceful integration of public schools and supported African–American families braving opposition and even violence to enrol their children in formerly all-white schools. Friends also opened at least four new intentionally integrated Quaker schools, in Virginia Beach, Virginia (1950), Westbury, New York (1957), Cambridge, Massachusetts (1961), and Detroit, Michigan (1961).

Many Quaker schools and colleges, however, hesitated to admit students of colour. After extended discussion, Oakwood School in New York and Media Friends School in Pennsylvania admitted their first African–American students in the 1930s. At Media, however, one-third of the white students then withdrew, causing a financial crisis that alarmed trustees of other schools. By the mid-1950s, however, pressure from pro-integration Friends and from students, as well as the 1954 US Supreme Court decision ordering integration of public schools, convinced most schools to revise their policies. Frequently they admitted only one African–American child per grade, keeping the numbers of students of colour small. Many maintained formal or informal policies against interracial dating. Guilford College in North Carolina decided to admit African–American students only after it invited Friends World Committee for Consultation (FWCC) to hold its 1967 World Conference there, which provoked concerns about how African Friends would be treated on a segregated campus. Only in the 1970s did most schools add a substantial number of non-white students, faculty, and staff, and explicitly include the African–American experience in the curriculum.

Quakers involved in desegregation work came together in National Conferences of Friends on Race Relations, organized by FWCC between 1956 and 1970, to discuss the civil rights movement, housing, and education. Several African–American Quakers served on the planning committees for these meetings, including Barrington Dunbar (1901–78), George Sawyer (1925–2002), Dwight Wilson, and Margot Adair.

There were numerous links between Friends and the black-led civil rights movement. African–American Bayard Rustin (1912–87) of New York Yearly Meeting worked with AFSC and the Fellowship of Reconciliation, advised Martin Luther King, Jr. and the Southern Christian Leadership Conference on the theory and practice of non-violent direct action, and was a lead organizer of the 1963 March on Washington. AFSC arranged for the first mass distribution of King's *Letter from the Birmingham Jail*. Civil rights leaders, including King, spoke at Friends General Conference Gatherings and at the 1967 Friends World Conference.

After the 1968 assassination of Martin Luther King, Jr., however, many African–Americans rejected non-violent campaigns to integrate blacks into mainstream American society. Black Power advocates accused white allies, including Quakers, of trying to maintain white dominance. Increasingly, groups such as the Black Panthers demanded that predominantly white institutions, including Quakers, relinquish leadership and simply donate money, as reparations, to black-led organizations. In response, several American Yearly Meetings committed to raising substantial sums for economic development projects in minority communities. AFSC responded to this pressure by hiring non-white, largely non-Quaker, staff for programmes serving communities of colour, instead of white Quakers. It eliminated programmes such as weekend workcamps that had promoted integration and cross-racial personal connections. These changes created considerable tension between AFSC and its Quaker constituency, and reduced opportunities for white middle-class Quakers to work with African American activists.

QUAKERS AND RACE IN THE TWENTY-FIRST CENTURY

Since the 1970s, the population of Quakers around the world, as well as in the United States, has become significantly more multi-racial. African Friends now constitute more than half the Quakers in the world. At the same time, a number of American meetings have engaged in outreach and evangelism in communities of colour. An evangelical worship group in the predominantly African–American Cabrini-Green public housing project in Chicago became a Monthly Meeting, the Chicago Fellowship of Friends, in 1986, although the project was laid down in 2005 following razing of the housing project. Evangelical Friends International has church-planting projects among Haitians in Florida and New York and among Central Americans (many of them already Quaker) in cities throughout North America. New York City Friends have established a programmed meeting for worship intended to serve Friends from Jamaica. Unprogrammed meetings throughout North America are challenged by engagement with local immigrants from Evangelical Meetings in Central America and Africa, whose language and worship styles differ from their own. Some white Friends have adopted children of colour, making young Friends' groups more diverse than their adult counterparts. Most American meetings, however, remain overwhelmingly white. In 2004 Ernestine Buscemi of New York became the first African–American clerk of a North American Yearly Meeting.

In the United States, a number of Friends of both African and European descent are engaged in explicit anti-racism work, such as Niyonu Spann's 'Beyond Diversity 101' workshops. The Ministry on Racism programme of Friends General Conference conducts anti-racism programmes in local meetings and arranges periodic gatherings of Friends of colour. Evangelical Quaker pastor Richard J. Foster has also called on Friends to work against racism 'that dehumanizes those for whom Christ died' (quoted in Hamm 2003, 157).

Changing Quaker demographics and concerted anti-racism work have altered the structures and functioning of many Quaker organizations. The 1937 Friends World Conference had only three African participants, reflecting the African Meetings' status as mission fields rather than full Yearly Meetings. Between 1956 and 1975, as Yearly Meetings were recognized and grew, FWCC's gatherings of African Friends became an organized African Section; Kenya hosted worldwide FWCC conferences in 1961, 1982, 1991, and 2012. Simeon Shitemi of Kenya and Duduzile Mtshazo of South Africa have served as clerks of FWCC. Friends United Meeting has also formed an African section of its General Board and held General Board and Triennial Meetings in Kenya. African–American Dwight Wilson served as General Secretary of the US-based Friends General Conference. In 2001 Friends representing a number of Quaker groups attended the UN-sponsored World Conference against Racism in Durban, South Africa.

Friends' history shows a complex pattern of engaging with issues of racial equity, as individuals and Meetings have grappled with both theory and practice in a context of slavery, segregation, and economic inequality. In recent years the changing racial composition of the Religious Society of Friends, due to international missions and multi-racial outreach within the United States, has significantly shifted that discourse.

Suggested Further Reading

Barbour, H. (ed.) (1985) *Slavery and Theology: Writings of seven Quaker reformers, 1800–1870.* Dublin, IN: Prinit Press.

Brown, C. L. (2006) *Moral capital: Foundations of British abolitionism.* Chapel Hill: University of North Carolina Press.

Drake, T. E. (1950) *Quakers and slavery in America.* New Haven: Yale University Press.

Frost, J. W. (ed.) (1980) *The Quaker origins of antislavery.* Norwood, PA: Norwood Editions.

Gary, A. T. (1935) *The political and economic relations of English and American Quakers (1750–1785).* D.Phil. Thesis, Oxford.

McDaniel, D. and Julye, V. (2009) *Fit for freedom, not for Friendship: Quakers, African Americans, and the myth of racial justice.* Philadelphia: Quaker Press of FGC.

Soderlund, J. R. (1985) *Quakers & slavery: A divided spirit.* Princeton, NJ: Princeton University Press.

Weaver, H. D. Jr., Kriese, P., and Angell, S. W. (eds.) (2011) *Black fire: African American Quakers on Spirituality and human rights.* Philadelphia: Quaker Press of FGC.

CHAPTER 24

QUAKERS, WAR, AND PEACEMAKING

LONNIE VALENTINE

INTRODUCTION

FROM its origins in the English Civil War of the seventeenth century, to this day of ongoing and interconnected warfare across the world, the Religious Society of Friends has struggled with the relationship between what was seen as the 'leadings of the Spirit' and civil government. Further, this tension entered the Religious Society of Friends as well, and Quakers disagreed on what that relationship ought to be. Friends neither accepted whatever governments demanded nor rejected government as of no concern to Friends, and Friends have found themselves continuously wrestling with how to engage with the world. This chapter explores Quaker thought and action against war and for peace in light of this tension.

IN THE BEGINNING: APOCALYPSE THEN

The genesis of Quaker perspectives on peacemaking was shaped in war and for the emerging Quaker movement, the way to peace was through war. In its beginning, Quakers were gripped in apocalyptic expectations that permeated England. Shortly before the formal Declaration to Charles II that the Quakers rejected fighting with 'outward weapons' for any human kingdom or even the Kingdom of God, George Fox (1624–91) wrote a pamphlet in 1659 to the army and political leaders urging them to a divine mission to conquer Rome. He wrote: 'And if ever you soldiers and true officers come again into the power of God which hath been lost, never set up your standard until you come to Rome, and it be atop of Rome, and there let your standard stand'

(Brock 1990, 15). Fox was not alone in seeing that the Lamb of God wielded the sword in Holy War. Hence, in the apocalyptic cauldron of the English Civil War, Friends generally embraced the cause. It was through Holy War that the Peaceable Kingdom would come.

During the English Civil War, there were many Quakers who joined the New Model Army, and their zealousness for a spiritual transformation of faith and politics by inward and outward means was often seen as too extreme and dangerous by those in political power. The Quakers and other dissenters were thought to be demanding too much of the army, expecting too much of the new government, and seeking too much transformation of individual hearts. Since this apocalyptic vision attracted many in the army to the Quakers, it caused the commanders to fear the Quakers. As Henry Cromwell reported in 1656, 'Our most considerable enemy now in our view are the Quakers. I think their principles and practices are not very consistent with civil government, much less with the discipline of any army' (Brock 1990, 11). Thus, during the period of Puritan rule, Quakers were sometimes pushed out of the army, often because they were too apocalyptic, not because they were pacifists (Hill 1984, 129). For Quakers the collapse of the spiritual and political revolution they sought was not at the restoration of Charles II in 1660, but the failure of those leading the revolution to be pure enough in faithful commitment.

However, before the Restoration in 1660 and the statement of Friends' refusal to participate in war, some Quakers, including leaders of the movement, had already embraced pacifism as a divine leading. George Fox combined a refusal to take up the sword with urging the government and army to pursue war for the sake of the kingdom. In a letter to Cromwell in 1654, Fox said that his own calling was to bring people to Christ rather than participate in warfare, but told Cromwell to wield the sword to restrain evil. In his *Journal*, Fox says that in 1651 he was twice offered military command to fight in the army for the Commonwealth. However, Fox says he told them that he 'was brought off from outward wars', and that he now lived 'in the virtue of that life and power that took away the occasion of all wars' (Fox 1995, 65). This may sound confusing, but the fulcrum of early Quakerism was a view that though some would spread the Gospel with spiritual weapons only, other Quakers were rightly called to take up the sword.

How is it that Fox could both support Cromwell's war and even support Quakers in the army, and yet refuse to join them in such a fight? Fox and early Friends often referred to Paul's Letter to the Romans, ch. 13:1–7. Here Paul writes that Christians ought be 'subject' to the governing authorities and those who resist government authority resist God. Rulers, then 'are not a terror to good conduct, but to bad' and the divinely ordained ruler 'does not bear the sword in vain' (Weddle 2001, 26). With this view of pacifism as vocation, it becomes easier to understand how Fox could both decline to participate in the Civil War and yet support not only Cromwell, but Quakers who served in his army. Thus, a war could be both divinely sanctioned while some were called by that same divine power to refuse all war.

George Fox was not alone in combining a personal commitment to refuse to participate in war while encouraging others to participate in such wars if they were so led. A
number of historians studying Quakerism have argued that Quaker pacifism was rare
before 1660 (Hill 1984, Reay 1985). Further, some historians see the Quaker rejection of
war in the statement to Charles II in that year as a self-protective measure (Ingle 1994).
However, there are records of a number of other Quakers who came to reject 'all wars and
fightings' well before 1660. Important early Quaker leaders such as William Dewsbury
(c.1621–88) and John Lilburne (1615?–57) had been soldiers, but were moved to pacifism. Also, there are records of many Quakers who were not leaders coming to put down
their weapons. For example, Quaker soldiers Peter Hardcastle and Robert Evans both
left the army and Evans' testimony says that his conscience moved him to reject war.
However many Quakers were becoming pacifists in the army, it is clear that there were
enough to worry the military in a new way. Rather than being too enthusiastic for the
militant cause, Quakers in the army were being persuaded to reject the use of arms.
General George Monck was informed of the Quaker danger in that 'these people's principles will not allow them to fight' (Braithwaite 1955, 229–30). The situation was similar
in the colonies before 1660. For example, there are records showing that about thirty
Quakers in Maryland in 1658 were punished for refusing to take up arms in the local
militia. Likewise Rhode Island, although the first colony to recognize conscientious
objection in 1657 because of Quaker influence, also passed legislation to fine those who
refused to join the militia.

For a detailed example of a military man moved to embrace Quaker rejection of war,
there is the testimony of Thomas Lurting (c.1632–1713) in his *Fighting Sailor Turned
Peaceable Christian* (Kuenning 2002, 1–31). He described the emergence of his 'scruple
of conscience' against fighting, and this occurred in the midst of a battle. He had come
to know Quakers on board his ship and was attracted to their message even though
those Quakers were punished for not joining the required worship on the ship. When
Lurting was convinced further that fighting is wrong, the other Quakers were not clear
on this aspect of Quakerism. Lurting presented this as a situation where it was God
leading him to reject arms, and so in this he was like Fox and others who believed
that this rejection of such outward fighting was the work of divine leading. Historian
Margaret Hirst sums up her view of these early accounts of Quakers being moved to
reject war in this way:

> Hence it was not primarily by the literal interpretation of certain verses in the
> Sermon on the Mount that their testimony against wars and fightings arose, but by
> an inward convincement that such practices were contrary to the Spirit of Christ.
> (Hirst 1923, 41)

Thus, Quakers came to a crisis point at the end of the 1650s and had to reconsider how
they were to relate to their holy expectations for bringing in the Kingdom of God and
the disappointment of these expectations. This crisis was a new apocalypse for Friends
and resulted in a movement that changed the way Quakers saw war and peace.

From Divine Revolution to Government Reformation

With apocalyptic fires dampened, the nascent Society of Friends emerged from the crisis with a sense of their calling to speak the Truth of the Spirit and lay down 'outward weapons' for spiritual weapons alone. In the Declaration to Charles II of 1660 (Kuenning 2002, 181–8), Friends stated that none of their members would participate in war any more 'either for the kingdoms of this earth or for the Kingdom of God'. While the rejection of war was now the position of the entire Society, not all Quakers who had participated in the Civil War accepted this position.

Though the organizational commitment to pacifism was established, questions of what exactly Friends were to do when wars came emerged. In the matter of warfare, Friends were clear that if government did not allow Friends to follow their conscience in rejecting participation in war, the Quaker standard was to refuse obedience to the government and take the consequences peaceably. In England as in the American colonies, there was no universal military obligation. Rather, there were differing obligations in time and place that required able-bodied men to train in the militia and to be ready to take up arms if required by the authorities. Quakers were nearly consistent in refusing to take up arms for such service, but there were related issues that emerged that required further discernment.

Often anyone called to service could provide payment for someone else to serve in their place or willingly pay a fine if they failed to appear when called. Until the close of the seventeenth century, Friends almost universally believed that taking this route was too close to direct military service and so refused to obey. They did not resist when government officials then seized their property as penalty. However, there were struggles over what the Quaker stance ought to be if tax money was collected for support of various military-related activities but not directly tied to their personal participation in war. Mostly, Quakers drew the line between anything directly and exclusively supporting the military and general taxes, following Fox and others who made this distinction based upon their reading of Romans 13. In 1676 Robert Barclay, the key Quaker theologian, wrote that Friends 'have suffered much in our country . . . because we neither could ourselves bear arms, nor send others in our place, nor give our money for the buying of drums, standards, and other military attire' (Barclay 2002, 473).

Following the formula laid down by George Fox, Friends generally refused to contribute to specifically war-related taxes, but usually did pay general taxes levied by the governing authorities even if it was clear that some money would be used for military purposes. In the records of 'Sufferings' between 1660 and 1700, there are noted many occasions where Quakers were imprisoned or had possessions taken for refusing to cooperate with demands to support the military. For example, Friend Philip Ford was brought to trial in London around the turn of the eighteenth century for refusing to pay the fine levied on him for refusing to participate in the London militia. Ford spoke clearly about how he 'received a summons from the Prince of Peace to march under his banner, which is love, who came not to destroy men's lives but to save them'. However, he indicated he was ready to pay all regular taxes, even when this money would in part be used for defensive military purposes, since this responsibility was Caesar's and Ford saw this as his duty to the governing authorities. Not all Quakers agreed and some rejected paying taxes required for defensive efforts. Thus, there was a struggle to discern where Friends would draw the line on the government demands related to war. This is a point of tension that persists for Quakers today in relation to government spending for the military.

This tension between Quaker pacifism and government demands for support of the military at times led Friends to support military efforts they had earlier refused. The militia was formed but twice from 1700 to 1750, once in 1715 and again in 1745 during the Jacobite uprisings, and during these times of stress Quakers did pay money demanded to support the militia and some even took up arms (Hirst 1923, 1889). Also, some Quakers enthusiastically supported the war-making of the governing authorities. For example, when the militia was called up during these two uprisings, some Friends expressed public support for the king's victory and sent gifts, including ten thousand wool waistcoats to keep the soldiers warm. Though they were apparently disciplined by their Meetings, nonetheless the tension there was made clear between Quakers serving Christ non-violently and so refusing to fight while also serving Caesar who was understood to have the role of God's political and sometimes coercive authority.

Along with this rejection of war and the emerging tensions among Quakers on what this meant, questions arose about how pursuing the gospel of peace was to be done. The 1660 Declaration says that not only were Friends called by the Spirit of Christ to reject all warfare with carnal weapons, they were to 'seek peace and ensue it'. The theological underpinnings of this position were given by Elizabeth Bathurst in her systematic theology, *Truth's Vindication* (1679). Bathurst writes: ' I now find (force) to be diametrically opposite to that Foundation Principle, upon which (Quaker) religion is built, which Principle is Christ, the Prince of Peace, who utterly disallows of all coercive compulsion, force, constraint or violence to be used in matters of religion' (Garman et al 1996, 418). Friends began to engage in many experiments to discern how they were to proceed to engage with the government and their larger society with only 'spiritual weapons'.

Central to this shift was the stress on the inward changes required of anyone to be led by the Spirit and to then manifest peaceableness in their actions. That is, rather than seeking to take over society by storm and thereby enforce peace, the Quakers relied on gathering together to seek the guidance of the Spirit of Christ and to preach this gospel without force. The understanding of 'the Lamb's War' was disjoined from seeking the coercive political means to enjoin it. However, the notion of seeking and preaching inward transformation was not limited to being evangelical witnesses for the Spirit. Friends sought to discern how the Spirit called them to reform society. Quakers claimed, citing the Letter of James, that wars arose from 'lust', which is human pride and self-seeking, and the anger that arose from the frustration of these lusts. Hence, the search for peace began as this inward struggle, and Friends invited others to join in this struggle. This was central to any claims to be peaceable and any work for alleviating the suffering of others. However, Friends did not withdraw from addressing social ills and so continued the effort to create larger social change. Rather than establishing a revolutionary theocracy, Friends sought social reform so that the Spirit might be able to work in the hearts of others.

In relations with the government about matters other than warfare, Friends also challenged aspects of government rule rather than always passively accepting suffering caused by the government. Sometimes passive suffering was what the Spirit called Friends to do; sometimes resisting non-violently was what was needed. After the Restoration of Charles II and in spite of the Quaker Declaration to him that they would not fight the monarchy, there were government actions that pressed upon Quakers and provided prison terms for disobedience. For example, the Quakers were faced with how to respond to direct government prohibitions upon their religious practices: these included the Corporation Act of 1661 requiring oaths and forbidding petitions to the government, the Quaker Act of 1662 prohibiting Friends' Meetings, and the Coventicle Acts of 1664 and 1670 that prohibited attendance at all religious services except the Church of England (Weddle 2001, 33). Friends now understood that they must sometimes obey the government but at other times non-violently resist the government.

As a central example of this approach, William Penn (1644–1718) sought to discern when to accept government punishment for disobedience and when to challenge the government. In Penn's prison term for questioning the concept of the Trinity he wrote *No Cross, No Crown* (1669) where he argued that one must 'listen to the Light' and 'daily bear the cross of Christ' in one's life. This meant that the world would reject you, as it did Christ, but this is the true Christian witness to the world. However, later Penn was arrested for preaching in front of a London meeting house that was declared an illegal place of worship and again locked up by the government. In his trial, Penn did not accept punishment passively, but argued for religious freedom of conscience. The jury refused to convict Penn and the judge then sentenced the jury to prison, but this sentence was overturned on appeal. Penn's trial is a vital expression of the right to trial by jury and Penn wrote *The Great Case of Liberty of Conscience* (1670) seeking to change the government's laws during this prison term (Dunn 1967, 14). So, in Penn's example we see how Friends held the centrality of spiritual practices that sometimes led to passive acceptance of the government's actions and at other times led to non-violent resistance to the government. Thus, the Friends tried to balance obedience to the government generally with resisting government in particulars, and this was the pattern in Quaker engagement with questions of warfare and peacemaking. This tension between sometimes suffering for the Spirit and sometimes resisting for that same Spirit was not without its difficulties on matters of war and peace, as would become clear in William Penn's colony itself.

The Holy Experiment: from Government Reformation to Political Witness for Peace

In the colonies, Quakers had the opportunity to attempt to reform government towards their peaceable testimony, since they became the dominant political force in Rhode Island and Pennsylvania and quite influential in other of the colonies. Here was a chance to reform government on Quaker ideals. As historian Rufus Jones puts it: 'Friends felt a profound responsibility laid upon them to work out their principle of the Light within the field of political life' (1923, 329). However, in these two colonies, they found it difficult to reject war as their Quaker beliefs held and still have responsibility to govern the colonies. In Rhode Island, King Philip's War in 1675 saw individual Friends and Quakers in government support military measures (Weddle 2001). In the 'Holy Experiment' of Pennsylvania, Penn was given an entire colony by the power of English crown. He sought to join the workings of the Spirit with a government that would work to make peaceable space for the expressions of the Spirit. However, working out how to live as a peaceable Quaker and govern created a fracture in Quakerism. William Penn recognized this problem in seeking a Quaker government. In his *Frame of Government for Pennsylvania* Penn wrote that:

> Government, like clocks, go from the motion men give them, and as governments are made and moved by men, so by them they are ruled too ... Let men be good and the government cannot be bad: if it be ill, they will cure it. But if men be bad, let the government be never so good, they will endeavor to warp and spoil it to their turn. (Barbour and Frost 1988, 75)

This was a radical experiment in democracy as a government established for the good growth of the human spirit, but the seeds of its own destruction were there because of the recognition of the primacy of conscience in democratic governance. As Penn had argued for government to respect his own claim to conscience in matters of worship and war, in the Holy Experiment of Pennsylvania, some Quakers argued for freedom of conscience in either advocating for war or advocating for peaceful resistance to the war-making of the government.

Though Friends generally sought to resolve conflicts peaceably and compromise with governments at times to keep the peace, they still stated that the guidance of the Spirit was overall. This applied even to the government of Pennsylvania. Some Friends argued that now that Quakers were in government, they needed to support the military in order to protect the citizens: Quakers were now the rulers as described in Romans 13, and now had to wield the sword to keep the peace. On the other hand, other Quakers, such as John Woolman, argued that when the choice becomes preserving ties to government or separating because of the leadings of the Spirit, the choice is clear even if Quakers were in the government. For example, Woolman and others in Pennsylvania sought relief from paying taxes to be used for the French and Indian War by setting up an alternative fund so that those who did not want to pay taxes for war purposes could have their tax payments directed towards financial efforts to seek peace with the Native Americans. In their petition to the colonial government, which included many Quakers, these Friends stated that if such provisions were not made, they would then refuse to pay taxes used for war.

Despite the tensions that beset the Holy Experiment, it survived for seventy-five years. The key pressures towards the end of Quaker influence in Pennsylvania in the 1750s came from settlers welcomed into the colony who then began encroaching on Native American territory, resulting in killings on both sides.

With the large movement of Quakers from England to the American colonies, the influence of Quaker notions on colonial governments was significant. So, as in England, many colonies came to recognize Quaker conscientious objection. From the mid-1750s to the Revolutionary War, important colonies such as New York, Massachusetts, Virginia, Rhode Island, and North Carolina provided exemptions from militia service for Quakers. As in England, Quakers had to deal with the question of paying another to serve in their place or paying fines and paying taxes used for the military. Rhode Island so understood liberty of conscience that it not only extended conscientious objection provisions for Quakers, it extended this to anyone who objected on reasons of conscience, including those who did so on non-religious grounds (Hirst 1923, 331). This broad influence in the colonies led James Madison to argue that conscientious objection ought to be enumerated in the Bill of Rights in the debates shaping the US Constitution. It was considered, but left to the separate states to decide.

Friends were coming to see that their convictions about government, war, and conscience were meant for the world, not only the English and their colonies. Penn argued in his *Essay Towards the Present and Future Peace of Europe* (1693) that an international structure of representatives from European governments could better the lives of their citizens by preventing wars and resolving the conflicts between states. Other Quakers subsequently made similar efforts to propose international structures for peacemaking, including John Bellers's *Some Reasons for a European State Proposed to the Powers of Europe* (1710).

In addition, there were Quakers who acted to prevent war and establish peace. For example, Joseph Sturge attempted to mediate a conflict in 1850 in Northern Europe and then formed a peace delegation to the Czar a few years later which sought to prevent the Crimean War. Not only did the ideas of war prevention by mediation and transnational structures echo down the centuries in Quaker work for international peacemaking, these efforts influenced work for peace on an international level by non-Quakers.

Therefore, Quaker efforts to join with others in governing had successes and failures. However, in the face of the loss of direct power in government, Friends sought to act for social change outside government channels. So, for example, when Woolman and other Quakers made efforts to secure an alternative to paying taxes for war, not only did some then refuse to pay those taxes, they formed their own 'Friendly Association for Regaining and Preserving Peace with the Indians By Pacific Measures' (Brock 1968,

140–1, 149). This was an early example, one could say, of a Quaker non-governmental organization. Such efforts became legion in the history of Friends, as they sought to influence government towards peace and the Quaker vision of social service as well as building their own non-governmental structures to address their concerns.

In 1765, Quakers engaged in widespread non-violent protests against the Stamp Act, enacted in the British Parliament without American representation. For example, eighty Quaker merchants in Philadelphia joined in a boycott of British goods in protest. However, as the crisis between Great Britain and the American colonies escalated, American Quakers, beginning in 1769, shifted towards neutrality in the impending conflict. In 1776, early on in the American Revolution, Philadelphia Yearly Meeting counselled Quakers not to enlist in either military, nor engage in business that would further war. Friends were to refuse payment of war taxes, withdraw from any activity related to government, and not vote in elections for public office. Quakers rendered humanitarian assistance to civilian victims of the war. Other American Yearly Meetings similarly took positions of neutrality. Quakers underwent a variety of 'sufferings' for this witness, most commonly fines, but also seizure of goods, and, in some cases, imprisonment or corporal punishment. In 1777, eleven prominent Philadelphia Friends suffered a year-long exile to Virginia. Some Friends did support the American patriotic cause, and paid taxes or joined the military. American Yearly Meetings exercised their discipline vigorously against those who took such a path. Nineteen per cent of military-age Quaker men in Pennsylvania and thirty-three per cent of the same cohort in New Jersey were disowned for war-related offences, along with lesser percentages in other parts of the American colonies (Mekeel 1979; Barbour and Frost 1994, 139–45).

In addition to maintaining a witness to governing authorities, Quakers built social service institutions meant to address a number of social problems. This was a blossoming of the Quaker commitment in the 1660 declaration to 'seek peace and ensue it'. Thus, through the nineteenth century, Friends generated many institutional efforts to address societal needs in addition to continuing to witness to the government. However, their influence on government in England and the new Untied States was receding.

FROM WITNESS FOR PEACE TO ASSIMILATION

The beginning of the twentieth century may be said to mark the beginning of the decline of distinctly Quaker ideas and actions for the transformation of society. Other denominations and other non-religious organizations were now doing what Quakers had been doing. However, it can be argued that the movements of Quakerism beyond the English and American settings was planting seeds of a spiritual Quakerism that would bloom, while the Anglo-American form of Quakerism became assimilated into the larger culture.

For example, pacifism was no longer a distinctly Quaker or radical Reformation notion since pacifist ideas had spread to other denominations. Further, like other denominations, the Society became divided about pacifism and Quakers were not unified on this issue any longer. This may have been first evident in the US Civil War (1861–65). Many young Quaker men, torn between pacifism and opposition to slavery, opted to join the Union Army; in Indiana, twenty-four per cent of military-age Quaker men did so, and Quakers in other states had a similar experience. American meetings deplored this deviation from their discipline, but, unlike their actions in the American Revolution in the previous century, there were no large-scale disownments for this reason (Barbour and Frost 1994, 197–200). Especially after the institution of a military draft in 1863, some Quaker men did undergo imprisonment or other sufferings for their conscientious objection to military participation (Pringle 1962).

Similar divisions and diversity of Friends' witness were evident in Britain and the United States during the two world wars. In England and the United States, from from thirty to fifty per cent of eligible Quakers accepted service in the First World War, and in that percentage grew in the US during the Second World War to some seventy-five per cent (Witte, 8). In these two conflicts, however, there was also moving witness by Quakers who were conscientious objectors, both those who served prison terms and those who engaged in some form of alternative service (Gara 1999; Pendle Hill 1998; Hopkins 2010).

The warnings of war were on the horizon before the turn of the twentieth century and Quakers did move to address the 'occasions of war' in examining the political and economic drivers of war. Also, Quakers sought to reconnect the various branches of Friends in order to consider what they could do. With the Boer Wars and the Spanish-American War, British and American society had cause to celebrate their colonial power as well as inklings of what warfare could become. In 1901, all Quaker branches in the United States met together in Philadelphia for the American Friends Peace Conference. In spite of the deep differences in theology and social perspectives, these American Friends were united in affirming that 'War in its spirit, its deeds, the persistent animosities which it generates, and the individual and social degeneration produced by it is the antithesis of Christianity' (in Hirst 1923, 450).

However, the plunge into the First World War in the most Christian area of the world decimated these efforts and, worse, led many Friends to embrace the war effort. In Britain, the Peace Society under the leadership of Quaker Joseph Pease (1860–1943) approved the declaration of war by the British government and he subsequently resigned as president of the Society. Similarly, in the United States, the American Peace Society that had declared in 1916, 'Jesus Christ was a pacifist', moved within a year to support the Wilson administration. Even the Liberal Friends of Philadelphia proclaimed: 'We do not agree with those who would utter sentimental platitudes while a mad dog is running amuck biting women and children or with those who would stand idly by quoting some isolated passage of scripture while an insane man murdered him, ravished his wife, bayoneted his babies or crucified his friends' (Barbour and Frost 1994, 251).

So the disaster of First World War revealed the loss of the unified peace testimony within the Religious Society of Friends and revealed the horrors of modern warfare. This crisis brought new efforts across the spectrum of Friends to address their internal divisions and the suffering of the larger world. In the All Friends' Conference of 1920, over 1,000 Quakers from around the world came to London to address the issue of warfare and the underlying issues of economic, racial, and spiritual roots of warfare. Nearly all Quaker Yearly Meetings were represented. Friends came from the United States, Britain and the Commonwealth, France, Germany, Austria, Switzerland, Norway, Denmark, China, Japan, India, Syria, and Madagascar. Reiterating the language of early Friends, this conference stated that war can be eliminated by taking away the 'roots of war'. This was a task for both individual spiritual work and corporate social change. Christ calls for inward cleansing of 'self-seeking' and 'domination' and such changes will overcome 'barriers of race and class' so that all humanity will become 'a society of friends' (Hirst 1923, 524–5).

Though the unified pacifist stance was now broken, the impact of these gatherings of Friends from all branches of Quakerism, was to seek to reconnect these diverse expressions of Quakerism. Further, Quakers now joined with like-minded individuals and organizations for peace and social service.

Though individual Quakers in Britain and the United States did enlist and support the war effort in the First World War, the official stance of the Society remained pacifist. The work in the previous century to establish recognition of conscientious objectors allowed those Friends and others in the pacifist denominations to gain recognition of their individual conscientious objection. Just after the mid-nineteenth century, Britain and the United States moved to an all-volunteer military. In both countries, recognition of religious pacifism was more or less established and with the reinstatement of the military draft in the face of twentieth-century conflicts, both countries made provision for conscientious objection by religious minorities. Though war fever swept Britain and young men rushed to enlist without any conscription legislation, Conservatives in the government demanded such a bill so that those who had less than full patriotic commitment would do their duty. However, the recognition of conscientious objection on the basis of religious belief was maintained. The same pattern held in the United States.

However, Quakers believed that maintaining a pacifist stance was no longer sufficient and the many experiments in addressing social concerns would now lead to the establishment of Friends Service Committees in Britain and the United States. In Britain in the late nineteenth century, Friends not only issued statements against the Franco-Prussian War, but began to organize war relief. Their appeals to join this effort were not only made within the Religious Society of Friends, but to all citizens. In 1914 when the London Yearly Meeting spoke out against universal conscription, but also stated there was a 'sense of the responsibility for true national service which attaches to citizenship in a civilized state'. Though the Yearly Meeting claimed that war was unlawful for the Christian, it affirmed that Quakers would join with others to do work to alleviate suffering and seek change in the conditions that lead to war. They said this work was of 'high value for the Kingdom of God' and that there was 'no more truly national service than the replacing of mutual suspicion between nations by mutual trust and helpfulness' (Hirst 1923, 487).

Several branches of British Quaker service were initiated during and just after the war: the Friends Ambulance Unit; the War Victim's Relief Committee; and the Emergency Committee for Assistance of Germans, Austrians, Hungarians, and Turks in Distress. These evolved and in 1927 joined with the Friends Foreign Mission Association to establish the Friends Service Council. In the United States, a parallel organization, the

American Friends Service Committee, was founded in 1917. As with its British counterpart, the American organization combined statements against war and the return of conscription with organizing alternative service in which Quakers and others could participate. One of the key figures in this development, Rufus Jones (1863–1948), declared the need to have people 'who believe in the conquering power of love and who express in deeds the conviction that Christ's Kingdom of God is something more than a dream or an illusion' (Jones 1920b, xiii–xiv).

Recognizing that the Religious Society of Friends was small—about 150,000 worldwide—the Service Committees made their appeal to any who shared their views of service. The AFSC reached out to all churches, welfare organizations, farm and labour organizations, business and professional societies. The Red Cross joined with the AFSC in making appeals and by 1921 over six million dollars and tons of material aid were raised. So, though the Quakers founded these service organizations, now they sought and found significant help from many others. Indeed, these other groups and individuals were required to make the goals of Quaker service a reality.

In 1943, with the Second World War raging, Quakers created a new organization in the United States, the Friends Committee on National Legislation, the first religious lobbying organization (Wilson 1975). Then in 1947, the AFSC asked the Friends World Committee for Consultation to establish a relationship with the newly formed United Nations, opening offices in Geneva and New York. Like the Service Committees, these new organizations relied on support from beyond the Society of Friends. All of these efforts would, in their turn, lead other religious and humanitarian bodies to form similar organizations. In 1947, the Nobel Peace Prize was awarded jointly to the Friends Service Council and the American Friends Service Committee. A Nobel Peace Prize had previously been awarded to Quaker Emily Green Balch in 1946 for her work with the Women's International League for Peace and Freedom. Later in 1959, Quaker Philip Noel-Baker (1889–1982) was awarded the Nobel Peace Prize for his lifelong work on disarmament efforts, including work for the League of Nations and the United Nations. Thus, these Quaker individuals and organizations were influencing and coordinating with those who shared their values in the larger society. Such efforts gained world recognition and the Society of Friends was no longer a peculiar people with clearly distinct views of war and peace.

A key element in widening Quaker ideals in the world and the diminishing of Quaker distinctiveness came with the emergence of the ecumenical movement's concern for peace. In the early 1920s, Quaker Wilbur K. Thomas and a member of the Schwenkfelder church issued a call for all denominations who 'profess discipleship of Jesus Christ and who hold that war has no place among Christens' to send representatives to conferences designed to further this notion beyond the pacifist sects. Though the first conference in 1922 drew only representatives from the Church of the Brethren, the Mennonites, Schwenkfelder Church, and Quakers, this effort continued into the mid-1930s. By the final conference in 1935, after failing to draw in the larger mainstream churches, these groups came to designate themselves as the 'historic peace churches' and continued to seek ways to work together for peace (Gibble 2006).

With this important but limited ecumenical connection, Brethren, Mennonites, and Quakers subsequently met with President Roosevelt in 1937 to appeal for recognition of conscientious objection to military service and the establishment of alternative service as Second World War loomed. In subsequent meetings with the US administration, the peace churches representatives had differences and so presented the administration with a list of requests they did not all agree to, such as making accommodation for pacifists who were not members of the peace churches and allowing objectors not to be required to register with the government in preparation for the draft. Though the government did not allow non-registration by those objecting to conscription as well as participation in war, it did recognize that all those who opposed war by 'religious training and belief' would be permitted to do alternate service under civilian direction. Hence, as the US began its first peacetime conscription in 1940, it also officially recognized conscientious objectors from all denominations and provided for civilian organized alternative service.

After the war other individuals from many denominations joined in efforts to heal the damages of war and seek ways to prevent continuing warfare. The peace churches were involved in the formation of the World Council of Churches (WCC) and the inaugural 1948 WCC assembly. Now on the world stage of Christian communions, the peace church position was considered of equal merit along with the two dominant views of Christians: that war was the decision and responsibility of governments with which Christians must consent; or the view of war as sometimes necessary but nonetheless falling far from God's justice. Thus, the vision of Christian pacifism upheld by small groups within the Church for centuries was now influencing the larger confessions, while at the same time the 'historic peace churches' were not entirely filled with pacifists. During the Vietnam War, all major Christian denominations and many smaller ones issued statements proclaiming that members of their confessions would be supported if they chose to be conscientious objectors (Boyle 1983). Indeed, peace work has spread far beyond the bounds of Christianity, and there are now activists among all the world's faiths who are working towards rejecting war and pursuing peace.

At the End: Apocalypse Again?

For a small religious group, the Religious Society of Friends developed a vast number of experiments in how to refuse involvement in warfare and incarnate peacemaking. It challenged and changed powerful governments and transformed widespread societal views about the place of conscientious objection, non-violent action, and a host of social attitudes and structures. However, the tension between maintaining a peace testimony and engaging in the larger world created problems for the Society of Friends. At times, the peace witness appeared confusing to outsiders; at times the witness was abandoned within the Society itself.

Along with such influence and struggles, Friends now find themselves less distinct from their neighbours and so have merged with larger cultural currents. As we have seen here, as pacifism spread beyond the Religious Society of Friends, Quakers themselves were less cohesive about their own Peace Testimony. Ironically, this has led both to a strengthening of peacemaking in the larger culture as well as inconsistency among Friends about their own Peace Testimony. Further, as creative efforts for peacemaking by the Religious Society of Friends spread to others, uniquely Quaker efforts diminished. Is this then the end of a distinctively Quaker witness against war and for experiments in peacemaking?

Maybe not. The spread of Quakerism to other parts of the world in the early twentieth century has opened a path that might rejoin the deep spiritual vision of Friends with their long history of conscientious objection to war and work for peace. For example, in conflict zones such as the West Bank and East Africa, Quakers have reunited active peacemaking with a strong sense of being led by the Spirit. Often the early missionaries reflected the nineteenth-century split within American Quakerism between Liberal and Evangelical Friends, and brought less of a Quaker perspective on peacemaking and more of Protestant evangelical theology.

Nonetheless, in recent decades in those regions of missionary work, the history of Friends in peacemaking is being revived. In turn, such developments beyond the Anglo-American Quaker world have returned where Quakerism began with a potential force for re-energizing Friends. For example, the conflict in the Middle East has connected Friends from across the Liberal and Evangelical branches to join with Quakers in the West Bank to seek peace (International Quaker Working Party).

In East Africa, Quakers in Rwanda are using education in alternatives to violence to further healing from the 1994 genocide, and Quakers in Kenya are using similar techniques to heal from their 2008 post-election violence and to work to prevent violence arising around future elections. So Quakers from the North have been connecting with the largest group of Quakers in the world to advance the work of peacemaking (Zarembka 2011). Thus, as Quakers experience conflict around the world and within their own Society, it may be a season for the rebirth of Quaker commitment to its own peace testimony and to creative experiments in international and interfaith peacemaking.

SUGGESTED FURTHER READING

Brinton, H. H. (2002) *Friends for 350 years.* Rev. ed. Wallingford, PA: Pendle Hill Publications.

Cooper, W. (2001) *A living faith: An historical and comparative study of Quaker beliefs.* Richmond, IN: Friends United Press.

Dandelion, P. (2008) *The Quakers: A very short introduction.* Oxford: Oxford University Press.

Brock, P. (1990) *The Quaker peace testimony, 1660–1914.* York, England: Sessions Book Trust.

Hirst, M. (1923) *Quakers in peace and war.* New York: George Doran.

Orr, E. W. (1974) *Quakers in peace and war, 1920–1967.* Sussex, UK: W. T. Oxford.

Smith-Christopher, D. (ed.) (2007) *Subverting hatred: The challenge of nonviolence in religious traditions.* Maryknoll, NY: Orbis Books.

Thompson, H. (1988) *World religions in war and peace.* Jefferson, NC: McFarland & Co.

CHAPTER 25

QUAKERS AND PENAL REFORM

MIKE NELLIS AND MAUREEN WAUGH

INTRODUCTION

WHILE Quakers cannot quite claim to have invented the concept of 'penal reform', they might legitimately claim to have institutionalized it. In the nineteenth century, both British and American Friends played a prominent part in campaigns against corporal and capital punishment, and for creating prisons better suited to reformative ends. In the twentieth century, Friends supported reductions in prison use, the search for constructive alternatives to imprisonment, and the pursuit of non-punitive, restorative responses to crime. The vectors, outcomes, and legacies of Quaker influence on penal practice in each country have differed, but even secular histories of imprisonment have attested to the prominence of Quakers in penal change, not always flatteringly (Ignatieff 1978; Sullivan 1990). Quaker work in penal reform has largely entailed four overlapping approaches, some corporate, some individual: a) establishing projects and services for offenders; b) championing good ideas and practices originating with others; c) establishing secular bodies to promote penal improvement; and d) expressing their faith through personal philanthropic work or paid employment, and volunteering in secular criminal justice and social work agencies.

In respect of both Britain and America—and even more so internationally—gaps remain in historical scholarship about Quaker involvement in penal reform, but it should not be assumed that Quakers have always and everywhere borne witness in this field. It has depended on context, priorities, and opportunities—on the social and personal capacities and inclinations of Friends in different times and places, on the amenability of governments and individual officials to influence, and on the presence or absence of other actors in the penal reform field. There is undoubtedly an Anglo-American Quaker 'tradition' of penal reform, an internally constructed narrative of events, aspirations, and achievements gives continuing impetus and legitimacy to contemporary work in penal reform, and thus renews itself. Friends in other countries can draw inspiration from the tradition, or from particular aspects of it, despite not having shared directly in the history that produced it. At different times in the past, Friends' work in penal reform has overlapped with work on temperance, anti-slavery, civil liberty, and asylum issues, and in the contemporary world some work on behalf of prisoners is undertaken under the rubric of 'human rights activism' rather than penal reform. A belief in universal redeemability and a perfectible social order, plus the various iterations of the peace testimony, and commitments to equality and non-violence have usually been the basis of Quaker concern for lawbreakers and for their antipathy to various forms of punishment. Some Yearly Meetings have advanced more specific Quaker positions on penal matters, which have had local significance, but no explicit testimony on penal reform, or to restorative justice, or against punishment has gained full and formal acceptance in the worldwide Religious Society of Friends.

EARLY FRIENDS, JUSTICE, AND CRIMINAL LAW

The root of Quaker involvement in what later became 'penal reform' lies in their seventeenth-century experience as a persecuted sect, and the distinct nature of the spirituality they sought to express. As seventeenth-century Quakers coalesced into a distinct spiritual movement, imprisonment (and sometimes other punishments—fines, whipping, stocking and pillorying, and ear mutilation) became a commonplace part of their experience, a consequence of upholding their faith, exercising their freedom of conscience, insisting upon their own style of worship, and challenging existing church practices. Friends learned to look after their own when their members were imprisoned, created support structures for them, and learned firsthand of the iniquities of the judicial and penal systems. George Fox (1624–91) himself was first imprisoned in 1649 (for interrupting a sermon); he appeared before magistrates on over sixty occasions and cumulatively his eight imprisonments claimed six years of his life. He wholly accepted the legitimacy of the state to deal effectively with genuine 'evildoers', but during or after periods of confinement he regularly indicted the secular authorities for imposing excessive punishments on ordinary, poor criminals, and for atrocious conditions in the jails themselves. While imprisoned in Derby in 1651, for example, Fox wrote to local magistrates 'concerning their putting men to death for stealing cattle or money and small things', reminding them 'what a sore thing it was that prisoners should lie so long in gaol, and how that they learned badness one of another in talking of their bad deeds, and therefore speedy justice should have been done...' (Fox 1995, 65–6). At the root of early Friends' confident engagements with the penal authorities of their day was an eschatological belief that a perfected social order was both possible and imminent, and that Christian love in a judicial context was best given practical expression through the application of fair procedures and the determination of just outcomes, proportionate to the seriousness of the offence, and mindful of the circumstances that had given rise to it. The belief in *imminent* perfectability—if not always perfectability as such—faded with time, but Braun (1950) convincingly suggests that early Friends' understanding of the way in which the sentiment of Christian love was to be translated into a dependable form of secular justice—the spiritual and secular being entwined and inseparable realms—lasted well into the twentieth century.

In what Gwyn (1995: 334) aptly calls the 'last Utopian vision offered by a seventeenth century English Friend', London cloth merchant John Bellers (1654–1725) imagined how a more perfect social order might be created, to which fair wages, proper training, and fulfilling work were central. Bellers understood that bad environments sapped personal responsibility, and urged the reclamation of homeless youth who roamed London's streets and turned to criminality. He envisioned prisons as places of reform through industrious work, combining moral exhortation with attention to the offender's material wellbeing. Regarding the death penalty, he took the Quaker sense of 'that of God in every man' to its limit, publicly opposing (unlike Fox) all executions, even for murder. Although not the first Christian thinker to take an absolutist line on the death penalty, his public demand for its complete abolition came many decades before the more famous Enlightenment case was made for it by the Italian jurist Cesare Beccaria (1764/1963; Megivern 1997).

In England, Bellers's tracts had negligible influence, even on Friends, but in William Penn's (1644–1718) 'holy experiment' in the American colonies begun in 1681, Quaker officials did pursue progressive penal ideals (in marked contrast with the more punitive practices of Puritan states such as Massachusetts, which banned Quakers from preaching and between 1659–61 hanged four Quakers on Boston Common). Pennsylvania's workhouse-prisons combined industriousness with religious instruction; Native Americans were allowed to sit on juries in cases involving one of their own; and capital punishment was restricted to the single offence of murder. Imperfect and short-lived as these arrangements were—corporal punishment and capital punishment (for twelve offences), were both restored after Penn's death—the interest of Pennsylvania Quakers in penal reform never completely faded, and their greatest influence was yet to come.

John Howard, American Quakers, and the Emergence of the Penitentiary

In the latter half of the eighteenth century, the High Sheriff of Bedford, John Howard (1726–90) (not a Quaker), fused his evangelical faith with Enlightenment thinking to argue that prisoners might better be reformed by austere discipline and appeals to their reason than by cruelty and contempt. First in his home county, then in the country as a whole and then abroad, he embarked on a personal mission against insanitary and disorderly conditions within prisons, sought classification and segregation of prisoners by type and reformability, opposed torture and required night-time solitary confinement for each prisoner. Howard's fame as a Christian reformer was eventually immense, but penal progress in Britain was slow. He lacked the temperament for building organizations to promote and consolidate change, but was fortunate in his friendship with John Fothergill (1712–80), a Quaker physician who had visited American prisons in 1744–5 and retained close relations with the Quaker-dominated Pennsylvania business elite who became early advocates of Howard's ideas.

The Philadelphia Society for the Relief of Distressed Prisoners, the world's first penal reform society, was established in 1786. Its Walnut Street Jail, opened in 1790, was the first of several 'penitentiaries' in America whose regimes experimented with various permutations of silence and solitude to effect repentance and personal reformation. Its less serious offenders worked in association with each other and slept in dormitories, while more dangerous felons were held in solitary cells. Quaker businessman and reformer Thomas Eddy (1758–1827) initially copied this regime in Newgate Prison in New York, but in his later prison at Auburn, opened in 1816, daytime association in workshops was permitted only on condition of complete silence, enforced by corporal punishment, while all prisoners slept in solitary cells (Winternitz et al 1995). The Eastern State Penitentiary, which opened at Cherry Hill, Philadelphia in 1829, opposed Auburn's 'silent system' with a 'separate system' in which prisoners both worked alone and slept in their cells, a practice that not only maximized time available for spiritual reflection but also, by dint of having no silent association, lessened the need for corporal punishments to enforce it. In terms of architecture, and some slight variations of ethos, Cherry Hill's 'separate system' became the model worldwide for several hundred prisons, despite early humanitarian worries about the deleterious impact of solitary confinement on fragile minds (Sullivan 1990).

Elizabeth Fry and the Institutionalizing of Penal Reform

Through thrift, industriousness, and mutually supportive family networks, and by dint of their exclusion from universities and professions, many eighteenth-century Friends became wealthy and influential as industrialists and business leaders. Their earlier sense of themselves as harbingers of a new social and religious order diminished, but through corporate and philanthropic efforts many still sought to improve society, contributing time and money to what they believed was moral and social progress in various fields of activity. In the early years of the nineteenth century, as the immiseration caused by the Industrial Revolution created new political anxieties for the elites, some now affluent Quakers turned again to the abolition of the death penalty, the improvement of prison conditions, and the spiritual reform of prisoners, speaking truth to power from a position of commercial and political influence that early Friends had not had.

Philadelphia Quaker Stephen Grellet (1773–1855), travelling in Europe and visiting prisons wherever he went, was particularly shocked by conditions in London's Newgate Prison and encouraged Elizabeth Fry (1780–1845), daughter of a wealthy banking family, to begin visiting there in 1816. The prison, in which men, women, and children mixed freely without occupation, was squalid, violent, and over-crowded, little improved from Howard's day. Fry and her assistants established a school for the prison children and in 1817, in the face of official scepticism, founded the 'Ladies' Association for the Reformation of the Female Prisoners in Newgate'. They improved material conditions, and introduced Bible study and paid work, setting prisoners' earnings aside for their use upon release. Fry pressed for the separation of men and women in prison, for women prisoners to have female wardens, and for classification to limit the mixing of murderers, prostitutes, and debtors. Unlike American Quakers, she was opposed to the cruelty of solitary confinement—it was seriously canvassed in England in the 1830s— but she acquiesced in transportation to the colonies, a major feature of the British state's response to crime, seeking only to ameliorate the shipboard conditions of convicted women sent to Australia (Rose 1980).

Fry's work was not specifically endorsed by London Yearly Meeting, but was financed by a network of wealthy Quaker relatives (brothers and brothers-in-law) and friends, including William Allen (1770–1843) and Peter Bedford (1780–1864) who were active penal reformers in their own right. William Allen established the Prison Discipline Society in 1817 to champion and extend Fry's work in Newgate, and he and Peter Bedford helped start a London-based Society for Lessening the Causes of Juvenile Delinquency, whose area-by-area investigation showed, as Bellers had done previously, that thousands of uneducated, unhoused, and workless hungry children lived rough (and by crime) on the city's streets. They sought to help these youngsters, and support those among them who were released from jail.

Sustained opposition to the death penalty, in alliance with other churches and reformers, was entwined with these activities. In 1808, Allen helped create the first of three associations seeking its complete abolition, and London Yearly Meeting pressed this case in its Epistles of 1818, 1830, and 1847. Bedford and Fry argued that capital punishment diminished the worth of human life, coarsened public sentiment, and ultimately could not deter crime among the impoverished urban poor, whose routine behaviour was governed by immediate and urgent need rather than fear of future consequences in this life or beyond. Such arguments, much mocked in their day, only had influence as more disciplinary alternatives became available: nonetheless, the number of capital offences fell from 150 in 1800 to just two (murder and treason) in 1861, and formerly public executions in England were sequestered behind prison walls in 1867 in the hope that this would undercut demands for full abolition. Some Christian churches were content with these achievements, and comfortably retained capital punishment for murder, but Quakers pressed on for total abolition, articulating the principle that, as Quaker MP John Bright (1868) eloquently put it, 'the real security of human life is to be found in a reverence for it' (*Quaker Faith and Practice* 1999, 23.96).

As her fame grew, Elizabeth Fry travelled extensively within Britain and Europe, promoting penal reform among its ruling elites and inspiring individuals from her own class and milieu to take up her cause. She corresponded with the Dutch Quaker Jean Etienne Mollet (1781–1851), who helped found the Netherlands Society for the Moral Improvement of Prisoners in 1832, to visit women prisoners and support them after their release. Theodore Fliedner (1800–62), a German Evangelical Pastor from Dusseldorf who observed her work in Newgate in 1820, founded the Rhenish-Westphalian Prison Society in 1826 to minister to prisoners (especially women), and to support both resettlement through agricultural colonies, and to promote refuges for the victims of alcohol. In America, a number of women—notably Abigail Hopper Gibbons (1801–93)—followed Fry into work with serving and discharged prisoners, and while Fry herself was not formally feminist—she did not support women's suffrage—she and her colleagues laid the foundations of an enduring association between middle-class women and penal reform (Bacon 2000).

Imperialist expansion spread Quaker penal concerns still further. In 1831 Quaker missionaries James Backhouse (1794–1869) and George Washington Walker (1800–58), travelled with London Yearly Meeting's blessing to the colonies in New South Wales and Van Diemen's Land (now Tasmania), reporting back on penal and aboriginal settlements, supplying medical assistance to convict ships in Australian waters, and encouraging prison visiting by the colony's women. In 1837 they met Alexander Maconochie, superintendent of the Norfolk Island prison colony, and endorsed his use of indeterminate task-based punishments rather than fixed-length, time-based sentences and his practice of rewarding prisoners for good behaviour rather than further punishing them for bad—approaches which, over time, became internationally influential in their own right (Hughes 1987). In the same year, Joseph Sturge and Thomas Harvey campaigning in the Caribbean on behalf of London Yearly Meeting for the emancipation of slaves, challenged plantation owners' infliction of brutal punishments, and complained to the governor of Barbados about conditions in Bridgetown Jail.

THE HOWARD ASSOCIATION AND THE SECULARIZATION OF PENAL REFORM

Compared with international peace work and temperance, penal reform did not figure prominently in the formal concerns of London Yearly Meeting in the late nineteenth century (Isichei 1970). Nonetheless, as secretary of the Howard Association (a secular penal reform body established in 1866 in part by Stoke Newington Meeting), one individual Quaker, William Tallack (1831–1908) became pre-eminent in the field. A previous secretary of the Quaker-led Society for the Abolition of Capital Punishment, he drew lifelong inspiration both from Cherry Hill's separate system, of which he had formed a favourable view as a young traveller in the US, and from the social witness of Peter Bedford whose belief that poverty produced criminality he largely shared. Nationally and internationally, Tallack was the public voice of the Howard Association for thirty-five years until his retirement in 1901, as well as being active in theological debate among British Friends, opposing modernizing tendencies within it. Tallack (1889) mostly supported progressive penal practices, championing residential schools to keep children out of prison, and advocating the American innovation of using 'probation' rather than prison for first-time adult offenders. However, his unswerving commitment to reform-by-deterrence for more incorrigible adults eventually placed him at odds with government attempts in the Gladstone Report of 1895, to take more of a reform-by-training approach. At the end of an otherwise illustrious career, outflanked by modernizers in both the Religious Society of Friends and in penal reform, Tallack was somewhat marginalized, and has been unfairly neglected in accounts of Quaker penal tradition.

His Quaker successor as Howard Association secretary, Edward Grubb (1854–1939), a leading figure in the ongoing modernization of London Yearly Meeting, fully aligned himself with the government's new rehabilitative stance on prisoners. His brief three-and-half-year tenure as secretary included a visit to the US to study penal methods which informed all the Howard Association's subsequent proposals. These included indeterminate sentences and early release under license for adult offenders on the recommendation of a parole board; the adoption of a probation system akin to that in Massachussetts; and reformatories for young adult offenders modelled on the Elmira experiment in New York State. After a twelve year non-Quaker secretaryship at the Howard Association, Cecil Leeson (1883–1949), a Quaker journalist/probation officer who wrote the first British handbook on probation (Leeson 1914), was its secretary between 1916–21. He left to create the Magistrate's Association (a voice for progressive sentencers, including numerous Friends) in the same year that the Howard Association merged with the Prison Reform League to become the Howard League for Penal Reform.

The Penal Reform Committee and the Creation of a Quaker Penal Tradition

By then British penal debate had been affected by the voices of those who had been imprisoned for conscientious objection during the first World War, many of whom had been Quakers. One of these, Stephen Hobhouse (1881–1951), worked with fellow socialist and pacifist Fenner Brockway to collate the testimonies of all such objectors for the Independent Labour Party. They showed that the supposedly liberalizing influence of the 1895 Gladstone Report had been limited, and their arguments for reform were to prove influential with a rising generation of prison administrators well into the 1930s (Hobhouse and Brockway 1922). The experience of imprisonment by conscientious objectors renewed the formal interest of British Friends in penal reform, and in

1921 London Yearly Meeting appointed a Penal Reform Committee (PRC) to stimulate new Quaker initiatives and to support the secular efforts of the Howard League whose parent organization it had helped create over a half-century before. The PRC pressed for fuller implementation of probation legislation and supported philanthropist Geraldine Cadbury's (1865–1941) efforts to provide juvenile courts with better remand and assessment services, sometimes at her and her husband's own expense. It also supported Quaker Roy Calvert (1898–1933), founder of the National Council for the Abolition of the Death Penalty in 1925, whose deployment of empirical evidence and telling international comparisons continued work that William Tallack had begun, confronting those whose moral confidence in capital punishment made them indifferent to its actual limited deterrent effect (Calvert 1927).

It was in 1930s Britain that a strong sense of there being a Quaker 'tradition' in penal reform first emerged, a vision which contemporary Friends were obliged to carry forwards, with Margery Fry as its leading light. It was stimulated, perhaps, not only by events (the emergence of the PRC) but by the publication of Auguste Jorns' *Quakers as Pioneers in Social Work* (1931), and Ruth Fry's *Quaker Ways* (1933), which both portrayed penal reform as a more defining and consistent feature of Friends' social concern than previous Quaker historians had done (for example, Grubb 1899). A distant descendant of Elizabeth and sister of Ruth, Margery Fry (1874–1958) had been a high-profile Howard League secretary (1921–6), and worked actively with the Home Office in the 1930s to create what would have been strikingly progressive criminal justice legislation had the Second World War not intervened to prevent its enactment (Forsythe 1990). Margery Fry had formally left the Religious Society of Friends but as a lifelong magistrate, prison visitor, and penal campaigner she never lost her 'Quaker conscience' (Fry 1951; Huws-Jones 1966), and although never quite as well known outside professional circles as her esteemed ancestor, her class background and style— engaged in practice, at ease with policymakers—was supremely emblematic in the mid-twentieth century, of the informed, idealistic, non-confrontational, and patrician approach to penal reform that earlier Quaker activity had set in place more than a century before (Logan 2008).

In Britain, the Second World War produced a further wave of conscientious objectors whose views on what needed to be done to make prisons more constructive were collated by the Howard League (Benney 1948; Brock 2001). The post-war Quaker Prison Ministry grew out of wartime visiting arrangements for imprisoned Quakers and cumulatively became entwined in the work of prison chaplaincies (Miller 2009). Some monthly meetings set up 'approved schools' for juvenile offenders. Acting out of personal concern, social worker David Wills (1903–80) pioneered a series of therapeutic communities for young people outside the auspices of the Religious Society of Friends; only in 1969 did Friends themselves (moved by a Quaker probation officer inspired by Wills) establish something similar at Glebe House in Cambridgeshire. The apotheosis of Quaker influence on Britain's penal system, the moment of greatest congruence between Quaker vision and official policy, arguably came with the appointment of prison governor Duncan Fairn (1906–86), a former Swarthmore lecturer and an ardent champion of the rehabilitative ideal, as overall head of the English Prison Service in 1964 (Fairn 1951; 1966).

While the Penal Affairs Committee (as the Penal Reform Committee was renamed in 1964) regarded official moves towards a more scientific, rehabilitative approach to prisoners as consistent with Quaker views on redeemability, they now began to question the overuse of imprisonment and to support other reformers in making the case for alternatives to custodial sentences. They also promoted Norman House, a resettlement hostel for released prisoners in London, established by a non-Quaker pacifist Merfyn Turner, and challenged the anomaly of military-style discipline in detention centres for young offenders (Friends Home Service Committee 1968, 1970). A significant cause for celebration came with the abolition of the death penalty in England in 1965: final victory in this ultimately interdenominational and secular struggle owed much to Friends' relentless witness (Potter 1993).

In mainland Europe, in the pre-Second World War era, such small-scale Quaker penal reform work as went on tended to claim inspiration from Elizabeth Fry. In France in the 1920s Friends at the Quaker International Centre in Paris were heavily involved in prison work. Phoebe Borghesio (1864–1937) became a regular visitor at the women's prison at St Lazare in 1924 and soon after Henri van Etten (1893–1968), together with Gerda Kappenburg (1896–date unknown), founded 'The Committee for the Diminution of Crime' which sought improvements in prison conditions and in society's response to young offenders. During the Second World War, French Quaker relief work saved many prisoners from starvation and disease (van Etten 1953). After the war, French Quaker women continued to visit prisons in Paris and Le Havre, and in Lyons a male Quaker supported discharged prisoners. Further afield, in the 1960s and 1970s, a Quaker minister in Kenya, Rasoah Mutuha (1906–96), undertook a programme of pastoral work among women prisoners on behalf of East Africa Yearly Meeting (McMahon 2006). The international profile of Quaker work in penal reform was raised when the Religious Society of Friends gained access to the United Nations Commission on Criminal Justice and Crime Prevention, and by the work of the Quaker United Nations Office (QUNO) in Geneva, some of which has had a penal focus.

NORTH AMERICAN QUAKERS AND THE RADICAL CRITIQUE OF IMPRISONMENT

Penal reform in post-war America lay firmly in the hands of secular liberal progressives who hoped that the establishment of several therapeutic prisons was a sign of a lasting shift towards scientific rehabilitation among penal policymakers. American Friends supported this trend, with Philadelphia judge Curtis Bok (1897–1962) confidently claiming that half the US prison population would willingly cooperate with psychiatric treatment in essentially open institutions if it was self-evidently for their own good. Bok (1953, 139) shared the equally mainstream view that some incorrigibles would 'have to be kept permanently in maximum-security fortresses, at least until we are wiser and surer in our treatment'. A major conference for American and Canadian Friends in Germantown, Ohio in 1959 reaffirmed the Quaker commitment to the abolition of capital punishment, and promoted probation, parole, and better facilities for rehabilitation in prisons.

In the 1960s, however, the actual practice of scientific rehabilitation in American prisons was called into question by the imprisonment of draft resisters during the Vietnam War, and of activists in the civil rights movement. The American Friends Service Committee (AFSC) established a committee of mostly non-Quaker experts which considered imprisonment in the broader context of social justice, condemned the oppressive practices (especially indeterminate sentences) carried out in rehabilitation's name and, in the context of a demand to use prison less, urged a qualified return to retributive principles and fixed sentence lengths. *Struggle for Justice* (American Friends Service Committee 1971) proved influential in wider penal debates, both in the US and in Britain, but inadvertently gave legitimacy to the 'back-to-punishment' demands of an ascendant political Right. The AFSC never wholly repudiated its depiction of prisons as a potent means of disciplining the poor, but over time it played down retributivism and reaffirmed rehabilitation. It has remained oppositional in respect of American penal policy, combining both practical work with serving and released prisoners, with openness to ideas for more radical change.

Fay Honey Knopp (1918–96), a peace and civil rights activist who had worked for the AFSC, supplied some of those. Having begun prison visiting in 1955, she visited hundreds of conscientious objectors during the Vietnam years, and in 1968 cofounded Prisoner Visitation and Support to extend such work. This experience deepened her radicalism, and in 1971 she founded the Prison Research Education Action Program (PREAP) and became a prison abolitionist, coproducing a handbook that set out an 'attrition strategy'—develop so many alternatives to prison that there would only be minimal need for the confinement of the dangerous few—for achieving this (Knopp 1976). She chastised Friends for accepting uncritically the social and political necessity of imprisonment, and pressed them to treat prisons as they had treated war and slavery, as endemically violent, counterproductive institutions whose rightness they should 'utterly deny'.

The AFSC accepted the long-term goal of abolition in 1978, proposed a moratorium on prison-building, and committed itself to identifying viable alternatives to prison (Knopp and Lugo 1987). Knopp reconstituted PREAP as The Safer Society Program to undertake research, training, and practice with offenders in the community, particularly sex offenders who, for largely obvious reasons, communities most wished to incarcerate (Knopp 1991). Although it gave expression to the latent utopianism of some Quaker social thought, her abolitionism seemed abstract and untimely to many Friends, and moved few. In the wake of the US Supreme Court decision to restore capital punishment in 1976, campaigning against the death penalty, and small-scale community-building projects such as the AFSC's Violence and Criminal Listening Project in West Virginia have seemed both more urgent and more feasible to local meetings (Wilson 1995).

Knopp's ideas were, however, taken up by the Canadian Quaker Committee on Jails and Justice (QCJJ), which also claimed the abolition of imprisonment as its long-term goal in 1978. Under the tutelage of social worker Ruth Morris (1933–2001) Canada Yearly Meeting itself reached precarious unity on prison abolition in 1981, although, as in the US, no movement developed among Friends to advance it. QCJJ remained committed to the practical provision of alternatives to custody, political action, and public education, and in the 1990s actively championed restorative justice. It founded the International Conference on Prison Abolition (ICOPA) as a secular, self-organizing body in 1983 whose periodic meetings around the world bring together activists, academics, and ex-prisoners to keep a radical ideal alive. It later renamed itself the International Conference on Penal Abolition to signify its outright opposition to punishment rather than just the institution of imprisonment: whether this made it more or less radical is a moot point (Morris 1995). Morris (2000) went on to espouse a strategy of 'transformational justice', insisting that reducing both crime and prison use was inseparable from wider political efforts to reduce social inequality, although since her death, there has been in Quakers Fostering Justice (as QCJJ is now called), a greater focus on the tangible potential of restorative justice and less emphasis on prison abolition.

No Quaker penal reformers in Britain in the 1970s and 1980s were as politically radical as Knopp and Morris; so long as dialogue with government was feasible, an oppositional, let alone an abolitionist stance towards penal policy seemed both unnecessary and counterproductive. Nonetheless, the group of Six Friends whom the Penal Affairs Committee asked to discern ways forward on crime and punishment came in large measure to reflect the considered view of its most renowned member, David Wills, that inflicting punishment on anyone was a form of violence, profoundly at odds with the peace testimony, and should no longer be publicly countenanced by the Religious Society of Friends. The Six Friends argued (against, for example, Braun 1950), that 'justice' was best expressed not as due process and the proportionate infliction of deserved pain, but as deserved 'love' that healed the emotional damage in which so much criminality originated. They wished to see more therapeutic interventions with offenders, both within residential institutions and in the community, and criticized the amount of violence in popular media, which they believed had a deleterious effect on behaviour and a debasing impact on culture (Wills et al 1979). Their study paper was published but not formally endorsed by the Penal Affairs Committee, which had rightly anticipated that it would prove controversial and divisive: British Friends did debate the case for a testimony against punishment in the years after Wills' death but never came to unity on it (*The Friend's Quarterly* 1985). Over time, however, the paper subtly effected a deepening of thought among some British Friends, prompting their first reflections on what one of the Six, Quaker magistrate Janet Arthur, had presciently called 'restorative action' towards crime victims.

Towards Restorative Justice
and Alternatives to Violence

In the mid-1980s, huge increases in the American prison population, its discrimina-tory impact on people of colour, and the intolerable conditions for all inmates in both jails and prisons led the AFSC's criminal justice panel to consider updating *Struggle for Justice*. What actually emerged from their deliberations was a national project entitled '200 Years of the Penitentiary: Breaking Chains, Forging Justice', and a plan to pose as challenging a set of questions to criminal justice in its era as the Philadelphia peniten-tiary builders had posed in theirs. The AFSC repudiated the concept and legacy of the penitentiary, regretted Quaker complicity in it, while insisting that in its day it had been *intended* as a better alternative to the-then prevailing forms of punishment (Marinissen 1990).

The AFSC subsequently established a commission on crime and justice, whose mem-bers were all drawn from ethnic minorities, and whose subsequent report attacked the poverty, inequality, and racial discrimination which underpinned crime in the US, challenged the death penalty, depicted a prison system which failed utterly to rehabili-tate, and asked what measures could be taken that actually made communities safer. This is a subtle reframing and widening of the question that Quakers had traditionally asked, which concentrated on what might best be done with offenders alone (Thurston 1993). In the same era, individual Friends associated with the AFSC specifically indicted the increasing use of solitary confinement in American prisons, and condemned the growth of 'supermax' institutions geared solely to control and deter (Kerness and Ehosi 2001; Magnani and Wray 2006). Empowering organizations to make these kinds of cri-tiques, and to enter political coalitions whose combined voice may one day effect struc-tural change, remained an important part of Quaker work, but at local meeting level, many Friends wished to do something practical for offenders and victims in their own communities. It has been in that context that restorative justice and the Alternatives to Violence Project (AVP) became significant forms of Quaker penal witness in the twenty-first century—they were small-scale activities within the gift of local meetings to arrange, and likely to have immediate, tangible benefits in a way that long-term political action did not.

Canadian Mennonites—a Christian peace church with many spiritual affinities with Quakers—had pioneered 'victim-offender reconciliation' projects in the 1970s, enabling offenders to make amends to victims in word or deed, and victims to better understand the person who harmed them (Zehr 1979). Within fifteen years Philadelphia Yearly Meeting was seeking to develop a testimony on 'restorative justice' (as the new approach came to be called), but few Friends realized at the time that the concept was latent within their own tradition, and could have been activated much earlier in penal debate if thought had been given to it. The eighteenth-century Quaker practice of resolving conflicts amongst themselves by arbitration rather than through courts of law was one precursor of 'restorative' thinking. George Fox, William Tallack, Margery Fry, and the Six Quakers had all in different ways recognized the potential of 'reparation' as a technique, if not necessarily as a comprehensive penal vision (see especially, Tallack 1900). Many contemporary Quakers have concluded that restorative justice is, in fact, a more rounded and authentic expression of their peace testimony than rehabilitation (which neglects the needs and interests of crime victims), and in Britain Marian Liebmann (2009) and Tim Newell (2000) have been exemplary exponents of its theory and practice. Quakers affected by violent crime—the mother and sister of murdered women—have also written movingly of their need to encounter those who had done their loved one's harm, to 'salvage the sacred' from the darkest of circumstances (Moreland 2001; Partington 2004). The Canadian Mennonites' 'restorative' practice of using Circles of Support and Accountability for released sex offenders was successfully introduced to England by British Quakers, stimulated in part by concern about the tabloid media's demonization of paedophiles, which was making rational debate about the provision of both constructive responses to offenders and viable protection for potential victims more hazardous (Nellis 2009).

Friends in Northern Ireland have been involved in conflict reduction throughout 'the Troubles', up to and beyond the Good Friday Agreement in 1998. Under the auspices of the Ulster Quaker Service Committee (UQSC), initially established to help those in Belfast driven from their homes by sectarian violence, Quakers set up the first Prison Visitors Centre in Northern Ireland in 1978. Monica Barritt (1921–99), who became manager of the scheme, began liaising with prisoner authorities on behalf of distressed families and in 1985 she set up pre-release groups to prepare both prisoners and families for eventual homecomings. Her successor, Martie Rafferty, became involved in dialogue with paramilitary leaders when bitter conflicts within the Maze Prison spilled over into the wider community, work with a restorative element that was later transferred to the Northern Ireland Prison Board in the early 1990s (Blair 2009). Wise words on 'mending hurts' and 'encounters with perpetrators' have been written by one particular Quaker who had undertaken peace work in Northern Ireland, whose personal background lay in therapeutic work with young offenders pioneered by David Wills (Lampen 1987; 2011).

Traditional Quaker peacemaking concerns also informed the birth of the Alternatives to Violence Project (AVP) in the United States in the mid-1970s. It began with long-term prisoners in Greenhaven Penitentiary in New York asking Lawrence Apsey (1902–1997), a lawyer with the Quaker Project on Community Conflict, to help prisoners become less violent. Apsey sought advice from Dr Bernard LaFayette, a veteran anti-war protester and former associate of Martin Luther King, and from Fay Honey Knopp. As a result, Apsey and LaFayette ran the first non-violence workshop in Greenhaven in March 1975. Something similar took place in Auburn Penitentiary shortly afterwards and by trial and error in both prisons, as well as dialogue with other groups involved in non-violence training, a distinct programme of activities evolved, and from this AVP emerged (Apsey 1991; Lugo and Cadbury 1995). Stephen L. Angell (1919–2011), a New York social worker who had become involved with the programme, 'took on AVP as a kind of ministry' spreading word about it across North America, as well as in Britain, Australia, New Zealand, and other countries (Sorel 1995:320). It has continued to grow internationally, often nurtured in the first instance by Quakers, sometimes becoming independent of them, and sometimes extending outwards from prisons into community reconciliation work. Starting in 2003, in Rwanda and Burundi under the auspices of the Africa Great Lakes Initiative, the Healing and Rebuilding Our Communities project, modelled on AVP, emerged to undertake trauma healing with individuals and communities in the aftermath of the Hutu-Tutsi conflict. Project participants included both victims and perpetrators of ethnic violence, some of whom have been released prisoners. The HROC programme has since been expanded to the Eastern Congo and to Kenya in the wake of the 2008 post-election disturbances in which considerable inter-ethnic violence occurred (Zarembka 2011).

CONCLUSION

To a greater or lesser degree, most Christian churches have had a penal witness from a specifically theological perspective that has been expressed as both practical concern for the wellbeing of prisoners and periodic critique of prevailing criminal justice practices. Quakers have been no exception to this, but uniquely in Britain in particular, they also contributed to the creation of a secular penal reform infrastructure that has lasted until the present day, and which has occasionally been the model for penal reform initiatives elsewhere in the world. More so than other churches, Quakers understood in the early eighteen century (and intuited before then) that making moral and social progress in penal reform required the articulation of their beliefs in terms of reason as well as faith and the influencing of political processes independently of a formally religious position. It can genuinely be said of Quakers in Britain, both in their corporate and individual work, that they generated a sensibility that constantly challenged notions of criminal behaviour as intractable, and its invariable corollary, the 'necessary evil' of harsh punishment. Quakers consistently infused their spiritual sensibility into secular debate on penal reform, rarely worrying that it was reframed in wider cultural debate as merely 'humanitarian' or 'liberal', so long as it positively affected hearts and minds. The abiding sense of other-worldly idealism which still imbues penal reform, its indelible optimism, may well be interpretable as a last surviving trace of the perfectionist spirituality that Friends brought to bear in this field.

There has been a distinct Quaker tradition in penal reform—a consistent, heartfelt, cross-generational application of principles to complex questions of crime and punishment—which has never quite coalesced into a testimony, although it has certainly approximated to one. Over time, the tradition has been self-correcting, willing to repudiate felt mistakes (most notably the penitentiaries), even if, at times, it has been overshadowed by the figure of Elizabeth Fry. Important and foundational as she was, the handing down of an unduly simplifed understanding of her success, which obscured the degree of derision she overcame and omitted her failures, channelled penal reform in Britain into a form of patrician social work, in which the wealthy and powerful were persuaded to soften the punishments of the poor. Some humanitarian benefit resulted from this approach, and even in contemporary democracies there remains much to be said for influencing elites on penal matters, and for caring social work with offenders and victims. It is significant, however, that in North America in the 1970s, where Quaker influence on penal practice—and liberal influence more generally—declined markedly, some Friends looked again at what traditional Quaker commitments to peacemaking and non-violence might mean in this context, and devised a more structurally informed critique of incarceration, attuned to its role in sustaining injustice and oppression. The prescient thinking of Fay Honey Knopp and Ruth Morris deserves to gain renewed critical attention. In the deeper deliberation on penal matters among Friends recently called for by Tony Taylor (2011), perhaps Friends will move beyond gradualist reformism by finding better ways of combining practical work with greater moral censure of prevailing penal trajectories.

SUGGESTED FURTHER READING

Knopp, F. et al (1976) *Instead of prisons: a handbook for abolitionists.* Orwell, VT: The Safer Society Programme.

Morris, R. (1995) *Penal abolition: the practical choice.* Toronto: Canadian Scholar's Press

Morris, R. (2000) *Stories of transformational justice.* Toronto: Canadian Scholar's Press.

Newell, T. (2000) *Forgiving justice: A Quaker vision for criminal justice.* London: Quaker Home Service (The Swarthmore Lecture 2000).

Thurston, L., ed. (1993) *A Call to action: An analysis of the United States Criminal Justice System, with recommendations.* Chicago: Third World Press.

Van Drenth, A. and de Haan, F. (1999) *The rise of caring power: Elizabeth Fry and Josephine Butler in Britain and the Netherlands.* Amsterdam: Amsterdam University Press.

CHAPTER 26

QUAKERS AND ASYLUM REFORM

CHARLES L. CHERRY

THE epithets 'mad' and 'enthusiast' tainted the Quaker movement from its outset. Born in a period of revolt and social chaos, Quakers early on worked to create an organizational structure that would transform a movement into a sect, one that would outlast the Ranters and other sects that thrived in the seventeenth century. Itinerant preachers with powerful messages, such as George Fox (1624–91), James Nayler, Richard Farnworth, and Edward Burrough, moved throughout England attracting many converts. But a body of believers open to ideas of perfectionism, apocalypse, and subjective revelation, while also being resistant to oaths and deferential hat honour, was vulnerable to attack. Individuals heeding inner voices and leadings from the 'Light', 'Seed', 'Christ', 'Spirit' (words often used interchangeably) embodied a potential theology of chaos, both personal and public. How should fellow Quakers deal with Solomon Eccles when he felt called by the Lord to place a pan of glowing coals on his head, or Martha Simmonds and Hannah Stranger, who decided with Nayler's complicity to re-enact at Bristol Christ's entry into Jerusalem, or those who would go 'naked as a sign', or who were moved to disrupt church services run by 'hireling ministers'? How in the face of public outrage to maintain a tolerance for ambiguity? How to discern spiritual leadings or eccentricity from neuroses or psychoses?

The Quaker appeal to direct experience rather than external authority may have been related to the mid-seventeenth-century empiricism of the New Philosophy, but Fox was alive to the risks of such subjectivity. He might assert wisely that 'Friends' minds should not go out from the spirit of God into their own notions' (Braithwaite 1955, 147) and concur with Catherine Phillips' counsel to young people 'to guard their own minds, lest they admit of any pleasing imagination and stamp it with the awful name of revelation' (Brinton 1972, 28), but he was also part of the problem. Consider 'The Book of Miracles', a catalogue of more than 150 cures attributed to George Fox (Cadbury 1948). Cadbury argues that the use of 'miracles' enabled Fox to inspire Seekers and deflate enemies who called him a 'false prophet', but they also made Fox and the movement vulnerable to charges of blasphemy and devil-worship while potentially aligning them with fanatical sects and Roman Catholics. Later Friends, such as Isaac Penington, Robert Barclay, and Thomas Ellwood, suppressed the 'Book' and 'scrubbed' (Reay 1985, 113) Fox's *Journal* of miracle accounts so that the 1694 edition included only twelve 'miracles', five of physical healing and seven of mental/emotional (Hodges 1995, 20; Lawrence 2009, 54). As Barclay said: 'We do not need miracles, because we preach no new gospel, but only what has already been confirmed by the numerous miracles of Christ and his Apostles' (2002, 189–90).

Nonetheless, it is significant that the majority of miracles in the 1694 edition concern Fox healing several individuals who were 'distracted', or 'moping', or 'troubled'. One such incident occurred in 1649 in Skegby at the home of Elizabeth Hooton, an early convert and formidable recruiter of other women to the cause (Moore 2000, 6). It concerned a woman 'possessed two and thirty years' who had been bothering Friends at meeting. Fox expressed concern about her aberrations:

At that time our meetings were disturbed by wild people, and both they and the professors and priests said that we were false prophets and deceivers, and that there was witchcraft amongst us. The poor woman would make such a noise in roaring, and sometimes lying upon her belly upon the ground with her spirit and roaring and voice, that it would set all Friends in a heat and sweat. And I said, 'All Friends, keep to your own, lest that which is in her get into you', and so she affrightened the world from our meetings. Then they said if that were cast out of her while she were with us, and were made well, they would say that we were of God. This said the world, and I had said before that she should be set free.

She was then healed:

She rose up, and her countenance changed and became white; and before it was wan and earthly; and she sat down at my thigh as I was sitting and lifted up her hands and said, 'Ten Thousand praise the Lord', and did not know where she was, and so she was well; and we kept her about a fortnight in the sight of the world and she was wrought and did things, and then we sent her away to her friends. And then the world's professors, priests, and teachers never could call us any more false prophets, deceivers, or witches after, but it did a great deal of good in the country among people in relation to the Truth, and to the stopping the mouths of the world and their slanderous aspersions. (Fox 1995, 43)

This is a significant moment, one in which Fox is conscious of an audience beyond those present (the 'world's people') and using only prayer and the force of his personality, appears to expel the woman's demons. At the same time, he exhorts Friends to be models of moderation 'lest that which is in her get into you'. Fox, anticipating later techniques of care, uses a focused kindness to restore a woman to sanity. One is also reminded of similar counsel in his 1658 letter to an ill and depressed Elizabeth Claypole, Cromwell's daughter: 'Be still and cool in thy own mind and spirit from thy own thoughts, and then thou wilt feel the principle of God to turn thy mind to the Lord God' (Nuttall n.d., 201).

Fox's empathy for the mentally disturbed doubtless emanated from his own problems. Early in the *Journal* he speaks about his dark night of the soul. At Barnet, when he was twenty, he felt a 'strong temptation to despair' and continued in this state so 'dried up with sorrow, grief, and troubles' that the doctors were unable to perform therapeutic bleedings. Plagued by bad dreams and finding no consolation from priests, Fox continued in despair for three years until he heard a voice saying, 'There is one, even Jesus Christ, that can speak to thy condition' (Fox 1995, 11). Rufus Jones notes that Fox 'discovered within the deeps of his own personality a meeting place of the human spirit with the Divine Spirit' (Cadbury 1948, 32). Boisen says that Fox 'succeeded in making certain insights which came to him in the disturbed period the organizing center of a socially valuable new self' (Boisen 1936, 82). William James was similarly struck by Fox's skirting a fine line between sanity and pathological behaviour. Had Fox not experienced an integration of personality through religion, James suggests, he would have suffered a breakdown (Trueblood 1968, 35).

It is not surprising that Fox was early interested in becoming a doctor. He owned a copy of Nicholas Culpeper's *The English Physitian Enlarged* (Cadbury 1948, 51) and once said: 'I was at a stand in my mind whether I should practice physic for the good of mankind, seeing the nature and virtue of the creatures were so opened to me by the Lord' (Fox 1995, 27). Still, he distrusted much of the physic practised by most contemporary physicians and relied more on herbal medicines, natural healing, and spiritual counsel.

Gradually Fox saw the need for a more formalized approach to care of the insane. In a 1669 epistle he urged Friends to 'have and provide a house for those that are distempered', a charge later amplified: 'That friends do seek some place convenient in or about ye City wherein they may put any person that may be distracted or troubled in mind, that so they not be put among the world's people or run about the streets' (Tuke 1825, 192). In 1673 there is a record of 'John Goodson offering to take a large house for distempered and discomposed persons'. Goodson, a surgeon, apparently set up the house in a 'quiet locality off Bartholomew Close', but beyond this there is no record. Auguste Jorns suggests that it was soon given up, prompting the placement of the Quaker mentally ill in asylums run by non-Quakers (Jorns 1931, 154). The problems associated with Friends being under the care of non-Friends led to the 1796 establishment by the Tukes of York Retreat.

Quakers continued to suffer physical and verbal attacks from religious opponents with a special theme being religious enthusiasm and madness. The more personal assaults on early Friends reflected the fierce rhetoric of a world turned upside down by political and religious chaos as well as bitter respect for the gains made by Quaker ministers. Richard Blome's *The Fanatick History* (1660), for instance, has a catalogue of aberrant Quaker conduct, as noted in the lengthy subtitle:

> An Exact Relation and Account of the Old Anabaptists, and New Quakers. Being the summe of all that hath been yet discovered about their most Blasphemous Opinion, Dangerous Practices, and Malitious Endevours to subvert all Civil Government both in Church and State. Together with their Mad Mimick Pranks, and their ridiculous

actions and gestures, enough to amaze any sober Christian. Which may prove the Death and Burial of the Fanatick Doctrine.

Chapter five lists forty-five instances of Friends going naked, bothering the worship of others, drugging people to attend Quaker meetings, possessing people, leading people to copulate with the Devil, assaulting Ministers, and claiming to perform miracles. Joseph Smith's *Bibliotheca Anti-Quakeriana* (1873), though by no means complete, contains hundreds of similar references to attacks on Friends.

Even though later Friends receded into Quietism and even though they managed through a system of communal restraint to avoid the moral and social anarchy of the Ranters to become a part of the commercial mainstream, the criticism did not abate. Later attacks reflect a changed world view. The Enlightenment—born out of Lockean empiricism with a cosmos modelled on the great chain of being, admiring satire with its implied moral and social standards, with order/disorder a more potent dualism than good/evil, promoting reason over imagination, piety over enthusiasm, reality over magic—viewed Quakers with suspicion. With Fox in mind, Jonathan Swift said that 'the two Principal Qualifications of a Phanatic Preacher are, his Inward Light, and his Head full of Maggots' (1958, 62). He equated enthusiastic preachers (for example, Quaker 'Female Priests') to the Aeolists, both inspired with subterranean vapours that 'overshadow the Brain' producing conceptions that smack of 'Madness or Phrenzy' (Swift 1958, 157). The brain, Swift affirmed, when in its 'natural Position and State of Serenity does not prompt anyone with a thought of drawing the masses to his own Power, his *Reasons* or his *Visions* ... But when a Man's Fancy gets *astride* on his Reason, when Imagination is at Cuffs with the Senses, and common Understanding, as well as common Sense, is Kickt out of Doors; the first Proselyte he makes, is Himself, and when that is once compass'd, the Difficulty is not so great in bringing over others; A strong Delusion always operating from *without*, as vigorously as from *within* (Swift 1958, 171).

John Locke and those he influenced (such as Swift) resented the excesses of the Quakers and other dissenting sects that had caused so much civil and religious chaos during the English Revolution. He attacked the notion of innate ideas and religious enthusiasm, which rises from 'conceits of a warmed or overweening brain'. Doubtless he had Quakers in mind when he disputed the idea of the 'internal Light', concluding 'It is a Revelation, because they firmly believe it; and they believe it, because it is a Revelation' (Locke 1975, 702). Even into the nineteenth century, Quakers were not immune from conventional attacks. The phrase 'Mad Quaker', for example, endured even up to Sydney Smith's benign use of it in his 1814 discussion in the *Edinburgh Review* of Tuke's *Description*. He noted that 'a mad Quaker belongs to a small and rich sect, and is, therefore, of greater importance than any other mad person of the same degree in life' (Smith 1814, 197). Less sympathetic was Francis Jeffrey's 1807 review of Thomas Clarkson's *A Portraiture of Quakerism*. He attacked Quakers for their spiritless faith, said Fox was 'exceedingly insane' and that Quaker doctrines were 'too high-flown for our humble apprehension' (Jeffrey 1807, 85, 102).

This legacy of their ancestors' antics perhaps made Quakers particularly sensitive to social disorder and to the mentally ill. They became a more guarded sect intent on monitoring and controlling each other's conduct. Members were disowned for a variety of offenses that would appear to bring dishonour or public shame to Friends. Public drunkenness, sexual misconduct, financial irregularities, marrying outside of meeting: these and other failings subjected meeting members to dismissal. Thus meetings became inbred both psychologically and physically. Whether this made Quakers more vulnerable genetically to mental disorder is an open question, but it is certainly the case that Friends like the Tukes sensed that Quakers needed to direct energies to personal and group development—thus the emphasis on 'family' in terms initially of religious exclusivity—and also needed grand goals to lift them from a culture of self-criticism and vacant formalism. Asylum reform was but one of these noble causes. Such humanitarian efforts provided creative outlets for an ambitious, intelligent segment of the population stifled in many other avenues of achievement. Such were the reasons for the establishment of York Retreat.

York Retreat

That the publication of Samuel Tuke's *Description of the Retreat* in 1813 'elevated a small, provincial experiment to something like a national monument' (Jones 1955, 41), and that subsequent attacks on its author led to Parliamentary investigations which 'laid the groundwork for the modern mental hospital era' (Tuke 1964, 6) are important parts of the story of Quakers and asylum reform. The details in *Description* are now familiar. Hannah Mills, a 42-year old Quaker widow from Leeds, had been placed in York Asylum, a public charity, by relatives who because they lived at a distance, asked Overseers of York Meeting to visit her. They attempted to do so, but were rebuffed and told that she was not in a 'suitable state to be seen by strangers' (22). She died on 30 April 1790 without the pastoral care of Friends. Samuel's grandfather William, a tea and coffee merchant in York, was then motivated by his daughter Ann to establish an asylum managed by Quakers *for* Quakers. In June 1792, York Quarterly Meeting passed a minute approving the establishment of 'A Friends Institute for Mentally Afflicted'. Samuel was more detailed:

> ...it was conceived that peculiar advantage would be derived to the Society of Friends, by having an Institution of this kind under their own care, in which a milder and more appropriate system of treatment, than that usually practiced, might be adopted; and where, during lucid intervals, or the state of convalescence, the patient might enjoy the society of those who were of similar habits and opinions. It was thought, very justly, that the indiscriminate mixture, which must occur in large public establishments, of persons of opposite religious sentiments and practices; of the profligate and the virtuous; the profane and the serious; was calculated to check the progress of returning reason, and to fix, still deeper, the melancholy and misanthropic train of ideas, which, in some descriptions of insanity, impresses the

mind. It was believed also, that the general treatment of insane persons was, too frequently, calculated to depress and degrade, rather than to awaken the slumbering reason, or correct its wild hallucinations. (Tuke 1964, 22–3)

Many objections to the project were raised: that the scheme was too bold for a Quarterly Meeting; that Friends should support local asylums rather than construct their own; that York was too distant a location for many Friends; that mental illness could not be helped and it was foolish to try. William persevered however. The Retreat opened on 11 May 1796 with three patients being admitted the following month. Timothy Maud, a Bradford Friend with medical experience, was named superintendent and with Dr Thomas Fowler as attending physician. Maud died within two months and was replaced by George Jepson as both superintendent and apothecary with Katharine Allen (later Mrs Jepson) as matron or female superintendent responsible for the domestic department and general care of the patients. By 1813 there were sixty-four patients—twenty-four men and forty women.

THE LIGHT WITHIN

Why did Quakers involve themselves in an activity demanding a substantial commitment of resources without a clear promise of positive results? Beyond being motivated by a sense of religious exclusivity, a sensitivity to a legacy of association with breaches of public and personal order, and a need for worthy outlets to overcome a sense of physical and psychological 'inbreeding', the concept of the Light Within (or Light of Christ) was perhaps most important. Quakers believe that there is God in every person, an indwelling power whose expression should not be hindered by any form of physical or mental oppression. That power may be described differently by believers, but it is central to Quakers' 'inward encounter with God' (Dandelion 2008b, 2). Even the most severely afflicted of the mentally ill, Quakers believe, retain some spark of that Light, which makes them God's children and part of a religious community. Philadelphia Friends claim that recognizing God's Light in all persons 'overcomes our separation and our differences from others and leads to a sympathetic awareness of their need and a sense of responsibility toward them' (*Faith and Practice* 2002, 16). Any bar to expression of the Light establishes an ethical need to remove it, thus the impulse for Friends to become engaged in many forms of social action.

HEROIC TREATMENT

What therapeutics were practised at the Retreat? One must first consider standard treatment provided most patients until this period. The model for such treatment was provided at Bethlem Hospital, London, in practices described in the now-infamous testimony of its chief physician Thomas Monro in his 1815 appearance before a Parliamentary committee investigating madhouses:

> They [the patients at Bethlem] are ordered to be bled about the latter end of May, or the beginning of May, according to the weather; and after they have been bled they take vomits once a week for a certain number of weeks, after that we purge the patients; that has been the practice invariably for years, long before my time; it was handed down to me by my father, and I do not know any better practice. (Hunter 1963, 702)

Eighteenth-century treatments were a blend of classical science and medieval cosmology. Especially important was the Galenic system of humoural pathology with its effort to achieve a balance of blood, phlegm, and yellow and black bile through vigorous ('heroic') purgings and bloodlettings. A later influential teacher was William Cullen 1710–90), Professor of Physics at the University of Edinburgh, the leading medical school during this period. In his *First Lines in the Practice of Physic* (1784), Cullen emphasized the effect on the brain from tension and spasm in the arteries; thus our modern terminology of 'high strung' or 'nervous tension'. Benjamin Rush, one of his students, espoused this theory in his *Medical Inquiries and Observations Upon the Diseases of the Mind* (1812), a work that earned him the title 'Father of American Psychiatry'.

Cullen's work and the experience of practitioners led to the widespread use of emetics (such as black hellebore), bleeding (through use of scarifiers, later leeches), blistering (using Spanish fly), drugs (especially laudanum and morphine), isolation (solitary confinement), and mechanical restraint that figured so prominently in the pharmacopeia of eighteenth-century physicians. Samuel Tuke, who had hoped to attend the Edinburgh School of Medicine (Dr Fowler's alma mater), had familiarized himself with the theory and practise of asylum care before writing the *Description*. He had read Philippe Pinel in particular, but also a wide spectrum of English theorists and practitioners. As Tuke notes, Jepson and Fowler tried the various therapeutics mentioned in these works, but determined by experiment and common sense that moral treatment was more effective.

Moral Treatment

As 'one of the first practical efforts to provide systematic and responsible care for an appreciable number of the mentally ill' (Bockoven 1963, 13), moral treatment was an emotional or psychological way to arouse dormant faculties and help patients regain control of their lives. No single common method was devised to achieve this. Beyond the basics of good food, clean living conditions, humane attendants, minimal restraint and force, there was close personal attention to each patient in order to identify specific therapeutic possibilities, such as manual labour, intellectual diversion, or religious worship. Health was achieved in a family or communal setting where every staff member and attendant was sensitive to patients' needs. It appeared to be a more successful therapy. Of course, its success at York Retreat and later at Friends Asylum depended in part on the setting (a pleasant, light-filled building designed to be both comfortable and secure), and a reassuring 'family' of managers and custodians, especially the attendants/nurses charged with the daily care of patients (Digby 1985; D'Antonio 2006).

Most physicians were children of the Enlightenment, Lockeans in their epistemology, and Cullenites/Rushites in their therapeutics. They believed in a mind/brain dualism and the influence of environment on their patients. They believed that mental problems were caused by physical disorders of the brain, but they were uncertain of and could not demonstrate the specific causes. Both York Retreat and later its counterpart in America, Friends Asylum in Philadelphia, had diagnostic categories of mania, melancholia, monomania, dementia, and idiocy. More intriguing was the list of causes. At Friends Asylum, for example, beyond generic categories of 'unknown, constitutional, hereditary, medical, emotional, intemperance, religion' we have under 'medical' for men 'fever, head injury, epilepsy, paralysis, inflammation, misc.' (miscellaneous could be 'measles, exposure, seminal discharge, asthma, ill health, cerebritis'); under emotional or moral, the largest percentage is 'financial anxiety', then ' masturbation, disappointment, domestic difficulty, business anxiety, grief'. For women, medical includes 'apoplexy, change of life, amenorrhea, parturition'; under emotional 'domestic difficulty, disappointment, fright, grief' (D'Antonio 2006, 198–9).

Moral treatment could help heal 'by removing emotional irritants and permitting—perhaps even assisting—the brain's natural restorative powers to operate' (Dain 1964, 71). That is, psychological methods could reverse minor somatic changes before brain lesions formed. One therapy was the creation of a positive environment through a 'family' atmosphere. If a patient lacked a background that stressed 'Christian self-denial, moderation and uprightness of character', the Retreat 'might provide a surrogate home and family in which to resocialize the patient' (Digby 1985, 34). The asylum superintendent functioned as a paterfamilias who might administer drugs for the body, but primarily established a non-threatening domestic, supportive atmosphere with religious overtones. Moral treatment was designed in part to have patients internalize proper conduct and self-control.

Charland's defence of moral treatment against Foucault and Scull underlines the Retreat's 'unique therapeutic legacy'. While acknowledging the use of fear and 'heroic' treatments in the Retreat's early days, he argues that with a small group of mostly Quakers patients and Quaker attendants, and seeing 'religious principles... as a means of cure' (Tuke), the Retreat not only was a Quaker 'family'; it 'was a religious institution in every sense of the word'. The 'Light Within' redeemed the patients, no matter how insane: 'the mad may have lost their minds, but not their hearts'. The premise of moral treatment was that 'core benevolent affections in humans remain mostly untouched by madness'. Tuke said that brain lesions left affective functions intact. Fear was used not as punishment, but 'to help to instill discipline and help the mad to regain control of themselves (Tuke 1964, 143). The Light Within was the source of the 'ethical and affective aspects of moral treatment at the Retreat' (Charland 2007, 78).

As noted by Charland, what was distinctive about the Retreat, beyond the promotional work done by Samuel Tuke in his *Description*—the first account of an asylum run on 'progressive lines' (Digby 1985, 238)—was the shared religious belief of its patients and use of therapy as a mode of living faith. During George Jepson's tenure as superintendent (1796–1823), 87.6 per cent of the patients were Quakers, 8.5 per cent were connected to the Society of Friends, and 3.9 per cent had other religious affiliations (Digby 1985, 174). The rates of cure were very appealing. As recounted by Tuke in a detailed analysis, from 1796 to 1811, 149 patients were admitted; of that number twenty-six died and eighty-five were 'recovered' or 'improved with no further need for confinement'. This success rate was undercut by patients with chronic mental illness and thus not as amenable to early treatment. These rates of cure, based on an intimate Quaker family environment with Quaker attendants, could not be easily duplicated. It would later yield to custodial care and a 'cult of pessimism' would come to replace 'a cult of curability' (Tomes 1984, 315).

THE INFLUENCE OF THE YORK RETREAT

The York Retreat was not the first or only asylum to provide a therapy of simple kindness, compassion, good diet, and useful labour. It had precedents in some private madhouses such as those run by Edward Long Fox and William Battie, in the treatment of patients at Pennsylvania Hospital, in the parallel work of Philippe Pinel at the Bicêtre and Salpêtrière in France, and by Chiarugi in Italy. But the dissemination of Samuel Tuke's *Description*, his personal visits to nearly all the asylums in the United Kingdom and many on the Continent, William Tuke's (1732–1822) testimony before Parliament's Select Committee on Madhouses of 1814–16, and the enthusiastic endorsements by the Retreat's important and diverse visitors—including physicians, architects, philanthropists, hospital administrators, royalty, even an Indian chief—from Russia, Switzerland, United States, Malta, Scotland, and Germany, made the Quaker asylum the 'alma mater of moral treatment' and 'a symbol of a new orthodoxy in the care of the insane' (Digby 1985, 256, 258).

Numerous asylums—Quaker and secular—are indebted to the York Retreat and to Samuel Tuke's (1784–1857) *Description* for their philosophy of care and architecture. In fact, it is difficult to exaggerate the impact the Retreat had on all kinds of institutions. For example, as a 'crude indication' of such influence, Kathleen Jones notes that a large number of private madhouses adopted the name 'Retreat' in homage to the York Retreat's celebrity, eleven of them in Yorkshire alone. Four of the seven voluntary hospitals created before 1800 (Bethlem, Liverpool, Manchester, York) and five of the nine county asylums established before 1830 (Nottingham, Bedford, Lancaster, West Riding, Cornwall) owed debts to the Retreat. Thomas Morris, superintendent of Nottingham, stayed at the York Retreat to study its methods. Two Quaker retreats were created at Loughall near Armagh and Bloomfield near Dublin (see Gillespie), followed by the public Richmond Asylum in 1815, modelled on the Retreat's moral management. Four of the five asylums built in Scotland between 1800 and 1830 were influenced by the Retreat (Digby 1985, 24253), as were those in Wales (Jones 1993, 845).

America was also fertile ground for such influence. In the first three decades of the nineteenth century, Quakers took special pride in the growth of asylums modelled on their care and the quality of their leaders, many of whom were Quakers or Quaker-influenced. For example, the first private, non-profit asylum in America, Friends Asylum in Philadelphia, had direct connections with the Retreat. An American Friend, Thomas Scattergood, visited York in 1799 and toured the Retreat, doing so again seven months later, when he was moved to worship with the patients. Scattergood was then instrumental in the 1813 founding of Friends Asylum. Four of the first eight private and corporate asylums built in the US were Quaker institutions modelled on the Retreat. These were Friends Asylum, PA (1813), McLean Asylum, MA (1818), Bloomingdale Asylum, NY (1821), and Hartford Retreat, CT (1824). Friends Asylum, McLean, and Hartford in particular 'served as model institutions for the practise of psychological medicine' (Dain 1964, 22). Visitors emulated their practices and many leading mad-doctors of the mid-nineteenth century received their training there. For example, Thomas Kirkbride (1809–83) (the first medical superintendent of Pennsylvania Hospital) and Pliny Earle (1809–92) (superintendent of Bloomingdale Asylum) both served as resident physicians at Friends Asylum. Clark and Elkinton's *The Quaker Heritage in Medicine* details the spider-web of Quaker relationships that runs through asylum work in America and how the work of these Friends related to the sixteen mental hospitals founded by 1841 based on moral treatment.

Also, of the thirteen original members of the Association of Medical Superintendents of American Institutions for the Insane (eventually the American Psychiatric Association), established in 1844, the following were Quakers or had association with Quaker mental hospitals: Thomas S. Kirkbride, Amariah Brigham, Pliny Earle, Luther V. Bell, John S. Butler, Samuel B. Woodward (Deutsch 1949, 91). Clark and Elkinton extend this list of Quaker connections beginning with early Quaker physicians (Cadwalader Evans, Caspar Wistar, Thomas Chalkley James, Samuel Emlen); British physician Edward Long Fox, who practised moral treatment at his private facilities Brislington House and Cleve Hill; Edward Wakefield, an important figure in the movement to reform mental hospitals; and Daniel Hack Tuke, son of Samuel Tuke and editor of the the *Journal of Mental Science* (1880–95) and co-author with John Charles Bucknill of *A Manual of Psychological Medicine* (1858), a popular textbook that marked an important step in establishing alienism.

CHANGE

Reaction to the work of York Retreat has not been uniformly positive. The concept of moral treatment came subject to attack, especially from Michel Foucault and Andrew Scull who led frontal assaults on the values of the Enlightenment and Whig historians who saw Victorian asylums as a triumph of science over superstition. Overlooking Quaker religious beliefs, especially the concept of the Light Within (*see* Lawrence, Stewart, Cherry), they charged Tuke and Pinel with imposing on their patients a kind of moral imprisonment and with subtly manipulating them to endorse a bourgeois value system of work and duty. Gerald Grob said that moral treatment lacked rigour and predictability, and became different things to different doctors and social norms (Grob 1973, 88). Later figures such as R. D. Laing, Erving Goffman, and Thomas Szasz agreed and interpreted such terms as 'mental illness' and 'treatment' not as realities but as value-laden social constructions. People are confined in asylums, they suggested, not because they are truly ill, but because they deviate in their conduct from accepted social norms.

Also, sharp increases in the number of patients necessitated custodial rather than curative care; it was impossible to maintain a family atmosphere with a large number of patients. Consonant with these changes was the gradual reassertion by the medical community of its supremacy in the care and treatment of the mentally ill. From the low point of Dr Monro's testimony before a Parliamentary committee ('the disease is not cured by medicine, in my opinion'), proponents of medical over moral treatment gradually gained ascendancy as doctors regained power from the 'amateurs'. They had more credibility with their professional association and were bolstered by reform acts mandating that asylums of a certain size be headed by medical superintendents (Scull 1993, 190–8). In fact, a group of Quaker scientists—led by Lister and Hodgkin—sought in 1839 to establish a Southern Retreat as an alternative to the moral management approach of York Retreat (Cherry 1989, 108–15). Important as well was a changing conception of mental illness. Madness came to be perceived either as an unavoidable hereditary disease or a weak-willed evasion of responsibility. The Quaker notion of the Light Within, the sense that individuals, though weakened, could still control and shape their own destiny, could recover, and become functioning members of civil society—the concepts that had underpinned much of the Quaker reform movement with the mentally ill—began to weaken. By 1850, lip service was still accorded these notions, but their influence on actual practice in asylums was less forceful and less convincing.

In an ironic cycle, the push for reform made famous by Pinel and Tuke was then forwarded mid-century by reformers such as Dorothea Dix and Lord Shaftesbury who agitated for a transition from small community/familial systems of care—including workhouses, jails, and private madhouses—to segregating 'lunatics' into large, purpose-built asylums. Some superintendents in the nineteenth century such as John Galt and Charles Bucknill, frightened by the growth in asylum numbers, argued for cottage systems similar to that at Gheel in Belgium or the farm of St Anne at Bicêtre (Grob 1983, 321.) But it was too late. Sadly, these structures proposed as models of moral treatment degenerated into warehouses of custodial care with little in the way of therapy; Colney Hatch, for example, treating the mentally ill of North London, had at one point over 3,500 patients (Hunter 1974). Asylums became 'bureaucratic monsters' (Jones 1993, 114) into the twentieth century with wards full of medicated 'perfect mental patients—dull, unmotivated, and helpless' (Aviv 2011, 60). As a result of 'asylum' novels, films, and documentaries about conditions and abuses of patients (*Titicut Follies, One Flew Over the Cuckoo's Nest, The Snake Pit*), psychiatrists and asylums alike became demonized with doctors once again being seen as a threat to the mentally ill. The result has been an attempt to return to smaller, more accessible forms of care, more 'family' structures. Large facilities have been shut down and their patients 'decarcerated' or 'deinstitutionalized'. In Britain, the number of patients in state asylums went from 148,000 in 1954 to fewer than 60,000 in 1989 (Scull 1993, 381), while in the United States that number went from 512,500 in 1950 to 132,200 in 1980 (Scull 1989, 313). Today there are even fewer.

The resulting care has been tangled and complex. It can be argued that asylums never really replaced community care and that 'care outside the walls of the asylum remained the primary response of industrial societies to the problem of the mentally disordered' (Bartlett viii). Also, the attempt to remove patients from seemingly ossified, anonymous institutions to a more personal, intimate 'community care', that is, to a network of social workers, psychologists, and psychiatrists to monitor patients in community centres, group homes, nursing homes, and halfway houses had been forwarded in Britain by legislation beginning in 1930 with the Mental Treatment Act and culminating in additions to the 1990 Community Care Act; and in America by the signing in 1963 by President Kennedy of the 'Community Mental Health Centers Act', designed to replace asylums with 'a humane network of behavioral-health centers and halfway homes'. These efforts have been marred by insecure funding and a 'tentative backlash', at least in the United Kingdom, in which some argue that institutional care may be needed for a group of patients 'dangerous as well as mad' (Bartlett 1999, 265). Budget cuts and lack of facilities have also resulted in many patients ending up in jail or homeless (Scull 1989, 302–26). Patient 'freedom' has too often become 'abandonment' (Aviv 2011, 61).

CONCLUSION

Moral treatment did not vanish, but rather has been revived or reconstituted in the more intimate, personal setting of milieu therapy, community hospitals, and therapeutic community. Although many of the Quaker asylums mentioned in this essay are still in existence, their mission and identity have changed, sometimes dramatically, with the private hospitals (in the US) establishing discrete private-pay units for treatment of more affluent patients (the 'Retreat' at Sheppard Pratt, the 'Pavilion', and '3 East' at McLean), yet the concept of moral treatment remains a constant. Janelle Stanley has explored how that approach remains strong today, from the dialogue between Jung and Quakers in the early twentieth century to 'how modern Friends integrate Quaker theology with modern psychological and pastoral care practices' (Stanley 2010, 548). In a broader approach, Annie Borthwick identifies basic principles of moral treatment (respect for individuals with mental problems and a 'pragmatic, non-doctrinaire' approach to treatment), and how these remain germane in the care of the mentally ill (Borthwick 2001).

Perhaps the greatest contemporary threat to the use of moral treatment is the under-standable temptation to resort to psychoactive drugs for immediate results. As noted in one study of a mental hospital, psychopharmacology now rules in a world of 'quick diagnoses, rapid drug prescriptions, and hopes for the best' (Beam 2001, 233). In a con-troversial article, former editor of *The New England Journal of Medicine* Marcia Angell notes that the latest *Diagnostic and Statistical Manual of Mental Disorders* (the 'bible of psychiatry') contains 365 diagnoses of mental disorders with no citations or scientific studies to support them, but with a plethora of drugs recommended to deal with them. She states: 'Our reliance on psychoactive drugs, seeming for all of life's discontents, tends to close off other options. In view of the risks and questionable long-term effects of drugs, we need to do better' (Angell 2011, 22). More than two centuries after the found-ing of York Retreat, 'cures' for mental problems remain elusive and we still seek answers to complex mind/body relationships. Dr Monro might well feel at home.

SUGGESTED FURTHER READING

Cherry, C. L. (1989) *A quiet haven: Quakers, moral treatment, and asylum reform.* London and Toronto: Associated University Presses.

D'Antonio, P. (2006) *Founding Friends: Families, staff, and patients at the Friends Asylum in early nineteenth-century Philadelphia.* Bethlehem, PA: Lehigh University Press.

Digby, A. (1985) *Madness, morality and medicine: A study of York Retreat.* Cambridge: Cambridge University Press.

Grob, G. (1983) *Mental illness and American Society, 1875–1940.* Princeton: Princeton University Press.

Jones, K. (1993) *Asylums and after: A revised history of the Mental Health Services, from the early 18th century to the 1990s.* London: The Athlone Press.

Lawrence, A. (2009) *Quakerism and approaches to mental affliction: A comparative study of George Fox and William Tuke.* A thesis submitted to the University of Birmingham for the degree of Master of Philosophy. School of Theology, Department of Quaker Studies.

Scull, A. (1993) *The most solitary of afflictions: madness and society in Britain 1700–1900.* New Haven and London: Yale University Press, 1993.

Scull, A. (1989) *Social order/mental disorder: Anglo-American psychiatry in historical perspective.* Berkeley and Los Angeles: University of California Press.

Stanley, J. (2010) 'Inner Night and Inner Light: A Quaker model of pastoral care for the mentally ill', *Journal of Religious Health,* 49:547–59.

Tomes, N. (1984) *A generous confidence: Thomas Story Kirkbride and the art of asylum-keeping, 1840–1883.* Cambridge: Cambridge University Press.

CHAPTER 27

QUAKERS AND EDUCATION

ELIZABETH A. O'DONNELL

QUAKER EDUCATIONAL THEORY AND PRACTICE

IT is generally agreed that the Religious Society of Friends has never actually had a clearly defined philosophy of education, and terms such as ethos, atmosphere, or tendency have been preferred (Lacey 1998, xvi–xvii). This chapter explores how coherent or consistent have been the fundamental principles underpinning three and a half centuries of educational provision, and how they have been adapted in response to new ideas or the pressure of historical events. Quaker educational institutions have varied greatly in their interpretations of Friends' principles, as has the extent to which they have been intertwined with the formal organization of the Society, especially in the United States, with its widely differing branches of Quakerism. On both sides of the Atlantic, some schools developed with formal oversight by a particular Meeting or group of Meetings, while others were founded by private individuals, with or without the direct support of their religious body.

Early Friends aimed to create an environment in which a child would be secluded from evil influences (Barbour and Frost 1994, 115). The avoidance of 'contagion' by 'the world' underpinned the Society's desire for a 'guarded education', which persisted widely until the late nineteenth century. Initially founded on a positive view of human perfectibility, developed through preparing children for an approved way of life within a special community, by the early eighteenth century the model had shifted to the enforcement of rigid conformity through an exclusive education (Stewart 1953, 31; Pratt 1985, 51). Principles identified as underlying the Society's educational provision arose from Quaker testimony, although the forms these took over the centuries changed. Quaker schools today commonly cite simplicity, equality, community, and non-violence as their founding principles. These can be traced back to the earliest period, but how consistently and coherently they have been applied is open to debate.

The testament to plainness, or simplicity, was expressed initially through a curriculum that was practical and 'In the Truth', and the suppression of extreme emotions to create a serious and serene individual. But for nearly two centuries, the attention paid to requirements such as plain dress, speech, and deportment, long after their original significance was lost, tended to make them mere badges of membership rather than evidence of an inward spiritual state (Brinton 1940, 94). In both Britain and America, these 'peculiarities' weakened in most schools from the 1860s.

Inspired by their belief in spiritual equality and the conviction that poverty, criminality, and other moral failings stemmed from a lack of education, Friends supported education for all, regardless of wealth, gender, or race. However, this did not automatically lead to equality in education, as seen in a report of the British Friends' Educational Society in 1839, which stated that 'the end object of instructing the poor should be to afford them the knowledge requisite to the due performance of the duties of their situations in life' (Stewart 1953, 74). Similarly, although American Friends were undoubtedly prominent in the extension of schooling to African–Americans from the late eighteenth century, it was many years before the Society's own schools and colleges became fully integrated (Lacey 1998, 124–5). The belief in spiritual equality also meant that, in theory, both genders were given the same educational opportunities, as seen in the cofounding of Meeting schools for girls as well as boys. More traditionally, women were seen as the nurturers of the next generation, responsible for socializing children into their community's values (Davies 2000, 119–22). However, in the past, female teachers were paid considerably less than their male counterparts and there were significant differences between the curricula for boys and girls.

Although non-violence or the peace testimony has been another fundamental principle, the level of physical punishment used in British Quaker schools in the early nineteenth century has been described as 'astonishing', in a Society devoted to many humanitarian concerns, with whipping, birching, caning, and solitary confinement widely deployed (Stewart 1953, 197). However, by 1839 the British Friends' Education Society announced that corporal punishment was no longer being used in Quaker schools, apparently putting the Society many decades ahead of other schools in the same period (Brinton 1940, 74).

As Quakerism has interacted with internal developments and trends in the wider world, its institutions have adjusted to meet new situations. Whereas in the past Friends were preoccupied with keeping outside influences at bay, a later dilemma was how far their schools should develop as centres of academic excellence, or, through closer adherence to Quaker principles, appeal to a more restricted constituency and thereby imperil their survival. Some have argued that Quaker schools have lost their way, departing from their original purpose of transmitting their distinctive cultural and spiritual heritage. Nevertheless, although the 'Quaker heritage' of institutions still claiming a connection with the Society may be hard to pinpoint, most still lay claim to a certain ethos, emphasizing not only intellectual achievement but also the importance of social service.

QUAKER EDUCATION IN THE LATE SEVENTEENTH AND EARLY EIGHTEENTH CENTURIES

Both practical and spiritual imperatives inspired the concern to educate the children of members, with an overarching objective to inculcate the Quaker way of life. Apparent ambivalence towards education amongst early Friends, which arose from hostility towards the classical training of clergy and mistrust of 'brain knowledge', did not mean they were against learning altogether. Evidence of Quaker involvement in education in England from the early 1660s includes, for example, the prosecution of Thurston Read of Colchester for teaching without a bishop's licence in 1663 and 1664 (Davies 2000, 124). In 1668, when British Quakers, facing renewed persecution following the Restoration of the monarchy, had begun to organize more effectively, George Fox (1624–91) founded two Quaker schools: Waltham Abbey for boys and Shacklewell for girls. By 1671, there were fifteen boarding schools kept by English Friends. The practice of sending members' children to Quaker schools was soon well-established, although as there were not enough schools run by Friends to cater for all, many attended schools run by non-members. In 1690, London Yearly Meeting urged Quarterly and Monthly Meetings to establish schools so that children would not be contaminated through association with non-Friends.

The blueprint for Quaker education was Fox's idea that education should be 'civil and useful', therefore the curriculum, which emphasized the vernacular, comprised fundamental subjects that everyone needed to know in order to be 'useful'. Literacy was important to members of the Society for a number of reasons: to allow oversight of their own business interests; to enhance employment prospects; to record the sufferings of members as a lesson to others; and to enable the reading of approved literature. In addition, with no specially educated clergy to interpret and mediate God's word and to enable the keeping of meticulous records, it was desirable that all members should be literate. Practical training was also valued as a statement of plainness, to acknowledge the dignity of labour, and avoid the temptations of idleness. Even wealthy Friends were urged to combine manual labour with intellectual learning for their children's education. Appreciation of the natural world was strongly encouraged and scientific subjects were taught in Friends' schools from an early date. The study of nature satisfied a commitment to being 'In the Truth', relying on factual knowledge rather than emotion or imagination, and was also treasured as a revelation of God's work as Creator of order and beauty (Cantor 1999, 4).

University education was not regarded as necessary to qualify for the ministry, being seen as over-emphasizing human, rational learning at the expense of divine inspiration. This has led to the view that the early leaders completely rejected a classical curriculum, but Fox, for one, never claimed that the existence of divine inspiration made learning unnecessary (Woody 1920, 7–12). Moral and religious training and the establishment of schools was promoted, while knowledge of Latin, Greek, and Hebrew was valued as a means of reading the Scriptures and a vehicle for global communication, promoting business success, and international understanding.

Artistic accomplishments, such as music, drama, fiction, and dance, seen as 'vain customs of the world', were all excluded from the curriculum. This remained the case until the second half of the nineteenth century. Children were constantly exposed to religious influences through bible readings, Meetings for Worship, and the use of Friends' writings as educational texts, rather than through formal religious instruction, which carried the danger of interference with the Light of Christ (Stewart 1953, 31; Brinton 1940, 57). However, as early as 1657, Fox published his first *Catechisme for Children*, followed by other instructional texts aimed at transmitting a more explicit but simple definition of Quaker faith and practice and reprinted many times in the ensuing century and a half ([http://quest.quaker.org/issue-9-angell-01.htm]).

From early in the Society's history, children were regarded as being in the care of their Meeting and great efforts were made to provide schooling for the children of poor members. Education would help them gain employment thus avoiding dependence on the Meeting, as well as discouraging idleness, which could lead to wanton behaviour. In 1674, London Friends set up a school at Devonshire House for the children of poor Friends, undertaking to provide free tuition for all those sent by their Monthly Meeting. In North America, a free school for the poor was established by Philadelphian Friends in 1697.

Towards the end of the seventeenth century, especially after 1681, when William Penn (1644–1718) received the charter to develop Pennsylvania, Quaker presence in the British colonies expanded rapidly. Schools were often set up immediately after the establishment of a Meeting (Hamm 2007, xii). Educational ideas circulated throughout Britain and America by means of Epistles and Advices emanating from Yearly Meetings, by travelling ministers and representatives to various meetings, and by books and pamphlets. Penn's letter to his wife and children, written when he left England for America in 1682, was an important influence on Quaker educational practice on both sides of the Atlantic. He strongly recommended practical training to develop diligence and frugality. Primers and elementary grammars commonly used in Friends' schools combined instruction with religious and moral precepts. Textbooks for classical languages were produced, illustrated with Scriptural examples rather than 'heathenish' stories.

By the middle of the eighteenth century, there were at least twenty boarding schools exclusively for Friends in Britain and Ireland. In Pennsylvania, about forty schools under the care of Monthly Meetings had been set up. During this era of Quietism, the Society's mission was to sustain and preserve rather than proselytize and expand, in contrast with the vigour of the early movement. In Britain, the number and quality of ministers fell and with theological teaching increasingly regarded as a barrier to the Light Within, religious training for Quaker youth was neglected (Wright 1995, 15). In North America, after 1740 new Quaker leaders emerged who, disturbed by the effects on members of increasing prosperity, called for a return to primitive purity through a tightening of discipline and more protection from 'the world' (Hamm 2003, 31–2). On either side of the Atlantic, the tendency of the religious community was to isolate itself, until the end of the eighteenth century brought calls for reform.

A New Concern for Education: the Late Eighteenth to Mid-Nineteenth Centuries

Increasing dissatisfaction with the state of Quaker education in Britain in the late eighteenth century was stimulated by a dwindling membership and a perception of spiritual 'deadness'. By the 1770s, attempts to revitalize Quakerism were underway, with education seen as playing a key role, by nurturing community solidarity, transmitting Quaker beliefs and attitudes, and responding to new social and economic demands. Across the Atlantic, the war years of the American Revolution brought hardship for Quaker communities, due to their close ties with Britain and anti-war stance (Hamm 2003, 35). Nevertheless, a renewed concern for education also gathered pace. The largest Yearly Meeting, Philadelphia, adopted an annual query in 1778 requiring Monthly Meetings to report on the state of education, and there was a rapid growth in Friends' schools in Pennsylvania and beyond.

The opening of Ackworth in 1779, a co-educational boarding school for the children of members 'not in affluence', partly funded by London Yearly Meeting, marked the start of a new phase in Quaker education in Britain, ending a period of decline during which the concern for education had mainly been kept alive by the efforts of dedicated individuals, who felt 'called' to educational service (Lacey 1998, 97). In the first few decades of the nineteenth century, more Quaker boarding schools under the care of local Meetings were established, including Sidcot (1808), Islington (1811), and Wigton (1815). Several schools, such as Ayton (1841), were set up to educate the children of parents disowned by the Society, in an attempt to reverse the decline in Members. Manual labour as part of an education continued to be important, both in Britain and North America. The rules of West Lake Friends' Boarding School in Canada, founded in 1841, stipulated that boys should labour for two hours a day (Brinton 1940, 107). In keeping with the commitment to education for both genders, parallel or dual establishments were usually set up, although accommodation and classes remained separate for most of the nineteenth century.

The number of private schools for the children of wealthier Friends also increased. Academic studies tended to replace manual labour, however, so that the presence of physical work on the curriculum effectively branded the school socially as well as economically inferior (Stewart 1953, 75). Esther Tuke (1727–94) established a girls' school in York in 1785, to provide an education 'rather superior to that of Ackworth'. Financial difficulties forced its closure in 1814 but it was revived in 1831 as the Mount School. Meanwhile, a private school for boys in York, Bootham's, had become a Quarterly Meeting school in 1829 (Sturge and Clark 1931, 4).

Whereas the earliest education efforts had been directed towards the establishment of elementary schools, many of them transitory, by the early nineteenth century American Friends began to found academies or high schools to allow Quaker children to continue their education and to ensure a supply of teachers for the lower schools. The first, in

1784, was in Rhode Island and was later called Moses Brown. Some grew out of elementary schools but developed into boarding schools, because of the difficulty in creating the desired religious environment in a day school. The majority offered education to both genders, although not co-educational in the fullest sense.

A lack of advanced training caused problems in securing teachers for Quaker schools. The profession was not highly regarded and because keeping costs down was always a priority, teachers were usually chronically underpaid (Lacey 1998, 90). It was hard for them to support a family, so in America a plot of ground was often included in the remuneration package to encourage longer service at a school. The monitorial system of Joseph Lancaster (1778–1838), with instruction placed in the care of older pupils to reduce expense, allowed schooling to be provided more cheaply and led to the development of the apprentice teacher (Hole 1978, 12). Increasing pressure to improve Quaker schools led to teacher training being taken more seriously. In Britain, the first male apprentice at Ackworth was given an extra year's tuition then articled to the school for six or seven years, receiving board and lodging plus a small payment, but in addition to teaching, was expected to have charge of about seventy boys outside the classroom. From 1836 at the Mount School in York, a few girls were admitted annually who, in return for lower fees, stayed on as trainee teachers, while in 1848 the Flounders Institute was established to prepare male teachers to teach at secondary level.

Despite the decline of the more extreme manifestations of Quietism within the majority of the Quaker community, a 'guarded education' was still desired. Many of the schools set up in this period were deliberately located in rural settings, seen as healthier but also to minimize contact with the 'world'. Westtown in 1799, for example, was deliberately located a day's journey from Philadelphia. In Britain, Ackworth scholars were not even allowed an annual holiday until 1847, to avoid bad influences. 'Plainness' had developed into a fetish, and to ensure the correct moral message was imparted, the Society produced its own textbooks and other reading material.

From the early nineteenth century, many American Friends migrated westwards, often from the slave states in the South, travelling to states such as Ohio and Indiana. They also left the east in search of better economic opportunities. Philadelphia remained a major centre of Quakerism, but the number of Friends in the east declined. Frontier life was difficult and isolated; reinforcing Quaker values without a concentration of Friends in the immediate neighbourhood made it even more important to establish schools, to instil the Society's values. By 1850, the Indiana Yearly Meeting noted ninety-six elementary schools in its environs, with academies also established. Most of these became part of the public school system and the Friends' Quaker Boarding School in Richmond eventually developed into Earlham College (Bacon 1986, 89).

Bitter schisms shook the Society in America from 1827. The divisions into Hicksite and Orthodox Friends had an impact on the provision of education, as each branch sought to safeguard the transmission of its message.

The Changing Character of Quaker Education in the Late Nineteenth and Early Twentieth centuries

By the second half of the nineteenth century in Britain, the Society was shedding some of its 'peculiarities'. Education had also become a national concern, to which many Friends gave service. Forster's Education Act in 1870, named after former Quaker William E. Forster (1818–86) who was responsible for carrying it through Parliament, paved the way for universal elementary education, while the opening up of Oxford and Cambridge to non-Anglicans in 1871 led to an increased demand for an education that would prepare pupils for university entrance.

Leighton Park School was set up by the Friends' Public School Company in 1890 to discourage affluent and ambitious parents from sending their sons to non-Quaker public schools and there was little in its curriculum to distinguish it from the latter. Other Quaker schools were also losing their distinctiveness, with severe 'Quaker dress' being phased out, and the plain speech that demanded teachers be addressed by both names giving way to the use of titles such as 'Miss' and 'Sir' (Stewart 1953, 226). The curriculum was widened to embrace the arts, with, for example, singing allowed from the 1860s. Friends were responding to competition from other educational establishments, especially as the number of non-Friends at Quaker schools increased. By 1901, only 55 per cent of pupils in British Quaker schools were the children of Friends. Moreover, a highly critical report in 1879 into the quality of girls' education in Quaker schools blamed the poor training and pay of women teachers, leading to pressure for improvements, as provision outside the Society was catching up (Stewart 1953, 236).

In America, too, a decrease in both the birth rate and membership of the Society meant more non-Quakers being admitted into their schools. By 1940, only Friends' Boarding School in Barnesville, Ohio maintained its Friends-only policy (Brinton 1940, 57). From the 1840s, splits occurred within Orthodox Friends, into Gurneyites and Wilburites. Gurneyites, in the majority, were more open to religious movements outside the Society, whereas Wilburites prioritized the retention of Quakerism's unique characteristics. These differences affected the way each understood its mission to educate; for example, no college was founded by the Wilburites, while in the Midwest, the participation of some Gurneyites in 'The Great Revival' introduced strong emotions and sudden conversion experiences into Quaker meetings, which producing further internal conflict (Barbour and Frost 1994, 188). In the early twentieth century, yet more disputes arose between Holiness Quakers and Modernists. The number and diversity of Quaker schools and colleges increased substantially in the last quarter of the nineteenth century, reflecting the divergent groups within American Friends. In areas where an evangelical tendency was foremost, the distinctiveness of Quaker education diminished, lessening the need for exclusivity, and allowing many schools to be absorbed into the public system. Friends' schools in the East were more likely to survive, albeit with a majority of non-Quaker students.

HIGHER EDUCATION AND THE RELIGIOUS SOCIETY OF FRIENDS

The Society's attitude towards higher education was initially influenced by hostility towards university training for 'hireling priests'. During the Quietist period, many feared that 'head knowledge' would obscure the leadings of the Light Within. By the early nineteenth century, however, a concern to develop opportunities for advanced learning was gaining momentum, although expressed differently within the various Quaker communities. In Britain until 1871 Friends were excluded from university education, which primarily prepared men for the Anglican ministry, while in America until the 1830s there was little interest in establishing Quaker colleges of higher education.

One common motivating factor in the development of higher learning for Friends was the perennial problem of finding suitably qualified Quaker teachers. As many Friends became more affluent, their higher social standing brought increased opportunities for mixing with 'the world', adding to pressures for better educational standards. Many parents chose to send their children to non-Quaker schools, despite frequent exhortations from London Yearly Meeting against allowing the Society's youth to mix with non-Quakers. Clearly, there was a need to train more teachers competent to teach at a higher level, leading to the establishment of the Flounders Institute in 1848, which, in 1858, adapted to the examination requirements of London University (Lacey 1998, 102). For other advanced learning, however, British Friends chose to support non-sectarian educational initiatives, such as the development of London University from 1836, rather than to establish institutions of their own.

In America, a tradition for religious bodies to found private colleges was well established, and this was the route taken by American Quakers. To understand the development of Quaker-born colleges, the separations occurring from the late 1820s must be taken into account. Oliver describes three phases in the establishment of Quaker colleges in the nineteenth and early twentieth centuries (Oliver 2007, 265–6). The first, in the 1830s and 1840s, saw the founding of Haverford (Pennsylvania), Earlham (Indiana), and Guilford (North Carolina), all originally Orthodox academies providing secondary education, only later officially becoming colleges, in 1856, 1859, and 1888 respectively. Second, three colleges set up between 1869 and the end of the century, William Penn (Iowa, 1873), George Fox (Oregon, 1891), and Whittier (California, 1896), had also begun as high schools, but the other three, Swarthmore (Pennsylvania, 1869), Wilmington (Ohio, 1870), and Bryn Mawr (Pennsylvania, 1885), were established as colleges from the start. Swarthmore was the only college set up by Hicksites. In the third phase, from 1892 to 1917, Malone (Ohio, 1892), Asuza Pacific (California, 1899), and Barclay (Kansas, 1917) began as Bible colleges or training institutions for Christian workers. Friends' University (Kansas) was set up in 1898 as a college from the start. In addition, Cornell (New York, 1868) and Johns Hopkins (Maryland, 1873), although not intended as Quaker institutions, were founded by Quakers.

The reasons for the establishment of colleges varied, although with one factor in common: the desire, through higher education, to strengthen the community of whichever tradition out of which the college had grown. Their development has largely followed mainstream trends towards a secular curriculum rather than maintaining a specifically Quaker education (Hamm 2007, xvi). Because of early financial difficulties in most colleges, non-Quakers had to be attracted, leading to the introduction of aspects of non-Quaker college life such as fraternities and athletics, and a subsequent weakening of Quaker 'peculiarities'. The exceptions, Malone and Barclay, were founded in reaction to the Modernist movement in the late nineteenth century, but were heavily influenced by non-Quaker religious fundamentalism. Overall, cultural shifts in the late nineteenth century meant that barriers between Quakers and the rest of American society were breaking down, with expertise rather than religious orthodoxy being demanded from their colleges.

Quakers of all types have played a significant role in the development of higher education for women. In *Reflections on the Present Condition of the Female Sex, with Suggestions for its Improvement* published in 1798, British Quaker Priscilla Wakefield (1751–1832) argued for a rational and moral system of education so that women could fulfil their obligation to be useful citizens and financially self-supporting (Leach and Goodman 2001, 166–8). Although her ideas had little impact at the time, in the second half of the nineteenth century, female Friends worked towards the realization of Wakefield's aspirations through the struggle to obtain higher qualifications for women on both sides of the Atlantic. For example, five out of the first eight students studying medicine at the Female Medical College of Pennsylvania in 1850 were Quakers, while in Britain, female Friends supported the establishment of Girton, the first Cambridge college for women (Bacon 1986, 151; O'Donnell 2001, 45). Moreover, in America, all the Quaker colleges, with the exception of Haverford (male) and Bryn Mawr (female), admitted students of both genders. Swarthmore was especially radical in terms of providing fully co-educational higher education from the start together with equal participation on its management board and the employment of female faculty (Densmore 2007, 57).

INVOLVEMENT IN EDUCATION OUTSIDE THE SOCIETY, LATE EIGHTEENTH AND NINETEENTH CENTURIES

From the beginning of Quakerism, individual Friends viewed the extension of learning to all, regardless of class, race, or gender, as a religious obligation. In nineteenth-century Britain, Quakers were associated with prison schools, the Ragged Schools movement, and the drive towards universal elementary education. As with other reform and philanthropic movements, Friends appear to have had an impact out of all proportion to their small numbers in the wider society, and whether as individuals or as a community have often been associated with educational ideals that appear years ahead of their time. However, the assumption that Friends were inevitably in the vanguard of new educational ventures must be treated with caution. Too narrow a focus on Quakers and education brings the danger of claiming the Society was inevitably at the forefront of all developments, but even during the Quietist period, Friends were affected and influenced by the social, cultural, and economic realities of the period in which they lived. By the end of the eighteenth century, they were just as likely to be collaborating with educationalists of other denominations as they were to be initiating exclusively Quaker institutions (Lunn 2007, 217). By examining the full context, their efforts can be viewed as part of a wider consciousness. Similar educational philosophies emerged in the same period apparently unrelated to each other, suggesting roots in a common culture (Lacey 1998, 176–204). For example, the views of Johann Amos Comenius (1592–1670) on the importance of learning through observation and investigation, and the educational philosophy of John Locke (1632–1704), which stressed the development of moral character over book learning and endorsed a practical and science-based curriculum, bore striking similarities to those of William Penn, although there is no evidence that Penn read either. John Griscom (1774–1852), a New York Quaker scientist and educator, travelled around Europe in the early nineteenth century, visiting a wide variety of institutions to observe their educational practices. His journal, published in 1824, influenced educational practices among Friends and others, for example, on the Reformatory movement.

Quaker Meetings first demonstrated their commitment to making education available to the poor by supporting less-affluent members, but the provision for poor children outside the Society was a favourite form of philanthropy. In New York in 1801, women Friends organized non-denominational schools for the poor; these were eventually adopted by the city and developed into the New York public school system. True to their ideals of spiritual equality, Quakers established schools for both genders, for example, Anthony Benezet (1713–84) founded the first public school for girls in the American colonies in 1754, teaching French, Latin, the classics, composition, and gymnastic exercises. Individual Friends also developed new educational strategies, some of which became very influential, to aid provision for the poor. John Bellers's (1654–1725) 'Colledge of Industry' (1696) advocated teaching trades to the unskilled unemployed within a self-sustaining community, combining manual training with careful moral supervision of the young (Brinton 1940, 94). Although his ideas were only partially realized in the Quaker Workhouse at Clerkenwell, others interested in changing society through education were influenced by them, most notably Robert Owen at New Lanark, Scotland between 1800 and 1825. The educational theories of Quaker Joseph Lancaster (1778–1838) were also widely applied. Concerned that the poor were denied education because of the cost of schoolmasters, he devised a method of teaching whereby a single teacher could be in charge of three hundred or more children in one schoolroom, the younger children being taught in small groups by the older, known as monitors.

The monitorial system dominated popular education in Britain and parts of America for decades. However, Quakers were not unique in displaying a religiously motivated interest in educating the poor; other denominations were similarly committed.

In 1671, George Fox, writing to Friends in Barbados, exhorted them to 'teach, instruct and admonish Negroes, Tawnies and Indians' (Brinton 1940, 87). Anthony Benezet (1713–1784), a convinced Friend originally from France, believed that education of the poor was a religious and social duty for the well-to-do, dedicating his life to this cause. He had already taught both freed and slave African–American children in the evenings for twenty years when he inspired the establishment of the Negro School in Philadelphia in 1770, providing a basic education free of charge and overseen by a committee appointed by the Monthly Meeting. In 1837, Philadelphia Quakers established the Institute for Coloured Youth, offering a more advanced curriculum, which later expanded to provide industrial, mechanical, and agricultural courses (Lacey 1998, 121–3). After the Civil War, some Quakers helped provide schools for freed slaves. In 1866, for example, there were nine new schools in Columbus, Mississippi (Barbour and Frost 1994, 198), while Indiana Yearly Meeting established and supported Southland College, an industrial and teacher-training school for black people in Arkansas.

Despite these pioneer efforts, the Society did not carry the doctrine of racial equality to its logical conclusion, generally favouring separate schools for the different races with few exceptions. In 1832, the admittance of black pupils to a girls' school in Connecticut led to the proprietor Prudence Crandall (1803–90), a Friend and abolitionist, being thrown into jail and the school almost destroyed by an angry mob (Brinton 1940, 91). The emphasis on practical training in the institutions which they established for African–Americans, moreover, suggests that Quakers subscribed to the accommodationist ideas of Booker T. Washington and even in the twentieth century, Quakers were slow to admit minority students into their own schools (Lacey 1998, 70). Earlham was apparently the first Quaker college to admit a black student, in 1880, while Malone, a Bible college established by Quakers in 1892, admitted African–American students from the start, but it was not until the 1920s that Haverford College began to do the same, and Wilmington College did not integrate until the 1950s (Hamm 2007, xx).

There is no evidence for Friends' involvement in the education of Native Americans until the late eighteenth century, despite Fox's encouragement. In 1796, three Friends established schools for Oneidas, training the children in gender-appropriate skills, such as smith work for the boys and spinning for the girls (Woody 1920, 263). Similar initiatives followed in the nineteenth century.

QUAKERS AND ADULT EDUCATION

It has been claimed that the greatest contribution of British Quakers in the field of education was to basic adult education (Wright 1995, 80). However, Lunn warns that the history of their involvement in the expansion of education has too frequently presented a partial 'insider account', focusing on their perceived distinctiveness rather than acknowledging that Friends were 'both riding and contributing to the wave of a wider tide of social concern and action' (Lunn 2007, 206). Adult education in Britain actually began in the 1660s, with Dissenting Academies providing university learning for non-conformists. The Society for Promoting Christian Knowledge was set up in 1699 by Anglicans to encourage literacy in adults, while the Methodist 'circulating schools' of the 1780s attracted adults as well as children. In the first half of the nineteenth century, subscription libraries, Mechanics' institutes, literary and philosophical societies, all added to the opportunities for non-sectarian education for working-class adults. Individual Friends contributed to these early forms of adult education, for example, in 1798 a Methodist minister and a Quaker formed the first adult Sunday school for women lace-makers. However, it was not until the 1830s that their own First-Day Schools, instigated by Evangelical Quakers, began to spread. Part of Home Mission Work, they were not necessarily seen as a way of direct recruitment into the Society, although it was hoped to bring some into the fold. Conservative Friends expressed reservations about adult schools but Jones saw them as the means by which the Society's social conscience was deepened (Jones 1921, 95). American Quakers showed a similar concern for adult education, including their provision targeted at African–American and Native American people.

The establishment of educational settlements by British Quakers in the early twentieth century grew out of the adult school movement, as fewer adults were attracted to Sunday classes providing only basic education and Bible study. The first two settlements were set up in 1909. By 1921, fourteen were affiliated with the Friends' Educational Settlements Association. Meanwhile, following a peak of 113,789 in 1910, membership of adult schools plummeted to 50,761 within a decade. Paradoxically, the emergence of educational settlements may actually have hastened the decline of Quaker adult schools, by offering a wider curriculum, professional teachers, and other activities (Freeman 2007, 195). Although clearly influenced by the university settlement movement of the later nineteenth century, where university students lived and worked amongst the urban poor, the Quaker initiative tended to have non-residential staff, focusing more narrowly on education. Some did perform broader functions, however, working to improve living conditions and providing material relief in areas of high unemployment during the Depression, particularly in South Wales. In the interwar years, with financial support from the Joseph Rowntree Charitable Trust, these settlements were significant providers of adult education, seen by their supporters as an important means to forge links between Quaker Meetings and the wider community, by promoting a sense of spiritual fellowship. From the late 1930s, there was increasing competition from other adult education providers with better resources, while the term 'settlement' became associated with Victorian paternalism. After the Second World War, many Quaker settlements were subsumed into community centres, which emphasized informal communal activities rather than formal educational provision, while others closed altogether, with just a few surviving as independent institutions. At the start of the twenty-first century, the Society still promotes 'lifelong learning' and some of its earliest 'settlements' continue to offer a community education service, albeit very different from that envisaged at the beginning of the movement.

As well as basic adult education as a social service or form of outreach, British Quakers also became concerned with religious education for members who had completed formal education. This could take the form of lectures, conferences, libraries, reading circles, and adult Bible classes, but at the beginning of the twentieth century there was a call on both sides of the Atlantic to establish permanent centres of study. The idea of a British Quaker college was first mooted in the late nineteenth century, to, in the words of George Cadbury, 'infuse a new spirit and energy into the Society' (Lunn 2007, 212). The 1895 Manchester Conference was an important stage in the readjustment of Quakers to the demands of the modern world. John Wilhelm Rowntree (1868–1905), a leading voice at the gathering, called for Friends to prepare to apply their Christian spirit to the needs of society and in 1903, Woodbrooke opened in a building donated by Cadbury in Selly Oak, Birmingham, supported by an endowment from Rowntree.

In America, the Haverford Summer Schools held in 1900 and 1904 marked the start of a new phase in religious education for adult members (Brinton 1940, 51). From 1918 the John Woolman School at Swarthmore offered courses in religious and social subjects, while in 1918 a graduate school for the study of religious subjects was set up at Haverford College. Pendle Hill was founded in 1930 at Wallingford, Pennsylvania, where in addition to attending lectures and discussion groups, students, in keeping with the ethos of earlier times, shared domestic duties. Adult Sunday Schools for members have also developed as an important function of programmed meetings in the twentieth century, as well as vacation Bible schools, retreats, and camps. Unprogrammed meetings of Wilburites and Hicksites, on the other hand, having been slow to embrace the First Day Schools movement in the nineteenth century, tend to offer religious education for adult members through discussion groups before or after meetings for worship (Hamm 2003, 118–19).

MISSION AS EDUCATION

Although the earliest Friends, including George Fox, exhibited missionary zeal, as the movement developed so did a reluctance to send missionaries overseas, partly because of opposition to a paid ministry. It was not until the second half of the nineteenth century that some urged members to follow the biblical injunction to take the Gospel message to the heathen. Rachel Metcalf was the first British Quaker missionary, working in India in 1866 and soon Quaker missionaries, from America as well as Britain, were travelling to other parts of the world, including China, Ceylon, the Middle East, Africa, and Latin America. In the absence of educational opportunities in these countries, an important part of the Society's mission was the provision of schools.

Quaker schools in the Middle East date back to the start of missionary activity in the 1860s. A girls' training school was first inaugurated at Ramallah, Palestine, in 1869, a boys' school following in 1901. Remarkably, both survived the disruption of multiple foreign occupations, world wars and intifadas, despite fluctuating school rolls, periods of closure, and influxes of refugees. In 1990 the schools became co-educational, the Girls'

School encompassing the kindergarten and elementary departments and the Boys' School becoming a high school ([www.quakersintheworld.org/quakers-in-action]). From the 1970s Friends have also provided support for a pre-school play centre and several kindergartens elsewhere in this troubled region, such as the Gaza Strip, as well as training adults to deal with the many cases of trauma seen in Palestinian children. Schools at Brummana, Lebanon, developed from the late 1860s through the efforts of Elijah G. Saleeby and Theophilus Waldmeier (1832–1915). Waldmeier, a German–Swiss missionary who became a Quaker in 1874, expanded educational provision at Brummana with the support of British Friends, making it available to both genders in separate schools until co-education was introduced in 1902. Like the schools at Ramallah, Brummana endured decades of disruption caused by conflict in the region. The school allows pupils to follow their own beliefs, but the ethos of the school has been based on the principles of the Religious Society of Friends, emphasizing non-violence, equality, respect for individuals, and service to the pupils' communities, as well as intellectual excellence ([http://www.quakersintheworld.org/quakers-in-action/150]).

The largest concentration of Quakers at the beginning of the twenty-first century outside the United States is in Kenya, where about 200 secondary and 1,000 primary schools have been founded, as well as a university. From the arrival of the first Quaker missionaries in 1902, Friends have played a major role in secondary education and vocational and agricultural training, centred on the mission established at Kaimosi, as well as establishing a theological college there ([http://www.quakersintheworld.org/quakers-in-action/37]). Elsewhere in Africa, the Great Lakes School of Theology at Bujumbura in Burundi, set up in 1999, provides theological training for students from Burundi, Congo, and Rwanda.

From the early twentieth century, Friends established schools in many countries in Central and Latin America and the Caribbean, including Guatemala, Mexico, and Cuba, although Cuban schools were taken over by the Castro government in 1959. Since 1920, Quakers have also been present in Bolivia, where membership comprised the third-largest Quaker population in the world by the early twenty-first century (Barbour and Frost 1994, 272–5). The Society has been important in providing schooling for the indigenous people, the Aymara Indians making up the majority of its members there, with further initiatives developing out of the Bolivian Quaker Education Fund which began operating formally in 2003. There are also individual schools in Japan, Australia, India, the Philippines, and Zimbabwe.

CONCLUSION

This chapter has offered only a brief account of the many ways in which the enduring commitment of the Religious Society of Friends to education has been expressed. Schools and colleges with roots in Quakerism continue to profess the importance of certain principles, despite Quakers usually being a tiny minority of those attending.

Quakers have also helped to develop educational opportunities for all and new forms of teaching, including an involvement in progressive education in the second half of the twentieth century, as well as developing resources for the wider educational community, for example, in peace studies and conflict resolution. Although it may be inaccurate to claim that Friends have stood alone as educational innovators, their reputation as significant educators deserves recognition.

Suggested Further Reading

Clarke, G. (1987) *John Bellers: His life, times and writings*. London: Routledge and Kegan Paul.

Davis, R. (1953) *Woodbrooke, 1903–1953: A brief history of a Quaker experiment in Religious Education*. London: Bannisdale Press.

Freeman, M. (2004) *The Joseph Rowntree Charitable Trust: a study in Quaker philanthropy and adult education 1904–1954*. York: William Sessions.

Havilland, M. M. (2006) 'Westtown's Integration: "A natural and fruitful enlargement of our lives"', in *Quaker History* 95:2, pp 19–33.

Heath, D. H. (1979) *The peculiar mission of a Quaker school*. Wallingford, Pennsylvania: Pendle Hill.

Kashatus, W. C. (1997) *A virtuous education: Penn's vision for Philadelphia schools*. Wallingford. PA: Pendle Hill.

Mather, E. P. (1980) *Pendle Hill: A Quaker experiment in education and community*. Wallingford, Pennsylvania: Pendle Hill.

Rasmussen, A. M. B. (1995), *A history of the Quaker Movement in Africa*. London: British Academic Press.

CHAPTER 28

....

QUAKERS, BUSINESS,
AND PHILANTHROPY

....

MARK FREEMAN

THE distinctive role played by Quakers and other non-conformists in the development of capitalism has been a long-standing theme in economic and social history. Although not the first to make the connection between religious and economic change, Max Weber is often seen as a starting point (Weber 1998). In *The Protestant Ethic and the Spirit of Capitalism* he showed how seventeenth-century English Puritans—who were also the early settlers in North America—saw their religious practices in worldly terms, and therefore brought Christian motivations to their economic and social activities. Because this encouraged rational rather than speculative commercial behaviour, it resulted in business success. However, this very success ultimately weakened their religious motivations, and the modern capitalist 'ethic'—Weber was writing at the turn of the twentieth century—had lost most of its religious dimension. Quakers were not central to Weber's argument, although he noted the importance of 'the connection of a religious way of life with the most intensive development of business acumen among those sects whose otherworldliness is as proverbial as their wealth', specifically including Quakers in this category (Weber 1998, 44). For Weber, Quaker and Baptist asceticism was intimately associated with a commercial ethic that emphasized honesty, 'conscientiousness', and the identification of work as a 'calling'; this religious motivation drew Friends into commercial activity (Weber 1998, 144–54, 161–2).

At the same time, Quakers were drawn into business because of their exclusion from other areas of English life. Their peace testimony excluded them from military service, while the refusal to take oaths effectively disqualified them from holding office and from many professions (Weber 1998, 150). As is often noted, Friends and other non-conformists (and Roman Catholics) were kept out of Parliament, the English universities, and professional life for the whole of the eighteenth and much of the nineteenth century: the seventeenth-century Test and Corporation Acts were repealed in 1828, and the university 'tests' abolished in 1871 (Pratt 1985, 19–20;

Raistrick 1993, 36–7). Some Friends evaded these prohibitions by taking advantage of 'occasional conformity', or by compromising their testimony against oaths, but, like other non-conformists in England, they were both pushed and pulled towards commercial and industrial activity. Indeed, despite being in a 'retreatist' phase for much of the eighteenth century, David H. Pratt notes that 'the Quakers remained the most favourably disposed of all the sects toward economic endeavours' in the mid- to late eighteenth century (Pratt 1985, 18).

THE GROWTH OF QUAKER BUSINESS IN ENGLAND

In England, Quakers were undoubtedly successful as industrial capitalists. One of the best-known Quaker industrial concerns was run by the Darby family of Coalbrookdale (Raistrick 1993, 122–46) Three generations of this family guided their ironworks through the eighteenth century, starting with Abraham Darby I, born in 1678, who started in the mill-making trade at the end of the seventeenth century but rapidly diversified, moving to Coalbrookdale in Shropshire, where the first iron furnace was running by 1709. Other furnaces were established in the region, and further afield in Wales, over time, and by the mid-eighteenth century the Darby enterprise—in which other Quaker families were also involved—was 'a flourishing concern', both innovative and profitable (Walvin 1997, 110). The famous cast-iron bridge, designed by Thomas Pritchard, was built in the 1770s, and remains a key landmark of Britain's first Industrial Revolution. Another example was the Pease 'dynasty' of Darlington (Pollard 2004; Kirby 1984). Edward Pease (1711–85) was a pioneer of the woollen industry, strengthening the firm that he had inherited from his father, and overseeing the transition from domestic proto-industrial production to the factory system, a common development in the textile industries of the eighteenth century (Kirby 1984, 2). Pease's grandson, also Edward (1767–1858), was also one of the promoters of the Stockton to Darlington railway, which opened in 1825, building on his Quaker connections to acquire the largest shareholding in the concern (Pollard 2004). Edward's sons Joseph and Henry followed him into the railway industry, the former as a manager of the Stockton and Darlington and the latter as a member of the board of the North Eastern Railway Company, following its takeover of the Stockton and Darlington in 1863 (Kirby 1984, 41–2). Joseph entered Parliament in 1832—refusing to take the oath, he was allowed to affirm (Pollard 2004)—and many other members of the family followed him into politics in subsequent years (Kirby 1984, 57ff). Supported by a close network of Quaker relatives, friends, and business associates, the Pease family had investments in a range of extractive and industrial concerns, and their history was 'inextricably linked to the rise of the British industrial economy' (Kirby 1984, xiii). More widely, almost half of the iron industry was Quaker-owned in the first half of the eighteenth century (Walvin 1997, 88). As Douglas Gwyn has emphasized, '[n]o group exceeded the Quakers in being lifted by the updrafts of the commercial revolution. Their network of communications and mutual aid...lent themselves to new purposes in joint ventures, shared contacts and pooled expertise' (Gwyn 1995, 286).

Early Quaker enterpreneurs acquired a reputation for fair dealing, especially with regards to their insistence on fixed-price trading rather than haggling, and on 'just weights and just measures', to which George Fox exhorted them in his 200th epistle. Other Protestant sects made the same insistence (Weber 1998), and in the case of Quakers, Methodists, and Baptists, it was often associated with simplicity in personal life and attachment to 'industry and frugality'. Their perceived trustworthiness—together with connections built up through other business activities—drew many Quakers into banking, in which they became remarkably prominent in the eighteenth and early nineteenth centuries, before the reform of the English banking system in 1826. Banks were created with the wealth accumulated in Quaker industrial concerns: many early Quaker bankers came from a background in mining or the iron industry (Raistrick 1993, 56). The second Edward Pease, for example, had strong connections among Quaker bankers, and his family established two banks: Pease Partners in the eighteenth century and later, in 1858, J. and J. W. Pease (Pollard 2004; Kirby 1984, 3–4, 43–4). Pratt estimates that a quarter of the English 'country banks' in the late eighteenth century were Quaker-owned businesses, along with a number in London (Pratt 1985, 76–7). Families such as Lloyd, Fox, and Gurney built a strong Quaker banking network, with half of all Quaker banks linked by intermarriage in some way (Pratt 1985, 77, 89; Walvin 1997, 70–2). Although family banking was somewhat undermined by the growth of joint-stock banking in England after the liberalization of the system in the 1820s, many notable Quakers remained associated with banking into the twentieth century; one example was Gillett and Company, which merged into Barclays in 1919. Another bank taken over by Barclays was J. and J. W. Pease, which failed in 1902 (Kirby 1984, 101–16).

The Quaker reputation for trustworthiness was enhanced by Meetings' oversight of their members' financial affairs. The Religious Society of Friends was concerned that business failures might reflect badly on other Quakers, and Meetings were able and willing to disown members for bankruptcy. Disownment sent a message that the Religious Society of Friends disapproved of members over-extending their investments, failing to pay their debts, and lacking in care for their business activities (Walvin 1997, 55–7). Meetings would usually be willing to disown a bankrupt Quaker only if his downfall was manifestly his own fault, and where disownment did take place it was done with reluctance, and as sensitively as possible (Pratt 1985, 115). Nevertheless, when fraud or impropriety was discovered, the Society could be quite ruthless, as in the case of Jonathan Richardson, managing director of the Northumberland and Durham District Bank, which failed in 1857. Richardson was found to have concealed the true state of the bank's affairs from shareholders, and—despite protests from his local Meeting—was disowned by Newcastle Monthly Meeting in 1858. Many of his relatives resigned their membership of the Society (O'Donnell 2003).

BUSINESS AND QUAKER PHILANTHROPY

While Quakers were associated with business acumen and fairness, the Religious Society of Friends was also known, even in the seventeenth century, for dealing both efficiently and charitably with its own members who had fallen upon hard times. Such a fate was not unusual among Quakers or others in a society where, according to Gregory King, half the population relied on 'some help beyond what they could earn' (Clarke 1987, 10–11). A number of historians (Tolles 1948, 82–4; Walvin 1997, 50) have noted a 'paradox' or 'implicit conflict' at the heart of Quaker business activity: their industriousness contrasted with their 'distaste' for material prosperity. One way out of this paradox was philanthropic activity. The Religious Society of Friends had a 'Box Fund', used to help poor Quakers to find work, and by the end of the seventeenth century had acquired a reputation for helping others where possible. In an influential pamphlet published in 1695, John Bellers (1654–1725), treasurer of the 'Box Fund' and a member of Meeting for Sufferings, proposed that the Society establish a subscription-funded 'Colledge of Industry' in which the poor could be given useful employment and acquire education. Male inmates would work on the farm or in various trades, while women and girls would work as cooks, dairy maids, spinners, and so on. Bellers insisted that his college would not be a workhouse, emphasizing the provision of education for the poor that was an integral part of the proposal (Bellers 1695, 14). This prefigured the later involvement of many Friends in adult education, which is discussed in O'Donnell's 'Quakers and Education', chapter 27 within this volume. Bellers's college never materialized, although there was a Quaker workhouse in Clerkenwell established in 1702, which quickly evolved into an educational institution for poor children (Raistrick 1993, 86). However, Bellers's proposals are an important example of the links between business, philanthropy, and education in early Quakerism. For Gwyn, they epitomize the accommodation with English society that Friends had reached by the end of the seventeenth century, playing an economic role that was aligned with the needs of early capitalism (Gwyn 2006, 334–5). As R. H. Tawney remarked, '[t]he Society of Friends…met the prevalent doctrine that it was permissible to take such gain as the market offered, by insisting on the obligation of good conscience and forbearance in economic transactions, and on the duty to make the honourable maintenance of his brother in distress a common charge' (Tawney 1938, 270).

The latter duty was pursued assiduously in the social activities of many early Quaker industrialists. The Darbys, along with their partner (and son-in-law of Abraham Darby II) Richard Reynolds, were also known for their 'contributions to social well-being', which Raistrick sees as 'a normal expression of their Quaker faith and practice' (Raistrick 1993, 142). The Darbys built cottages and a meeting house for their workers, stopped the furnaces weekly so that employees did not have to work on Sundays, and refused to profit unnecessarily from the increased prices during the American wars of the late eighteenth century. Meanwhile, Reynolds allowed free public access to the local woodland, which he purchased along with the lordship of the manor; more significantly in the Quaker context, he also built two Sunday schools and a day school, and contributed funds for Quaker schools in other parts of the country. Reynolds spent up to £8,000 a year on charitable objects, much of it in Bristol, although his name was not widely associated with this expenditure (Raistrick 1993, 145). The Pease family's local political power in Darlington was often resented in the community (Kirby 1984, 58–72), and they are usually associated more with politics than philanthropy, but they nevertheless sponsored a number of local educational and charitable projects (Pollard 2004). Their involvement in matters of traditional Quaker concern, such as the Peace Society, reflects the ongoing importance of Quakerism in the lives of many such capitalist dynasties. Examples could be multiplied among early British Quaker industrialists: the Sturge and Gurney families, among others, gained a reputation for supporting workplace welfare and wider philanthropic projects.

Perhaps the best known of all Quaker employers are those who made and sold cocoa and chocolate in the nineteenth and twentieth centuries. The Cadburys of Birmingham, Frys of Bristol, and Rowntrees of York all gained prominence in this area, expressing what Gillian Wagner has called the 'chocolate conscience' in their industrial and philanthropic practices (Wagner 1987). Joseph Rowntree (1836–1925) established a small family business in York in 1869; this company grew from a modest 200 employees in 1883, to 900 in 1894, and 4,000 in 1906 (Freeman 2004, 2; see Vernon 1958). Under Joseph and his son Seebohm Rowntree (1871–1954), the company established various employee welfare initiatives, including canteens, welfare officers, continuation classes, and a works magazine. All these were part of a strategy designed, in Joseph's words, to furnish his factory 'with those amenities which might make it easier for men and women to "develop all that is best and most worthy in themselves"' (quoted in Vernon 1958, 102–03). These practices could be seen as a deliberately paternalistic strategy devised in order to ward off industrial militancy—Joseph Rowntree in particular was suspicious of trades unions—but they also reflected a broadly benevolent vision of workplace welfare that exercised a strong influence in twentieth-century Britain. Many of the Rowntree initiatives were also followed in the Cadbury factory, and although relations between the two leading Quaker chocolate firms were sometimes characterized by competitive tension (Wagner 1987, 103–23), there was also collaboration, fostered—as in earlier Quaker business networks—by intermarriage between the families (see for example Freeman 2004, 187). By the early twentieth century, the influence of companies such as Rowntree and Cadbury brought business issues to Yearly Meeting, where they had rarely been discussed before, and the first conference of Quaker employers was held in 1918 (Wagner 1987, 47).

Beyond the workplace, Joseph Rowntree and his contemporaries followed a coherent philanthropic strategy, using the mechanism of the charitable trust to deliver both charitable and political outcomes. In 1904 Rowntree placed a large proportion of his personal wealth at the disposal of three trusts (Freeman 2004). The Joseph Rowntree Social Service (now Reform) Trust was designed to follow explicitly political objectives, while the Joseph Rowntree Charitable Trust supported Quaker and other educational initiatives. The largest was the Joseph Rowntree Village Trust, which was established under the influence of the Bournville Village Trust, created by George Cadbury in the preceding year. The development of the model villages at Bournville, near the Cadbury factory, and New Earswick, near York, was overseen by these two trusts. Rowntree's new village was influenced by Ebenezer Howard and the Garden City movement, as well as by William Lever, whose Port Sunlight community had been built in 1888, although Rowntree wanted to avoid what he saw as the stultifying paternalism of Lever's model village (Wagner 1987, 68–72). The community at New Earswick was supposed to embody democratic decision-making, although in practice the Village Trust was able to veto the decisions of the residents (see Davies and Freeman 2004). These model communities reflected the wider conception of philanthropy that motivated Quakers of Rowntree and Cadbury's generation. In a much-quoted memorandum written on the establishment of his trusts in 1904, Joseph Rowntree—using terms borrowed from Cadbury—noted (quoted in Freeman 2004, 20):

> I feel that much of current philanthropic effort is directed to remedying the more superficial manifestations of weakness or evil, while little thought or effort is directed to search out their underlying causes... The Soup Kitchen in York never has difficulty in obtaining adequate financial aid, but an enquiry into the extent and causes of poverty would enlist little support.

Thus Rowntree's trusts, as well as building and running New Earswick, supported the social research carried out by Seebohm Rowntree in the first half of the twentieth century, as well as contributing to educational objectives, reflecting the long-standing Quaker involvement in this area. The trusts also owned a large proportion of the shares in Rowntree and Company, and were therefore in a position to exercise a continuing influence over the culture of the company into the second half of the twentieth century, until Nestlé took over Rowntree Mackintosh in 1988. Although, as Wagner points out, 'by the end of the Second World War Quaker influence in the business world had further declined' (Wagner 1987, 47), some of the biggest names in British industrial capitalism retained their Quaker associations.

Although many early British business histories tended to emphasize the role of 'great men' and their work—M. W. Kirby's study of the Pease family is, revealingly, entitled *Men of Business and Politics* (Kirby 1984)—Quaker historians have often noted the importance of women in business and in the maintenance of networks. Arthur Raistrick, for example, pointed out the work of wives and children in running the businesses of early male Friends who were imprisoned by the state, and later the role of marriage within the Religious Society of Friends in strengthening business networks (Raistrick 1993, 55–6, 80–1, 119–20 and *passim*). More recently, Sandra Stanley Holton's book *Quaker Women* details the interlinked public and private lives of a group of Quaker families, including the Brights, Priestmans, Bancrofts, and Clarks, from the late eighteenth century to the early twentieth (Holton 2007). Throughout the book, Holton documents examples of women's importance in Quaker economic life, even where they were not directly involved in the day-to-day running of businesses. For example, when Margaret

Wheeler married Arthur Tanner in the mid-1850s, she was enabled to exercise an influence over the running of the Tanner family's struggling paper mill in Cheddar, Somerset. Although she did not actively intervene in the management of the mill, she was able to insist on certain arrangements between members of the Tanner family, and thereby to ensure Arthur's position as an equal partner in the enterprise. She also enhanced his social standing in the neighbourhood (Holton 2007, 119–23). Other women took more active roles in business. Margaret Wood (1783–1859) was a spinster and sister-in-law of John Bright, and ran a confectionery shop in Rochdale before retiring to live off her capital in the mid-1820s. In her frugal habits, Wood epitomized the Quakerism of the early nineteenth century, but she also kept up a regular correspondence with Friends in Britain and America. Wood was at the centre of a successful business network, based on family connections and strengthened by intermarriage; this was typical of women's position in Quaker society in this period (Holton 2007, 46). It is tempting to relate women's important position in Quaker business networks to the relatively privileged place that they enjoyed in the hierarchy of the Religious Society of Friends compared with other denominations. However, much modern scholarship has emphasized the importance of women in business across the early capitalist economy (e.g Laurence et al 2009); it may be, therefore, that middle-class Quaker women were not untypical in this respect.

QUAKERS IN AMERICA

Wood's American connections emphasize the international dimensions of Quakerism, and Frederick B. Tolles and other historians have noted the emergence of a series of Anglo-American Quaker links during the eighteenth century (Tolles 1948, 29–32, 89–93). Given these links, it is not surprising that the early history of American Quakerism echoes many of the themes found in the British story. There were, of course, some significant differences: most notably under William Penn's 'Holy Experiment' starting in 1681, Quakers were permitted to take a full role in government and many did so, although in the later eighteenth century a new period of 'Quietism' reduced Friends' involvement at this level. Exclusion from political activity and the professions, therefore, cannot be used to explain Quaker business success in the United States. Tolles pointed out that Friends would exclude themselves from military careers, and there was some suspicion of the legal profession, although in Pennsylvania a number of Friends achieved prominence in this sphere (1948, 49–51). However, as in Britain, Quakers in Pennsylvania and elsewhere in the United States met with success in commerce and industry, and with it wealth: although comprising only a seventh of the population of Philadelphia in 1769, Quakers made up half of those paying more than £100 a year in tax (Tolles 1948, 49). Gwyn quotes a Quaker adage: 'Friends came to Philadelphia to do good—and they did very well'. For Gwyn, this adage encapsulates the paradox at the heart of Quaker economic success: while making money enabled them to 'work for social betterment' under spiritual guidance, the process of making money involved an accommodation with capitalism that potentially compromised Quaker values. Some even owned slaves, and many more profited, directly or indirectly, from the institution of slavery. Nevertheless, they retained a reputation as fair-dealing and reliable business people, and this enabled them to make their mark on the development of American capitalism (Gwyn 2006, 341–2).

One example of a successful American Quaker merchant was Isaac Hicks of New York, a cousin of Elias Hicks, who became a key figure in the separation of American Quakerism in the 1820s. Isaac Hicks, born in 1767, began as a wholesale grocer, diversified into dry goods and eventually developed a successful shipping and commission agent business. Retiring from business at the age of 38, Hicks offered practical assistance to his cousin Elias, often travelling with him around the country (Davidson 1964, 135–6, 139, 142ff). As for many English Friends, Hicks's Quakerism was a useful business asset: not only did he benefit from the 'public reputation' enjoyed by Friends in business, but he also transacted most of his business with fellow members of the Society (Davidson 1964, 20, 28–9). For Tolles, however, the 'fundamental explanation' of Quaker business success in the American colonies lay in their 'economic ethic', which they shared with their transatlantic coreligionists and which also explained many other aspects of Quaker business practice (Tolles 1948, 51–62). As in Britain, American Yearly Meetings—both Hicksite and Orthodox—criticized 'the evil of speculation' in stocks and shares throughout the nineteenth century, although Philip S. Benjamin suggests that bankrutpcy was stigmatized less within Hicksite Meetings (Benjamin 1976, 52, 57).

The potential conflicts between the necessity of industry and Quaker opposition to acquisitiveness prompted self-reflection among American Friends, and could result in three outcomes. First, many American Quakers, like Hicks, retired early from business, devoting the rest of their lives to religious and social service. Second, many devoted much of their wealth and time to philanthropic projects: one example was Justus Clayton Strawbridge (1838–1911), an Orthodox Friend from New Jersey, who cofounded the the department store Strawbridge and Clothier in Philadelphia in 1868. Strawbridge was a trustee of both Haverford and Bryn Mawr colleges and president of the City Parks Association (Lief 1968, 92–6). His business partner, the Philadelphia Hicksite Friend Isaac H. Clothier (1837–1921), was also known for 'his long service in philanthropic work and civic movements' (Lief 1968, 79). It is worth noting that business partnerships such as this could also perform a service to Quakerism itself: by drawing together prominent representatives of the Hicksite and Orthodox sects, such activity could help to heal the divisions within American Quakerism (Benjamin 1976, 55–6). A third dimension of the 'Quaker ethic' in America, as in Britain, was a sense of corporate responsibility that often resulted in pioneering approaches to workplace relations. Strawbridge's contemporary Jonathan Wright Plummer (1835–1918), a Hicksite Friend from Richmond, Indiana, who moved to Chicago, became a leading figure in and eventually the president of the wholesale drug firm Morrisson Plummer and Company, which towards the end of the nineteenth century introduced a pioneering profit-sharing scheme among its employees (Warren 2006, 30–31). This was just one element of Plummer's approach to business and philanthropy: he acquired a reputation for safe and honestly labelled drugs, and was active in the Quaker philanthropic community, establishing the Friends Union of Philanthropic Labor under the auspices of Illinois Yearly Meeting in 1882 (Warren 2006, 38–44).

Profit-sharing and Labour Relations

Plummer's innovative approaches to labour relations were further developed by twentieth-century Quaker business people. In Britain, the Swiss-born entrepreneur Ernest Bader (1890–1982) and his wife Dora Scott provide an example of Quaker influence on business practice in Britain in the second half of the twentieth century. Theirs is not an exclusively Quaker story, as Bader did not become a Friend until 1945 (Hoe 1978, 51, 72–3). In 1920 Bader and Scott established Scott Bader Ltd, a chemical company that became a leading innovator in polyester and similar products. In the early post-war years Bader initiated a short-lived 'Fellowship', which was influenced by Rowntree and Cadbury—Rowntrees had established a profit-sharing scheme in 1923 (Vernon 1958, 189–91)—and involved the representation of employees at various levels in Scott Bader Ltd, funded by dividends on the main shareholdings in the company (Hoe 1978, 79–89). The Scott Bader Fellowship has been described as 'a naïve experiment in management-staff relations outside unionization' (Corina 2004), and Bader's biographer Susanna Hoe has contrasted its democratic rhetoric with the autocratic reality of management at Scott Bader in this period (Hoe 1987, 55–6, 67–9, 97–8). Subsequently Bader established the Scott Bader Commonwealth, a more radical attempt at profit- and power-sharing, in which the Chemical Workers' Union was directly involved, and which ultimately amounted to an industrial cooperative owned by the workers: by 1963 Bader had sold all his shares in the company (Hoe 1978, 105–19). The Commonwealth succeeded where the Fellowship had failed, and influenced similar ventures elsewhere, which were given legislative sanction by the Common Ownership Act in 1976, although Bader never managed to persuade the Religious Society of Friends to adopt common ownership as a policy (Hoe 1978, 107–8, 161, 208–10).

As in the case of Scott Bader, Quaker businesses' commitment to profit-sharing did not necessarily result in a peaceful relationship with organized labour. On both sides of the Atlantic, Quaker attitudes to trades unionism have ranged from broad support through mistrust to outright hostility. Seebohm Rowntree, although less suspicious of organized labour than his father Joseph, was concerned about militant trades union activity in the 1920s, and the Joseph Rowntree Charitable Trust supported initiatives that promoted 'industrial peace'. Nevertheless, industrial militancy *could* be linked with Quaker values, and some Friends gave practical support to the miners following the general strike of 1926 (Freeman 2004, 103–5). In the US, the former miner, coal trader, and labour and socialist activist Hank Mayer, although brought up a Baptist, attended Quaker Meetings. However, he was concerned that his 'affluent' Quaker congregation had little instinctive sympathy for progressive causes; in general, American Friends endorsed arbitration to prevent strikes (Mayer 1989, 152–3; Warren 2006, 41). On both sides of the Atlantic, members of the Religious Society of Friends have often had a difficult relationship with organized labour, and even socialist Quakers have prioritized the avoidance of workplace conflict and expressed unease about restrictive practices, notably the 'closed shop', although some Friends supported the latter (FSRC 1977, 1–2, 12). At a conference on 'Trade Unions and the New Social Order', held at Woodbrooke in 1977, the Industry and Work Committee of the Friends Social Responsibility Council emphasized the need to 'control and humanise' the power held by trades unions, especially by ensuring that individual liberty of conscience was maintained in workplaces (FSRC 1977, 12–13). In practice, this has often resulted in Quaker support for industrial arbitration, profit-sharing, and workers' councils, and an emphasis on mutual responsibility in the workplace. The Quakers and Business Group, noting the historic role of Quaker employers in pioneering aspects of workplace relations that were considered normal in the early twenty-first century, advised Quaker employers to 'cultivate a mutual trust' between themselves and trades unions, and to have clear procedures for resolving workplace disputes (Quakers and Business Group 2000, 24–33).

Quakers in Business Today: Challenges for a World Religion

During the twentieth century, Pink Dandelion has noted that 'in general Quakers have moved away from such direct involvement in industrial capitalism' (Dandelion 2007, 79). This has been true on both sides of the Atlantic: it is notable that Thomas D. Hamm's survey of modern American Quakerism contains very little on Friends' business activities (Hamm 2003). In Britain, Quakerism is a middle-class religion, in which professionals are over-represented. Early twenty-first-century surveys by David Rubinstein and Paul F. Burton of York and Scotland respectively offer some insight into the occupational profile of modern British Quakers. In York 39.5 per cent and in Scotland 31.1 per cent of Friends were in the educational professions, with other significant groupings in the medical and community professions. 'Business and related' occupations accounted for little more than a tenth in either York or Scotland (Rubinstein 2001, 201–4; Burton 2007, 243–8). Teaching, academia, and social work have become popularly associated with Quakerism. As the editor of a directory of Quaker business in Britain remarked in 1992 (Quaker Social Responsibility and Education 1992, editorial):

> A caricature of a Friend in middle years is a person employed in the caring professions. In comparison with the image we have of Quaker industry from earlier centuries, the image of Friends in business today seems to sit less easily within the Society...to some Friends the world of business is a little tainted.

Although this directory did list many Quaker businesses, most were sole traders or small proprietors, and the sectors traditionally associated with Quakerism—heavy industry and banking—were not represented. More typical of late twentieth-century Quaker businesses were the four printers and publishers, six typesetters, and eight consultants listed in the directory, which also contained the details of two counsellors/psychothera- pists, three solicitors, a builder, an insurance broker, and even a detective agency! Of course, Quaker economic and professional activity has evolved with the wider context, as manufacturing industry declined and the service sector—including education and public service—expanded in the second half of the twentieth century.

There remains, however, a strong sense of a distinctively Quaker approach to busi- ness and commerce, one which is often out of step with modern shareholder capital- ism. Early Quaker entrepreneurs were suspicious of the joint-stock company, preferring to keep management and ownership within their families and communities wherever possible (Tolles 1948, 91–2; Pratt 1985, 75–6). This style of management retains consid- erable cultural and political purchase in modern Britain, where the Nestlé takeover of Rowntree Mackintosh in 1988 and the Kraft acquisition of Cadbury Schweppes in 2010 both provoked a public outcry, inflected with national sentiment in the face of an emerg- ing global order that appeared to threaten the unprotected British worker and capitalist. The Nestlé takeover in 1988 was an important moment in the exposure of British manu- facturing to the realities of globalization, and was intensified by the ethical dimension: Nestlé had been criticized since the mid-1970s for its role in marketing formula milk to mothers in the Global South. As at Cadbury, a large proportion of the Rowntree shares were owned by the family charitable trusts, ensuring the centrality of 'Quaker values' to the company; as one member of the Cadbury family has commented, British Quaker chocolate firms were run in 'a strong collaborative style of management that had evolved over more than a century' (Cadbury 2010, 270–71, 277–9). In 1988 and 2010, reactions in the popular press emphasized the association between Rowntree and Cadbury and the Religious Society of Friends, suggesting that Quakerism remains associated with a particular form of benign capitalism that is under threat in the global age. Along with many others, contemporary Quakers face the challenge of doing business ethically in the global economy.

This challenge is highlighted by the spread of Quakerism in the Global South, a key feature of the modern period. By 2005, of 367,808 Friends affiliated to the Friends World Committee for Consultation (FWCC), 157,153 were in Africa with several thousand more in Central and South America. There were other significant groups in Cambodia, Indonesia, and the Philippines (Dandelion 2007, 177–9). International and intercontinental links between Friends have raised awareness of issues of economic development and global inequalities that often have an intimate relationship with Quaker efforts in the promotion of peace. The Quaker United Nations Office (QUNO), with a presence in Geneva and New York, has engaged with a range of international issues: it participates in the traditional Quaker activities of peacebuilding and provid- ing relief for displaced persons, but also, through its Global Economic Issues (GEI) programme, promotes a Quaker perspective on development economics. In the past,

GEI has considered intellectual property in agriculture—in the context of support-ing food sustainability—and the movement of labour, while current priorities include biodiversity and agricultural trade networks ([www.quno.org]). In 2009 the FWCC launched its Consultation on Global Change, headed by a list of queries in the tradi-tional Quaker format, including, most fundamentally, 'How has global change affected our communities and ourselves?' (*Friends World News*, no. 170, 2009, 7; [www.fwcc globalchange.org]).

The contemporary politics of environmentalism underpin many of these Quaker efforts in the Global South. Friends claim a long heritage of concern in this area, reflect-ing their historical attachment to simplicity in personal behaviour and the avoidance of conspicuous consumption. Gwyn quotes the early Friend Thomas Taylor, who imag-ined God inveighing in environmental terms against mid-seventeenth-century English greed: 'And the Multitudes of People who are as Grasshoppers in thy Bowels devour-ing every green thing and spending my Creatures upon their Lusts, not regarding my Glory at all, shall be as heaps of fuel for the fire of my Jealousy' (Gwyn 2006, 247). A vision of a somewhat less jealous God lies behind modern initiatives such as the Friends Committee on Unity with Nature in the US and Quaker Green Concern in Britain. It is clear that 'environmental witness' is considered by many Friends to be a key aspect of their Quakerism. The QUNO and other international organizations have raised aware-ness of climate change among Friends, and many of the projects promoted by Quaker groups in the Global South have environmental sustainability at their heart: one exam-ple is Right Sharing of World Resources ([www.rswr.org]), founded in 1967, which supports projects in Kenya, Sierra Leone, and southern India. In the United States the Northwest Yearly Meeting Book of Discipline contains the query (quoted in Valentine 2003, 90): 'As a Christian steward, do you treat the earth with respect and with a sense of God's splendour in creation, guarding it against abuse by greed, misapplied technology, or your own carelessness?'

There are many examples of specific Quaker or Quaker-inspired projects. One is the Friends Rural Service Centre at Hlekweni in Zimbabwe, run under the auspices of Bulawayo Monthly Meeting. This contains an experimental farm and a centre of alter-native technology. Supported by charitable donations from some British Meetings, Hlekweni provides entrepreneurship training with an emphasis on sustainable tech-niques, as well as basic food relief to impoverished Zimbabweans (CSAYM 1995, 8; [www.hlekweni.org]). The FWCC's African section supports a Rwandan scheme called Women in Dialogue, where groups of women—including genocide widows and the wives of genocide suspects—are supported with loans to run their own small businesses (*Friends World News*, no. 170, 2009, 13). Here the links between reconciliation and busi-ness development are particularly clear, demonstrating the important role that entre-preneurship often plays in Friends' conceptions of relief and development work. Other important efforts have been made in Bolivia, where several projects have been funded by Quaker Bolivia Link (QBL), with contributions to educational and social welfare ini-tiatives by American and British Friends (Garver 2001a, 2001b). Established in 1995, QBL has supported projects including education and 'community empowerment', and economic development schemes based on proposals made by indigenous Bolivians. In Bolivia—where there are somewhere between 30,000 and 40,000 Friends—an independent culture of Quaker service has emerged with the early support of QBL: a group of professional Quakers in La Paz established the *Comité de Servicio Cuáquero en Bolivia*, which is similar to the British Quaker Peace and Social Witness or the American Friends Service Committee. Like Quakers elsewhere, Bolivian Friends have focused heavily on educational projects in their philanthropic work: the Bolivian Quaker Education Fund is an example. In 2011, one of its events included a workshop on Quaker values in small business ([www.bqef.org]).

It is clear, then, that a distinctive Quaker conception of business and philanthropy continues to exist, albeit in the very changed circumstances of the early twenty-first-century global economy. While some of the emphases have shifted, Quaker business practices remain underpinned by the ethos that early Friends brought to the development of capitalism. Many Friends in the developed world have supported fair trade organizations, in what one activist has described as 'an act of solidarity with the [Global] South' (Brewer 1993, 4). In Britain, the importance of Quaker corporate economic witness is confirmed by the existence of groups such as the Quaker Network for Economic Change and the Quakers and Business Group. The latter has set out detailed guidance for the ethical pursuit of business, emphasizing traditional Quaker concerns regarding fair prices, honest advertising, and compliance with the law, as well as relationships between employers and employed (Quakers and Business Group 2000). Recognizing the belief of some Quakers that 'business itself is unethical', encouraged by the excesses of modern global capitalism, the Group argues that it is possible for Friends to engage in beneficial business activities without compromising their testimonies on peace, social justice, and the environment (Quakers and Business Group 2000, 3–4). Yet, for many, the 'paradox' at the heart of Quaker business remains. The tensions between economic success and the distaste for material prosperity that characterized Quaker entrepreneurship during the Industrial Revolution are echoed in responses to multinational commodity capitalism in the early twenty-first century. Concluding his study of the economic role of early Quakers, Gwyn considers the position of contemporary Friends in the developed world (Gwyn 2006, 341):

> Modern Friends . . . feel a satisfaction with our economic accomplishments and social respectability. Yet we also feel a twinge of conscience that our success somehow mocks our intentions. Clearly, this is not the despair of an oppressed people. It is more the nagging sense of some failed calling.

This blend of satisfaction and conscience continues to animate the spirit of Quaker service, and to enhance the social contribution of Quakers across the world. Although conditions have changed immeasurably since the emergence of Quakerism in the seventeenth century, Quaker approaches to business and service continue to mark out the Religious Society of Friends as a distinctive religious and social force in the modern world.

Suggested Further Reading

Cadbury, D. (2010) *The chocolate wars: From Cadbury to Kraft—200 years of sweet success and bitter rivalry*. London: Harper Press.

Davies, J. S. and Freeman, M. (2004) 'A case of political philanthropy: The Rowntree Family and the Campaign for Democratic Reform', *Quaker Studies*, vol. 9, pp. 95–113.

Gwyn, D. (2006 [1995]) *The covenant crucified: Quakers and the rise of capitalism*. London: Quaker Books.

Holton, S. S. (2007) *Quaker women: Personal life, memory and radicalism in the lives of Women Friends 1780–1930*. London: Routledge.

Pratt, D. H. (1985) *English Quakers and the first Industrial Revolution: A study of the Quaker community in four industrial counties, Lancashire, York, Warwick and Gloucester 1750–1830*. New York, London: Garland.

Walvin, J. (1997) *The Quakers: Money and morals*. London: John Murray.

CHAPTER 29

QUAKERS AND THE FAMILY

EDWINA NEWMAN

INTRODUCTION: ISSUES OF DEFINITION AND SCHOLARLY APPROACHES TO THE SOURCES

IN the seminal history of the formation of the English middle class, Quakers are represented as acting as 'a kind of religious "family"' providing emotional and material support to their members (Davidoff and Hall 2002, 100), while in 2007, in considering the prospects for the continuation of distinctive commonalities among Quakers worldwide, Pink Dandelion writes, in terms of 'The Quaker Family'. This use of the word family is by no means unusual, indicating a group bound together by some common tie of assent, as opposed to the more usual definition of a group of people interrelated by descent (or some other form of cohabitation within a household). What is understood as 'family' therefore is by no means straightforward, and when considering Quakers and the family, religious affiliation might, historically, be seen as equally important with heredity and domestic duty. Thus while historians of the family identify a tendency in Western society towards the discrete, private family with that 'special sense of solidarity that separates the domestic unit from the surrounding community' (Shorter 1976, 205), the historian of the Quaker family needs to take into account the additional layer of the Quaker community between the individual family and wider society.

In the historiography of the late seventeenth to mid-nineteenth centuries, the identification of a distinctive Quaker family is possible because of the practice of endogamy, Quakers being identified as a clan, all coming from 'the same general genetic pool' (Vann and Eversley 1992, 176). The impression of Quakers as a group set apart is compounded by the 'hedge', which they set up around themselves. Contemporary Quaker commentators see them as establishing a 'familied monasticism' (Abbot et al 2003, 99), with each household mirroring the Benedictines in forming a little 'colony of heaven' (Boulding 1989, 185). However, neither the isolation nor the homogeneity should be exaggerated. Households were inextricably tied up with the trades and industries that sustained them, and there was an inevitable effect on family life. Even eighteenth-century Irish Quakers who were 'as sharply distinguished from the rest of Irish society as they could have been without living in a separate territory with a self-sufficient economy', had to 'mingle' at times (Vann and Eversley 1992, 51). In colonial America, Quakers remained an integral part of public life until the mid-eighteenth century, so that Barry Levy is able to argue that Pennsylvanian Quakers' vision of a 'morally self-sufficient household' had a defining influence on the formation of a national republican identity (Levy 1988, 18, 22), in marked contrast with Irish and English Quakers who, in spite of sharing the same vision, were seen as countercultural.

With the ending of the practice of endogamy in the mid-nineteenth century, Quakers became increasingly 'diluted' within society, and when the comparatively unified trans-atlantic culture itself became divided, then we must reverse Levy's perspective on a distinctive Quaker domestic legacy and look instead at the way Quakerism was influenced by a dominant Evangelical discourse of 'family values', a complex ideological concept which, over time, has been subject to developing interpretations.

The study of Quaker families has particular pitfalls for the family historian seeking to identify patterns of behaviour, and requires careful attention to the specific context of the religious underpinning of domesticity. Nevertheless, the comparative richness of the source material makes for rewarding investigation. Quakers kept records of births, marriages, and deaths, equivalent to parish registers in England, but also somewhat more usefully, recording births soon after the event (compared with the practice of recording Anglican baptisms). As early as 1668 Fox had encouraged Friends to 'buy convenient books for registering the births and marriages and burials', although in fact registers seem to have been kept already by at least some meetings, and this was likely to have been necessary given disputes over inheritance and the need to relieve those in distress (Vann and Eversley 1992, 15). Meticulously kept 'registers' allow historical demographers to use family reconstitution methods to produce data that can be compared against a wider sample of the population, particularly in terms of fertility and family limitation strategy (Vann and Eversley 1992 and Wells 1971). This approach, however, has limitations in terms of understanding individual familial behaviour.

What Michael Anderson describes as the 'sentiments approach' makes use of a wider range of sources, such as the autobiographical accounts and material evidence which a comparatively affluent and literate minority such as Quakers produced in quantity. Leonore Davidoff and Catherine Hall, writing Family Fortunes in 1987 from a feminist perspective, made use of a wide range of family papers and life writings in order to explore the formation of individual identities within middle-class households between 1780 and 1850. As they note in the introduction to the revised edition in 2002, since then post-Modern influence has shifted their 'big picture' approach to the study of local communities at a micro level (Davidoff and Hall 2002, xvi). Sandra Holton's study of the Priestman–Bright–Clark circle is the outstanding example of this kind of study. Holton's methods and sources provide an insight into the nature of Quaker networked families, the strength and coherence of which depended in large part on the creation of 'family memory'. Leading Quaker families effectively created a family archive that served to 'preserve extensive bonds of kinship, despite physical separation and the passage of time'. Such archives were an expression of shared values as well as a 'chronicle of family life and its connections with larger economic, social and political processes' (Holton 2007, 2).

In practice, historians have tended to use a combination of approaches and as wide a range of sources as possible. Just as 'total history' has, paradoxically, to be local history in order to be manageable, so, even given the comparative coherence of the community, it is difficult to reconstruct an overview of Quakers and the family that satisfactorily spans continents as well as centuries.

EARLY QUAKERS AND 'GOSPEL FAMILY-ORDER'

If, as Levy argues, Quakerism became noted for its domesticity, it certainly did not start out as such. In the days when Quakers saw themselves in the vanguard of the end times, family life was an irrelevance or impediment. James Nayler (1618–60) simply walked away from his home on an immediate religious impulse, without even taking leave of his wife and children. The founder of the first Irish Quaker meetings, William Edmundson (1627–1712) and his wife (who died in 1691 the victim of religious persecution), had seven children, two of whom they named Hindrance and Tryal. To some early Quakers, celibacy was regarded as a virtue, and the fact that George Fox (1624–91) and Margaret Fell (1614–1702) married in 1669 when Fell was past child-bearing age has been offered as evidence that Quakers valued love between men and women that was not based on reproductive imperatives (Vann and Eversley 1992, 162).

It was when he was in Barbados and confronted by the reality of slave-holding, that George Fox articulated a Quaker 'family policy', recorded at a Mens' Meeting of plantation owners and slave holders; this was subsequently published as *Gospel Family-Order* (1676). This 'order' was both conservative in stressing a patriarchal model of family life—(the patriarchy is perhaps exaggerated because Fox was concerned primarily with making male slave owners aware of their responsibilities)—but also radical in effectively defining humanity as one family (Angell 2011a, 17–19). The husband's duty was not just to wife and children, but to servants and apprentices, and to slaves too. 'Preach Christ Jesus to them in your Families, that so each may come to know Christ and their way to salvation' (Fox 1676, 15).

This might be seen as the formal genesis of the move to universalize and spiritualize the Quaker family (Angell 2011a, 18). All the distinctive elements of Quaker marriage were here for everyone within the household: '[L]et them take one another before witnesses, in the presence of God, and the Masters of the Families, in the name of Jesus, the restorer of all things to the beginning [...] and so to record it in a book, which was and is the practice of [...] such as denyed debauchery, whoredom, fornication and uncleanness' (Fox 1671, 17–18).

The pressures of the 1660s and 1670s required further formalization in the ordering of the family and of membership. The need to relieve poverty in the face of persecution that

often involved periods of imprisonment and distraint of goods meant that it was important to know who was and was not the responsibility of individual Meetings. Birthright
membership, whereby the children of members were automatically accepted into the
Society was recognized by London Yearly Meeting in 1737, and by Yearly Meetings in
America between 1762 and 1790. The development of the Quaker discipline circumscribing behaviour might be seen as a direct response to obviate a nominalism which, it
was feared, might otherwise result from conferring membership on those who had not
formally espoused the beliefs.

To leave or be disowned by the Society and lose this membership must have been
very isolating to those who had been brought up as Quakers, even though they might
still retain ties with their birth families and carry on attending Meetings for Worship.
Disownment of only one parent meant that membership was denied to any new infant
even though the birth was still recorded. A strong sense of belonging would have been
replaced by an unsettling limbo state; Mary Wright Sewell who left Quakers in the
mid-nineteenth century testified to the ensuing sense of loneliness (Davidoff and Hall
2002, 87).

NUPTUALITY, FERTILITY, AND CHILD-CARE IN THE AGE OF ENDOGAMY

In England, Quaker marriage was not formally legalized until the Marriage Act of
1836, although the right to perform weddings had effectively been recognized since
Hardwicke's Marriage Act of 1753 when Quakers and Jews were specifically exempted
from the legal requirement that marriages be celebrated by an Anglican clergyman.

A Quaker marriage followed the comparatively simple form laid down by Fox in
Gospel Family-Order, where two people married each other in the presence of witnesses,
before God. However the whole process of embarking on married life involved a lot
of effort. 'If you incline to marry, then marry your inclination', William Penn advised
his children, 'but be not hasty, but serious; lay it before the Lord, proceed in his fear,
and be you well-advised' (1726b, 54–5). The responsibility for ensuring the suitability
and legality of the match belonged to the Meeting. Care was taken that the couple was
well-matched, not close relatives, and that the man could support the family in the manner to which he and his wife were both accustomed. Among wealthier Quakers 'marriages were frequently prudently dynastic and contracted in search of business capital
and connections' (Vann and Eversley 1992, 55). However, contrary both to popular perceptions, and indeed common practice among the commercial classes in the eighteenth
and nineteenth centuries, Quaker discipline forbade marriage between first cousins,
and although it did happen, it was rare (Anderson 1995, 36–7 and Vann and Eversley
1992, 122). Equal care was taken with servants and apprentices in Quaker households,
and a manservant was expected to have set himself up in some trade or occupation

before marrying. There is evidence, too, that account was taken of individual feelings, and 'observers noted the unusual sociability of Quaker spouses with one another', suggesting 'affectionate, if not romantic, marriage' (Vann and Eversley 1992, 243–2). Both spouses, moreover, were expected to show high levels of tolerance within the family, being exhorted to avoid misunderstanding, to allow for weaknesses and differences of disposition, and to overlook failings (Penn 1726b, 55–6).

Many members were lost to the Society for 'marrying out', and particularly after 1760 when the discipline became more vigorously enforced. Perhaps unsurprisingly, given the strictures and lack of suitable partners, the age of first marriage of men and women began to rise in England from the mid-eighteenth century; in England there was a sharp decline in women marrying under the age of twenty and an increase in those marrying over the age of thirty. This differed from the wider national tendency and from the Irish Quaker experience where it was more likely for Quaker girls to marry as teenagers and where marriage after the age of thirty was relatively uncommon. By the first half of the nineteenth century, it is calculated that around twenty per cent of English Quaker women never married. Among English and Irish Quakers, there was a significant number of marriages where the woman was older than her husband, in marked contrast to American Quakers (Vann and Eversley 1992, 90–108, 127).

The nature of Quaker birth registers means that historical demographers have been able to do valuable comparative work on fertility in the eighteenth and nineteenth centuries, and to explore areas of family life on which the more autobiographical sources are silent. The statistical data show that Quakers in the British Isles experienced a rise in fertility from the mid-eighteenth century, with a marked growth between 1775 and 1825. (This trend would hardly have been noticeable since the overall numbers of Quakers declined as a result of disownment and emigration.) Thereafter there is some evidence of family limitation achieved largely by family spacing, and with a notable gap between marriage and the birth of the first child. Richard Vann and David Eversley claim that this was without precedent in Europe at this time; they argue that 'periodic abstinence from intercourse could demonstrate a freedom from fleshly concerns while at the same time helping to see that all children born could be adequately loved and provided for'(1992, 162).

American Quakers in the same period tended to have larger families overall. Robert Wells, however, in his study of Quaker families in New York, New Jersey, and Pennsylvania identifies a similar but earlier decline in fertility, evident by the end of the eighteenth century. Given that fertility rates of Quakers in the late eighteenth and early nineteenth centuries were lower than in the American population in general, it would seem that again deliberate family limitation was being practised (1971, 73). This can be linked to Jerry Frost's identification of child-centred American Quaker families and the desire to treat each child as an individual (1973, 70).

Whether the limitation was achieved through abstinence or some other method is hard to determine. Were Quaker women particularly likely to have breastfed their infants as a means of reducing fertility? William Edmundson, Thomas Chalkley, and Sophia Hume all defended the benefits of maternal breastfeeding, against the increasingly fashionable practice of employing wet nurses (Frost 1973, 71–2). On the other hand, Vann and Eversley show that the death of the immediately previous child had little effect on the timing of the next conception, suggesting that abstinence was the more likely strategy of limitation, regardless of views on maternal breastfeeding (Vann and Eversley 1992, 169–74).

Family limitation in both Britain and America may certainly have been part of the same pattern of Quaker behaviour, but since the pattern established itself at different times, the specific national context must have been influential too, and so should warn us against assuming too much in the way of Quaker isolation.

By the eighteenth century, children had become of great importance to the Society simply in terms of ensuring the continuity, and in order 'to adopt, preserve, and pass the faith on to their descendants' (Frost 1973, 73). If this was to be achieved, education and moral training of the young was also of critical importance. At a time when there was a general Christian feeling that children were 'creatures [...] who needed discipline to ensure the innate evil was suppressed' (Anderson 1995, 44), Quakers, by contrast, did not accept that their children were tainted by original sin, and their upbringing was accordingly distinctive, marked, too, by the ways in which their future within the Society was in large part already planned.

This is perhaps best illustrated by *A Map of the Various Paths of Life* (1794), a novel example of the kind of guidance that might be given to Quaker children (specifically boys). It shows a variety of routes away from 'Parental Care Hall', across an imagined landscape that has echoes of *Pilgrim's Progress*. As well as some seriously crooked byways, there is more than one reasonably direct path to 'Happy Old Age Hall', but the accompanying commentary by 'Parens' directs the children through 'Love Learning Garden' over 'Manly Hill' to 'Many-Friends City' where they might become 'tradesmen, much esteemed for their piety and sobriety'. The snares do not end there, however, and further direction is given through the 'Steady Plains' and 'Serenity Province', avoiding 'Temptation Gate' which in turn leads to such places as 'Self's Corner' where they might deny those who 'once remembered them in Many-friends City'. However, as the map shows, having once been diverted onto one of the 'strange paths', there are always ways back, no matter how tortuous. Even on the very shore of the 'Bottomless Pit' there is a way back to the 'Peaceful Ocean' through 'deep repentance valley'.

Given all the strictures of Quaker discipline, including the care and foresight that went into Quaker marriage, family life would have been plain but largely comfortable. The practice of living close to places of trade or manufactory, in less than salubrious environments took its toll on health; infant and child mortality remained a serious concern in London until after 1775, even though Quakers did not object to medical advances such as inoculation against smallpox (Vann and Eversley 1992, 220–2).

In the nineteenth century, there was something of a retreat to the suburbs. For example, the success of Richard Tapper Cadbury's drapery business in Bull Street in Birmingham meant that in 1812 he was able to rent a second house in Edgbaston. His son John set up his coffee and tea merchant's shop in Bull Street in 1824 and lived above the shop with his wife, but on the birth of their first child he moved to Edgbaston, close to his parents where, as one of his daughters wrote, 'home was the centre of attraction to us all' (Davidoff and Hall 2002, 57). And although heads of the household continued to take an active role in the business, there was a notable interest taken by all members of the family in domestic life (there were, after all, few other outlets for entertainment open to Quakers). Members of the networked family, male as well as female, could be intimately caught up in the *minutiae* of everyday home life; for example, when the young Helen Bright's relationship with her new stepmother was troubled, her aunt's concern was communicated to other family members, and her husband was sufficiently involved to suggest that the child's fondness for rice pudding could usefully be indulged to ease the tensions (Holton 2007, 99).

The strength of the family networks ensured that households would continue to run smoothly in the event of crisis or when mothers needed to fulfil a public duty. Elizabeth Fry may have experienced criticism for the neglect of her children, but it is misleading to generalize too much from her experience when other evidence does not suggest Quakers generally disapproved of women's role as ministers (Davidoff and Hall 2002, 139). Women's spiritual narratives attest to the agonizing internal conflicts experienced by those torn between their powerful concerns and the care of their children; Elizabeth Stirredge (1634–1706) is a good example of this, although, in the seventeenth and eighteenth centuries, she was by no means an isolated case of a mother leaving children at home in order to travel in the mininstry (Boulding 1989, 134). But the call to fulfil a religious duty was generally accepted and in this, as in the not-uncommon event of maternal mortality, other family member stepped into the breach of domestic and child-care duties (as shown in the examples of Abraham and Abiah Darby and John and Elizabeth Bright).

The Worldwide Quaker Family in the Age of Evangelicalism

When endogamy was finally abandoned in Britain in 1860, it was driven by concerns about declining membership, whereas in 'Revival' Quakerism, endogamy was simply abandoned as an irrelevance. The sense of Quakers as a 'gathered remnant' supporting each other in their own domestic monasticism was untenable in the kind of context where those wishing to join outnumbered those who 'knew the ropes' and were able to spend time on duties of oversight. Such was markedly the case in the Midwest of the United States and in the destinations of Quaker missionaries where, from the last decades of the nineteenth century onwards, Quakerism became part of a wider Evangelical movement with its own 'family values' (Dandelion 2007, 107, 110–11).

'Family values' in this context are by no means easy to define, and have undergone shifts in emphasis over time. The term is usually connected with a nuclear or close family unit, which is identified as the repository of society's moral standards. As the Evangelical movement in Britain and America became increasingly ascendant in the nineteenth century, 'family values' were strongly patriarchal but in the context of a reinterpretation of 'manliness', encompassing piety and domesticity as well as attention to business (Davidoff and Hall 2002, 113). The father took the role of the morally upright head of the family, to whom the rest of the household owed obedience, and the mother was expected to remain firmly in the domestic sphere, idealized as the 'angel in the house'. A telling mark of an Evangelical family was for the patriarch regularly to lead the household (including servants) in prayer and Bible reading. Parents were expected to be models for their children's behaviour.

From a Quaker perspective in the nineteenth century, espousing such Evangelical 'family values' linked the Society to a wider ecumenical movement, and thus marks a break from the essentially sectarian isolation that Quaker families had heretofore sought. The extent to which Quakerism was absorbed into a wider Evangelical culture in the nineteenth century is hard to gauge, especially in regions where communities were well established. Growing up in New England in the 1860s, in a household where his mother played the dominant role in family worship, Rufus Jones (1863–1948) was very conscious of the distinctiveness of his Quaker family, and the 'dignity' accorded to his 'little life' by feeling that he 'belonged to God's own people' (1903, 26–9). A 'turning point' in Jones's life occurred when, on upsetting his parents severely by his behaviour, his mother took him into a room to kneel and pray with him, making him see 'just what I was and no less clearly what I ought to be'. The impact of the incident may, however, have been particularly strong because he had clearly been expecting, 'the severe punishment which was administered with extreme infrequency in our home' (1903, 72).

The espousal of a more conventional domestic ideal among Quakers, albeit patchy, did have a notable effect; since it was Evangelical Quakers who participated in the missionary movements of the late nineteenth and early twentieth centuries, it is their 'family values' which were disseminated in worldwide Quakerism. In Africa, in common with Western missionary activity in general, Quakers failed to deal perceptively with the specific cultural context and could not understand the very different ideas of household and family that pertained, thereby producing some strange anomalies. Faced with polygamy among the Abaluyia, the Quaker missionary Edna Chilson insisted that a man should have only one wife and therefore put away his secondary wives, thereby not only effectively justifying divorce but also doing great harm to the second and third wives whose identities were defined in their own society in terms of their marriage and childbirth, and who were effectively made into single mothers and outcasts. Less punitive (although still markedly patriarchal) values were evident by the 1930s when men with second and third wives could be afforded half-membership, while in 1950 the East Africa Yearly Meeting ruled that, while only a first wife could be a full Quaker, second and third wives could be admitted to worship (Mombo 1998, 135–9).

While in the nineteenth century a shift to 'respectable' domesticity was not the cause of serious division within Quakerism, division has been more marked in the twentieth century. As a definition of 'family values' has increasingly become associated with advocacy of two-parent families and heterosexuality, and the censure of divorce and abortion, so differences between Evangelical, Holiness, Conservative, and Liberal Quakers have been brought into focus. In Meetings affiliated to Evangelical Friends International, for example, where marriage resembles any other Protestant wedding ceremony, the pastors see no biblical justification for divorce and refuse to marry divorced people, while at the other end of a wide spectrum, divorce is celebrated in some American Liberal Meetings as the welcome break-down of patriarchy (Hamm 2003, 197).

In a *Report from the Middle*, Douglas Gwyn suggests that, rather than conforming to—or wholly rejecting—societal norms of marriage and parenthood, Quakers should be aware of their spiritual roots and the belief that 'Christ's work' will be 'through whomever he wills' (Gwyn 2005, 33). The Quaker tradition of non-conformity is seen as allowing for a creative reassessment of what constitutes the family (Boulding 1989, 6). These views certainly acknowledge shifting (Western) social *mores*, but at the same time argue not from a secularized perspective but from long-held Quaker religious aspirations. A developing view of 'gospel family-order' coupled with a wariness of any 'preset moral code' should not, however, be confused with the idea that some Quaker Meetings hold that 'anything goes'; within all Yearly Meetings, licentious behaviour is no more sanctioned in the twenty-first century than it was by Fox in 1671 (Dandelion 2007, 230).

In other respects, practical considerations have set the agenda for Quaker responses to family issues. In the mid-twentieth century, Friends General Conference's Committee on Religious Education thought in terms of 'the Quaker family as a *unit*, not with either of its components—children or parents—as a separate entity' but as 'a family unit functioning "for the glory of God" [...] bound together by ties of more than blood and law' (Clement 1950, 3–4). However, while families were once the fundamental unit of Quakerism, it is notable that in twenty-first-century America (and Britain), marriages where both partners are Quakers are 'exceptional' (Hamm 2003, 194). In addition, of course, patterns of work as well as patterns of relationship have affected 'familial groupings', which have taken on different dimensions and 'recombined', so that individual meetings might include the families of same-sex couples and of single parents (Boulding 1989, 3–7). In addition, in Philadelphia Yearly Meeting, a 'Quaker Parenting Initiative' project recognized a need to be helpful to those unfamiliar with historical Quakerism as much as to those who were new parents (Heath 2009).

Overall, there has been a shift to the idea of 'parenting', and a focus on the needs of family members as individuals. Quakers in Britain and the US have corporately addressed 'parenting skills' as a means of coping with the competing needs and confrontations that are seen as inevitably and increasingly a part of family life. It has been argued that advice on 'parenting' is directed not so much to the spiritually influenced family unit as to the anxieties of adults who have the care of children and young people (Redfern and Collins 1994, 9, 23). Resolution of generational tensions is sought in the practice of Quaker testimonies within family life; the exploration and practice of testimonies on peace and simplicity, for example, are seen as a way of helping family members to care for each other as well as providing a 'metaphor for claiming responsibility for the state of the planet' (Boulding 1989, 7; Heath 2009). There has been a shift from the explicit belief that 'the service of God is the family's reason for being' (Clement 1950, 4), to a more implicit expression of historical Quaker mission.

In spite of the pressures, Hamm argues that 'virtually all Friends' still consider the family 'a fundamental institution' (2003, 194–5). The nurture of children within family continues to be seen in the early twenty-first century as a defining characteristic of the Society, and although the family unit itself might be more loosely understood and the spiritual function of it less clearly articulated, nevertheless the sense of an overarching Quaker family pertains. The Friends General Conference website in 2011 states that 'the foundation of spiritual life is laid in the family [...]. A Quaker family, whatever its configuration is rooted in the wider community of Friends' and 'we bear corporate and individual responsibility for children within the meeting' ([www.fgcquaker.org/what-are-quakers/quakers-and-children], accessed 12.08.11).

CONCLUSION

With the ending of endogamy and Quaker separations, the mid-nineteenth century marks a watershed not so much in altering the perceived importance of the idea of family to Quaker values, so much as in the historiography. The Quaker family from at least as early as 1676 up to the mid-nineteenth century was something uniquely identifiable, the basic building block of 'a coherent and self-conscious community' (Davidoff and Hall 2002, 56). Thereafter the picture becomes less clear and reflects continuing tensions between different strands of Quakerism, with a spectrum of emphases on what is acceptable in the configuration of family, and 'family values' being a matter of defining difference between Yearly Meetings. Overall, however, and in spite of a growth of individualism, within every branch of Quakerism it appears that it remains the ideal, of a 'family of Friends' who are regarded as having equal responsibility in the pastoral care and spiritual nurture of each other.

SUGGESTED FURTHER READING

Angell, S. W. (2011a) 'Gospel family order: George Fox's ministry in Barbados and the development of a Quaker testimony of family' in *Keeping us honest, Stirring the pot. A festschrift in Honor of H. Larry Ingle*, ed. by Chuck Fager. Fayetteville, North Carolina: Kimo Press, pp. 17–34.

Anderson, M. (1995 [1980]) *Approaches to the history of the western family*. Cambridge: Cambridge University Press.

Boulding, E. (1989) *One small plot of Heaven. Reflections on family life by a Quaker sociologist*. Wallingford, Pennsylvania: Pendle Hill Publications.

Davidoff, L. and Hall, C. (revised ed. 2002) *Family Fortunes*. London and New York: Routledge.

Frost, J. W. (1973) *The Quaker family in colonial America: A portrait of the Society of Friends.* New York: St Martin's Press.

Holton, S. S. (2007) *Quaker women: Personal life, memory and radicalism in the lives of women Friends, 1780–1930,* London and New York: Routledge.

Levy, B. (1988) *Quakers and the American family: British settlement in the Delaware Valley.* New York and Oxford: Oxford University Press.

Vann, R. T. (1969) *The social development of English Quakerism, 1655–1755.* Cambridge, MA: Harvard University Press.

Vann, R. T. and Eversley, D. (1992) *Friends in life and death. The British and Irish Quakers in the demographic transition.* Cambridge: Cambridge University Press.

Wells, R. V. (1971) 'Family size and fertility control in eighteenth century America: A study of Quaker Families', *Population Studies* 25, pp. 73–82.

CHAPTER 30

QUAKERS AND SEXUALITY

PETRA L. DOAN AND ELIZABETH P. KAMPHAUSEN

THE Religious Society of Friends' relationship with sexuality has been peppered with accusations and misunderstandings since its birth. Beginning in seventeenth-century England, Quakers' dramatic language and actions were interpreted by critics as explicitly sexual rather than biblical. Even George Fox (1624–91) and Margaret Fell's (1614–1702) 'helpsmeet relationship' raised questions about unacknowledged sexuality, discipline, and rightly ordered behaviour. Conflicts about sexual morality have continued to permeate Friends' history through the centuries, resulting in contemporary disagreements about sexuality, sexual orientation, gender identity, marriage, and committed same-sex partnerships. This chapter provides a summary of Quakers' relationship with sexuality for the past 350-plus years, including an overview of different perspectives that have emerged during the twentieth century within Friends General Conference (FGC), Friends United Meeting (FUM), and Evangelical Friends Church International (EFCI).

SEXUALITY AND SEVENTEENTH-CENTURY QUAKERS

Early Friends were accused of sexual immorality because their ministry challenged traditional social norms. George Fox urged his followers to control their passions and to 'Keep your bodies clean from all fornication, adultery and uncleanness ... [which] defiles and is out of the Truth' (Jones 1989, 128). However, this cautionary view of sexuality was balanced by 'a highly affectionate style of expression' (Gwyn 2000, 323) among the first Quakers. Believing themselves to be magnifying the indwelling Christ, Friends understood their bodies to be sites of sacred witness, embodying perfection on earth. Their experience of a 'concrete, substantial, and visceral convincement' resulted in a 'new relationship to language, to prophecy, and above all, to God, in and through the testament of celestial flesh' (Tarter 2001, 150). Messages from both women and men in early Quaker worship were filled with sexual and maternal imagery, opening Friends to unfounded accusations of 'demonic possession and sexualised perversion' (Myles 2007, 118).

The Song of Songs was regularly used by early Quakers of both sexes to describe their relationships, as in one surviving letter from Thomas Camm to Fox in which Camm dreams of Fox embracing and kissing him 'with the kisses of thy mouth' (Moore 2000, 77). In another letter, Francis Howgill laments separation from yokefellow Edward Burrough, referring to the words of David and Jonathan in 2 Samuel 1:22: 'Thy love to me was wonderful, passing the love of women' (Damrosch 1996, 124). Such intense spiritual friendships—including the bond between James Nayler and George Fox in the movement's beginnings—were startling to observers (Ingle 1994). Friends' sense of their unity with the Divine led to a strong experience of unity with one another, which may have contained an 'unexpressed sexuality', according to Quaker historian Rosemary Moore (2000, 77).

In addition to their erotic language, seventeenth-century Friends challenged dualistic male/female roles because the presence of the Light Within each believer undermined the gendered hierarchy of orthodox theology (Damrosch 1996, 122). Since Quaker women's prophetic witnessing was visibly gender non-conforming according to societal expectations of the time, anti-Quaker pamphlets frequently accused Friends of sexual misbehaviour (Moore 2000, 117). Friends who travelled in the ministry in same-sex or non-marital pairs were particularly troublesome to onlookers, such as the missionary pair of Katherine Evans and Sarah Chevers who identified as 'Yoak-Mates' and spoke of their partnership in marital language: 'The Lord hath joined us together, and wo be to them that should part us' (Myles 2007, 123). The apparent freedom of itinerant Quakers was interpreted as a sexualized threat to the stability of traditional families as well as to 'orderly' society.

Fox's Teaching on Helpsmeet Relationships

The biblically based helpsmeet relationship was foundational to the early Friends' movement. Being 'helps-meet' for seventeenth-century Quakers was a radical return to the condition of Adam and Eve's tri-relationship with each other and with God in the Garden of Eden, based on Genesis 2:18: 'And the LORD God said, It is not good that the man should be alone; I will make him an help meet'. Fox believed that it was possible through Christ to reverse the condition when 'man' had been placed over 'woman' in the Fall, such that the original state of perfection could be regained: men and women could once again be 'equal helpmates'. In addition to Adam and Eve, Fox gave several examples of helpsmeet relationships in his Epistles, such as Abraham and Sarah as well as Ruth and Naomi, who were 'meet-helps and fellow laborers together in the work and service of the Lord' (Jones 1989, 329).

The spiritually grounded nature of a helpsmeet partnership was not restricted to a marriage or sexual relationship for the early Friends, although certainly two meet-helps could be married, as eventually happened with Fell and Fox. Rather than emphasizing sexual relations, however, the focus was on individuals helping each other to keep the Gospel Order, always being mindful of the 'First Love, the First Bridegroom'. Fox considered that 'all Christians, regardless of sex, are married to Jesus Christ' (Jones 1989, xv), as Fox wrote in this 1653 Epistle: 'Dear Friends, prize your heavenly calling...Break not wedlock with the Lord Jesus Christ....Keep marriage with him, the holy One, the Just One' (Jones 1989, 28–9).

Helpsmeet Marriages as Modelled by Fox and Fell

The relationship of George Fox and Margaret Fell is illustrative of the tension between appearance and propriety for early Quakerism. After hearing Fox preach in 1652, Fell brought the itinerant preacher back to the house she shared with her husband, Judge Thomas Fell. For the next several years Margaret and George became very close spiritual Friends in ways that were not socially acceptable for a commoner and the married wife of a landed aristocrat. After the death of Judge Fell, Fox and Fell were wed in 1669, setting the precedent for marriage as a spiritual union initiated by God, rather than primarily a sexual relationship. Specifically, when questioned by a Puritan who understood marriage as justified only by the aim of procreation, Fox 'asserted he had married in response to a *leading* to testify to a new order of marriage and not to have children' (Whitbeck 1989, 15, emphasis added). Fell and Fox were clear that marriage was in essence a religious covenant, divinely led and joined, rather than a legal or procreative relationship (Hoffman 1989). As Fox writes in 1669:

> For the right joining in marriage is the work of the Lord only and not the priests nor magistrates. For it is God's ordinances and not man's. Therefore, Friends cannot consent that they should join them together. For we marry none, it is the Lord's work and we are but witnesses. (Jones 1989, 247)

Fell and Fox's marriage provided a model for early Friends' helping one another—as helpmates—to be faithful to their individual leadings, even if that meant periods of physical separation. In fact, George and Margaret were called apart many times during their twenty-two years of matrimony, raising questions for some observers about the nature of their relationship, including whether their marriage was ever consummated. Given Fox's assertion that 'his marriage *and the sexual union within it* [Fox's term is the marriage 'bed'] were honorable' (Whitbeck 1989, 15), it can be argued that Fox and Fell did not have a celibate marriage. Furthermore, Fell apparently believed she was pregnant after the nuptials, although her condition was actually a false or imaginary pregnancy (Ingle 1994, 228).

SEXUALITY AND EIGHTEENTH- AND NINETEENTH-CENTURY FRIENDS: QUIETISM, RENEWAL, REVIVAL

Eighteenth-century Quakerism shifted away from the early Friends' belief in perfectibility and coagency with God, to being a God-fearing Religious Society focused on sin (Dandelion 2007, 60). Seeking to strengthen the protective hedge against worldly entanglements by 'bearing the cross' that obliterated every carnal desire, Quietist Friends viewed passions as the chief objects of discipline (Hamm 1988, 7–10). Fornication, incest (referring usually to sexual relations between first cousins), and adultery were grounds for disownment for these plain Friends, as well as Friends marrying non-Quakers, or two Friends marrying in a non-Quaker ceremony. Attitudes towards sexuality reflected Friends' general concern about being faithful, such as Catherine Phillips who waited twenty-three years before being sure 'that her intended was truly God's choice and not just her own' (Dandelion 2007, 60). In addition, travelling ministers of this period rarely referred to marital helpmeets left at home. For example, abolitionist Friend John Woolman mentioned his wife and child only once in his journal, 'not because he did not love them, but because to write of them would be to put self, the creature, forward' (Bacon 1994, 14). Nevertheless, the same strong spiritual companionships witnessed among the early Friends continued to be quietly recorded among eighteenth-century travelling ministers such as Elizabeth Shipley and Elizabeth White who were known for their 'lifelong devotion to one another' (Bacon 1994, 9).

After the Hicksite–Orthodox split in 1827—and with the later rise of the Renewal and especially the Revival/Holiness movements—Orthodox Friends abolished endogamy and allowed Quakers to marry other Christians (Dandelion 2007, 112). Similar to non-Quaker evangelicals of the time, Orthodox Friends of the late nineteenth century increasingly used the Bible as the basis for Quaker beliefs, practice, and testimonies, resulting in the 'outward cross [supplanting] the inward one' (Hamm 1988, 86). Many of these Bible-based Orthodox members of the Religious Society would become twentieth-century Evangelical Friends associated with programmed churches or semi-programmed meetings within Evangelical Friends Church International and/or Friends United Meeting. Their emphasis on the primacy of biblical authority and interpretation laid the groundwork for increasingly heated clashes about sexuality and sexual morality with the heirs of nineteenth-century Hicksite Friends—who in the twentieth century would become associated primarily with Friends General Conference and unprogrammed meetings.

Sexuality and Twentieth-century Quakers: Acknowledging Diverse Identities

Quaker historian Thomas Hamm writes, 'For the first three hundred years of the [Religious] Society of Friends, sexuality was not an issue' in that Friends 'embraced the sexual ethics other Christians endorsed' (2003, 137). However, the turbulent social and cultural upheavals in the 1960s—epitomized by protests against the Vietnam War, expansion of civil rights, feminist conscious-raising, and increased sexual freedoms—led to an influx of dialogue and conflict among twentieth-century Quakers. Although many Friends were in sympathy with the anti-war, anti-racist, and anti-sexist sentiments that echoed traditional Quaker testimonies, Friends' responses to the sexual revolution and gay liberation movements became more divisive.

The printing of *Towards a Quaker View of Sex* (1963) by Friends Home Service Committee in Britain was an influential first public discussion of the subject of sexuality among Friends, characterizing it as a 'glorious gift from God' (Heron 1963, 12). Ten years later in 1973, Mary Calderone's (1904–98) Rufus Jones Lecture on 'Human Sexuality and the Quaker Conscience' at Friends General Conference's Gathering continued the conversation, emphasizing that 'because there is that of God in every human, and because sexuality is an innate part of the human being, then there surely must be that of God in human sexuality' (Calderone 1973, 1).

Towards a Quaker View of Sex also initiated the first—and controversial—discussion about homosexuality within the Religious Society of Friends. Whereas 'doubtless, there have always been gay Friends', same-sex relationships were simply not mentioned by Quakers before the twentieth century, with the possible exception of an 'oblique' reference by Fox to sodomy (Hamm 2003, 137–9). *Towards a Quaker View of Sex* affirms that the divine gift of sexuality is not limited to heterosexuality, and that homosexuality is not 'morally worse' (Heron 1963, 41), a viewpoint shared by Calderone, who advocated for 'simple acceptance of homosexuality as one variant of sexual life style' (1973, 12–13).

David Blamires' *Homosexuality from the Inside*, published in 1973, is a notable early example of a British Friend describing the experiences of gay and lesbian Friends. Similar publications would follow, including *Each of Us Inevitable* (1989, later expanded in 2003), which compiles keynote presentations given by gay, lesbian, and bisexual Quakers in North America—and their allies—in support of Friends seeking to live faithfully to their sexual orientations. *Part of the Rainbow*, printed in the UK in 2004, also sought to help Britain Yearly Meeting understand same-sex relationships. This publication highlights gay and lesbian *families* by writing, 'We see lesbians and gays in loving and faithful relationships; living lives of great service to others; as devoted parents rearing happy and sane children', emphasizing that 'Being gay is neither good nor bad of itself—it is what we do with our lives that matters' (Quaker Lesbian and Gay Fellowship 2004, 7).

TWENTIETH-CENTURY SEXUALITY
AND BIBLICAL AUTHORITY

The twentieth century witnessed severe conflicts among Friends over biblical authority regarding sexual relationships and sexual orientation, particularly homosexuality. Walter Barnett's 1979 Pendle Hill pamphlet, *Homosexuality and the Bible*, argues that Biblical texts used by Evangelical Friends to condemn homosexuality have been misused and/or misinterpreted. Specifically, he writes that the sin of Sodom and Gomorrah (Gen. 19:1–19) was inhospitality, not homosexuality; that Deuteronomy 23:17–18 refers to prostitutes, not gay or lesbian people; and Leviticus 18:22, 20:13 refers to practices of idolatry, not homosexuality. Barnett also writes that homosexual behaviour was never discussed by Jesus, concluding that 'on the subject of homosexuality as an orientation, and on consensual behavior by people who possess that [sexual] orientation, [the Bible] is wholly silent' (Barnett 1979, 6–7). He suggests that heterosexual Christian Quakers who are quick to judge homosexual acts as sinful should leave the judging to God, since 'God's own spirit within each of us is capable of doing whatever convicting of sin needs to be done' (Barnett 1979, 30). This viewpoint is later echoed by Elizabeth Watson (1914–2006) in her pamphlet *Sexuality: A Part of Wholeness*, where she wonders whether the violence she witnessed toward gay and lesbian Friends reflects a lack of wholeness: 'How many [of us] live with a mask on, because [we] dare not reveal [our] sexual preference?' (1982, 17). Watson also affirms that condemnation of gays and lesbians is 'archaic', that to 'base one's attitude toward gay and lesbian people today on ancient codes in the Bible, set forth in a vastly different time, is to ignore continuing revelation' (1991, 79).

Evangelical Friends generally disagree with these Liberal Quakers. As Richard Foster (1942–) writes in *Money, Sex & Power: The Challenge of the Disciplined Life*, the 'notion that homosexuality is merely a special form of normal sexuality is unthinkable from a biblical perspective' (1985, 108). Similarly, in the Quaker Theological Discussion Group's *Sexual Ethics: Some Quaker Perspectives*, Ben Richmond states that there is no place in the Restoration [Return to the Garden] for practising homosexuals, citing Fox's writing in 1682 that 'surely there ought not to be a whore, nor a Sodomite amongst them that are called Christians' (Cooper and Fraser 1990, 2). In his response to Richmond, Robert Fraser states that contemporary understandings of homosexuality only arose during the twentieth century and therefore cannot be the set of behaviours referenced by Fox (Cooper and Fraser 1990, 27), thereby suggesting the question: if the sins of Sodom were the sins of inhospitality rather than homosexuality, who might contemporary Sodomites be? Comparable debates continued during the late twentieth century, with numerous articles written in Friends' publications such as *Friends Journal*, *Quaker Life*, and *Evangelical Friend*.

Biblical scholar and Quaker meeting attender Walter Wink (1935–2012) raised cautions about becoming 'mired in interpretative quicksand' (1999, 33) in applying biblical injunctions to contemporary experiences of sexuality. While he stated that indeed there are 'unequivocal condemnations' of homosexuality (Lev. 18:22, 20:13, Rom. 1:26–27), he lists sexual attitudes, practices, and restrictions 'that are normative in Scripture but that we no longer accept as normative' such as stoning adulterers (Deut. 22:22), non-virgin brides (Deut. 22:13–21), and sanctioning slavery (Wink 1999, 47). Wink also asked why homosexuality is a greater sin than divorce, 'especially considering the fact that Jesus never even mentioned homosexuality but explicitly condemned divorce [Mark 10:1–2]' (Wink 1999, 41). Instead, he wrote that there is no biblical sex ethic, thereby encouraging Friends to critique sexual practice by the love ethic exemplified by Jesus:

> Christian morality, after all, is not an iron chastity belt for repressing urges, but a way of expressing the integrity of our relationship with God. It is the attempt to discover a manner of living that is consistent with who God created us to be. For those of same-sex orientation, as for heterosexuals, being moral means rejecting sexual mores that violate their own integrity and that of others, and attempting to discover what it would mean to live by the love [commandment] of Jesus ... [including asking] What does it mean to love my gay neighbor? (Wink 1999, 45–6)

Wink concluded that 'what is clear, utterly clear, is that we are commanded to love one another. Love not just our gay sisters and brothers who are often sitting beside us, acknowledged or not ... but all of us who are involved in this debate' (Wink 1999, 49).

EARLY TWENTY-FIRST-CENTURY QUAKERISM AND SEXUALITY

While early twenty-first-century Friends generally agree with Philadelphia Yearly Meeting's 2002 *Faith and Practice* that sexuality is a gift from God; that sexual relations be 'equal, not exploitative'; that sex be an 'act of love, not of aggression'; and that sexual relationships dependent upon the Spirit are sacramental (Dandelion 2007, 229), there is less agreement regarding sexual codes of conduct and acceptance, especially of non-heteronormative partnerships. Among unprogrammed Yearly Meetings within Friends General Conference there is greater openness to departing from traditional sexual morality in terms of both heterosexual and homosexual intimate relationships. Many Liberal Quakers believe that the Religious Society of Friends needs to adjust to changing contemporary times and to rely on integrity rather than on strict moral codes. That said, there is also discomfort among these Friends with sexual promiscuity because '[e]ven with its respect for individual leadings, Quakerism does not sanction license in sexual behaviour' (Dandelion 2007, 229).

Evangelical Friends typically hold traditional Christian views on sexuality, sharing the belief of many non-Quaker evangelicals that sexual activity (including homosexuality) outside traditional heterosexual marriage is sinful. These Friends claim that homosexuality is 'a horrendous crime against God, nature, and humanity' (Hamm 2003, 141).

Reflecting evangelical missionary efforts during and after the colonial era, the belief that homosexuality is biblically sinful remains especially strong among Yearly Meetings in Africa within Friends United Meeting (FUM) and Evangelical Friends Church International (EFCI). These differences in openness, acceptance, and welcome provide 'the biggest block to Evangelical Friends seeing Liberal Quakers as Friends', resulting in some Evangelicals' refusal to use the term 'Quaker' as a self-description (Dandelion 2007, 245).

Evangelicals within certain Friends churches have also prevented lesbian, gay, bisexual, and transgendered (LGBT) Friends who are 'out of the closet' from joining the Religious Society formally or taking up positions of responsibility. This has resulted in a 'a new kind of sanction, where a portion of the population [is] explicitly excluded from applying for Quaker membership, or from service as part of the priesthood of all believers' (Dandelion 2007, 238). For example, two Friends in Mid-America Yearly Meeting were stripped of their recording as ministers because they questioned the Yearly Meeting's condemnation of homosexuality (Hamm 2003, 141–2).

EARLY TWENTY-FIRST-CENTURY QUAKERS: MARRIAGE AND HELPSMEET RELATIONSHIPS

Regarding sexuality and marriage in the early twenty-first century, Quakers generally agree that a good marriage is loving, respectful, faithful, and ideally a covenant relationship rooted in seeking divine guidance (Hamm 2003, 196). However, as exemplified by the 2000 *Faith and Practice: The Book of Discipline* of Evangelical Friends Church (Eastern Region), many Evangelical Friends adhere to traditional Christian values—specifying that 'sexual relations take place . . . only within heterosexual marriage' (Hamm 2003, 137–8). Likewise, while maintaining the covenant nature of wedded relationships, the 2001 *Faith and Practice of Evangelical Friends Church Southwest* affirms that 'a [heterosexual] marriage covenant . . . is the only appropriate context for sexual fulfilment and procreation' (Dandelion 2007, 225).

In contrast, Liberal Friends have wrestled—sometimes for decades—with how to respond to requests for commitment ceremonies and marriages from same-sex couples. The first same-sex 'union' under the care of a Friends Meeting was celebrated at University Friends in Seattle in 1981; the first to use the label 'marriage' took place at Morningside Meeting in New York City in 1987 (Hamm 2003, 140). *Seeking God's Will on Same-Sex Relationships: The Experience of Cleveland Friends Meeting* (Grundy 2010) documents the clearness process for 'witnessing' the marriage of Nancy Reeves and Lynn Clark in 1994, although Cleveland Meeting was subsequently disowned by Ohio Yearly Meeting for its discernment. Part of the changing acceptance and eventual celebration of same-sex marriage among these Quakers is linked to their desire to uphold the Religious Society's equality testimony, as articulated by this minute by Bloomington Friends Meeting (Ohio Valley Yearly Meeting) on 2 Twelfth Month, 2002:

> With the understanding that Christ has given us as Quakers today, we cannot accept actions or attitudes that diminish the humanity of lesbians, gay men, or bisexual persons, assign to them an inferior status within the Religious Society of Friends, or the wider world, or suggest that their covenant relationships are in any way less sacred, less valid, or the cause for less joy than those of other persons. ([http://flgbtqc.quaker.org/marriageminutes.html])

Other meetings have emphasized Friends' historic testimonies against discrimination, prejudice, and oppression, such as this minute by Concord Friends Meeting (New England Yearly Meeting) in 2002:

> We celebrate marriage for all couples after the manner of Friends if we find them clear in their commitment to be faithful to each other . . . Friends have never accepted the primacy of the written word over religious experience and, while the weight of tradition cannot be ignored, it cannot rule. Profound experiences of divine love moved early Friends to oppose slavery and the subjugation of women to their husbands, even though these practices were supported by Scripture and ancient tradition. ([http://flgbtqc.quaker.org/marriageminutes.html])

Likewise, University Friends Meeting (North Pacific Yearly Meeting) sent this message to officials in the Washington state government in 1997: 'Arguments denying same sex marriage based on assertions of poor parenting and inappropriate modeling are simply unfounded . . . [reflecting] a flaw in society, not a flaw in homosexual parents'. The Quaker Lesbian and Gay Fellowship (QLGF) in the UK was influential as well in seasoning this issue among British Friends. *We Are But Witnesses* documents Britain Yearly Meeting's leading 'to treat same sex committed relationships in the same way as opposite sex marriages' (2009, 4), including lobbying their government to extend the civil rights enjoyed by heterosexual married couples to all.

Conservative Friends have also struggled with how to respond to requests by same-sex couples for clearness to marry within their Yearly Meetings. Callie Marsh's *A Lively Faith: Reflections on Iowa Yearly Meeting of Friends (Conservative)* records the 'long and sometimes harrowing' process of working towards Truth—and letting God lead through the pain, injustice, and fear—as her West Branch Monthly Meeting found clearness for taking same-gender marriages and civil unions under its care (2011, 55–65).

Although 'helpsmeet' language is not used as frequently as recorded by seventeenth-century Quakers, written accounts of late twentieth- and early twenty-first-century Liberal Friends' marriages—whether same-sex or not—testify to the same Spirit underlying Fell and Fox's spiritual partnership: namely, helping one another to live faithfully to God, as led, with Divine assistance. For example, Leslie

Hill's *Marriage: A Spiritual Leading for Lesbian, Gay and Straight Couples* describes John Calvi and Marshall Brewer's marriage in 1989 under the care of Putney Meeting in Vermont in terms paralleling Fox/Fell's marriage: 'Like George and Margaret, who married to serve God and follow their leadings, John and Marshall openly attended to their responsibility to the Divine Spirit by seeking to carry out their spiritual leadings' (1993, 20). Even though Fox wrote of God joining 'one male and one female' in the Restoration/Return to the Garden (Jones 1989, 246), Liberal Friends generally consider Fox's language to be culturally bound and therefore not a present-day barrier to same-sex marriages.

DISCERNMENT WITHIN FRIENDS' INSTITUTIONS: FGC, FUM, AND EFCI

While there is not unity about sexuality within all branches of Friends at the beginning of the twenty-first century, there has been substantial movement over the past fifty years towards acknowledgment and inclusion of lesbian, gay, bisexual, and transgendered (LGBT) people. The largest support for same-sex relationships is found among Liberal Quakers in Friends General Conference, as seen by the number of minutes approved by Yearly and Monthly Meetings listed on the FLGBTQC website ([http://flgbtqc.quaker.org/marriageminutes.html]). Many Yearly Meetings in Friends United Meeting and Evangelical Friends Church International continue to voice their opposition to homosexuality, although there are supportive Friends within FUM and EFCI who have been moved by the lives and witness of LGBT Quakers.

Friends General Conference (FGC) has provided significant affirmation for gay, lesbian, bisexual, transgendered, and queer Friends, beginning in 1972 when a handful of gay American Quakers began meeting as the 'Committee of Concern' at FGC's annual Gathering. With increased feelings of safety and growing acceptance from FGC, this group evolved into 'Friends Committee on Gay Concerns' in 1975 and later to 'Friends for Lesbian and Gay Concerns' (FLGC) in 1978. The first decades of FLGC's existence were both wrenching and powerful for this community of faith due to many gay Quakers dying of HIV/AIDS. The grief, need for spiritual accompaniment, and an enduring love among these Friends led to powerful meetings for worship that still provide deep sustenance and spiritual comfort for worshippers—including heterosexual allies. After lengthy discernment in 2003, FLGC was led to change the name to 'Friends for Lesbian, Gay, Bisexual, Transgender, and Queer Concerns' (FLGBTQC) to include bisexual and transgendered Quakers—acknowledging that sexual orientation (to whom one is attracted, men and/or women) is different than gender identity (how one identifies as a person).

As Doan (2002) describes, FLGBTQC is a vitally important place for LGBT Quakers who are seeking to live their spiritual journeys with integrity. An oasis for people who have been spurned by the world at large, FLGBTQC welcomes family members of LGBT people, straight allies, Friends feeling led to explore or question their sexuality, and any Quaker committed to honouring, affirming, and upholding 'that of God' in all people:

> We are learning that radical inclusion and radical love bring further light to Quaker testimony and life. Our experience with oppression in our own lives leads us to seek ways to bring our witness to bear in the struggles of other oppressed peoples. ([http:// flgbtqc.quaker.org/whatis.html])

Friends General Conference's Central Committee has also recorded their support for LGBT Friends, as demonstrated by the following minute, approved in 2004:

> Our experience has been that spiritual gifts are not distributed with regard to sexual orientation or gender identity...We will never go back to silencing those voices or suppressing those gifts. Our experience confirms that we are all equal before God, as God made us. ([www.fgcquaker.org/library/fgc-news/lgbtq-minute.php])

While FGC does not set policy for its affiliated meetings, such a discerned statement of support is in contrast to Evangelical Yearly Meetings in EFCI, all of whom have adopted statements that homosexuality is sinful (Hamm 2003, 141).

Friends United Meeting (FUM), which encompasses a broad range of unprogrammed and programmed American Quakers as well as East African, Cuban, and Jamaican Friends, has been particularly challenged by sexual issues in the late twentieth- and early twenty-first centuries. An early example is recorded in *Each of Us Inevitable*, where Tom Bodine describes his choosing to be a closeted gay man while serving as FUM's presiding clerk from 1972 to 1975, during which time he experienced FUM Board members speaking strongly of the 'sin of homosexuality' in his presence. By keeping his sexual orientation private, Bodine had hoped to build bridges of understanding between Evangelical and Liberal Friends, notwithstanding the hurtful ramifications personally (Leuze 2003, 100–1).

Disagreement among FUM Friends increased when their General Board adopted a personnel policy in 1988 (amended in 1991) that banned 'non-celibate homosexuals and heterosexuals in non-marital sexual relationships' from working for FUM (Dandelion 2007, 167). This hiring policy effectively prohibited employment by FUM to anyone having a sexual relationship outside heterosexual marriage (understood to be between one man and one woman) or to non-celibate homosexuals. Many Friends within Yearly Meetings dually affiliated with Friends General Conference and Friends United Meeting were upset by this policy, resulting in Southeastern Yearly Meeting withdrawing its membership from FUM in 2010. Yearly Meetings that are solely affiliated with FUM and almost entirely composed of pastoral meetings have generally endorsed this 1988 General Board decision.

Indiana Yearly Meeting (FUM) was also challenged by West Richmond Friends Meeting's approval in 2008 of a 'welcoming and affirming minute' that reflected their understanding of Christ's call to love everyone ([http://www.westrichmondfriends.org/ affirming.htm]). Acknowledging the absence of legal or denominational provisions for lesbian and gay couples, West Richmond Friends stated that 'we regard same sex couples who are in committed relationships as families'. In addition, this minute affirmed persons who were openly gay or lesbian to be members of West Richmond Meeting and encouraged their accepting leadership positions. In response, Indiana Yearly Meeting eldered West Richmond Friends in 2008 for their 'lack of submission' to the Yearly Meeting's minute of 1982 that declared 'homosexual practices' as 'contrary to the intent and will of God for humankind', citing Leviticus 18:22, 20:13 and Romans 1:21–32. Other FUM Friends consider West Richmond's 'coming out' as prophetic, akin to Woolman's witnessing against slavery (Angell, 2010–11). North Carolina Yearly Meeting (FUM) was also threatened with splits in 1994 and 1995 because of 'demands from fundamentalist Friends that some ministers who had expressed sympathy for gay rights be silenced' (Hamm 2003, 142).

Open dialogue among Friends within EFCI about the presence of LGBT individuals in their programmed churches began occurring in the early twenty-first century. Although many members of EFCI Yearly Meetings assert that gays and lesbians can be 'welcomed' but not 'affirmed' within their congregations, these Friends deny that LGBT persons can assume leadership roles therein, again citing biblical authority. However, some Evangelical Friends have confronted long-held beliefs and policies of EFCI as well as institutions under its care. For example, over 400 'lesbian, gay, transgendered, queer, and allied' alumni of George Fox University—one of the leading Friends' universities serving Evangelical Friends—have formed an organization called OneGeorgeFox that brings a 'message of hope' by advocating support of same-sex marriage and responsible same-sex relationships. These alumni have written an open letter to their university, affirming that 'Making acceptance of LGBTQ people within the George Fox community contingent on celibacy is not loving or responsible' ([http://www.onegeorgefox.org]).

In preparation for the Sixth World Conference of Friends held in Kenya in 2012, the Friends World Committee for Consultation (FWCC) sent representatives of FUM, EFCI, and FGC-affiliated Yearly Meetings materials that stated 'homosexuality has been a deeply divisive issue among Friends worldwide'. Recognizing that 'Some Friends can not accept homosexuality, believing it is contrary to God's will', whereas 'Other Friends hold that all loving relationships are reflections of God's love', FUM, EFI, and FGC representatives were strongly invited to work together so that the gathering 'be a safe place for expression of [Friends'] views in an atmosphere of mutual respect and Christian love'. By the conclusion of this 2012 World Conference, a summary of the proceedings noted that 'Friends yearn for healing of divisions and conflicts among us, especially on the subjects of racism, human sexuality, gender equality, and other hidden unspoken inequalities'. The final Epistle also reported that while there is not unity among contemporary Friends regarding sexuality, it asked, 'Can we end our internal strife? Can we reach out in love to one another as Jesus commanded?' ([http://saltandlight2012.org]). Other contemporary Quakers around the world are making similar attempts to build connections—rather than separations—within the Religious Society of Friends, trusting in God's presence and guidance.

Conclusions: Helpsmeet Relationships at the Foundation

Members of today's Religious Society of Friends continue to wrestle with experiences of sexuality and complexities of relationships that were not discussed among seventeenth-century Quakers, such as sexual intimacy outside marriage, sexual orientation, and gender identity. Although heterosexual, homosexual, bisexual, and transgendered Friends are now talking more openly about the generally acknowledged gift of sexuality, divisive issues continue—including the role of biblical authority, understandings of sinfulness, nature of continuing revelation, sexual morality, discipline, and right-ordered sexual behaviour. Disagreements are often heated regarding whether to create a welcoming and affirming community for all, irrespective of sexual orientation and gender identity; whether sexual orientation is a lifestyle choice or a relatively fixed identity; whether acceptance of non-married committed heterosexual partnerships and same-sex marriage is divinely led; whether witnessing to the testimonies of equality, honesty, and integrity means celebrating LGBT individuals, couples, and families without exclusion, oppression, and fear; and to what extent biblical passages used to discredit or dishonour homosexuality are culturally bound.

The history of Quakers' relationship with sexuality has also included a testimony to upholding helpsmeet relationships, as modelled by Margaret Fell and George Fox's relationship. As this chapter has shown, their helpsmeet spiritual partnership provides a shared foundation for all branches of the Religious Society of Friends in helping one another witness to Truth as experienced. Fox was fond of reminding the early Quakers, 'Whom God joins together, let no man [or Friend] put asunder' (Mark 10:9). Therein lies the touchstone for FGC, FUM, and EFCI Friends seeking to live authentic lives that reflect their sexuality as led by God. For as Margaret and George witnessed in their lives, their partnership was spiritually grounded in God's leading and primarily focused on God's *work* in the world—a powerful example for contemporary Liberal and Evangelical Friends seeking to answer to 'that of God in everyone'.

Suggested Further Reading

Heron, A. (ed.) (1963) *Towards a Quaker view of sex: An essay by a group of Friends*. First Edition. London: Friends Home Service Committee, London Yearly Meeting.

Hill, L. (1993) *Marriage: A spiritual leading for lesbian, gay, and straight couples*. Pendle Hill Pamphlet 308. Wallingford, PA: Pendle Hill Publications.

Leuze, R. (ed.) (2003) *Each of us inevitable: Some keynote addresses at Friends for Lesbian and Gay Concerns and Friends General Conference Gatherings, 1977–1993*. New York: Published by Friends for Lesbian, Gay, Bisexual, Transgender and Queer Concerns.

Watson, E. (1982) *Sexuality: A part of wholeness*. Philadelphia: Published by Philadelphia Yearly Meeting's Family Relations Committee.

CHAPTER 31

QUAKERS, YOUTH, AND YOUNG ADULTS

MAX L. CARTER AND SIMON BEST

YOUTH AND QUAKER ORIGINS

QUAKERISM began, in large part, as a youth movement (youth is defined here as young adults aged 18–35). Dissatisfied with the lack of integrity in the established Church, caught up in the spirit of the English Civil War, and appalled by the devastation of violent responses to questions of legitimate authority, many young people joined the non-conformists, some of whom became known as Quakers. Early leaders were typically in their twenties and thirties, some were even in their teens. George Fox (1624–91) was only twenty-eight when he had his vision of a great people to be gathered, and preached to a thousand people on a hillside near Sedbergh in Cumbria. Edward Burrough died in prison in 1663 at the age of twenty-nine having been a minister for ten years. James Parnell (1636–56) was fifteen when he was convinced, having met George Fox in prison, he 'came to be a very fine minister...and turned many to Christ' (*Quaker faith and practice* 19.26). Parnell died before he turned twenty. Two decades later, Robert Barclay (1648–90) became a major Quaker author while still in his twenties, publishing *An Apology for a True Christian Divinity,* still the most significant work of Quaker systematic theology, in 1676 at the age of twenty-eight.

Quaker theology held that children were not born with 'original sin' and that humans could be perfected through turning to the Light of Christ Within, but the early movement did not concern itself greatly with the spiritual formation and education of children, as there was an expectation that the 'inward apocalypse' of Christ in the first Friends was a precursor to an eschatological reign of Christ on earth. That expectation faded in the 1660s with the Restoration of the Crown, the enactment of anti-Quaker laws, the Fire of London, and the Great Plague. Only then did Quakers turn to concern about the formation of their youth. Even without a systematic approach to youth, younger Friends captured the essence of worship, and could be committed to maintaining Quaker practices apart from adults. The 1662 Quaker Act prohibited Quaker worship, and when Friends in Reading and Bristol were arrested, everyone over the age of sixteen was in prison. Children continued to keep the Meeting until the adults were released.

George Fox himself encouraged the establishment of schools for children in 1668. The first Quaker schools in America followed soon thereafter. The transformational experience of the first Friends set them apart as a 'peculiar people', and schools were needed to provide a 'guarded education' for Quaker children and an upbringing in Friends' ways.

YOUTH FORMATION IN THE EIGHTEENTH AND NINETEEN CENTURIES

As Quaker culture developed in the period of Quietism, patterns of Quaker family life emerged. Attitudes about youth were characterized by practising love and affection, resisting corporal punishment, and using the nuclear family and the extended family of the Quaker community to model expected behaviour and dependence on the Light in their consciences rather than arbitrary authority.

Rufus Jones (1863–1948) recalled that as a child in a Quietist Quaker family in Maine, in the US, every day began with a reading from Scripture at the breakfast table and a long period of silence during which the Spirit was expected to reveal the meaning of that passage. He noted in his autobiography that: 'I was not "christened" in a church, but I was sprinkled from morning to night with the dew of religion' (Jones 1902, 23). Beyond the family, worship in the local meeting and frequent visiting ministers and elders provided models of what a devout and holy life might look like.

It was typical for the young people to sit together in a section of the meeting house—sometimes in the 'children's gallery' in the balcony. This sometimes made them the object of ministers' messages or the stern gaze of an elder or overseer from the facing bench if there was youthful misbehaving.

Little formal religious instruction was given, lest it lead to formal worship and then an ordained clergy! Youth who experienced an inward spiritual movement were often left to fend for themselves, as even parents—if not 'recorded' as ministers—were hesitant to pray vocally or offer a message. Allen Jay (1831–1910) recalled a time of deep religious wrestling during his youth when his mother noticed that something was amiss; she 'wanted to say more, but her training, like that of most Friends of that time (1840s), was to repress all religious conversation' (Jay 2010, 11).

INFLUENCE OF YOUTH IN EMBRACING NEW UNDERSTANDINGS OF QUAKERISM

In the 1850s, young Friends such as Allen Jay in Indiana, in the US, began organizing literary societies, practising family home worship, and Bible studies in each other's homes—even as the Quietist culture discouraged such 'creaturely' activities. In 1860, Charles (1823–1916) and Rhoda Coffin (1826–1909) in Richmond, Indiana, opened their home during sessions of Indiana Yearly Meeting (Orthodox) to nearly 500 young Friends who were discouraged by the lack of spiritual vitality in the Religious Society of Friends, encouraging them to be open to the movement of the Holy Spirit—even if it manifested itself in vocal prayer and praise, expressions rare among Friends at that time. A powerful worship ensued.

In 1870, Allen Jay, who had become superintendent of the work of the Baltimore Association to Advise and Assist Friends in the Southern States and had moved to North Carolina, faced the challenge of young Friends' attendance at lively Methodist revivals. Their parents and elders discouraged such violation of Quietist restrictions, which prompted some youth to consider leaving Friends. Jay responded by gaining the young people's agreement to remain Friends if he could gain the permission of the elders and ministers for them to continue attending the revivals. The bargain helped usher in major changes in Friends' worship practice among Gurneyite Quakers in the US.

Later on a trip through England, Jay was impressed by the energy and vision of young adult Friends to bring Quakerism out of Quietism and into the modern world. An influential essay, *Quakerism, past and present* by John Stephenson Rowntree who was one of these young adult Friends, in 1859 had led to the loosening of restrictions on marriage and other aspects of the 'plain' life. Returning to the United States, Jay launched the Young Friends Fellowship Movement.

Similar to Jay's earlier experience in Indiana, Young Friends in Massachusetts organized a Whittier Literary Association named after the Quaker poet John Greenleaf Whittier (1807–92), and around the same time young Friends in Ontario, Canada, also organized a literary society.

In the 1880s, Orthodox Friends in Philadelphia established a reading room for young Friends visiting in the city; later, when the property was sold, proceeds funded a Friends Institute endowment, which supported young adult Friends' programmes. Study groups on Quaker history and testimonies organized by young adult Friends in the 1880s in Philadelphia Yearly Meeting (Hicksite) led to the formation of a Young Friends Association, with Young Friends on the programme at the first gathering in 1900 of Friends General Conference.

Before and while a systematic Quaker youth work was developing, some turned to other Christian organizations. There were active YMCA programmes on many Quaker college campuses (Guilford College even built a YMCA building on campus in the late 1800s). In 1881 the Young People's Society of Christian Endeavour was founded in Maine by non-Friends. Its purpose was to bring youth to accept Christ. Christian

Endeavour societies provided structure for much of Quaker youth involvement among Orthodox Friends into the 1920s, when they were replaced by particular Young Friends groups.

In 1907 the recently formed Five Years Meeting of Friends endorsed the idea of a national young Friends organization. A national conference was held in 1910 at Winona Lake in Indiana, continuing periodically for several years.

In 1914 Thomas Elsa Jones (1888–1973) was named national youth secretary for FYM, serving in that position until 1917. He was followed by Clarence Pickett (1884–1965) and a succession of young men and women into mid-century, many of whom went on to significant leadership positions among Friends. Friends General Conference Young Friends Campouts began in 1919. While both national organizations had boards of Young Friends Activities, FYM discouraged cross-branch activities.

Jones observed that among British and American young people there was a common interest in new life and power coming to Friends. There were, however, tensions between activist, evangelical, and intellectual approaches. In the Midwest he encountered the attitude that Hicksite Friends could not be trusted, that modern thinkers were destroying the Bible, and he was confronted by a professor of Theology at Friends University in Kansas with the statement, '... you and those Quakers over East talk about the "Inner Light." Nothing could be more wrong or sinful. Salvation cannot come from within man who is lost in sin; redemption can come only from the shed blood of Christ as revealed by the Holy Ghost' (Jones 1973). For their part, Hicksite Friends expressed concern about their young people's becoming involved in Christian Endeavour.

Such differences in approach to the theology of the Light and of losing Quaker distinctives in too-close association with other Christian bodies continued to divide Friends through the twentieth century and into the twenty-first. But already in 1911 Orthodox, Hicksite, and Wilburite young Friends came together in New Hampshire around a pilgrimage to 'Whittier land'. British young Friends at the same time felt a concern to be involved in helping bring together divided Friends in America.

The American Friends Service Committee was founded in 1917, offering young Friends opportunities for alternative service to the military and providing relief and reconstruction efforts which brought Friends from various branches and nations together, serving as a seedbed for leadership development—and to later attempts at reuniting Friends. As happened in the American Civil War, though, many youth were caught up in the war spirit of the Second World War and served in the military.

In 1920 the first young Friends world conference was called, meeting at Jordans, England. FYM held young Friends conferences periodically through the 1920s and 1930s, discontinuing them when fuel rationing in the Second World War made travel difficult. Also in the 1920s several American Yearly Meetings established positions of Field Secretary or Executive Secretary for youth work.

Individual Friends and Yearly Meetings began establishing summer camps for youth in the 1920s, influenced by patterns in the broader Christian community that went back to revival camp meetings, YMCA summer camps, and denominational summer camps for youth in the nineteenth century. Pastoral Yearly Meetings used the camps evangelistically; later, the philosophy of the camps was characterized as bringing campers closer to God and acquainting them with Jesus Christ. Unprogrammed Friends saw the camping programmes as inculcating Quaker values and spirituality and emphasized quiet worship in nature, community building, developing a sense of responsibility, and turning campers inward to the Light.

PROFESSIONAL YOUTH WORKERS

While Five Years Meeting of Friends developed professional youth positions early in the twentieth century, Friends General Conference was a network of volunteers who shared concerns and strategies, one area of concern being youth.

By 1970, this volunteer network had gradually been replaced by professional staff, serving particular committees, one of which was the Religious Education Committee, which had its first professional staff in the 1950s. In the 1980s, FGC focused young adult Friends work in a Youth Ministries Committee.

The first American Yearly Meeting paid staff in youth work was Edwin Hinshaw (1934–), experienced in youth leadership training as a student at Earlham College and in service in Kenya. He became Youth and Education Secretary of New England Yearly Meeting in 1963.

The Second World War disrupted youth work on national levels, but Civilian Public Service camps in the US served to connect several thousand conscientious objectors in networks that fed into Quaker schools, colleges, service, and leadership after the war. Some went to prison; other British and American Friends served in the Friends Ambulance Unit. A majority of those of military age in Britain and America served in the armed forces. German youth were faced with the dilemma of execution or military service, with some opting for the latter and others quietly left out of call-ups by sympathetic officials.

In 1947, nationwide young Friends conferences were resumed through the collaboration of Clarence Pickett (1884–1965), then General Secretary of the AFSC and Charles Thomas, FYM Young Friends Secretary. Conferences continued through the 1950s and into the early 1960s, with the 1953 conference giving birth to the Young Friends of North America.

YFNA was dominated by unprogrammed Friends but sought to be inclusive and continued with its own young adult Friends'-run annual conferences until ever-narrowing interests led to a decreasing number of attendees, and the group became inactive in the 1990s. YFNA reflected the chaos experienced in youth culture in the West during the 1960s, especially in the intensity of the anti-war movement, the new liberation movements, and sexual freedom. From 1969–74, a number of young Friends, most from YFNA, lived communally at New Swarthmoor, a Quaker farm near Clinton, New York. Formed to revive the vital nature of the early Quaker movement, it also served as a countercultural centre, with a variety of liberties taken that led many veterans of the community later to endorse more conservative moral and theological views.

Young Friends pioneered in alternative views during the Cold War. YFNA had an 'East–West Contacts Committee' and promoted understanding of Russia and China. As the century progressed, however, fewer and fewer of military age upheld the traditional peace testimony of Friends, only a minority becoming conscientious objectors.

In 1959, the Friends World Committee for Consultation sponsored its first Quaker Youth Pilgrimage, bringing together Friends from many nations and branches for a summer of service work, pilgrimage, and education in England. Meanwhile, Yearly Meetings and national Friends bodies organized programmes for young Friends through the Friends Committee on National Legislation in Washington, DC and the Quaker United Nations Office in New York and Geneva.

Individual Yearly Meetings developed their own youth programming, growing out of the volunteer work of Christian Education Committees of local meetings. Youth groups were brought together for activities at the Quarterly and Yearly Meeting level. Over the years, this emphasis on youth work at the local level evolved especially in the unprogrammed Yearly Meetings into Yearly Meeting-based activities: retreats throughout the year and at Yearly Meeting sessions, encouragement to participate in national youth programmes, and reliance on summer camps.

Yearly Meetings hired staff to direct youth and religious education programming. Approaches to curriculum changed as membership—and the ability to support staffing and curriculum development—declined through the latter part of the twentieth century. In many instances, as more households depended on two incomes outside the home, young people became involved in more activities outside the family and meeting, and were not reliably in attendance at worship and youth activities. However, many Evangelical Friends continued to hire youth pastors in their churches and to design extensive youth programmes, including missionary trips and outreach ministries in addition to social activities

For some Yearly Meetings, such as Baltimore Yearly Meeting (affiliated both with Friends United Meeting and Friends General Conference) and Northwest Yearly Meeting (affiliated with Evangelical Friends Church International), camping programmes have become a strong vehicle for spiritual formation. Northwest Yearly Meeting's Twin Rock camps on the Oregon coast have been quite successful in developing youth leadership and engaging in spiritual nurture.

In the liberal Yearly Meetings, less comfort in teaching the Bible and Christian thought became apparent. Teaching about other religions, the environment, Quaker testimonies, and 'heroes' of the Quaker faith were the norm. In the evangelical Yearly Meetings, it was more typical for standardized, non-Friends Bible and Christian materials to be used in programming for youth and to emphasize fun activities that could compete with popular culture.

In evangelical Yearly Meetings, youth have their own Youth Yearly Meeting, electing officers and doing much of their own programming. In Northwest Yearly Meeting annual sessions, one evening session is largely youth-led. Youth are often involved in music and worship leadership.

As young Friends moved into the young adult Friends category (typically 18–35), they became more independent and provided their own organization and programming. As technologies developed, more and more communication and 'community' occurred by way of the Internet and electronic media.

Young Friends and Liberal Quakerism in Britain

In 1893 John Wilhelm Rowntree (1868–1905) gave a very powerful ministry at London Yearly Meeting in which he pleaded for greater understanding of the spiritual struggles of young Friends who were attempting to reconcile their Quakerism with modern life (Young Friends Sub-committee 1911, 5). Younger Friends were instrumental in finding a way forwards for Friends to embrace the world of modernity while remaining committed to the Religious Society of Friends. A key event was the Manchester Conference held in 1895, which ushered in an age of liberalism in Britain Yearly Meeting and helped empower a generation of young adult Friends with new ideas about the world around them and its problems, and about the nature of the human and the divine. Amongst the speakers were John Wilhelm Rowntree who was twenty-seven, John William Graham who was thirty-six, and John T. Dorland who was thirty-five.

A major concern arising out of the conference was the religious education of members of the Religious Society of Friends. Education was seen as vital to an intelligent evaluation of faith, and Rowntree believed that the lack of solid historical knowledge was one of the gravest dangers to the Religious Society of Friends at that time (Kennedy 1984, 44). Starting in 1897, Summer Schools were organized to encourage religious education within the Religious Society of Friends. The success of these Summer Schools, especially among the youth, led to a desire to establish a permanent summer school to foster the gifts of those called to ministry (Rowntree 1905, 135–50). In 1903 the establishment of Woodbrooke in Birmingham addressed this need, and Woodbrooke continues to this day. In 1897 Rowntree (twenty-nine at the time) met Rufus Jones (thirty-four), an American Quaker and kindred spirit. Together they developed the idea of a series of books on Quaker history. This idea led to the Rowntree History Series, published in seven volumes between 1909 and 1921 (Southern 2010, 2).

In 1911 a conference for Young Friends was held at Swanwick in Derbyshire. Over 400 young people attended. This conference included lectures on Quaker history, theology, spirituality, Quaker service, the peace testimony, and the ethical application of the Quaker message. A generation of young and gifted Friends began leading Quakers into the modern era and towards an engagement with the world around them. This group included the social reformer Seebohm Rowntree (1871–1951), famous for his research into poverty in York as well as absolutist conscientious objectors who served in prisons for their refusal to fight in the First World War, and others who served in the Friends Ambulance Unit or Friends' War Victims Relief Committee.

THE CHANGING NATURE OF THE YOUNG FRIENDS MOVEMENT

The Swanwick conference led to the establishment of a special sub-committee charged with coordinating Young Friends activities with the Yearly Meeting's Home Mission and Extension Committee (Young Friends Sub-committee 1911, 16). Although clearly not the intention of those at the time (Young Friends Sub-committee 1911, 14–16), it was the beginnings of a separate organization for young Friends that was marked by increasing independence from the adult movement, especially after 1960, and the consequent marginalization of the young Friends movement from organizational Quakerism.

Up until 1963 Young Friends Central Committee was made up only of representatives from the Monthly Meetings within London Yearly Meeting, but in 1963 Young Friends Central Committee once again became an open meeting with a number of appointed officers. After then, its primary function changed from a formal committee to a general forum and meeting place for young Friends (Deacon 1974, 5). In the 1960s and 1970s it provided 'a very necessary social contact among Young Friends' groups and for isolated Young Friends' (Deacon 1974, 5), although the group consisted of 'young people who relate to the Society of Friends in a number of different ways of which [YFCC] is only one and no longer a particularly significant one' (Deacon 1974, 14).

After this change, attendance rose (Deacon 1974, 19) and by the 1980s the tri-annual gatherings regularly drew in excess of a hundred participants. In 1993 YFCC changed its name to Young Friends General Meeting to reflect the change from a representative committee to an open community (Young Friends General Meeting [http://yfgm.quaker.org.uk/wiki/images/d/d7/Yfgm-user-friendly-guide.pdf]). YFGM is constitutionally part of Britain Yearly Meeting and appoints representatives to Meeting for Sufferings as well as occasionally to other Quaker committees. Although many Area Meetings still appoint representatives it is now open to all; members, attenders, those who have been connected with Friends all their lives, and those new to Quakerism, and Area Meeting representatives have dwindled to a minority of those attending.

Over the past forty years Young Friends have supported a number of concerns and, often have led the way in relation to Quaker witness on particular issues such as East–West relations (until the late 1960s when the work was transferred to the Friends Service Council), ethical investment (Young Friends Central Committee 1980), and membership of the Religious Society of Friends. The last of these is illustrative of the inter-relationship between the 'adult' Quaker group and the youth movement.

Membership, Belonging, and the Separation of Young Friends

Within Britain Yearly Meeting formal membership rests with Area Meetings and 'the origins of the development of what it is to be a Friend lie with our Monthly Meetings' (Dandelion 1996, 275). The meaning of membership is influenced by the method of its administration, and because membership is of individual Monthly Meetings this necessarily requires an association with a local Meeting. However, there are obstacles to this type of belonging:

> Many Young Friends are not members although very involved...in its present form membership can make attenders feel excluded.... Many Young Friends are committed to the Society of Friends without wishing to become members...because in the present system of joining a specific local meeting they feel excluded because many of us are fairly itinerant. (Young Friends Central Committee Minute 90/34 in Young Friends General Meeting 1998, 165–7)

In a recent survey of 141 sixteen- to eighteen-year-old Quakers, almost 70 per cent self-identified as Quakers despite only 23 per cent of these individuals being in formal membership (Best 2010), and in one group of adolescents over half indicated informally that they would become members if it was possible to join Britain Yearly Meeting centrally without having to join an area meeting (Best 2010, 143).

In 2001 Britain Yearly Meeting established a small group to consider, amongst other issues, whether 'it might be made possible for membership...to be held in a way that is not specific to a geographic meeting' (Britain Yearly Meeting 2001, Minute 30) which has been a particular concern on young Friends. In the event the group limited their consideration to the process of membership rather than examining its meaning (*Quaker Life* 2004, 2) and stated that: 'We do not see any practicable ways to implement non-geographically held membership' (*Quaker Life* 2004, 1). This has served to maintain the status quo in terms of membership being administered through Area Meetings and has prevented the accommodation of sectarian adolescents who affiliate with exclusively adolescent groups and whose sense of belonging is through these groups. Although meetings were encouraged to 'contact an applicant's wider Quaker networks...such as...a young people's Link Group' (*Quaker Life* 2004, 7), this report did not address the way in which young Friends hold their belonging to Quaker groups. In the case of those involved in Young Friends General Meeting this is recognized by the Yearly Meeting to the extent that those who are 'members' of YFGM (in effect anyone who attends an event) can get permission from the Clerks of YFGM to attend the Yearly Meeting sessions, a privilege that is otherwise only open to those in formal membership or attenders in good standing of local Quaker Meetings. In contrast with their marginalization regarding formal membership, Young Friends General Meeting has a strong and positive reputation in relation to the practise of the Quaker business method to the extent that they have been asked to introduce, and provide teaching to the whole Yearly Meeting on this (Young Friends General Meeting annual report 2010).

CROSS-BRANCH AND INTERNATIONAL YOUTH CONFERENCES

'YouthQuake!' began in California Yearly Meeting in 1975 as an event primarily for CYM youth and five years later was expanded to include other Yearly Meetings. In 1986 a YouthQuake! was held in Mexico to encourage international participation. Subsequent YouthQuake! gatherings were held throughout the 1990s and into the early years of the twenty-first century, with an expanding base of Yearly Meetings, including programmed and unprogrammed branches.

As the circle of Yearly Meetings widened, inevitable tensions developed. A workshop in 1988 that included issues of homosexuality led to concerns from some Evangelicals. One Evangelical Yearly Meeting withdrew from YouthQuake! in the early 1990s because the event was not seen as 'Christ-centred' or evangelistic enough. Reports back to liberal Yearly Meetings told of Evangelical youth who pressured attendees to accept Jesus Christ as their saviour; youth returning to Evangelical Yearly Meetings told of Friends who didn't believe in God, Jesus, or the Bible.

As adult Friends began expressing concern about 'exposing' their youth to opposing opinions, participation in YouthQuake! waned, it became less diverse, and it was finally put 'on hold'.

In 1985 a World Gathering of Young Friends was held at Guilford College. Fifty-seven Yearly Meetings in thirty-four countries were represented, with 500 in attendance. Young Friends raised the funds for participants from Africa, Asia, and Central and South America. The theme of 'Unity in Diversity' was taken seriously; tough theological differences were not swept under the rug but were tackled openly—leading to a remarkable sense of community by the conference's end. Much of the future leadership in the Society around the world came out of the conference.

A second World Gathering of Young Friends was held in 2005 at the University of Lancaster, England. Unfortunately, despite careful planning and reassurances, many participants, particularly from Africa, were denied entry into the UK. The Gathering decided to hold a second, smaller gathering later in the year in Kenya for those unable to come to England.

Learning from the tensions of cross-branch engagement at the first conference, much preparation went into introducing Friends to theological and cultural differences before the second conference. Two young adult Friends, Coleman Watts (from the unprogrammed tradition) and Betsy Blake (from the programmed tradition) prepared a DVD 'Can We ALL Be Friends?' for wide distribution; it depicted the differences between FUM, FGC, Evangelical, and Conservative Friends in one city, Greensboro, North Carolina.

New Models of Community for Young Adult Friends

As enormous shifts in the West occurred in the last quarter of the twentieth century, the loss of young adult Friends from meetings and churches became an increasing concern. The Christian Education Director in one Yearly Meeting associated with both FUM and FGC noted that changing cultural norms in North America rendered obsolete the 'one hour once a week' model of religious education. Quaker parents were not as grounded anymore; many were products of religious scepticism. Options for youth involvement proliferated, sidelining the meeting/church as the social centre of life. Parent/youth relationships were stressed, and the 'battle' over attendance at worship and youth activities was often an easy one to give up. When youth did continue to attend meeting, many found the spirituality lacking or unfulfilling. Perhaps most daunting of all, the pervasive Western youth culture offered almost overwhelming competition to Friends' activities.

To address these issues, new strategies were developed. Retreats were used for intensive conversation, programming, and mentoring. Service trips introduced youth to intergenerational modelling and the reality that their problems were often trivial in comparison with those being assisted. Intergenerational programmes were added to the annual sessions of Yearly Meetings.

Similar issues faced young adult Friends (YAFs). The outgoing YAF coordinator for Philadelphia Yearly Meeting wrote in 2011 that these Friends needed advocacy in spiritual discernment, an experience of vital spirituality, and community. As with youth programming, providing retreats and mentoring were typical responses, but other initiatives included the development of an Emerging Leadership Scholarship Programme to encourage keeping YAFs connected with the wider Quaker community, cross-branch collaborations over the Internet, and in occasional conferences, leadership institutes, the development of a Quaker Volunteer Service programme, and the creation of intentional communities of YAFs as Friends moved to urban areas for education, job opportunities, or simply the need for such community.

Two young adults from the Atlanta Friends Meeting described in 2010 what was needed to address the particular needs of their generation: community, mentors, and encouragement to be involved; listening to young adult concerns with empathy;

involvement of young adults in meaningful leadership; peer groups at the local level; and authenticity in the lives Quakers lead—with the Spirit evident in their lives (S. and M. Hallward 2010).

Young Friends in Evangelical Yearly Meetings expressed more interest in Bible study, growing in Christ, service, and lively worship. Programming often de-emphasized Quaker distinctives in favour of Evangelical Christianity and personal moral questions rather than social justice issues.

In the early 2000s, numerous young adult Friends who had experienced vibrant spiritual community in programmes at Quaker colleges expressed concern about their upbringing in liberal, unprogrammed meetings. They had not been given adequate exposure to the Bible, a basic understanding of Christianity, or even a grounding in their Quaker faith.

One programme that sought to address such concerns was the Quaker Leadership Scholars Programme initiated at Guilford College in 1992. It intentionally recruited Friends from all the branches and offered a systematic, four-year cocurricular programme of Quaker studies, spiritual formation, leadership development, and mentoring. It was created to mimic the Quaker culture that served for 300 years to provide such formation through vital meeting communities, Quaker education, and home life—but which began disappearing in the mid-twentieth century. Its success in creating such a culture of Quaker community produced a new generation of YAFs equipped to provide leadership for the broader RSOF. Other Quaker colleges in the United States, such as George Fox and Earlham, have recently established similar programmes, to some extent modelled after Guilford's programme.

The term 'Convergent Friends' was first applied as a term for a cross-boundary Quaker renewal group by Robin Mohr in 2006. Described as comprised of the politically liberal end of the Evangelical spectrum, the Christian end of the Unprogrammed spectrum, and the outgoing end of the Conservative spectrum, Convergent Friends utilized social media especially to form a 'virtual community' that bridged all Quaker boundaries and promoted a deeper understanding of Quaker heritage and authentic religions life. In some cases, young adult Friends created real communities, one notably emerging in West Philadelphia in the early 2000s, with many of its members assuming leadership roles in Friends institutions. In the United States, a Quaker Voluntary Service organization was developed in 2012, with a first unit in Atlanta staffed by Quakers recently graduated from college; the first executive director of QVS, Christina Repoley, was in her early thirties. Participants came from across the Quaker spectrum.

A BRITISH CASE STUDY OF YOUTH COMMUNITY

Simon Best spent five years researching teenage Quaker religiosity and ran surveys, group interviews, and individual interviews with 418 teenage British Quakers attending residential events and set to analyse his data (Best 2010). These were committed Quakers,

85 per cent stating that their involvement in Quakerism was either quite important or very important to them. However, nearly 60 per cent also said that other adolescents were the group of Quakers with whom they felt most affinity. Meeting together at residential events was thus key for the nurture and affirmation of this faith identity, technology allowing those networks to be sustained between-times across the miles, what Best calls a 'continuing community' (Best 2008a, 195).

Worship and ritual is very important to these young Quakers. It is based in silence and seated in a circle as it is for the adult group, but without some of the formalization of the worship process developed by the adults, such as standing to 'offer ministry', or the role of (only) the elders to end worship. Young Quakers hardly ever stood up to speak and the formal handshake at the end of adult worship was replaced by hugs and by the whole group joining hands. Worship ritual is thus less differentiated between participants. It is also more fluid in its form and gave more place to dance, song, and music generally. Unlike the adult group, speech or non-silence is given equal value to silence. Best concludes that a 'culture of contribution' operates rather than a 'culture of silence'.

This culture of contribution affects patterns of believing. Rather than belief being a marginal and often invisible category as in the older Quaker group, only uncovered when sociologists run belief surveys, the freedom to share belief-stories increases the acceptance and knowledge of theological diversity. Changes in theology are overt. Belief is not so much marginal as not relevant as a discrete category of conversation. Adolescent Quakers are post-doctrinal (and as it happens non-Christian). Of the 41 per cent who claimed they believed in God and the 40 per cent who said they were not sure, participants gave twenty-seven different descriptions of God in response to a single survey question. Questions of belief, so enthusiastically discussed by sociologists of adult Quakerism, become irrelevant in the study of youth Quakerism. Key terms to older Quakers such as the idea of 'that of God in everyone' have been reinterpreted in a variety of ways.

Values have taken the place of belief in the creation of Quaker identity for these young people but these are also individualized. A commitment to their mutual wellbeing was a value shared by all and Best has developed the concept of a 'community of intimacy' to describe the social dynamic within the group:

> The core features of a Community of Intimacy are that: 1) the members of the group feel a sense of belonging and affiliation to the group; 2) the group has a set of shared values which are expressed in internal and external behaviour; 3) this behaviour contributes to feelings of difference between the Community of Intimacy and other groups which it is juxtaposed to; 4) this results in the group occupying separate physical and psychological spaces. (Best 2008a, 192)

Community is highlighted and encouraged to create a self-identity that is self-policed and is perceived as countercultural or non-worldly, potentially world-rejecting (Wallis 1984).

This sense of sectarian difference is shared with the older Quaker group but, critically, these young Quakers also feel different from adult Quakers, who, of course, are no longer bullied for their beliefs and who, to the younger Quakers, do not live their faith so openly or radically. It appeared as if the habitus of older Quakers was less differentiated from wider society and less developed in discrete terms than the younger Quaker one. Older Quakers went to Meeting (worship) and talked about God, younger Quakers lived their ideas and beliefs in every-day networked community. As Best writes:

> The adolescent Quaker group has both a high level of internal integration and a high degree of differentiation from other groups (Fenn 1997, 41). Adolescent ritual involves the creation of a separate space that reflects an ideal social order and the transformation of individuals to being members of the adolescent Quaker group, the Community of Intimacy. (Best 2008a, 209)

Best identifies a 'triple culture' amongst the younger group formed by 'ritual', 'networked community', and 'narrative and behaviour'. This triple culture creates and preserves a sense of separate space, and maintains and sustains the community of intimacy. Thus adolescent Quakers are not Quakers by reference to their older coreligionists but with reference to their own sense and creation of a distinctive Quaker identity. They are Quaker because they say they are. In other research, Best shows that both older and younger Quaker groupings operate sect-like characteristics in relation to the world, but that the adolescent group is more demanding, more sectarian, and maintains a sectarian attitude even towards the adult group—it is not just world-rejecting but parent-body–rejecting. It is a 'hidden sect', a sect within a sect (Best 2008b, 112). However, this sectarian attitude is hidden by the rhetoric of the older group claiming that youth and adults are part of the same large group, that the young are the future Quakers of tomorrow.

Best argues that the older Quaker group idealizes 'their' young as part of the same cultural and doctrinal formation without listening to the concerns and aspirations of these young people. Best called this process 'empty co-option' (2008b, 110).

YOUNG FRIENDS IN THE GLOBAL SOUTH

In areas of the world where Quaker missionary activity established a Friends presence—Africa, Latin and Central America, and the Pacific Rim—young people were typically served in the manner introduced by the culture of the missionaries. In Kenya, an industrial school was begun shortly after Friends arrived in 1902; at mid-century, a theological school was begun to train leadership; by 2011, there were nearly 1,400 primary and secondary schools started by Friends in the country.

There are no summer camps or 'vacation Bible schools' in Kenya as in the United States. Youth conferences are held, but not in all Yearly Meetings. Congregational youth groups and a Kenya-wide young adult group (Young Quakers Christian Association) have prepared young Friends for sharing leadership with their elders, but it continues to be almost exclusively male, restricted to worship leading on occasion, and youth are excluded from decision-making.

Although Quakers in Africa overwhelmingly practise a programmed form of worship, it is still strongly influenced by the less 'lively' form introduced by the early missionaries. As Pentecostal and charismatic groups have spread, they have attracted large numbers of Quaker youth. Meetings have slowly adapted to try to keep their youth—and where Kenyans themselves have started new missions, local customs such as clapping, dancing, and exuberant expression have been encouraged in worship. Youth in programmed African meetings have also formed their own associations, both for experiencing a more 'spirited' worship and for outreach. The theology continues to be orthodox and evangelical, with an emphasis on Jesus Christ as Saviour; more liberal forms of Quakerism, with their openness to diverse (or no!) theologies and more tolerant views of social issues, are foreign.

Similar to the Quietist period, when recorded ministers, elders, and overseers determined the parameters of Quaker faith and practice, and in Kenya, where similar authorities maintained the faith that Western missionaries had brought, youth in Bolivia have chafed at the control exercised over them. One young Bolivian Friend has written, '... in the years 1999 and 2000 the youth... got together for the purpose of strengthening ourselves and strengthening the Quaker community, but none of the elders wanted to take responsibility for us... they only spoke about this "no" and that "yes"' (Conti et al 2010, 295). Not unlike the revivals in the Midwest and South in the mid-1800s, Bolivian youth gathered themselves apart from the elders, and began worshipping together and assuming their own leadership.

Several young female Bolivian Quaker teachers have made connections with North American Quaker schools through the Quaker Bolivia Link and, in spite of the primarily liberal orientation of the schools, these evangelical women have gained leadership skills and an openness to the wider Quaker world that have been taken back to their home country. Many young people from Asian, African, and other Latin American mission fields have also sought educational opportunities in European and North American institutions, where they are exposed to different interpretations of Quakerism and often struggle to interpret that back to the more homogenous Quakerism of their countries of origin.

CONCLUSION

For its first two hundred years, the Religious Society of Friends enjoyed a nearly uniform transatlantic culture. Similar books of discipline, travelling ministers, elders, and overseers, and a seamless integration of home, school, and Meeting provided a 'guarded' formation of Quaker youth. Separations in the early nineteenth century began a process, which, along with momentous social changes in the West, led to growing divisions in the understanding of preparing youth for their role among Friends. Evangelical Quakers saw the need for personal conversion, the authority of the Bible, and growth in Christian beliefs. Those who began in opposition to Evangelical influences and later were labelled as 'liberal' emphasized the sufficiency of the Inward Light, the authority of the Spirit, and a more social and political focus on the meaning of the traditional testimonies of Friends.

Without a religious hierarchy of bishops and ordained clergy, Friends were influenced by the prevailing culture, their provincial understanding of Quaker doctrine, and the proclivities of local leadership. Quaker schools, youth activities, camping programmes, First-day (Sunday) School curricula, and even national and international conferences took on varying social and religious emphases, depending on the dominant leaders and cultural influences.

Evangelical Friends view the young person as needing salvation through the work of the historical Jesus Christ, with Quaker distinctives secondary to an Evangelical Christian faith. Liberal Friends see 'salvation'—if they even use such a term—as an organic process of living up to the Inward Light and letting one's life 'preach' the integrity of the Quaker testimonies. Historical biblical and Christian teaching is not emphasized. When they come into contact with each other in settings that promote open and sustained worship, community, and dialogue, sometimes each feels short-changed by what was missing in their upbringing.

Occasional attempts at bridging the differences through cross-branch activities succeeded for a time but typically foundered on non-negotiable beliefs and practices. Growing absolutism in the wake of the enormous cultural upheaval of the 1960s led to further splintering of the practices and attitudes of Quaker youth and young adults. Whether the Convergent Friends movement of the early twenty-first century or programme models such as Guilford College's Quaker Leadership Scholars Programme will prove to be exceptions remains to be seen.

SUGGESTED FURTHER READING

Blake, B. and Watts, C. *Can We ALL Be Friends?* Personally produced DVD, 2005. Available through Quaker Books.

Conti, A., Curtis, C., Daniels, C. W., Hart, H., Hoggatt, S. K., Jadin, E., Lomuria, J. E., Mamani, E. C., McQuail, K., and Miller, R. A. (eds.) *Spirit rising: Young Quaker voices*. Philadelphia: Quakers Uniting in Publications and Quaker Press of Friends General Conference, 2010.

Hallward, S. and Hallward, M. *Young Adult Friends, the 'present' of Quakerism*. Southeastern Yearly Meeting, annual Michener Lecture, 2010.

Homan, W. J. *Children and Quakerism*. Berkeley, California: Gillick Press, 1939.

Jay, A. *The autobiography of Allen Jay*. Richmond, Indiana: Friends United Press, 2010.

Jones, T. E. *Light on the horizon*. Richmond, Indiana: Friends United Press, 1973.

Levy, B. *Quakers and the American Family*. Oxford: Oxford University Press, 1988.

Young Friends General Meeting. *Who do we think we are? Young Friends commitment and belonging*. London: Quaker Home Service, 1998.

PART IV

....

QUAKER EXPRESSION

....

CHAPTER 32

QUAKERS AND PRINT CULTURE

BETTY HAGGLUND

THE 1640s and 1650s in England saw a remarkable burgeoning of printed books and pamphlets and the fledgling Quaker movement took full advantage of and added to this growth. Quakers began to publish their ideas in tracts, broadsheets, and books in late 1652; by the end of 1656 nearly 300 Quaker titles had been issued (Peters 2005, 1). This chapter focuses on the distinctive ways in which Quakers made use of the opportunities afforded by contemporary developments in print culture during the earliest period of Quakerism; it then discusses some significant features of the later periods.

SEVENTEENTH-CENTURY PUBLISHING

Religious publishing in the 1630s had predominantly focused on large runs of officially approved publications such as the Authorized Version of the Bible, the Book of Common Prayer, psalters, and catechisms. In the 1640s, however, 'this production was either severely curtailed or brought to an abrupt end' (Green and Peters 2002, 67). The political and religious turbulence during the Civil War and the period immediately following it meant that for many publishers it was both easier and more lucrative to concentrate on publishing the many shorter works produced by the new political and religious groups that were springing up on an almost daily basis.

An analysis of extant books printed in Britain and printed overseas in the English language between 1475 and 1665, measured by titles:

> ...shows a steady growth until about 1640, followed by a sharp and sustained increase, one that is shaped by fluctuations for the following quarter-century.... The years 1641–60 reflect the fierce and contestatory book culture of the civil wars in Britain, and the use of books by parties in involved in those wars in order to recruit public opinion. (Raymond 2011, 60; see also Barnard and Bell 2002)

While many people saw these pamphlets and broadsheets as ephemeral items to be read one day and then used the next day to line cake tins, to light fires, or as toilet paper, there were those who saw them as evidence of the political and religious changes happening all around them and chose to collect that evidence before it disappeared.

From late 1640 until 1661, the Presbyterian bookseller George Thomason (1602–66) systematically collected books, pamphlets, and newspapers issued in London, and as many as he could obtain from the provinces and abroad. His collection of printed material, now at the British Library, contains between 22,000 and 30,000 items Although the collection does not include every item published during those years and is far from comprehensive as far as Quaker books and tracts are concerned, it does give a good indication of the range and scope of publications and provides an insight into contemporary feeling, opinion, interests, and events (Fortescue 1908; Spencer 1958). Similarly, the London wood-turner Nehemiah Wallington (1598–1658) collected godly petitions to Parliament; the military administrator Sir William Clarke (1623–66) collected newsbooks (Mendle 2002, 202). From the 1670s, Quakers systematically collected and catalogued two copies of every book published by Quakers and one copy of every anti-Quaker book, a collecting policy that forms the basis of the library of Britain Yearly Meeting today. While the activities of the collectors provide useful access to the pamphlets of the 1640s and 1650s, they may also distort the numbers, giving the sense that the increase in publication and printing in the 1640s was larger than it was in actuality. Even with the collections, survival rates for books and other printed material are difficult to assess. As suggested above, the timeliness and immediacy of much ephemeral publication may lead it to be rapidly discarded. Repeated readings of fragile pamphlets may damage them beyond usefulness. Events such as the Great Fire of London in 1666 may have destroyed entire print runs. Joad Raymond has suggested that perhaps as few as two-thirds of the items printed in this period survive today (2011, 60).

Raymond has further argued that to measure print output purely by numbers of titles is a crude measure that may not accurately reflect the situation and that the changes in output had more to do with types of publication than with quantity:

> The increase in the number of titles indicates a move away from substantial works, long octavos and folios towards shorter quartos and broadsides. The number of square inches of paper may have varied little but the way that paper was employed changed considerably. Bookstalls were filled with small inexpensive pamphlets and newsbooks.... In other words the peaks ... reflect a move towards pamphlets and an increase in the words spilling from the presses. (Raymond 2003, 168)

A number of factors have been suggested as reasons for the apparent explosion of print. Printing press technology had improved greatly since the fifteenth century. The earliest presses were capable of producing 300 impressions a day; by the 1620s, some presses were able to produce 250 impressions an hour (Achinstein 2001, 52; see also Moran 1973). The collapse of state censorship and control of the press was certainly a factor, although it has been argued that it was less significant than historians such as Christopher Hill and Keith Thomas have claimed (McKenzie 2002, 560; Hill 1985; Thomas 1986). Another factor was the spread of literacy and of book ownership. The Protestant religion was committed to the principle of universal and democratic access to Scripture. The numbers of Bibles and other religious books published grew steadily from the sixteenth century onwards and they were produced at prices that made them available to large segments of the population. Children who did not go to school were taught to read by parents or neighbours and those who could not read themselves listened to those who could. There is considerable evidence that even men and women of modest means frequently owned at least one or two religious books, especially Bibles (Laqueur 1976; Spufford 1981, 19–45).

QUAKER PUBLISHING IN THE SEVENTEENTH CENTURY

From the earliest days of the movement, Quakers actively used print and the written word as one of the ways they communicated their message and it contributed to the speed with which the movement spread. 'This is the day of thy Visitation, O Nation', wrote Edward Burrough in 1654, 'wherein the Lord speaks to thee by the mouth of his Servants in word and writing' (cited in Corns and Loewenstein 1995, 1). Alongside their use of the written word to proselytize, it served to help the early movement establish its own identity, bringing together a geographically dispersed membership. Print was equally important when it came to refuting opponents and answering the many attacks upon them and 'pamphlet debates' occupy a substantial place in the printed output of early Friends.

The first Quaker tracts appeared in late 1652 or early 1653. According to Moore, there are no surviving Quaker pamphlets that can be definitely dated to 1652, although a letter from Richard Farnworth to Margaret Fell dated December refers to 'the printing of three hundred books that were now in use and being publicly read'. The 291 titles by nearly a hundred named authors that had appeared by the end of 1656 represent an average of more than one a week. By 1666 approximately 1300 texts had appeared, varying from single-page broadsheets to substantial books, and between 1666 and 1699 they continued to publish at a rate of approximately seventy-five items per year (Peters 2005, 3, 21; Moore 2000, 20, 231, 241–2; Green and Peters 2002, 70–1).

While many Quakers, both women and men, wrote and published, and writings by Quaker women contributed in significant numbers to Quaker publications, George Fox was by far the most prolific writer over the entire period 1652–66, although before the Bristol incident of 1656, James Nayler published more books and tracts each year than did Fox. Most authors wrote fewer than three works. As Ian Green and Kate Peters have shown, there was a close relationship between manuscript and print. 'Many early printed tracts originated as manuscript letters written by itinerant ministers to meetings they had visited or to each other, letters offering encouragement and providing news of how other Meetings were faring.... As they travelled, establishing Meetings and appointing local figures to continue their work, they carried each other's books and manuscripts and wrote more of their own; as they were imprisoned for their preaching, they encouraged local sympathizers and fellow prisoners to join with them in helping to secure publication of their "sufferings"' (Green and Peters 2002, 71–2). A 1653 multi-authored tract, *A Brief Discovery of a Threefold Estate of Antichrist, now extant in the World* included a copy of a long letter sent by James Nayler in October 1652 to 'friends', and thereafter, printed letters containing Quaker news became commonplace. A collection of letters written by travelling ministers was published in late 1654 as *Severall letters written to the saints most high* (Peters 1995, 13).

In the early years, prophetic works and proclamations addressed to those outside the movement formed the largest proportion of Quaker printed works. Alongside these were epistles to Friends or Meetings, disputes with other groups, and responses to attacks, accounts of persecutions and sufferings, and appeals to the government including petitions. Books were used as part of missionary work in Britain and Ireland and abroad in Barbados, Holland, and Germany during the 1650s. Later in the century more autobiographical works and an increasing number of memorial volumes and volumes of collected works were printed (Runyon 1973; Bell 1988; Gill 2005; O'Malley 1979).

Like *A Brief Discovery,* many Quaker texts were multi-authored. Work by two or more single authors might be published in a single pamphlet or book; single-handed writing could be embedded within a larger work by another author; sometimes texts were written collaboratively and signed by multiple authors. Catie Gill has argued that these collaborative accounts produced a sense of community through print, 'implicitly unit[ing] Friends around an issue, or a series of concerns, within a single work' (2005, 7; see also Bell 1990, 260–2). Luella Wright has spoken of the 'group consciousness', which permeated the writings of early Friends (1966, 10).

Early Quaker books were printed in relatively small numbers, 'in runs of 300 or even 100 for a pamphlet specific to a locality, though by 1656, runs of 600 were agreed' (Green and Peters 2002, 73). The production and distribution of the printed works were controlled by a small group of men and women. One of the most significant in the earliest days was Thomas Aldam (1616–60), who spent 1652 to 1654 in prison, organizing the printing and distribution of books. From the beginning, Aldam urged Friends to take advantage of the potential of printing, arguing that 'Bookes [are] very servisable for weake friends, and Convinceing the world', and suggesting that Friends should make efforts to 'keepe the markets in your County with Bookes ... Make some Contribution amongst you'. Prior to the establishment of a London Quaker base, Thomas Aldam and Margaret Fell between them coordinated most Quaker publications; once there was a central London office, most of the management of the process of publishing and printing was based there (Peters 1995, 50–1).

Seventeenth-century Printers and Publishers of Quaker Works in England

From the beginning, virtually all English Quaker pamphlets were printed in London. Early printers and publishers of Quaker works included Giles Calvert (c. 1612–63) and Elizabeth Calvert (d. 1675?), Thomas Simmonds (b. 1618?), Robert Wilson, Mary Westwood (d. 1667), Andrew Sowle (1628–95), and Tace Sowle (1666–1749). The Calverts were well-known publishers of radical and sectarian literature through the 1640s and 1650s. Although not Quakers themselves, they produced a sizeable quantity of Quaker literature and organized networks of distribution, forwarding letters and parcels to travelling ministers, and dispatching books to provincial distributors. After the death of Giles Calvert in 1663, Elizabeth Calvert continued the business until her own death in 1675.

From 1656, an increasing amount of Quaker publishing was handled by Thomas Simmonds (sometimes spelled Simmons), a Quaker who worked from the main Quaker meeting house in London called the Bull and Mouth. His wife Martha Simmonds (1624–65), the sister of Giles Calvert, was a Quaker writer and activist disowned by Fox for her involvement in James Nayler's 1656 ride into Bristol and her general involvement in factional disputes. In December 1656 Giles Calvert was one of eighty-seven signatories to a petition for remitting the remaining part of James Nayler's punishment (Hessayon, 2004). By 1657 Simmonds was printing more than Calvert, including most of Fox's works and in 1659 Simmonds' total production for Friends was nearly 120 items. After the Restoration, Simmonds' output fell away, although he continued publishing Quaker works until 1662. As Simmonds began to print less, Robert Wilson became the main Quaker publisher, publishing over 200 works for Friends over the next seven years. Mary Westwood published work by Quakers from the southern counties from 1659 to 1663, including the women's tithe petition of 1659 and writings by those imprisoned at Winchester (Bell 1988).

Andrew Sowle began printing for Friends around 1672. His daughter Tace Sowle succeeded to the business in 1691 and became the leading Quaker printer and bookseller of her generation. She printed and distributed works by virtually all of the founders of Quakerism, including Fox, Fell, Barclay, Nayler, Penn, and Penington, and continued to print Friends' books until the 1740s. Alongside this she handled virtually all the routine business printing for Quakers, such as the Yearly Meeting Epistle, printed in a run of 1,000 copies annually. She took responsibility for both national and international distribution, shipping Quaker books and tracts throughout Britain and Ireland, to continental Europe, to the American colonies, and the Caribbean. In 1736 she employed a relative, Luke Hinde; in 1739 he became her partner in the business, succeeding her after her death at the age of 84 in 1749 (McDowell 2004).

Printers and booksellers issuing Quaker books in the early decades ran considerable risks. Robert Wilson spoke of having been very often 'plundered by the Rulers of my goods' who burned his books both 'at home and abroad'. In 1661 he was jailed for selling 'seditious pamphlets' and the books in his shop were seized. Andrew Sowle's shop was repeatedly searched and his printing press broken to pieces (Wright 1966, 95; Anonymous 1908).

SEVENTEENTH- AND EARLY EIGHTEENTH-CENTURY QUAKER BOOKS IN AMERICA

From the mid-1650s Quaker missionaries travelled from England to New England carrying tracts and books. These were initially unwelcome; Mary Fisher and Anne Austin had their books confiscated when they arrived in Boston in 1656. Despite this, Quaker missionaries produced handwritten texts, copying out letters and tracts, and circulating them among converts and sympathizers. Copies of some of these letters were carried back to England and subsequently published (Hall 2008, 67–9). Quaker books, some sent personally by George Fox, continued to arrive in the colonies (Hall 2000, 127).

As the decade went on and Quaker settlements were established, American Quakers published far less than English Quakers. From 1683 until 1776, only thirty-four Pennsylvania and New Jersey Quakers published tracts, journals, or broadsides (Frost 1991, 3). Some English Quaker books were republished in America, having first been approved by a Philadelphia Yearly Meeting committee called 'Overseers of the Press', set up in 1691:

> In theory the Overseers received copies of all English Quaker books. They were then free to decide which were suitable for reprinting and contracted with printers to whom they guaranteed a certain number of sales at a given price. These books the Yearly Meeting passed out to monthly and quarterly meetings on either a quota or subscription basis. (Frost 1991, 7)

For the most part, however, American Quaker colonists relied on the importation of books from England. The colonists had the choice of either buying books through a local bookseller or ordering directly from England. The mark-up added by colonial booksellers was high—Virginia booksellers, for example, added up to 41 per cent to the original price—but buying directly from England was slow, with shipments taking up to six months to arrive.

There were seven lending libraries within the geographical area of Philadelphia Yearly Meeting and these, along with Meeting libraries, were a major source of reading material for local Quakers. By the 1740s, members of most Meetings would have had access to copies of Sewel's *History*, Barclay's *Apology*, a few autobiographical accounts by English Friends, Ellwood's *Scriptural History*, and Penn's *No Cross, No Crown* (Frost 1991, 12–15).

SELF-REGULATION OF PUBLISHING

From the earliest days, Quakers took some corporate responsibility for what was published in their name. As time went on, local Friends' Business Meetings increasingly took on responsibility not only for the regulation of publishing but also arrangements for printing, proofreading, finance, and distribution. During the Restoration, the Quakers were the most heavily prosecuted non-conformist sect in England, with over fifteen thousand Friends sent to prison (McDowell, 1996, 252). Friends became more cautious; concern grew for the reputation of the Society and, as David Hall has argued, 'Quaker enthusiasm had to be curbed ... as it became evident that intemperate, inaccurate, repetitive works could discredit Friends' (1992, 60).

In 1672, Yearly Meeting appointed ten Friends to control the publishing of books under the name of the Society. All books were to be carefully corrected; no new book or new edition of an old book could be published without approval. The committee was to decide the number of books that were to be sent to each county and to whom they were to be sent. Books were to be sent abroad only when a printer had been instructed by the committee to do so.

The work of this small committee was limited to seeing books through the press, but in 1673, upon returning from America, George Fox set up the Second Day Morning Meeting (Quakers used numbers rather than names for days of the week and months of the year; the Second Day Morning Meeting therefore met on Mondays). This group of influential male Friends supervised and censored printing, and controlled ministry in the London area (Braithwaite 1921, 279–81, 495). The members of the Second Day Morning Meeting were to formulate replies to attacks from Quaker opponents, and they were to judge the diction, rhetoric, and acceptability of the manuscripts submitted to them (Wright 1966, 97). Manuscripts were read aloud during the meeting, with the committee deciding line by line which passages were to be altered or omitted (McDowell 1996, 252). Books rejected for immediate publication were either sent back to the author for revision or rejected outright. Quaker printers were to be advised against printing or advertising books not approved by the Meeting (Coudert 1999, 262).

In 1675, in response to the large-scale imprisonment of Friends, Meeting for Sufferings was established to record and respond to the sufferings of Friends. This group also became involved in coordinating the practicalities of the printing and distribution of the books approved by the Second Day Morning Meeting.

These three bodies, Yearly Meeting, Second Day Morning Meeting, and Meeting for Sufferings, together controlled the Quaker press, a control that reflected the changes being directed by Fox, Fell, and other leading Friends after 1668, as they attempted to give the movement greater institutional and organizational strength and structure (see chapter 2 within this volume by Richard Allen entitled 'Restoration Quakerism, 1660–1691'). Critics, both inside and outside the movement, commented on these changes. Writing in 1675, former Quaker William Mucklow (1630?–1713) complained that 'the

Quakers have for some years formed themselves into a kind of Politic-Ecclesiastick Body, and have held their Meetings for matters of Government, every Monday, or Second day of the Week' and referred to a 'Paper' which stated that:

> ...if any person had (as he thought) a command from God, to do a thing, or to put forth a thing in Print, he must first come and lay it before the Body, and as they judg, he must submit ...Herein the ground of our Liberties is taken from us (to wit) To live, act and judg according to the Law within. (1675, 18)

William Rogers (d. 1711?) was a significant Bristol Quaker who, during the 1670s, challenged Fox principally on the grounds that the activities of the Friends in Westmorland were being restricted by the movement's leaders in London (Gill 2004). Rogers denounced the Second Day Morning Meeting as 'uncertain Numbers, of uncertain qualified Persons, who ...pretend themselves to be vested with spiritual power to correct or suppress what is brought before them' (1681, 7–8). Mucklow, Rogers, and other opponents of the organizational changes were answered in books and pamphlets by Fox's supporters, including George Whitehead, Thomas Ellwood, Anne Whitehead, and Mary Elson (Gill 2004), and a pamphlet war grew up within the Quaker movement, paralleling those between Quakers and other sects.

Thomas O'Malley suggests that at least one third of Quaker publications between 1674 and 1688 were considered by Second Day Morning Meeting and/or Meeting for Sufferings before publication. Between 1674 and 1688, approximately 20 per cent of the manuscripts submitted to the committees were rejected, usually by Second Day Morning Meeting (Meeting for Sufferings tended to focus more on practical aspects of printing and publication) (O'Malley 1982, 83). A survey of the later period, 1691 to 1695, shows '73 titles accepted, 19 not accepted and 7 where reservations were expressed' (Hall 1992, 65). During the same period 236 Quaker publications seem to have appeared—a similar ratio to that suggested by O'Malley for the earlier period. (The calculation of numbers of Quaker publications is based upon David Runyon's analysis of types of Quaker writings by year as cited in Hall 1992, 66.)

Many of the works that were accepted for publication were still recommended for further revision or editing. In 1680, for example, the Second Day Morning Meeting minutes record:

> Richard Robinsons paper to the unmarried hath been read And Friends Judgment is that it is unsafe for it to goe as it is, But is the Advice of the meeting he be writ to, that if he will leave it to friends to correct it hee may write his mind thereon and Friends may correct it. (Minutes, Second Day Morning Meeting. 31st of 11th month, 1680/81; cited in Hall 1992, 67–8)

Texts already printed by Friends could be suppressed if the committee no longer felt them appropriate, or sent for correction and re-editing. New editions of previously printed texts were reread and reassessed. When Isaac Penington's works were being reprinted in 1680–1, it was ordered that a number of underscored lines in one text must 'be wholly left out of all Impressions; Ben Clarke to take care therein' (McKenzie, 1976, 33, cited in Hall 1992, 64). Benjamin Clark[e] was a Quaker printer who was cautioned on several occasions about printing only what was approved by Second Day Morning Meeting (Mortimer 1948, 38–41; Coudert 1999, 262–3).

Even George Fox's works were reviewed by the Second Day Morning Meeting, a fact that caused him considerable annoyance when a paper of his on the Wilkinson-Story controversy was refused circulation in 1676:

> I was not moved to set up that meeting to make orders against the reading of my papers; but to gather up bad books that was scandalous against Friends; and to see that young Friends' books that was sent to be printed might be stood by; and to see where every one had their motion to the meeting that they might not go in heaps; and not for them to have an authority over the Monthly and Quarterly and other Meetings or for them to stop things to the nation which I was moved of the Lord to give forth to them. (Fox to London Women Friends, 28 April 1676, cited in Braithwaite 1919, 280)

It is difficult to ascertain with certainty the extent of the influence that Second Day Morning Meeting had on Quaker writing. Only a few manuscripts have survived as they were when submitted to the Meeting. Changes in prose style need to be seen within a broader context. As Luella Wright has argued, 'the simplification noted in the writing of the Friends in respect to word choice and sentence structure accords with tendencies also observable in contemporary writers in the last half of the age of Dryden and of the Queen Anne period' (1966, 100).

Nonetheless, there is considerable evidence in both the minutes of the Morning Meeting and in changes that can be tracked in style and subject matter of Quaker literature to suggest that the internal controls exercised by the Meeting were wide-ranging and extensive:

> By the beginning of the eighteenth century, the old fantastic titles, such as *A Handful after the Harvest-Man* and *A Wren in the Burning Bush, Waving the Wings of Contraction to the Congregated Clean Fowls in the Ark of God* entirely disappear in favour of such carefully considered and officially approved nomenclatures as *The Collected Gospel Labours of John Whitehead*... By 1725 a certain piquancy of style due to the picturesque and homely phrasing, characteristic of the earliest Quaker writers, is lost.... A greater degree of accuracy supplants, comparatively speaking, the former complexity of style. (Wright 1996, 100–1)

Prophetical and mystical texts fell out of fashion. So too did texts by Friends who were critical of other Quakers or their writings. History, biography, autobiography, and doctrinal writing gradually took their place. It has been suggested by many scholars that Quaker women were disproportionately affected by the activities of the Morning

Meeting (see Trevett 2000 and 2004; Tarter 2004; Gill 2005, ch. 5; Wilcox 1995; Larson 1999, ch. 1; Hobby 1988, ch.1). Certainly the increasing opposition to the publishing of prophecy silenced the prophetic voices of Quaker women, which had been such a feature of both writing and speaking during the first decade of the movement. There is evidence for works by specific women being rejected by the Second Day Morning Meeting (Wright 1966, 105–6; McDowell 1998, 156–67; see also Gill 2005, 172–81). Women did, however, continue to publish throughout the seventeenth century. Anne Docwra (1624–1710), for example, described by Paula McDowell as 'an ardent polemicist for religious toleration, the separation of church and state, and women's right to prophesy and testify in public' (1998, 146), published at least seven tracts between 1682 and 1700, and her publisher, Tace Sowle, printed books and tracts by a number of other Quaker women authors. Maureen Bell has argued that the changes in Quaker women's writing at this time reflect the wider changes in Quaker writing more generally (Bell 1990, 260).

Similar mechanisms for controlling what could be published in the name of Quakers existed in the American Quaker colonies. When the English Quaker publisher and printer William Bradford (1663–1752) set up his press in Pennsylvania, he brought with him a letter from George Fox, giving him permission both to print Friends' books and to import them from London for the use of the faithful throughout New England. The letter asked Friends to give Bradford 'encouragements' by arranging for each Meeting to take a certain number of the books he printed and to order their books through him. At the same time, however, Fox ordered that Friends at Philadelphia should act on behalf of the London Second Day Morning Meeting and maintain strict control over Bradford's publishing work.

> You may make an order that he shall not permit any Friend's Books among you but what Friends in the ministry do there approve of; as they do here in England. (McMurtrie 1936, 407; cited in Green 2000, 200)

As soon as Bradford had printed his first work, an almanac, he was called before the Pennsylvania Council and ordered to make changes to all copies of the work and to print nothing 'but what shall have Lycence from ye Councill'. In 1687 he was required by Philadelphia Monthly Meeting to 'show what may concern friends or Truth before printing to the Quarterly Meeting of Philadelphia, and if it require speed then to the monthly meeting where it may belong', and the following year he was directed to collect and destroy all copies of an almanac he had just printed because it contained 'several light and frivolous paragraphs which Friends found offensive' (Johns 1994, 24–5).

Bradford's conflicts with the Philadelphia Quaker establishment continued, culminating in a major dispute over his publishing of works by the controversial Quaker preacher and writer George Keith; in 1692 he was tried and jailed for printing works without an imprint (Winton 2004).

QUAKER PUBLISHING DURING THE EIGHTEENTH AND NINETEENTH CENTURIES

As Russell Mortimer has argued, 'The story of Quaker [publishing] after the seventeenth century is at once less heroic and more complex than that which the Stuart period affords' (1963, 101). With the lapse of the Licensing Act in 1695, the English printing trade, which had previously been limited almost entirely to London, Oxford, and Cambridge, spread into the provinces. By 1850, Quaker books had been published in almost every county in England and Wales. Toleration meant that publishing Quaker books was no longer a risky occupation.

Collectively written deathbed testimonies which sought both to remember the life and to record the death of Quakers had been a significant part of Quaker publishing since the Restoration (Gill 2005, 147–64). In 1701 John Tomkins published a compilation of the deathbed scenes of pious Friends under the title *Piety promoted, in a collection of dying sayings of many of the people called Quakers*. The volume was so successful that a second volume was published in 1702 and by 1740 several compilers had produced seven Parts, which were frequently reprinted. The tenth volume, published in 1810, was reprinted in 1811, 1821, and 1838. As J. William Frost has shown:

> Production of each volume was a collective enterprise. The families and friends of the dying gathered around the bedside for parting advice. The monthly meeting commissioned someone to write a memorial to the deceased which was read in the meeting and then forwarded to London where it might be read aloud in a session of the Yearly Meeting. Eventually, the memorial might be incorporated into the next book. (1991, 18)

By contrast, only one minor compilation of American Quaker deathbed scenes was published before the Revolution and the first American edition of memorials of public Friends was not published until 1787.

Piety Promoted was succeeded by the *Annual Monitor*, a list of British Quakers who died each year between 1813 and 1920, including over 20,000 records, compiled from information supplied by Monthly Meetings. Most entries are confined to basic data but some entries include a testimony to the life of the individual, sometimes running to several pages. An American *Annual Monitor* was published from 1858 to 1863.

Much effort went into the collating and publishing of Joseph Besse's *Sufferings* in 1753, a major two-volume collection of accounts of Friends' sufferings and persecutions from the beginning of the movement until the Toleration Act (Knott 1995; Anonymous 1926).

Improvements in printing technology in the nineteenth century made printing much cheaper. Technical improvements in papermaking using steam power meant that large quantities of paper were now available at a lower price than had been the case in the eighteenth century; parallel improvements in printing technology meant that multiple copies could be produced quickly and cheaply. The new technologies, coupled with the schisms and theological controversies in Britain and North America, led to a new increase in Quaker publishing. Friends reissued collections of the writings of early Friends such as the *Works of George Fox*, the *Friends Library*, and the *Friends Miscellany* for their own uses; and the move towards evangelicalism led to a desire to publish material that could be used for proselytization. In the early nineteenth century, Friends began to establish tract associations to print and distribute their texts. The evangelical Religious Tract Society had been founded in 1799, and Friends' tract associations were a Quaker parallel. The Tract Association of the Society of Friends (London) was founded in 1813; so, too, was the Religious Tract Association of Friends in Newcastle-upon-Tyne, and there were dozens of others across the country. The Dublin Tract Association began in 1814. The London group continued until 1935 when it merged with the Literature Committee of London Yearly Meeting. The Newcastle group stopped printing in the mid-nineteenth century. Little is known about the Dublin Tract Association but it is said to have published 250,000 copies of tracts by 1831 (Bronner 1967, 343; Mortimer 1963, 108–9).

In the United States, the Tract Association of Friends was founded in 1816 in Philadelphia and several others soon followed—New York in 1817, Baltimore in 1818, and one covering the western counties of the state of New York in the same year. Friends at Richmond, Indiana started one a few years later. As Edwin Bronner has shown:

> The tract movement originated in a period when there was a shortage of printed material on the frontier and in many foreign lands there was virtually nothing to read. Tracts stood a good chance of acceptance because there was little else available. Friends belonging to Philadelphia Yearly Meeting were receiving virtually no printed material from the Meeting in 1816 ... There was no periodical. Friends did publish some books, but it is clear that a minimum of Quaker printed material reached Friends' homes. (1967, 345)

The American Tract Association of Friends is still in existence, and still printing and distributing Friends' books and pamphlets.

The move towards evangelicalism during the nineteenth century also led to a new interest in Bible reading and distribution. While the Bible had always been read by Friends, the emphasis had primarily been on the ongoing work of revelation, with the Scriptures seen as a declaration of the source and not the source itself. Convinced, however, that 'a want of proper scriptural knowledge' had been one of the primary causes of the Hicksite–Orthodox split among American Friends, the promotion of Bible reading took on a new significance among Evangelical Friends. The Bible Association of Friends in America, founded in Philadelphia at the time of the separation, aimed to place a Bible in every Quaker family and to ensure that every Friend owned at least a copy of the New Testament; by 1840 it was able to report almost complete success in this endeavour (Hamm 1992, 25).

QUAKER PERIODICAL PUBLISHING

The nineteenth-century improvements in printing technology that led to the increase in reprints and tracts also led to an increase in serial and periodical publishing among Quakers. The first edition of the British Quaker periodical *The Friend*, was published on 15 February 1843. Its appearance at that point reflects a general increase in newspaper and magazine production and availability. The 4d tax, which had placed magazines and newspapers out of the reach for many people, had been cut to 1d per copy in 1839. The building of the railways had transformed print distribution networks, giving publishers access to the whole of the country; improvements in the postal services simplified the processes of ordering and payment (Feather 1991, 131–5).

The Friend was not the first or the only Quaker periodical to be produced in the nineteenth century. The scientist and philanthropist William Allen (1770–1843) edited and published the *Philanthropist* (1811–19), and the *Lindfield Reporter* (1835–42), both covering a range of political, educational, and philanthropic issues. While not aimed specifically at a Quaker readership, these magazines circulated widely among Friends. *The Irish Friend*, published from Belfast, targeted a mainland Quaker readership:

> Its opposition to the prevailing evangelical outlook of the Society and its support for radical American anti-slavery groups gave it a minority flavour. Nevertheless it had a wide circulation and in its political fervour and enthusiasm it spoke for a younger generation of provincial Friends who felt increasingly alienated from London Yearly Meeting. (Morton 1993, 7)

The Irish Friend ceased publication at the end of 1842. Two rival monthly publications sprang up almost at the same time. *The British Friend*, published in Glasgow by the Smeal brothers who were supporters of *The Irish Friend*, became the mouthpiece of the more conservative members of the Religious Society of Friends, while the London-based *The Friend* took a more evangelical line. Although the political and theological positions of the two magazines differed, much of the content overlapped. Alongside a wide variety of articles dealing with theological and social concerns, book reviews, and letters to the editor, they carried announcements of births, deaths, and marriages, regular reports from Friends travelling in the ministry, and reports of Quaker missionary activities overseas. Yearly Meeting and Women's Yearly Meeting were given extensive coverage and notices of other meetings of interest to Friends—those relating to anti-slavery, temperance, peace, or adult school activities, for example—were included (Beck 2003, 551; Barber 1993, 71).

In 1867 a third British Quaker periodical, the *Friends' Quarterly Examiner*, was founded, focusing on substantial signed articles rather than short news items and welcoming contributions from all sections of the Quaker community.

The *British Friend* ceased publication in 1913. The *Friends' Quarterly Examiner* became *Friends' Quarterly* in 1947 and is still published as a quarterly; *The Friend* is still published as a weekly magazine for British Quakers.

In the United States, the Philadelphia-based *Friend* began publication in 1827. The *Friends Intelligencer,* a Hicksite publication, began in 1844; the *Friends Review,* a moderate Gurneyite publication, began in 1847; the *Christian Worker,* a Revivalist publication, began in 1871. Other shorter-lived Quaker periodicals included Benjamin Lundy's *Genius of Universal Emancipation* (1821–33) and *The Philanthropist* (1817–22), a weekly magazine published by Charles Osborn and then Elisha Bates.

American Quaker women had their own publications. The longest-lived and most substantial was *The Friends' Missionary Advocate,* which began publication in 1885 and was oriented toward Orthodox Gurneyite Quaker women. In 1976, the name was changed to simply *The Advocate*; it remains in publication today.

The *Friends Review* and the *Christian Worker* merged in 1894 under the editorship of the young Rufus Jones (1863–1948). From 1894, the publication was called the *American Friend* and was targeted at the entire range of American Gurneyite Quakerism. Given the Modernist–Holiness disputes, such breadth did not seem to be entirely workable, so some Evangelical Friends split off to begin the *Soul-Winner* magazine in 1902. This subsequently changed its name to the *Evangelical Friend,* and a journal by this name was published at least sporadically from about 1905 until the publication was discontinued in 1994. In 1955, the *Friend* (Philadelphia) and the *Friends Intelligencer* merged to form the *Friends Journal.* The *American Friend* ceased publication in 1960 and was replaced by *Quaker Life.* Of these publications, only *Friends Journal* and *Quaker Life* are published as of 2012. *Quaker Life* is the denomination organ for Friends United Meeting; *Friends Journal* is not officially aligned with any branch of American Quakerism, but it is published in Philadelphia and is broadly sympathetic to liberal strands of American Quakerism.

Twenty-first Century Quaker Print Culture

Quaker publishing is gradually taking advantage of the possibilities offered by online communications. While initially Friends tended to use the World Wide Web as a means of publicizing their print publications, they are increasingly publishing material directly online. Quaker study centres such as Woodbrooke in England are beginning to develop online study materials; individual blogs and online forums provide new venues for discussion; Quaker publishers are beginning to experiment with e-books and other electronic media.

A number of Quaker bodies either subsidize or control a press, among them Britain Yearly Meeting; Australia Yearly Meeting; North Carolina Yearly Meeting;

Friends General Conference (USA); Pendle Hill (USA); and Friends United Meeting (international; includes Yearly Meetings in North America, East Africa, Cuba, and Jamaica). Other privately run Quaker presses such as Barclay Press, Quaker Heritage Press, and Inner Light Books in the US, and Pronoun Press, the New Foundation Fellowship, and Quacks Books in the UK reflect the wide diversity of worldwide Quakerism today. Begun informally by a small group of Quaker publishers and booksellers in 1983, Quakers Uniting in Publication is an international network of over fifty Friends organizations and individuals concerned with the ministry of the written word.

Twenty-first-century Quakers continue to be prolific periodical publishers. The Quaker library at Friends' House in London currently receives over 200 titles that are mainly Quaker related, ranging from academic titles such as *Quaker Studies, Quaker History,* and *Quaker Religious Thought,* to special interests such as *Towards Wholeness* (Friends Fellowship of Healing), to the newsletters and journals of Yearly Meetings from around the world. Current major periodical titles include *Quaker Life* (Five Years Meeting), *Friends Journal* (liberal American), *The Conservative Friend, The Friend* (BYM), and *Friends Quarterly* (BYM). There are national Quaker periodicals in Kenya, France, Australia, Canada, Nigeria, and elsewhere (Chijioke 2011, 403).

While financial cutbacks and the global recession have affected some Quaker presses and publishing projects adversely, Quakers today nonetheless continue to use the written word in ways and for purposes very similar to those of their seventeenth-century forbears: to communicate their message, to establish their identity and distinctiveness, to bring together a worldwide membership, to explore and debate ethical and spiritual issues. The medium may be changing; the significance of the written word to Quakers remains the same.

Suggested Further Reading

Corns, T. N. and Loewenstein, D. (eds.) (1995) *The emergence of Quaker writing: Dissenting literature in seventeenth-century England.* London: Frank Cass.

Green, I. and Peters, K. (2002) 'Religious publishing in England 1640–1695' in J. Barnard and D. F. McKenzie (eds.) *The Cambridge History of the Book in Britain, vol. IV: 1557–1695,* pp. 67–96. Cambridge: Cambridge University Press.

Hall, D. (2010) 'Spreading Friends Books for Truths Service: the distribution of Quaker printed literature in the eighteenth century', *Journal of the Friends Historical Society,* 62 (1), pp. 3–24.

Hall, D. J. (1992) '"The fiery Tryal of their Infallible Examination": self-control in the regulation of Quaker publishing in England from the 1670s to the mid 19th century', in R. Myers and M. Harris (eds.) *Censorship & the control of print in England and France 160–1910,* 59–86. Winchester: St Paul's Bibliographies.

Mortimer, R. S. (1963) 'Quaker printers, 1750–1850', *Journal of the Friends Historical Society,* 50 (1), pp. 100–133.

Peters, K. (2005) *Print culture and the early Quakers.* Cambridge: Cambridge University Press.

....

CHAPTER 33

QUAKERS AND VISUAL CULTURE

....

ROGER HOMAN

THIS chapter is an exploration of the visual culture of Friends with the principal focus on two-dimensional figurative art and on the architecture and interior décor of meeting houses. From their earliest days and through the subsequent centuries, Quakers have applied a restraint on visual expressions in keeping with other aspects of lifestyle and demeanour. In recent years former taboos have been relaxed along with a reappraisal of what it means to be plain and simple.

THE VIRTUE OF PLAINNESS

....

The early meeting houses conform to no prototype. Many started life as cottages and were adapted for worship. Those that were purpose-built do not exceed such cottages in scale or pretension, and yet, as we may view from the comprehensive set of illustrations offered by Kenneth Southall (1974), there was a ubiquitous character before the emergence of a style.

Attempts to define this normative character are expressed in a limited vocabulary that is sometimes patronizing. Meeting houses are typified by epithets that tell us more about the effect than the intention, such as 'charming', or 'quaint', or 'delightful'. These accolades, which are equally applied to the products of Quaker artists such as Edward Hicks (1780–1849) (Weekley 1999, 212), tell us about the impact but not the rationale. After all, there is no intention to charm or provide a curiosity. A meeting house such as Jordans (1688) in Buckinghamshire or Come-to-Good (1710) in Cornwall is now conspicuously picturesque, not because it was built to be so but because its contemporaries have since vanished.

To identify the normative Quaker aesthetic on the basis of the early Meetings we should look not for the surface of style but for the depth of spirit. We may come to

Quaker visual culture not with formally schooled notions of what constitutes beauty but with a readiness to value externals as the products of internals and to discern the spirit of the community in which it is generated.

Such an attitude to visual culture is associated with leading Victorian writer and critic John Ruskin (1819–1900) who surveyed the architecture of a very different age and culture. For Ruskin and for his collaborator William Morris (1834–96), the dignity of work and the self-esteem of the worker were capacities that Morris aimed to restore in the practice of his company. Good art and craft, they believed, were the products of contented souls. Though seemingly naïve when thus understated, Ruskin elaborated this theory in terms of a cluster of moral and spiritual principles in his *The Seven Lamps of Architecture* (1845).

It is in this way, and not as critics or connoisseurs of art, that we may approach the visual culture of Quakers and note the thinking of George Cadbury in founding the model village of Bournville. The early meeting houses were designed and constructed by faithful people, in the local manner, offering their best skills and the most worthy available materials. They are not distinguished by innovation but they are imbued with Ruskinian virtues such as honesty and integrity. And in time they take on an additional character that cannot be articulated in technical terms: they are hallowed by use. The early meeting house becomes, in the words of the poet T. S. Eliot (1888–1965), a place where prayer has been valid. Meeting houses of the generation of Come-to-Good and the Blue Idol in Sussex have the capacity to calm and rest the spirit of those who visit, be they accustomed to Quaker usage or not.

Descriptions such as 'charming' are particularly deficient in respect of the early period before there was a consciousness of either being visual or constituting a culture. They represent feeble attempts to take intellectual control of the character of meeting houses on the basis of their outward appearance, and not for the values and sensibilities of those who fashioned them. As these inner promptings come to be negotiated, authorized, and legislated, the prospect of an intelligent descriptive vocabulary is more appropriate

The application of fundamental principles will be explored in respect of Quaker behaviour including speech and dress. The focus here is on the dynamic relation of the inward self and the outward expression.

EXPRESSIONS

In the early years (though not always in later times nor among Quakers in countries other than England) it is recognized that simplicity is a desirable interior condition which has as its correlate the behavioural habit of plainness: with implicit approval, London borrowed from North Carolina Yearly Meeting a time-honoured formulation of the ethic of simplicity that is expressed more in terms of an inner quest than of observable habits:

> The heart of the Quaker ethic is summed up in the word 'simplicity'. Simplicity is forgetfulness of self and remembrance of our humble status as waiting servants of God. Outwardly, simplicity is shunning superfluities of dress, speech, behaviour, and possession, which tend to obscure our vision of reality. Inwardly, simplicity is spiritual detachment from the things of this world as part of the effort to fulfil the first commandment: to love God with all of the heart and mind and strength. (Britain Yearly Meeting 2009: 20.27)

It is, however, as a disapproval of the arts that the ethic of simplicity combines with other virtues to impact on visual expression. In the United States, the Quaker sculptress Sylvia Shaw Judson (1982, 2) recognizes that Quakers 'have traditionally held art in distrust'; she attributes this to the norms of representation in the formative years of Quakerism when Englishmen wore ruffs and these were included in their stone effigies. There has been an aversion to art and ornament, and an inhibition of Quakers who, in spite of the exclusion of art and music from the curriculum of Quaker schools, discovered in themselves talents in these pursuits. Barnes (1984, 7) reminds us that as late as 1906 the Book of Discipline severely condemned all the vain pursuits of the arts.

By the beginning of the nineteenth century Friends notice and regret among their number 'a declension from the simplicity of truth' (Homan 2006a, 94). The criterion for this moral judgement was the demise of a former stricture governing outward expressions:

> It is matter of exceeding grief and concern to many of the faithful among us, to observe, how far that exemplary plainness of habit, speech and deportment, which distinguished our forefathers, and for which they patiently underwent reproach and contradiction, is now departed from by too many under our name. (London Yearly Meeting 1802, 134)

The visual culture of any group of believers is subject to a cluster of factors including its core beliefs, the skills and resources of its members, the visual culture of the host society, and the possible desire to assert an independent identity.

It is commonly supposed that the early period was marked by an austere simplicity that was an act of witness against the superfluities of the world: such, for example, is the interpretation of panels C4 and D2 of the Quaker tapestry held at the Friends' meeting house at Kendal in the English Lake District. But even in its heyday, the plain had its dissidents. Margaret Fell (1700) protested that the taboo on colour in dress was 'a silly poor gospel'. Notwithstanding either this view or the standing of its author, this habit of plain dress persists as a stereotype in American cinema. In Harry F. Millande's *The Quack Quaker* (1916) Rosie Pinkhum, who is promoting her talent as a dancer in New York, dresses in a grey gown, screens the pictures in her home, and drapes the statuary to prepare for the visit of her rich Quaker uncle Ezra (Ryan 2009, 65).

The popular stereotypes of the Quaker meeting house are faintly sentimental and attest to a dutiful regard for a moral condition underlying the visual effect. The meeting house is described as simple and modest, as quaint and charming, or as 'plain, dignified and beautiful' (Southall 1974, viii). Not only are these perceptions predominantly visual but they imply a norm from which the Meeting subtracts: this tendency is evident in Robert Sefton's typification of the Quaker meeting houses of New England:

> Simple wood frame, shingled exterior, covered porch at one side, residential in scale, it is unassuming, quaint, passive. It seems to express so well the simple, non-authoritarian, introspective faith of the Friends. The interior is furnished only with the barest wooden pews. There is no altar, no pulpit, no choir, no music, no cushions, nothing worldly to distract them from a *vis-à-vis* connection with God. (Sefton 1972: 206–7)

That these properties of Quaker visual culture are intrinsic to Quaker life and worship is articulated by Sylvia Shaw Judson who characterizes the plain integrity of Quaker meeting houses, with their good proportions, quiet colour, and restful lighting, and the purity of line of their honestly fashioned furniture (Judson 1982: 3).

The interior of the English meeting house is governed not by taste but by purpose. Extremism, whether of opulence or austerity, is not conducive to the resting of the spirit in worship. Accordingly, colour and comfort are moderate and there is a general but not universal absence of pictures and other potential distractions. There are instances in which the budget may have yielded to other considerations in the acquisition of a rug or table, prompting the characterization of meeting-house furnishings as 'typically Quaker: simple, plain and very costly' (Homan 2006b). A conflict of principle arises when an English Meeting is given a wall hanging by African Friends symbolizing the Spirit of the Earth and desires to validate the intentions of its donors without compromising the tradition of its own visual culture (Homan 2006b).

The early meeting houses provide a prototype for subsequent meeting-house design and a model for Quaker aesthetic. Simplicity is expressed in restraint but not in meanness. We have noted that non-Quaker connoisseurs have tended to characterize meeting houses by style rather than by motive, by outward effect, and not by intention.

REGULATION

To the extent that core values are internalized and consensual they produce effects in harmony with the conscientious principles of individuals. The complexion of early Quaker meeting houses attests to this tendency independently of the imposition of what might be called a style. In due time, local and individual manners yield to the negotiated conventions of the wider community. This evolution of religious aesthetic is common to many reformed traditions. It is evident in the departure from Gothic style in the rebuilding of London after the Great Fire of 1666, in the formulated disciple of American Shakers, in the uniformly dignified modesty of Calvinist chapels (Homan 1997). It is partly dictated by liturgical function and partly by the desire within a denominationally differentiated society to present a distinctive profile.

In England there are very few meeting houses that exhibit Gothic features such as a high-pitched roof, pointed windows or bell tower: Exeter and Bournville are rare exceptions. In recent years English meeting-house designs have ventured further from the time-honoured model in such places as Scarborough and Blackheath, while in Houston there is a particularly innovative design at Live Oaks. These departures contrast with the practice of other Christian denominations in which national controls and prescriptions have prevailed over local initiative. Where Quaker Meetings adopt the organizational term 'church' and revert to the corresponding sociological type, a brand emerges: so in America and in missionary fields such as Kenya we may find a tower surmounting the main entrance to the building, albeit without the bell which church towers were originally built to support.

It has not been conformity to a corporate image but the ubiquitous desire to establish meeting houses that would serve the practical purpose of utility and the core value of simplicity. These intentions governed the designs and yielded the distinctive complexions of early Meetings in England and subsequently of New England. They prevail, too, in the thriving churches that follow missionary activity in, for example, Kenya, Honduras, Cuba, and Guatemala. They are typically simple, clean, with white-washed walls, and innocent of gratuitous decoration. Favoured biblical texts and the memorable sayings of early Quakers are sometimes found on the walls, where appropriate translated into Spanish. Here and there in Cuban churches are small pictures remembering those who survived persecutions. If there is a platform, it is for the purpose of amplification rather than hierarchy as it had been in the early English meetings. Outwardly, many meetings have the character of church buildings and a small number of the earliest Meetings (including Kaimosi, Lugulu, and Lirhanda) built by American missionaries have a tower presiding over the main door. In Kenya, seating accommodation is often divided by a central aisle, affording the custom for men and women to sit on different sides. However, more recently some churches have favoured a polygonal design enabling the effect of the circle: examples include Malava, Vokoli, Friends Theological College at Kaimosi, and Friends International Centre in Nairobi.

Among Quakers the most energetic exercise of an aesthetic discipline has been the procedure known as 'plaining', usefully documented by Peter Collins (1996, 2001). He has argued that plainness is the critical element of a Quaker aesthetic, that it has a coherent moral basis, that in the early years plaining was the principle of group identity, and that it continues to be a prominent theme of discourse, even unconsciously, whenever Quakers congregate (Collins 2001, 123).

There are thus two dimensions in the circumspection with which Quakers have approached art and architecture. The one is a consensual ethic of plainness and the other a sectarian rejection of the world and of established religion. In the application of aesthetic principles Quakers have been both rigorous and meticulous.

Detachment from the established order in this context is expressed as a disdain for fashion. It implies a detachment for its own sake from the habits of the world as vices in themselves, such as vanity or superfluity. In the elegant words of the contemporary observer Thomas Clarkson (1760–1846) (2006, 290), 'the adoption of taste instead of utility in this case, would be considered as a conscious conformity with the fashions of the world'.

The rejection of habits for their worldliness endorses the development of plain taste. Ornament itself is offensive and Friends are disturbed to discover it in the homes of their own kind (Homan 2006a, 89). In the early 1690s Joseph Pike of Cork and his cousin Samuel Randall were appointed to inspect homes for 'gospel order': they began by purging their own:

> As to our own clothing we had but little to alter, having both of us been pretty plain in our garb, yet some things we did change to greater simplicity. But my dear cousin, being naturally of a very exact and nice fancy, had things in a more curious order as regards household furniture than I had. Our fine veneered and garnished cases of drawers, tables, stands, cabinets, escritoires, &c, were put away or exchanged for decent plain ones of solid wood without sumptuous garnishing or ornamental work; our wainscots and woodwork we had painted of one plain colour ... Our curtains, with valences, deeply fringed that we thought too fine, we put away or cut off; our large looking-glasses with decorated frames we sold or made them into smaller ones. (Braithwaite 1919, 507)

The tension between the validation of inner light and the external control of visual culture is not peculiar to Quakers. And among the American Shakers, who migrated from English Quakerism and established several communities in the eastern United States, a denominational aesthetic evolves from inward disposition to the realization of a consensus to organizational discipline. For the Shakers too, simplicity has been deeply rooted in the spirit, even celebrated in their hymnody as a 'gift'. Their communal lifestyle was frugal, celibate, uncluttered; their craft and meeting houses were singularly unfussy and serene. Once the aesthetic emerged it came to be legislated in a set of Millennial Laws' in 1821. For the most part, however, Shaker style is claimed as the effect of an inner spiritual condition more than the conformity to consensual principles:

> Beadings, mouldings and cornices, which are merely for fancy, may not be made by Believers. Old or fanciful styles of architecture may not be used among Believers, neither should any deviate widely from the common styles of building among Believers, without the union of the Ministry. The meeting house should be painted white, and of bluish shades within. Houses and [work]shops should be uniform in color as consistent; but it is advisable to have shops of a little darker shade than dwelling houses. Floors in dwelling houses, if stained at all, should be of a reddish yellow, and shop floors should be of a yellowish red. It is unadvisable for wooden buildings fronting the street, to be painted red, brown or black, but they should be of a lightish shade. No buildings may be painted white, save the meeting houses. (Andrews 1953, 285–6)

It is notable here that while the aesthetic of plainness requires the elimination of excess, it simultaneously dignifies what is 'decent' and 'solid'. It is a taste to which the furnishings of many Friends' meeting houses bear witness.

Writing in the early nineteenth century John Barclay expressed some embarrassment at the abiding lack of plainness in Quaker homes:

> I have been almost ready to blush for some, at whose houses I have been, where pier-glasses with a profusion of gilt carving and ornament about them, delicately papered rooms with rich borders, damask table-cloths curiously worked and figures extremely fine, expensive cut glass, and gay carpets of many colours, are neither spared nor scrupled at. (Isichei 1970, 183)

Clarkson, who was not a Quaker but knew many Friends through his involvement with them in the campaign to abolish slavery, evidently visited their homes often. In his reports of the detail and rationality of Quaker habits, he stresses utility and decency as the basic aesthetic principles. It is the purpose 'to be adjudged by the rules of decency and usefulness, but never by the suggestion of show' (Clarkson 2006, 290).

The possession of pictures or portraits was viewed with disfavour well into the nineteenth century: a report of London Yearly Meeting for 1847 has it that these things were considered 'utterly at variance with the known principles of the body' (*The British Friend* 1847, 128). A mirror, of course, is a stumbling-block not merely for its ornamental gilt frame (Isichei 1970, 183) but for the focus it affords upon the self. If a looking glass is the window of vanity, the portrait is the freezing of its image.

During the reign of the profligate King Charles I (1625–49), the royal patronage of distinguished international artists such as Rubens and Van Dyck had been deployed to convey exuberant images of the divinity and grandeur of the monarch, not always to the assent of his subjects. When he was executed the Puritans disposed of his paintings in two ways: those that affected to indentify the monarch with God were deemed idolatrous and were destroyed by being thrown into the Thames, while those that were merely vain were sold abroad to pay the king's debts and ended up in museums such as the Prado in Madrid (Dixon 1996, 71–9).

On the other side of the Atlantic, Johnson (2003) discovers among colonial Quakers of the eighteenth century a widespread practice of sitting for painters, albeit with subtle concessions to the expectation of plain dress. Johnson in Philadelphia and Isichei (1967) in England recognize the tendency of prospering Quaker merchants to assimilate in degrees the habits appropriate to their position in the world. Gathered as testimonies in, for example, the portrait gallery of Bull Street Meeting in Birmingham, Southall's work is to be understood not as deferential portraiture but as Quaker iconography.

The aesthetic attitude embodied in the early meeting houses yields norms which are then given authority and standardized. Excesses are restrained by the practice of 'plaining' for which Meetings appoint members to visit and inspect the homes of other members and direct the removal of gratuitous decoration. This evolution of expression from the individual level to the corporate, parallels the experience of the American Shakers for whom simplicity started out as a gift and was in time formulated as a disciplinary code.

In certain respects, such as the disapproval of portrait-painting on account of the vanity of the sitter, Quakers connected with the Puritan principles in an earlier century and carried this disdain into the nineteenth. The Millennial Laws of Shaker and the Quaker practice of plaining both aim to regulate design by the specification of visual effects such as colour. Both have been preceded by fundamental moral principles which they are intended to protect: in Shaker, for example, 'tis the gift to be simple'. Particularly in the Shaker case, this has evolved a corporate image, which is institutionalized in the Laws.

In Quaker practice, an explicit formulation of the moral basis of design may be found in the instructions given by George Cadbury (1839–1922) to the architect William Alexander Harvey (1875–1951), to whom he entrusted the planning and design of Bournville village. Here in Birmingham were to be the cottages for workers in the chocolate factory. Chocolate, it has to be said, was in itself a philanthropic mission undertaken in England by a number of Quaker families and promoted in its liquid form as an antidote to socially destructive beverages such as gin. Observing that throughout the Industrial Revolution the accommodation of factory workers had been mean, Cadbury's philanthropic mission was to provide homes and gardens that would enhance their dignity and self-respect (Harvey 1906). Architectural details were carefully crafted and a century later these cottages are much sought after. Such enhancements to the complexion of cottages as allowed by Cadbury's principles are not prescribed for the sake of pretension but as a tribute by the sponsor to the residents. They have to do with giving dignity to the factory workers, with the removal from the city to the countryside, with providing an alternative to its amusements, with fresh air and growing vegetables, and in accommodating manual workers alongside 'brain workers' (Harvey 1906, 9–15). To a significant extent, aesthetic restraint concedes to a philanthropic vision.

In common with its direct opposite—ceremony—plaining has the function, conscious at first and subsequently habitual, of impressing upon peers and observers the nature of one's piety and of registering a cultural distance from other human groups. The tendency of outward expression to supplant inward quest has long been a concern of the faithful. Margaret Fell (Glines 2003, 470) famously warned of the danger of supposing that one could become a true Christian by getting into an outward garb. In the analysis of Frost (2003) and Lapsansky (2003) the practice of plaining as a formal discipline with sanctions such as exclusion has been abandoned, not because standards have been relaxed, but because the ethic of plainness has matured in the aesthetic of simplicity.

The paradox of plaining is memorably captured in the succinct words of Margaret Fell: attention to outward expressions will not necessarily guarantee or impact upon the inner life. And outer show that is not underpinned by the qualities it expresses is counted as hypocrisy. On the other hand habitual usage engenders a preference for desirable values: in recent years the discouragement of racist and sexist language has attested to this effect.

The exclusion of cumber is achieved by a rather more radical strategy in the recent work of the Quaker installationist James Turrell (1943–). To the extent that he is not operating by behavioural prescriptions but is seeking a focus upon 'the Light Without', his work may be said to be rather more theological than moral. Turrell has been occupied from childhood with the relationship of the Inner Light and its outwardly visible correlate. In his installations he captures not so much images as effects. They have names such as *Acton* and *The light inside*, and his 1999 exhibition in Jerusalem was entitled *Space that sees*. Most famously he designed the Live Oak meeting house in Texas with a roof space for the observation of the sky, and in 1979 acquired a dormant volcano, the Roden crater, to be adapted as a massive observatory. In his work he attempts to achieve 'a clarity that clears out the dust' and to use 'the light Without [to remind] us of the Light Within' (Mann 1999, 9; Sox 2000, 110–11).

The conscious connection with the effect of light is a purpose in the design of some modern meeting houses, contrasting with earlier prescriptions to exclude distractions (Alexander 1820).

Restraint and laxation

Shifting attitudes in the aftermath of collective discipline may be variously interpreted as the loss of control, the maturing of plainness as simplicity, the accommodation of a burgeoning materialist subculture (Isichei 1964), or the triumph of inward virtues over outward signs.

Some Quakers were to make a career of trimmings and to establish themselves among the more distinguished of Victorian architects. Thomas Rickman (1776–1841) was to be 'the man whose name is most notoriously associated with the era of the 'Commissioners' churches' that followed the Church Building Act of 1818: he designed twenty-one Anglican church buildings (Port 1961, 67). Anglicans cannot easily believe that he was not of their number. He also stands as a significant architectural theorist for it was he who classified and named the orders of Gothic ecclesiastical architecture, which we know as Early English, Decorated, and Perpendicular. His departure from the Society was not altogether the consequence of his art: he wanted to marry his cousin Lucy and had to remove to the Church of England whose table of kindred and affinity allowed such a union.

As a successful architect much patronized by the Established Church, he practised in the Gothic style and for that reason he was less of a loss to Quakers. Hubert Lidbetter, a Quaker architect of the twentieth century, observed:

> It is perhaps fortunate for the Society that he exercised his medieval proclivities in quarters more sympathetic thereto than a Friends Meeting House could be. (Lidbetter 1961, 8)

There are, indeed, several documented cases of Friends in Britain and America who in the nineteenth century encountered a lack of sympathy for their artistic talents and sought it elsewhere or diverted their skills to a more acceptable profession. Alfred Waterhouse (1830–1905), for example, turned architect. He was born near Liverpool in 1830, brought up in a Quaker family and married a Quaker Elizabeth Hodgkin of Lewes in 1858. His inclination was to pursue a career in painting but his parents dissuaded him and he turned to architecture (Smith 1976: 102–21). The civic grandeur for which Waterhouse is celebrated within his profession had no place in the Society: it is exemplified in such designs as the Prudential Assurance Building and University College Hospital in London, Manchester's Town Hall and Assize Court, Brighton's Metropole Hotel, the former Hove Town Hall, and a number of imposing churches (Smith 1976, 102–21).

The rigour of plain taste has not been absolute, nor have exemptions necessarily implied the compromise of simplicity. Exceptions to a hard-and-fast rule include the repeal of a taboo on art education in Quaker schools and the production of sometimes-opulent furnishings by Quaker firms in America.

Samuel Lucas (1805–70) of Hitchin regarded himself to be a born painter, saying that if he had no hands he would have painted with his feet (Isichei 1970, 153): yet for want of commissions by Quaker peers he was obliged to abandon his art and return to the family brewery business. Nor was the virtual discipline of non patronage confined to England. Carolyn Weekley documents the case of the erstwhile painter Edward Hicks (1780–1849). He learnt the skills as a carriage and sign painter and graduated to the easel. It was with the identity of artist that in the early years of the nineteenth century he was admitted to the Society of Friends in Bucks County, Pennsylvania, in due course becoming a valued Gospel minister. But when his former trade failed to secure a sufficient income, he set up business as an ornamental painter. This work was regarded by Quakers as too ostentatious and he was obliged to forsake art for farming. He later declared, 'If the Christian world was in the real spirit of Christ, I do not believe there would be such a thing as a fine painter' (Weekley 2003, 219). Farming also failed him and he returned to art. His rehabilitation within the Society owed something to the avowed rejection of the vanity or portraiture that he had once practised and to his epoch-making *The Peaceable Kingdom*. In his sixty-one versions of this work, vision becomes visual image: the Utopian poem of Isaiah 11 is energized in figurative form and is barely resistible as a witness for peace (Brzostoski 2000).

Changes in attitude may be largely attributed to the leading of particular individuals. The case of Joseph Southall is studied further on in this chapter. Among American Friends Lapsansky looks to the luminary Rufus Jones (1863–1948) for his rejection of the early anti-aestheticism of American Quakers: she notes that in 1932, Philadelphia Yearly Meeting warned against the undervaluing of material culture. Lapsansky (2003, 4) notes that in 1971 a fine arts programme was finally introduced at Haverford College.

NORMS AND DEVIATIONS

The Quaker regard for the material aspects of buildings is distinctive of its Western meetings. In England and the United States there have been meticulous architectural studies of meeting houses (Lidbetter 1946, 1961; Butler 1999). Nowadays, tours are arranged around 1652 Country and the meeting houses of New England. Antiquarian interest is the means of engaging the piety of early Friends. In Africa and Latin America, by contrast, it is not the image of the church building but its current vibrant life that is featured on the website of the Meeting. To that extent, there is not the Western awareness of Friends' accommodation as visual culture.

When two or three are gathered together in silent worship, they are likely to be more aware of and affected by their physical setting than when there are five hundred in chorus. The floor covering, for example, is more apparent to a small contemplative group than to a charismatic congregation. In large-scale programmed worship, a distinctively Quaker visual culture may not be evident, let alone relevant. And if we look too hard for it we will be inappropriately imposing a Western intellectual construct.

Moreover, the notion of culture implies a degree of homogeneity emanating from a particular type. Being driven by the same needs and motives as the early English Friends—opportunism and utility—the scale and complexion of meeting houses are diverse. Whereas the mainstream churches of the colonial powers brought their prototypes with them and commissioned architects from back home, Quaker missionaries such as the three Cleveland Friends who sailed to Mombasa in 1902 and William Abel who sold Bibles in La Paz in 1919 were not committed to a corporate image, although they drew upon familiar motifs.

Thomas Clarkson, who in the early nineteenth century noticed and respected the restraint with which English Quaker homes were furnished, might have discovered less austerity had he ventured into contemporary households in Pennsylvania and the Delaware valley, from which Lapsansky and Verplanck (2003) illustrate extravagant furnishings. Susan Garfinkel (2003) studies the case of Thomas Affleck, a maker of lavish mahogany cabinets with rococo ornamentation. In the 1770s Affleck was 'treated with' by the Monthly Meeting not for his offence against the ethic of plainness but for transgressing the 'Rules of our Discipline and Christian Testimony' by allowing a priest to conduct his marriage. Nor was he the only maker of fine cabinets to be so treated for that transgression. The conspicuous offence against the code of plain speech, dress, and furniture, however, was not treated and Susan Garfinkel speculates on the circumstances of this omission; the patronage of wealthy Quaker merchants may have had something to do with it.

The norms of Quaker aesthetics established in the Western world represent a response to a particular social and cultural milieu. It was therefore not surprising that in England art was provocative of Quaker sensibilities. Before the seventeenth century, art in Europe had centred round a narrow range of biblical themes. In southern and northern Europe respectively, the renowned artists of the Renaissance favoured the themes of the Madonna and the Crucifixion. A more primitive form was to be found as images of saints, angels, and Doom paintings in the parish churches. The royal and aristocratic families then commissioned extravagant and flattering portraits, which hung in their homes.

But these were not the uses to which the visual media have been applied elsewhere outside Europe. At the same time as Friends were adapting cottages as meeting houses or building new ones in a similar modest, domestic, and vernacular style, they were also distancing themselves from the manner of the Established Church. Modesty was itself a protest, albeit a less conspicuous one than habits of dress and speech. In later years Wesleyans and others were to rival the scale and number of parish churches with new buildings of their own, but Friends did not play such a game.

Thus the reticence of the early English archetype of a Quaker meeting house would not serve a more evangelistic movement such as Africa Quaker Vision (Muhanji 1999) or the programmed traditions of Bolivia and Guatemala. The aesthetic sensibilities of the early Quakers were shaped by concerns that were prevalent in and to some extent peculiar to England in the seventeenth century. Elsewhere in the world, colourful dress and personal ornament were not and are not distinctive of privileged or elite groups.

If the prevailing norm for religious buildings in seventeenth-century England had been Gothic, the architectural inheritance for Quakers who settled in Latin America was the sumptuous Baroque of Spain and Portugal, a manner particularly inimical to plain taste (Castedo 1969): neither suited, nor was a contrary corporate style cultivated.

To a significant extent early Quaker practice in Britain provides the foundation of a Quaker aesthetic. Departures from the norm are prompted by the evolution from a sectarian to a denominational tendency (Isichei 1970), to the migration of the aesthetic, and its assimilation throughout the world, and to the tension between the sanctions of the group and the aspirations to self-fulfilment of individuals within it.

From the textual and photographic references assembled by Amelia Mott Gummerle (1901) it is evident that the phenomenon of Quaker plain dress is of long standing but it has not been universally observed. What is of interest in the context of this chapter is not merely the diversity of opinion and practice, but the factors affecting the emergence of a denominational complexion and thence of a stereotype.

While plain dress has been represented as a norm the reality has been more complex. What is at issue is not merely the outward effect but the desirability of a leading from within. If dress is plain, Fell contends, let it be by a leading from within rather than by dint of reproofs by Monthly and Quarterly Meetings: 'We must look at no colours, nor make anything that is changeable colours as the hills are, nor sell them, nor wear them, but we must all be in the one dress and the one colour. This is silly poor gospel.' To challenge the method of collective discipline was not to deride the conscientious practice: George Fox (1698) had urged Friends not to 'run after...every fashion of apparel that gets up; but mind that which is sober and modest'. So plain dress survived as a distinctive marker of Quaker affiliation. At the outset of the nineteenth century, Thomas Clarkson (1807) observes a uniformity of outward appearance not known in the laity of any other denomination and matched only by the Anglican clergy.

A PROFILE

The Birmingham Quaker Joseph Edward Southall (1861–1944) withstood the negative attitudes of his day in the way that Edward Hicks could not, and maintained a high profile both as a painter and as a peace campaigner. Like Rickman and Waterhouse before him, his Quaker parents guided him to the safer option of architecture but he retreated from the office to his own studio.

Southall epitomizes the emancipation of two-dimensional figurative art among English Quakers and he does so by transcending the principled taboos that had formerly acted upon it. Among Friends he had a national profile as a peace campaigner, using art for propaganda purposes in the forms of drawings, posters, and cartoons (Breeze 2005). In the art world, he took a leading role in the revival of tempera painting, for which his reputation endures.

Southall associated closely with the Arts and Crafts movement with its emphasis on the integrity of the artist. He identified himself as 'artist-craftsman'and in his writings and records, was more studious of the process than, say, the attention and patronage he enjoyed from Picasso. Indeed, tempera painting lends itself to the definition of craft and Southall was especially painstaking in his approach to it. The gesso surface was prepared and burnished by him. Needing egg yolks to bind the pigment, he kept his own hens.

The particular properties of tempera painting are significant in Southall's statement of himself as artist-craftsman. The emphasis is less on expression than on technique; painters in tempera engage fully in the preparation of their materials; the process is laborious; and for those who worked in tempera its special [un-Quakerly] appeal was the intensity of colour (Sprague 2005, 24). The colour is applied in several layers over a period of time. And the elaborate gilded frames that distinguish many of his works were the craft of his wife Bessie Southall. Southall studied and applied the principles of decorative effect but his religious paintings are not offered as ornaments, nor are they narrative. The key to Southall's religious art is to be found not in the norms of artistic expression but in the Quaker practise of 'ministry', by which Friends in Meeting frequently take historical or contemporary incidents and explore them as parables. His subjects prompt reflections, illustrate virtues, and make allegorical statements of Quaker testimony. In its title and explicit narrative *St Dorothea and her two sisters refusing to worship the idol* (1902) is about a third-century Christian martyr of Cappadocia who declined to bow down to the image of a Roman deity: the authorities engaged her two sisters to persuade her to comply but she converted them to the Christian faith and was made to watch their execution before her own. The painting is already about conscience and the priority of principles over self-interest. It is about the effectiveness of personal resistance against organized authority, here symbolized by the classical architectural framing of the picture surmounted by a pediment. It is about themes that transcend and survive the trials of Christians in the third century. Southall's choice of idol is evidently Mars, the god of war, and this is therefore a peace testimony. But still more, when it was painted Southall was much exercised by the imposition in the 1902 Education Act of a tax to subsidize the schools of the Established Church: this he persistently refused to pay, suffering the distraint of certain of his goods and buying them back in auction rather than paying the tax voluntarily and conventionally. His court appearances, at each of which he seized the opportunity for verbal ministry, continued for over forty years (Massey 1945, 4). Thus St Dorothea triggers a cluster of contemporary concerns, which are explored visually in the way that a spoken ministry might explore them verbally.

Southall's *The Mount of Olives* (1922) similarly takes a narrative, this time biblical, and from it makes an impassioned plea in the form of the peace testimony. The picture is one of harmony and composure. Jesus occupies the foreground; the gnarled olive tree and the sheep grazing safely celebrate the achievement of peace on earth. But it is in that sense that the painting is poignantly idealistic rather than realistic. This painting was executed for the convent of Notre Dame des Anges in Fort Courtrai, Belgium, where it has served as a memorial to ninety-two men, women, and children who were asphyxiated by poison gas. It is a statement against the effects of war and is dedicated 'in the hope that all who look upon it may be inspired to do everything in their power to prevent future wars, and to hasten the day when on Earth there shall be universal Peace among men' (Homan 2006a, 104).

In the early nineteenth century Thomas Clarkson had reported that in the course of many visits to Quaker homes he never saw more than one picture displayed on the walls, and he recalls only ever seeing three types: one was of William Penn's treaty with the Indians, another of a slave ship, and the third a plan of the building of Ackworth school (Clarkson 1806, 292–4). All of these images, we may note, were in some measure didactic and affirmative of the denominational affiliation of the residents. At Southall's home in Edgbaston, however, cumber was back with a vengeance. A surviving photograph of the drawing room in the 1930s (Crawford 1984: 69) evidences the unilateral rehabilitation of cumber: we discover opulent furnishings, a square piano, and several paintings in his beloved gilded frames.

Disapproval of portrait painting on the grounds of the intrinsic vanity of the sitter did not disappear with the Puritans of the seventeenth century. Notwithstanding, Southall was a prolific portraitist. His principle was to disconnect the vice of vanity from the moment of observation. The sitter shows no pleasure in the act of being regarded. For example, although the directors of Cadbury Brothers commissioned from Southall the portrait of their chairman Barrow Cadbury that now hangs in the boardroom of the chocolate factory, he is shown hurrying to a meeting, affecting an almost hostile glance towards the artist as though he has been caught by the paparazzi. Subjects are seldom shown full-face, but more often in semi-profile, and as a feature in the landscape of their respective ministry. In the portrait of his mother, the feature that commands attention is her crocheted hat. While Southall produced a number of self-portraits, it is clear from his own notes (Birmingham 1980, 55) that he is more interested in discovering the process of tempera painting than capturing the person, from whom he deflects with such titles as *Man with a sable brush* or *The coral necklace*.

Whereas in former times black or dark dress was the language of sobriety, by Southall's day it was assumed as the uniform of the City of London and thereby the dominance of capital. Colour, then, was a liberation and Southall rejoiced in it, in his seaside paintings at breezy Southwold, in his narrative works, in his mural that survives in Birmingham City Museum, and in the un-Quakerly flamboyance of his own sartorial manner:

CONCLUSION

The ambivalent disposition of Quakers to the visual arts has evolved extensively since the eighteenth century. The seminal value of simplicity has implied a taste for plainness and a distaste for excess or 'cumber'. Indulgence in interior décor as well as the fine arts has at times been regulated and exercised by monitors appointed by Meetings. Conscientious Quakers with talents in the arts have not always been able to develop these. In the twentieth century, however, there was some softening of the Quaker attitude, evident in the form of art education in Quaker schools, and in the regard for a number of practitioners whose work has found favour in the wider world.

Art finds its way slowly into the Quaker experience. Initially it is subject to a comprehensive disapprobation on the basis of its notional attachment to various bad habits: ostentation, vanity. There was neither need nor sense to restrain art once these associations did not apply as in the Quaker experience in Kenya and South America, and in the radical and conscientious approach of Joseph Southall.

SUGGESTED FURTHER READING

Barnes, K. C. (1984) *Integrity and the arts*. York: Sessions.

Butler, D. M. (1995) *Quaker meeting houses*. Kendal: Quaker Tapestry Booklets.

Collins, P. J. (1996) '"Plaining": the social and cognitive process of symbolization in the Religious Society of Friends (Quakers)', *Journal of Contemporary Religion* 11 (3), pp. 277–88.

Lapsansky, E. J. and Verplanck, A. (eds.) (2003) *Quaker aesthetics: reflections on a Quaker ethic on American design and consumption*. Philadelphia: University of Pennsylvania Press.

Marmer, N. (1981) 'James Turrell: the art of deception' *Art in America* (May), pp. 90–99.

Nicholson, F. J. (1968) *Quakers and the arts*. London: Friends Home Service.

Southall, K. H. (1974) *Our Quaker heritage: early meeting houses built prior to 1720 and in use today*. London: Quaker Home Service.

Sox, D. (2000) *Quakers and the arts: 'Plain and fancy': an Anglo-American perspective*. Richmond, Indiana: Friends United Press.

CHAPTER 34

....

QUAKERS, PHILOSOPHY, AND TRUTH

....

JEFFREY DUDIAK AND LAURA REDIEHS

QUAKERS AND PHILOSOPHY

QUAKERISM'S beginning in the middle of the seventeenth century coincided with the philosophical reconsiderations of knowledge and reality that gave rise to the emergence of modern science. While the early Quakers were not engaged in academic philosophy as such, some of their work intersected with the important philosophical questions of the time. Because of the persecution they faced, they were forced to clarify their religious views, and many wrote to defend their ideas, engaging in debates with those who opposed their views. These views had important philosophical implications. Thus, while the Quakers did not construct a systematic academic philosophical system (nor did they always agree with each other), their views can be connected to epistemological, metaphysical, and ethical themes that concerned the philosophers of this period. Since there is a separate chapter on Quakers and ethics, this chapter will focus especially on epistemology and metaphysics.

Epistemologically, Quakers can be said to have emphasized a practical wisdom for bringing forth God's Kingdom. The debate among philosophers during the seventeenth century is often characterized as a debate between rationalism and empiricism. The Quakers were unusual in implicitly grounding their religious views in experience rather than rational proofs for God's existence. Quakers also maintained an interest in science throughout their history (Cantor 2005).

Metaphysically, during the seventeenth century, vitalism was waning in favour of either matter–spirit dualism or an emerging materialism, but there were many philosophical problems with both dualism and the theory of matter. The Quakers never accepted a physicalist materialism; indeed, Quaker philosopher Anne Conway (1631–79) explicitly argued against materialism.

It is important to keep in mind that philosophy, theology, and science were not yet strictly separated during this period. Nor was academic philosophy fully professionalized yet. Major contributors did not necessarily see themselves as primarily or exclusively philosophers, and some women as well as men were participating in philosophical discussions. While not all Quakers were well-educated, there were Quakers who were aware of the philosophical and scientific discussions of the day and who did try to defend the Quaker faith in light of those broader discussions. There was, however, suspicion towards too much education in Quaker circles, and a belief that the hubris it could engender could distract people from the most important matters of faith. 'Disentangling science and religion in the seventeenth century is impossible', writes historian David Byrne. 'The Puritan and Anglican contributions to natural theology have been well documented, but even . . . groups like the Quakers contributed to the wealth of new ideas which together forged "the new science"' (Byrne 2007, 33).

CONNECTIONS BETWEEN QUAKERS, PHILOSOPHERS, AND SCIENTISTS

Viscountess Anne Conway (1631–79) provided one important connection between the Quakers and well-known philosophers and scientists of the early modern period. She herself was a philosopher, and also became Quaker. She brought Quakers and philosophers into conversation with each other. Conway's brother John Finch and her husband Edward Conway, First Earl of Conway, were both members of the Royal Society of London. Because Anne Conway suffered frequent severe headaches, members of the Royal Society would try to treat her headaches, including Robert Boyle (Hutton 2004, 121). Conway's husband was a close friend of Boyle's brother, Roger, Lord Orrery (Hutton 2004, 124–5).

Through John Finch, Anne Conway came to know the Cambridge Platonist philosopher Henry More (1614–87), and the two developed a close friendship and an intellectual collaboration (Hutton 2004, 78). More was also a Fellow of the Royal Society and a teacher of Isaac Newton (Byrne 2007, 26). Both More and Conway disapproved of the philosophy of Thomas Hobbes and others who during this time were developing and promoting materialism, determinism, and atheism. More, who was very much influenced by Descartes, although not entirely in agreement with him, 'dedicated his intellectual talents to the defence of religious beliefs in a rational and sceptical age' (Hutton 2004, 81), believing that religious belief was fully compatible with reason. Conway, in her *Principles of the Most Ancient and Modern Philosophy*, developed a non-materialist metaphysics that influenced the philosopher Gottfried Leibniz (Hutton 2004, 232–234). Francis Mercury van Helmont (1614–98) shared with Conway a growing interest in Quakerism. He came to the Conway residence, Ragley Hall, to treat her headaches and became her resident physician. He had first met Quakers in 1659 or 1660 at the court of the Elector Palatine in Heidelberg (Hutton 2004, 178; Hull 1941, 106), and either converted to Quakerism or at least considered himself Quaker from around 1676 (Hutton 2004, 178; Hull 1941, 109). Noted Quaker leaders Fox, Keith, Penn, Penington, and Barclay, among others, came to visit Conway and van Helmont. Conway herself became Quaker in 1677 (Hull 1941, 108).

While Fox and Barclay had their disagreements with aspects of van Helmont's metaphysical views, such that van Helmont's hermetic, Kabbalistic, alchemical philosophy cannot be said to be representative of Quaker philosophy, van Helmont's and Conway's involvement in conversations with and between Quakers and More certainly had an influence in shaping the subsequent development of Quaker thought.

According to Richard Bailey and Sarah Hutton, Anne Conway may well have played a key role in encouraging the Quakers in the 1670s to tone down the more extreme Quaker beliefs, casting their views in a more philosophically respectable framework (Bailey 1992, 245). Conway's family and friends (including Henry More) were scandalized at her becoming Quaker (Hutton 2004, 184–5). Henry More at first was somewhat sympathetic towards Quakerism, admiring the work and friendship of George Keith, himself trained in philosophy and divinity (Nicholson 1930, 39), but tried to dissuade Conway from joining. Conway encouraged continued conversations between More and the Quakers (Hutton 2004, 187–8), seeing compatibilities in their views. Robert Barclay was closely involved in the Ragley circle (Hutton 2004, 229), and 'Barclay's *Apology* in effect codified Quaker doctrine, and ensured that a milder, less radical version of Quaker beliefs prevailed' (Hutton 2004). This work was published in Latin in 1676 and in English in 1678.

After Conway's death in 1679, van Helmont found her *Principles of the Most Ancient and Modern Philosophy*, and had a Latin version published in 1690. He was friends with Leibniz and was probably van Helmont who showed her work to Leibniz. Leibniz respected Conway's work; he was also curious about the Quakers because of van Helmont's interest, and read Barclay's *Apology* and Penn's *Travails in Holland and Germany* (Rescher 1955), but did not have much respect for the philosophical grounding of their views. Writing to Thomas Burnet in 1696, he said, 'There are very few who know what this Light is. I doubt very much if your Quakers know it, however much they may talk of it' (quoted in Hull 1941, 119). It is possible that Leibniz was inspired by Conway or van Helmont to use the term 'monad'. Scholars have also noted that Conway's ideas 'at least anticipated the spiritual monism of [George] Berkeley' (Byrne 2007, 33).

Another site for connections between Quakers and philosophers was Holland. Early in Quaker history, some Friends went to Holland, because it was more religiously tolerant than England (although the Quakers still met with difficulties there), and because the Quakers found seekers receptive to their message in that country. In 1653 the first Quaker missionaries, William Caton and John Stubbs, visited Middelburg and Vlissingen. A few years later, in 1656, William Ames arrived in Amsterdam and soon gained recognition as an important Quaker leader.

In addition to reaching out to seekers and to Christians, such as the Dutch Collegiants and Mennonites who were sympathetic to their message, the Quakers were also trying to convert Jews to Christianity in anticipation of what they thought was the coming

Millennium. While unsuccessful in converting Jews, some Quakers, including William Ames, did meet the Jewish philosopher Baruch Spinoza, who had been excommunicated from his synagogue in 1656. Margaret Fell asked another Quaker, Samuel (bap. 1604, d. 1665), to translate some of her writings into Hebrew. Once in Holland, Fisher handed over this project to a recently excommunicated Jew, probably Spinoza (Popkin 1985, 220). Part of the evidence that Fisher and Spinoza knew each other is that many themes from Fisher's 1660 work *Rusticus ad Academicos* appeared in Spinoza's 1670 *Tractatus Theologica-Politicus* (Popkin 1985, 219, 221).

Another site for intellectual discussions in Holland was Rotterdam. Benjamin Furly (1636–1714) was an English Quaker merchant who moved to Holland and lived in Rotterdam for much of his life. He played a key role in bringing the writings of the English Quakers to the Dutch- and German-speaking countries. He hosted English Quakers when they visited, including Fox, Penn, Barclay, and Keith, and also played an important role in finding settlers for Pennsylvania. He and other Quakers visited and corresponded with Princess Elizabeth of Bohemia (famous for her correspondence with Descartes). But Furly was especially close to the English philosopher John Locke, who lived in Holland during his political exile from 1683 to 1698. They remained friends for the rest of Locke's life.

While in Holland Locke spent most of his time in Amsterdam, but spent 1687–8 in Rotterdam, 'residing frequently in Furly's house' (Hull 1941, 83). During his time in Holland, he worked on his *An Essay Concerning Human Understanding*, which he finished in Rotterdam (Hull 1941, 83). While it is impossible to determine exactly how much his friendship with Furly and his contact with Quakers may have influenced his thinking, Hull notes, 'it is significant that during the time when he was largely engaged upon his great *An Essay Concerning Human Understanding*, he made frequent and friendly use of Furly's home and splendid library' (Hull 1941, 90).

Furly's house was also the meeting place of an informal society called the 'Lantern'. According to Hull, Locke's letters indicate that this society was probably not solely a Quaker group but 'included non-Quaker members and was for the purpose of discussing in a free and congenial atmosphere philosophical and scientific questions' (Hull 1941, 87–8). Van Helmont attended these meetings when he was in Holland (Hull 1941, 118).

Furly and Locke had similar political views, although no political letters survive, since Locke arranged for his political correspondence to be destroyed before his death, perhaps to protect his friends (Hull 1941, 83). Locke also knew Penn, and his influence on both Penn and Furly helps explain how Locke's political ideas found some expression in Pennsylvania's government (Hull 1941, 100). Furly and Locke also shared a concern for religious toleration. Locke wrote his famous 'A Letter Concerning Toleration', which was published in Latin in 1689, the year he returned to England. After Catholic King James II of England fled the country and was replaced by Protestants William of Orange and Mary (James's daughter), Furly spent eleven months in England advocating religious toleration. The Act of Toleration was indeed passed that year.

Connections between Quakers, philosophers, and scientists continued beyond the early modern period and extend into the present day. Some of the more notable later connections include Arthur Stanley Eddington (1882–1944), the astronomer famous for experimentally confirming Einstein's *Theory of General Relativity* during the solar eclipse of 1919. Eddington, influenced by his Quaker background, presented his own synthesis of science and religion in his 1929 Swarthmore Lecture, *Science and the Unseen World*. And some noted twentieth-century Quaker philosophers who wrote specifically on questions concerning religious epistemology include Rufus Jones, Douglas Steere, Elton Trueblood, Gerald Hibbert, and Calvin Keene.

QUAKER EPISTEMOLOGY

The Quaker sense of knowledge is broader and richer than the typically philosophical sense—in any biblically resonant tradition 'knowledge' includes, beyond cognitive matters, a sense of 'intimate familiarity.' There is still a sense, however, in which one could state that Quakers have developed something like an epistemology, in the broadest sense of a theory of how we come to know. This theory was articulated in theological rather than philosophical terms.

This account of knowledge has as its centrepiece the very simple but revolutionary claim of George Fox: 'Christ has come to teach people himself' (Fox 1995, 104). Exactly what this claim means has been the subject of much interpretation, affected by the various cultural, intellectual, and theological cross-pressures that have forged the varieties of Quakerism found today. Quakers have not agreed on what should be understood as the referent of Fox's 'Christ', and they have disagreed about what kind of 'teachings' Friends can expect to receive in this manner. What is clear is that for Fox himself, this teacher, Christ, provided spiritual direction and discernment, direct factual information, and the means of correctly 'opening' the Scriptures. Of central importance here is the immediacy of the illumination. When Fox made this message the core of his preaching, he was bypassing, undercutting, and undermining the centrality for religious significance of the 'mediating' terms that the historical Christian churches had interposed between God and individual human beings. These included the institutional Church itself, its priestly class, the Scriptures (which had replaced the Church as the principal mediator of God's revelation in the predominant Protestantism of Fox's time), and even the community of believers. The severity of this prohibition against mediating terms led to some theological ambiguity around the necessity of the historical Christ as mediator. Even Friends' careful clarifications that they had never doubted the equivalence of the Light of Christ and the historical Christ (e.g., Penn's response to George Keith [Braithwaite 1979, 486]), probably encouraged their detractors to believe that they *had* doubted such an equivalence. Thus there was an ambiguity at the heart of Quakerism that would create further hermeneutical ambiguities as the movement developed over time.

Friends assigned these terms, which other Christians had believed to be mediating relationships between individual and God, to what Friends took to be their proper place. The Church was no longer taken as our Mother. Rather, it was the community of those attentive to and transformed by the power of the Light of Christ (which is why Friends opted for the name 'meeting houses' for their buildings rather than 'church'). Similarly, they abolished any priestly class in favour of a priesthood of all believers. This transformed epistemology and ecclesiology presented its own problems for the construction of a viable religious community over the long term. The James Nayler episode (see Chapter 1), and claims by Quakers who followed John Perrot that meetings should not be held at set times but only according to 'the immediate leadings of the Spirit' (see Chapter 2; Braithwaite 1979, 237), accentuated the prospect of anarchy seemingly inherent in a doctrine of non-mediational, revelational knowledge-acquisition. In recognition of such risks, both the Scriptures and the Quaker community became a 'check' on individual eccentricity or extravagant ideas being taken as true teachings of Christ.

Friends did not understand the Scriptures to be a closed and comprehensive canon limiting or forbidding future revelation. However, early Friends did believe themselves to be in the same Spirit out of which the Scriptures were given; thus 'whatsoever doctrine is contrary unto their testimony, may therefore justly be rejected as false' (Barclay 1678, 77) lest the Spirit of Christ contradict itself. These further revelations were, moreover, very often illuminations on how to properly interpret the Scriptures, as 'it is only the spiritual man who can make a right use of them' (Barclay 1678, 77). For Evangelical Friends today, the ongoing revealing work of the Spirit is often largely limited to this function.

The Quaker community played a similar role of discernment, as the weight of the meeting provided a ballast in terms of which revelations to individuals were deemed more or less sound; 'the sense of the Meeting' was given greater authority than individual revelation. The convention of testing leadings with the Meeting remains an established Quaker practice. It provides an interesting parallel with the scientific practice of validating new scientific findings through peer review.

THE LIGHT WITHIN AND THE LIGHT OF REASON

Many early Quakers were highly biblically literate and remarkably theologically sophisticated, despite the fact that few, including Fox, possessed much formal education or familiarity with the intellectual discourses of the times. Nevertheless, they were undoubtedly influenced by what was going on around them, by what was 'in the air' as much as by what was 'at hand'. But as in any age, new ideas are always in active competition with more long-established ones. The latter also exert their influence, often even more forcefully, as they tend to function as 'default positions' unless explicitly challenged. Thus, early Quakers were influenced by the radically new and the very old, as summed up in William Penn's telling description of the movement as 'primitive Christianity revived', but revived under new circumstances. They believed that, after a millennium and a half of apostasy, the Church was finally being renewed; though all things were in the process of being made genuinely new, the touchstone for this new age— its inspiration and point of reference—was biblical eschatology. Douglas Gwyn (1986) has perhaps done the most to illustrate this point.

Seventeenth-century Quakerism was almost certainly a unique configuration of a number of contemporary influences—English radical Puritans, continental mystics, political Levellers and Diggers, religious Seekers, the Dutch Collegiants—all of whom in turn were influenced by the ubiquitous Western tradition of Latin (including Protestant) Christianity in thoroughgoing if different ways. The Canadian philosopher Charles Taylor is right when he claims that history is hermeneutically messy. This certainly holds true for the history of Quaker thought.

Clearly, early Friends' ideas about the acquisition of knowledge reflect and resist the emerging Modernism that was the intellectual and cultural backdrop for nascent Quakerism. The germination of Quakerism corresponds chronologically with what we now categorize as the 'Early Modern' period. The great French thinker and intellectual known as the 'Father of modern philosophy', René Descartes died in 1650, roughly coinciding with the emergences of Quakerism. Quakerism germinated in the context of this emerging modern world, when the ideas we now think of as 'modern' were in the ascent, but had not yet attained full ascendancy

Indeed, there are interesting convergences but also divergences between the 'Light of Reason' as employed by the modern philosophers and the Quaker 'Light Within'. Under both formulations, the Light functions as a primary source of truth and the final judge of the truth of traditions and authorities. Within both conceptis, the individual on his or her own has immediate access to the Light (the Light Within or the Light of Reason) in an unmediated way. Within modern philosophy, the primacy and role of the Light of Reason was disputed as empiricism gained ascendancy. Its exact definition varied from philosopher to philosopher, although the empiricists were as critical of authority and tradition as were their rationalist counterparts. While some Quakers seemed to have an understanding of the Light Within close to empiricism (as is discussed below), Anne Conway had rationalist leanings, influenced as she was by Henry More, who in turn was influenced by Descartes. More sometimes preferred to think of reason as an 'exalted' spiritual faculty rather than merely an intellectual faculty (Nicholson 1930, 40). More believed that reason, properly applied, led inevitably to Christianity. Even before his interest in Quakerism, he referred to 'the light within', which is how reading More led George Keith to convert to Quakerism (Nicholson 1930, 39–42). The Dutch Collegiant movement also took seriously the concept of the Light Within. Consequently, the Quakers and Dutch Collegiants were initially attracted to each other, but over time, perhaps under the influence of Spinoza, the Collegiant view of the Light Within eventually merged with the natural Light of Reason (Fix 1991). The early Quakers, in contrast, generally maintained a distinction between the Light Within and reason.

The relationship between the Quaker Light Within and the Modernist Light of Reason is anything but straightforward. This is partly because Modernism itself is difficult to define; it has interrelated political, social, ethical, aesthetic, and anthropological aspects as least as important as the philosophical ones. For present purposes, the Modern can be best characterized by highlighting the core idea that the rationally endowed human is capable of attaining truth by means of rationality alone, if properly disciplined and attended to outside the corruptions of traditions and authorities. Taking form in a world already moving towards modern values and sensibilities, Quakerism was and remains conversant with them. It might even be taken as making a significant contribution to them, for example, in William Penn's contributions to the ideas behind American democracy, the early Quaker promotion of religious tolerance, and later Quakers' efforts at institutional reform. In certain ways, Quakerism can appear quintessentially modern, even if a broader view of its origins and history paint a more complex picture.

Over time, some Quakers increasingly identified the Light Within with the Light of Enlightenment reason. Friends inclined to see Christ in terms of the fulfilment of an inherent human potential (and not as divine intervention) increasingly adopted this position, one that resonated with emerging liberal theologies. This trajectory was consolidated and made more mainstream after the Manchester Conference of 1895, the nexus of a self-conscious, explicit attempt to 'modernize' Quakerism, to bring it into line with scientific rationality and the correlative confidence in human progress. This more optimistic, humanistic trajectory within Quakerism took the Light Within (rebranded as the 'Inner Light' by Rufus Jones to reflect this new emphasis) as a natural human endowment. 'That of God in everyone' was highlighted as a positive part of human nature, and it functioned increasingly as the basis for human rights advocacy and peace testimony based on a doctrine of the inviolability of this divine core in each person. It also became the basis for a conscience-based ethics, since the natural human conscience is to be trusted, if not corrupted by outside influences. Most important for our discussion here, these Quakers saw the conscience as providing reliable access to truth. If natural reason is not inherently corrupt, and so can and should be trusted, then 'revelation' becomes more a matter of developing and trusting one's own capacities that are considered 'spiritual'. William James's famous designation of the 'once-born', against the 'twice-born' religious character type, comes to mind here.

But for almost all early Friends (and for the statistical majority of Friends to this day) a sharp distinction was drawn between the 'natural light' (of Reason) and the 'Light Within' (or Light of Christ). The human being in her or his natural condition was not oriented to God but to 'the world', and a profound internal struggle ('the Lamb's war') had to be waged between 'the Light' and one's 'natural' darkness. Indeed, the first function of the Light was to illuminate the corrupted 'natural' (selfish and worldly) tendencies of the individual, or sin, and the tenacity of those tendencies to resist the appeal of 'that of God' to salvation and sanctification. The Light Within, the immediate appeal of God to the heart, is not spoken of as a pure intervention contingent upon divine prerogative, as in Reformed theology, but as a description of the universal human 'spiritual' condition, as 'the true Light, which lighteth every man that cometh into the world' (Jn 1:9).

For early Quakers, the Light was therefore not purely 'inner' in the sense of being merely human, nor was it purely 'outer' in the sense of being foreign to the human condition and thus needing to be imposed from some 'supernatural' outside. Early Friends seem to have had a view of the Light as a kind of 'outside that is always already inside' that resists a reading that emphasizes one side at the expense of the other. Whether that view is, philosophically speaking, highly sophisticated or simply confused, it remains religiously challenging, and it may well be one of the most important contributions of Quaker thought.

As the optimistic view of humanity characteristic of the modern period has become questionable again over the last century, early Quaker views seem increasingly pertinent. After two world wars that were anything but wars to end all war, techno-environmental crisis, and ongoing oppressions at the heart of the most 'civilized' societies, faith in the 'modern' is no longer contemporary. Friends, like everyone else, will have to find a way to deal with the 'post-Modern' challenge, and they might well benefit from reconnecting with an earlier Quaker sensibility, not as a way of going back, but of finding a new way forwards.

Knowledge and Experience

Another possible launch pad for what might count as a Quaker epistemology is one of Fox's celebrated phrases: 'This I knew experimentally' (Fox 1995, 11). The terms 'experimental' and 'experimentally' were also used by Robert Barclay in his *Apology* (2002 [1678]) and by George Keith (*Of Divine Immediate Revelation and Inspiration*, 1684). The usage by Fox is probably the earliest of the three, likely written or dictated by Fox sometime between 1675 and 1676. While present-day Quakers tend to translate this term as 'experientially', and scholars are divided on the use of this term in early Quakerism, the fact that the early Quakers were writing during the rise of modern science raises the question of whether they were intentionally using a word that would echo the strong interest in the new experimental method being developed in science during this time. The experimental method represented a shift from Aristotelian science that focused on observation and classification to a method that was more interactive: a dialogue with nature. Furthermore, learning about nature was in principle available to everyone. The Quakers, in parallel, seemed to shift from a passive 'observational' relationship with theology, requiring the mediation of priests or the Bible, to a more interactive, dialogical relationship with the divine. This direct interaction with the divine was also, in principle, available to everyone. Because of Barclay' and Keith's association with the Conway circle, they may well have consciously used the term 'experimental' to move towards a more dynamic way of thinking about knowledge. Anne Conway was well connected to scientists and philosophers of the time and encouraged discussions between the Quakers and the philosophers. The writings of Keith and Barclay, moreover, may have been partly the product of Conway's request to make Quakerism more philosophically respectable. The question of Fox's famous usage of the term is more difficult to answer, as he seems to have used the term before meeting Conway but still late enough that he was most likely in conversation with others who were familiar with this term in its scientific context. In any case, whether we think of 'experimental' in terms of the new vision of science emerging in this period, or as a synonym of 'experiential', the emphasis here is on knowledge, especially religious knowledge, being tied to a personal encounter with God, and not suspended in some abstract set of doctrines that one can 'know' without living them. Doctrines not backed up by experience are derisively referred to as 'notions' by Quakers.

There is a deeper sense of how knowledge functions here, and a variety of interpretations find support. Whereas Orthodox and Evangelical Friends are inclined to take experimental knowledge as backing up and confirming doctrinal claims, Liberal Friends often understand this experiential knowledge as superseding and replacing doctrine, and providing a mystical means of apprehending sacred reality.

The idea that knowledge is dependent upon experience is suggestive of two philosophical schools of thought: empiricism and existentialism. Should Quaker epistemology be thought of as a species of one of these? Empiricism was a prominent trajectory within the larger Modernist *zeitgeist*, especially strong on the British Isles. Its programme, in concert with an emerging commitment to scientific method as *the* singularly reliable means to truth, was only to accept as knowledge that which could be supported by the evidence of the senses. It should be noted that what counted as the 'senses' was broader in the early modern period than it is now. Both Locke and Hume included both the 'outer' five senses, and the 'internal' senses of our awareness of our thoughts and feelings. While their understanding of the internal senses did not allow for a direct sensing of divine truth, it does show that early empiricism rested upon a broader experiential base than empiricism does today. Considering this context, we find the more philosophically inclined Quakers carving out a unique theory of knowledge that grounds the possibility of religious knowledge more in experience than in reason. In the face of growing philosophical and scientific emphases on external empiricism and materialism during the modern period, most philosophers who wanted to maintain a place for religious belief increasingly relied upon rationalism to do so. Some philosophically inclined Quakers, in contrast, were an exception. Penn, Barclay, and Keith interpreted the Light Within almost as an additional sense. Penington, Fox, Nayler, and Lawson distinguished the Light Within from mere reason (Barbour 1973, 250; Penington 1668; Lawson 1680). Penn offered a moderate position, allowing some role for reason (Barbour 1973, 251–4; Endy 1973). Barclay and Keith used sensory language to describe the epistemological functioning of the Light Within, although they were careful to make clear that they used this language metaphorically and not literally. There is much to recommend a view that would identify early Quaker epistemologies with the emerging empiricism of the age that gave birth to Quakerism. The Quaker distrust of 'notions' corresponds, in many essential ways, with the empiricists' distrust of metaphysics, that is, of systems of thought that cannot be verified by reference to concrete experience. This sensibility is reflected in the general suspicion among Quakers towards theological systems, and in the fact that no systematic Quaker theology of any comprehensive nature has been produced since the appearance of Barclay's *Apology*. Yet, if one thinks of Quaker epistemology as an empiricism, then it would have to be an expanded empiricism, one that includes far more than the data issuing from the senses, which itself is relativized in the face of a very different kind of experience. What counts as experience here are the spiritual forces to be found in the experiences internal to each human being and within the world outside oneself. George Fox frequently expressed the conviction that 'the power of the Lord is over all', intending this phrase to encompass both kinds of experience. Quakers did make a clear distinction between divine revelation and knowledge gained by empirical observation or experiment. Both can be described as 'experiential' and thus the early Quakers were distinctive in justifying religious knowledge in a way that parallels more closely an epistemology of empiricism (in its seventeenth-century sense) than of rationalism.

Along with empiricism, the philosophical school of existentialism (and existential phenomenology) also puts experience at the centre of the pursuit of truth, offering a richer view of experience than empiricism traditionally has. It may thus also accord with Quaker views. In contrast, existential phenomenology takes lived experience as the reality, where scientific and causal explanations are the abstraction. The latter are useful if in the service of such experience, but reductive if taken as true in themselves. In existential phenomenology, a description of life, as meaningfully lived from the inside out, grounds and checks explanatory frameworks. This is not dissimilar to the way in which Quaker religious life grounds and checks even Quaker theology, and where what is personally meaningful, not just that which is objectively demonstrable, becomes the compass for truth. Since existentialism is a twentieth-century movement in philosophy and theology, early Friends were not influenced by existentialists. Nor is there any evidence that Quaker ideas were important to early existentialists. But there are similarities. For example, perhaps the Haverford College philosopher and Quaker ecumenist Douglas V. Steere (1901–95) translating and editing Kierkegaard's *Purity of Heart* (1938) reflects such a resonance.

QUAKERS AND TRUTH

In philosophy, particularly mainstream modern philosophy, there are three predominant and competing theories of truth: correspondence, coherence, and pragmatic. In the first, truth is defined as the *correspondence* between some ideal mental meaning and some external non-mental 'state of affairs'. The second refers to truth as the logical *coherence* of a series of propositions with each other in an internally consistent system. The third holds that something is true if it accomplishes or facilitates the use for which it is employed, or is *pragmatically* effective.

For Friends, particularly earlier Friends, the term 'truth' was all but ubiquitous, and functioned in a number of interrelated ways. Early Friends *did* speak of the truth as a matter of fact, as when George Fox 'declared the truth' in preaching or in disputations (both orally and in writing), such that others were 'convinced' of it. Early Friends certainly had something to say, something they took to be true, in the sense of 'factually the case'. And yet in seventeenth-century idiom the term 'convinced' is closer to what we might today think of as 'convicted'. Being convinced was no mere giving of intellectual assent to something; it named an event of spiritual struggle with Truth. Seeing *the truth* about oneself, i.e., that one was not oriented within and towards '*the Truth*' but 'the world' (which is in its ways not turned towards the truth), way was made for the Light Within (or the Seed of God) to grow in one and *exert its power* over the former, natural person and from there over the world. Truth thus had transformative power over individuals and in the world. Truth in this sense is therefore not something merely 'known' (in the cognitive sense) but something humans participate in, or more precisely, something in which people are taken up within as they give themselves over to it. Additionally, Truth in early Quaker writings can refer to the 'Source of this power', to God or to Christ, who, after the testimony of John's ('the Quaker') gospel, *is* 'the way, *the truth*, and the life' (Jn 14:6).

'Truth' in earlier Quaker discourse, therefore, while often 'accenting' one or the other of these aspects, is perhaps best understood as the simultaneous evocation of (1) the Source of the Power, (2) the Power and the participatory experience that the Children of Light had of it, and (3) the teachings about this Power, united into a gestalt the aspects of which could not be separated out from each other without distortion. Teachings separated from this Power were rejected as mere 'notions', even when they were true in the factual sense. And yet, while recognizing, in an apophatic way, that the Power was 'beyond words', Quakers nevertheless gave expression to this Power in articulations that they took to be true. The inseparability of Christ (and God) from the Power that acted in them led to an ambivalence in their discourse about the historical Christ over the Christ Within, opening them up to a charge of atheism by their detractors.

So while knowledge of the truth was a constituent of the truth for early Friends, truth was taken as much more than a matter of knowledge. While knowledge of one's true condition was a necessary condition for one's subsequent participation in the Truth, it was not a sufficient condition. Rather, a surrender to the Truth was required (via 'the Lamb's war', the internal battle between the prideful 'self' and the Light Within), a matter not just of the head but also of the will and the heart. Early Friends gave themselves over to and participated in the Spirit of God, thus experiencing God's Spirit dwelling within them. At its most intense, certain early Quakers claimed an experience of 'celestial inhabitation'; that is, they felt that their bodies were inhabited by Christ (Bailey 1992, 111; Tarter 2001, 149). Almost at the opposite extreme of disinterested, objective matters of cognition, this manifestation of Quaker concern for truth is closer to ecstatic possession.

This being in the Life, in the Truth, reflecting a 'root', religious (re-)orientation, was comprehensive in its reach and effects. It found expression in every aspect of Quaker life, and in every mode of truth. Thus 'theological' truths, most systematically formulated in Barclay's *Apology*, pointed to and gave expression to the experience of the Light Within, in dialogue with the Scriptures, which were taken themselves to have done the same. The celebrated Quaker 'testimonies' were precisely a 'witness' to this event of Truth in the life of the Quaker, who henceforth lived not after the ways of the world, but as a participant in Truth, for example, when Fox claimed to live 'in the virtue of that life and power that took away the occasion of all wars' (Fox 1995, 65).

'Quaker truth' thus included the correspondence, coherence, and pragmatic theories of truth. It included the correspondence view (though not with a concern for strict philosophical precision) because Quaker doctrines were taken as a faithful expression of the reality of Christ in their lives. It included the coherence theory, evinced in a concern for dialectics in, for example, Barclay's argument for the coherence of Quaker teachings with Biblical testimony. And it included a certain pragmatism, in the adherence to a Truth that has to be enacted to be realized, and which cannot be true in the abstract. Thus a functional idea (as opposed to a theoretically oriented one) of truth emerges that while faithful (true!) to the religious experience of the Quakers, and rigorously so, is yet 'broader' or 'richer' than the analytically more precise senses of truth that are generally the standard in philosophy.

SUGGESTED FURTHER READING

Barclay, R. (2002 [1678]) *An apology for the true Christian divinity*, ed. Peter D. Sippel. Glenside, PA: Quaker Heritage Press.

Cantor, G. (2005) *Quakers, Jews, and science: Religious responses to modernity and the sciences in Britain, 1650–1900*. Oxford: Oxford University Press.

Eddington, A. S. (2007 [1929]) *Science and the unseen world*. London: Britain Yearly Meeting.

Fix, A. C. (1991) *Prophecy and reason: the Dutch Collegiants in the early enlightenment*. Princeton, NJ: Princeton University Press.

Fox, G. (1995 [952]) *Journal of George Fox*, (ed.) J. L. Nickalls. Philadelphia: Religious Society of Friends.

Gwyn, D. (1986) *Apocalypse of the Word: The life and message of George Fox*. Richmond, IN: Friends United Press.

Hutton, S. (2004) *Anne Conway: A woman philosopher*. Cambridge: Cambridge University Press.

Jones, R. M. (1914) *Spiritual reformers in the 16th and 17th centuries*. Whitefish, MT: Kessinger Publishing.

Trueblood, D. E. (1988 [1939]) *The trustworthiness of religious experience*. Richmond, IN: Friends United Press.

CHAPTER 35

···

QUAKERS AND SCIENCE

···

GEOFFREY CANTOR

INTRODUCTION

THE Quaker scientific heritage includes such eminent scientists as the chemist John Dalton (1766–1844), the astrophysicist Arthur Stanley Eddington (1882–1944), and the crystallographer Kathleen Lonsdale (1903–71). Although this chapter acknowledges the scientific contributions made by these and other leading Quaker scientists, it also addresses the far broader question of how Quakers have engaged with the sciences. It considers the many different types of scientific endeavour pursued by Quakers including not only the highly theory-laden physics practised by Eddington but also the local botanical studies that attracted many eighteenth- and nineteenth-century Friends, the teaching of science subjects at Quaker schools, and both the acceptance and the rejection of Darwin's theory of evolution by some Quakers.

'Science' is a problematic and historically relative term. Quaker participation in science over the past three and a half centuries, therefore needs to be set within the context of the changing understandings of the natural world during the same period, beginning with the 'Scientific Revolution' of the seventeenth century. During the latter decades of that century the notion of science was repeatedly contested; thus in the next section we shall see that seventeenth-century Quakers engaged the natural world from a religious perspective, which placed them in opposition to the increasingly successful mechanical philosophy championed by such writers as Robert Hooke, Robert Boyle, and Isaac Newton. Although Quakers have often claimed that the pursuit of science is thoroughly compatible with their religion, the final section of this chapter argues that the study of the natural world has nevertheless repeatedly been in tension with other aspects of Quakerism.

EARLY QUAKER ATTITUDES TO NATURE AS GOD'S CREATION

Quaker attitudes to the study of nature are addressed in this section, covering the period prior to c.1691, a period previously discussed in Rosemary Moore's chapter 1 within this volume, entitled 'Seventeenth-century Context and Quaker Beginnings' and Richard C. Allen's chapter 2 within this volume entitled 'Restoration Quakerism 1660–1691'. With few exceptions early Quakers paid scant attention to the new forms of natural knowledge being discussed by the elite Royal Society of London. One of those exceptions is the schoolmaster Thomas Lawson (c.1630–91) who kept a detailed diary in which he noted and described the botanical specimens he encountered while travelling in the Quaker cause. By contrast, George Fox's *Journal* contains very few references to the landscape and flora through which he travelled, let alone the emerging scientific culture of his day. For him, as for many Quaker contemporaries, it was far more important to disseminate a spiritual message leading to salvation than to contemplate the behaviour of the material world.

Biblically informed discussions of the spiritual state of humankind nevertheless sometimes addressed the natural world. One example is the account of God's creatures given in Edward Burrough's *A standard lifted up* (1658). Here Burrough (1633–63) insisted that the state of the 'creatures'—a term that would certainly encompass 'brutes' but probably also other parts of creation—depended on the spiritual state of 'man'. Thus while 'no creature was evill or defiled in its [original] creation', after the Fall 'man' had infected the other creatures with his evil and corruption: 'he makes all creatures evill in his exercise of them, and he corrupts them and perverts them to another end than wherefore they were created, and by the creatures, dishonours the Creator'. However, with the advent of the new covenant prophesied in the Bible, Burrough envisaged that the creatures would also be restored:

> …and all creatures are seen to be the Lords, and the whole earth is his and the fulnesse thereof, and the abuse of all creatures is ceased, and they are enjoyed in their pure vertue to feed and to cloth the creature, and not to be destroyed upon the lust. (Burrough 1658b, 17–18)

Thus their purity and the harmony of the world are restored to their pre-lapsarian state. Many variants on this theme can be found in early Quaker writing. For example, in William Smith's *New creation brought forth* (1661) the Fall involved the dissolution of the harmonious natural order, such that 'the Serpent hath weakned him [man], and set the Creatures over him, and then leads him to commit evil in the use of the Creatures'. With the establishment of the new creation announced in Smith's title, 'man' would again acquire his rightful place and re-establish his dominion over the rest of creation (W. Smith 1661, 13).

The dominant theme in these early Quaker creation narratives is the complete harmony and unity that existed after the initial creation. After the Fall, this harmony had to be re-established—sometimes completely, sometimes incompletely—with a new creation. Although writers such as Burrough, Smith, George Fox, and Francis Howgill paid no attention to the physical process of creation—a subject that attracted a number of non-Quakers—they articulated the necessary harmony that originally existed between humankind and the rest of creation, one that will be re-established through faithfully following the Quaker way. While it would be anachronistic to see here a form of modern environmentalism, these early Quaker writers maintained an idealized vision of harmony between humankind and nature, with humans having dominion over nature, which should be used for the benefit of humanity.

Quakers such as these were also united in their opposition to the ancient Greek authorities in science and medicine. Although Aristotelian physics and Galenic medicine were at that time being displaced in the British universities by innovative scientific theories, Quakers criticized Greek notions principally on religious grounds. Thus Lawson condemned Aristotelian and Platonic philosophies of nature as heathen and as opposed to the biblically based Christian understanding of creation. Likewise, in a small tract the Bristol apothecary Charles Marshall (1637–98) attacked Galenic medicine as being far more dangerous than the iatrochemical cures that he concocted for his patients; such cures were, he argued, also more effective because they addressed not only the body but also the soul (Marshall 1670). This was important because illness afflicted both body and soul.

By contrast to their opposition to Aristotelian and Galenic ideas, a number of early Quakers, including Fox, were attracted to the mystical hermetic form of natural philosophy, especially the views of Johannes Baptista van Helmont (1579–1644) and his son Francis Mercury van Helmont (1614–98), who may himself have converted to Quakerism. In keeping with writers in the Quaker tradition, the two van Helmonts opposed Aristotelianism and the medical philosophy of Galen, and instead offered a spiritually based understanding of the world. Like their Quaker contemporaries they stressed the essential goodness and unity of creation. Moreover, in their medical practice they prescribed iatrochemical substances similar to those adopted by Marshall and several other Quaker medical men.

Most early Quakers repudiated the pursuit of science as practised in the fledgling Royal Society of London, which they viewed as irreligious. As Isaac Penington (1616–79) argued in his attack on the Society, the study of physical nature did not lead to Truth, and those who pursued science were not merely wasting their time but by pursuing a false path they were renouncing the opportunity to gain salvation. Science had no place in the religious odyssey (Penington 1668). The repeated emphasis on the ultimate importance of the spiritual path and the recurrent repudiation of the physical and the sensual would seem to imply that most early Quakers were disinclined to study the physical world, unless it was viewed through the kind of spiritual lens provided by Helmontian natural philosophy.

Observing the Natural World

Although Penington's views probably reflected the outlook of most contemporary Quakers, a few individuals positively sought to engage with the new developments in science. Of these William Penn (1644–1718) was the most prominent and he even sought membership of the Royal Society (although the admission process was never completed). Moreover, in a letter from Pennsylvania to John Aubrey in 1683 he claimed that 'I am a Greshamist throughout', indicating his enthusiasm for the Society (which met at Gresham College) and its activities (Dunn and Dunn 1981–7, II, 394–6). In his writings, particularly his *Some fruits of solitude* (1693), Penn advocated the view that Quakers—especially young Quakers—should study nature. Echoing the widely held view that the natural world is the divinely authored Book of Nature, he urged that 'the *World* is a great and stately *Volume* of natural Things ...[and it] ought to be the *Subject* of the Education of our *Youth*, who, at [the age of] 20, when they should be fit for Business, know not anything of it' (Penn 1693, 2). Penn urged that study of the Book of Nature was far more worthwhile educationally than studying grammar, rhetoric, or foreign languages. Studying the natural world was also religiously uplifting, since nature displays 'an *Eternal Wisdom, Power, Majesty* and *Goodness*' (Penn 1693, 5). Unlike those seventeenth-century Quakers who considered the physical world to be corrupt and the external senses to be channels that admitted evil, Penn insisted that students should use their senses to appreciate the physical world and also to acknowledge that it is God's creation.

These arguments advanced by Penn enabled the student to appreciate the existence and qualities of the Creator from the study of nature. Thus for Penn and many later Quakers reflecting on the natural world became a spiritual exercise. To take two examples among many: in an early article on astronomy in the *Friend*, the author asserted that the study of the heavens is 'calculated to awaken and inspire emotions of admiration and reverence' for God. '[W]e shall find abundant proofs of wise and exquisite design in the construction of our [astronomical] system, of the nicest adjustment of laws and application of contrivances' (R. 1843). This is a form of the popular argument from design. A less formal appreciation of the spiritual value of the natural world appeared in a letter written in 1806 by Joseph Gurney Bevan (1753–1854) in which he expressed his enjoyment of autumn walks. These enabled him to revere God's works, since the 'mind does not stop at Creation, without being led by it to the Creator' (Anon. 1821, 93–4). When illuminated by the Light Within, nature could become a source of spiritual enlightenment. Such arguments also helped to legitimate the empirical study of nature among Quakers.

In the late seventeenth century and throughout the eighteenth an increasing number of Quakers reiterated Penn's views concerning not only the religious but also the utilitarian value of studying the natural world. For example, the schoolmaster and botanist Thomas Lawson who, like Penn, had received a university education, provided a long list of 'Useful and Necessary' topics about which young people should become familiar, such as 'Trees, Birds …the Rules of Gardening, Agriculture …Medicine …[the] Improvement of Lands … [and the] Propagation of Plants'. In typical Quaker fashion these serious and valuable activities were contrasted with such frivolous and ungodly pursuits as reading 'Lascivious Poems' and studying 'Pagan [i.e., Aristotelian] Philosophy' (Lawson 1680, 41). While Lawson insisted that knowledge of the creation was secondary in importance to the spiritual appreciation of God, he accepted that the natural world provided training in skills that would be of use to Quakers in maintaining themselves, their families, and their communities.

The value of science, especially botany, for education was recognized by some Quakers, including George Fox who famously instructed one of his followers to establish a school for teaching languages, 'together with the nature of herbs, roots, plants and trees' (Braithwaite 1979, 528). Later, science featured in the curricula of Quaker schools such as Ackworth (f. 1779), where a garden was soon established to enable pupils to study horticulture. At Bootham School (f. 1823) in York, which attracted boys from the more affluent Quaker families, a flourishing Natural History Society was founded in 1834, with a herbarium and library. Astronomy also proved popular and in the early 1850s a well-equipped observatory was built within the school grounds. Meanwhile girls at the Mount—Bootham's sister school—participated in nature walks and attended occasional science lectures. Such was the interest in science subjects, especially botany, that a consortium of Quaker schools founded their own monthly periodical, the *Natural History Journal* in 1877, to which staff and pupils contributed. Natural history was deemed of educational value because it taught careful observation and the classification of specimens. According to one pupil who had studied at Sidcot School, it had also been valuable in 'keep[ing] us from idleness', had formed 'an agreeable amusement and is calculated to expound the ideas of the wisdom, power and goodness of our Heavenly Father' (Knight 1908, 90).

Quakers not only introduced science subjects into their schools but they also contributed to scientific education in the wider community. For example, in several of her books of advice for women, Priscilla Wakefield (1750–1832) stressed the importance of knowing about contemporary science. She even wrote an illustrated *Introduction to botany* (1796), which passed through twelve editions. This book, which was written in a conversational style, portrayed botany as a suitable subject for upper-middle-class women to study. It was a healthy, interesting, and intellectually stimulating subject as well as being a source of innocent enjoyment. Nor did Wakefield ignore botany's value in teaching of the 'Infinite Wisdom and Intelligence, [manifested] in the structure of every leaf and every blossom' (Wakefield 1796, 43). Several Quakers edited popular science periodicals, including the *Botanical Magazine* (f. 1787 by William Curtis) and several of Edward Newman's titles including the *Entomologist* (f. 1840), the *Zoologist* (f. 1843), and the *Phytologist* (f. 1844). During the early years of *Nature* (f. 1869)—probably the most celebrated general scientific weekly of the period—one of the assistant editors was the botanist Alfred Bennett (1833–1902), who had previously edited the *Friend*, which itself carried scientific articles and even at times included a section variously entitled 'Literary and Scientific' or 'Scientific Notes'.

Quaker amateur scientists encountered science in the *Friend* and, less frequently, in the *British Friend*, and also subscribed to such periodicals as the *Botanical Magazine* and the *Zoologist*. They were active in local scientific societies and in the British Association for the Advancement of Science (BAAS), which functioned as an umbrella organization and held an annual meeting. Amateur interest in science long predates the BAAS; indeed, as early as 1678 Robert Barclay (1648–90) had listed '*Gardening*' and '*Geometrical and Mathematical Experiments*' among the 'innocent divertisements, which may sufficiently serve for relaxation to the mind' (Barclay 1678, 370). Many Quakers enjoyed gardening and laid out impressive gardens in which they cultivated rare species. John Fothergill's garden at Upton (where he lived from 1762 to 1780) and, in the middle decades of the nineteenth century, Robert Were Fox's at Penjerrick near Falmouth, were outstanding examples. Country walks were also encouraged and provided an opportunity for relaxation, enjoyment, and the enhancement of natural history collections. Many Quakers expressed their joy and enthusiasm for nature study, including Arthur Lister (1830–1908), a wine merchant by trade who made significant contributions to botany. According to his obituary in the *Annual Monitor*, Lister 'was never happier than when in intervals of leisure, he could get away among the wild life of the woods and the fields' (Anon. 1909). There are even examples of Quakers ignoring or abandoning their businesses because they found botanizing far more congenial.

Astronomy was another popular pursuit. For example, early in the nineteenth century the manufacturing chemist William Allen recorded in his diary his pleasure at retiring to the observatory at his home in Stoke Newington in order to find peace and spiritual solace at the end of a busy working day. Astronomy, he affirmed, was his 'favourite recreation' (Anon. 1846–7, I, 155). A later example is provided by the banker Joseph Gurney Barclay (1816–98), who was a Fellow of the Royal Astronomical Society. He constructed a well-equipped observatory at his family home in Leyton and even employed an assistant to make regular observations, which were published in four volumes entitled *Astronomical observations taken … at the private observatory of Joseph Gurney Barclay, Esq., FRAS, Leyton, Essex* (1865–78).

Meteorology also attracted a number of Quakers, including John Dalton, Elihu Robinson (1734–1809), John Fletcher Miller (1816–1856; a tanner from Whitehaven), and the pharmaceutical chemist Luke Howard (1772–1864). Dalton's first book *Meteorological observations and essays* (1793), to which many Quakers subscribed, indicates that he made observations three times a day at Kendal. Howard likewise made extensive meteorological observations over many years and also published an impressive two-volume work entitled *The climate of London* (1818–20). Here he tried to ascertain the (divinely framed) laws governing climate and, more famously, he proposed the classification and nomenclature for cloud types still widely used today.

Travel undertaken in the Quaker cause has sometimes been combined with a lively interest in botany and other sciences. For example, the nurseryman and botanist James Backhouse (1794–1869) was directed by York Monthly Meeting to travel to Australia and Tasmania in order to minister to the inhabitants and to investigate the penal system. His journal, which was published in 1843, records the people he met on his travels, with specific references to the conditions of the convicts. But it also contains detailed descriptions of the plants he encountered, including their Latin names and information about their habitats. He saw his role not only as spreading the Christian message but also as chronicling God's creation in a land whose botanical treasures were little known.

Some Quakers have pursued careers or business ventures that pertained directly to their botanical interests. For example, in the mid-eighteenth century Peter Collinson (1694–1768) became a leading importer of exotic plants from America. His collectors and correspondents in America included the Quakers John and William Bartram and he often used Quaker-owned ships to transport specimens back to England. An impressive number of Quakers became gardeners or seedsmen; in the period up to 1790 the minutes of the Edinburgh Yearly Meeting recorded nineteen Scottish Friends who were employed as gardeners, many of whom were members of the influential Miller family. For a thirty-five year period Quakers staffed the herbarium at Kew Gardens: Daniel Oliver (1830–1916), who was also Professor of Botany at University College, London, held the post of Keeper from 1864 until his retirement in 1890. He was then succeeded by his assistant John Gilbert Baker (1834–1920), who retained the position until 1899.

With the increasing professionalization of science Quakers pursued careers in many branches of science, some of which bore little connection with their commitments to Quaker values. Yet the Quaker tradition in botany was carried into the twentieth century by such scientists as Edgar Anderson (1897–1969), who worked at the Missouri Botanical Garden and Washington University, St Louis, and published his influential study *Introgressive hybridization* in 1949, and the eminent botanist, plant taxonomist, and historian of botany William Thomas Stearn (1911–2001), who worked as principal scientific officer at the British Museum (Natural History). Another example is Joseph Burtt Hutchinson (1902–88) who made outstanding contributions to crop cultivation, using the emerging science of genetics to improve the production of crops, especially cotton. He not only invigorated crop cultivation in Britain but travelled widely, using his expertise to assist growers in Trinidad, India, Uganda, and the Sudan. In 1956 he was knighted for his services to the agriculture of East Africa.

QUAKERS AND THE PHYSICAL SCIENCES

By contrast with the observational sciences discussed in the previous section, eighteenth- and nineteenth-century Quakers paid relatively little attention to what we would now call physics. Given the historic importance of Isaac Newton's mechanics and his immense impact on our culture it is significant that Quakers ignored his work. In part this is because dissenters were not admitted to Oxford nor allowed to graduate from Cambridge until the 1850s, and also because of their own distaste for these Anglican universities, which were the loci of Newtonianism. In part, too, Quakers were averse to creeds, while the Newtonian system of natural philosophy was often portrayed as dogma by its advocates. Moreover, the mathematical systematization of nature that

Newton formulated far transcended experience of nature and of its Creator, both of which were greatly valued by Quakers.

Although John Dalton deployed some of Newton's ideas in articulating the behaviour of gases composed of atoms, the first Quaker who can justifiably be called a physicist was the Bootham-educated Silvanus P. Thompson (1851–1916), who was trained at the Royal School of Mines and subsequently taught physics at Bristol University before being appointed as Principal and Professor of Electrical Engineering at the City and Guilds Finsbury Technical College. He made significant contributions to the study of electricity and optics and was a staunch advocate of technical education. He also argued that a natural alliance existed between Quakerism and the sophisticated physical science of his day. In a paper provocatively entitled 'Can a scientific man be a sincere Friend?' (Thompson 1896), which he delivered at the 1895 Manchester Conference, and in his 1915 Swarthmore Lecture, appropriately entitled *The quest for truth*, he portrayed both science and Quakerism as rational, open-ended, and parallel activities that equally sought truth as their primary aim. Thus science and Quakerism were not merely reconcilable but were parallel forms of investigation.

In another Swarthmore lecture delivered fourteen years later the relationship between Quakerism and science was again addressed, this time by astrophysicist Arthur Stanley Eddington (1882–1944). Like Thompson he portrayed Quakerism as commensurate with modern science; indeed, in an often-quoted passage from *Science and the unseen world* (1929) he portrayed the search for Truth as the basic objective underpinning both the Quaker approach to religion and the proper method for the pursuit of science. As an undergraduate Eddington had taken the mathematics tripos examination in his second year at Cambridge and achieved the remarkable accolade of Senior Wrangler. Later he was appointed Plumian Professor of Astronomy and Director of the Cambridge University Observatory. He is best known for his participation in the 1919 expedition to Principe (an island off the west African coast and close to the equator) to observe the solar eclipse. Despite the visibility of the sun being impaired by cloud cover, the resulting observations from Principe and from a similar observatory in Brazil subsequently confirmed Einstein's general theory of relativity, which predicted a specific bending of light rays passing close to the sun.

Eddington's participation in the 1919 expedition had a direct connection with his Quakerism. During the First World War the British authorities were confronted with the problem of how to deal with this awkward Cambridge scientist who refused to be inducted into the military service. Sending him on a scientific expedition to a remote island circumvented this difficulty. And there is another significant link. At a time when many British scientists openly expressed antipathy towards their German counterparts, Eddington was keen to provide an empirical test of a theory proposed by a German (Einstein), since as a Quaker he believed that science is an international venture that should be used to promote peaceful and unifying ends.

As Matthew Stanley has effectively demonstrated, the connections between Eddington's science and his Quakerism went well beyond his pacifist and internationalist commitments (Stanley 2007). Most importantly, a form of mysticism provided the common grounding for both his science and his religion. Unlike many other religious traditions, the Quaker emphasis on the Light Within encouraged Eddington to reject dogmatism and to embrace an openness to experience, especially religious experience, that enabled the individual to grow spiritually and to gain a greater sense of relationship with God. Similarly Eddington advocated a non-dogmatic, open-ended vision of the scientific method, which he described as mystical. Thus in his 1927 Gifford Lectures, published as *The nature of the physical world*, he addressed the two most important modern developments in physics, quantum theory and relativity, and also articulated a philosophy of science that included the conscious observer as part of the experimental situation.

The historical line from Thompson to Eddington has continued into our own day with Jocelyn Bell Burnell (*b*.1943), the astrophysicist who discovered radio pulsars. In a recent interview she argued that:

> Quakerism and research science fit together very, very well. In Quakerism you're expected to develop your own understanding of God from your experience in the world. There isn't a creed, there isn't a dogma.... [I]t also means that you keep redeveloping your understanding as you get more experience, and it seems to me that's very like what goes on in 'the scientific method'... Nothing is static [in science], nothing is final, everything is held provisionally. (Bell Burnell 2010)

Following the work of Bell Burnell and others on pulsars, an American Quaker, Joseph Hooton Taylor, Jr. (*b*. 1941), discovered the binary pulsar—a rapidly spinning neutron star orbiting around a companion star. For this discovery Taylor shared the Nobel Prize for physics in 1993 with his graduate student and he is currently Professor of Physics at Princeton University.

In the related field of cosmology George Ellis (*b*. 1939), of the University of Cambridge and more recently the University of Cape Town, made important contributions especially to the theory of spacetime. He has also been active in the anti-apartheid movement and, in 2004, received the Templeton Prize for Progress Toward Research or Discoveries about Spiritual Realities.

Compared with physics (and its parent field often called natural philosophy), Quakers have been far more visible in the area of chemistry, especially pharmaceutical chemistry. In the eighteenth century a number of Quaker pharmacies were established. In part this reflected the Quaker reputation for honesty at a time when pharmacists had acquired a negative reputation for adulterating medicines. The most notable Quaker pharmacy was at Plough Court in the City of London, founded by Silvanus Bevan in 1715. In 1795 William Allen became a partner in the firm and he subsequently entered into partnership with Luke Howard. When that partnership was dissolved Allen joined forces with members of the Hanbury family to form Allen and Hanburys, which remains a household brand name despite being taken over by Glaxo (now GlaxoSmithKline) in 1958.

CONFRONTING THE HUMAN CONDITION

The Quaker impulse to alleviate human suffering is manifest in Quakers' contributions to medicine and its allied sciences, such as pharmacy. Quaker participation in medicine is itself a major topic and one that cannot be addressed here adequately. It should, however, be noted that in the late seventeenth century and early decades of the eighteenth, the medical school at Leiden attracted a number of Quakers students. Subsequently, the medical school at Edinburgh University, with its strong reputation and absence of religious tests, became the favourite place for Quaker students not only from Scotland but also from Ireland, England, and America. In 1734 John Fothergill (1712–80) was the first Quaker to enter the medical school at Edinburgh, and over the ensuing century nearly a hundred Friends followed. These students would not only have attended lectures on medical topics, including *materia medica* (which spanned chemistry and botany), but would also have studied chemistry, natural philosophy, and possibly other scientific subjects.

The links between medicine and Quaker social initiatives are exemplified by the biography of George Newman (1870–1948). Educated at Sidcot and Bootham schools, he studied medicine at Edinburgh and King's College London before being appointed a district medical officer. In his *Infant mortality: a social problem* (1906) he offered an incisive analysis of the connection between social deprivation and infant deaths. He was subsequently appointed Chief Medical Officer to the Board of Education and held a similar position at the Ministry of Health. An untiring advocate of public health, he was particularly active in developing the Schools' Medical Service, for which he was knighted in 1911.

The role of Quakers in the development of nineteenth-century anthropology sheds light on Quaker participation in the human sciences, beginning with James Cowles Prichard. In his 1808 Edinburgh University dissertation, which formed the basis of his later publications, Prichard sought to explain human diversity from a close study of the evidence gleaned by travellers and others about the different races around the globe. Although he had joined the Anglican Church by the time his major book was published—*Researches into the physical history of man* (1813)—his research was underpinned by a commitment to the idea of the unity of the human races based on the biblical view that all races were descended from Adam and Eve. Human diversity therefore did not arise from innate differences between the races but was to be explained by such differential effects as climate and culture. Prichard's emphasis on the unity of humankind was reiterated by several other Quakers with anthropological interests, especially the Edinburgh-trained Thomas Hodgkin.

Quakers were also very prominent in the Aborigines' Protection Society (f. 1833), at a time when settlers and foreign powers were voraciously exploiting 'aborigine' people, often pursuing policies that we would now identify as ethnic cleansing. In response to such inhumanity, the Aborigines' Protection Society compiled information about the conditions of 'aborigines' and tried to influence both public opinion and administrators to behave humanely towards these groups. The society's motto 'Ab uno sanguine' indicates its monogenic orientation, which stood in direct contrast to the widespread polygenic stance that justified the view of Caucasians as a vastly superior race that could legitimately exploit other, and necessarily inferior, races. The conflicting views about whether other races were inferior surfaced in the 1850s in the Ethnological Society, which sought to advance the scientific study of ethnology. This resulted in a schism; its Quakers members (among others) supporting the monogenist camp within the Ethnological Society, while the polygenists seceded and founded their own society—the Anthropological Society.

A bus journey in Havana in 1856 proved a turning point in the life of a young Quaker who was to become a leading figure in British anthropology: Edward Burdett Tylor (1832–1919) encountered a fellow Quaker, Henry Christy (1810–65), an ethnologist who invited him to join an expedition to Mexico. This experience persuaded Tylor to immerse himself in the study of anthropology with the result that he later published work that helped establish anthropology as a science. His most important book was *Primitive culture* (1871) which offered an insightful and carefully documented account of the development of cultures, broadly conceived, including the progress of religion. Tylor had ceased being a Quaker some years earlier and was subsequently appointed keeper of the Oxford University Museum and Reader in Anthropology. In 1896 he became Professor of Anthropology, the first to hold a Chair of Anthropology at Oxford.

In his anthropological researches Tylor accepted that Darwin's theory of evolution applied to the development of humankind. During the closing decades of the nineteenth century, Quakers—especially Quaker naturalists—had come round to accepting Darwin's theory. Following the publication of *On the origin of species* in 1859, Friends had shown little interest in the theory, and when they did comment on it they did not engage in the vicious polemic that has marked much opposition to Darwin—both then and today. One of the Quaker critics of evolution was Edward Newman (1801–76), who reviewed the *Origin* in the *Zoologist* (which he edited) in 1861. While Newman asserted that evolution was incompatible with special creation, he and some of the older Quaker botanists who were principally concerned with taxonomy considered the theory to be inadequate for explaining the vast diversity of species. By contrast, over the ensuing decades a rising generation of Liberal Quakers was keen to adopt Darwin's ideas in their scientific investigations and they also published pro-evolutionary works. Their attitude to Darwinism was coloured by the view that Quakerism had become too inward-looking and should engage the new currents of Victorian thought, such as evolution. Thus, for example, George Stewardson Brady (1832–1921, Professor of Natural History at Armstrong College, Newcastle) contributed an essay to the *Friends Quarterly Examiner* with the title 'The modern spirit in the study of nature' in which he argued the need to accept Darwin's theory (Brady 1886). Evolutionary ideas also cohered well with the increasing emphasis on progressive revelation adopted by Liberal Quakers and engendered a new way of appreciating the unity of humankind.

Strands of environmentalist thought can be found throughout Quaker history, such as the emphasis on the unity of creation. In recent years Quakers have responded to the increasing concern over environmental issues by founding such groups as the Friends Committee for Unity with Nature (f. 1987) and, in the UK, the Living Witness Project which aims to support the development of Quaker corporate witness to sustainable living and explore ways of bringing it to the wider community.

While Quakers have frequently supported environmental initiatives, a few Quaker scientists have pursued research on environmental issues. For example, Timothy Charles Whitmore (1935–2002) was among the pioneers of forest ecology. Having studied forestry in the Far East (especially Malaysia), in Ecuador, and the Solomon Islands, and served for seven years as botanist at the Forest Research Institute of Malaysia, Whitmore worked at the Commonwealth Forestry Institute in Oxford and later returned to Cambridge where he taught rainforest ecology and biogeography. In publications such as *Tropical rain forests of the Far East* (1975) and in numerous papers he advanced the understanding of the dynamics of forests and he also undertook extensive consultancy work to promote improved management of forests. A rather different career path was followed by Ian Prestt (1929–95), whose early research at Monks Wood Experimental Station centred on demonstrating the impact of pesticides on birds, and thus on the food chain. He later assisted the Department of the Environment in the UK in framing its policies and worked for the Nature Conservancy Council. However, he is best known for his effective advocacy of protecting birds and their habitats, and also as the influential Director General and later President of the Royal Society for the Protection of Birds. A further example of a Quaker conservationist is Wolf Guindon (*b*.1920), from Alabama, who was jailed as a conscientious objector in 1949 and subsequently moved to Costa Rica, where he undertook conservation work and later helped establish the Monteverde Cloud Forest Reserve.

In the Scientific Community

Quakers have played a significant role in the scientific community and contributed to its organization. For example, a number of Quakers were elected to the Royal Society of London, probably the most prestigious scientific society in the English-speaking world. Although a few eighteenth-century Quakers were elected, including Peter Collinson and John Fothergill, the highest proportion of Quaker Fellows occurred in the latter half of the nineteenth century and early decades of the twentieth century. These included a few amateurs, such as the lawyer Sir Edward Fry, but more significantly a number of Quakers who had been appointed to academic positions, including Daniel Oliver (1830–1916), George Stewardson Brady, Silvanus Thompson, and Arthur Eddington. Several Fellows from Quaker backgrounds held important administrative positions in the society, including Thomas Birch (1705–66), who served as one of its secretaries for a thirteen-year period in the middle of the eighteenth century and produced its four-volume history; and Joseph Lister (1827–1912) who was President of the Royal Society at the end of the nineteenth century. Throughout most of the Society's long history women were excluded from membership. However, as part of its attempt to restructure itself after the Second World War, the society opened its fellowship to women in 1945. Kathleen Lonsdale was one of the two women elected in that year and she was subsequently awarded the Society's Davy Medal (1957) and also served on the Society's council.

Not surprisingly, Quakers have been active in learned societies that relate to their scientific expertise; for example, Lonsdale was Vice President and later President of the International Union of Crystallography. Of broader significance is her long-time involvement in the BAAS, where she was the first woman to hold the post of President. As a fairly egalitarian organization seeking to bring science to a wider public, the BAAS has proved particularly congenial to Quakers. John Dalton attended the inaugural meeting in 1831 and served as a Vice-President in 1833 and 1842. Moreover, significant numbers of Quakers, including women, attended the association's annual meetings throughout the nineteenth century and beyond. These meetings are held in a different city each year and local Quakers have often participated and helped with the local organization.

As a Quaker and pacifist Kathleen Lonsdale was one of the scientists who both sought to redirect the government's science policy to address significant human needs and opposed its use for military purposes. She was a founding member of the Pugwash Conferences (which are dedicated to reducing the danger of armed conflict and encourage cooperative solutions for global problems) and was active in the British Atomic Scientists' Association, serving both as its Vice-President and President. Among the other Quaker scientists who have been active in pacifist causes were the Scottish radiation physicist Jack Boag (also a founder of the Pugwash Conferences who served for a number of years as the British secretary), while Lionel Penrose (whose publications spanned genetics, psychiatry, mathematics, and chess) was a founder member of the Medical Association for the Prevention of War and served as its President for over ten years.

QUAKER AMBIVALENCES TOWARDS SCIENCE

It would appear that many Quakers have been strongly attracted to the natural world and keen to study it. The attraction of science arises principally because it addresses two significant aspects of Quakerism. The first is theological: the Creator can be appreciated by studying the creation. Thus the Book of Nature has been an apt subject for religious contemplation. Although modern Quakers have often moved away from earlier notions of divine creation and design, the study of the natural world continues to exert a strong attraction as a source of reflection. The second is utilitarian and relates to Quaker service: science offers power over nature and thus the ability to use natural materials for the benefit of humankind. Although Quaker engagement with science has varied significantly, depending on both the particular science and the historical context, these two issues have repeatedly been raised to justify Quaker participation in science.

However, the above argument masks two important problems that Quakers have encountered in trying to reconcile science with Quaker values. On closer inspection both the religious significance of science and its potential utility turn out to clash with other aspects of Quakerism. The first of these difficulties was apparent to the early Quakers and relates to their repeated emphasis on the primacy of the spiritual world. The exploration of the material world was frequently in tension with this outlook. Hence Quakers have expressed concern that they would lose their state of grace if their involvement in science took precedence over their religious commitments. For example, the eighteenth-century Dublin apothecary and Quietist John Rutty recounted in his spiritual diary that at one Quaker Meeting for Worship he had reflected: 'Lord, remember not the sin of my youth and age, even that of idolizing nature! O give me now to redeem the time, the precious time!' (Rutty 1776, I, 256). Although he pursued science diligently he (like a number of other Quakers) appreciated the danger of 'idolizing nature' and thus providing a distraction from his more important spiritual activities.

Secondly, there has been recent and widespread recognition that science is not pursued in a social vacuum but possesses immense implications for society. Power over nature is not an unmixed blessing. In particular, with the threat of nuclear war, Quakers have been very active in the peace movement and in trying to influence science policy in order to ensure that science is used for the good of humankind. The environmental crisis has likewise raised the important question of whether the use of science, especially by industry, government, and the military, is not a boon to humankind but rather a threat to human existence. This mounting social criticism of science is probably a significant factor in explaining why over the past few decades Quakers have been less attracted to science than were their Victorian forebears.

In recent decades scientific research has forged ahead, yet its findings have not always been used wisely and for the benefit of humankind. Science can and should play a significant role in addressing global warming, environmental degradation, overpopulation, and other problems facing the world. As Friends possess not only a strong tradition in scientific innovation but are also committed to humane values, Quaker scientists share a particular responsibility to moderate and direct science for humanitarian ends.

SUGGESTED FURTHER READING

Adams, A. (ed.) (1996) *The creation was open to me: An anthology of Friends' writings on that of God in all creation*. Wilmslow: Quaker Green Concern.

Cantor, G. (2005) *Quakers, Jews, and science: Religious responses to modernity and the sciences in Britain, 1650–1900*. Oxford: Oxford University Press.

Eddington, A. S. (1929) *Science and the unseen world*. London: George Allen & Unwin.

Kass, A. M. and Kass, E. H. (1988) *Perfecting the world: The life and times of Dr Thomas Hodgkin 1798–1866*. Boston: Harcourt Brace Jovanovich.

O'Neill, J. and McLean, E. P. (2008) *Peter Collinson and the eighteenth century natural history exchange*. Philadelphia: American Philosophical Society.

Raistrick, A. (1950) *Quakers in science and industry: being an account of the Quaker contribution to science and industry during the 17th and 18th centuries*. London: Bannisdale Press.

Slaughter, T. P. (1996) *The natures of John and William Bartram*. New York: Alfred A. Knopf.

Stanley, M. (2007) *Practical mystic. Religion, science, and A. S. Eddington*. Chicago: University of Chicago Press.

Whittaker, E. J. (1986) *Thomas Lawson 1630–1691: North Country botanist, Quaker and schoolmaster*. York: Sessions Book Trust.

CHAPTER 36

QUAKERS AND ETHICS

JACKIE LEACH SCULLY

When we speak of 'ethics', we mean something like the set of ideas governing what an individual or community thinks is right or wrong, and good or bad. This background of ideas generates the individual's and community's moral codes of conduct. Ethics as a discipline can also be thought of as the systematic examination of everyday, often taken for granted, moral codes. This chapter considers the extent to which a form of ethics can be identified as 'Quaker', distinct from secular ethics and the ethics of other churches or faith groups. Membership of a religious community, such as the Religious Society of Friends, is often taken as synonymous with adherence to a moral code peculiar to that religion. In reality, though, the moral codes of religious groups are usually quite similar to the everyday morality of the culture in which they are set. As a religious movement that arose within Western Judaeo-Christian culture, many of Quakerism's beliefs and practices are effectively indistinguishable from those of other churches within the Christian tradition (Scully and Dandelion 2007). There are, however, some features that mark Quaker ethics out as distinctive. They include the ethical resources and authorities that Quakers draw on; the processes by which ethical (and other) decisions are reached, individually and corporately; and the place that Testimony holds as a central ethical principle underpinning the Quaker vision of a good life.

The other chapters within this volume explain in detail the unity and diversity of modern Quakerism. In this chapter I use the simplest three-way typology of Liberal, Evangelical, and Conservative Friends. 'Liberal' indicates the unprogrammed tradition of Yearly Meetings found in Britain, the United States, continental Europe, Australasia, and some parts of Africa; 'Evangelical', the (largely) programmed tradition found within Friends United Meeting in the US and elsewhere, which tends to take a more traditional view of religious authority and ethics, and whose members use the moral language of sin, evil, redemption, and so on in a way that most Liberal Friends do not; and 'Conservative', the small number of Yearly Meetings, mostly from the US, that have in common the unprogrammed form of worship and 'conservatism' in many of their practices.

This chapter does not attempt to delineate all the ways in which each branch of Quakerism differs from the others in its ethical stance. It looks at the features that are central to contemporary Quaker ethics, in most cases starting with western Liberal Quakerism, and then turns to the points at which Evangelical or Conservative Friends have different beliefs or practices. Liberal Quakerism is in some ways the most distinctive of the branches in its handling of ethical issues. Broadly speaking, it has shifted significantly away from many of the traditional scriptural and pastoral sources of Christian guidance, while still maintaining that it has religious rather than secular ethics. Evangelical and to a lesser extent Conservative Quakerism sit closer to other well-characterized traditions within mainstream Christianity. (Much more detail on branches of Quakerism can be found in the other chapters.) Throughout this chapter 'Quaker' usually means Western Liberal Quaker, but everything should be broadly applicable to other strands of Quakerism except where clear differences are highlighted.

SOURCES OF MORAL AUTHORITY

The central, revolutionary feature of early Friends was the authority they allowed to a person's 'inward revelation'. In stark contrast with most of Western Christendom at the time, in which ethical claims were based on appeals to Scripture and church tradition, and where the authority for interpreting the text or the tradition was held by an elite group of clergy, the Religious Society of Friends believed and continues to believe in unmediated communication with God, including guidance on ethical matters. While seventeenth-century Friends certainly never discounted the claims of Scripture or church tradition, Fox and his contemporaries appear to have thought that Scripture 'did not need to be prescribed as an authority because the inward revelation [since it came from God] was so reliable' (Dandelion 2007, 185).

Friends continue to place greater emphasis on the experience of guidance by the Spirit than on theological formulations. Liberal Quakerism places least reliance on the authority of Scripture or tradition, so that the individual conviction on moral issues is given more weight. This tendency became marked in the twentieth century, which saw a move away from a belief in Scripture as the inerrant word of God and towards the greater credibility of experience-based spiritual (and hence also moral) claims. Individual Liberal Friends today have a high degree of autonomy in terms of ethical judgements, and their ethical stances are likely to be grounded primarily in personal judgement.

This does not mean that Friends in the Liberal tradition are free to develop their own idiosyncratic moral framework. Rather, it means that moral significance will be grasped through the spiritual experience of guidance by the Inward Light or 'Light Within', and not by reference to a scriptural text or the statements of a church elite.

Friends of the Evangelical tradition place more reliance on Scripture, and on the teaching of the Friends' Meeting or Church, for ethical guidance. For some Evangelical Friends the Bible is the written word of God, and therefore whatever Scripture says (or is believed to say) on a particular moral issue must be binding. Even those Meetings that hold less stringent views would still consider that while individual Friends' 'leadings' may well be inspired by the Spirit, they must nevertheless still be 'checked with the Scriptures' (Dandelion 2007, 185). For these Friends, a person's experience may be legitimate but its ethical content can only be understood within a larger spiritual context, and for most Evangelicals this context is provided principally by Scripture (Punshon 2001, 31).

Alongside personal experience and Scripture, the tradition of Quakerism as a whole also provides an ethical framework for all branches, again to differing degrees. Willcuts, an Evangelical writer, describes the guidance found in various Books of Discipline as representing 'the efforts by our forebears and approved spiritual leaders and representative bodies under the corporate guidance of the Spirit and study of the Scriptures' (Willcuts 1984, 42). Liberal Friends, too, do not ignore Quaker tradition completely: like Evangelical and Conservative Friends, they continue to draw on the collected wisdom of their Yearly Meeting, encapsulated in its Book of Discipline. Nevertheless, how this is done in practice and the force with which the guidance of a Book of Discipline (or 'Faith and Practice') is applied to Friends within the Meeting differs between traditions. The ethical guidance of Liberal Yearly Meetings' Books of Discipline is generally more exploratory and interrogative, and significantly less prescriptive, than that of Evangelical Yearly Meetings.

Individual and Corporate Ethical Decision-making

The Quaker reliance on individual ethical discernment carries the risk of producing moral judgements that are too personalized for the community to endorse, leading to fragmentation of the group. The process of ethical judgement and decision-making, by which individual moral convictions or concerns are 'tested' against the judgement of the Meeting as a whole, can be seen as a structural safeguard against this.

The Meeting for Worship for Business, sometimes known as the Meeting for Worship for Church Affairs, is where collective decisions are reached. The decision-making procedure in Business Meetings is strictly laid down, peculiar to Quakers, and, in principle at least follows a defined protocol. Business Meetings begin and end in silence and are conducted as an occasion of worship. The Meeting is not 'trying to reach a decision' but 'seeking divine guidance on a matter'. If divine guidance is not forthcoming or at least cannot be found on that occasion, then on matters of major ethical importance the Meeting may prefer to hold back from making any decision if the 'sense of the Meeting' is that unity is not yet possible.

The Book of Christian Discipline of Philadelphia Yearly Meeting (a Liberal Yearly Meeting) says, 'We consider ourselves to be in unity when our search for Truth is shared; when our listening for God is faithful; when our wills are caught up in the presence of Christ; and when our love for one another is constant. A united meeting is not necessarily all of one mind, but it is all of one heart' (Philadephia Yearly Meeting, 2002). Similarly, Ohio Conservative Yearly Meeting says, '…Friends …continue in a spirit of search for divine guidance. It naturally follows that there can be no rightful or satisfactory decision of a matter until there is large measure of unity in it' (Ohio Yearly Meeting of Friends, 1992, 6).

Business Meetings are as likely to address matters of major moral weight as issues of no or minor ethical significance (stereotypically, the colour of the meeting-house carpet). However, the Meeting for conduct of business, at least in principle, has similar form and objective as a Meeting for Worship, which means that little formal distinction is made between moral and practical discernment in terms of the processes that Friends collectively go through in order to come to a conclusion (see chapter 16 within this volume by Birkel, entitled 'Leadings and Discernment'.) This is in line with the general Quaker disinclination to separate particular times, places, or activities as having more spiritual significance than others. (In practice, of course, Friends should sense that certain issues are more serious than choosing meeting-house décor.)

All this binds ethical discernment very strongly to a model in which the individual Quaker is a moral agent only if he or she is embedded within the collective body. To exercise proper discernment requires guidance from the gathered Meeting, via one practice or another (Scully 2007), such as the 'Meetings for Clearness' where a Quaker facing difficulty may gather a group of trusted Friends, to listen to him or her in a spirit of worship before offering comments that will, ideally, guide the Friend towards greater clarity. Quakerism acknowledges, 'that no one person sees the whole truth and that the entire meeting, as the Body of Christ, can see more accurately than one person can see any part of it' (Willcuts 1984, 76). Traditionally, ethical discernment would have been done in the context of a strong and clearly defined Quaker community in which family, friends, acquaintances, and often work colleagues would all have been Quakers. Today most Friends do not live in this kind of community, and the traditional view sees this as placing the lone Friend at risk of error. While contemporary thinking in Quakerism credits the individual Friend with significant moral capacity, there have also been efforts within world Quakerism to devise forms of Quaker community (such as online Meetings) that take account of contemporary Quaker lifestyles.

Leadings, Concern, and Discernment

The interwoven concepts of leadings, concerns, and discernment are crucial to Quaker ethics. *Leadings* refer to the sense that Friends have of being guided by God, towards a particular ethical stance, for example. In keeping with the Quaker belief in the indivisibility of the divine and mundane, a leading can be about almost anything. Liberal Friends tend to restrict their claims to being divinely led to a serious ethical or political decision, for instance, or a life-changing shift in employment. Conservative Friends have retained the early Quaker practice of waiting for a leading on a wider diversity of events, believing that God will steer the path of a person's life via small nudges just as much as through dramatic crises: 'there is no aspect of our life,' says one Conservative author, 'that may not be the subject of a divine leading or prompting' (Wilson 2001, 181).

The notion of a *concern* is particularly relevant to developing the policy of the Yearly Meeting, or initiatives that a local Meeting may be asked to support. An individual Friend who feels prompted by the Spirit on an ethical issue should formally bring it to the attention of others ('lay the concern before the Meeting'). The Meeting may decide to support the Friend's concern in whatever way is appropriate, or may respond that the issue is not one on which the Meeting is united. But as Willcuts notes, 'If the concern is held deeply or perhaps is brought up again and again in spite of previous inaction or even opposition, the meeting may finally acquiesce even though a degree of hesitation was felt at first by some' (1984, 75). The most famous (or notorious) example of this concerns John Woolman's first attempts to convince New England Friends that slavery was wrong: the 'slowly changing stance' (Wilson 2001, 134) of American Yearly Meetings on the issue can be traced through the evolving guidance given by the Minutes instructing Friends on the slaves they then owned and ultimately what their stance on slave owner-ship should be. This process may be nothing more elevated than the wearing down of opposition by determined moral attrition; nevertheless, the Quaker theology of divine guidance effectively encourages decisions (including those decisions that stick to the status quo rather than challenge it) to be revisited, to check whether new insight that was not previously available may change a Meeting's understanding of God's will.

The final component in Quaker ethical and spiritual judgement is *discernment*. Discernment is the skill of identifying the right course of action, not through a cognitive exercise but through the ability to attend to the 'promptings of love and truth' (*Britain Yearly Meeting* 2009, 1.02). According to *Quaker Faith and Practice* of Britain Yearly Meeting, 'Throughout the discernment process there should be one overriding prin-ciple before the hearts and minds of all: is this individual or group right to believe this action or service has been 'laid upon them' by God?' (Britian Yearly Meeting 2009: 13.06). Discernment has to do with making ethical choices, but also the formation of the attitudes that shape them (Punshon 2001, 231). Punshon argues that the focus on discernment provides an explanation for the apparent lack of an explicit moral the-ology in the Religious Society of Friends. Writing within the Evangelical tradition he notes that Friends regard individual and collective behaviour as reflecting the state of the relationship with God. Moral knowledge comes from the Inward Light; morally good action entails obedience to what the Light requires. Such a pattern of discernment and response cannot occur outside a spiritual framework, and so ethical judgement is not about the application of abstract principles or the calculation of consequences, but rather an opportunity to discern and respond to the divine call (Punshon 2001, 240–1).

A Procedural Ethics

Liberal Friends in particular are likely to assess an ethical judgement through the proc-ess by which it is reached rather than the conclusion to which it comes. (Process is not the whole story for Evangelical and Conservative Friends, because of their different sources of moral authority.) In other words, Liberal Quakerism today is oriented towards a procedural rather than a substantive ethics (Scully 2007). The criterion for whether an action or stance is morally right is not in the first instance whether it accords with a given set of statements about right or wrong, but whether it has been arrived at through right processes that ensure as far as possible that it is God's will.

The discernment procedures used across Quakerism acknowledge the significance of individual perception, to greater or lesser extents, but they also systematically counterbalance that with church tradition and with corporate discernment. Hence all branches of Quakerism have institutionalized forms of corporate testing. Because Liberal Quakerism is less counterbalanced by text or tradition, the corporate testing by the body of the Meeting is even more important, in principle at least. Thus once an individual Quaker has experienced a moral intuition or come to a reasoned conclusion via individual discernment, the procedure becomes a collective one located within corporate practices.

In the early-to-middle history of Quakerism many decisions that would today be considered private and personal would be held up to corporate discernment. As Dandelion and others have noted, there was a need to ensure that the line between Quakers and 'the world' was kept firm, and that Quaker behaviour was perceived by outsiders as exemplary: vigorous policing of private Quaker behaviour helped to ensure this (Skidmore 1993). Later, growing accommodation to the norms of the world meant that practices of corporate disciplining became less common and more perfunctory among Liberal Friends; these practices have been retained to a greater extent by Conservatives and Evangelicals. For all Friends, significant decisions on Quaker ethical policy continue to be taken through the formalized discernment procedures of the Meeting for Worship for Business at local and national levels.

One of the commonest criticisms levelled against communitarian forms of ethics (Taylor 1989; MacIntyre 1984) is that they are inherently resistant to change. Interestingly, Quaker discernment practice not only tolerates, but in principle actively requires ongoing receptiveness to insights that come from God, prior to any exercise of collective judgement. This opens up the possibility of moral insights that radically challenge community norms. For Quakers, the presence of God can provide a kind of Archimedean point disrupting the conservative reliance on Scripture or church tradition. A potentially closed-off system can in theory be troubled through a moral insight that neither individual nor the collective, constrained by their horizons of understanding, could have imagined.

THE VISION OF THE GOOD LIFE

The principles, values, frameworks for evaluation, and so on of philosophical ethics are means to the end of working out the right way(s) to live. To achieve this, behind the principles and values must rest some theory of what constitutes the morally good life. Where secular visions of the morally good life are framed in terms of particular ethical acts, or through the characteristics of moral agents, theological ethics articulates its vision through the notion of the right relationship to God.

Central to the Quaker vision of the good life is 'gospel order'. This is sometimes understood narrowly as the structure of the embryonic Quaker church set down by early Friends; today it also refers to a broader metaphysical claim about the meaning of the good life. Gospel order is indeed about the shape of a faithful community, but the reason why this is what such a community looks like is because it facilitates Friends' discernment of how God wants them to live.

To fully grasp the significance of the idea of gospel order to Quaker ethics, it must be placed in the context of Quaker eschatology (see chapter 13 within this volume by Gwyn, entitled 'Quakers, Eschatology, and Time'). Quaker theology holds that the Kingdom of God is already present (in the sense that it is available to believers, rather than that the current state of the world is just as God would want it to be). Friends consider that it is possible to live the new life in the present moment. Gospel order indicates 'the right relationship of every part of creation, however small, to every other part and to the Creator' (Wilson 2001, 3). The various practices that Friends have developed help discern the course of action (or sometimes inaction) that is in keeping with gospel order.

Early Friends believed that conversion to the Quaker way produced such an extraordinary cognitive shift, an 'epistemic break' with old ways of thinking, that it became possible for newly converted Friends to intuit the life that gospel order required them to follow. Liberal Friends today are less likely to express this through the concept of conversion than of enduring disposition: everyday behaviours and practices that over time habituate Friends to the consciousness of the right thing to do. Wilson describes gospel order as 'an organizing principle' (Wilson 2001, 4): not a set of rules, but an entire conceptual framework within which Friends make sense of the world through understanding the relationship with God 'in all of the divine manifestations and the responsibilities of that relationship' (Wilson 2001).

Quakers believe that living in accordance with the divine will is possible now, and that what is discerned are acts and choices that will place a Friend in harmony with gospel order now, rather than offering a vision of a form of life to come. This claim makes a stringent combination of spiritual and ethical demands: life as a Quaker is not about making verbal statements of justification but about living in ways that witness to the presence of God.

THE ROLE OF TESTIMONY

The concept of testimony encapsulates the Quaker view of the relationship between spiritual and everyday life. It is ethical inasmuch as it is a statement of how the good life should be lived. For early Friends, 'the whole of life was testimony to the inward spiritual experience' (Dandelion 2007, 221), and Quakerism continues to see the way of life as the primary evidence of an inward orientation towards God. Over time, and also between and within branches of Quakerism, the meaning of testimony has changed, Punshon argues that some ecclesiological or theological testimonies (such as the rejection of clergy and of defined sacraments) have become less important or been reinterpreted, while modes of behaviour held to be characteristic of Quaker life have increased in significance (2001, 249–50)—although it is also true that the details of such behaviours and the firmness of their contours have shifted too.

Especially in Liberal Quakerism the global term of 'testimony' is often broken down into discrete testimonies: to peace, justice, truth, simplicity, equality, and (sometimes) community. Expressed like this they are more easily used as moral guides in everyday life. Indeed, they can be seen as ethical principles, although some more closely resemble virtues than formal ethical principles. But however they are defined, individual testimonies need to be viewed as aspects of the overall testimony that is inseparable from its theological background. The testimonies are not primarily about ethics: they are fundamentally theological statements about the Quaker relationship with God, thereby making ethical statements about how to live out that relationship.

Quaker traditions today differ in the theological basis they use to support testimony. Like early Friends, Evangelical Quakers focus on changes in outward forms of life as testifying to an inward conversion. Liberal Friends by contrast are more likely to talk about testimonies as guides to living a good life. This is one place where a difference in language may lead to an overstatement of the difference in the underlying concept. Although fewer Liberal Friends would articulate the testimonies as being about bearing 'witness to the reality of Christ's Inward Presence and lordship', they would agree that living in accordance with the testimonies witnesses to their own attempts to follow the guidance of the Inward Light; and while they may not invoke Christ's lordship, they would agree that the desire to live as a Quaker responding to 'promptings of love and truth' determines both 'what we want to do and what we are able to do; how we want to live and how we are enabled to live' (Wilson 2001, 164).

But branches of Quakerism can differ significantly in the precise delineation of a good Quaker life in gospel order, particularly on contentious issues of sexuality and simplicity. Dandelion (2007, 222–223) gives the example of an Evangelical Bible College that provides a detailed code of conduct, including forms of dress, that its students should adhere to as a sign of their spiritual commitment. Liberal Friends would be very unlikely to produce an equivalent list. Liberal Yearly Meetings do have ways of indicating to their members the aspects of their lives that the Meeting considers ethically important, but these indicators are often couched as 'queries', provocations to ethical reflection, rather than binding rules. So, for example, where the Bible College code mentioned above forbids the 'patronage of professional sports events, motion picture theaters, and the viewing of television' (Dandelion 2007, 222), query 39 of Britain Yearly Meeting's *Advices & Queries* says only: 'Consider which of the ways to happiness offered by society are truly fulfilling and which are potentially corrupting and destructive. Be discriminating when choosing means of entertainment and information.'

Although the branches of Quakerism can differ in their theological articulation of testimony and the details of how lives are lived, there is still a large degree of unity. All branches would be likely to agree that prioritizing either the inward change or the outward behaviour is misleading. Ideally, there is no divide: 'our outward and inward natures are so integrally connected that each reflects and influences the other. Our inward condition shapes our outward behaviour, and vice versa' (Wilson 2001, 181). There is also a great degree of commonality about the (named) testimonies. This is in part because they are not separate building blocks that can be dropped from or added to a moral code. The testimonies come as a bundle because they are the 'necessary outcome of our understanding of church and the basis of corporate not just individual morality' (Punshon 2001, 253).

Hence, there is often strong internal resistance to any change in the agreed set of testimonies. For example, from the 1990s onwards Liberal Quakerism has been discussing a testimony to 'sustainability', 'creation', or 'stewardship' (of natural resources). The arguments against are primarily that there is no need to add a perspective that might turn out to be historically contingent to the testimonies, which are seen as timeless. Moreover, everything that a testimony to sustainability or creation implies could equally well be contained within the existing testimonies: for example, a testimony to simplicity could be interpreted in such a way that it covered the concerns of sustainability. Some Yearly Meetings, such as Canada, have had a particularly strong engagement with environmental issues, which Canadian Friends frame in terms of trying 'to understand this work through our social justice and human rights lenses' (Canadian Friends Service Committee 2011)—perspectives that are themselves derived from the foundational testimonies to equality and justice.

Other voices, however, argue that a testimony to sustainability expresses a new spiritual insight about the intrinsic value of the natural world, one not available to early Friends. Thus Australia Yearly Meeting prepared a 'Quaker Earthcare Statement' in 2008 (Australia Yearly Meeting 2010). In Britain Yearly Meeting overt calls for a new testimony to creation diminished in the early twenty-first century, yet the wording of the *Framework for Action* reflected how Liberal Friends saw the issue as part of their witness: 'Sustainability is an urgent matter for our Quaker witness. It is rooted in Quaker testimony and must be integral to all we do corporately and individually' (*A Framework for Action 2009–2014*). At Britain Yearly Meeting Gathering at Canterbury in 2011 a Minute recording the decision to move corporately towards being a low-carbon sustainable community gave 'care for the environment' as one of the testimonies.

This exemplifies the way in which Quaker ethics, while resistant to change for its own sake, is open to the idea of fresh divine guidance, so that behaviours acceptable to people in one circumstance (such as slavery) may later be perceived as morally wrong. This is not the same, however, as saying that something is morally right in one age and wrong in another. Quakers will argue that slavery was always wrong, and that although every human being's moral perception is contextually limited, those Friends who could not see the moral wrong of slavery in the seventeenth and eighteenth centuries were still at fault even if the fault is understandable.

Moral Action

The ideas that Quaker lives are testimony to the inner orientation towards God and that Quakers live within an existing gospel order underpin Quaker engagement with the world. That Quakerism requires its members to work actively to put right, or at least make better, various kinds of social evils, not in order to win converts but because this constitutes Quaker spirituality, is encapsulated in William Penn's 1682 assertion that 'True godliness don't turn men out of the world but enables them to live better in it and excites their endeavours to mend it' (Britian Yearly Meeting 2009 23.02). The activist tradition has been stronger or weaker at different times and across the different Quaker branches. It is relatively strong today, indicated by the emphasis on social justice work of many Yearly Meetings. Social engagement (or 'good works') is practised by many faith groups, but the key point of Quaker ethics is that the motivation for moral action is provided by a theological framework peculiar to Quakerism.

Relationship to Secular Ethics

Like most lay ethical discourse, Quaker approaches to making moral judgements form a 'collage', drawing on a number of frameworks derived from more than one ethical tradition (Scully 2002, 211–12). The driving force is not the production of a consistent and coherent philosophical argument, but rather the need to articulate a personal understanding of the situation at each stage of working towards a conclusion about the best way forward. Elements from ethical traditions are reinterpreted and combined, where necessary, with innovation. Coherence is maintained by drawing on unifying 'concepts, analogies, metaphors, and symbols' (Stout 1990, 169) that unite Friends' moral intuitions with their religious lives.

Religious groups commonly have a deontological basis to their ethics: their ethical thinking is organized around commandments that become moral imperatives because of their perceived status as articulations of the will of God. However, as I have argued in more detail elsewhere (Scully 2002, 2007), this does not seem to weigh so heavily for Liberal Quakers. Evangelical and Conservative Quakers are more likely to take deontological, scripturally based moral statements as a large part of their collage. Deontological claims about moral rules that duty requires one to obey are effectively credal, and therefore unlikely to appeal to the branch of Quakers whose identity is so strongly connected with the rejection of written creeds as sources of authority. But at the same time the desire to place a more transcendent criterion than good or bad outcomes behind moral claims, leads to the rejection of purely consequentialist reasoning as well. It may also be that the 'utilitarian calculus', in other words the maximization of benefit for the greatest number of people, will never be compelling to a group that has rejected quantitative decision-making (Scully 2007).

Averse to both deontological and consequentialist approaches, the Liberal Quaker collage is dominated by a form of virtue ethics (Crisp and Slote 1997; Hursthouse 1999). (This is a generalization, and even within Liberal Quakerism there are those who hold something closer to a deontological stance about the intrinsic wrongness of a particular practice, based on Scripture or classic Quaker writings.) Virtue ethics is an agent-centred theory in which the right act is not found by following a defined rule or process, but by identifying what a virtuous person in that situation would do. There seem to be two main reasons for the popularity of virtue ethics among Liberal Friends. First, an ethical framework based on interior character, and necessarily contingent on the moral insight available to an embodied individual at a particular place and time, resonates with a number of powerful epistemological concepts in contemporary Liberal Quakerism about the partiality of truth, revelation as contextual and limited, the spiritual life as an ongoing search, and so on. By contrast, both deontological and consequentialist ethics operate around an assumption of epistemic closure—that the (moral) truth can be known by following the rule or undertaking the evaluation of outcomes.

Virtue ethics makes a strong connection between the inward nature of a person and his or her outward behaviour, in that outward acts are generated by the internal moral habitude, and an analogous strong continuity between inner and outer life is found in the Quaker concept of testimony. As Dandelion has argued (1996), religious identity for Quakers is demonstrated in terms of behaviour rather than statements of belief. The virtues are more than contingent personality traits; they are enduring dispositions towards actions, reflecting a commitment to a particular view of the good life. Similarly the testimonies can be considered as establishing enduring dispositions towards actions, reflecting a background commitment to a Quaker view of the good life in gospel order. Virtue ethics' focus on the right act as necessarily a reflection of the actor's inner commitments, and as part of a consistent pattern of right action, clearly has more in common with the model of right living given by testimony than do ethical theories that evaluate the outward act detached from the moral identity of the actor. A corollary is that Quaker values are as embedded in the means by which particular moral goals are pursued as in the goals themselves, a feature which again echoes the structure of virtue ethics: if all life is a statement of inner spiritual/ethical stance then individual steps towards a goal must also be, in themselves, morally justifiable.

Positioning an individual's actions as equivalent to his or her statement of faith connects moral life with religious identity in an unusually direct way. Of course, other faith groups also expect spiritual commitment to be evidenced in outward actions. But most religious identities are primarily defined through belief statements, and in doing so an ontological gap is inserted between religious and moral life. This cannot be the case for a Friend claiming to be a good Quaker, even among Evangelical and Conservative traditions where doctrinal statements carry more weight, and certainly not among Liberal Friends.

Although Liberal Friends, and to a lesser degree Conservative and Evangelical Friends, take an approach that resembles virtue ethics, they also make use of what I have called a 'deontological tether' in which virtue-related statements are grounded in the ultimately non-negotiable claim to the value of human personhood. In contemporary Quakerism this is expressed in the phrase 'that of God in everyone' (Scully 2002). As many commentators have pointed out, this is probably the single theological statement shared by all branches of Quakerism. For George Fox, who originated the phrase, it did not signify something about the absolute value of human personhood; rather, for Fox, probably following Romans 1:18–20, 'that of God' stood in judgement of the evil within each human being as well as in affirmation of the good. The current meaning of the phrase among Liberal Quakers has as much to do with the early twentieth-century Modernists as it does with classic Quaker thought. But however interpreted, it sets the normative standard for Friends in their dealings with others. Like 'love your neighbour as yourself', or Kant's categorical imperative that people should be treated as ends in themselves and not solely as means to (someone else's) ends, it provides the minimum normative core around which the virtues of the good Quaker cohere. In terms of secular ethics it is a foundational ontological claim about the nature of human beings, coupled to a deontological command for Quakers to answer that of God in everyone. From the point of view of Liberal Quaker theology, however, the command is not strictly speaking deontological, since its force is not based on duty (to respond to that of God in everyone) but rather on the desire to respond to God (within others) in a way that reflects the relationship Friends would wish to have with God; that is, with love.

This phrase remains peculiar to Quakers, even if the Quaker traditions have different interpretations of how 'that of God' is made manifest in individual lives. As the normative core, it shapes a Quaker ethical anthropology, whereby people are essentially good because of this element of the divine nature they carry. From this perspective, it also underpins a meta-ethical claim about the nature of evil. Evil becomes a deviation from the fundamentally good human ontology into moral pathology. Thus in Quaker ethics, moral goodness is attributed to the intrinsically good nature of the agent, while moral wrong is more likely to be described in terms of actions that are separable from the fundamental being of the actor.

CONTEMPORARY ETHICAL ISSUES

Quaker history, theological diversity, and local culture all affect the ethical responsiveness of Quakers around the world, determining which issues they hold to be most ethically troubling, and how they feel it right to react. The diversity within Liberal Quakerism alone means that Yearly Meetings frequently struggle to make unequivocal statements on ethical issues. On more contentious moral questions, Yearly Meetings, especially Liberal and Conservative ones, will acknowledge openly that the experiences and opinions of their members differ rather than attempting to give an artificially unified view.

The relationship between the Religious Society of Friends and 'the world' has evolved though its 360-year history, going through periods of confrontation, Quietism, and accommodation to the standards of society at large. Many Liberal Friends in Western democracies today feel a responsibility to maintain the tradition of radical dissent, 'speaking truth to power', and rejecting the standards of the non-Quaker world. Elsewhere, Friends of other traditions will also feel this call to challenge secular moral failings. Evangelical or Conservative Friends will commonly pay more attention to regulating the internal moral behaviour of the group than Liberal Yearly Meetings are likely to; on the other hand some Yearly Meetings are also located in parts of the world where it is unsafe to be too openly critical of, for example, government policies, and therefore may hold back from public ethical statements.

It is hard to generalize about the ethical issues with which contemporary Quakers concern themselves, and the details would rapidly go out of date. However, it would be broadly true to say that ethical issues are often identified and framed in terms of their conflict with named testimonies. Thus various kinds of peace-building and efforts to prevent conflict remain of paramount importance to Friends, because of the special place that the peace testimony holds within Quaker tradition. In one recent example of local peacekeeping, Friends in Kenya formed the Friends Church Peace Teams in response to the violence following Kenyan elections in 2007, aiming to foster immediate reconciliation, but also to 'build lasting peace' through local social justice initiatives (American Friends Service Committee 2011). Liberal, Conservative, and Evangelical Friends are united in seeing global inequalities, materialism, corruption, and so on, as ethically as well as spiritually wrong in themselves, because they conflict with testimonies to equality, justice, and integrity. Historically, Liberal Friends have been provoked to action against long-standing social evils such as poverty or addiction through seeing them as either based in or exacerbated by unjust social arrangements, and in conflict with the Quaker claim that the marginalized of society are equally of ethical concern and are moral subjects who matter as much as the more powerful, this conviction in turn being rooted in the testimony to equality. Friends increasingly argue that the roots of conflict and violence also lie in inequalities, and therefore see their work against inequality as part of the peace testimony.

Today's issues are often political or global, especially when they are to do with conflict, economic injustice, or sustainability. So, for example, in November 2011 the American Friends Service Committee (AFSC) and Quakers in Britain issued statements in support of the Occupy Wall Street and the Occupy London Stock Exchange activists who had protested against 'the decisions of powerful business and political leaders' (American Friends Service Committee 2011). The statement of BYM directly linked the Quaker vision of a transformed world with ethical action: 'The idea that another world is possible is crucial for us [Quakers] too. We cannot accept the injustice and destructiveness of the economic system as it is' ([http://www.quaker.org.uk/news/news-release-quakers-express-support-occupy-london]).

Liberal Friends tend to be progressive on matters of sexual ethics, resisting prescriptive statements and emphasizing the nature of the relationship. Thus Philadelphia Yearly Meeting's Book of Christian Discipline says that, 'Friends are led in part by our testimonies: that sexual relations be equal, not exploitative; that sexual behavior be marked by integrity; and that sex be an act of love, not of aggression ... Friends are wary of a preset moral code to govern sexual activity', but goes on to add, 'Even with its respect for individual leadings, Quakerism does not sanction license in sexual behavior' (Philadelphia Yearly Meeting 2002, 70–1). Conservative and Evangelical Friends are more likely to find issues such as abortion, sex outside marriage, and homosexuality to be morally wrong. But having said that, there is diversity of opinion and of practice around these issues even within non-Liberal Quakerism, with Evangelical Friends more likely to preserve unity within the Meeting by stating their position as non-negotiable, and Conservative Friends more likely to submit questions around these issues to Quaker business procedures to discern the way forward (Angell 2011b).

Liberal Friends will take a corporate stance on sexual ethical issues where they perceive injustice to be present. An example is Britain Yearly Meeting's conclusion in 2009 that the legal ban on marriage between partners of the same sex was unjust. British Friends at this point felt called to make a stand against this as part of their testimony to equality. At Yearly Meeting Gathering that year, Quakers in Britain agreed to call for a change in the law so that 'same-sex marriages can be prepared, celebrated, witnessed, reported to the state, and recognised as legally valid, without further process, in the same way as opposite sex marriages are celebrated in Quaker meetings'. The Minute recording that decision recognized not only that 'We have heard dissenting voices during the threshing process which has led us to this decision' but also that 'We will need to explain our decision to other Christian bodies, other faith communities, and, indeed to other Yearly Meetings, and pray for a continuing loving dialogue, even with those who might disagree strongly with what we affirm as our discernment of God's will for us at this time'. This concern, which was tested in Meetings over many years, brought to the collective discernment of the gathered Yearly Meeting, considered with scrupulous attention to dissenting voices, set within the context of testimony, and where the final Minute articulates the provisional, dialogical, and ongoing nature of ethical discernment, elegantly exemplifies the goal, processes, and theological background of Quaker ethics and ethical decision-making.

SUGGESTED FURTHER READING

Meilaender, G. and Werpehowski, W. (eds.) (2005) *The Oxford handbook of theological ethics.* Oxford: Oxford University Press.

Lafollette, H. (ed.) (2000) *The Blackwell guide to ethical theory.* Blackwell Philosophy Guides. Oxford: Blackwell.

Scully, J. L. and Dandelion, P. (2007) *Good and evil: Quaker perspectives.* Aldershot: Ashgate.

Scully, J. L. (2007) 'The secular ethics of Liberal Quakerism', in J. L. Scully and P. Dandelion (eds.) *Good and evil: Quaker perspectives,* 219–31. Aldershot: Ashgate.

Scully, J. L. (2008) 'Virtuous Friends: morality and Quaker identity' in P. Dandelion and P. Collins (eds.) *The Quaker condition: the sociology of a liberal religion,* 107–23. Newcastle: Cambridge Scholars.

CHAPTER 37

GLOBAL QUAKERISM AND THE FUTURE OF FRIENDS

MARGERY POST ABBOTT

THE FALLIBILITY OF PROJECTIONS

THE Religious Society of Friends, the second smallest of the twenty-three members within the Conference of Christian World Communions with perhaps 507,000 members worldwide (Barrett et al 2009, 31), continues to bring its distinctive form of Christianity to the table at the start of the twenty-first century. In 1966, Roland H. Bainton wrote that the 'future of Quakers depends plainly in part upon the future of Christianity'. He noted that Christianity is a minority religion and likely to remain so, and commented on the effect of urbanization on faith and the shift this brought in Christian liturgy and ethics as well as thought. His view of the Quaker future suggested two alternatives—survival as a driblet of [North American and British] sophisticated folk, or as militant leader of a social and religious rejuvenation that might cause Friends to fragment further (Bainton et al 1966, 1–9). The half-century since Bainton's observations has brought a slight increase in the numbers of the unprogrammed Friends, hints of a potential for social and religious rejuvenation in disparate parts of the globe, new connections among different traditions of Friends, and a dramatic growth in East Africa, South America, and other parts of the world far from the 'driblet' of sophisticated folks he referenced.

Trying to predict the future has its problems, as Bainton's example suggests, and trying to predict actual numbers makes even less sense. In the seventeenth century it looked briefly as if Quakers could become the primary religion in England. By the twentieth century pessimists were projecting that Quakers, at least in Britain, would be gone within 50 years (Murgatroyd 2010, 13, 14). The most consistent set of historic figures show about 164,000 Quakers in the world in 1950 and 199,000 by 1980 (Russell 1950; FWCC 1980). While other sources suggest larger numbers—507,000 as noted above—the numbers reported in 2010 total 450,000. This includes 233,000 Quakers in Kenya,

Table 1 **Friends by Region**

	1950	1980	1999	2010
Africa	13%	21%	40%	56%
North America	70%	59%	34%	23%
Central & South America	4%	7%	17%	12%
Europe & Middle East	12%	11%	7%	5%
Asia/Pacific	1%	2%	2%	4%

Source: Russell 1950; FWCC 1980, 1999, Abbott, 2010.

19,000 in the rest of Africa, 53,000 in Latin America, 19,000 in Asia, as well as 102,000 in North America, and 24,000 in Europe (Abbott et al 2011, 393–6). Thus, the best guess is that the Religious Society of Friends will continue to grow, but not enough to make it numerically significant among world religions.

It is most helpful to look at Quaker distribution worldwide and the significant trends that occurred in the twentieth century. Demographics have shifted rapidly away from the historic domination by North Americans and Europeans. Membership patterns by region indicate the largest challenges for Quakers today: How do Friends in the Global South see their faith and name it for the world? And how willing are Friends in the Global North to listen rather than dictate the terms of the conversation?

In the first years of the twenty-first century, North American and British Friends are just beginning to come to terms with being a smaller and smaller minority within the larger Religious Society of Friends. Kenya now has by far the largest community of Friends in the world. The global growth of Friends has come from a combination of missionary activity, once largely from North America, but increasingly originating from African, Latin American, and Asian churches, as well as natural population growth, particularly in the Global South. As a result, worship with hymns, Bible readings, and sermons has become the norm.

In North America, the situation is quite different. Actual membership in North America peaked in the middle of the twentieth century, and by 2010 membership had fallen to the levels of the early twentieth century, although in some Meetings, attenders are over half the congregation. Non-pastoral Friends accounted for 32 per cent of North American Quakers in the early 1980s, but were almost 40 per cent by 2010 as a result of a precipitous decline of membership within the pastoral churches of Friends United Meeting. This was partially offset by growth in Evangelical Friends Church (North America), which is part of Evangelical Friends Church International (EFCI), a worldwide association of Evangelical Friends; nonetheless, decline in pastoral Meetings accounts for almost all the loss in North American Quaker membership between 1980 and 2010. Worries about decline has been motivating greater evangelizing among Friends' churches as well as causing unprogrammed Friends to reach out through such programmes as Quaker Quest after many decades of strong discomfort with active outreach.

NEW LIFE AND ENERGY FROM THE FORMER MISSION FIELDS

As Yearly Meetings outside the US and Britain mature, it is not always clear how they might challenge the older bodies and what leadership they might exert among Friends (and others) in Europe and North America. There are some indications that these newer Quaker bodies could provide a valuable corrective to the relative ease and comfort of those Quaker communities with long histories.

Friends have long done much to provide education with an emphasis on excellence that has made Friends schools in many areas around the world, such as the one in Ramallah, Palestine, a magnet for many influential families. The Lindi Friends School in Kenya and Belize Friends School provide two examples where educational efforts reach out to children of the slums and those caught up in gang violence. Here, as in their many schools serving academically elite students, Friends provide leadership in teaching non-violence. In Kenya, a peace curriculum for all Friends' secondary schools began implementation in 2011, with hopes of also reaching out to non-Quaker institutions.

Mission efforts in Africa, in addition to spreading the Gospel and providing education, offer medical care along with basic sanitation, clean water projects, and care for HIV/AIDS orphans. The last is critical for these children in a culture where relatives rather than institutions are expected to step in, but where the devastation of AIDS may leave no options. At Friends Theological College, students are required to complete workshops in HIV/AIDS prevention and awareness, as well as in peace and conflict resolution skills. New churches are often planted in areas of extreme poverty and in places where there is significant potential for violence. The lives of members of such churches are a counterpoint to those Friends in the northern hemisphere who dwell in relative wealth and comfort despite efforts to live simply.

In the Democratic Republic of the Congo, where new members were attracted by the peace witness of the few Friends there, membership has grown despite the massive refugee camps and the constant threat of ongoing civil war. This is a country where sexual assault is regularly used as an instrument of terror by those with guns and power, yet Friends are present teaching skills in sewing, marketing, and other ways to provide income, as well as trauma healing, to widows who are marginalized in many African cultures. In nearby Rwanda and Burundi, some have noted that no Friends participated in the genocides. While expatriate European and American Quakers were evacuated during the worst of the violence, Kenyan Quakers stepped in to offer aid and refuge. In the years since, Rwandan and Burundian Friends have taken a strong lead in trauma healing and reconciliation work.

Further examples abound worldwide. New Friends Evangelical churches are being opened in the Republic of Ireland amid serious pockets of poverty. In India, Friends pray for ways to reach faithfully across rigid caste and economic disparities. In countries such as Indonesia and Nepal, Friends seek to find a way to exist and grow in a predominantly Muslim or Hindu or Buddhist culture, and to profess their faith knowing they may be treated harshly for being a Christian.

These circumstances seem to increase the importance of the Quaker understanding of the Gospel message as one that reaches out with a message of truth, hope, equity, love, humility, simplicity, and non-violence in a world that places much too little value on such things. For instance, the realities of a world climate change and the possibility of significant upheaval as sea levels rise, weather patterns change, economies are threatened, and growing seasons shift, mean that Friends will be challenged to speak to the poorest of the poor and know what message of hope they have to offer. This issue was a priority for Asian Quakers and was brought for consideration at the 2012 World Gathering of Friends. The members of the many new FUM and EFCI Meetings in Africa, Latin America, Asia, and elsewhere will have day-to-day experience in these conditions and a real capacity to empathize with all who are caught in these upheavals. To the degree they embody the fullness of Jesus teachings and way of being, they can demonstrate ways to live in difficult circumstances and among people of foreign beliefs and culture.

In 1980, Jack Willcuts and Stanley Perisho identified the key feature of Quakerism as being Spirit-led, honestly and actively searching for reality and Truth, rather than relying on tradition or cultural influences. They took seriously Jesus' command to 'be in the world but not of the world' and named peacemaking and social concern as part of the fire burning in the heart (Willcuts 1980, 4–6). Their message was for Friends looking to the future in 1980, yet this message is relevant thirty years later as Evangelical Friends spread into new corners of the globe. There is evidence that these are part of the witness as South American Friends live in lands where illegal drugs are grown. These Friends must find ways to witness against the resulting violence and direct threats against anyone who opposes the drugs trade. Friends in India provide aid for those who are HIV positive and work to relieve the oppression of women. In Hungary, much of Friends work is with the Roma people who are often poor and despised by the wider community. There are many other such examples of new life among Friends in unexpected places.

As Friends missions have been established amid the varied cultures of the world, each area poses new issues and understandings. For instance, Director of the EFCI Council Ron Stansell argues for increased tools for sorting out the true work of the Holy Spirit as a crucial dimension of Friends work, particularly in areas where Animism remains widely believed. Teaching that faith sets aside fear and that one can trust God in prayer is new in cultures where manipulating gods through magic is common. In these cultures he sees separating magic from prayer as central to discernment. A similar challenge is to name the sovereignty of God in a way that leads to hope and empowerment rather than to a fatalistic attitude. Humility in this work is essential as well as a commitment to Christ and knowing that His way is often one of apparent paradox.

The shift in Quakerism's centre of gravity has created tensions along with opportunities. Over the past century, readjusting relationships between the North American Yearly Meetings and those in the southern hemisphere have often been most visible in the flow of money (north to south), expectations on accounting for that money, and leadership of institutions. In Kenya, the new centre of Quakerism, where East Africa Yearly Meeting was established in 1946, Yearly Meetings have proliferated under the umbrella of Friends United Meeting but have struggled with increasing success to work cooperatively, but have not clearly defined their relationship to their sister Meetings in North America.

The tensions between the administrative control of institutions and the access to financial resources held by Westerners and the growing awareness of the authority rising up within other communities of Friends is far from being resolved. The direction in which these newer Yearly Meetings might lead the entire body is only now being hinted at. At the broadest, clearest level, the majority of Friends in the world are adamantly Christian, naming belief in the saving power of Christ Jesus as essential to membership, and essentially Protestant in their form of worship—that is, having someone (often the pastor) designated in advance to preach the message, select the hymns sung, and the Bible readings offered, but without the use of the outward sacraments of the bread and wine of communion.

When looking to see what distinctive dimensions of the Quaker way are important, most often the answer seems to come back to the local conditions. In Cuba, as in Bolivia and other Latin American countries, Friends are pushed hard on the question of how they can be Christians if they do not use the physical sacraments, particularly water baptism and the bread and wine of communion. This has led to requests for more Spanish language translations of Barclay's *Apology* as well as clear explanations of Friends understanding. This is happening at a time when some Evangelical Friends congregations in the US offer the outward sacraments.

Similar questions about the meaning of global partnership can be asked of peace work. In locations as diverse as Rwanda, Burundi, Central America, Colombia, and Indonesia, Friends Peace Teams—an organization founded by North American Friends—have become a visible presence and are boosting Quaker action with programmes for reconciliation in divided lands, healing from the trauma of extreme violence, and teaching tools for local peacemakers. Friends are also active in Christian Peacemaker Teams, a group founded by Mennonites, Church of the Brethren, and Quakers that work primarily in the Middle East. Some African Friends are taking leadership in work to establish peaceful responses to potentially violent situations, yet as in the US, some are reluctant to participate with others who are not committed to work to save souls. As often is the case wherever Christian and non-Christian edges of Friends come together, there is a clash when some insist on peace work without an explicit religious component and others want to focus on spreading the Gospel. In the African context, occasional concerns are raised as to whether work for peace has become popular because it provides access to Western money and programmes. The long history of imperialism raises such questions despite awareness of the problems created and sincere attempts to shift leadership of African, Asian, and Latin American work to the people who live in these communities.

In Peru and Bolivia, for instance, indigenous leadership within the Yearly Meetings is shifting to the next generation, a shift that offers hope for lessening the fragmentation of Friends there as the predominantly Aymara congregations take ownership of programmes, and sense that they can no longer defer decisions, funding, training of pastors, and other core activities to foreign missionaries. This leadership change is in part geographic from the rural Altiplano to the cities and the coastal regions. Also, the Aymara people are becoming more fully integrated into Peruvian life. Like all Friends, Bolivians and Peruvians are challenged to form a reflective community that would examine the dominant cultural perspectives in the light of who they are as the People of God. Old tensions with North American Friends are perhaps easing in some areas, but the long-standing distrust of outside authorities often seems projected onto the younger urbanizing generation as the older culture is threatened. And there is yet little evidence that those from the north look to non-English speaking Friends as role models.

A LIFE LIVED WELL: IS IT ENOUGH?

> I think that one of the greatest things that Quakerism did for us Kenyan Friends was to introduce a new type of family relationship in our communities. When I was growing up in the village of Lugala, you could tell which were Quaker villages. How could you tell? There was no wife beating.

These words were spoken by Miriam Were at the Fifth World Conference of Friends in 1991. (Were 1992, 203) She went on to put this in the context of an old African saying, that men show their love by beating their wives and noted how her father would be called a coward for treating the family gently. In a continent where many women die young and children do not consistently have enough food or medicine, building a stable community is essential.

The Quaker missionaries who brought the Gospel to Kenya came from the Midwest of the US and brought with them a deep love of Christ and a concern for everyday living and love of one's neighbour that was in right order with Biblical teachings. The connections between these regions remain strong and at the heart of Friends United Meeting. Yet in the US as well as in Kenya, these Friends are facing hard issues as they look to the future. Several forces seem to be at play here, weakening the Friends Churches along with the demographic shifts as Friends move away from agricultural areas, or young people are lured in other directions leaving smaller and/or older congregations behind. In Bolivia, Friends are discouraged by the lack of sufficient resources for developing strong youth programmes and worry that their children will not follow in the faith.

In preparation for the Sixth World Conference of Friends in 2012, the author was in communication with individuals from around the globe asking about the changes they were facing. One theme was the pull of materialism. African Friends, in particular, lamented the inability or unwillingness of many to pay tithes to support the church, along with the temptation to spend time and energy pursuing consumerism rather than attending to God's will. In his book on Quakers in Kenya, Zablon Malenge of Nairobi Yearly Meeting writes 'Friends Meetings in Kenya today spend most of their time gossiping and struggling for leadership and looking for material gains' (Malenge 2003, 48). He also notes the lack of Quaker pastors, absence of sufficient training in Christian discipline, as well as suspicion among members or between churches among the pressures that distract Friends Meetings from being 'living witnesses to God's truths' (Malenge 2003, 48).

Traditional Friends' testimonies that are at odds with the practices of a more generic evangelicalism is a factor in many parts of the world. Testimony to the ministry of women, the commitment to non-violence, or living simply can be seen as potential obstacles to bringing people to Jesus rather than integral to salvation. When pastors have no experience or training in Friends' understanding of the Gospel (a regular issue in the US), they preach out of the tradition they know. Saving souls is their business, not perpetuating a denomination. This is an attitude prevalent among evangelicals of many persuasions where denominationalism is downplayed. In this world view, core allegiance to Jesus Christ, the inerrancy of the Bible, and the moral values of the tradition are non-negotiable (Wellman 2008, 227).

Refusal to hire pastors at all distinguished the first two centuries of Friends' existence. As a result, many Friends churches are led by individuals who have no Quaker training, and this more than a century after wide acceptance of paid leadership became the norm in the US and in the rest of the world through American evangelizing. This ambiguity about pastors meant that while there were several Quaker Bible colleges, the first Quaker seminary in the US wasn't formed until 1960, and it faced distrust in many circles as a result of the complexity of the divisions among Friends. Africans and South Americans have been more deliberate about establishing leadership-training programmes than North Americans. The Friends Theological College in Kaimosi, Kenya, was founded in 1942, and the Instituto Biblico de Formación Teológica Jorge Fox opened in 1980 in Honduras, both specifically to train pastors. However, churches worldwide face economic obstacles to funding those who are called to a pastoral ministry, as well as a shortage of individuals trained in Quaker theology and practice. The congregational nature of Friends polity also adds to this in some regions where churches select their own leadership.

In the US, in Evangelical Friends Church Southwest there are provisions for the establishment of community churches that do business by voting rather than by sense of the Meeting. Within Friends United Meeting, serious disagreement arose in the early twenty-first century about homosexuality (is it a sin or is it a natural condition akin to skin colour or gender?), as well as about the divinity of Jesus, and the nature of salvation. Disownments and separations over these questions are part of the early twenty-first-century condition of Western and Indiana Yearly Meetings.

Some churches also struggle with the testimony to the equality of women. For instance, in Northwest Yearly Meeting of Friends Church, after decades of recognizing women ministers, it largely abandoned the practice in the mid-twentieth century because of interactions with other evangelical denominations that felt Scripture forbade women in the ministry. For several decades few women were accepted as pastors. It was only towards the end of the twentieth century that the Yearly Meeting Board of Ministry explicitly began to shift the process of recording ministers to raise up the historic acceptance of women in ministry, the peace testimony, and other practices Friends have long held as central to their understanding of the Gospel. The first woman superintendent was named in 2011.

Each culture has its own particular pressures which affect the character of mission-based churches. Often the issue of women in leadership is an important one for Friends churches. The pressure for recognition of women as leaders may come from international organizations expressing the expectation that Yearly Meetings send women as well as men to represent them, an expectation backed by financial support. Or the issue may rise up internally as women find the opportunity to serve in ways unacceptable in the broader culture or in other evangelical bodies. Nepal is one such case where the Quaker welcoming of women's ministry, opportunities for self-expression, and value as gifted human beings stands out in a culture that limits their roles, and also stands out among other denominations that do not challenge the culture.

The desire to save souls by bringing individuals and communities to Jesus is central to the majority of Friends. Yet a focus on demonstration of the transformed life focused on personal morality has often been at odds with a concern for transformation of secular and government institutions. This was true when Indiana Yearly Meeting split over strategies for the abolition of slavery in the nineteenth century and when, a century later, Quakers argued over public protests and marches against war. There is no reason to believe such disagreements will not be present for decades to come or longer. But there are indications that in the non-Western world, this is less a factor as individuals are less likely to focus on such dichotomies.

In North America there also appears to be a shift as individuals and Meetings from all branches gradually spend less energy defining themselves by who they are not (e.g. those Friends!), and more frequently stepping forward to embrace the Sermon on the Mount as a guide for living, not just a description of a future Kingdom of God. Increasingly, voices within the evangelical tradition are heard articulating a vision of integrating proclamation and demonstration in their message not only in matters of personal morality, but also in seeking justice for those without power. This mirrors more closely the early generations of Friends who strongly believed that proclamation of faith in Jesus held no value unless the reality of the living Christ was visible in one's words and actions, including taking active stances against unjust government actions. Nonetheless, most EFCI Friends and many from FUM elect not to join in lobbying with Friends Committee on National Legislation, which actively advocates for peace and justice in the US Congress.

A Passion for Justice: What of Faith?

Most unprogrammed Meetings in Europe, North America, South Africa, Australia, and New Zealand share a common passion for justice and peace, and find many newcomers arriving when war breaks out. In these Meetings, where Friends worship without a formal message being offered and without paid pastoral leadership, the range of beliefs of individual members and attenders is substantial. The assertion by early Friends that the spirit of Christ and the Inward Light were at work within the hearts of all humanity, whether or not they had heard of Jesus, has inspired a sense of acceptance and openness to all faiths (or to those with none). These Friends emphasize living in accord with the testimonies. It is easy to see this approach as a matching bookend to the priority evangelicals place on salvation.

Unprogrammed Friends are arguably closely related to mainstream Protestants in the US and Britain, a broad grouping of churches which has seen sharp declines in membership and attendance since the mid-twentieth century. Within this broad grouping belief in the unique contribution of Christianity to the world has lost its hold as articulate and popular theologians such as Wilfred Cantwell Smith, John A. T. Robinson, Harvey Cox, and Reinhold Niebuhr raised up values they saw as transcending Christianity (Hollinger 2011, 44). Other voices, such as Martin Marty, pressed for recognition of Jewish and secular voices as well as Catholic voices as legitimate within the American context, challenging the long-held notion of Protestantism as the American national religion (Hollinger 2011, 25). As these views were raised, the gap between some evangelicals and ecumenists grew. Often, this was accompanied by a growing gap between leaders and their congregations, and a concomitant decline in the mainsteam churches in the later twentieth century.

The shift away from Christianity within parts of the Quaker world parallels change within the mainstream denominations as intellectuals, in particular, distance themselves from an evangelical stance, and seek to respect the integrity of other faiths. In the past century, particularly within these unprogrammed Meetings, Hinduism, Buddhism, Judaism, and Wiccan practices are among those increasingly seen as having much to offer. The book *Honest to God*, by the Anglican bishop John A. T. Robinson, which distances Christianity from the supernatural and concepts of God in human form, was widely read, especially by British Friends.

The tendency to reject any assertion of Jesus as Lord and Saviour, while very strong in the late twentieth century, has lessened in more recent years as some Meetings seek to create an atmosphere where every individual can speak in words authentic to their own spiritual experience. The unprogrammed Meetings, in particular, have offered a refuge for individuals who have been deeply hurt by hypocritical practices in Christianity, find the biblical story impossible to believe, see only the violence in the history of the Christian church, or are convinced that no one religion holds all truth.

Both a desire for inclusiveness and a distrust of Christianity has left some Friends holding that Quaker beliefs are only the five testimonies of simplicity, peace, integrity, community, and equality. They find any suggestion of a corporate belief in the Christian sense totally unacceptable. Such expansiveness of belief has given rise to many threads such as Kenneth Boulding (1910–93) and evolutionary Quakerism, Howard Brinton's (1884–1973) exploration of the commonalities between Christianity and other faiths, and a feminist approach which has become one of the givens of Quaker thought (God is named as both he and she or genderless). In the early years of the twenty-first century, voices have been raised advocating for acceptance of non-theism as a legitimate dimension of the Quaker spectrum, describing this as 'taking leave of an idol for the sake of the values and the truth the idol has been held to represent', much as described by Don Cuppitt in *Taking Leave of God* (Boulton 2006, 6). Thich Nhat Hanh's (1926–) Buddhist teachings and articulation of non-violence have been another strong influence. An unwillingness to name who Friends are and say what Friends believe with any certainty has been labelled the 'absolute perhaps' (Dandelion 2007, 152) and leaves many frustrated with the uncertainty.

Yet British and continental European Friends, in particular, are putting much energy into revitalization, both in terms of outreach and in terms of willingness to articulate who Friends are and what they believe. Some voices challenge older Friends to step back and welcome those in their twenties and thirties to come forwards and reinvent Quaker organization and practice. One question posed is 'Do we need to become liquid again?', that is, rediscovering and focusing on the spiritual ground which is the basis of all Quaker testimony and become more like the first generation of Quakers (Best 2011, 49–63).

Unprogrammed Friends, nonetheless seek to offer a place for people of all persuasions to worship together and a form of worship hospitable to that view. As the twenty-first century unfolds, these Friends, like their evangelical counterparts are testing the ways they might speak more directly about who they are and be more honest about some of the painful ways in which they do not live up to their ideals. Some are stepping forwards in recognition that God—or whatever word they use to describe the centre of all being—is at once beyond all description or human comprehension, and close within the human heart and can be spoken of with joy. This is among the many paradoxes which seem to be shifting Friends.

CONVERGENT FRIENDS AND RECONCILIATION WORK OR A RETURN TO THE HEDGE?

How to correctly interpret the Bible is an underlying point of contention among North American Friends in the twenty-first century. The presenting issue may be the welcoming of gays and lesbians, or the efforts within Western Yearly Meeting to remove the recording of Phil Gulley (1961–) as a minister because of his questions about the divinity of Jesus (Gulley 2009).

Indiana Yearly Meeting (IYM) in 2012 was moving towards separation as significant numbers of Friends found they could not accept ongoing fellowship with Meetings welcoming to gays and lesbians. All Meetings within IYM name themselves as Christian and embrace the Bible, yet some raise up 'Avoidance of creeds, particularly when used as purity tests' and others 'believe in the concept of subordination... [as] a means of common protection'. The protection is to ensure that no one takes stances 'contrary or offensive' to IYM (Angell 2012, 35, 39). The latter approach echoes the establishment of 'the hedge' among eighteen-century Friends to keep themselves pure from the world's influences. Because the disagreements are within the Quaker community, the options when intractable disagreement arises are too often laid out as disownment or division as happened in 1827 and numerous times since.

A contrasting phenomenon of the early twenty-first century is a loose grouping, 'convergent Friends', who are not tied to any one place or Quaker institution. The often Web-based connections that are separate from the centuries-old divisions find particular appeal among younger Friends. Convergent Friends seem a natural offshoot and complement to the work of Friends World Committee for Consultation and other twentieth-century efforts to break down the barriers within Quakerism.

Blogging is one of the phenomena of the Internet age and Quakers have enthusiastically participated in writing online, sharing their personal spirituality, and their interpretation of Friends. The word 'convergent' was coined to describe those Friends committed to theological hospitality among the branches of the Quaker family tree (Mohr 2006, 18). Convergent Friends might see themselves as Christian, but socially liberal, with many wanting to recover the dynamism of the first generation of Friends.

The term 'convergent' points to affinity with both Conservative Friends and the Emergent Church movement, which is often non-denominational and tends to emphasize lived experience, the importance of narrative theology, and seeking both support and accountability within the community. Relationships are central, not structure, as these Friends seek to reclaim understandings and practices that might have been lost in the particular Quaker tradition where they worship.

A movement towards reconciliation among Friends and putting an end to our very human and often ugly separations, has its roots in Africa. Individuals and churches in Ruanda and Burundi are moving towards a new way of relating to one another after the horrors of the genocides in Central Africa. They are applying the skills of healing and forgiveness to all dimensions of their communities. Similarly, Kenyan Friends, beginning in the late 1980s with a strong nudge from the women, are increasingly working together with integrity. The nationwide Quaker peace group, Friends Church Peace Team, has set up a mediation committee to create space to address the long-standing hostilities there. This kind of work, sometimes referred to in Central Africa as the Reconciliation Project, has also spread to the US with some individuals taking unusual steps to end the defensiveness and hostility that are still all too pervasive. While not facing the consequences of physical violence prevalent in much of the world, American divisions among Friends have lasted for decades or more, and new separations continue.

One instance of this reconciliation work in the US was at the 2010 gathering of Yearly Meeting superintendents and secretaries when Friends attending from Northwest Yearly Meeting were moved by the Spirit to ask forgiveness for the fear, mistrust, and arrogance that were among the causes of the split from Five Years Meeting in 1926 (Wood 2011, 1). The extent of the wounds is indicated in this one example as the repercussions from separations almost a century ago still temper relationships among Friends today. This work highlights the need for forgiveness to occur around actions that may have happened yesterday, as well as those from the nineteenth century, and many instances in between, if cooperative and respectful relationships are to replace ongoing patterns of separation.

Ongoing Witness for Peace and Justice

New initiatives for bringing peaceful solutions to violent or potentially violent civic affairs continually arise as with the Quaker United Nations Office work to end the practice of child soldiers or with the individual action of Bernardino Ramírez who secretly fed Guatemalan soldiers who had been condemned to starvation. There are hundreds of examples of Friends whose faith calls them to respond to injustice day to day. New areas of concern continually arise as individuals attend to the movement of the Spirit as they engage in the world around them.

An ambitious international study of human behaviour published in 2011 (Norenzayan 2011, 1041–2) has found that violence, natural disaster, conflict, starvation, and upheaval, cause communities to regulate behaviour more tightly and to punish those who are different. In societies under stress, religion also thrives, in contrast with wealthier, more secure communities. Studies such as these easily lead one to project that a future dominated (as some predict) by major climate change, water shortages, or other disruptions will quickly become more rigid, perhaps under totalitarian regimes, perhaps under religious fundamentalism of any number of different forms. It is easy to name examples around the world that reinforce this pessimistic view.

Can the Religious Society of Friends be an example to the contrary? Quakers are inconsistent in the importance they place on the testimonies of truth, equality (including recognition of women in Quaker leadership), peace, and simplicity. A strict non-violent stance is just one testimony that is seen as central to faith by many and unrealistic by others. Friends, along with the Church of the Brethren and the Mennonites continue to build on their reputation as the Historic Peace Churches. Individual Quakers put themselves in harm's way to mediate between leaders in violent conflicts or to accompany people at risk of harm as members of Christian Peacemaker Teams and other organizations devoted to justice and non-violence. In the US, Friends Committee on National Legislation is a leader in advocating peace issues before the US Congress.

As noted earlier, many Quaker communities experience a surge in attendance from people each time the US government declares war. In contrast, some Friends Churches in the US downplay the peace testimony, have members who serve in the military, and argue what is essentially a just war position. Those formerly in the military who attend unprogrammed Meetings have usually been disillusioned about military solutions and are looking to live, in the words of George Fox, 'in the virtue of that life and power that took away the occasion of all wars' (Fox 1995, 65).

In the Altiplano of Bolivia and Peru, Quakerism initially took root among impoverished Aymara people. Agricultural work, the provision of clean water, and basic health care were integral parts of mission work, and the formation of new Churches depended on individuals willing to walk or bike many miles to deliver the message of Friends. In wealthier nations, individual Quakers and Meetings raise up simplicity and sustainability as goals for their own lives, and may work in soup kitchens or otherwise act to relieve poverty, but are less likely to have direct relationships with those who are truly poor in the communities where they live.

Yearly Meetings everywhere face major internal pressures to fracture and the challenge of how to witness to the call to love one another despite disagreements ranging from language, to treatment of marginalized people, to the correct way to read the Bible. Kenya is a country of many tribes and, for many years Quakerism grew largely among the Luhya peoples. The divisions of East Africa Yearly Meeting have often been along tribal lines, including the formation of Tongaren Yearly Meeting, which was accepted as the newest member of FUM in 2011. Yet one mark of the work to build cross-tribal relationships is the renaming of Nandi Yearly Meeting to Tuloi, a name that connects two groups in the region. Learning to live as one nation, treating the people of other tribes justly (this often has urban/rural dimensions as well as access to resources) has been an important theme nationally as well as among Friends.

Following the Kenyan national elections in 2007, widespread violence was often fed by tribal loyalties. While most Quakers were not of members of the tribes of the presidential candidates, they were caught up directly or indirectly in the burnings, rapes, and waves of internal refugees. These Friends felt called to engage with the gospel message of peace, which had not previously been a priority for them in this generally stable nation. In 2008, the Friends Church in Kenya (with support from many American Friends) made a strong joint statement to the government and the public about the need for an end to the violence that followed the national elections, and stepped in with active programmes. Ongoing efforts contributed to the peaceful 2013 elections.

In response to the violence, not only did Friends gather to confer on possible actions, the Friends Church Kenya wrote an open letter to the president demanding truth-telling, just treatment of all, and a fair election system. Kenyan Friends also undertook direct action working with internally displaced people missed by the Red Cross and the Kenyan government efforts, including welcoming some of these refugees into their church compounds, schools, and private homes. They also set up active training programmes for non-violent communications and violence prevention.

An equally significant challenge for Friends is the commitment to truth-telling. The honesty that distinguished seventeenth-century Quakers has been tested severely in some nations where corruption is rampant. In the US, there seems to be an ambiguity about this. Integrity is not always listed among the testimonies, yet many boast of a Quaker tradition of speaking truth to power, sometimes conflating unpopular opinion with truth. In Kenya, which has been listed among the most corrupt nations on the globe, some of this attitude has infected the Yearly Meetings. As numerous Kenyans have and are serving at many levels of government, they have the double challenge of bringing integrity into the administration of their religious home and the national arena.

Trauma healing, reconciliation, and offering dignity and livelihood to the many HIV/AIDS widows and orphans have been a major Quaker witness in Central Africa as well, following the genocides of the late twentieth century. In Asia, Friends churches have largely formed among the dispossessed such as the Nepali refugees in Bhutan as well as in Nepal. In India, where caste differences shape life, Quakers, as is true with many other Christian denominations, are mainly drawn from the lowest castes. Quaker witness in Bundelkhand began largely around establishment of an orphanage and EFCI Friends in South India work largely among children of the temple prostitutes. Friends seek to provide these children with opportunities in life other than following the example of their mothers. They also have created training programmes around HIV prevention and obtained grants for providing medical care.

Friends in many corners of the globe such as Canadian and Aotearoa/New Zealand Yearly Meetings, in addition to taking a leadership role in peace issues, have also focused on race relations and treatment of indigenous peoples. They have taken actions such as seeking to rectify the many injustices dealt the First Nations and supporting the land claims of the Maori people.

In parts of the world where Friends are a growing presence, there is at least anecdotal evidence that Quakers are a mix of individuals who have taken advantage of the tradition of education and medical care brought by the missionaries, and have thus become successful in their careers. This is true particularly in Guatemala, Bolivia, and East Africa, where there are long-established Friends churches. At the same time, the message being offered still speaks to those who have nothing or who face oppression based on tribal, caste, or other distinctions that have nothing to do with human worth. When Friends gave refuge to Kikuyu or Luo people in 2007/8, they did so with the awareness that the result might be for other neighbours to burn Friends' homes or churches.

The economic, theological, and cultural diversity of Friends means that no simple description or example applies to every Yearly Meeting. Economic justice looks very different from a well-to-do British home than it does in a Honduran village. Peace work in the US may mean lobbying Congress or standing in protest at a nuclear arms facility, while in Ramallah it takes on a day-to-day reality that affects every aspect of life.

SUMMARY AND CONCLUSIONS

Numerically, the future of Friends is in the hands of the growing African and Latin American bodies. They have much energy and a devotion to mission work, but lack the financial and educational resources of their North American and European counterparts. In many Yearly Meetings concerns arise about the coming generation of leadership. Availability of training in Quaker ways is limited and the pressures to conform to the society and the predominant religious practices around them are strong in every part of the globe. In the US, where the greatest theological diversity is evident, these broader pressures tend to push the branches of the Quaker family tree apart. In other places, such pressures seem to pull Friends away from a distinctive witness to God's work in the world. For all Friends, sorting out God's will from cultural norms is an ongoing concern and education about our faith is part of that solution.

However, the signs of vitality are numerous around the globe and show promise that the reputation of Friends will take new shape as individuals, Meetings, and churches work to evangelize, to witness to Jesus' commandment to love one's neighbours. Many of these people are also committed to establish the conditions of non-violent alternatives in situations where conventional wisdom calls for destructive action. The witness to integrity and truth-telling takes courage in cultures where corruption is rampant or where individuals are said to be faithful when they obey what the clan demands of them (Simiyu 2001, 10).

Within the Religious Society of Friends/Friends church, the forces pressuring towards fracture are very real and complex. Some communities stand firm as 'Christian Orthodox...with a commitment to mutual accountability', others are committed to raising 'penetrating spiritual questions to challenge all to greater devotion to Christ', and a third group that defines Quaker faith more in terms of practice than belief (Angell 2012, 39, 35; Dandelion 2011, 202). Varied tolerance for uncertainty of belief shapes individual Quaker communities as much or more than the variation in specific beliefs. The future of Friends will in many ways depend on how widespread the willingness is to stand in a place of tension between knowing Jesus as Lord and knowing the Light as universally present in many articulations of faith. Similarly, approaches to questions of morality and biblical interpretation can either tear Friends apart or bring Friends into a place of mutual respect and listening.

The twenty-first century could see the dissolution of the Religious Society of Friends as this small body splinters into tiny meaningless groups. Yet while further separations will most likely occur, there are too many signs otherwise to be certain of dissolution. Some of these separations are a natural consequence of growth. The future of European Yearly Meetings seems most at risk since several number fewer than a hundred members and these members are often elderly. Mission work now underway may change the distribution of Friends in Europe as dramatically as it has in the rest of the world.

Looking for new ways of interacting with each other, some Quakers urge Friends to create a 'bigger tent'—a space where individuals and Meetings/churches might engage one another with respect and work together on common goals despite divergent theologies or tribal heritage. If there is the desire to create this tent, what are the ways this might happen? Radical acts of reconciliation are one piece that might allow Friends to demonstrate a form of 'militant leadership' without the fragmentation that Roland Bainton once suggested as inevitable.

Early Quakers set a high standard for aligning belief, words, and behaviour. For example, the Kenyan women from all Yearly Meetings who decided to join together in prayer despite the disagreements among the male leadership, and the Kenyans who welcomed strangers into their homes in a time of violence all acted in accord with a vision of God's Kingdom on Earth.

This high standard of integrity means, for some, that they hold true to their core beliefs by separating themselves from those who do not accept these precepts, just as Quakers separated themselves from secular society in the eighteenth century. They treasure their communities. Within this group are both those who are committed to the Bible as they know it and use it to guide their lives, and those who find the Bible obsolete or incomprehensible. These churches, Meetings, and individuals are convinced that separating themselves from others who disagree is the way to unity, to salvation, and to growth.

Another possibility for the future is that Friends follow the path of convergence, a path that some Friends today would applaud. In this scenario, Friends offer a way for people from many faith traditions or secular backgrounds to be able to live together and demonstrate a reconciling community. Heredio Santos, pastor of a Friends church in Cuba spoke to this vision when he said, 'Yes, when we love one another, we find unity in our diversity!' in response to the query from a Friend who is a follower of Jesus but did not accept Jesus as Lord and Saviour (Sanders 1991, 13).

The underpinning of whatever future happens is hinted at by those committed to translating the writings of the first generation of Quakers and others who look to know what George Fox and so many others knew: the immediate presence and guidance of God. It is that encounter and internal knowledge, tested in community, which has been the ground and life-blood of this small group and allowed them to be a counterforce to the corruption and arrogance of so many in the world. To what degree this will happen will have to unfold.

SUGGESTED FUTHER READING

Kimball, H. and B. (2002) *Go into all the world: A centennial celebration of Friends in East Africa.* Richmond, IN: Friends United Press.

Maathai, W. (2009) *The challenge for Africa.* New York: Anchor Press.

Madrid Morales, É. A. (1997) *Doctrinas distintivas de los Amigos.* La Paz, Bolivia: Comité de los Amigos Latinoamericanos.

Mombo, E. (1998) 'A historical and cultural analysis of the position of Abaluyia women in Kenyan Quaker Christianity, 1902–1979' PhD dissertation, University of Edinburgh.

Rasmussen, A. M. R. (1995) *The Quaker movement in Africa.* London: British Academic Press.

Stansell, R. (2009) *Missions by the Spirit: Learning from Quaker examples.* Newberg, OR: Barclay Press.

Tórrez L. J. (1997) *La puerta: Estudio Bíblico sobre los fundamentos de le fe Cristiana.* La Paz, Bolivia: Editorial Logos.

BIBLIOGRAPHY

Abbott, M. P. (1995) *An experiment in faith: Quaker women transcending differences*, Wallingford, PA: Pendle Hill Publications.

Abbott, M. P. (2010) *To be broken and tender: A Quaker theology for today*, Portland, OR: Friends Bulletin Corporation.

Abbott, M. P. & Parsons, P. S. (eds.) (2004) *Walk worthy of your calling: Quakers and the traveling ministry*, Richmond, IN: Friends United Press.

Abbott, M. P., Chijioke, M. E., Dandelion, P. & Oliver, J. W. (eds.) (2003) *The historical dictionary of Friends (Quakers)*, Lanham, MD: Scarecrow.

Abbott, M. P., Chijioke, M. E., Dandelion, P. & Oliver, J. W. (eds.) (2011) *The historical dictionary of the Friends (Quakers)*, 2nd Edn., Lanham, MD: Scarecrow Press.

Achinstein, S. (2001) 'Texts in conflict: the press and the Civil War' in N. H. Keeble (ed.) *The Cambridge companion to writing of the English Revolution*, pp. 50–68, Cambridge: Cambridge University Press.

Adams, A. (ed.) (1996) *The creation was open to me: An anthology of Friends' writings on that of God in all creation*, Wilmslow: Quaker Green Concern.

Africa Great Lakes Initiative>About AGLI>History, http://aglifpt.org/About/history.htm. Accessed 20 October 2012.

Ahivah (1660) *A Strange Prophecie presented to the Kings Most Excellent Majesty…* London: Aaron Banaster.

Alexander, W. (1820) *Observations on the construction and fixing up of meeting houses*, York.

Allen, J. & Allen, R. C. (eds.) (2009) *Faith of our fathers: popular culture and belief in post-Reformation England, Ireland and Wales*, Newcastle: Cambridge Scholars Press.

Allen, M. & Holton, S. S. (1997) 'Office and services: Women's pursuit of sexual equality within the Society of Friends, 1873–1907', *Quaker Studies*, vol. 2, pp. 1–29.

Allen, M. (1998) 'Matilda Sturge, Renaissance Woman', *Women's History Review*, vol. 7, no. 2, pp. 209–226.

Allen, R. C. (2003) '"Mocked, scoffed, persecuted, and made a gazeing stock": The resistance of the Religious Society of Friends (Quakers) to the religious and civil authorities in post-toleration south-east Wales c.1689–1836', Nice, Cycnos: Publications de la Faculté des Lettres de Nice.

Allen, R. C. (2004a) 'Establishing an alternative community in the North-East: Quakers, morals and popular culture in the long Eighteenth Century', in Helen Berry and Jeremy Gregory (eds.) *Culture in North-East England, 1660–1832*. Aldershot: Ashgate, pp. 98–119.

Allen, R. C. (2004b) 'In search of a New Jerusalem: a preliminary investigation into Welsh Quaker emigration to North America c.1660–1750', *Quaker Studies*, vol. 9, pp. 31–53.

Allen, R. C. (2007a) *Quaker communities in early modern Wales: from resistance to respectability*, Cardiff: University of Wales Press.

Allen, R. C. (2007b) '"Turning hearts to break off the yoke of oppression": the travels and sufferings of Christopher Meidel c.1659–c.1715', *Quaker Studies*, vol. 12, pp. 54–72.

Allen, R. C. (2009) 'An Alarm Sounded to the Sinners in Sion: John Kelsall, Quakers and Popular Culture in eighteenth-century Wales', in J. Allen and R. C. Allen (eds.) *Faith of Our Fathers: Popular Culture and Belief in post-Reformation England, Ireland and Wales*, Newcastle: Cambridge Scholars Press, pp. 52–74.

Allinson, Sybil (2nd Mo 2, 1828) to Margaret H. Hilles, box 1, Gulielma M. Howland Papers, Haverford College, PA: Quaker Collection.

American Friend, Richmond, IN: Friends Publication Board.

American Friends Peace Conference (1902) *American Friends' peace conference, Philadelphia, 1901*, Philadelphia, PA.

American Friends Service Committee (1971) *Struggle for justice*, New York, NY: Hill and Wang.

American Friends Service Committee, 2011, website http://afsc.org/event/quakers-building-pe ace-and-preventing-violence-kenya. Accessed 20 October 2012.

American Friends Service Committee website http://afsc.org/story/afsc-continues-support-oc cupy-wall-street. Accessed 20 October 2012.

Amugamwa, B. K. (2008) 'Quakerism and the Isukha culture: The impact of Quakerism on the culture of the Isukha people of western Kenya', MA Thesis, Earlham School of Religion, IN.

Anderdon, J. (1659) *God's proclamation*, London: Calvert.

Anderson, M. (1995 [1980]) *Approaches to the history of the western family*, Cambridge: Cambridge University Press.

Anderson, P. N. (2000) *Navigating the living waters of the Gospel of John: On wading with children and swimming with elephants*, Pendle Hill Pamphlet 352, Wallingford, PA: Pendle Hill Publications.

Anderson, P. N. (2006) 'The Meeting for Worship in which business is conducted—Quaker decision making as a factor of spiritual discernment', *Quaker Religious Thought*, vol. 106–7, pp. 26–47.

Anderson, P. N. (2007) 'An incarnational sacramentology', *Quaker Religious Thought*, vol. 109, pp. 30–45.

Andrews, E. D. (1953) *The people called Shakers*, New York, NY: Oxford University Press.

Angell, M. (2011) 'The psychiatry', *The New York Review of Books*, New York, NY: Rea S. Hederman.

Angell, S. W. (1992), 'William Penn, Puritan moderate', in M. L. Birkel & J. W. Newman (eds.), *The lamb's war: Quaker essays to honor Hugh Barbour*, Richmond, IN: Earlham College Press, pp. 76–90.

Angell, S.W. (2000) 'Rufus Jones and the laymen's foreign mission inquiry: how a Quaker helped to shape modern ecumenical Christianity', *Quaker Theology*, vol. 3, pp. 167–209.

Angell, S.W. (2003) 'The catechisms of George Fox: why they were written in the first place, what was contained in them, what use was made of them, and what we can learn from them today', *Quaker Theology* 9 http://quest.quaker.org/issue-9-angell-01.htm accessed 16 October, 2012.

Angell, S. W. (2006a) 'Bunji and Toshi Kida and Friends missions to Japanese in California', *Quaker History*, vol. 95, pp. 1–25.

Angell, S. W. (2006b) 'Universalising and spiritualising the Gospel: how early Quakers interpreted the epistle to the Colossians.' *Quaker Studies*, vol. 11, pp. 34–58.

Angell, S. W. (2006c), 'Quaker women in Kenya and human rights issues', in R. D. Smith (ed.) *Freedom's distant shores: American Protestants and post-colonial alliances with Africa*, pp. 111–130, Waco, TX: Baylor University Press.

Angell, S. W. (2009) 'Howard Thurman and Quakers', *Quaker Theology*, vol. 16, pp. 28–54.

Angell, S. W. (2010–11) 'Two current conflicts in Midwestern Friends Meetings', *Quaker Theology*, vol. 18, pp. 1–33.

Angell, S. W. (2011a) 'Gospel Family-Order: George Fox's ministry in Barbados and the development of a Quaker testimony of family', in C Fager (ed.), *Keeping us honest, stirring the pot. A festschrift in honor of H. Larry Ingle*, pp. 17–34, Fayetteville, NC: Kimo Press.

Angell, S.W. (2011b) 'Lopping off a limb?' *Quaker Theology*, vol. 19, http://quaker.org/quest/QT-19.pdf. Accessed 20 October 2012.

Angell, S. W. (2012) 'The impending split in Indiana Yearly Meeting', *Quaker Theology*, vol. 20 pp. 11–40.

Anon. (1675). *The Quakers Farewel to England… Their Voyage to New Jersey.* Wood 416 (129). Ballads. Oxford: Bodleian Library.

Anonymous (1653/4) Swarthmore mss 2.17 and 3.19, papers on the setting up of meetings.

Anonymous (1653a) *Querers and Quakers.* London: Printed by I.G. For Nath. Brooke.

Anonymous (1653b) Swarthmore mss 2.74, 'To Friends in the Truth'.

Anonymous (1654) *An answer to the book which Samuel Eaton put up to the Parliament*, London.

Anonymous (1821) *Extracts from the letters and other writings of the late Joseph Gurney Bevan*, London.

Anonymous (1843) 'G. F. White', *National anti-slavery standard*, vol. 4 no. 94.

Anonymous (1846–7) *Life of William Allen, with selections from his correspondence*, (3 vols.) London: Gilpin.

Anonymous (1848) 'Biographies', *British Friend*, vol. 7, pp. 70–71.

Anonymous (1849) 'A new religious society', *Friends' Intelligencer*, vol. 6 no. 100.

Anonymous 1864, 'Circular meetings', *Friends' Intelligencer*, vol. 21 no. 264.

Anonymous (1866) 'Disciplinary action towards those who have violated our testimony against war', *Friends' Intelligencer*, vol. 23 no. 393.

Anonymous (1874) 'Nottingham Quarterly Meeting', *Journal*, vol. 2, no. 275.

Anonymous (1875) 'Scraps from unpublished letters', *Friends' Intelligencer*, vol. 32 no. 663.

Anonymous (1879) 'Friends mind the light', *Journal*, vol. 7, no. 394.

Anonymous (1887) 'News of Friends', *Friends' Intelligencer*, vol. 44, no. 829.

Anonymous (1889) 'The Cleveland conference', *Friends Missionary Advocate*, vol. 5, no. 85.

Anonymous (1908) 'Quaker printers and booksellers in the seventeenth century, 1652–1667', *Bulletin of the Friends' Historical Society of Philadelphia*, vol. 2, no. 2, pp. 73–77.

Anonymous (1909) 'Arthur Lister', *Annual Monitor*, pp. 76–80.

Anonymous (1926) 'The story of a great literary venture', *Journal of the Friends Historical Society*, vol. 23, no. 1–2, pp 1–11.

Anonymous (2009 [1832]) *An appeal to the Society of Friends on behalf of the Bible Association of Friends in America.* n.p.: General Books.

Anonymous (ed.) (1823) *Letters of Paul and Amicus.* Wilmington, OH: Robert Porter.

Anthony, R. (1830) *The mirror, or Quaker orthodoxy explained*, Wilmington, OH: W. H. P. Denny.

Apsey L. S. (1991) *Following the Light for Peace*, Katonah, NY: KIM Pathways.

Ashbridge, E. (1807) *Some account of the early part of the life of Elizabeth Ashbridge*, Philadelphia, PA: H. and T. Kite.

Australia Yearly Meeting of the Religious Society of Friends (Quakers) (2003) *This we can say: Australian Quaker life, faith, and thought.* Queensland: Kenmore.

Australia Yearly Meeting, 2010, website http://earthcarequaker.wordpress.com/earthcare-state
ment-australia-yearly-meeting/. Accessed 20 October 2012.

Aviv, R. (2011) 'God knows where I am', *The New Yorker,* May 30, pp. 57–65.

Backhouse, J. (1828) 'Memoirs of Francis Howgill with extracts from his writings', York: W.
Alexander & Son.

Bacon M. H. (2000) *Abby Hopper Gibbons: penal reformer and activist,* Albany, NY: State
University of New York Press.

Bacon, M. H. (1980) *Valiant Friend: the life of Lucretia Mott,* New York, NY: Walker and
Company.

Bacon, M. H. (1985) *The quiet rebels: the story of the Quakers in America,* Philadelphia, PA: New
Society Publishers.

Bacon, M. H. (1986) *Mothers of feminism: the story of Quaker women in America,* San Francisco,
CA: Harper & Row.

Bacon, M. H. (1987) *Let this life speak: the legacy of Henry Joel Cadbury*. Philadelphia, PA:
University of Pennsylvania.

Bacon, M. H. (1988) 'Quaker women in overseas ministry', *Quaker History,* vol. 77, no. 2, pp.
93–109.

Bacon, M. H. (1994), *Wilt thou go on my errand? Three 18th-century journals of Quaker women
ministers,* Wallingford, PA: Pendle Hill Publications.

Bacon, M. H. (2001) 'New light on Sarah Mapps Douglass and her reconciliation with Friends',
Quaker History, vol. 90, no. 1, pp. 28–49.

Bacon, M. H. (2003) 'The Motts and the Purvises: A study in interracial friendship', *Quaker
History,* vol. 92, no. 2, pp. 1–18.

Bailey, R. (1992) *New light on George Fox and early Quakerism: The making and unmaking of a
God,* San Francisco, CA: Mellen Research University Press.

Bailyn, B. (1964) *The New England merchants in the seventeenth century,* Cambridge, MA:
Harvard University Press.

Bainton, R. H., Cattell, E. L., & Maurice A. C. (1966) 'The future of Quakerism: Friends World
Conference issue', *Quaker Religious Thought,* vol. 8, no. 2, pp. 2–24.

Baker, F. (1949) *The relations between the Society of Friends and early Methodism,* London:
Epworth Press.

Baltimore Yearly Meeting (2001 [1988]) *Faith and practice of Baltimore Yearly Meeting of the
Religious Society of Friends.* rev. edn., Sandy Spring, MD: Baltimore Yearly Meeting.

Baltimore Yearly Meeting of Friends (1877) *Discipline of the Yearly Meeting of Friends held in
Baltimore for the Western Shore of Maryland, Virginia, and the adjacent parts of Pennsylvania,
as revised and adopted in 1876,* Baltimore, MD.

Banks, J. (1674) *To all the women's Meetings,* London.

Barber, M. (1993) 'The Friend: the first 50 years', *The Friend,* vol. 151, no. 3, pp. 71–3.

Barbour, H & Roberts A. O. (eds.) (2004 [1973]) *Early Quaker writings, 1650–1700,* Wallingford,
PA: Pendle Hill Publications.

Barbour, H. & Frost, J. W. (1994 [1988]) *The Quakers* (2d ed.) Richmond, IN: Friends United
Press.

Barbour, H. (ed.) (1985b) *Slavery and theology: Writings of seven Quaker reformers, 1800–1870,*
Dublin, IN: Prinit Press.

Barbour, H. (1979) 'William Penn, model of Protestant liberalism.' *Church History* 48 (2), pp.
156–73.

Barbour, H. (1985a [1964]) *The Quakers in Puritan England*, Repr. with a new preface by the author, Richmond, IN: Friends United Press.

Barbour, H. (1991) *William Penn on religion and ethics* (2 vols.), Lewiston, NY: Edwin Mellen Press.

Barbour, H., Densmore, C., Moger E. H., Sorel, N. C., Van Wagner, A. D., & Worrall, A. J. (1995) *Quaker crosscurrents: Three hundred years of Friends in the New York Yearly Meeting*, New York, NY: Syracuse University Press.

Barclay, R. (2001 [1673]) *A catechism and confession of faith*, Edited by D. Freiday and A. O. Roberts, Newberg, OR: Barclay Press.

Barclay, R. & Keith, G. (1676) *Quakerism confirmed, or, a vindication of the chief doctrines and principles of the people called Quakers...* Aberdeen.

Barclay, R. (1675) *Theses theologicæ, or the theological propositions*, London.

Barclay, R. (1678) *An Apology for the... Quakers: being a full explanation and vindication of their principles and doctrines...* Aberdeen.

Barclay, R. (1692) 'The possibility and necessity of the inward and immediate revelation of the spirit of God', Truth triumphant in the... writings of... Robert Barclay, London.

Barclay, R. (2002 [1678]) *An Apology for the true Christian divinity*, Peter D. Sippel (ed.), Glenside, PA: Quaker Heritage Press.

Barclay, R., of Reigate (1876), *The inner life of the religious societies of the commonwealth: considered principally with reference to the influence of church organization on the spread of Christianity*, London: Hodder and Stoughton.

Barnard, J. & Bell, M. (2002) 'Statistical tables: Annual book production 1475–1700' in J. Barnard and D. F. McKenzie (eds.), *The Cambridge history of the book in Britain Vol. IV: 1557–1695*, pp. 779–785, Cambridge: Cambridge University Press.

Barnes, K. C. (1984) *Integrity and the arts*, York: Sessions.

Barnett, W. (1979) *Homosexuality and the Bible: An interpretation*, Pendle Hill Pamphlet 226, Wallingford, PA: Pendle Hill Publications.

Barrett, D. B., Johnson, T. M. & Crossing, P. F. (2009) 'Christian world communions: five overviews of global Christianity, AD 1800–2025' *International Bulletin of Missionary Research*, vol. 33, no. 1, January, pp. 25–32.

Barry, J. (1998) 'Bristol as a "reformation city" c.1640–1780', in N. Tyacke (ed.) *England's long reformation 1500–1800*, pp. 261–64, London: UCL Press.

Bartlett, P. & Wright, D. (1999) *Outside the walls of the asylum: the history of care in the community 1750–2000*, London and New Brunswick, NJ: The Athlone Press.

Bates, E. (1875 [1824]) *The doctrines of Friends*, Mount Pleasant, OH.

Bathurst, E. (1683) *The sayings of women, which were spoken upon sundry occasions, in several places of the Scriptures*, Shoreditch: Andrew Sowle.

Bathurst, E. (1996 [1679]) "Truth vindicated" in M. Garman, et al (eds.), *Hidden in plain sight: Quaker women's writings*, Wallingford, PA: Pendle Hill, pp. 339–429.

Bauman, R. (1983) *Let your words be few: symbolism of speaking and silence among seventeenth-century Quakers*, Cambridge and New York, NY: Cambridge University Press.

Beam, A. (2001) *Gracefully insane: the rise and fall of America's premier mental hospital*, New York, NY: Public Affairs, the Perseus Books Group.

Beamish, L. K. (1967) *Quaker ministry, 1691–1834*, 76c Woodstock Road, Oxford: published by the author.

Beccaria C. (1764/1963) *On crimes and punishments*, Indianapolis: Bobbs-Merrill.

Beck, B. (2003) 'The Friend and the British Friend as sources for Quaker family history in the 19th Century', Genealogists' Magazine, vol. 27, no. 12, pp. 547–554.

Beck, W. & Ball, F. T. (1869) The London Friends' Meetings, showing the rise of the Society of Friends in London, London: Kitto.

Beebe, R. K. (1968) Garden of the Lord: A history of Oregon Yearly Meeting of Friends Church. Newberg, OR: Barclay Press.

Bell Burnell, J. (2010) Beautiful Minds documentary by the BBC, http://www.bbc.co.uk/programmes/b00ry9jq Accessed 20 October 2012.

Bell, E. A. (2003a) 'Discipline and Manhood in the Society of Friends: A Study with Particular Reference to Durham c.1650–1750', Unpublished PhD dissertation, University of York.

Bell, E. A. (2003b) '"Vain unsettled fashions": The early Durham Friends and popular culture, c.1660–1725', Quaker Studies, vol. 8, no. 1, September, pp, 23–35.

Bell, E. A. (2008) 'Eighteenth-Century Quakerism and the rehabilitation of James Nayler, Seventeenth-Century radical', Journal of Ecclesiastical History, vol. 59, no. 3, pp. 426–46.

Bell, M, Parfitt, G., & Shepherd, S. (1990) A biographical dictionary of English women, 1580–1720, Hemel Hempstead: Harvester Wheatsheaf.

Bell, M. (1988) 'Mary Westwood, Quaker publisher', Publishing History, vol. 23, pp. 5–65.

Bell, M. (1990) 'Quaker Women Writers' in M. Bell, G. Parfitt, & S. Shepherd, A biographical dictionary of English women writers 1580–1720, pp. 257–62, Hemel Hempstead: Harvester Wheatsheaf.

Bellers, J. (1695) Proposals for raising a colledge of industry of all useful trades and husbandry. London: T. Sowle.

Benedict & Fry, T. (1982) RB 1980: the Rule of St. Benedict in English, Collegeville MN: Liturgical Press.

Benezet, A. (1778) Some considerations on several important subjects, Digital Quaker Electronic Collection, Richmond, IN: Earlham College.

Benezet, A. (1780) An Extract from a Treatise on the Spirit of Prayer or The Soul rising out of the Vanity of Time into the Riches of Eternity with some Thoughts on War: Remarks on the Nature and bad effects of the use of Spirituous Liquors and Considerations on Slavery, Joseph.

Benjamin, P. S. (1976) Philadelphia Quakers in the industrial age 1895-1920, Philadelphia, PA: Temple University.

Benney, M. (1948) Gaol delivery: a searchlight on the state of English prisons and their future (published for the Howard League for Penal Reform), London: Longmans, Green and Co Ltd.

Benson, L. (1944) Prophetic Quakerism, N.p.

Benson, L. (1966) Catholic Quakerism: a vision for all men. Philadelphia, PA: Philadelphia Yearly Meeting Book Service Committee.

Bernet, C. (2006) 'Quaker missionaries in Holland and northern Germany in the late seventeenth century: Ames, Caton, and Furly', Quaker History, vol. 95, pp. 1–18.

Berryman, P. (1987) Liberation theology: essential facts about the religious movement in Latin America and beyond, New York, NY: Pantheon.

Besse, J. (1753), A collection of the sufferings of the people called Quakers (2 vols), London: L. Hinde.

Besse, J. (1773) An abstract of the sufferings of the people call'd Quakers. London: J. Sowle.

Best, S. (2008a) 'Adolescent Quakers: a community of intimacy', in P. Dandelion and P. Collins, eds. *The Quaker condition: the sociology of a liberal religion*, pp. 192–215, Newcastle: Cambridge Scholars Press.

Best, S. (2008b) 'Adolescent Quakers: a hidden sect', *Quaker Studies*, vol. 13, pp. 103–13.

Best, S. (2010) 'The Community of Intimacy: The Spiritual Beliefs and Religious Practices of Adolescent Quakers.' Unpublished PhD dissertation, University of Birmingham.

Biddle, W. C. (1883) 'Swarthmore College', *Friends' Intelligencer*, vol. 40, pp. 4–5.

Biddle, Ester (1660) *A warning from the Lord of life and power*. London: Robert Wilson.

Bieber, N. L. (1997) *Communion for a Quaker*. Pendle Hill Pamphlet no. 331, Wallingford, PA: Pendle Hill Publications.

Bieber, N. L. (2010) *Decision making and spiritual discernment: the sacred art of finding your way*, Woodstock, VT: SkyLight Paths.

Bill, J. B. (2008) *Sacred compass: the way of spiritual discernment*. Brewster, MA: Paraclete Press.

Birkel, M. L. (2003) *A near sympathy: the timeless Quaker wisdom of John Woolman*, Richmond, IN: Friends United Press and Earlham Press.

Birkel, M. L. (2004) *Silence and witness: the Quaker tradition*, Maryknoll, NY. Orbis Books.

Birkel, M. L. (2005) *Engaging scripture: reading the bible with early Friends*, Richmond, IN: Friends United Press and Earlham Press.

Birkel, M. L. (2008) *The messenger that goes before: reading Margaret Fell for spiritual nurture*, Wallingford, PA: Pendle Hill Publications.

Birmingham Museums and Art Gallery (1980) *Joseph Southall 1861–1944: Artist-craftsman*, Birmingham.

Bitterman, M. G. F. (1973) 'The early Quaker literature of defence', *Church History*, vol. 42, pp. 203–28.

Blackborow, S. (1658) *A visit to the Spirit in Prison*, London: Simmonds.

Blair R. (2009) 'Ulster Quaker service', in A Le Mare & F McCartney (eds.) *Coming from the silence; Quaker peacebuilding initiatives in Northern Ireland 1969–2007*, York: William Sessions.

Blake, B. and Watts, C. (2005) *Can We ALL Be Friends?* Personally produced DVD, available through Quaker Books of Friends General Conference, Philadelphia, PA.

Blamires, D. (1973) *Homosexuality from the inside*, London: Social responsibility council of the Religious Society of Friends.

Blome, R. (1988 [1660]) *The fanatick history; or, an exact relation and account of the old*, Bloomington, IN.

Bockoven & Sanbourne, J. (1963) *Moral treatment in American psychiatry*, New York, NY: Springer Publishing Company.

Boehme, J. (2010), *Genius of the transcendant: Mystical writings of Jakob Boehme*, trans. M. L. Birkel and J. Bach, Boston: Shambala.

Boisen, A. T. (1936) *The exploration of the inner world: a study of mental disorder and religious experience*, Chicago, IL: Willet, Clark.

Bok, C. (1953) 'Crime and punishment' in Kavanaugh J (ed.) *The Quaker approach*, pp. 137–42. London: George Allen and Unwin.

Borthwick, A., et al (2001) 'The relevance of moral treatment to contemporary mental health care', *Journal of Mental Health*, August, pp. 427–39.

Bossuet, J. B. (1698) *Quakerism, a-la-mode, or a history of quietism*, London: printed for J. Harris and A Bell.

Boulding, E. (1989) *One small plot of heaven. Reflections on family life by a Quaker sociologist.* Wallingford, PA: Pendle Hill Publications.

Boulton, D. (2006) *Godless for God's sake: nontheism in contemporary Quakerism*, Hobson's Farm, Dent: Dales Historical Monographs.

Bownas, S. (1795 [1756]) *An account of the life, travels, and Christian experiences in the work of the ministry of Samuel Bownas*, London: J. Phillips.

Bownas, S. (1989 [1750]) *A description of the qualifications necessary to a Gospel minister*, Wallingford, PA: Pendle Hill.

Boyle, B. E. (1983) (Tenth ed.) *Words of conscience: Religious statements on conscientious objection.* Washington, DC: National Interreligious Service Board for Conscientious Objectors.

Brace, H. W. (ed.) (1948–51) *The First Minute Book of the Gainsborough Monthly Meeting of the Society of Friends*, Hereford, England: Lincoln Record Society Publications 38, 40, 44.

Bradley, A. D. (1979) New York Yearly Meeting at Poplar Ridge and Primitive Friends, *Quaker History*, vol. 68, no. 2, pp. 75–82.

Brady, G. S. (1886) 'The modern spirit in the study of nature', *Friends Quarterly Examiner*, vol. 20 pp. 63–84.

Brailsford, M. (1915) *Quaker Women, 1650-1690*, London: Duckworth and Co.

Braithwaite, A. W. (1966) 'Early Friends and informers', *Journal of the Friends' Historical Society*, vol. 51, no. 2, pp. 107–14.

Braithwaite, A. W. (1969) 'Early Friends' testimony against carnal weapons', *Journal of the Friends Historical Society*, vol. 52, no. 2, pp. 101–5.

Braithwaite, J. B. (1909) *A Friend of the nineteenth century*, London: Hodder and Stoughton.

Braithwaite, W. C. (1919) *The second period of Quakerism*, London: Macmillan.

Braithwaite, W. C. (1909) *Spiritual guidance in the experience of the Society of Friends*, London: Published for the Woodbrooke Extension Committee by Headley Brothers.

Braithwaite, W. C. (1955 [1912]) *The beginnings of Quakerism*, Macmillan, London, 2nd edn. H. J. Cadbury, Cambridge: Cambridge University Press,

Braithwaite, W. C. (1979 [1919]) *The second period of Quakerism*, York: William Sessions.

Branson, A. (1892) *Journal of Ann Branson: a minister of the Gospel in the Society of Friends*, Philadelphia, PA: Wm. H. Pike's Sons, Printers.

Braun, K. (1950) *Justice and the law of love*, The Swarthmore Lecture, London: George Allen and Unwin.

Brayshaw, A. N. (1953) *The Quakers: their story and message* (3rd ed.), London: Friends Home Service Committee.

Brayshaw, A. N. (1982 [1905]) *The Quakers: their story and message*, York: William Sessions.

Breeze, G. (2005) 'Joseph Southall and the pursuit of peace', in A. N. Sprague, G. Breeze, & P. Skipwith, *Joseph Southall 1861-1944*, pp. 45–54. London: Fine Arts Society.

Brendlinger, I. A. (2007) *To be silent... would be criminal: The antislavery influence and writings of Anthony Benezet*, Lanham, MD: Scarecrow Press.

Brewer, A. (1993) 'Why Be a Traidcraft Rep?', *Quaker Network for Economic Change Newsletter*, Library of the Society of Friends, no. 1, pp. 4–5.

Brindle, S. K. (2000) *To learn a new song: A Quaker contribution towards real reconciliation with the earth and its people*, The James Backhouse Lecture. Armadale, Australia: Australia Yearly Meeting of the Religious Society of Friends.

Brinton, H. H. (1940) *Quaker education in theory and practice*, Wallingford, PA: Pendle Hill Publications.

Brinton, H. H. (1952) *Friends for 300 years; The history and beliefs of the Society of Friends since George Fox started the Quaker movement,* New York, NY: Harper.

Brinton, H. H. 1(958) *Quaker education in theory and practice.* Pendle Hill Pamphlet Number 9 (revised), Wallingford, PA: Pendle Hill Publications.

Brinton, H. H. (1972) *Quaker journals: Varieties of religious experience among Friends,* Wallingford, PA: Pendle Hill Publications.

Brinton, H. H. (2002 [1952]) *Friends for 350 years,* Wallingford, PA: Pendle Hill Publications.

Britain Yearly Meeting (2001) Minute 30. *Proceedings of the Yearly Meeting of the Religious Society of Friends (Quakers) in Britain for the year 2001.* London: Britain Yearly Meeting of the Religious Society of Friends (Quakers).

Britain Yearly Meeting (2004) Minute 39 Minute of 16 to18 year olds group. *Proceedings of the Yearly Meeting of the Religious Society of Friends (Quakers) in Britain for the year 2004.* London: Britain Yearly Meeting of the Religious Society of Friends (Quakers).

Britain Yearly Meeting (2009) *Quaker Faith and Practice* (4th edn.) London: The Religious Society of Friends (Quakers) in Britain.

Britain Yearly Meeting (2011)([http://www.quaker.org.uk/news/news-release-quakers-express-support-occupy-london]), accessed 2011

Brock, P. (1968a) *Pacifism in the United States: from the colonial era to the First World War.* Princeton, NJ: Princeton University Press.

Brock, P. (1968b), *Pioneers of the peaceable kingdom,* Princeton, NJ: Princeton University Press.

Brock, P. (1990) *The Quaker Peace Testimony 1660 to 1914,* York, England: Sessions Book Trust.

Brock P. (2001) *The black flower: One man's memory of prison sixty years after,* York: William Sessions.

Brock, P. & Young, N. (1999) *Pacifism in the Twentieth Century,* Syracuse, NY: Syracuse University Press.

Bronner, E. B. (1967) 'Distributing the printed word: the Tract Association of Friends, 1816-1966,' *Pennsylvania Magazine of History and Biography,* vol. 91, no. 3, pp. 342–54.

Brook, M. (1774) *Reasons for the necessity of silent waiting, in order to the solemn worship of God,* London: Mary Hinde.

Brown, C. L. (2006) *Moral capital: Foundations of British abolitionism.* Chapel Hill, NC: University of North Carolina Press.

Brown, J. (ed.) (2010) *Autobiography of Allen Jay (1831–1910),* Richmond, IN: Friends United Press.

Bruyneel, S. (2010) *Margaret Fell and the end of time: The theology of the mother of Quakerism,* Waco, TX: Baylor University Press.

Brzostoski, J. (2000) 'Hicks's Peaceable Kingdom,' *Friends Journal,* February, pp. 6–8.

Buckley, P. & Angell, S. W. (eds.) (2006) *The Quaker Bible reader,* Richmond, IN: Earlham Press.

Buckley, P. (ed.) (2009) *The journal of Elias Hicks,* San Francisco, CA: Inner Light Books.

Buckley, P. (2011) *Dear Friend: Letters and essays of Elias Hicks.* San Francisco, CA: Inner Light Books.

Bucknill, J. C. & Tuke, D. H. (1858) *A manual of psychological medicine,* Philadelphia, PA: Blanchard & Lee.

Burnet, G. B. (1952) *The story of Quakerism in Scotland 1650–1850, with an epilogue on the period 1850–1950 by William H. Marwick,* London: James Clarke & Co. Ltd.

Burrough, E. (1654), A. R. Barclay mss, 161.

Burrough, E. (1657a) *A declaration to all the world of our faith,* London.

Burrough, E. (1657b) *A standard lifted up*, London: Calvert.

Burrough, E. (1659a) *To the Parliament of the Commonwealth of England,* London.

Burrough, E. (1659b) *A message to the present rulers of England,* London.

Burrough, E. (1659c) *A declaration from the people called Quakers to the present distracted nation of England,* London.

Burrough, E. (1660a) *The everlasting gospel of repentance*, London: Wilson.

Burrough, E. (1660b) *A general epistle to all the saints,* London.

Burton, P. F. (2007) *A social history of Quakers in Scotland 1800–2000,* Lampeter: Edwin Mellen Press.

Butler, D. M. (1999) *The Quaker meeting houses of Britain,* 2 vols. London: Friends Historical Society.

Butler, J. (1978) 'Power, authority and the origins of denominational order: the English churches in the Delaware Valley 1680–1730', *Transactions of the American Philosophical Society,* New Series, vol. 68 no. 2, pp. 1–85.

Butterworth, C. (1882) *Diary,* Friends collection, Nov. 26, Richmond, IN: Earlham College.

Byrne, D. (2007) 'Anne Conway, early Quaker thought, and the new science', *Quaker History* vol. 96 pp. 24–35.

Cadbury, D. (2010) *The chocolate wars: from Cadbury to Kraft—200 Years of sweet success and bitter rivalry,* London: Harper Press.

Cadbury, H. J. (1952). 'First Settlement of Meetings in Europe', *Journal of the Friends' Historical Society,* vol. 44, no. 1(1), 11–12.

Cadbury, H. J. (1936), 'Negro Membership in the Society of Friends', *Journal of Negro History,* vol. 21, pp. 151–213.

Cadbury, H. J. (1948b), *George Fox's Book of Miracles,* Cambridge: Cambridge University Press.

Cadbury, H. J. (1953) 'A Quaker approach to the Bible', Ward Lecture, Guilford College. http://www.universalistfriends.org/cadbury-1.html accessed 12 October 2012.

Calderone, M. (1973) *Human sexuality and the Quaker conscience,* Philadelphia, PA: Friends General Conference.

Calvert, E. R. (1927) *Capital Punishment in the 20th Century,* London: Putnam.

Calvert, P. (2005) 'Reflections on Quaker Mestizaje' *Quaker Religious Thought,* vol. 104, pp. 5–13.

Canadian Friends Service Committee, 2011, http://quakerservice.ca/our-work/economics-and-ecology/ accessed 16 October 2012.

Canadian Yearly Meeting (2004. *A history of Canadian Yearly Meeting.* [Online] Available through The Quaker Archives and Library of Canada at http://archives-library.quaker.ca/en/historyofCYM.html accessed 12 October 2012.

Canadian Yearly Meeting (2008) *The Religious Society of Friends: an introduction.* [Online] Available at http://www.quaker.ca/ContactInfo/Intro/intro.html accessed 12 October 2012.

Cantor, G. (1997) 'Quakers in the Royal Society', *Notes and Records of the Royal Society of London,* vol. 51, no. 2, pp. 175–93.

Cantor, G. (1999) 'Aesthetics in science, as practised by Quakers in the eighteenth and nineteenth Centuries', *Quaker Studies,* vol. 4, pp. 1–20.

Cantor, G. (2004) 'Friends of science? The role of science in Quaker periodicals' L. Henson, G. Cantor, et al (eds.) *Culture and science in the nineteenth-century media,* pp. 83–96, Aldershot, Ashgate.

Cantor, G. (2005) *Quakers, Jews and science: Religious responses to modernity and the science in Britain, 1650–1900,* Oxford: Oxford University Press.

Capp, B. S. (1972) *The Fifth Monarchy men: A study in seventeenth century English Millenarianism*, London: Faber.

Carpenter, J. A. (1997) *Revive us again: The reawakening of American fundamentalism*, Oxford: Oxford University Press.

Carroll, K. L. (1971) 'John Perrot: early Quaker schismatic', *Journal of the Friends' Historical Society*, Supplement 33, London.

Carroll, K. L. (2010) 'Persecution and persecutors of Maryland Quakers, 1658–1661', *Quaker History*, vol. 99, no. 1, pp. 15–31.

Carter, C. F. (1967) 'Unsettled Friends: Church Government and the Origins of Membership', *Journal of the Friends' Historical Society*, vol. 51, 3, 143–53.

Carter, M. L. (1989) 'Quaker relations with Midwestern Indians to 1833', Unpublished PhD dissertation, Temple University, PA.

Case, J. R. (2012) *An unpredictable gospel: American evangelicals and world Christianity, 1812-1920*. New York: Oxford University Press.

Cassian, J. & Ramsey, B. (1997) *John Cassian, the Conferences*, New York, NY: Paulist Press.

Castedo, L. (1969) A history of Latin American art and architecture, London: Pall Mall Press.

Caton, W. (1658) *Report to Margaret Fell on the deployment of ministers*, Caton mss 3.29.

Cazden, E. (1997) 'The modernist reinventon of Quakerism: the independent meeting in New England, MA thesis, Andover Newton Theological School.

Central and Southern Africa Yearly Meeting (CSAYM) (1995) *Who are the Quakers? An introduction to the Religious Society of Friends (Quakers) in Southern Africa*, Cape Town: CSAYM.

Chace, E. B. (1937, [1891]) 'My anti-slavery reminiscences', *Two Quaker Sisters*, (ed.) M. R. Lovell, New York, NY: Liveright Publ. Corp.

Chalkley, T. (1866 [1751]) *Journal*, Philadelphia, PA: Friends' Bookstore.

Chamberlain, J. S. (2005, [2004]) 'Keith, George (1638?–1716)', *Oxford dictionary of national biography*, Oxford: Oxford University Press.

Champion, J. A. I. (1992) *The pillars of priestcraft shaken: the church of England and its enemies 1660–1730*, Cambridge: Cambridge University Press.

Chandler, W. (1827) to Benjamin Ferris, 5th Mo. 23, box 12, Ferris Family Papers. Swarthmore College, PA: Friends Historical Library.

Charland, L. C. (2007) 'Benevolent theory: moral treatment at the York Retreat', *History of Psychiatry*, vol. 18, no. 1, pp. 61–80.

Chenard, J. (2005) 'The three yearly meetings prior to 1955', *The Canadian Friend*, vol. 101, No. 3, July–August, pp. 4–5. [Online] Available at http://www.quaker.ca/Publications/cfriend/CF_V101_3/CF.V101.03.04to05.pdf Accessed 20 October 2012.

Cherry, C. L. (1989) *A quiet haven: Quakers, moral treatment, and asylum reform*, London and Toronto: Associated University Presses

Chijioke, M. E. (2011) 'Bibliography: Introduction', in M. P. Abbott, M. E. Chijioke, P. Dandelion, & Oliver, J. William Jr. (eds.), *Historical Dictionary of the Friends (Quakers)*, 2nd ed., pp. 402–5, Lanham, MD: Scarecrow Press.

Christian Faith and Practice in the Experience of the Society of Friends (1960) London Yearly Meeting of the Religious Society of Friends, London.

Christian Fundamentals: a Testimony to Truth, (n.d.) Chicago, IL: Testimony Publishing Company.

Christian Worker (periodical) Chicago, IL, 1871–94.

Clark, R. A. & Elkinton, J. R. (1978) *The Quaker heritage in medicine*, Pacific Grove, CA: The Boxwood Press.

Clark, R. I. (1988) 'The Quakers and the Church of England, 1670–1720: A study in ecclesiastical and intellectual history'. PhD dissertation, University of Lancaster.

Clarke, G. (1987) *John Bellers: his life, times and writings*, London: Routledge and Kegan Paul.

Clarkson, T. (1806) *A portraiture of Quakerism*, London: Samuel Stansbury, Hurst, Reece and Orme.

Clement, J. T. (1950) *Religious growth in the Quaker Family*, Committee on Religious Education, Philadelphia, PA: Friends General Conference.

Coffin, E. C. (1920) 'Women as Preachers and Pastors', *American Friend* XXVII, vol. 31, pp. 679–83.

Coffin, W. (1975) 'Women's liberation and Friends Testimonies: Profession or possession?' *Quaker Life*, vol. XVI, no. 8, pp. 16–17.

Coleridge, S. T. (1825) *Aids to reflection*, London: Taylor and Hessey.

Collins, P. J. (1996) '"Plaining": The social and cognitive process of symbolization in the Religious Society of Friends (Quakers)', *Journal of Contemporary Religion*, vol. 11, pp. 277–88.

Collins, P. J. (2001) 'Quaker plaining as critical aesthetic', *Quaker Studies*, vol. 5, pp. 121–39.

Comly J. (1853) *Journal of the life and religious labours of John Comly*, Philadelphia, PA: Chapman.

Concern (1959–1962) vol. I–IV, The Association of Evangelical Friends.

Condori M. E. (2011) Personal Interview, 4 April, Original in author's possession.

Conti, A., Curtis, C., Daniels, C. W., Hart, H., Hoggatt, S. K., Jadin, E., Lomuria, J. E., Mamani, E. C., McQuail, K., & Miller, R. A. (2010) *Spirit rising: Young Quaker voices*, Philadelphia, PA: Quakers Uniting in Publications and Quaker Press of Friends General Conference.

Conway, A. (1692) *Principles of the most ancient and modern philosophy*, London.

Coole, B. 1696, *The Quakers cleared from being apostates or the hammer defeated*, London: T. Sowle.

Cooper, K. & Gregory, J. (eds.) (2005) *Signs, wonders, miracles. Representations of Divine power in the life of the Church*. Studies in Church History 41. Woodbridge: Boydell Press.

Cooper, W. & Fraser, B. (eds.) (1990) *Sexual ethics: Some Quaker perspectives*, Greensboro, NC: Quaker Theological Discussion Group.

Cooper, W. (1985) *The Earlham School of Religion story: a Quaker dream come true 1960-1985*, Richmond, IN: Earlham School of Religion.

Cooper, W. (2001 [1990]) *A living faith: An historical and comparative study of Quaker beliefs*, 2d. ed., Richmond, IN: Friends United Press.

Cooper, W. A. (2005) 'Reflections on Rufus Jones', *Quaker History*, vol. 94, no. 2, pp. 25–43.

Corina, J. G. (2004) 'Bader, Ernest (1890–1982)', *Oxford dictionary of national biography*, Oxford University Press.

Corns, T. N. and Loewenstein, D. (eds.) (1995) *The emergence of Quaker writing: Dissenting literature in Seventeenth-Century England*, London: Frank Cass.

Cotton, A. (1656) *Request for travelling ministers*, Swarthmore mss 4.163.

Coudert, A. (1999) *The impact of the Kabbalah in the seventeenth century: The life and thought of Francis Mercury Van Helmont (1614–1698)*, Leiden: Brill.

Crawford, A. (ed.) (1984) *By hammer and hand: the arts and crafts movement in Birmingham*, Birmingham: Birmingham Museums and Art Gallery.

Creasey, M. (1962) *'Inward' and 'outward'*, London: Friends' Historical Society.

Creasey, M. (1963) 'Quakers and the sacraments', *Quaker Religious Thought*, vol. 5, pp. 2–25.

Creasey, M. (1969) *Bearings or Friends and the new reformation*, The Swarthmore Lecture, London: Friends Home Service.

Crisp, R. & Slote, M. (eds.) (1997) *Virtue ethics*, Oxford: Oxford University Press.

Crisp, S. (1822 [1694]) 'An epistle of tender love and brotherly advice', The Christian experiences, gospel labours and writings of...Stephen Crisp, Benjamin & Thomas Kite, Philadelphia.

Cronk, S. (1991) *Gospel order: a Quaker understanding of faithful church community*, Pendle Hill Pamphlet no. 297. Wallingford, PA: Pendle Hill Publications.

Cullen, W. (1789) *First lines of the practice of physic*, 4 vols, Edinburgh: Printed for C. Elliott.

Cummings, G. N. (1996) 'Exercising goodness: the antislavery Quaker in American writing, 1774–1865', Unpublished PhD Dissertation, University of Virginia, VA.

Cummings, G. N. (1998) 'Walt Whitman and Elias Hicks', *Modern language studies*, vol. 28, no 2, pp. 69–86.

D'Antonio, P. (2006) *Founding Friends: families, staff, and patients at the Friends Asylum in early nineteenth-century Philadelphia*, Bethlehem, PA: Lehigh University Press,

Dain, N. (1964) *Concepts of insanity in the United States, 1789–1865*, New Brunswick, NJ: Rutgers University Press.

Damiano, K. A. (1988) *On earth as it is in heaven: eighteenth century Quakerism as realized eschatology*. Unpublished PhD dissertation, Cincinnati, OH: Union of Experimenting Colleges and Universities.

Damrosch, L. (1996) *The sorrows of the Quaker Jesus: James Nayler and the Puritan crackdown on the free spirit*, Cambridge, MA: Harvard University Press.

Dandelion, B. P. (2010) *Confident Quakerism*, Pendle Hill Pamphlet 410, Wallingford, PA: Pendle Hill Publications.

Dandelion, B. P., Gwyn, D., & Peat, T. (1998) *Heaven on earth: Quakers and the second coming*, Birmingham: Curlew Productions and Woodbrooke College.

Dandelion, P. (1996) *A sociological analysis of the theology of Quakers: The silent revolution*. Lewiston, NY: Edwin Mellen Press.

Dandelion, P. (2005) *The liturgies of Quakerism*, Ashgate, Aldershot.

Dandelion, P. (2007) *An introduction to Quakerism*, Cambridge: Cambridge University Press.

Dandelion, P. (2008a) 'The creation of coherence: The "Quaker double culture" and the "absolute perhaps"', P. Dandelion & P. Collins (eds.) *The Quaker condition: the sociology of a liberal religion*, pp. 22–37, Newcastle: Cambridge Scholars.

Dandelion, P. (2008b) *The Quakers: A very short introduction*, Oxford: Oxford University Press.

Dandelion, P. (2010) 'Guarded domesticity and engagement with "the world": The separate spheres of Quaker Quietism', *Common Knowledge*, vol. 16, no. 1, pp. 95–109.

Dandelion, P. (2011) 'Liberal Friends', in M. P. Abbott, M. E. Chijioke, P. Dandelion, & J. Oliver, *Historical dictionary of the Friends (Quakers)*, 2nd edn., pp. 201–2, Lanham, MD: Scarecrow Press.

Dandelion, P. & Collins, P. (2008) *The Quaker condition: The sociology of a liberal religion*, Newcastle: Cambridge Scholars Publishing.

Dart, M. (1995) *Transcending tradition: Excerpts from the writings and talks of Marjorie Sykes*. York, Birmingham: William Sessions and Woodbrooke College.

Dart, M. (1999) *Quaker friendship: Letters from Marjorie Sykes*. York: William Sessions.

Dart, M. (1993) 'Marjorie Sykes: Quaker-Gandhian, Hyderabad', The Academy of Gandhian Studies in Collaboration with Nai Talim Samithi, Sevagram, with special permission, Birmingham.

Dartmouth (Mass.) Monthly Meeting, *Minutes (men's)*, Rhode Island Historical Society.

Davidoff, L. & Hall, C. (2002) *Family Fortunes*, (rev. edn), London: Routledge.

Davidson, C. N. (2004 [1986]) *Revolution and the word: The rise of the novel in America*, New York, NY: Oxford University Press.

Davidson, R. A. (1964) *Isaac Hicks: New York Merchant and Quaker 1787–1920*, Cambridge, MA: Harvard University Press.

Davie, M. (1997) *British Quaker theology since 1895*, Lewistown, NY: Edwin Mellen Press.

Davies, A. (2000) *The Quakers in English society, 1655–1725 (Oxford Historical Monographs)*, Oxford: Clarendon Press.

Davies, J. S. & Freeman, M. (2004) 'A case of political philanthropy: The Rowntree family and the campaign for democratic reform', *Quaker Studies*, vol. 9, pp. 95–113.

Davis, G. L. (1985) *I got the word in me and I can sing it, you know: A study of the performed African-American sermon*, Philadelphia, PA: University of Pennsylvania.

Davis, R. (1953) *Woodbrooke, 1903–1953: a brief history of a Quaker experiment in religious education*, London: Bannisdale Press.

Deacon, R. (1974) *Young Friends Central Committee: a study of a Church Youth Organisation.* Available from Young Friends General Meeting. Unpublished.

Dellheim, C. (1987) 'The creation of a company culture: Cadburys, 1861–1931', *The American Historical Review*, vol. 92, pp. 13–44.

Densmore, C. (2007) 'Swarthmore College', J. W. Oliver, C. L. Cherry, & C. L. Cherry, (eds.), *Founded by Friends: the Quaker heritage of fifteen American colleges and universities*, Lanham, MD: Scarecrow Press.

Deutsch, A. (1949) *The mentally ill in America: A history of their care and treatment from colonial times*, (2nd ed.) New York, NY:Columbia University Press.

Dewsbury, W. (1655) *The discovery of the great enmity of the serpent*, London: Calvert.

Dewsbury, W. (1653) *A true prophecy*, London: Calvert.

Digby, A. (1985) *Madness, morality and medicine: A study of York Retreat*, Cambridge: Cambridge University Press.

DiGiacomantonio, W. C. (1995) '"For the gratification of a volunteering society": Antislavery and pressure group politics in the First Federal Congress', *Journal of the Early Republic*, vol. 15, pp. 169–97.

Ditchfield, G. M. (1985) 'Parliament, the Quakers and the tithe question 1750–1835', *Parliamentary History*, vol. 4, pp. 87–114.

Dixon, A. G. (1996) *A history of British art*, London: BBC.

Doan, P. L. (2002) 'Gender, integrity and spirituality: A personal journey', *Friends Journal*, vol. 48, pp. 40–3.

Docwra, A. (1683) 'Spiritual community, vindicated amongst people of different persuasions in some things', London, s.n.

Doherty, R. W. (1965) 'The growth of Orthodoxy', *Quaker History*, vol. 34, no. 1, pp. 24–34.

Doherty, R. W. (1967) *The Hicksite separation.* New Brunswick, NJ: Rutgers University Press.

Dorgan, H. (1987) *Giving glory to God in Appalachia: worship practices of six Baptist sub-denominations*, Knoxville, TN: University of Tennessee.

Dorland, A. G. (1968) *The Quakers in Canada: A history*, Toronto: Ryerson.

Dorrien, G. J. (2003) *The making of American liberal theology*, vol. 2, Louisville, KY: John Knox Press.

Dorsey, B. (1998) 'Friends becoming enemies: Philadelphia benevolence and the neglected era of American Quaker history', *Journal of the Early Republic*, vol. 18, pp. 395–428.

Dougherty, R. M. (1995, *Group spiritual direction: community for discernment*. New York, NY: Paulist Press.

Drake, T. E. (1950) *Quakers and slavery in America*, New Haven, CT: Yale University Press.

Dudley, J. (1946) *The life of Edward Grubb 1854–1939*, London: James Clark.

Dugdale, J. A. (1850) 'Reform among the Quakers', *Indiana True Democrat*, March 27, Centerville, IN.

Dunn, M. M. (1967) *William Penn: politics and conscience*, Princeton, NJ: Princeton University Press.

Dunn, M. M. (1986) 'The personality of William Penn', in R. S. Dunn & M. M. Dunn (eds.), *The world of William Penn*, pp. 3–14, Philadelphia, PA: University of Pennsylvania Press.

Dunn, R. S. & Dunn, M. M. (eds.) (1981–7) *The papers of William Penn* (5 vols.) Philadelphia, PA: University of Pennsylvania Press.

Dunn, R. S. (1986) 'Penny wise and pound foolish: Penn as businessman', in R.S. Dunn & M.M. Dunn (eds.) *The world of William Penn*, Philadelphia, PA: University of Pennsylvania Press.

Dunn, R. S. and Dunn, M. M. (eds.) (1986) *The world of William Penn*. Philadelphia, PA: University of Pennsylvania Press.

Dunn, R. S. & Dunn, M. M. (eds.) 'Founding elite', in *The world of William Penn*, pp. 337–362, Philadelphia, PA: University of Pennsylvania Press.

Durham, H. F. (1972) *Caribbean Quakers*, Hollywood, FL: Dukane Press.

E. S. (1880) 'Some things we need in our First Day schools', *Journal*, pp. 182.

Eccles, P. J. (2009) *The presence in the midst: reflections on discernment*, The Swarthmore Lecture, London: Quaker Books.

Eddington, A. S. (1929) *Science and the unseen world*, London: George Allen & Unwin.

Eddington, A. S. (2007 [1929]) *Science and the unseen world*, London: Britain Yearly Meeting.

Edwards, G. W. (1968) 'Quakers as churchwardens and vestrymen', *Journal of the Friends' Historical Society*, vol. 58, no. 1, pp. 48–53.

Edwards, I. (1955) 'The women Friends of London, the two weeks and box meetings', *Journal of the Friends' Historical Society*, vol. 47, pp. 3–21.

Edwards, T. (1646) *Gangraena or a catalogue... of the errors, heresies of the... sectaries of this time*, London: Smith.

Elliott, E. T. (1969) *Quakers on the American frontier*. Richmond, IN: Friends United Press.

Elliott, M. K. (1991) 'You can get there from here', *Friends Journal*, December, pp. 7–13.

Ellis, S. S. (1858) *Friends at their own fireside: or, pictures of the private life of the people called Quakers*, London: Richard Bentley.

Emerson, E. H. (1952) *Walter C. Woodward, Friend on the frontier: A biography*. N.p.

Emlen, S. (1828) *to James Emlen*, 8th Mo. 7, Emlen Papers, Swarthmore College, PA: Friends Historical Library.

Endy, M. B., Jr. (1973) *William Penn and early Quakerism*, Princeton, NJ: Princeton University Press.

Endy, M. B., Jr. (1981) 'The interpretation of Quakerism: Rufus Jones and his critics', *Quaker History*, vol. 70, no. 1, pp. 3–21.

Endy, M. B., Jr. (2004) 'George Fox and William Penn: Their relationship and roles within the Quaker Movement', *Quaker History*, vol. 93, no. 4, pp. 1–39.

Evans, E. J. (1969) 'Our faithful testimony. the Society of Friends and tithe payments 1690-1730', *Journal of the Friends Historical Society*, vol. 52, no. 2, pp. 106–21.

Evans, E. J. (1976) *The contentious tithe: the tithe problem and English agriculture, 1750–1850*, London: Routledge and Kegan Paul.

Evans, J. (1837) *Journal*, Philadelphia, PA.

Evans, T. (1828) *An exposition of the faith of the Religious Society of Friends: Commonly called Quakers, in the fundamental doctrines of the Christian religion, principally selected from their early writings*, Philadelphia, PA: Kimber and Sharpless.

Extracts from the Minutes and Advices of the Yearly Meeting of Friends held in London from its first institution, 1783, London: James Phillips.

Fager, C. (2004) 'Lucretia Mott, liberal Quaker theologian.' *Quaker Theology*, vol. 6, no. 1, pp. 1–27.

Fager, C. (2011) 'From detoxification to godwrestling: Three stages of Bible study.' *Reclaiming a resource: Papers from the Friends Bible Conference*, www.kimopress.com accessed 14 October 2012.

Fairn, R. D. (1951) *Quakerism: a faith for ordinary men*. London: George Allen and Unwin.

Fairn, R. D. (1966) 'Prisons: 1866–1966' H. J. Klare (ed.) *Changing concepts of crime and its treatment*, pp. 155–70, London: Pergamon Press.

Farnham, S. G. (1991) *Listening hearts: discerning call in community*, Harrisburg, PA: Morehouse.

Farnham, S. G., Hull, S. A., & McLean, R. T., *Grounded in God: listening hearts discernment for group deliberations*, Harrisburg, PA: Morehouse Publishing.

Farnworth, R. (1653) *An Easter reckoning*, London.

Farnworth, R. (1654) *The heart opened by Christ*, London.

Faulkner, C. (2011) *Lucretia Mott's heresy: abolition and women's rights in nineteenth-century America*, Philadelphia, PA: University of Pennsylvania Press.

Feather, J. (1991) *A history of British publishing*, London: Routledge.

Fell, M. (1660a) *A declaration and an information from us the people of God called Quakers, To the present governors, the king and both houses of Parliament*, London: Thomas Simmons and Robert Wilson.

Fell, M. (1660b) *A true testimony from the people of God: (Who by the world are called Quakers) of the doctrines of the prophets, Christ, and the apostles*, London: Printed for Robert Wilson.

Fell, M. (1664) *A call to the universall seed of God*, N.p.

Fell, M. (1666) *Womens speaking justified*, London, n.p.

Fell, M. (1667) *A touch-stone: Or, a perfect tryal by the scriptures, of all the priests, bishops, and ministers, who have called themselves the ministers of the gospel. . . .* London, [s.n.].

Fell, M. (1710) *A brief collection of remarkable passages and occurrences . . .*, London: J. Sowle.

Fell, M. (1989 [1666]) *Womens speaking justified, proved and allowed by the scriptures*, C. Trevett (ed.), London: Quaker Home Service.

Fendall, L., Wood, J., & Bishop, B. (2007) *Practicing discernment together: finding God's way forward in decision making*, Newberg, OR: Barclay Press.

Fénelon, F., Guyon, J., & Molinos, M. (1816) *A guide to true peace: or a method of attaining to inward and spiritual prayer*, New York, NY: Samuel Woods & Sons.

Ferris, B. (1851) *to Joseph Foulke*, 3rd Mo. 20, box 2, Ferris Papers, Swarthmore College, PA: Friends Historical Library.

Fine Arts Society (2005) *Sixty works by Joseph Southall (1861–1944) from the Fortunoff Collection*, London: Fine Arts Society.

First Friends Church (2011), 'Justice League', http://www.firstfriends.org/ministries/justice-league. Accessed 20 October 2012.

Fisher, S. (1679 [1660]) '*Rusticus ad academicos in exercitationibus expostulatoriis, apologeticis quatuor* (the rustick's alarm to the rabbies)', in *Testimony of truth exalted*, London.

Five Years Meeting of Friends in America, official minutes of the session, 1940, Richmond, IN.

Fix, A. C. (1991) *Prophecy and reason: the Dutch collegiants in the early enlightenment*, Princeton, NJ: Princeton University Press.

Fletcher, A. (1984) 'The enforcement of the Conventicle Acts 1664–1679', in W. J. Sheils (ed.) *Studies in church history, 21: persecution and toleration*, pp. 235–46. Oxford: Basil Blackwell.

Forbes, S. S. (1982) 'Quaker Tribalism', in M. Zuckerman (ed.) *Friends and neighbors: group life in America's first plural society*, pp. 145–173, Philadelphia, PA: Temple University Press.

Forbush, B. (1973) *A history of Baltimore Yearly Meeting of Friends: three hundred years of Quakerism in Maryland, Virginia, the District of Columbia, and Central Pennsylvania*, Sandy Springs, MD: Baltimore Yearly Meeting.

Forster, Josiah (1860) *Reflections on the Gospel of Christ*. London: A. W. Bennett.

Forsythe W. J. (1990) *Penal discipline, reformatory projects and the English Prison Commission 1895–1989*, Exeter: University of Exeter Press.

Fortescue, G. K. (1908) *Catalogue of the pamphlets, books, newspapers, and manuscripts relating to the Civil War, the Commonwealth, and Restoration, collected by George Thomason, 1640–1661*, 2 vols, London: British Museum.

Fosdick, H. E. (ed.) (1951) *Rufus Jones speaks to our time*, New York, NY: Macmillan.

Foster, R. J. (1978) *A celebration of discipline: The path to spiritual growth*, San Francisco, CA: Harper and Row.

Foster, R. J. (1981) *Freedom of simplicity*, San Francisco, CA: Harper and Row.

Foster, R. J. (1985) *Money, sex & power: the challenge of the disciplined life*, San Francisco, CA: Harper and Row.

Foster, R. J. (2011) *Sanctuary of the soul: Journey into meditative prayer*, Downers Grove, IL: IVP Books.

Fothergill, J. (1971) *Chain of friendship: selected letters of Dr. John Fothergill of London, 1735–1780*, C. C. Booth and B. C. Corner (eds.), Cambridge, MA: Belknap Press.

Fothergill, S. (1812) 'Samuel Fothergill, meeting of elders, 1760', in M. Andrews (ed.), *Book of Extracts*, 18th of 6th Month, MS Box 28 (1), London: The Library of the Religious Society of Friends.

Foucault, M. (1965) *Madness and civilization: a history of insanity in the age of reason*. R. Howard (trans), New York, NY: Vintage Books.

Fox, G. (1653) *A paper sent forth into the world from them scornfully called Quakers, why they deny the teachers of the world*, London.

Fox, G. (1654a) *To all that would know the way to the kingdom*, N.p.

Fox, G. (1654b) Swarthmore mss 3.82.

Fox, G. (1655) Swarthmore mss. 2.28.Fox, G. (1656) *A testimony of the true light*, London: Calvert.

Fox, G. (1658a) *A reply to the pretended vindication*, London: Simmonds.

Fox, G. (1658b) *The pearl found in England*, London: Simmonds.

Fox, G. (1659a) *To the Parliament of the Commonwealth of England, fifty-nine particulars laid down for the regulating things, and the taking away of oppressing laws, and oppressors, and to ease the oppressed*. London: Thomas Simmons.

Fox, G. (1659b) *To the council of officers of the armie, and the heads of the nation*, London.

Fox, G. (1660a) *A distinction between the phanatick spirit*, London: Wilson.

Fox, G. (1660b) *The promise of God proclaimed*, London: Simmonds.

Fox, G. (1671) *Some principles of the elect people of God in scorn called Quakers*. London.

Fox, G. (1676) *Gospel family-order, being a short discourse concerning the ordering of families, both of whites, black, and Indians*, London: s.n.

Fox, G. (1698) *A collection of many select Christian letters, epistles and testimonies*, London: T. Sowle.

Fox, G. (1990 [1831]), *The works of George Fox*. 8 vols. New York: Gould, Philadelphia & Hopper, Repr. with new introductions. Pennsylvania: New Foundation Publications, George Fox Fund, ed. T. H. S. Wallace.

Fox, G. (1952) *The Journal of George Fox*, J. L. Nickalls, (ed.), Cambridge: Cambridge University Press.

Fox, G. (1995 [1952]) *The Journal of George Fox*, J. L. Nickalls, (ed.), Philadelphia, PA: Religious Society of Friends.

Fox, G. and R. Hubberthorne (1661) *A declaration from the harmless and innocent people of God, called Quakers, against all sedition, plotters, and fighters in the world*... London: Robert Wilson.

Frank, N. (2002) 'Producing men: Work, manhood, and capitalism in the early American republic' Unpublished PhD. Dissertation: Brown University, RI.

Freeman, M. (2004) *The Joseph Rowntree Charitable Trust: A study in Quaker philanthropy and adult education 1904–1954*, York: William Sessions.

Freeman, M. (2007) 'The magic lantern and the cinema: adult schools, educational settlements and secularisation in Britain, c.1900–1950', *Quaker Studies*, vol. 11, pp. 192–203.

Freiday, D. (1984), *Nothing without Christ: some current problems in the light of seventeenth century thought and experience*, Newberg, OR: Barclay Press.

Friend, The, (1890) *Editorial in The Western Friend, 4/1890*. reprinted in *The Friend* 63 (43) [May 24 1890] p. 343.

Friends Home Service Committee (1968), *Detention centres: A report by a subcommittee of the Friends Penal Affairs Committee*, London: Friends Home Service Committee.

Friends Home Service Committee (1970) *Why prison? A Quaker view of imprisonment and some alternatives*, London: Friends Home Service Committee.

Friends' Scripture School (1869), *Hymns for first day schools*. New York: Friends' Scripture School Press.

Friends Social Responsibility Council (FSRC) (1977), *Trade unions and the new social order: Report of a conference organised at Woodbrooke in co-operation with the industry and work committee of the FSRC*, Library of the Society of Friends, Box L.46/5.

Friends United Meeting (1981) *Friends and the sacraments*, Richmond, IN: Friends United Press.

Friends United Meeting in East Africa (2002) *Christian faith & practice in the Friends church*, Kisumu: National Printing Press Ltd.

Friends World Committee for Consultation (1937) 'Methods of Achieving Racial Justice', Report of Commission III B, *Friends World Conference Official Report*. Philadelphia, PA.

Friends World Committee for Consultation (2007) 'Finding Quakers around the world', http://www. fwccamericas.org/publications/images/fwcc_map_2007_sm.gif. Accessed 20 October 2012.

Friends World Committee for Consultation (2010) *Friends Around the World, 2010 Edition*, London: Friends World Committee for Consultation.

Friends' Quarterly (1985) *Special Issue: Towards a Testimony on Penal affairs*, vol. 23, no. 10. *Friends' Review* (periodical).

Frost, J. (2003b) 'John Woolman and the Enlightenment,' in M. Heller (ed.) *The tendering presence: essays on John Woolman*, pp. 167–89, Wallingford, PA: Pendle Hill Publications.

Frost, J. W. & Moore, J. M. (eds.) (1986) *Seeking the light: essays in Quaker history*, Wallingford, PA: Pendle Hill Publication.

Frost, J. W. (1973) *The Quaker family in colonial America. A portrait of the Society of Friends*, New York, NY: St Martin's Press.

Frost, J. W. (1980a) *The Keithian controversy in early Pennsylvania,* Norwood, PA: Norwood Editions.

Frost, J. W. (1986) 'The affirmation controversy and religious liberty', in R. S. Dunn & M. M. Dunn (eds.) *The world of William Penn,* pp. 303–22, Philadelphia, PA: University of Pennsylvania Press, pp. 303–22.

Frost, J. W. (1990) *A perfect freedom: religious liberty in Pennsylvania,* Cambridge: Cambridge University Press.

Frost, J. W. (ed.) (1980b) *The Quaker origins of antislavery.* Norwood, PA: Norwood Editions.

Frost, J. W. (1991) 'Quaker books in colonial Pennsylvania', *Quaker History* vol. 80, pp. 1–23.

Frost, J. W. (1992) '"Our deeds carry our message", the early history of the American Friends Service Committee', *Quaker History,* vol. 81, no. 1, pp. 1–50.

Frost, J. W. (2001) *Sex is not a shortcut to spirituality: Liberal Quakers confront the 20th-century sexual revolutions.* Friends Historical Library, Swarthmore College, PA. http://www.swarthmore.edu/Library/friends/sexspirituality.htm accessed 15 October 2012.

Frost, J. W. (2003a) 'From plainness to simplicity: changing Quaker ideals for material culture', in E. J. Lapsansky & A. A. Verplanck (eds.), *Quaker aesthetics: reflections in American design and consumption,* pp. 16–40, Philadelphia, PA· University of Pennsylvania Press.

Frost, J. W. (2012) 'Quaker antislavery: from dissidence to sense of the meeting', *Quaker History,* vol. 101. no. 1, pp. 12–33.

Fry A. R. (1933) *Quaker ways,* London: Cassell and Company.

Fry M. (1951) *Arms of the law,* London: Gollancz.

Fyrth, J. (1993) 'The aid Spain movement in Britain, 1936–39', *History Workshop,* vol. 35, pp. 153–64.

Gara, L. & Gara, L. M. (1999) *A few small candles: war resisters of World War II tell their stories,* Kent, OH: Kent State University Press.

Garfinkel, S. (2003) 'Quakers and high chests', in E. J. Lapsansky & A. A. Verplanck (eds.), *Quaker aesthetics: reflections in American design and consumption,* pp. 50–89, Philadelphia, PA: University of Pennsylvania Press.

Garman, M., Applegate, J., Benefiel, M., & Meredith, D. (1996) *Hidden in plain sight: Quaker women's writings 1650–1700.* Wallingford, PA: Pendle Hill Publications.

Garver, N. (2001a) 'Quakers in Bolivia', *Friends Journal,* vol. 47, no. 2, pp. 10–13.

Garver, N. (2001b) 'Quaker Bolivia Link', *Friends Journal,* vol. 47, no. 2, pp. 19–24.

Gary, A. T. (1935) *The political and economic relations of English and American Quakers (1750–1785),* Unpublished DPhil. Thesis, Oxford.

Geiter, M. K. (2000) *William Penn.* Harlow: Longman.

General Conference of Friends (1887) *Proceedings, including declaration of Christian doctrine, of the General Conference of Friends, held in Richmond, Ind., USA, 1887.* Richmond, IN: Nicholson & Bro.

Genesee Yearly Meeting (1862) *Minutes.*

Gerona, C. (2004) *Night journeys: the power of dreams in transatlantic Quaker culture,* Charlottesville, VA: University of Virginia Press.

Gibble, H. L. (2006) *Ecumenical engagement for peace and nonviolence: experiences and initiatives of the historic peace churches and the Fellowship of Reconciliation,* Elgin, IL: Historic Peace Churches/FOR Consultative Committee.

Gill, C. (2004) 'Rogers, William (d. 1711?)', *Oxford dictionary of national biography,* Oxford: Oxford University Press.

Gill, C. (2005) *Women in the seventeenth-century Quaker community: a literary study of political identities, 1650–1700,* Aldershot: Ashgate.

Gillespie, J .E .O'N. (1988) '"Every material of the best quality": the foundation of Bloomfield Hospital, Dublin', *Journal of the Friends Historical Society,* vol. 55, pp. 185–9.

Glines, E. F. (2003) *Undaunted zeal: The letters of Margaret Fell,* Richmond, IN: Friends United Press.

'God's Revelation in the Scriptures,' *Northwest Yearly Meeting of Friends Faith and Practice.* Accessed by internet 14 October 2011.

Goffman, E. (1961) *Asylums: essays on the social situation of mental patients and other inmates,* New York: Anchor-Doubleday.

Gorman, G. (1973) *The amazing fact of Quaker worship.* London: Friends Home Service Committee.

Gough, J. (1781) *Memoirs of the life,* Dublin.

Gould, Marcus T. C. (1827–30) *The Quaker.* Philadelphia, PA: Gould.

Gragg, L. (2009) *The Quaker community on Barbados: challenging the culture of the planter class,* Columbia, MS: University of Missouri Press.

Graves mss. Michael P. Graves' collection of 17th-, 18th-, and 19th-century Quaker sermon texts.

Graves, M. (2009) *Preaching the inward Light: early Quaker rhetoric,* Waco, TX: Baylor University Press.

Greaves, R. L. (1986) *Deliver us from evil: The radical underground in Britain, 1660–1663,* Oxford: Oxford University Press.

Greaves, R. L. (1992a) *Secrets of the kingdom: British radicals from the Popish plot to the revolution of 1688–1689,* Stanford, CA: Stanford University Press.

Greaves, R. L. (1992b) 'Shattered expectations. George Fox, the Quakers and the restoration state', *Albion,* vol. 24, no. 2, pp. 237–59.

Greaves, R. L. (1998) *Dublin's merchant Quaker: Anthony Sharp and the community of Friends, 1643–1707,* Stanford, CA: Stanford University Press.

Greaves, R. L. (2001) 'Seditious sectaries or "sober and useful inhabitants"? Changing conceptions of the Quakers in early modern Britain', *Albion,* vol. 33, no. 1, pp. 24–50.

Greaves, R. L. (2004a) 'Edmundson, William (1627–1712)', *Oxford dictionary of national biography,* Oxford: Oxford University Press.

Greaves, R. L. (2004b) 'Farnworth, Richard (c.1630–1666)', *Oxford dictionary of national biography,* Oxford: Oxford University Press.

Green, I. & Peters, K. (2002) 'Religious publishing in England 1640–1695', in J. Barnard & D. F. McKenzie (eds.), *The Cambridge history of the book in Britain, vol. IV: 1557-1695,* pp. 67–96, Cambridge: Cambridge University Press.

Green, J. N. (2000) 'The book trade in the middle colonies, 1680–1720' in H. Amory & D. D. Hall (eds.) *A history of the book in America, vol. I: the colonial book in the Atlantic world,* pp. 199–223, Cambridge: Cambridge University Press.

Greenwood, J. O. (1975–78), *Whispers of truth: Quaker encounters,* 3 vols. York: W. Sessions.

Grellet, S. (1874) *Memoirs of the life and gospel labours of Stephen Grellet.* B. Seebohm (ed.), Philadelphia, PA: Henry Longstreth.

Griffiths, J. (1764) *Some brief remarks,* Philadelphia, PA.

Griffith, J. (1779) *A journal of the life, travels and labours in the work of the ministry of John Griffith,* London: James Phillips.

Grob, G. (1972) *Mental institutions in America: social policy to 1875,* New York, NY: Free Press.

Grob, G. (1983) *Mental illness and American society, 18751940,* Princeton, NJ: Princeton University Press.

Grubb E. (1899) *Social aspects of the Quaker faith.* London: Headley Brothers.

Grubb, S. L. (1863) *A brief account of the life and religious labors of Sarah Grubb (formerly Sarah Lynes)*, Philadelphia, PA: Tract Association of Friends.

Grundy, M. (ed.) (2010) *Seeking God's will on same-sex relationships: The experience of Cleveland Friends Meeting,* Cleveland, OH: Printed for Cleveland Friends Meeting by Createspace. com.

Grundy, M. P. (2001) 'The Bethany mission for Colored People: Philadelphia Friends and a Sunday school mission', *Quaker History*, vol. 90, no. 1, pp. 50–82.

Guiton, G. (2005) *The growth and development of Quaker testimony*, Lewiston, NY: Edwin Mellen Press.

Guiton, G. (2012) *The early Quakers and the 'kingdom of God'*, San Francisco, CA: Inner Light Books.

Gulley, P. (2009) 'If the church were Christian, Jesus would be a model for living rather than an object of worship', *Quaker Theology*, no. 16, Fall-Winter, pp. 3–20.

Gummere, A. M. (1883) 'Friends in Burlington', *Pennsylvania Magazine of History and Biography*, vol. 7, no. 3, pp. 249–67.

Gummere, A. M. (1901) *The Quaker: A study in costume*, Philadelphia, PA: Ferris and Leach.

Gurney, J. J. (1832) *Sermons and prayers, delivered by Joseph John Gurney in the Friends meeting house, Liverpool, 1832*, Liverpool: Thomas Hodgson.

Gurney, J. J. (1834) *Essay on the habitual exercise of love to God*, Gurney's works, London.

Gurney, J. J. (1840) *Brief remarks on impartiality in the interpretation of scripture.* New York, NY: Isaac T. Hopper.

Gurney, J. J. (1848 [1834]) *Observations on the distinguishing views and practices of the Society of Friends*, Gurney's Works (7th ed).

Gurney, J. J. (1848) *Puseyism traced to its root*, Norwich: Josiah Fletcher.

Gwyn, D. (1986) *Apocalypse of the word: The life and message of George Fox,* Richmond, IN: Friends United Press.

Gywn, D. (1992) 'Can Our Branches Be Olive Branches?' *Friends Journal*, December, pp. 14–17.

Gwyn, D. (2000) *Seekers found: Atonement in early Quaker experience*, Wallingford, PA: Pendle Hill Publications.

Gwyn, D. (2005) *Report from the middle: Reflections on divisions among Friends today*, Boston, MA: Beacon Hill Friends House.

Gwyn, D. (2006 [1995]) *The covenant crucified: Quakers and the rise of capitalism,* Wallingford, PA: Pendle Hill Publications.

H. R. (1843) 'Astronomy', *Friend*, vol. 1, no. 76.

Hadley, H. M. (1991) *Quakers world wide: a history of the Friends World Committee for Consultation.* London: Friends World Committee for Consultation in association with William Sessions.

Hagglund, B. (2005) 'Sackcloth and ashes; Robert Barclay's "sign"', *Journal of the Friends' Historical Society*, vol. 60, no. 3, pp. 180–90.

Hall, D. D. (2000) 'Readers and writers in New England, 1638-1713' in H. Amory & D.D. Hall (eds), *A history of the book in America, vol. I: The colonial book in the Atlantic world*, pp. 117–51, Cambridge: Cambridge University Press.

Hall, D. D. (2008) *Ways of writing: The practice and politics of text-making in Seventeenth-Century New England*, Philadephia, PA: University of Pennsylvania Press.

Hall, D. J. (1992) '"The fiery tryal of their infallible examination": self-control in the regulation of Quaker publishing in England from the 1670s to the mid-19th century', R. Myers & M.

Harris (eds.) *Censorship and the control of print in England and France 1600–1910.* pp. 59–86, Winchester: St Paul's Bibliographies.

Hall, D. J. (2010) 'Spreading Friends' Books for Truths Service: the distribution of Quaker printed literature in the eighteenth century', *Journal of the Friends Historical Society*, vol. 62, no. 1, pp. 3–24.

Hall, F. (ed.) (1978) *Quaker worship in North America*, Richmond, IN: Friends United Press.

Hallward, S. and Hallward, M. (2010) *Young Adult Friends, the 'Present' of Quakerism.* Michener Lecture. Melbourne Beach, FL: Southeastern Yearly Meeting.

Hamm, T. D. (1988) *The transformation of American Quakerism: Orthodox Friends, 1800–1907.* Bloomington, IN: Indiana University Press.

Hamm, T. D. (1994) 'Hicksite Quakers and the antebellum nonresistance movement', *Church History*, vol. 63, pp. 557–69.

Hamm, T. D. (1995) *God's government begun: the Society for Universal Inquiry and Reform*, Bloomington, IN: Indiana University Press.

Hamm, T. D. (1997) *Earlham College: a history, 1847-1997*, Bloomington, IN: Indiana University Press.

Hamm, T. D. (2000) 'The Hicksite Quaker world, 1875–1900', *Quaker History*, vol. 89: pp. 17–41.

Hamm, T. D. (2002) '"A Protest against Protestantism": Hicksite Friends and the Bible in the Nineteenth Century', *Quaker Studies*, vol. 6, pp. 175–94.

Hamm, T. D. (2003), *The Quakers in America*, New York, NY: Columbia University Press.

Hamm, T. D. (2006) 'New light on old ways', *George Fox's Legacy: Friends for 350 Years*, 53–67. Philadelphia, PA: Friends Historical Association.

Hamm, T. D. (2007) 'Introduction: The search for a Quaker College', J. W. Oliver, C. L. Cherry & C. L. Cherry (eds.) *Founded by Friends. The Quaker heritage of fifteen American Colleges and Universities.* Lanham, MD: Scarecrow Press.

Hamm, T. D. (2008) 'Quakerism, ministry, marriage, and divorce: the ordeal of Priscilla Hunt Cadwalader', *Journal of the Early Republic*, vol. 28, no. 3, pp. 407–31.

Hamm, T. D. (2009a) '"Chipping at the landmarks of our fathers": the decline of the testimony against hireling ministry in the nineteenth century', *Quaker Studies*, vol. 13, pp. 136–59.

Hamm, T. D. (2009b) 'Friends United Meeting and its identity: an interpretive history', *Quaker Life*, January/February.

Hansen, R. (2005) '"Hungering and thirsting for the contact with kindred spirits": Henry Wilbur and the Committee for the Advancement of Friends' Principles, 1900–1914', *Quaker History*, vol. 94, pp. 44–55.

Hanson, J. W. (ed.) (1894) *The World Congress of Religions*, W. B. Conkey Co.

Harris, T. (2005) *Restoration: Charles II and his kingdoms 1660–1685*, London: Allen Lane.

Harris, T., Seaward, P., & Goldie, M. (eds.) (1990) *The politics of religion in Restoration England.* Oxford: Blackwell.

Harrison, R. S. (ed.) (2008) *A biographical dictionary of Irish Quakers* (2nd ed.), Dublin: Four Courts Press.

Hartshorne, S. V. (2010) *Elfrida: Elfrida Vipont Foulds 1902 to 1992*, York: Quacks Books,

Harvey, W. A. (1906) *The model village and the cottages*, London: Batsford.

Haviland, M. (1994) 'Beyond women's sphere: young Quaker women and the veil of charity in Philadelphia, 1790-1810', *William and Mary Quarterly*, vol. 51, pp. 419–46.

Havilland, M. M. (2006) 'Westtown's integration: "A natural and fruitful enlargement of our lives"', *Quaker History*, vol. 95, no. 2, pp. 19–33.

Healy, T. & Sawday, J. (eds.) (1990) *Literature and the English Civil War,* Cambridge: Cambridge University Press.

Heath, D. H. (1979) *The peculiar mission of a Quaker school,* Wallingford, PA: Pendle Hill Publications.

Heath, H. (ed.) (2009) *Paths to Quaker parenting. Using Quaker beliefs, testimonies and practices,* Haverford, PA: Conrow Publishing House.

Hedstrom, M. S. (2003) 'Rufus Jones and mysticism for the masses', *Cross Currents,* vol. 54, no. 2, pp. 31–44.

Heiss, W. (1963) *A brief history of Western Yearly Meeting of Conservative Friends and the separation of 1877.* Indianapolis, IN: John Woolman Press,

Heller, M. A. (ed.) (2003) *The tendering presence: essays on John Woolman,* Wallingford, PA: Pendle Hill Publications.

Heron, A. (ed.) (1963) *Towards a Quaker view of sex: an essay by a group of Friends,* Friends Home Service Committee, London: London Yearly Meeting.

Heron, A. (1995) *Quakers in Britain: a century of change, 1895–1995.* Kelso: Curlew Graphics.

Hessayon, A. (2004) 'Calvert, Giles (*bap.* 1612, *d.* 1663)', *Oxford dictionary of national biography,* Oxford: Oxford University Press.

Hetherington, R. (1996) *The defining marks of Quakerism,* Quaker Universalist Fellowship, Bismarck, ND. http://universalistfriends.org/quf-rh.html Accessed 20 October 2012.

Hewitt, N. (1989) 'Fragmentation of Friends: Consequences for Quaker women in antebellum America' in E. P. Brown & S. M. Stuard (eds.) *Witnesses for Change,* pp. 93–119. New Brunswick, NJ: Rutgers University Press, pp. 93–119.

Hibbert, G. (1924) *The inner light and modern thought,* London: Swarthmore Press Ltd.

Hickey, D. D. (1997) *Sojourners no more: The Quakers in the new South, 1865–1920.*

Hicks, E. (1824) *A letter... to Edwin A. Atlee.* N.p.

Hicks, E. (1831) *Two sermons and a prayer,* New York, NY: Isaac T. Hopper.

Hicks, E. (1832) *Journal of the life and religious labours of Elias Hicks.* New York, NY: Isaac T. Hopper.

Hicks, E. (1834) *Letters,* New York, NY: Isaac T. Hopper.

Hicks, E. (1861) *Letters of Elias Hicks. including also observations on the slavery of the Africans and their descendants, and on the use of the produce of their labor,* Philadelphia, PA: T. Ellwood Chapman.

Hicks, E. (1969 [1832]) *Journal of Elias Hicks,* New York, NY: Arno.

Higgins, L. H. (1980) 'The apostatized apostle, John Pennyman: heresy and community in seventeenth century Quakerism', *Quaker History,* vol. 69, no 1, pp. 102–18.

Hill, C. (1972) *The world turned upside down: radical ideas during the English revolution,* London: Temple Smith.

Hill, C. (1984) *The experience of defeat: Milton and some contemporaries,* London: Faber and Faber.

Hill, C. (1985) 'Censorship and English literature' in *The Collected Essays of Christopher Hill,* 2 vols. Brighton: Harvester: vol. 1, 32–71.

Hill, L. (1993) *Marriage: a spiritual leading for lesbian, gay, and straight couples,* Pendle Hill Pamphlet 308, Wallingford, PA: Pendle Hill Publications.

Hilty, H. H. (1977) *Friends in Cuba,* Richmond, IN: Friends United Press.

Hinderaker, E. (1997) *Elusive empires: constructing colonialism in the Ohio Valley, 1673-1800,* Cambridge: Cambridge University Press.

Hinds, H. (2011) *George Fox and early Quaker culture,* Manchester: Manchester University Press.

Hinshaw, M. E. & Hockett, R. R. (eds.) (1981) *Growth, development, service unlimited: the story of the United Society of Friends Women*, N.p.

Hinshaw, S. B. (1987) *The spoken ministry among Friends*. Davidson, NC: North Carolina Yearly Meeting.

Hinson, E. G. (1998) *Love at the heart of things: a biography of Douglas V. Steere*, Wallingford, PA and Nashville, TN: Pendle Hill Publications and the Upper Rooms Books.

Hirst, M. (1923) 'The Balby Seekers and Richard Farnworth', *Quakers in peace and War*, New York, NY: George Doran.

History of Central Yearly Meeting of the Friends Church (1976), Westfield, IN: Central Yearly Meeting.

Hixson, R. (1981) *Lawrie Tatum, Indian agent: Quaker values and hard choices*, Pendle Hill pamphlet 238, Wallingford, PA: Pendle Hill Publications.

Hoag, J. (1861) *Journal of the life of Joseph Hoag, an eminent minister of the gospel in the Society of Friends*, Auburn, NY: Knapp & Peck, Printers.

Hoare, Richard J. (2004) 'The Balby Seekers and Richard Farnworth', *Quaker Studies*, Vol. 8, Issue 2, p. 194.

Hobby, E. (1988) *Virtue of necessity: English women's writing 1649–88*. London: Virago.

Hobby, E. (1995) 'Handmaids of the Lord and mothers in Israel: early vindications of Quaker women's prophecy', in T. N. Corns & D. Loewenstein (eds.) *The emergence of Quaker writing: dissenting literature in Seventeenth-Century England*, pp. 88–98, London: Frank Cass.

Hobhouse, S. (1972) *William Law and Eighteenth Century Quakerism, including Some Unpublished Letters and Fragments of William Law and John Byrom*. New York, NY: Benjamin Blom, Inc.

Hobhouse S. and Brockway F. (1922) *English prisons today*, London: Longmans Green and Co.

Hodges, D. (1995) *George Fox and the healing ministry*, Guilford: Friends Fellowship of Healing.

Hodgson, W. (1875–6) *The Society of Friends in the nineteenth century*, 2 vols. Philadelphia, PA: Smith, English & Co.

Hoe, S. (1978) *The man who gave his company away: a biography of Ernest Bader, founder of the Scott Bader Commonwealth*, London: Heinemann.

Hoffman, J. (1989) 'On marriage: no safe dallying with truth', address given at North Pacific Yearly Meeting, reprinted in *Friends Bulletin*, vol. 60.

Hole, H. G. (1973) 'The two oceans', *Friends Journal*, vol. 19, pp. 582–3.

Hole, H. G. (1978) *Things civil and useful. a personal view of Quaker education*, Richmond, IN: Friends United Press.

Hollinger, D. A. (2011) 'After cloven tongues of fire: ecumenical Protestantism and the modern American encounter with diversity', *The Journal of American History*, June 2nd, pp. 21–48.

Holton, S. S. (2007) *Quaker Women: personal life, memory and radicalism in the lives of women Friends, 1780-1930*. London: Routledge.

Homan, R. (1997) 'Mission and fission: the organization of Huntingtonian and Calvinistic Baptist causes in Sussex in the 18th and 19th centuries', *Sussex Archaeological Collections*, vol. 135, pp. 265–282.

Homan, R. (2006a) *The art of the sublime*, Aldershot: Ashgate.

Homan, R. (2006b) 'The aesthetics of Friends' meeting houses', *Quaker Studies*, vol. 11, pp. 115–28.

Homan, W. J. (1939) *Children and Quakerism*. Berkeley, Ca: Gillick Press.

Hooton, E, (1650) Swarthmore mss 2.43.

Hopkins, M. R. (2010) *Men of peace: World War II conscientious objectors*, Caye Caulker, Belize: Producciones de la Hamaca.

Horle, C. W. (1988) *The Quakers and the English legal system, 1660–1688*, Philadelphia, PA: University of Pennsylvania Press.

Horle, C. W. (1986) 'Changing Quaker attitudes towards legal defense: the George Fox case, 1673–75, and the establishment of the Meeting for Sufferings', in J. W. Frost and J. M. Moore (eds.) *Seeking the Light: Essays in Quaker history*, Wallingford, Pennsylvania, PA: Pendle Hill Publications.

Hoskens, J. (1837 [1771]) *The life of Jane Hoskens*, in W. Evans & T. Evans (eds.) *The Friends Library*, Vol. I. pp. 460–73, Philadelphia, PA: Joseph Rakestraw.

Howgill, F. (1656) *A lamentation of the scattered tribes*, London: Calvert.

Howgill, F. (1658) *Some of the mysteries of God's kingdom*, London: Simmonds.

Howgill, F. (1659) *The invisible things of God*, London: Simmonds.

Howgill, F. (1661) *The glory of the true church*, London: Calvert.

Howgill, F. (1662) *A testimony concerning Edward Burroughs*, London: Warwick.

http://www.quaker.org/quest/progres1.htm accessed 16 October 2012.

Hubberthorne, R. (1656) Caton mss. 3.116.

Hughes, R. (1987) *The Fatal Shore: A history of the transportation of convicts to Australia 1787–1868*. London: Collins Harvill.

Hull, W. (1941) *Benjamin Furly and Quakerism in Rotterdam*, Swarthmore College, PA: Swarthmore College Monographs on Quaker History, Number Five.

Hunt, N. (1858) *Brief memoir*, Philadelphia, PA: Uriah Hunt, Philadelphia, PA.

Hunter, J. (1989) *Gospel of gentility: American women missionaries in turn-of-the-century China*. New Haven, CT: Yale University Press.

Hunter, R. & Macalpine, I. (eds.) (1963) *Three hundred years of psychiatry 1535–1860*, London: Oxford University Press.

Hunter, R. & Macalpine, I. (1974) *Psychiatry for the poor: 1851 Colney Hatch Asylum Friern Hospital 1973: A medical and social history*, London: Dawson.

Hursthouse, R. (1999) *On virtue ethics*, Oxford: Oxford University Press.

Hutchison, W. R. (1987) *Errand to the world: American Protestant thought and foreign missions*, Chicago, IL: University of Chicago Press.

Hutton, R. (1985) *The restoration: a political and religious history of England and Wales 1658–1667*, Oxford: Oxford University Press.

Hutton, S. (2004) *Anne Conway: a woman philosopher*, Cambridge: Cambridge University Press.

Huws-Jones, E. (1966) *Margery Fry: the essential amateur*, Oxford: Oxford University Press.

Ignatieff, M. (1978) *A just measure of pain: the penitentiary and the industrial revolution 1750–1850*. London: MacMillan.

Ignatius & Ganss, G. E. (1991) *Ignatius of Loyola: The spiritual exercises and selected works*, New York, NY: Paulist Press.

Illick, J. E. (1971) '"Some of our best Friends are Indians…:" Quaker attitudes and actions regarding the Western Indians during the Grant administration', *The Western Historical Quarterly*, no. 2, pp. 283–294.

Indiana Yearly Meeting (Orthodox) 1886, 1922, *Minutes.*

Ingle, H. L. (ed.) (1984) '"A ball that has rolled beyond our reach": The consequences of Hicksite reform, 1830, as seen in an exchange of letters', *Delaware History*, vol. 21, pp. 127–37.

Ingle, H. L. (1991) 'A Quaker woman on women's roles: Mary Penington to Friends, 1678', *Signs*, vol. 16, no. 3, pp. 587–96.

Ingle, H. L. (1994) *First among Friends: George Fox and the creation of Quakerism*, Oxford: Oxford University Press.

Ingle, H. L. (1998 [1986]) *Quakers in conflict: the Hicksite reformation.* Wallingford, PA: Pendle Hill Publications.

Institute of Quaker Studies (1971) *The three m's of Quakerism: meeting, message, mission,* Richmond, IN: Earlham School of Religion.

International Quaker working party on Israel and Palestine Conflict (2004) *When the rain returns: toward justice and reconciliation in Palestine and Israel,* Philadelphia, PA: American Friends Service Committee.

Inter-relationship, Philadelphia, PA and Chicago, IL: The John Winston Co.

Ireland Yearly Meeting (2000) *Organisation and Christian discipline of the Yearly Meeting of the Religious Society of Friends in Ireland (Quakers),* Dublin: The Yearly Meeting of the Religious Society of Friends in Ireland.

Irish Quaker Faith in Action (2011) 'Faith in Action', http://www.quakers-in-ireland.ie/about-us/concerns/faith-in-action-concerns Accessed 20 October 2012.

Isba, A. (2010) *The excellent Mrs. Fry, unlikely heroine,* London: Continuum.

Isichei, E. (1964) 'From sect to denomination in English Quakerism, with special reference to the nineteenth century', *British Journal of Sociology,* vol. 15, no. 3 (Sept 1964), pp. 207–22.

Isichei, E. (1970) *Victorian Quakers,* London: Oxford University Press.

Jackson, B. (2010) '"As a musician would his violin": The oratory of the Great Basin prophets', R. H. Ellison (ed.) *A new history of the sermon: the nineteenth century,* pp. 489–520, Boston, MA: Brill.

Jackson, M. (2009) *Let this voice be heard: Anthony Benezet, father of Atlantic abolition,* Philadelphia, PA: University of Pennsylvania Press.

Jantzen, G. (2010) 'Choose life! Early Quaker women and violence in modernity', *A place of springs: Death and the displacement of beauty,* pp. 75–92. London: Routledge.

Jay, A. (1910) *Autobiography of Allen Jay,* Philadelphia: John Winston Co.

Jay, A. (2010 [1910]) *Autobiography of Allen Jay.* Richmond, IN: Friends United Press.

Jeffrey, F. (1807) 'Thomas Clarkson's *A Portraiture of Quakerism.*' Review in *Edinburgh Review* 10, pp. 85–102.

Jenkins, G. H. (1985) 'The early peace testimony in Wales', *Llafur,* no. 4, pp. 10–19.

Jennings, J. (1986) 'The journal of Margaret Hoare Woods: "Bow me in deep humility of soul …"', *Quaker History,* 75 (1), pp. 26–34.

Jennings, J. (1997) *The business of abolishing the British slave trade, 1783–1807,* Portland, OR: Frank Cass.

Jennings, J. (2006) *Gender, religion, and radicalism in the long eighteenth century: The 'ingenious Quaker' and her connections,* Aldershot: Ashgate.

Jones, R. Tudur (ed.), Long, A., & Moore, R. (2007) *Protestant Nonconformist Tests,* Volume 1, Aldershot: Ashcroft.

Johns, D. L. (1992) 'Convincement and disillusionment: printer William Bradford and the Keithian controversy in colonial Philadelphia', *Journal of the Friends Historical Society* vol. 57, pp. 13–32.

Johns, D. L. (1998) 'Ritual management of absence and presence: the liturgical significance of silence', *Quaker Religious Thought,* vol. 28, pp. 31–42.

Johns, D. L. (2007) '(Re)visioning sacramental theology: a response', *Quaker Religious Thought,* vol. 109, pp. 56–61.

Johns, D. L. (ed.) (2011) *Collected essays of Maurice Creasey, 1912–2004,* Lewiston, NY: Edwin Mellen Press.

Johnson, J. (1860) *Essays on some of the testimonies of truth,* Philadelphia, PA: T. Ellwood Zell.

Jones, C. H. (1946) *American Friends in world missions*, Richmond, IN: Brethren Publishing House for American Friends Board of Missions.

Jones, J. R. (1986) 'A representative of the alternative society of restoration England?' in R. S. Dunn & M. M. Dunn (eds.) *The world of William Penn*, pp. 55–70, Philadelphia, PA: University of Pennsylvania Press.

Jones, K. (1955), *Lunacy, law, and conscience, 1744–1845: The social history of the care of the insane*, London: Routledge and Kegan Paul.

Jones, K. (1993) *Asylums and after: A revised history of the mental health services: From the early 18th Century to the 1990s*, London: The Athlone Press.

Jones, M. H. (1937) *Swords into plowshares*, New York, NY: Macmillan.

Jones, R. M. (1903) *A boy's religion from memory*, London: Headley Brothers.

Jones, R. M. (1904), *Social law in the spiritual world: Studies in human and divine inter-relationship*, Philadelphia, PA: John C. Winston Co.

Jones, R. M. (1909) *Studies in mystical religion*, London: Macmillan.

Jones, R. M. (1911) *The Quakers in the American colonies*, London: Macmillan.

Jones, R. M. (1914) *Spiritual Reformers in the Sixteenth and Seventeenth Centuries*, London: Macmillan.

Jones, R. M. (1917) 'Quietism', *The Harvard Theological Review*, vol. 10 no. 1, pp. 1–51.

Jones, R. M. (1920a) *The nature and authority of conscience*, London: Swarthmore Press.

Jones, R. M. (1920b) *A service of love in war time: American Friends' relief work in Europe, 1917–1919*, New York, NY: Macmillian.

Jones, R. M. (1921) *The later periods of Quakerism*, 2 vols., London: Macmillan.

Jones, R. M. (1927) *The faith and practice of the Quakers*, London: Methuen.

Jones, R. M. (1922) *Spiritual energies in daily life*. New York, NY: Macmillan.

Jones, R. M. (1931) *Pathways to the reality of God*, New York: Macmillan.

Jones, R. M. (1943) *New eyes for invisibles*, New York: Macmillan.

Jones, R. M. (1948) *A call to what is vital*, New York: Macmillan.

Jones, R. M. (1970 [1921]) *The later periods of Quakerism*, 2 vol., Westport, CT: Greenwood Press.

Jones, R. T., Long, A. & Moore, R. (eds.) (2007) *Protestant nonconformist texts*, vol. 1, Aldershot: Ashgate.

Jones, S. (1853) *Recollections of a prayer and sermon, by Sybil Jones, of Maine, New England, U.S., at the Friends' meeting house, Birmingham, on 1st day morning, 1st of 5th Month, 1853*, Birmingham: B. Hudson and Son, Printers.

Jones, T. C. (ed.) (1989) *The power of the Lord is over all: The pastoral letters of George Fox*, Richmond, IN: Friends United Press.

Jones, T. C. (1955) *George Fox's teaching on redemption and salvation*, Unpublished PhD thesis, Yale University, CT.

Jones, T. E. (1973) *Light on the Horizon*. Richmond, IN: Friends United Press.

Jordan, R. P. (2000) 'The Indiana separation of 1842 and the limits of Quaker anti-slavery', *Quaker History*, vol. 89, no. 1, pp. 1–27.

Jordan, R. P. (2007) *Slavery and the meetinghouse*, Bloomington, IN: Indiana University Press.

Jorns A. (1931) *Quakers as pioneers in social work*, New York, NY: Macmillan.

Judson, S. S. (1982) *The quiet eye: a way of looking at pictures*, London: Aurum.

Juterczenka, S. (2007) 'Crossing borders and negotiating boundaries: the seventeenth-century European missions and persecution', *Quaker Studies*, vol. 21, pp. 39–53.

Kashatus, W. C. (1997) *A virtuous education: Penn's vision for Philadelphia schools*, Wallingford, PA: Pendle Hill Publications.

Kass, A. M. & Kass, E. H. (1988) *Perfecting the world: The life and times of Dr Thomas Hodgkin 1798-1866*, Boston, MA: Harcourt Brace Jovanovich.

Keeble, N. H. (2002) *The restoration: England in the 1660s*, Oxford: Blackwell.

Keene, C. (1981) 'God in thought and experience', *Quaker Religious Thought*, vol. 52, pp. 3–22.

Keith, G. (1684) *Of divine immediate revelation and inspiration*, London.

Keith, G. (1692) *Some reasons and causes of the late separation*, Philadelphia, PA.

Keith, G. (1693) *An exhortation & caution to Friends concerning buying or keeping of Negroes*, New York, NY: William Bradford.

Kelley, D. B. (1986) 'Joshua Evans, 1731–1798: A study in eighteenth-century Quaker singularity', *Quaker History*, vol. 75, no. 2, pp. 67–82.

Kelly, T. (1941) *A testament of devotion*, New York: Harper & Brothers.

Kelly, T. (1988 [1966]) *The eternal promise*. Richmond, IN: Friends United Press.

Kelsall, J. (1682) *A testimony against gaming, musick, dancing, singing, swearing and people calling upon God to damn them. As also against drinking to excess, whoring, lying and cheating...*, London.

Kelsey, R. W. (1917), *Friends and the Indians, 1655–1917*, Philadelphia, PA: Associated Executive Committee of Friends on Indian Affairs.

Kennedy, T. (1984) 'History and Quaker renaissance: The vision of John Wilhelm Rowntree.' *The Journal of the Friends Historical Society*, vol. 55, no. 2, pp. 35–56.

Kennedy, T. C. (2001), *British Quakerism, 1860–1920: the transformation of a religious community*, Oxford: Oxford University Press.

Kennedy, T. C. (2009) *A history of Southland College: The Society of Friends and Black education in Arkansas*, Fayetteville, AR: University of Arkansas Press.

Kerness, B. & Ehosi, M. (2001) *Torture in US prisons: Evidence of US human rights violations*, New York: American Friends Service Committee.

Kersey, J. (1851) *Narrative*, Philadelphia, PA: T. Ellwood Chapman.

Keser, R. M. & Moore, R. (eds.) (2005) *Knowing the mystery of life within: selected writings of Isaac Penington in their historical and theological context*, London: Quaker Books.

Kierkegaard, S. (1948) *Purity of heart*, transl. D.V. Steere, New York: Harper Brothers.

Kilham, H. (1837) *Memoir*, London: Darton and Harvey.

Kimball, H. & Kimball, B. (2002) *Go into all the world: A centennial celebration of Friends in East Africa*, Richmond, IN: Friends United Press.

Kimber, E. (1822) *The church of Christ, and way of salvation universal*, Philadelphia, PA: E. Littell.

Kirby, E. W. (1942) *George Keith, 1638–1716*, London & New York, NY: D. Appleton-Century Co.

Kirby, M. W. (1984) *Men of business and politics: The rise and fall of the Quaker Pease Dynasty of North-East England 1700-1943*, London: Allen and Unwin.

Knight, F. A. (1908) *A history of Sidcot School*, London: Dent.

Knight, S. & McNemar, R. (1991) *Celebrating the Past, Claiming Our Future: A History of the First One Hundred Years of Wilmington Yearly Meeting of the Religious Society of Friends*. Sabina, OH: Wilmington Yearly Meeting.

Knopp, F. H. (1991) 'Community solutions to sexual violence: Feminist/abolitionist perspectives', in Pepinsky, H. (ed.) *Criminology as peacemaking*, Bloomington, IN: Indiana University Press, pp 181–93.

Knopp, F. H. et al (1976) *Instead of prisons: a handbook for abolitionists*, Orwell, VT: The Safer Society Programme.

Knopp, F. H. & Lugo J. (1987) 'The slavery of penal servitude: Quaker concerns about prisons and prisoners', Kenworthy L. (ed.) *Friends face the world: continuing and current Quaker concerns*, Richmond, IN: Friends United Press, pp. 147–57.

Knott, J. R. (1995) 'Joseph Besse and the Quaker culture of suffering', in T. N. Corns & D. Loewenstein (eds.) *The emergence of Quaker writing: Dissenting literature in seventeenth-century England*, pp. 126–41, London: Frank Cass.

Kohrman, A. (1995) *New England Yearly Meeting of Friends, 1945–1995*. N.p.

Kolp, A. (1984) 'Friends, sacraments, and sacramental living', *Quaker Religious Thought*, vol. 20, pp. 36–52.

Kuenning, L. (ed.) (2002) *Historical writings of Quakers against war*, Glenside, PA: Quaker Heritage Press.

Kunze, B.Y. (1994) *Margaret Fell and the rise of Quakerism*, Stanford, CA: Stanford University Press.

Labouchere, R. (1988) *Abiah Darby of Coalbookdale*, York: William Sessions.

Labouchere, R. (1993) *Deborah Darby of Coalbrookdale, 1754 1810: her visits to America, Ireland, Scotland, Wales, England and the Channel Isles*, York: William Sessions.

Lacey, P. A. (1985) *Leading and being led*, Wallingford, PA: Pendle Hill Publications.

Lacey, P. A. (1998) *Growing into goodness: essays on Quaker education*, Wallingford, PA: Pendle Hill Publications.

Lafollette, H. (ed.) (2000) *The Blackwell guide to ethical theory*. Oxford: Blackwell.

Laing, R. D. (1959) *The divided self: an existential study in sanity and madness*, London: Tavistock Publications.

Lakey, G. (1971) *Revolution: a Quaker prescription for a sick society*, Philadelphia, PA: A Quaker Action Group.

Lampen J. (1987) *Mending hurts*, The Swarthmore Lecture, London: Quaker Home Service.

Lampen J. (2011) *Answering the violence: encounters with perpetrators*, Pendle Hill Pamphlet 412, Wallingford, PA: Pendle Hill Publications.

Landes, J. E. (2010) *London's role in the creation of a Quaker transatlantic community in the late Seventeenth and early Eighteenth Centuries*, Unpublished PhD dissertation, Centre for Metropolitan History, University of London.

Landsman, N. (1986) 'William Penn's Scottish counterparts: The Quakers of "North Britain" and the colonization of East New Jersey', in R. S. Dunn & M. Maples (eds.) *The world of William Penn*, pp. 241–58, Philadelphia, PA: University of Pennsylvania Press.

Langdale, J. & Skidmore, G. (1999) *Josiah Langdale, 1673–1723: A Quaker spiritual autobiography*. Reading: Sowle Press.

Langford, M. J. (1997) *The fairest island: history of Jamaican Friends*, Richmond, IN: Friends United Press.

Lapsansky, E. J. & Verplanck, A. A. (eds.) (2003) *Quaker aesthetics: reflections on a Quaker ethic in American design and consumption*, Philadelphia, PA: University of Pennsylvania Press.

Lapsansky-Werner, E. J. & Bacon, M. H. (eds.) (2007) *Back to Africa: Benjamin Coates and the colonization movement in America, 1848–1880*, University Park, PA: Pennsylvania State University Press.

Laqueur, T. (1976) 'The cultural origins of popular literacy in England 1500–1850', *Oxford Review of Education*, vol. 2 no. 3, pp. 255–75.

Larson, R. (1999) *Daughters of Light: Quaker women preaching and prophesying in the Colonies and abroad, 1700–1775,* New York: Alfred A. Knopf; Chapel Hill, NC: University of North Carolina Press.

Laurence, A., Maltby, J., & Rutterford, J. (eds.) (2009) *Women and their money 1700–1950,* London: Routledge.

Lavoie, C. C. (2002) 'Quaker beliefs and practices and the Eighteenth-Century development of the Friends Meeting House in the Delaware Valley', in E. J. Lapsansky & A. A. Verplanck (eds.), *Quaker aesthetics: Reflections on a Quaker ethic in American design and consumption, 1720–1920,* pp. 156–87, Philadelphia, PA: University of Pennsylvania Press.

Law, W. (1856 [1776]) *An address to the clergy,* Philadelphia, PA: John Townsend.

Lawrence, A. (2009) 'Quakerism and approaches to mental affliction: A comparative study of George Fox and William Tuke', Unpublished MPhil dissertation, University of Birmingham.

Lawson, T. (1680) *A mite into the treasury,* London.

Leach, C. & Goodman, J. (2001) 'Educating the women of the nation: Priscilla Wakefield and the construction of national identity, 1798', *Quaker Studies,* vol. 5, pp. 165–82.

Leachman, C. L. (1998) 'From an "unruly sect" to a society of "strict unity": The development of English Quakerism c.1650–1689', Unpublished PhD dissertation, University of London.

Leachman, C. L. (2004a) 'Audland, John (c.1630–1664)', *Oxford dictionary of national biography.* Oxford: Oxford University Press.

Leachman, C. L. (2004b) 'Mucklow, William (bap. 1630? d. 1713)', *Oxford dictionary of national biography.* Oxford: Oxford University Press.

Leachman, C. L. (2004c) 'Pennyman, John (1628–1706)', *Oxford dictionary of national biography.* Oxford: Oxford University Press.

Leeson, C. (1914) *The probation system,* London: P. S. King and Son.

LeShana, D. C. (1969) *Quakers in California,* Newberg, OR: Barclay Press.

Leuze, R. (ed.) (2003) *Each of us inevitable: some keynote addresses at Friends for Lesbian and Gay Concerns and Friends General Conference Gatherings, 1977–1993,* New York, NY: Friends for Lesbian, Gay, Bisexual, Transgender and Queer Concerns.

Levenduski, C. (1996) *Peculiar power: a Quaker woman preacher in eighteenth-century America.* Washington, DC: Smithsonian Institution Press.

Levy, B. (1978) '"Tender plants:" Quaker farmers and children in the Delaware Valley, 1681–1735', *Journal of Family History,* vol. 3, no. 2, June, pp. 116–135.

Levy, B. (1988) *Quakers and the American family: British settlement in the Delaware Valley,* New York, NY: Oxford University Press.

Library of the Society of Friends, London (LSF), Great Book of Sufferings (GBS).

Lidbetter, H. (1946) 'Quaker meeting houses, 1670–1850', *Architectural Review,* May 1946. London.

Lidbetter, H. (1961) *The Friends meeting house,* York: Sessions.

Liebmann M. (2009) *Restorative justice: how it works,* London: Jessica Kingsley.

Lief, A. (1968) *Family business: a century in the life and times of Strawbridge and Clothier 1868–1968.* New York, NY: McGraw Hill.

Littleboy, W. (1945) *The appeal of Quakerism to the non-mystic,* London: Friends Book Centre.

Lloyd, H. (1975) *The Quaker Lloyds in the industrial revolution,* London: Hutchinson & Co.

Locke, J. (1975 [1689]) *An essay concerning human understanding,* P. H. Nidditch (ed.), Oxford: Clarendon Press.

Locke, J. (1983 [1689]) *A letter concerning toleration,* Indianapolis, IN: Hackett Publishing Company, Inc.

Locke, J. (1998 [1690]) *An essay concerning human understanding*, London: Penguin Classics.

Logan A. (2008) *Feminism and criminal justice: a historical perspective*, London: Palgrave.

London Yearly Meeting (1802) *Extracts from minutes and advices*, London: Religious Society of Friends.

London Yearly Meeting (1818) *Epistles from the Yearly Meeting of Friends, held in London, to the Quarterly and Monthly Meetings in Great Britain, Ireland and elsewhere, from 1681–1817*, London: W. & S. Graves.

London Yearly Meeting (1821) *A collection of the epistles from the Yearly meeting of Friends in London, to the Quarterly & Monthly Meetings in Great Britain, Ireland, and elsewhere, from 1675 to 1820; Being from the first establishment of that Meeting to the present time*, New York: Samuel Wood & Sons.

London Yearly Meeting (1836), *Report of the proceedings of London Yearly Meeting of Friends*, London: John Stephens.

London Yearly Meeting (Society of Friends) (1896) *Report of the proceedings of the conference of members of the Society of Friends, held, by direction of the Yearly Meeting, in Manchester from the eleventh to the fifteenth of eleventh month, 1895*, London: Headley Brothers.

London Yearly Meeting (1906, 1917, 1931) *Church Government*, London. London Yearly Meeting.

London Yearly Meeting (1922) *Christian life faith and thought in the Society of Friends*, London: London Yearly Meeting.

London Yearly Meeting (1925) *Christian practice*, London: London Yearly Meeting.

London Yearly Meeting (1959) *Christian faith and practice*, London: London Yearly Meeting.

London Yearly Meeting (1978) *Unity in the Spirit*, London: Quaker Home Service.

London Yearly Meeting (1987) *To Lima with Love*, London: Quaker Home Service.

London Yearly Meeting of the Religious Society of Friends (1994) *Documents in advance*, London: Religious Society of Friends.

Lord, M. (2008) 'Claiming the Peace Testimony: my experience with Kenyan Friends', *Friends Journal*, April, pp. 24–5.

Loring, P. (1992) *Spiritual discernment: The context and goals of clearness committees*, Wallingford, PA: Pendle Hill Publications.

Loring, P. (1997) *Listening spirituality*, 2 vols. Washington Grove, MD: Openings Press.

Louis, J. H. (2004) 'The "desert" society in Languedoc (1686–1704) as popular culture and the roots of French Quakerism', *Quaker Studies*, vol. 9, pp. 4–67.

LSF, Portfolio MS. vols. 10, 19, 41.

Lugo J. L. and Cadbury M. F. (1995) 'Prison Worship Groups', in Barbour, H., Densmore, C., Moger, E. H., Sorel, N.C., Van Wagner, A.D., and Worrall, A. J. (eds.) *Quaker crosscurrents: Three hundred years of Friends in New York Yearly Meetings*, pp. 344–6, New York, NY: Syracuse University Press.

Lunn, P. (1997) 'You have lost your opportunity': British Quakers and the militant phase of the women's suffrage campaign: 1906–1914', *Quaker Studies*, vol. 2, pp. 30–55.

Lunn, P. (2007) 'Woodbrooke in wider context: The enduring thread of adult education' *Quaker studies*, vol. 11, pp. 204–233.

Luther (1827), '11th Mo. 27, 1827 Letter', *Friend*, vol. 1, pp. 38–9.

MacIntyre, A. (1984 [1981]) *After virtue*, Notre Dame, IN: University of Notre Dame Press.

Mack, P. (1989) 'Gender and spirituality in early English Quakerism, 1650–1665', E. P. Brown & S. Stuard (eds.), *Witnesses for Change: Quaker Women over three centuries*, pp. 19–45. New Brunswick, NJ: Rutgers University Press.

Mack, P. (1992) *Visionary women: Ecstatic prophecy in Seventeenth-century England*, Berkeley, CA: University of California Press.

Mack, P. (2003) 'Religion, feminism, and the problem of agency: Reflections on Eighteenth-century Quakerism', *Signs: Journal of women in culture and society*, vol. 29, no. 1, pp. 149–77.

MacMaster, R. (1979) *Conscience in crisis: Mennonites and other peace churches in America 1739-1789*, Scottdale, PA: Herald Press.

Magnani L. & Wray, H. I. (2006) *Beyond prisons: A new interfaith paradigm for our failed prison system*, Minneapolis, MN: Fortress Press.

Magnani L. (1990) *America's first penitentiary: A 200 year old failure*, National California Ecumenical Council, American Friends Service Committee Pacific Mountain Region. San Francisco, CA: Criminal Justice Committee of Philadelphia Yearly Meeting.

Malenge, Z., Sakamoto, H., Clausen, C., Marroquin, C., & Swift, L. (1982) 'Five regional perspectives', *Friends Journal*, November 15, pp. 16–19.

Malenge, Z. I. (2003) *Quakerism in the perspective of Friends Church in Kenya*, Nairobi: Dianas Books Library Services.

Malone, J. W. (1993) *J. Walter Malone: The autobiography of an evangelical Quaker*, J. W. Oliver (ed.) Lanham, MD: Scarecrow Press.

Mangus, M. S. (1999) '"A cruel and malicious war": The Society of Friends in Civil War Loudoun County, Virginia', *Quaker History*, vol. 88, no. 1, pp. 40–62.

Mann, M. (1999) 'James Turrell: spirit and light', *Friends Journal*, March 1999, unnumbered pages. Philadelphia.

Manners, E. (1914) *Elizabeth Hooten: First Quaker woman preacher, 1600-1672*, London: Headley Brothers.

Manning, D. (2009) 'Accusations of blasphemy in English anti-Quaker polemic, c.1660–1701', *Quaker Studies*, vol. 14, pp. 27–56.

Manning, E. (1664) *The mask'd devil... of the seven Quakers which were lately convicted and to be transported ...*, London.

Manousos, A. (2010) 'Howard Brinton and the World Council of Churches: the theological impact of ecumenism on Friends', *Quaker Theology*, vol. 17, pp. 1–14.

Map of the various paths of life 1794, Box LL2/25 LSF/34791), London: W. Darton and J. Harvey.

Marietta, J. D. (1974) 'Wealth, war and religion: the perfecting of Quaker asceticism, 1740-1783', *Church History*, vol. 43, no. 2, pp. 230–241.

Marietta, J. D. (2007 [1984]) *The reformation of American Quakerism, 1748–1783*, Philadelphia, PA: University of Philadelphia Press.

Marinissen, J. (1990) *America's first penitentiary: a 200 year old failure*, National California Ecumenical Council, American Friends Service Committee Pacific Mountain Region. San Francisco, CA: Criminal Justice Committee of Philadelphia Yearly Meeting.

Marsh, C. (2011) *A lively faith: reflections on Iowa Yearly Meeting of Friends (Conservative)*. Philadelphia, PA: Quaker Press of Friends General Conference.

Marshall, C. (1675) *An epistle to Friends coming forth in the beginning of a testimony and of the snares of the enemy therein*. N.p.

Marshall, C. (1704) *Sion's travellers comforted and the disobedient warned*, London: T. Sowle.

Marshall, C. (1670) *A plain and candid relation of the nature, use, and dose of several approved medicines*. N.p.

Martin, C. J. L. (2003) 'Controversy and division in post–restoration Quakerism: The Hat, Wilkinson-Story and Keithian Controversies and comparisons with the Internal Divisions of Other Seventeenth-Century nonconformist groups'. Unpublished PhD dissertation, Open University.

Martin, M. (2003) *Invitation to a deeper communion*. Pendle Hill Pamphlet 366. Wallingford, PA: Pendle Hill Publications.

Massey, V. (1945) *A testimony to the life of Joseph Edward Southall,* Warwickshire Monthly Meeting.

Mather, E. (1980) *Pendle Hill: a Quaker experiment in education and community,* Wallingford, PA: Pendle Hill Publications.

Mayer, C. H. (1989) *Continuing struggle: autobiography of a labor activist,* Northampton, MA: Pittenbruach Press.

McCown, C. (1927) 'The beatitudes in the light of ancient ideals', *Journal of biblical literature,* vol. 46, no. 1, pp. 50–61.

McDaniel, D. & Julye, V. (2009) *Fit for freedom, not for friendship: Quakers, African Americans, and the myth of racial justice,* Philadelphia, PA: Quaker Press of Friends General Conference.

McDowell, P. (1998) *The women of Grub Street: Print, politics and gender in the London literary marketplace 1678–1730,* Oxford: Clarendon Press.

McDowell, P. (2004) 'Tace Sowle (1666–1749)', *Oxford Dictionary of National Biography.* Oxford: Oxford University Press.

McDowell, P. J. (1996) 'Tace Sowle; Andrew Sowle', in J. K. Bracken & J. Silver (eds.) *The British literary book trade, 1475–1700, Dictionary of Literary Biography,* vol. 170, pp. 249–57, Detroit, MI: Gale Research.

McKenzie, D. F. (1976) 'The London book trade in the later seventeenth century', Unpublished Sandars lectures. Cambridge: Cambridge University Library.

McKenzie, D. F. (2002) 'Printing and publishing 1557–1700: Constraints on the London book trades' J. Barnard & D. F. McKenzie (eds.), *The Cambridge history of the book in Britain, vol. IV: 1557–1695,* pp. 553–567, Cambridge: Cambridge University Press.

McMahon E. (2006) 'A "spiritual pilgrim": The life of Rasoah Mutuha, and East African Quaker.' *Quaker History,* vol. 95, no. 1, pp. 45–56.

McMurtrie, D. C. (1936) *A history of printing in the United States: Middle and South Atlantic States.* New York, NY: R. R. Bowker.

Megivern, J. J. (1997) *The death penalty: a historical and theological survey,* Mahwah, NJ: Paulist Press.

Meilaender, G. & Werpehowski, W. (eds.) (2005) *The Oxford handbook of theological ethics,* Oxford: Oxford University Press.

Mekeel, A. J. (1979) *The relation of the Quakers to the American Revolution,* Washington, DC: University Press of America.

Mendle, M. (2002) 'Preserving the ephemeral: reading, collecting and the pamphlet culture of seventeenth-century England' in J. Anderson and E. Sauer (eds.), *Books and readers in early modern England: Material studies,* pp. 201–216, Philadelphia, PA: University of Pennsylvania Press.

Meredith, D. (ed.) (1991) *Proceedings of the First International Theological Conference of Quaker Women, held at Woodbrooke, England, July 24_31, 1990,* Woodbrooke, Birmingham.

michiganquakers.org/indexhtml/the_scriptures_as_understood_and_used_by_conservative_friends. Accessed 20 October 2012.

Mielke, A. (1997) '"What's here to do?" An inquiry concerning Sarah and Benjamin Lay, abolitionists', *Quaker History,* vol. 86, no. 1, pp. 22–44.

Migne, J. (1879 [1844]) *Patrologiae cursus completus…: [Series Latina],* vol. 73, Parisiis: Migne.

Miller M. (2009) *A heart to help: An introduction to the work of Quaker prison chaplains,* Manchester: Hardshaw and Mann Area Meeting.

Miller, J. (2005) '"A suffering people": English Quakers and their neighbours c.1650–c.1700', *Past and Present,* vol. 188, no. 1, pp. 71–103.

Milligan, E. (1968) *The past is prologue: 100 years of Quaker overseas work, 1868–1968*, London: Friends Service Council.

Milner, C. A. Jr. (1982), *With good intentions: Quaker work among the Pawnees, Otos, and Omahas in the 1870s*, Lincoln, NE: University of Nebraska Press.

Minear, M. (1987) *Richmond, 1887: A Quaker drama unfolds*, Richmond, IN: Friends United Press.

Minutes of Central Yearly Meeting of Friends, 1927, 1927, N.p.

Minutes of Friends United Meeting, 1966, 1966, N.p.

Minutes of Indiana Yearly Meeting of Friends, 1890, 1890, Richmond, IN.

Minutes of Kansas Yearly Meeting of Friends, 1890, 1890, Lawrence, KS.

Minutes of Kansas Yearly Meeting of Friends, 1891, 1891, Lawrence, KS.

Minutes of the Canada Yearly Meeting of Friends, 1900, 1900, Toronto.

Minutes of the Canada Yearly Meeting of Friends, 1902, 1902, Toronto.

Minutes of the Canada Yearly Meeting of Friends, 1907, 1907, N.p.

Minutes of the Canadian Yearly Meeting, 1988, 1988, N.p.

Minutes of the Eighty-Eighth Ohio Yearly Meeting of the Friends Church, 1900, 1990, Damascus, OH.

Minutes of the Five Years Meeting of Friends in America, 1912, 1912, Richmond, IN.

Minutes of the Five Years Meeting of Friends in America, 1922, 1922, Richmond, IN.

Minutes of the Five Years Meeting of Friends in America, 1945, 1945, Richmond, IN.

Minutes of the Five Years Meeting of Friends, 1950, 1950, Richmond, IN.

Minutes of the Five Years Meeting of Friends, 1955, 1955, Richmond, IN.

Minutes of the Five Years Meeting of Friends, 1960, 1960, Richmond, IN.

Minutes of the Five Years Meeting of Friends, 1963. 1963, Richmond, IN.

Minutes of the Friends United Meeting, 1972, 1972, N.p.

Minutes of the Friends United Meeting, 1993, 1993, N.p.

Minutes of the Friends United Meeting, Triennial Sessions, 1987, 1987, N.p.

Minutes of the New York Yearly Meeting of the Religious Society of Friends, 1986, 1986, N.p.

Moger, E. H. (2003) 'Quakers as abolitionists: the Robinsons of Rokeby and Charles Marriott', in *Quaker History*, vol. 92, no. 2, Fall 2003, pp. 52–9.

Mohr, R. (2006) 'A convergence of Friends', *Friends Journal*, October, pp. 18–19.

Mombo, E. (1999) 'Haramisi and Jumaa: The story of the women's meetings in East Africa Early Meeting, 1902–1979', *Woodbrooke Journal*, Autumn, pp. 1–26.

Mombo, E. (2006) 'Rape: The invisible crime', in P. Buckley & S. W. Angell (eds.), in *The Quaker Bible Reader*, Richmond, IN: Earlham School of Religion Press.

Mombo, E. M. (1998) 'A historical and cultural analysis of the position of Abaluyia women in Quaker Christianity: 1902–1979', Unpublished PhD dissertation, University of Edinburgh.

Moore, J. (ed.) *Friends in the Delaware Valley 1681–1981*, Haverford, PA: Friends Historical Association.

Moore, R. (1995) 'Reactions to persecution in primitive Quakerism', *Journal of the Friends' Historical Society*, vol. 57, no. 2 pp. 123–31.

Moore, R. (2000) *The light in their consciences: the early Quakers in Britain 1644–1666*, University Park, PA: Pennsylvania State Univ. Press.

Moore, R. (2001) 'The epistle from the Elders of Balby', *Friends Quarterly*, vol. 32, no. 5, pp. 215–18.

Moore, R. (2005) 'Late Seventeenth Century Quakerism and the miraculous: A new look at George Fox's 'book of miracles', K. Cooper & J. Gregory (eds.), *Studies in church history 41: Signs, wonders, miracles. Representations of divine power in the life of the church*. Woodbridge: Boydell Press.

Moran, J. (1973) *Printing presses: History and development from the fifteenth century to modern times,* Berkeley, CA: University of California Press.

Moreland L. (2011) *An ordinary murder,* London: Aurum Press.

Moretta, J. A. (2007) *William Penn and the Quaker legacy,* New York & London: Pearson Longman.

Morgan, N. J. (1980) 'Lancashire Quakers and the oath 1660–1720', *Journal of the Friends' Historical Society,* vol. 54, no. 5, pp. 235–54.

Morgan, N. J. (1993) *Lancashire Quakers and the establishment, 1660–1730,* Halifax: Ryburn.

Morley, B. (1993) *Beyond consensus: Salvaging sense of the meeting.* Wallingford, PA: Pendle Hill Publications.

Morning Meeting (1699, 1702), MS minutes of the Second Day Morning Meeting of London, LSF: London Yearly Meeting.

Morris, R. (1995) *Penal abolition: the practical choice,* Toronto: Canadian Scholar's Press.

Morris, R. (2000) *Stories of transformational justice.* Toronto: Canadian Scholar's Press.

Morrisson R. (1828) 'Letter', *The Friend, or advocate of truth,* vol. 2, pp. 38–9.

Mortimer, R. S. (1948) 'The first century of Quaker printers', *Journal of the Friends Historical Society,* vol. 40, pp. 37–49.

Mortimer, R. S. (1963) 'Quaker printers, 1750–1850', *Journal of the Friends Historical Society,* vol. 50, no. 3, pp. 100–33.

Morton, V. (1993) 'The launch of *The Friend,* 1843: Two celebrations or one?', *The Friend,* vol. 151, no. 1, pp. 7–8.

Mott, E. (1943) *Christ preeminent,* Oregon Yearly Meeting Publication Board.

Mott, L. (1846) 3rd Mo. 23 letter to R.D. and H. Webb, Anti-slavery Manuscripts (Rare Books Department, Boston Public Library).

Mott, L. (1980) *Lucretia Mott: her complete speeches and sermons,* ed. by Dana Greene. Lewiston, NY: Edwin Mellen Press.

[Mucklow, W.] (1673) *The Spirit of the Hat,* London: printed for F. Smith.

Mugatroyd, L., Best, S., & Kall, F. (2010) 'The future of The Religious Society of Friends' *Britain Friends Quarterly* 2.

Muhanji, John. Personal Interview, 12 Dec. 2011. Original in Michael Birkel's possession.

Mullett, M. (1978a) '"The assembly of the people of God": The social organization of Lancashire Friends' in M. Mullett (ed.) *Early Lancaster Friends,* pp. 12–21, Lancaster: Centre for North-West Regional Studies.

Mullett, M. (ed.) (1978b) *Early Lancaster Friends,* Lancaster: Centre for North-West Regional Studies.

Mullett, M. (1984) 'From sect to denomination? Social developments in Eighteenth-Century Quakerism', *Journal of Religious History,* vol. 13, December, pp. 168–91.

Munn, M. M. (1999) 'James Turrell: Spirit and light', *Friends Journal,* March, pp. 6–8.

Myles, A. (2007) 'Border crossings: The queer erotics of Quakerism in seventeenth-century New England', in Thomas Foster (ed.) *Long before Stonewall: Theories of same sex sexuality in early America,* pp. 114–143, New York, NY: New York University Press.

Nash, G. B. (1968) *Quakers and politics: Pennsylvania, 1681–1726,* Princeton, NJ: Princeton University Press.

Nash, G. B. (1986) 'The early merchants of Philadelphia: The formation and disintegration of a founding elite', in in R. S. Dunn & M. M. Dunn (eds.) *The world of William Penn,* pp. 337–51. Philadelphia, PA: University of Pennsylvania Press.

Nayler, J. (1653a) *A discovery of the first wisdom,* London: Calvert.

Nayler, J. (1653b) *The power and glory of the Lord,* London: Calvert.

Nayler, J. (1653c), 'The Examination of James Nayler', *Saul's Errand to Damascus*, pp. 29–33.

Nayler, J. (1655), Swarthmore mss 3.80.

Nayler, J. (1656) *Love to the lost*, London: Calvert.

Nayler, J. (1657) *The Lamb's War*, London: Simmonds.

Nayler, J. (1716) *A collection of sundry books, epistles and papers*, ed. by G. Whitehead, London: J. Sowle.

Neale, M. P. (1860 [1795]) *Some account of the life and religious discourses of Mary Neale.* Philadelphia, PA: Friends' Bookstore.

Nebraska Yearly Meeting of Friends, 1956, 1956, N.p.

Nebraska Yearly Meeting of Friends, 1957, 1957, N.p.

Nebraska Yearly Meeting of Friends, 1958, 1958, N.p.

Neelon, D. (2009) *James Nayler: revolutionary to prophet*, Becket, MA: Leadings Press.

Neill, S. (1964) *A history of Christian missions*, Hardmondsworth: Penguin Books.

Nellis, M. (2009) 'Circles of support for sex offenders in England and Wales: their origins and implementation 1999–2005', *British Journal of Community Justice*, vol. 7, no. 1, pp. 23–43.

Nesbitt E. (2003) *Interfaith pilgrims*, London: Quaker Books.

New England Yearly Meeting (Westerly), Canada Yearly Meeting (Pickering), Ohio Yearly Meeting (Stillwater), Western Yearly Meeting (Plainfield), Iowa Yearly Meeting (West Branch), Kansas Yearly Meeting (Spring River) and North Carolina Yearly Meeting (Cedar Grove) 1912, *A brief synopsis of the principles and testimonies of the Religious Society of Friends, with minutes of adoption from the Yearly Meetings of New England, Canada, Ohio, Western, Iowa, Kansas, and North Carolina*, adopted 1912, issued 1913, http://snowcamp.org/brief/brief.html accessed 16 October 2012.

New England Yearly Meeting (1966 [1950]) *Faith and practice of New England Yearly Meeting of Friends.*

Newell, T. (2000) *Forgiving justice: a Quaker vision for criminal justice*, The Swarthmore Lecture 2000, London: Quaker Home Service.

Nicholson, M. (1930) 'George Keith and the Cambridge Platonists', *Philosophical Review*, vol. 39, pp. 36–55.

Nixon, E. A. (1985) *A century of planting: a history of the American Friends mission in India*, Newberg, OR: Barclay Press.

Niyonzima, D. & Fendall, L. (2001) *Unlocking horns: forgiveness and reconciliation in Burundi*, Newberg, OR: Barclay Press.

Norenzayan, A. (2011) 'Explaining human behavioral diversity', *Science* 332, May 27, pp. 1041–2.

North Carolina Yearly Meeting (Conservative) (1943) 'Friends Peace Testimony', *Minutes.*

Nuttall, G. (1946) *The Holy Spirit in Puritan faith and experience*, Oxford: Basil Blackwell.

Nuttall, G.F. (n.d.) *Early Quaker letters from the Swarthmore MSS to 1660.* Calendared, Indexed, and Annotated by G. F. Nuttall, Haverford College Copy, PA.

O'Donnell, E. (2003) 'Deviating from the path of safety: The rise and fall of a nineteenth-century Quaker Meeting', *Quaker Studies*, vol. 8, pp. 68–88.

O'Donnell, E. A. (1999) 'Woman's rights and woman's duties: Quaker women in the nineteenth century, with special reference to Newcastle Monthly Meeting of Women Friends.' Unpublished PhD dissertation, University of Sunderland.

O'Donnell, E. A. (2001) '"On behalf of all young women trying to be better than they are": feminism and Quakerism in the nineteenth century: the case of Anna Deborah Richardson', *Quaker Studies*, vol. 6, pp. 37–58.

O'Malley, T. (1979) 'The press and Quakerism, 1653–1659', *Journal of the Friends' Historical Society*, vol. 54, pp. 169–84.

O'Malley, T. (1982) '"Defying the powers and tempering the spirit": a review of Quaker control over their publications 1672–1689', *Journal of Ecclesiastical History*, vol. 33, pp. 72–88.

O'Neill, J. & McLean, E. P. (2008) *Peter Collinson and the eighteenth-century natural history exchange*, Philadelphia, PA: American Philosophical Society.

Ohio Yearly Meeting of Friends (1992) *The book of discipline of Ohio Yearly Meeting of the Religious Society of Friends (Conservative)*, Barnesville, OH: Ohio Yearly Meeting of Friends.

Ohio Yearly Meeting of Progressive Friends (1852), *Minutes*.

Oliver, J. W., Cherry, C. L., & Cherry, C. L. (eds.) (2007) *Founded by Friends. The Quaker heritage of fifteen American colleges and universities*, Lanham, MD: Scarecrow Press.

Olney Friends School (*c*.2011) *History*.

Olson, A. G. (1992) *Making the empire work: London and American interest groups, 1690–1790*. Cambridge: Cambridge University Press.

Orr, E. W. (1974) *The Quakers in peace and war 1920–1967*, Eastbourne, Offord.

Outhwaite, R. B. (1995) *Clandestine marriage in England 1500–1850*, London: The Hambledon Press.

P[hipps], J. (1754) *A summary account of an extraordinary visit to this metropolis, in the year 1753, by the ministry of Ann Mercy Bell*, London.

Packer, I. (2003) 'Religion and the new liberalism: the Rowntree family, Quakerism, and social reform', *Journal of British Studies*, vol. 42, pp. 236–57.

Pagitt, E. (1645) *Heresiography*, London.

Painter, L. K. (1966) *The hill of vision: the story of the Quaker movement in East Africa, 1902–1965*, Nairoba: East Africa Yearly Meeting of Friends .

Palmer, B. W. (ed.) (2002) *Selected letters of Lucretia Coffin Mott*, Urbana & Chicago, IL: University of Illinois Press.

Palmer, P. J. (2008) *A hidden wholeness: the journey toward an undivided life: welcoming the soul and weaving community in a wounded world*, San Francisco, CA: Jossey-Bass.

Palmer, T. V. (2006) 'Did William Penn diverge significantly from George Fox in his understanding of the Quaker message?', *Quaker Studies*, vol. 11, pp. 59–70.

Palmer, T. V. (2011) *Friends, God, and the Bible*, Unpublished book manuscript.

Parker, S. (2005) *Faith on the homefront: aspects of church life and popular religion in Birmingham, 1939–1945*, Bern: Peter Lang.

Parnel, J. (1655) *A shield of the truth*, London: Calvert.

Partington, M. (2004) *Salvaging the sacred: Lucy, my sister*, London: Quaker Home Service.

Pedigo, M. M. (1988) *New church in the city*, Richmond, IN: Friends United Press.

Pemberton, J. (1785) *The following extracts from the writings of pious men of different denominations and at different periods of time exposing the evil and pernicious effects of stage plays and other vain amusements*, Dublin: Robert Jackson.

Pencak, W. & Richter, D. K. (2004) *Friends and enemies in Penn's Woods: Indians, colonists, and the racial construction of Pennsylvania*, University Park, PA: Pennsylvania State University Press.

Pendle Hill (1998) *Friends in civilian public service: Quaker conscientious objectors in World War II look back and look ahead*, Wallingford, PA: Pendle Hill Publications.

Penington, I. (undated) *The Light within and selected writings*, Philadelphia, PA: Tract Association of Friends.

Penington, I. (1658) *The way of life and death*, London: Lloyd.

Penington, I. (1659a) *The axe laid to the root*, London: Lloyd.

Penington, I. (1659b) *The outward Jew*, London: Lloyd.

Penington, I. (1660) *The consideration of a position*, London: Wilson.

Penington, I. (1663) *Some of the mysteries of the kingdom,* London.

Penington, I. (1668) *Some things relating to religion proposed in the consideration of the Royal Society (so termed) to wit, concerning the right ground of certainty therein. . . . ,* London.

Penington, I. (1997 [1680]) *The works of the long-mournful and sorely-distressed Isaac Penington,* 4 vols. Glenside, PA: Quaker Heritage Press.

Penington, I., Fox G., & Penn, W. (1784) *The Works of the Long-Mournful and Sorely-Distressed Isaac Penington, Whom the Lord, in His Tender Mercy, at Length Visited and Relieved by the Ministry of That Despised People Called Quakers . . .* London: Printed and sold by J. Phillips.

Penn, W. (1679) *An address to Protestants upon the present conjuncture.* London.

Penn, W. (1693) *Some fruits of solitude,* London.

Penn, W. (1694) *An account of William Penn's travails in Holland and Germany anno 1677,* London: T. Sowle.

Penn, W. (1726a) *A collection of the works of William Penn. To which Is prefixed a journal of his life, with Many original letters and papers not before published,* London: J. Sowle.

Penn, W. (1726b) *Fruits of a father's love: being the advice of William Penn to his children, relating to their civil and religious conduct,* London: J. Sowle.

Penn, W. (1877 [1682]) *No cross, no crown: a discourse showing the nature and discipline of the holy cross of Christ,* Philadelphia, PA: Friend's Book Store.

Penn, W. (1991 [1682]) *No cross, no crown,* N. Penney (ed.), York: Sessions.

Penn, W. (1993) 'The peace of Europe, the fruits of solitude and other writings', E. Bonner (ed.) London: Everyman.

Pennington, S. (2010) 'The scriptures as understood and used by Conservative Friends' ' Accessed by internet 14 February 2010.

Pennsylvania Yearly Meeting of Progressive Friends (1853) 'Exposition of sentiments.'

Pennyman, J. (1670a) *Begin. Oh people! My bowels yearn, etc. [An exhortation to faith in Jesus Christ.] End . . . ,* London.

Pennyman, J. (1670b) *The people called Quakers having printed and published a paper against mee: or rather against the Lord, whose servant I am . . . ,* London.

Pennyman, John, (1670c) *The Ark is begun to be opened, (the waters being somewhat abated) . . . ,* London.

Pennyman, J. (1696) *A short account of the life of Mr John Pennyman,* London.

Pestana, C. G. (1991) *Quakers and Baptists in Colonial Massachusetts,* Cambridge: Cambridge University Press.

Peters, K. (1995) 'Patterns of Quaker authorship, 1652–1656' in T. N. Corns & D. Loewenstein (eds.), *The emergence of Quaker writing: Dissenting literature in seventeenth-century England,* pp. 6–24, London: Frank Cass.

Peters, K. (2005) *Print culture and the early Quakers,* Cambridge: Cambridge University Press.

Philadelphia Yearly Meeting (Hicksite) (1830) *Minutes.*

Philadelphia Yearly Meeting (Hicksite) (1910) *Rules of discipline of the Yearly Meeting of Friends held in Philadelphia,* Philadelphia, PA.

Philadelphia Yearly Meeting (Orthodox) (1926 [1910]) *Rules of discipline of the Yearly Meeting for Friends for Pennsylvania, New Jersey, and the eastern part of Maryland.* Philadelphia, PA: Friends Book Store.

Philadelphia Yearly Meeting (1997) *Faith and practice: a book of Christian discipline,* Philadelphia, PA: Philadelphia Yearly Meeting.

Philadelphia Yearly Meeting of the Religious Society of Friends (2002), *Faith and Practice: A Book of Christian Discipline,* Philadelphia, PA.

Phillips, C. P. (1797) *Memoires of the life of Catherine Phillips, to which are added some of her Epistles,* London: James Phillips and Son.

Phillips, C. P. (1798) *Memoirs of the life of Catherine Phillips,* Philadelphia, PA: Budd and Bartram.

Phipps, J. (1767) *Observations on a late anonymous publication, intituled, a letter to the author of a letter to Dr. Formey,* London: Mary Hinde.

Pike, J. & Oxley, J. (1837) *Some account of the life of Joseph Pike... also, a journal of the life... of Joseph Oxley,* J. R. Barclay (ed.), London: Darton and Harvey.

Pinel, P. (1806) *A treatise on insanity,* D. D. Davis (Trans.), London: Prichard, James Cowles.

Plank, G. (2012) *John Woolman's path to the peaceable kingdom: a Quaker in the British empire.* Philadelphia, PA: University of Pennsylvania Press.

Pollard, A. F. (2004) rev. Charlotte Fell-Smith and M. W. Kirby, 'Pease, Edward (1767–1858), *Oxford dictionary of national biography.* Oxford: Oxford University Press.

Pomfret, J. E. (1953) 'The proprietors of the province of East New Jersey, 1682–1702', *Pennsylvania Magazine of History and Biography,* 77, pp. 251–93.

Pomfret, J. E. (1956a) *The province of West New Jersey, 1609–1702,* Princeton, NJ: Princeton University Press.

Pomfret, J. E. (1956b), 'The first purchasers of Pennsylvania, 1681–1700', *Pennsylvania Magazine of History and Biography* vol. 80, no. 2, pp. 137–163.

Poole, W. ([11th Mo. 1824]) to Benjamin Ferris, William Poole Letters. Swarthmore, PA: Friends Historical Library.

Popkin, R. (1985) 'Spinoza and Samuel Fisher', *Philosophia* 15, pp. 219–36.

Port, M. H. (1961) *Six hundred new churches: a study of the church building commission 1818 to 1836 and its church building activities,* London: SPCK.

Potter H. (1993) *Hanging in judgement: religion and the death penalty in England* London: SPCK.

Pratt, D. H. (1985) *English Quakers and the first industrial revolution: a study of the Quaker community in four industrial counties—Lancashire, York, Warwick and Gloucester, 1750–1830,* London & New York: Garland.

Preston, M. H. (2004) *Charitable words: women, philanthropy, and the language of charity in Nineteenth-Century Dublin,* Westport, CT: Praeger Publishers.

Pringle, C. G. (1962) *Civil War diary of Cyrus Pringle,* Pendle Hill Pamphlet 122, Wallingford, PA: Pendle Hill Publications.

Prior, A. (1997) 'Friends in business: The interaction of business and religion within the Society of Friends 1700–1830', Unpublished PhD dissertation, University of Lancaster.

Proceedings of Baltimore Yearly Meeting, 1973, 1973, N.p.

Proceedings of the Conference of Friends of America, 1892, 1892, Richmond, IN.

Proceedings of the Conference of Friends of America, 1897, 1897, Philadelphia, PA.

Proceedings of the Five Years Meeting of the American Yearly Meetings of Friends, 1907.

Pryce, E. (2010) '"Negative to a marked degree" or "an intense and glowing faith"?: Rufus Jones and Quaker Quietism', *Common Knowledge,* vol. 16, pp. 518–31.

Punshon, J. (1984) *Portrait in grey: A short history of the Quakers,* London: Quaker Home Service.

Punshon, J. (1987) *Patterns of change: The Quaker experience and the challenges of the contemporary world,* Richmond, IN: Friends United Press.

Punshon, J. (2001) *Reasons for hope. The faith and future of the Friends church,* Richmond, IN: Friends United Press.

Punshon, J. (2006) 'Miss Wilson's legacy: How my early schooling taught me to read the Letter to the Hebrews', in P. Buckley & S. W. Angell (eds.), *The Quaker Bible reader,* pp. 251–72, Richmond, IN: Earlham School of Religion Press.

Quaker Committee for Christian and Interfaith Relations (2009, *We are but witnesses,* Quaker Committee for Christian and Interfaith Relations (QCCIR) of Britain Yearly Meeting of the Religious Society of Friends (Quakers), London.

Quaker Lesbian and Gay Fellowship (2004), *Part of the rainbow: A plain look at lesbian, gay and bisexual lives,* Harrogate: Published by Quaker Lesbian and Gay Fellowship.

Quaker Life (periodical), Richmond, IN: Friends United Press.

Quaker Life (2004) *Quaker Life Membership Procedures Group Consultation Document for Monthly Meetings.* London: Quaker Life.

Quaker Social Responsibility and Education (1992) *Directory of Friends in business,* Durham: QSRE Work and Society Committee.

Quaker Women's Group (1986) *Bringing the invisible into the Light; some Quaker feminists speak of their experience* London: Quaker Home Services.

QuakerInfo.com 2010, 'Online Books of Faith and Practice'.

Quakers and Business Group (2000) *Good business: Ethics at work, advices and queries on personal standards of conduct at work,* London: QBG.

Quakers in the World (2008) Education in Africa. Chilterns Area Quaker Meeting, The New Jordans Programme.

Raistrick, A. (1938) *Two centuries of industrial welfare: The London (Quaker) lead company. 1692–1905,* London: Friends' Historical Society.

Raistrick, A. (1993 [1950]) *Quakers in science and industry, being an account of the Quaker contributions to science and industry during the 17th and 18th Centuries,* York: William Sessions.

Rasmussen, A. M. B. (1995) *A history of the Quaker movement in Africa,* London: British Academic Press.

Raymond, J. (2003) *Pamphlets and pamphleteering in early modern Britain,* Cambridge: Cambridge University Press.

Raymond, J. (2011) 'The development of the book trade in Britain' in J. Raymond (ed.) *The Oxford history of popular press culture, vol. I: Cheap print in Britain and Ireland to 1660,* pp. 59–75, Oxford University Press.

Reay, B. (1983) 'The authorities and early Restoration Quakerism', *Journal of Ecclesiastical History,* vol. 34, pp. 69–84.

Reay, B. (1985) *The Quakers and the English Revolution,* New York: St. Martin's; London: Temple Smith.

Redfern, K. & Collins, S. (eds.) (1994) *Relative experience. A contemporary anthology of Quaker family life,* London: Quaker Home Service.

Rescher, N. (1955) 'Leibniz and the Quakers', *The Bulletin of the Friends Historical Association,* vol. 44: pp. 100–107.

Report of the proceedings of the conference of members of the Society of Friends, held, by the direction of the Yearly Meeting in Manchester . . . (1896). London: Headley Brothers.Restaino, G. M. (1994) 'Quaker in Canton: Dr. William Warder Cadbury's Mission, 1909–1949', *Quaker History,* 83, pp. 1–17.

Rhode Island Monthly Meeting, *Minutes (men's),* Newport (RI) Historical Society.

Richmond, B. (2005) *Signs of salvation: new life where grace and truth meet,* Richmond, IN: Friends United Press.

Riney, C. J. (1963) 'Emergence and development of a ministry of music within the Society of Friends', Unpublished PhD dissertation, University of Southern California, CA.

Roberts, A. O. (1967) *Move over, Elijah: sermons in poetry and prose,* Newberg, OR: Barclay Press.

Roberts, A. O. (1975) *Association of Evangelical Friends,* Newberg, OR: Barclay Press.

Roberts, A. O. (1992) 'John Frederick Hanson', in M. Birkel and J. Newman eds., *The Lamb's War, Quaker essays to honor Hugh Barbour,* Birkel, M. & Newman, J. (eds.), Richmond IN: Earlham College.

Roberts, A. O. (2006a) 'Corresponding with George A. Fox', *Quaker History,* vol. 96, pp. 143–72.

Roberts, A. O. (2006b) *The sacred ordinary: Sermons & addresses,* Newberg, OR: Barclay Press

Roberts, H. (2004) 'Friends in business: Researching the history of Quaker involvement in industry and commerce', *Quaker Studies,* vol. 8, pp. 172–93.

Rocky Mountain Yearly Meeting of the Friends Church, 1957, 1958. N.p.

Rogers, W. (1680) *The Christian Quaker distinguished from the apostate and innovator,* London.

[Rogers, W.] (1681) *The sixth part of The Christian-Quaker.* London: Printed for W. R.

Rose G. (1961) *The struggle for penal reform,* London: Stevens.

Rose, J. 1980, *Elizabeth Fry: A biography,* London: Macmillan.

Rothman, D. (1971) *The discovery of the asylum: Social order and disorder in the new republic,* Boston, MA: Little, Brown.

Rowntree, B. S. (1921) *The human factor in business,* London: Longmans.

Rowntree, J.S. (1859) *Quakerism, Past and Present: Being an inquiry into the causes of its decline in Britain and Ireland.* London: Smith, Elder & Co.

Rowntree, J. W. (1905) 'A plea for a Quaker settlement' in Joshua Rowntree (ed.), *John Wilhelm Rowntree: Essays and Addresses,* pp. 135–150. London: Headley Bros.

Rubinstein, D. (2001) *Faithful to ourselves and the outside world: York Quakers during the Twentieth Century,* York: William Sessions.

Ruether, R. R. (1990) 'Prophets and humanists', *Journal of Religion,* vol. 70, pp. 1–18.

Runyon, D. (1973) 'Types of Quaker writings by year—1650-1699', in H. Barbour & A. O. Roberts (eds.) *Early Quaker writings 1650-1700,* pp. 567–576, Wallingford, PA: Pendle Hill Publications.

Rush, N. (1944) *A bibliography of the published works of Rufus M. Jones.* Waterville, ME: Colby College library.

Rushby, W. F. (2000) 'Cyrus Cooper's memorial and the free gospel ministry', *Quaker History,* vol. 89, no. 1, pp. 28–46.

Ruskin, J. (1925 [1845]) *The seven lamps of architecture,* London: Allen and Unwin.

Russell, E. (1928) *Separation after a century,* Philadelphia, PA: Reprinted from *Friends Intellegencer.*

Russell, E. (1942) *The History of Quakerism,* New York, NY: Macmillan.

Russell, E. (1950) *Friends at mid-century,* Richmond, IN: Five Years Meeting of Friends.

Russell, E. (1979 [1942]) *The History of Quakerism,* Richmond, IN: Friends United Press.

Rutty, J. (1776) *Spiritual diary and soliloquies,* (2 vols), London: James Phillips.

Ryan, J. E. (2009) 'Staging Quakerism in American theatre and film', *Quaker Studies,* vol. 14, pp. 157–71.

S. M. Stuard (eds.) *Witnesses for change: Quaker women over three centuries,* pp. 31–63, New Brunswick, NJ: Rutgers University Press.

Sanders, P. (1991) 'En espititu y en verdad…le fe en accion', *Friends Journal,* November.

Sanneh, L. (2008) *Disciples of all nations: Pillars of world Christianity,* New York, NY: Oxford University Press.

Sansbury, R. (1988) *Beyond the blew stone. 300 years of Quakers in Newcastle,* Newcastle: Newcastle upon Tyne Preparative Meeting.

Sassi, J. D. (2011) 'With a little help from the Friends: The Quaker and tactical contexts of Anthony Benezet's abolitionist publishing', *Pennsylvania Magazine of History and Biography*, vol. 135, pp. 33–71.

Schmidt, L. (2005) *Restless souls: The making of American spirituality from Emerson to Oprah*, San Francisco, CA: Harper.

Schmitt, H. (1997) *Quakers and Nazis: Inner light in outer darkness* Columbia, MO: University of Missouri Press, pp. 205–20.

Scott, J. (1797) *Journal, of the life, travels, and gospel labours of that faithful servant and minister of Christ, Job Scott*, New York, NY: Isaac Collins.

Scott, J. (1824a) *The knowledge of the Lord, the only true God. To which Is added, remarks upon the doctrine of perseverance*, Philadelphia, PA: Emmor Kimber.

Scott, J. (1824b) *A treatise on church discipline*, Philadelphia, PA.

Scott, J. (1831), 'Journal, of the life, travels, and gospel labours of that faithful servant and minister of Christ, Job Scott.' *Works of… Job Scott*, Philadelphia, PA: J. Comly.

Scott, J. (1860 [1817]) *The baptism of Christ*, London: A. W. Bennett.

Scott, J. (1980) *What canst thou say? Towards a Quaker theology*, The Swarthmore Lecture, Quaker Books.

Scott, J. (2001 [1824]) *Essays on salvation by Christ*, Farmington, ME: Quaker Heritage Press.

Scull, A. (1989) *Social order/mental disorder: Anglo-American psychiatry in historical perspective*, Berkeley & Los Angeles: University of California Press.

Scull, A. (1993) *The most solitary of afflictions: madness and society in Britain 1700-1900*, New Haven, CT & London: Yale University Press.

Scully, J. L. (2002) *Quaker approaches to moral issues in genetics*, Lampeter: Edwin Mellen Press.

Scully, J. L. (2007) 'The secular ethics of liberal Quakerism', in J. L. Scully & P. Dandelion (eds.), *Good and evil: Quaker perspectives*, pp. 219–31, Aldershot: Ashgate.

Scully, J. L. (2008) 'Virtuous Friends: morality and Quaker identity', in P. Dandelion & P. Collins (eds.), *The Quaker condition: The sociology of a liberal religion*, pp. 107–23, Newcastle: Cambridge Scholars Publishing.

Scully, J. L. & Dandelion, P. (eds.) (2007) *Good and evil: Quaker perspectives*, Aldershot: Ashgate.

Sefton, R. (1972) 'The church in North America', *The decorative arts of the Christian* Church, G. Frere-Cook (ed.), London: Cassell.

Sell, A. P. F. (1992) 'Robert Barclay (1648–1690), the fathers and the inward, universal saving Light: a tercentenary reappraisal', *Journal of the Friends' Historical Society*, vol. 56, no. 3, pp. 210–26.

Selleck, G. (1976) *Quakers in Boston: Three centuries of Friends in Boston and Cambridge*, Boston, MA: Friends Meeting in Boston.

Semple, R. A. (2003) *Missionary women: Gender, professionalism, and the Victorian idea of Christian mission*, Woodbridge: Boydell Press.

Senn, F. C. (1997) *Christian liturgy: catholic and evangelical*, Minneapolis, MN: Fortress Press.

Sharp, I. & Norman P. (eds.) (1903/4) 'The case of William Gibson' in *Journal of the Friends' Historical Society*, vol. 1, pp. 22–6.

Sheeran, M. J. (1983) *Beyond majority rule: Voteless decisions in the Religious Society of Friends*, Philadelphia, PA: Philadelphia Yearly Meeting of the Religious Society of Friends.

Sheffield Archives, SpSt/81/3, 12 (January 1661) Nicholas Bowdon, London, to Thomas Barnby, Barnby Hall, Yorkshire.

Sheils, W. J. (ed.) (1984) *Studies in church history, 21: Persecution and toleration*, Oxford: Basil Blackwell.

Shellens, H. (2004) *Was the invisible brought into the light?* Birmingham: Woodbrooke Occasional Paper.

Shorter, E. (1976) *The making of the modern family,* London: Collins.

Silf, M. (1999) *Inner compass: An invitation to Ignatian spirituality,* Chicago, IL: Jesuit Way.

Simiyu, O. K. (2001) 'Integrity', *Quaker Life,* July/August, pp. 10–11.

Sippel, P. (ed.) *Quaker homiletics online anthology,* http://www.qhpress.org/quakerpages/qhoa/ Accessed 30 January 2012.

Skidmore, G. (ed.) (2003) *Strength in weakness: Writings by eighteenth-century Quaker women,* Walnut Creek, CA: Altamira Press.

Skidmore, G. (1993) 'Watch over one another for good: an introduction to elders and overseers.' *Friends Quarterly,* vol. 27, no. 6, pp. 257–70.

Skidmore, G. (2005) *Elizabeth Fry: a Quaker life,* New York, NY: Altamira Press.

Slack, K. (1967) *Constancy and change in the Society of Friends.* The Swarthmore Lecture. London: Friends Home Service.

Slaughter, T. P. (1996) *The natures of John and William Bartram,* New York, NY: Alfred A. Knopf.

Slaughter, T. P. (2008) *The beautiful soul of John Woolman, apostle of abolition.* New York, NY: Hill and Wang.

Smedley, K. (1987) *Martha Schofield and the re-education of the South, 1839–1916,* Lewiston, NY: Edwin Mellen Press.

Smith, H. (1657) *The first and second priesthood,* N.p.

Smith, H. W. (1875) *The Christian's secret of a happy life.* New York, NY: Fleming H. Revell.

Smith, H. W. (1903) *My spiritual autobiography or how I discovered the unselfishness of God,* New York, NY: Fleming H. Revel Company.

Smith, J. (1873) *Bibliotheca Anti-Quakeriana,* London: J. Smith.

Smith, N. (1990) 'Exporting enthusiasm: John Perrot and the Quaker epic', in T. F. Healy & J. Sawday (eds.), *Warre is all the World About: Literature and the English Civil War,* Cambridge: Cambridge University Press, pp. 248–64.

Smith, N. (1998) *George Fox: The Journal,* London: Penguin.

Smith, N. (2004) 'Perrot, J. (d. 1665)', *Oxford dictionary of national biography,* Oxford: Oxford University Press.

Smith, N. (2004) 'Whitehead, George (1637–1724)', *Oxford dictionary of national biography.* Oxford: Oxford University Press.

Smith, R. (1687) *The foundation of true preaching asserted,* London: Andrew Sowle.

Smith, S. (1814) 'Samuel Tuke's *Description of the Retreat'.* Review in *Edinburgh Review* 23, pp. 189–98.

Smith, S. A. (1976) 'Alfred Waterhouse: civic grandeur' in J. Fawcett (ed.), *Seven Victorian architects,* London: Thames and Hudson.

Smith, T. L. (1980) *Revivalism and social reform: American Protestantism on the eve of the Civil War.* Baltimore, MD: Johns Hopkins.

Smith, W. (1661) *New creation brought forth,* London.

Smuck, H. (1987) *Friends in East Africa.* Richmond, IN: Friends United Press.

Snyder, M., Gibbs, C., Hillmann, S. A., Peterson, T. N., Schofield, J., & Watson, G. (2001) *Building consensus: Conflict and unity,* Richmond, IN: Earlham Quaker Foundations of Leadership Program.

Soderlund, J. R. (1983) *William Penn and the founding of Pennsylvania. A documentary history.* Philadelphia, PA: University of Pennsylvania Press.

Soderlund, J. R. (1985) *Quakers and slavery: A divided spirit,* Princeton, NJ: Princeton University Press.

Somervell, J. (1924) *Isaac and Rachel Wilson, Quakers, of Kendal, 1714–1785,* London: Swarthmore Press.

Sorel, N. (1995) 'Peace and social Concerns: The last forty years 1955–1995', in H. Barbour, C. Densmore, E. H. Moger, N. C. Sorel, A. D. Van Wagner, & A. J. Worrall (eds.), *Quaker crosscurrents: Three hundred years of Friends in New York Yearly Meetings,* pp. 276–320, New York, NY: Syracuse University Press.

Southall, K. H. (1974) *Our Quaker heritage: Early meeting houses built prior to 1720 and in use today.* London: Quaker Home Service.

Southern, A. (2010) 'The Rowntree history series and the growth of liberal Quakerism: 1895–1925.' Unpublished MPhil dissertation, University of Birmingham.

Southern, A. (2011) 'The Rowntree history series and the growth of liberal Quakerism', *Quaker Studies,* vol. 16, pp. 7–73.

Sox, D. (2000) *Quakers and the arts: 'Plain and fancy': an Anglo-American perspective,* Richmond, IN: Friends United Press.

Spears, J. & Spears, L. (1990) *Friendly Bible study,* Philadelphia, PA: Friends General Conference.

Specht, N. (2002) 'Removing to a remote place: Quaker certificates of removal and their significance in trans-Appalachian migration', *Quaker History,* vol. 9, no. 1, pp. 45–69.

Spencer, C. D. (2007) *Holiness: the soul of Quakerism: a historical analysis of the theology of holiness in the Quaker tradition,* Milton Keynes: Paternoster.

Spencer, L. (1958) 'The professional and literary connexions of George Thomason', *The Library,* 5th ser., vol. 13, pp. 102–18.

Spinoza, B. (1670) *Tractatus theologico-politicus,* Amsterdam: Jan Rieuwertsz.

Spoon, P. (1953) 'Our responsibility in Kenya', *American Friend,* vol. 60, no. 20, pp. 312–18.

Sprague, A. N. (2005) 'The British tempera revival' *Fine Arts Society,* pp. 22–36.

Spufford, M. (1981) *Small books and pleasant histories: Popular fiction and its readership in seventeenth-century England,* Cambridge: Cambridge University Press.

Standing, H. (1964) *Iowa Yearly Meeting (Conservative): A historical sketch,* unpublished paper, Drake University Divinity School, IA.

Stanley, J. (2010) 'Inner night and inner light: A Quaker model of pastoral care for the mentally ill', *Journal of Religious Health,* vol. 49, pp. 547–59.

Stanley, M. (2007) *Practical mystic. religion, science, and A. S. Eddington,* Chicago, IL: University of Chicago Press.

Stansell, R. (2009) *Mission by the spirit: learning from Quaker examples,* Newberg, OR: Barclay Press.

Stanton, M. (1830) 3rd Mo. 5 to Isaac Walker, box 23, Miscellaneous Manuscripts, Swarthmore, PA: Friends Historical Library.

Stassen, G. (2009) 'The sermon on the mount as realistic disclosure of solid ground', *Studies in Christian Ethics,* vol. 22, no. 1, pp. 55–75.

Steele, I. K. (1986) *The English Atlantic, 1675–1740: An exploration of communication and community.* New York, NY: Oxford University Press.

Steere, D. V. (1984) 'Letter from I. Penington to T. Walmsley', 1670. P. 143, *Quaker Spirituality,* New York, NY: Paulist Press.

Stephen, C. E. (1891) *Quaker strongholds,* Philadelphia, PA: H. Longstreth.

Stevenson, C. (1987) *The millionth snowflake: The history of Friends in South Australia,* Australia: Charles Stevenson.

Stewart, K. A. (1992) *The York retreat in the light of the Quaker way. Moral treatment therapy: humane therapy or mind control?* York: William Sessions.

Stewart, W. A. C. (1953) *Quakers and education,* London: Epworth Press.

Stout, J. (1990) *Ethics after Babel: The languages of morals and their discontents*. Princeton, NJ: Princeton University Press.

Sturge, H. W. & Clark, T. (1931) *The Mount School, York. 1785–1814; 1831–1931*, London: J. M. Dent and Sons Ltd.

Swain, E. D. (2001) 'From benevolence to reform: the expanding career of Mrs. Rhoda M. Coffin', *Indiana Magazine of History*, vol. 97: pp. 190–215.

Swatzler, D. (2000) *A Friend among the Senecas: The Quaker mission to Cornplanter's people*. Mechanicsburg, PA: Stackpole Books.

Swift, D. E. (1962) *Joseph John Gurney: banker, reformer, & Quaker*, Middletown, CT: Wesleyan University Press.

Swift, J. (1958 [1704]) *A tale of a tub*. A. C. Guthkelch & D. N. Smith (eds.), Oxford: Clarendon Press.

Switzerland Yearly Meeting (2009) *Swiss Quaker life, belief, and thought*, York: William Sessions.

Szasz, T. (1961) *The myth of mental illness: Foundation of a theory of personal conduct*, New York, NY: Dell.

Taber Jr., W. P. (1985) *The eye of faith: a history of Ohio Yearly Meeting, Conservative*. Barnesville, OH: Representative Meeting of Ohio Yearly Meeting.

Taber, Jr., W. P. & Taber, F. (2004) 'The witness of Conservative Friends. Plenary address to 2004 sessions North Carolina Yearly Meeting (Conservative)', reprinted in 2010 by Friends World Committee Section of the Americas. Available online at http://www.fwccamericas. org/publications/wqf/2010_spring/wqf_taber_printer%20spreads_052510.pdf accessed 16 October 2012.

Taber, W. P. (2010) *The mind of Christ: Bill Taber on meeting for business*, ed. by M. L. Birkel, Wallingford, PA: Pendle Hill Publications.

Tallack, W. (1861) *Friendly sketches in America*, London: A.W. Bennett.

Tallack, W. (1889) *Penological and preventive principles: With special reference to Europe and America, and to crime, pauperism and prevention*. London: Wertheimer, Lea and Co.

Tallack, W. (1900) *Reparation to the injured and the rights of the victims of crime to compensation: A paper prepared, by request for the Quinquennial International Prison Congress AD 1900*. London: Wertheimer, Lea and Co.

Tarter, M. L. (1993) *Sites of performance: theorizing the history of sexuality in the lives and writings of Quaker women, 1650–1800*, Unpublished PhD dissertation, Boulder, CO: University of Colorado.

Tarter, M. L. (2001), 'Quaking in the light: the politics of Quaker women's corporeal prophecy in the Seventeenth-Century transatlantic world', in J. M. Lindman and M. L. Tarter (eds.), *A centre of wonders: The body in early America*, pp. 145–62, Ithaca, NY: Cornell University Press.

Tarter, M. L. (2004) '"Go north!" The journey towards first-generation Friends and their prophecy of celestial flesh', in P. Dandelion (ed.), *The creation of Quaker theory: Insider perspectives*, pp. 83–98, Aldershot: Ashgate.

Tarter, M. L. (2005) 'Reading a Quaker's book: Elizabeth Ashbridge's testimony of Quaker literary theory', in *Quaker Studies*, vol. 9, pp. 176–90.

Tawney, R. H. (1938 [1926]) *Religion and the rise of capitalism: A historical study*, Harmondsworth: Penguin.

Taylor, C. (1989) *Sources of the self: the making of the modern identity*, Cambridge: Cambridge University Press.

Taylor, Ernest E. (1994) *The Valiant Sixty*. Reprint of 3rd ed., 1988. York: Sessions Book Trust.

Taylor T. (2011) *Changing the prison system*, 2011 Quaker Lecture, Christchurch, NZ: Religious Society of Friends.

Thomas, A. B. (1938) *Story of Baltimore Yearly Meeting from 1672 to 1938*, Baltimore, MD.

Thomas, A. C. (1920) 'Congregational or progressive Friends: A forgotten episode in Quaker history', *Bulletin of Friends' Historical Society*, vol. 10, pp. 21–32.

Thomas, H. (2009) 'The future of Quakers in South America: Challenges and temptations in the 21st Century', unpublished paper presented to the Quaker Theological Discussion Group.

Thomas, K. (1986) 'The meaning of literacy in early modern England' in G. Baumann (ed.), *The written word: Literacy in transition*, pp. 97–131, Oxford: Clarendon Press.

Thomas, K. H. (2002) *The history and significance of Quaker symbols in sect formation*, Lewiston, NY: Edwin Mellen Press.

Thomas, S. S. (1999) 'Gender and religion on the mission station: Roxie Reeve and the Friends Africa mission', *Quaker History*, vol. 88, no. 2, pp. 24–46.

Thomas, S. S. (2000) 'Transforming the gospel of domesticity: Luhya girls and the Friends African mission, 1917–1926', *African Studies Review*, vol. 43, pp. 1–27.

Thompson, M. J. A. (1991) 'The post-restoration peace testimony: Quakers and the Kaber Rigg plot', in M. Mullett (ed.) *New light on George Fox 1624–1691*, York: Sessions.

Thompson, S. P. (1896) 'Can a scientific man be a sincere Friend?', in *Report of the proceedings of the conference of members of the Society of Friends, held, by the direction of the Yearly Meeting in Manchester . . . ,* pp. 227–39, London: Headley Brothers.

Thorne, J. Z. (1999) 'Earnest and solemn protest: Quaker anti-slavery petitions to Congress, 1831–1865', *Quaker History*, vol. 88, no. 2, pp. 47–50.

Thurston, L. M. (1993) *A call to action: An analysis and overview of the United States criminal justice system, with recommendations: A report from the National Commission on Crime and Justice*, Chicago, IL: Third World Press.

Tolles, F. B. (1938) 'Emerson and Quakerism', *American Literature*, vol. 10, pp. 142–65.

Tolles, F. B. (1945), 'Quietism versus enthusiasm: The Philadelphia Quakers and the Great Awakening', *The Pennsylvania Magazine of History and Biography*, vol. 69, pp. 26–49.

Tolles, F. B. (1948) *Meeting house and counting house. The Quaker merchants of colonial Philadelphia 1682–1763*, Chapel Hill, NC: University of North Carolina Press.

Tolles, F. B. (1952) *The Atlantic community of early Friends*, London: Friends Historical Society.

Tolles, F. B. (1960), *Quakers and the Atlantic culture*, New York, NY: Macmillan.

Tolles, F. B. (1963 [1948]) *Meeting house and counting house. The Quaker merchants of colonial Philadelphia 1682–1763*, New York, NY: W. W. Norton & Company, Inc.

Tomes, N. (1984) *A generous confidence: Thomas Story Kirkbride and the art of asylum-keeping, 1840–1883*, Cambridge: Cambridge University Press.

Tonsing, B. K. (2002) *The Quakers in South Africa: A social witness*, Lewiston, NY: Edwin Mellen Press.

Tousley, N. C. (2008) 'The experience of regeneration and erosion of certainty in the theology of second-generation Quakers: no place for doubt?', *Quaker Studies*, vol. 13, pp. 6–88.

Trevett, C. (1990) 'The women around James Nayler, Quaker: A matter of emphasis', *Religion*, vol. 20, pp. 249–73.

Trevett, C. (1991) *Women and Quakerism in the Seventeenth Century*, Sessions Book Trust, York: Ebor Press.

Trevett, C. (1997) *Previous convictions*, The Swarthmore Lecture. London: Quaker Home Service.

Trevett, C. (2000) *Quaker women prophets in England and Wales, 1650–1700*, Lampeter: Edwin Mellen Press.

Trevett, C. (2004) '"Not fit to be printed": the Welsh, the women and the Second Day's Morning Meeting', *Journal of the Friends Historical Society*, vol. 59, pp. 115–44.

Trowell, S. (1994) 'George Keith: Post-Restoration Quaker theology and the experience of defeat', *Bulletin—John Rylands University Library of Manchester*, vol. 76, pp. 119–37.

Trueblood, D. E. (1948) *Alternative to futility*, New York, NY: Harper & Row.

Trueblood, D. E. (1966) *The people called Quakers,* New York, NY: Harper & Row.

Trueblood, D. E. (1968) *Robert Barclay,* New York, NY: Harper & Row.

Trueblood, D. E. (1988 [1939]) *The trustworthiness of religious experience,* Richmond, IN: Friends United Press.

Tual, J. (1988) 'Sexual equality and conjugal harmony: the way to celestial bliss. A view of early Quaker matrimony', *Journal of the Friends' Historical Society,* vol. 55, pp. 161–74.

Tucker, R. (1971) 'Revolutionary faithfulness', *Quaker Religious Thought,* vol. 9, no. 2, pp. 2–30.

Tuke, S. (ed.) (1825) *Selections from the epistles, etc. of George Fox.* York, England.

Tuke, S. (1964 [1813]) *Description of the retreat: An institution near York for insane persons of the Society of Friends. Containing an account of its origin and progress, the modes of treatment, and a statement of cases,* R. Hunter & I. Macalpine (eds.), London: Dawson's of Pall Mall.

Ullmann, R. K. (1959) *Between God and history: The human situation exemplified in Quaker thought and practice.* London: Allen and Unwin.

Underwood, T. L. (1997) *Primitivism, radicalism, and the Lamb's war: The Baptist-Quaker conflict in seventeenth-century England.* Oxford: Oxford University Press.

Updegraff, A. T. (10th Mo. 7, 1844) *Diary,* Updegraff Papers. Quaker Collection, Haverford, PA.

Updegraff, D. B. (1892) *Old corn; or, sermons and addresses on the spiritual life,* Boston, MA: McDonald and Gill.

Updegraff, James and Mary (3rd Mo. 28, 1829), to Elias Hicks, box 30, Elias Hicks Papers. Swarthmore, PA: Friends Historical Library.

Valentine, L. (2003) 'Environment', *Historical dictionary of the Friends (Quakers),* M. P. Abbot, M. E. Chijioke & P. Dandelion (eds.), pp. 90–1, Lanham, MD: Scarecrow Press.

Van Drenth, A. & De Haan, F. (1999) *The rise of caring power: Elizabeth Fry and Josephine Butler in Britain and the Netherlands,* Amsterdam: Amsterdam University Press.

van Etten, H. (1953) 'Prisons and prisoners', J. Kavanaugh (ed.) *The Quaker approach,* London: George Allen.

van Etten, H. (2009) *Chronique de la vie Quaker Francais.* Congeries, France: Editions Ampelos.

Van Wagner, A. D., & Barbour, H. (1995) 'Reunion,' in Barbour, H., Densmore, C., Moger E. H., Sorel, N. C., Van Wagner, A. D., and Worrall, A. J. *Quaker crosscurrents: Three hundred years of Friends in the New York Yearly Meeting,* pp. 257–75, New York: Syracuse University Press.

Vann, R. T. (1969a) 'Nature and conversion in the early Quaker family', *Journal of Marriage and Family,* vol. 31, pp. 639–643.

Vann, R. T. (1969b) *The social development of English Quakerism, 1655-1755,* Cambridge, MA: Harvard University Press.

Vann, R. T. & Eversley, D. (1992) *Friends in life and death. The British and Irish Quakers in the demographic transition.* Cambridge: Cambridge University Press.

Vernon, A. (1958) *A Quaker business man: The life of Joseph Rowntree 1836-1925,* London: George Allen and Unwin.

Vining, E. G. (1958) *Friend of life: the biography of Rufus M. Jones,* Philadelphia, PA: Lippincott.

Vipont, E. (1954) *The story of Quakerism,* London: Bannisdale Press.

Vokins, J. (1691) *God's mighty power magnified as manifested and revealed in his faithful handmaid,* London: Thomas Northcott.

Wacker, G. (2001) *Heaven below: early Pentecostals and American culture,* Cambridge: Cambridge University Press.

Wagner, G. (1987) *The chocolate conscience,* London: Chatto and Windus.

Wakefield, P. (1796) *Introduction to botany,* London: E. Newberry.

Walker, P. O. (2006) *One heart and a wrong spirit: The Religious Society of Friends and colonial racism*. James Backhouse Lecture. Kenmore, Australia: Backhouse lecture committee.

Walton, Joseph S. (1848) 8th Mo. 24, to George Martin, box 4, Margaretta Walton Papers. Swarthmore, PA: Friends Historical Library.

Walvin, J. (1997) *Quakers: Money and morals*, London: John Murray.

Warren, E. (2006) *Jonathan Wright Plummer: Quaker Philanthropy*, Bloomington, IN: Author House.

Watkins, O. (1972) *The Puritan experience*, London: Routledge.

Watson, E. (1979) *Guest of my life*, Burnsville, NC: Celo Press.

Watson, E. (1982) *Sexuality: A part of wholeness*, Philadelphia, PA: Philadelphia Yearly Meeting's Family Relations Committee.

Watson, E. (1991) 'New occasions teach new duties', in *Realignment: Nine views among Friends*, Wallingford, PA: Pendle Hill Publications.

Watts, M. (1978) *The dissenters. vol. I: From the Reformation to the French Revolution*, Oxford: Oxford University Press.

Weaver, H., Kriese, P., & Angell, S. W. (2011) *Black fire: African American Quakers on spirituality and human rights*, Philadelphia, PA: Quaker Press of Friends General Conference.

Webb, B. (1831) *The authenticity of the Scriptures*, Wilmington, DE: W. M. Naudain.

Weber, M. (1998 [1905]) *The Protestant ethic and the spirit of capitalism*, Los Angeles, CA: Roxbury Publishing.

Weddle, M. B. (2001) *Walking in the way of peace: Quaker pacifism in the Seventeenth Century*, Oxford: Oxford University Press.

Weekley, C. (1999) *The kingdoms of Edward Hicks*, New York: Harry N. Abrams.

Wellman, Jr., J. K. (2008) *Evangelicals vs. liberals: the clash of Christian cultures in the Pacific Northwest*, Oxford and New York: Oxford University Press.

Wells, R. V. (1971) 'Family size and fertility control in Eighteenth-Century America: A study of Quaker families', *Population Studies*, vol. 25, pp. 73–82.

Were, M. (1992) 'Faith in action' *Faith in action: Encounters with Friends*, London: Friends World Committee for Consultation.

Wharton, W. (1828) 8th Mo. 25, to Benjamin Stokes, box 22, Miscellaneous Manuscripts. Swarthmore College, PA: Friends Historical Library.

Whitbeck, C. (1989) 'Friends historical testimony of the marriage relationship', *Friends Journal*, vol. 35, pp. 13–15.

Whitehead, G. (1674) *Enthusiasm above atheism: or, divine inspiration and immediate illumination ... asserted*. London.

Whitehead, G. (1704) *An evangelical epistle to the people of God, in derision call'd Quakers*, London: T. Sowle.

Whitehead, G. (1725) *The Christian progress of that ancient servant and minister of Jesus Christ, George Whitehead*, London.

Whittaker, E. J. (1986) *Thomas Lawson 1630–1691: North Country botanist, Quaker and schoolmaster*, York: Sessions Book Trust.

Wiggins, R. C. (ed.) (1996) *Captain Paul Cuffe's logs and letters*. Washington, DC: Howard University Press.

Wiggins, R. C. (2001) 'Paul and Stephen, unlikely friends', *Quaker History*, vol. 90, pp. 8–27.

Wilbur, J. (1845) *A narrative and exposition of the late proceedings of New England Yearly Meeting, with some of its subordinate meetings and their committees, in relation to the doctrinal controversy now existing in the Society of Friends*. New York, NY: Piercy & Reed.

Wilbur, J. (1859) *Journal of the life of John Wilbur*, Providence, RI: G. H. Whitney.

Wilbur, J. (1895) *Republication of the letters of John Wilbur to George Crosfield*, Providence, RI: Meeting for Suffering of New England Yearly Meeting of Friends.

Wilcox, C. M. (1995) *Theology and women's ministry in seventeenth century English Quakerism: Handmaids of the Lord*, Lampeter: Edwin Mellen Press.

Willcuts, J. L. & Perisho, S. (1980) 'Quakers in the eighties: a spirit-moved People', *Friends Journal*, January 1/15, pp. 4–6.

Willcuts, J. L. (1984) *Why Friends are Friends: some Quaker core convictions*, Newberg, OR: Barclay Press.

William and Mary (1819 [1688]) 'An Act for exempting their majestyes Protestant subjects dissenting from the Church of England from the penalties of certaine lawes. [Chapter XVIII. Rot. Parl. pt. 5. nu. 15.]', J. Raithby (ed.) *Statutes of the Realm: volume 6: 1685–94*, pp. 74–6.

Williams, W. R. (1987 [1962]) *The rich heritage of Quakerism*, P. Anderson (ed.), Newberg, OR: Barclay Press.

Wills, David et al (1979) *Six Quakers look at crime and punishment: a study paper by a group of Friends*, London: Quaker Social Responsibility and Education and Quaker Home Service. Wilson R. (1995) *Breaking the cycle: Violence and criminal justice West Virginia listening project*, Philadelphia, PA: American Friends Service Committee.

Wilson, E. R. (1975) *Uphill for peace: Quaker impact on Congress* Richmond, IN: Friends United Press.

Wilson, L. L. (1996) 'Why do you still read that old thing?' Philadelphia, PA: Wider Quaker Fellowship.

Wilson, L. L. (2001 [1993]) *Essays on the Quaker vision of gospel order*, Philadelphia, PA: Quaker Press of Friends General Conference.

Wilson, L. L. (2005) *Wrestling with our faith tradition: Collected public witness, 1995–2004*. Philadelphia, PA: Quaker Press of Friends General Conference.

Wilson, L. L. (2006) *Holy surrender: New England Yearly Meeting keynote address*, Worcester, MA: New England Yearly Meeting.

Wilson, L. L. (2009) '"The remnant of like faith": The first 50 years of North Carolina Yearly Meeting (Conservative)', Unpublished MA thesis, Earlham School of Religion.

Wilson, T. & Dickinson, J. (1847) *Journals of the lives, travels and gospel labours of Thomas Wilson and James Dickinson*, London: C. Gilpin.

Wilson, W. E. (1948) 'Quaker and evangelical', *Friends' Quarterly*, October, pp. 3–15.

Winchester, A. J. L. (1991) 'Ministers, merchants and migrants: Cumberland Friends and North America in the Eighteenth Century', *Quaker History*, vol. 80, pp. 85–99.

Wink, W. (ed.) (1999) 'Homosexuality and the Bible', in *Homosexuality and Christian faith*, pp. 33–49, Minneapolis, MN: Augsburg Fortress Publishers.

Winternitz, R., Barbour, H., and Wosh, P. (1995) 'Thomas Eddy' in Barbour, H., Densmore, C., Moger E. H., Sorel, N. C., Van Wagner, A. D., and Worrall, A. J. *Quaker Crosscurrents: Three Hundred Years of Friends in the New York Yearly Meeting*, pp. 79–84, New York, NY: Syracuse University Press.

Winton, C. (2004) 'Bradford, William (1663–1752)', *Oxford dictionary of national biography*, Oxford: Oxford University Press.

Witte, W. D. S. (1954) 'Quaker pacifism in the United States, 1919–1942'. PhD dissertation, Columbia University, NY.

Wood, J. (2011) 'Quaker reconciliation project', *Seeds*, January.

Woodard, L. *Historical sketch of the schism in the Friends Church in the years 1827–28*, Plainfield, IN: Caller Publishing Company.

Woodward, W.C. (1927) *Timothy Nicholson: Master Quaker*, Richmond, IN: Nicholson Press.

Woody, T. (1920) *Early Quaker education in Pennsylvania*, New York, NY: Teachers' College, Columbia University.

Woolman, J. (1754) *Some considerations on the keeping of Negroes recommended to the professors of Christianity and every denomination*, Philadelphia, PA: James Chattin.

Woolman, J. (1775) *The works of John Woolman*, London: J. Phillips.

Woolman, J. (1989 [1971]) *The Journal and Major Essays of John Woolman*, P. P. Moulton (ed.), Richmond IN: Friends United Press.

Woolman, J. & Gummere, A. M. (1922) *The journal and essays of John Woolman*, A. M. Gummere (ed.) New York, NY: Macmillan Company.

World Council of Churches (1982) *Baptism, eucharist and ministry*, Geneva.

World Council of Churches (2005) *The nature and mission of the church*, Geneva.

World Council of Churches website: www.oikumene.org

Worrall, A. J. (1980) *Quakers in the colonial Northeast*, Hanover, NH: University Press of New England.

Wright, L. M. (1966 [1932]) *The literary life of the early Friends 1650–1725*, New York, NY: AMS Press.

Wright, S. W (1995) *Friends in York: The dynamics of Quaker revival, 1780–1860*, Newcastle under Lyme: Keele University Press.

Wright, S. W. (2003) '"Gaining a voice": An interpretation of Quaker women's writing, 1740–1850', *Quaker Studies*, vol. 8, pp. 36–50.

Yarrow, C. H. M. (1978) *Quaker experiences in international conciliation*, New Haven, CT: Yale University Press.

Young Friends Central Committee (1980) *Responsible investment: a challenge to Quakers*. London: Quaker Home Service.

Young Friends General Meeting (1998) *Who do we think we are? Young Friends Commitment and Belonging*. London: Quaker Home Service.

Young Friends General Meeting (2010) 'Annual Report 2010.' http://yfgm.quaker.org.uk/wp-content/uploads/2012/01/2010-Annual-Report.pdf accessed 16 October 2012

Young Friends General Meeting (Undated) 'A user-friendly guide to YFGM.' http://yfgm.quaker.org.uk/wiki/images/d/d7/Yfgm-user-friendly-guide.pdf, accessed 16 October 2012.

Young Friends' Sub-committee of the Friends' Home Mission and Extension Committee. (1911) *Swanwick 1911: being the Report of the Conference of Young Friends held at Swanwick from August 28th to September 4th 1911*. London: Friends Home Mission Committee.

Young, M. B. (1939) *Functional poverty*, Pamphlet 6, Wallingford, PA: Pendle Hill.

Young, M. B. (1941) *A standard of living*, Pamphlet 12, Wallingford, PA: Pendle Hill.

Zarembka D. (2011) *A peace of Africa: reflections on life in the Great Lakes Region*. Washington, DC: Madeira Press.

Zarembka, D. (2012) 'The candlelight of peace', *The Friend*, vol. 170, no. 5, pp. 10–11.

Zehr H. (1979) *Changing lenses: a new focus on crime and justice*, Scottdale, PA: Herald Press.

INDEX

Lightning Source UK Ltd.
Milton Keynes UK
UKOW04f0811050117

291439UK00002B/4/P